BARRON'S

HOW TO PREPARE FOR THE

TOEIC®

TEST OF ENGLISH FOR INTERNATIONAL COMMUNICATION

2ND EDITION

Lin Lougheed

®TOEIC is a registered trademark of Educational Testing Service. There is no connection between Barron's and Educational Testing Service. This publication has not been reviewed or endorsed by ETS.

Photo Credits
The author gratefully acknowledges the following institutions that granted permission to reproduce the respective photos:

Australian Consulate General, New York, NY
LCRP #7, 13, 14, 15, 17; LRE #4, 8, 9; MT1 #1, 2, 3, 5, 6, 9, 12, 17; MT2 #1, 6, 8, 12, 18, 19; MT3 #2, 10, 12; MT4 #4, 10, 13; MT5 #10, 12, 14, 15; MT6 #9, 16

Embassy of The State of Kuwait, Washington, D.C.
MT2 #17

French Press and Information Service, French Embassy, Washington, D.C.
MT1 #11; MT2 #14; MT6 #6

Instructional Design International, Washington, D.C.
LRE #1; MT2 #16; MT3 #9, 17; MT4 #2, 7, 11, 15; MT5 #6, 8, 9, 11, 18; MT6 #4, 17, 19

Inter-American Development Bank, Washington, D.C.
LCRP #2, 4, 6, 16, 18; LRE #6, 7; MT1 #7, 13, 16, 18; MT2 #3, 11, 15; MT3 #1, 4, 7, 15, 18; MT4 #14, 16, 19; MT5 #1, 3, 4, 19; MT6 #1, 3, 8, 14

Japan Airlines, New York, NY
LCRP #5; MT1 #3; MT3 #3; MT4 #1, 12; MT5 #2, 17

Japan Information and Culture Center, Washington, D.C.
LCRP #1, 3, 8, 9; MT1 #4, 8, 10, 14, 19, 20; MT2 #2, 7, 9, 13, 20; MT3 #6, 8, 14, 19; MT4 #6, 8, 20; MT5 #1, 7, 16; MT6 #5, 7, 10, 12, 13, 15, 20

Malaysia Airlines, Los Angeles, CA
LCRP #10; MT4 #17; MT5 #5; MT6 #11, 18; LCRP #10;

Merck & Co., Inc., Whitehouse Station, NJ
MT4 #5, 9

Royal Netherlands Embassy, Washington, D.C.
LRE #3; MT1 #15; MT2 #4; MT3 #11; MT4 #3, 18; MT5 #13; MT6 #6

Swissair; LRE #2, 10

Swiss National Tourist Office, New York, NY
LRE #5; MT2 #10; MT3 #13, 16, 20

© Copyright 1999 by Lin Lougheed.
Prior edition copyright © 1995.

All rights reserved.

No part of this book may be reproduced in any form, by photostat, microfilm, xerography, or any other means, or incorporated into any information retrieval system, electronic or mechanical, without the written permission of the copyright owner.

All inquiries should be addressed to:

Barron's Educational Series, Inc.
250 Wireless Boulevard
Hauppauge, New York 11788
http://www.barronseduc.com

Library of Congress Catalog Card No.: 98-39883

International Standard Book No. 0-7641-0877-8 (Book only)
　　　　　　　　　　　　0-7641-7266-2 (Book with four CD's package)

Library of Congress Cataloging-in-Publication Data
Lougheed, Lin, 1946–
　　How to prepare for the TOEIC test : test of English for international communication / Lin Lougheed. —2nd ed.
　　　　p.　　cm.
　　ISBN 0-7641-7266-2
　　1. Test of English for International Communication—Study guides.
　2. Communication, International—Examinations—Study guides.
　3. English language—Textbooks for foreign speakers.　4. English language—Examinations—Study guides.　I. Title.
PE1128.L64　1999
428'.0076—d21　　　　　　　　　　　　　　　　98-39883
　　　　　　　　　　　　　　　　　　　　　　　　CIP

PRINTED IN THE UNITED STATES OF AMERICA
9

CONTENTS

Overview of the TOEIC vi
To the Teacher vi

INTRODUCTION
Questions and Answers Concerning the TOEIC 3
Study Plan for the TOEIC 6

LISTENING COMPREHENSION REVIEW
Overview—Parts I, II, III, and IV 11
TOEIC Sample Questions 11
Types of Problems in the Listening Comprehension Section 15
Problems Analyzing Pictures 16
Strategies for Analyzing Pictures 27
Problems Analyzing Answer Choices 28
Strategies for Analyzing Answer Choices 53
Problems Analyzing Question Types 54
Strategies for Analyzing Question Types 77
Problems Analyzing Language Functions 78
Strategies for Analyzing Language Functions 85
Mini-Test for Listening Comprehension Parts I, II, III, and IV 86
Strategies to Improve Your Listening Comprehension Score 96

READING REVIEW
Overview—Parts V, VI, and VII 99
TOEIC Sample Questions 99
Types of Problems in the Reading Section 100
Problems Analyzing Vocabulary 104
Strategies for Analyzing Vocabulary 120
Problems Analyzing Grammar 120
Strategies for Analyzing Grammar 198
Mini-Test for Reading Parts V and VI 199
Reading Comprehension Tips 202
Types of Questions Found on the TOEIC 202
Types of Information Sought on the TOEIC 202
The PSRA Strategy 204
Strategies for Reading Comprehension 206

iv CONTENTS

    Problems Analyzing Reading Passages   206
  Mini-Test for Reading Part VII   226
    Strategies to Improve Your Reading Score   237

TOEIC MODEL TESTS
Model Test 1   243
Model Test 2   281
Model Test 3   319
Model Test 4   355
Model Test 5   391
Model Test 6   429

ANSWER KEYS FOR THE TOEIC REVIEW EXERCISES, MINI-TESTS, AND MODEL TESTS
Answer Key for Listening Comprehension Review   465
  Problems Analyzing Pictures   467
  Problems Analyzing Answer Choices   467
  Problems Analyzing Question Types   467
  Problems Analyzing Language Functions   467
Answer Key for Mini-Test for Listening Comprehension Parts I, II, III, and IV   467
Answer Key for Reading Review   468
  Problems Analyzing Vocabulary   468
  Problems Analyzing Grammar   468
Answer Key for Mini-Test for Reading Parts V and VI   471
  Problems Analyzing Reading Passages   471
Answer Key for Mini-Test for Reading Part VII   471
Answer Key for TOEIC Model Tests   271
  Model Test 1   471
  Model Test 2   473
  Model Test 3   474
  Model Test 4   475
  Model Test 5   476
  Model Test 6   477

EXPLANATORY ANSWERS FOR THE TOEIC REVIEW EXERCISES, MINI-TESTS, AND MODEL TESTS
Explanatory Answers for Listening Comprehension Review   479
  Problems Analyzing Pictures   481
  Problems Analyzing Answer Choices   481
  Problems Analyzing Question Types   484
  Problems Analyzing Language Functions   487
Mini-Test for Listening Comprehension Parts I, II, III, and IV   488

Explanatory Answers for Reading Review 491
- Problems Analyzing Vocabulary 491
- Problems Analyzing Grammar 492
- Mini-Test for Reading Parts V and VI 501
- Problems Analyzing Reading Passages 503
- Mini-Test for Reading Part VII 506

Explanatory Answers for TOEIC Model Tests 508
- Model Test 1 508
- Model Test 2 519
- Model Test 3 529
- Model Test 4 539
- Model Test 5 549
- Model Test 6 559

APPENDIX: Transcripts for Listening Comprehension Exercises, Mini-Test, and Model Tests 1–6

Transcripts for the Listening Comprehension Sections 573
- Listening Comprehension Exercises 573
- Mini-Test for Listening Comprehension Parts I, II, III, and IV 587
- Model Test 1 Listening Comprehension 595
- Model Test 2 Listening Comprehension 608
- Model Test 3 Listening Comprehension 621
- Model Test 4 Listening Comprehension 634
- Model Test 5 Listening Comprehension 647
- Model Test 6 Listening Comprehension 660

Answer Sheets
- Mini-Test for Listening Comprehension Parts I, II, III, and IV 673
- Mini-Test for Reading Parts V and VI 673
- Mini-Test for Reading Part VII 673

Overview of the TOEIC

There are two sections on the TOEIC exam: Listening Comprehension and Reading. Specific information about each section is given in detail in this book. The kinds of questions asked and strategies you'll need to master in order to perform well are provided in the respective chapters. The timetable for the TOEIC is as follows:

Timetable for the TOEIC
Total Time: 2 hours

Section 1 (45 minutes)	Listening Comprehension	
	Part I: Picture	20 Questions
	Part II: Question-Response	30 Questions
	Part III: Short Conversations	30 Questions
	Part IV: Short Talks	20 Questions
Section 2 (75 minutes)	Reading	
	Part V: Incomplete Sentences	40 Questions
	Part VI: Error Recognition	20 Questions
	Part VII: Reading Comprehension	40 Questions

To the Teacher

Rationale for a TOEIC Preparation Course

Barron's *How to Prepare for the TOEIC® Test* may be used as either a self-study course or a class course. In a class situation, this text will provide an excellent structure for helping the students improve their English language skills and prepare for the TOEIC exam.

Adult learners of English are very goal-oriented. For many adults who are required to take the TOEIC exam, their goal is, obviously enough, a high score. Having a goal that can be easily measured will be very motivating for your students.

Many teachers do not like to "teach to the test." They feel that developing a general knowledge of English will be more useful to the students than reviewing test items. But students want to "study the test." They don't want to "waste their time" learning something that might not be tested.

Both arguments ignore what actually happens during a TOEIC preparation course. General English is used to discuss how the exam is structured, what strategies should be used, and what skills should be developed. General English is used to explain problems and to expand into other areas. By helping students prepare for an exam, you can't help but improve their general knowledge of English.

A TOEIC preparation course gives the students what they want: a streamlined approach to learning what they think they need to know for the exam. The course gives the teachers what they want: a scheme to help them improve the English language ability of their students.

Organization of a TOEIC Preparation Course

Timetable

Every test-preparation course faces the same dilemma: how to squeeze a total review of English into a class timetable. Some of you may have an afternoon TOEIC orientation; others may have a one-week intensive class; some may have a ten-week session. However long your class time, one thing is true: no class is ever long enough to cover everything you want to cover.

As a guideline, you might want to follow this plan and expand it as your time allows.

- First period: Study Chapter 1, Introduction
- Next period: Take a Model Test.
  Evaluate answers; determine the weak areas of the class.
- Subsequent periods: Review Listening Comprehension.
  Take the Mini-Test.
  Review Reading.
  Take the Mini-Test.
  Take additional Model Tests.
- Last Period: Take a final Model Test and note the improvement in scores.

After students have completed the exercises, the Mini-Tests, or the Model Tests, they can look in the Answer Key (Chapter 5) for quick access to the correct answer or in the Explanatory Answers (Chapter 6) for reasons why the correct answer is right and the incorrect answers are wrong.

These abbreviations are used in the exercises and Explanatory Answers.

adjective	(adj)	noun	(n)
adverb	(adv)	preposition	(prep)
article	(art)	pronoun	(pron)
auxiliary	(aux)	subject of a sentence	(sub)
conjunction	(conj)	verb	(v)
interjection	(interj)		

The symbol ≁ is also used, to mean "is not the same as," "is different from," and "does not equal."

Teaching Listening Comprehension

The more students hear English, the better their listening comprehension will be. Encourage a lot of discussion about the various strategies mentioned in the Listening Comprehension activities. Have the students work in pairs or small groups to increase the amount of time students will spend listening and speaking.

All tests require the students to choose a correct answer. This means the students must eliminate the incorrect answers. There are common distracters (traps) on an exam that a student can be trained to listen for. And coincidentally, while they are learning to listen for these traps, they are improving their listening comprehension.

The Listening Comprehension activities in this text are a gold mine. You can use them for the stated purpose, which is to help students learn how to analyze photos, answer choices, question types, and language functions. In addition, you can use them for a variety of communicative activities.

Using the Picture Exercises

The photos can be used to help students develop their vocabulary. There are over 140 photographs in this text. Have the students pick a photograph and, in pairs or small groups, name everything they can see in the picture.

Then, in the same small groups (or individually) have them use those words in a sentence. They can write a short description of the photograph or, even better, they can write a short narrative. The narratives can be extremely imaginative—the more imaginative the better. Have the students describe what happened before the picture was taken and what might happen afterwards.

Once students have the vocabulary under control, they can make an oral presentation. The other students or groups will then have to retell the narrative. This will help them evaluate their own listening comprehension.

Using the Question-Response Exercises

In this section, there is one short question, followed by an equally short answer. This is not the way people communicate. Have the students establish a context for the short question. Where are the speakers? Who are they? What are they talking about? What were they doing before? What will they do next? What did they say before? What will they say next?

Have them create a short skit that a pair of students can act out. Then have others in the class try to summarize the dialogue. Again you are helping them evaluate their own listening comprehension.

Using the Short Conversation Exercises

The same technique can work here. Actually, it will be easier, because there is more dialogue for the students to use as a basis. This time have the students listen to the skit created by their colleagues and ask "wh" questions. Have them learn to anticipate *who, what, when, where, why,* and *how*.

Using the Short Talks Exercises

There are a variety of short talks: some are about the weather; others are public service announcements; some are advertisements. Have the students take one of the small talks and rewrite it. If it is a weather announcement, have them take a rainy day and make it sunny; have them change an advertisement for a TV to an advertisement for a car.

Then, as with the other activities, have the other students create the "wh" questions. See if they can stump their colleagues. Have them make these talks challenging.

Teaching Reading

Again, the best way for students to improve their reading is to read, read, read. On the TOEIC exam, even the grammar activities focus on reading. They demand that students understand the whole context of the statement, not just an isolated part. That is why the structure tests are in the Reading section.

As in the Listening Comprehension section, it is as important to know why an answer is wrong as it is to know why an answer is right. Training your students to use the strategies mentioned in these sections will make them more efficient readers.

Using the Vocabulary Exercises

All students want to know words and more words. Remind them that it is important to know how to use them. They will learn more by reading and learning words in context than they will from memorizing word lists.

They can and should create their own personal word lists. Every time they encounter an unfamiliar word, they should write it down in a notebook. They should try to use it in a sentence, or even better in a dialogue. Have the students create their own skits using the words in their own personal word lists.

If the students insist on lists, show them all the charts of words in the various sections of both the Listening and Reading sections. Have the students use these words to learn how to use words in context.

Using the Grammar Exercises

The grammar reviewed in this text covers those areas that are most likely to be found on the TOEIC and that most likely will give students the most problems. You can help students focus their attention by having them analyze their mistakes in the Model Tests.

Use a Model Test as a diagnostic. If the students have several errors on questions testing prepositions, you would suggest they concentrate on the problems dealing with prepositions. Lists in the front of Chapter 2 and Chapter 3 provide an easy way for you to find the specific exercises your students need. (See pages 15 and 100–101.) By focusing on problem areas, they will be able to study more efficiently and effectively.

Using the Reading Exercises

The strategies emphasized in the Reading Review are not only for reading on the TOEIC exam. They can be, and should be, applied to all reading a student might have to do. Use outside reading materials such as English news magazines and newspapers. Have the students read not only the articles but also the ads, announcements, subscription forms, and Table of Contents. In fact, have them scan and read the entire magazine. Everything found in a news magazine, including charts and graphs, is found on the TOEIC.

As the students did in the Listening Comprehension Review, have them create "wh" questions for the articles, graphs, tables, etc., they find. Let them try to stump their colleagues. To make the lesson even more communicative, have the students give an oral presentation of what they have read. Let the "wh" questions be oral, too.

Teaching Is a Group Effort

This text was the result of the ideas and suggestions of teachers and TOEIC administrators who have used my materials in Japan, Korea, Thailand, Malaysia, France, Switzerland, Canada, and the United States. As the TOEIC test widens its footprint, I would like to hear from other teachers in other countries. The more help I have from you, the more the subsequent editions will contain just what you need for your own teaching situation. You may contact me by e-mail or in care of Barron's at the address below. I look forward to hearing from you. Good luck and enjoy your class.

Lin Lougheed
TOEIC Editorial
c/o Barron's Educational Series
250 Wireless Blvd.
Hauppauge, NY 11788
USA

E-mail: books@lougheed.com

INTRODUCTION

WHAT TO LOOK FOR IN THIS CHAPTER
- Questions and Answers Concerning the TOEIC
- Study Plan for the TOEIC

INTRODUCTION

WHAT TO LOOK FOR IN THIS CHAPTER

- Design and Advance Conceptions of the
  Study Plan for the TQM.

Questions and Answers Concerning the TOEIC

Over 1,200,000 people take the TOEIC test each year, and this number is growing. The TOEIC is administered in Europe, Asia, North America, South America, and Central America. Since the test is relatively new (compared to the TOEFL, which was first given in 1963), many test-takers are unfamiliar with the TOEIC. The following are some commonly asked questions about the TOEIC. You can also learn more at the TOEIC web site <http://www.toeic.com> or at my web site <http://www.lougheed.com>

What Is the Purpose of the TOEIC?

Since 1979, the TOEIC (the Test of English for International Communication) has been used internationally as a standard assessment of English-language proficiency. The TOEIC has been developed by linguists, language experts, and staff at the The Chauncey Group International Ltd. to evaluate the English language skills of nonnative speakers of English in the field of business.

What Skills Are Tested on the TOEIC?

The TOEIC test consists of two sections: Listening Comprehension (100 multiple-choice questions) and Reading (100 multiple-choice questions). An audiotape is used to test Listening Comprehension.

The content of the TOEIC test is not specialized; the vocabulary and content are familiar to those individuals who use English in daily activities.

Who Uses the TOEIC?

Government agencies, multinational corporations, and international organizations use the TOEIC to ascertain the English-language capabilities of employees and prospective employees. The scores are used as an independent measure of proficiency and can be helpful in identifying personnel capable of handling language-specific responsibilities, in placing personnel in language-training programs, and in promoting personnel to positions where reliable linguistic standards are met.

Language-training programs use the TOEIC to establish language-training goals and to assess students' progress in overall English ability.

Who Takes the TOEIC?

In addition to the staffs of the companies and organizations above, individuals take the TOEIC to document their abilities for personal and professional reasons.

What Is the Format of the TOEIC?

The TOEIC consists of two sections:

Listening Comprehension

Part I: Picture	20 questions
Part II: Question-Response	30 questions
Part III: Short Conversations	30 questions
Part IV: Short Talks	20 questions

Reading

Part V: Incomplete Sentences	40 questions
Part VI: Error Recognition	20 questions
Part VII: Reading Comprehension	40 questions

There are a total of 200 items; total time allowed for the test (including administrative tasks) is approximately 2½ hours. The Listening Comprehension section takes 45 minutes; the Reading section takes 75 minutes.

How Is the TOEIC Score Determined?

Separate scores are given for Listening Comprehension (5 to 495) and Reading (5 to 495). These two sub-scores are added to arrive at the total score. The TOEIC score is represented on a scale of 10 to 990 and is based on the total number of correct answers.

What Do TOEIC Scores Mean?

There is no established minimum passing score; each institution, through experience, sets up its own acceptable score.

How Are TOEIC Scores Obtained?

TOEIC test-takers who are sponsored by companies, institutions, or organizations receive their scores from their sponsors. Those examinees who register individually to take the TOEIC receive their scores directly.

What If I Think My Score Is Incorrect?

You should contact your local representative, who can score your answer sheet by hand and give you a second report. You may have to pay for this service.

How Long Are TOEIC Scores Kept?

TOEIC representatives keep individual test scores for two years.

When and Where Can I Take the TOEIC?

The TOEIC test is offered worldwide and is generally available upon demand. The dates, times, and locations of the test sites are determined by the local TOEIC representatives. For test fees, test dates, and locations, contact the TOEIC office in your country or contact ETS in the USA. The TOEIC representative offices are listed on page 5.

TOEIC Representative Offices
List of Authorized Sites (by region)

WORLDWIDE HEADQUARTERS
TOEIC Service International
The Chauncey Group International Ltd.
664 Rosedale Road
Princeton, NJ 08540, USA
Tel: 1/609-720-6647
Fax: 1/609-720-6550
toeic@chauncey.com
http://www.toeic.com

THE AMERICAS

Argentina
Instituto Cultural Argentino
Norteamericano
Maipú 686
Buenos Aires, Argentina
Tel: 54/1-322-4557
Fax: 54/1-322-2106
icana@arg.siscotel.com

Canada
ICI Communications Canada Inc.
133 Princess Street Suite 212
Kingston, ON, K7L 1A8, Canada
Tel: 1/613-542-3368
Fax: 1/613-542-2907
info@ici-canada.com
http://www.ici-canada.com

ICI Communications Canada Inc.
Bureau du Québec
C.P. 69044
Lval, QC, H7X 3M2, Canada
Tel: 1/514-689-3151
or 1-888-689-3151
Fax: 1/514-689-2790
sylvieici@videotron.ca
http://www.ici-canada.com

Colombia
Centro Cultural Colombo Americano
Calle 13 Norte, No. 8-45
Cali, Colombia
Tel: 57/2-6673 539,
676 849 or 675 001
Fax: 57/2-6684 695

Mexico
English Testing de México,
S.A. de CV
Av. Nuevo León No. int. 304
Col. Hipódromo Condesa
México, D.F. 06100, México
Tel: 52/5-553-5930/4752
Fax: 52/5-211-5434
aqocean@infosel.net.mx

United States of America
International Communications
Incorporated (ICI)
3301 Country Club Road,
Suite 2205
Endwell, NY 13760, USA
Tel: 1/607-748-9500
Fax: 1/607-748-9614
usici@aol.com
http://www.toeic-usa.com

Venezuela
Asociacion Venezolano-Americana de
Amistad
Av. Casanova, Edif. Blandín 2 Piso
Apartado 60835, Chacaito
Caracas 1060, Venezuela
Tel: 58/2-951-0394
Fax: 58/2-951-0592
avaa@trve.net

Centro Venezolano Americano del Zulia
Calle 63 No. 3E-60
Apartado 419
Maracaibo, Estado Zulia, Venezuela
Tel: 58/61-911 436 880/980
Fax: 58/61-921 098

ASIA

Hong Kong
Institute of International Education
Shatin Central
PO Box 1298
Shatin, New Territories,
Hong Kong
People's Republic of China
Tel: 852/2603-5771
Fax: 852/2603-5765
leemarsha@cuhk.hk

Indonesia
PT RIMA Tritunggal
Plaza Bapindo II, 27th Floor
J1 Jend. Sudirman Kav. 53-55
Jakarat 12190, Indonesia
Tel: 62/21-527-2222
Fax: 62/21-527-3333
toeic@centrin.net.id

Japan
Institute for International Business
(IIBC)
TOEIC Steering Committee
Sanno Grand Building
2-14-2 Nagata-cho, Chiyoda-ku
Tokyo 100, Japan
Tel: 81/3 3581-5663
Fax: 81/3 3581-5608
iibc@mx2.nisiq.net
http://www.toeic-fc.co.jp

Korea
International Communication Foundation
Si-sa-yong-o-sa, Inc.
#55-1, Chongno 2-ga,
Chongno-gu
Seoul 110, Korea
Tel: 82/2-274 0509
Fax: 82/2-277 2610
toeic@bora.dacom.co.kr
http://www.ybmsisa.com

Malaysia
Kassim Chan Management Consultants,
Sdn. Bhd.
11th Floor
No. 3 Cangkat Raja Chulan
50200 Kuala Lumpur, Malaysia
Tel: 60/3-328 0133
Fax: 60/3-232 4585

Taiwan
The Language Training and Testing Center
(LTTC)
170 Hsin-hai Road, Section 2
Taipei, Taiwan 106, R.O.C.
Tel: 886/2-2362-6385
Fax: 886/2-2362-2809
gts@lttc.ntu.edu.tw
http://www.lttc.ntu.edu.tw

Thailand
TOEIC Center Thailand
Suite #1305
Bangkok Business Building
54 Asoke Road, Sukhumvit 21
Bangkok 10110, Thailand
Tel: 66/2-260-7061, or 260-7189
Fax: 66/2-260-7061
toeic@email.ksc.net

TOEIC Center Thailand—Northern Region
Nawarat Building 3rd Floor
Kaeo Nawarat Soi 3
Amphur Muang
Chiangmai 50000, Thailand
Tel: 66-053-248-408
Fax: 66-053-248-408
toeic@email.ksc.net

EUROPE

France
Council on International Educational
Exchange (CIEE)
66, Avenue Champs-Elysées (Bâtiment E)
75008 Paris, France
Tel: 33/1-40 74 05 21
Fax: 33/1-42 56 65 27
toeicfrance@ciee.org
http://www.france.toeic.com

Council on International Educational
Exchange (CIEE)
60 Rue Masenon
69003 Lyon, France
Tel: 33/4-78 60 48 25
Fax: 33/4-78 60 46 48
toeiclyon@ciee.org
http://www.france.toeic.com

Italy
O.S. Consulting
Via Fra' Paolo Sarpi 7
50136 Firenze, Italy
Tel: 39/55-672 580/581
Fax: 39/55-669 446
O.S.@iol.it

Spain
TEA Ediciones, S.A.
Calle Fray Bernardino de
Sahagún, 24
28036 Madrid, Spain
Tel: 34/1-345-7026 or 359-8311
Fax: 34/1-345-8608
teadic@nexo.es
http://www.cop.es/test/dll.htm

Switzerland
TOEIC Language Consulting, S.A.
Route de Moncor 14—P.O. Box 49
CH-1752 Villars-sur-GLâne 1
Fribourg, Switzerland
Tel: 41/37 41 26 26
Fax: 41/37 41 26 27

United Kingdom
International Communications
(UK), Ltd.
TOEIC House
129 Wendell Road
London W12 9SD, England
Tel: 44/181-740-6282
Fax: 44/181-740-5207

MIDDLE EAST AND AFRICA

Egypt
AMIDEAST
4 & 6 Kamel El Shennawy Street
Garden City
Cario, Egypt
Tel: 20/2-355-3170, 354-2726
Fax: 20/2-355-2946
egypt@amideast.org
http://www.amidest.org

Madagascar
Centro Culturel Americain
USIS-American Embassy
14 and 16 rue Raintovo
Antsahavola
Antananarivo, Madagascar
Tel: 261/20-20 238
Fax: 261/20-22 213 978
psaxton@usaid.gov

Yemen
AMIDEAST
Beit Al-Showaee, 15 Street (off Baghdad Street)
P.O. Box 15508, Sana'a, Yemen
Tel: 967/1-203-588
Fax: 967/1-416-975
yamen@amideast.org
http://www.amideast.org

How Can I Prepare for the TOEIC?

If you plan to take the TOEIC test, make a concerted effort to use English as much as possible, and in many different situations.

The best preparation is using a book/tape combination such as this—a program designed to help you specifically with the TOEIC. Following through with this book will:
- make you aware of certain test-taking skills;
- make you familiar with the format of the test; and
- improve your total score.

Additional suggestions are found in the next section, entitled "Study Plan for the TOEIC."

How Can I Get a Better Score on the TOEIC?

Assuming you have prepared well for the TOEIC, you can maximize your score on the test day by following these suggestions:
- Read the directions carefully.
- Work quickly.
- Do not make notes in the test booklet.
- Guess if you're not sure.
- Mark only one answer.

Additional suggestions are found in the next section, "Study Plan for the TOEIC."

Study Plan for the TOEIC

There is an English expression: You can lead a horse to water, but you can't make him drink. Similarly, this book can lead you through the TOEIC test, but it can't make you think. Learning is a self-motivated activity. Only you can prepare yourself for the TOEIC.

It takes a lot of discipline to learn a foreign language. The following suggestions will help you develop this discipline and improve your English at the same time.

Studying Before the Test

1. *Study regularly.* Pick the same time of day to practice. If you don't develop a routine, you won't develop good study habits. Tell yourself that you can't watch TV at 7:30 because that is your TOEIC time. If you do miss your scheduled time one day, don't worry. Try to make it up later in that day. But don't study at a different time every day. You will never get any studying done.
2. *Do a little at a time.* Tell yourself that you will study for ten minutes on the train every morning or ten minutes just before you go to bed. It is better to learn one thing very well in a short period of time than to spend long periods trying to study everything.
3. *Budget your time.* The TOEIC is a timed test, so time your study sessions. Give yourself ten minutes to study and then stop. You must use your time effectively. Learn how to take advantage of short periods of time.
4. *Write out a study schedule.* If you put something in writing, you are more likely to do it.
5. *Listen to as much English as you can.* The best way to improve your listening comprehension is by listening. As you listen, ask yourself these questions:

Who is talking?
Who are they talking to?
What are they talking about?
Where are they talking?
Why are they talking?

As you answer these questions, you will improve your ability to understand English through context.

6. *Read as much English as you can.* It should be no surprise that the best and easiest way to improve your reading comprehension is by reading. Concentrate on weekly news magazines. Look at the tables of contents, the advertisements, the announcements, and the articles. Read anything in English you can find: want ads, train schedules, hotel registration forms, etc. Again, always ask yourself questions as you read.

   Use the PSRA reading strategy technique discussed on pages 204–206. That will help you on the TOEIC and every time you read anything—even reading material in your own language!

7. *Keep a vocabulary notebook.* Don't bother learning long lists of words. That will not help you as much as learning words in context. Look at the suggestions in the "Problems Analyzing Vocabulary" section on page 104.

   If you are addicted to lists, there are lists in Chapter 2, Listening Comprehension Review, and in Chapter 3, Reading Review. Study the lists and the examples given in context.

8. *Know your goal.* Why are you taking the TOEIC? If it's to qualify for a better position in your company, picture yourself in that job. What kind of score will you need? Work for that score (or a higher one).

9. *Develop a positive attitude.* Before Olympic athletes enter the competition, many shut their eyes and imagine themselves skiing down the mountain, running around the track, or swimming the fastest and passing the finish line first. They imagine themselves performing perfectly, scoring the best, and winning. This is the power of positive thinking. It is not just for athletes. You can use it, too.

   You must have a positive attitude when you take the TOEIC. Every night just before you fall asleep (when the right side of the brain is most receptive) repeat the following sentence ten times. "I understand English very well, and I will score very high on the TOEIC." The subconscious mind is very powerful. If you convince yourself that you can succeed, you are more likely to succeed.

10. *Relax.* Don't become anxious about the exam. Your mind will be more receptive if you are calm. Relax before, during, and especially after the exam.

Using Barron's *How to Prepare for the TOEIC® Test*

1. *Become familiar with the TOEIC questions and directions.* Read the sections on the TOEIC and the introductions to the Listening Comprehension and Reading chapters carefully. They contain information and advice that will help you raise your score.

2. *Take a Model Test.* Use the Explanatory Answers as a guide to help you determine your weaknesses. If you miss more questions about prepositions than about adverbs of frequency, then you should spend your time studying prepositions. Use the lists of problems found on pages 15 and 100–101 to easily find the exercises you need most.

3. *Study efficiently.* When time is limited, concentrate on what you really need to study. Don't try to do everything if you don't have enough time.

4. *Study and use the strategies.* This book lists many strategies that will help you score well on the exam. A strategy is a technique to use to help you approach a problem. In this case, a strategy will help you comprehend spoken and written English.

5. *Study all the potential problems.* Know what to look for in the Listening Comprehension and Reading sections. You should learn how to recognize an incorrect answer.

6. *Do the exercises, Cumulative Review Exercises, and Mini-Tests*. All of the exercises are designed like those on the TOEIC. You will develop both your English ability and your test-taking skills by studying these exercises.
7. *Review the Explanatory Answers*. All of the answers for the review exercises, Mini-Tests, and the Model Tests are explained thoroughly in Chapter 6. Studying these explanations will sharpen your ability to analyze a test question. Knowing why you made an error will help you avoid the error the next time.

    Chapter 5 contains Answer Keys. You can use these keys to quickly find out which questions you did not answer correctly. Then, go to the Explanatory Answers to learn where you went wrong. This will help you to focus your studies on the areas in which you need the most practice.
8. *Do a little every day*. It is worth repeating this advice. Following a consistent study routine will help you prepare for the TOEIC. You may not have to study everything in this book. Study the types of questions for which you need additional practice. But do it every day!

Taking the Test

1. *Be early*. You should avoid rushing on the test day. Leave yourself plenty of time to get to the testing center.
2. *Be comfortable*. If you can choose your own seat, pick one that is away from distractions. You don't want to be near an open door where you can watch people pass outside. On the other hand, you might want to be near a window to get good light. Try, if you can, to sit near the audio cassette player. If you can't hear well, be sure to tell the test administrator.
3. *Bring what you need*. Your test site may provide pencils with erasers, but to be safe you should bring three or four No. 2 pencils with erasers. You may find a watch useful, too.
4. *Listen to the directions*. Even though you will know the format after using this book, you should listen to the directions carefully. Listening to the familiar directions will help you relax.
5. *Answer all questions*. Even if you do not know an answer, you should mark your best answer. But try to make it an educated guess. When time is running out, just blacken any letter for the questions you have not answered—even if you didn't have time to read the question. You may be right.
6. *Match the numbers*. Make sure that the number on your answer sheet matches the number in your test book.
7. *Mark only one answer per question on the answer sheet*. Only one black mark will be counted. If you make a mistake and erase, do it completely. Do not make any other marks on the answer sheet.
8. *Answer the easy questions first*. In the Reading section, you can pace yourself. If you do not immediately know an answer to a question, skip that question and go to one you can answer. At the end of the section, come back and do the more difficult questions. This will give you an opportunity to answer as many questions as you can.
9. *Pace yourself*. The cassette player will keep you moving in the Listening Comprehension section. But in the Reading section you will be able to adjust your own pace. You will have less than 45 seconds for each question in the Reading section.
10. *Leave time at the end*. If you can, try to leave a minute at the end to go over your answer sheet and make sure you have filled in every question.
11. *Celebrate after the exam*. Go ahead. Have a good time. You deserve it. Congratulations on a job well done.

LISTENING COMPREHENSION REVIEW

WHAT TO LOOK FOR IN THIS CHAPTER
- Directions for the Listening Comprehension section, Parts I, II, III, and IV
- Examples of TOEIC Listening Comprehension questions
- Types of Problems in the Listening Comprehension section
    - Problems analyzing pictures
    - Problems analyzing answer choices
    - Problems analyzing question types
    - Problems analyzing language functions
- Mini-Test for Listening Comprehension Parts I, II, III, and IV
- Strategies to Improve Your Listening Comprehension Score

OVERVIEW—PARTS I, II, III, AND IV

There are four parts to the Listening Comprehension section of the TOEIC test. You will have approximately 45 minutes to complete this section.

Part I: Picture   20 Questions
Part II: Question-Response   30 Questions
Part III: Short Conversations 30 Questions
Part IV: Short Talks   20 Questions

TOEIC Sample Questions

This section will show you the kind of questions you will have to answer on Parts I–IV. You should familiarize yourself with the actual directions used on the TOEIC before you take the exam. You can find these directions in the Model TOEIC Test and the TOEIC Bulletin. You can get these publications from the TOEIC offices listed on page 5.

SECTION I: LISTENING COMPREHENSION
Part I: Picture

Directions: In your test book, you will see a picture. On the compact disc, you will hear four statements. Choose the statement that most closely matches the picture and fill in the corresponding oval on your answer sheet.

SAMPLE QUESTIONS

Question 1

You will hear: Look at the picture marked number 1 in your test book.
                        (A) They're waiting at the bus stop.   Ⓐ Ⓑ Ⓒ ●
                        (B) They're leaving the building.
                        (C) They're selling tickets.
                        (D) They're getting off the bus.

Statement (D), "They're getting off the bus," best describes what you see in the picture. Therefore, you should choose answer (D).

12 LISTENING COMPREHENSION REVIEW

Question 2

You will hear: Look at the picture marked number 2 in your test book.
　　　　　　　　(A) The men are all smiling.
　　　　　　　　(B) All are wearing ties.
　　　　　　　　(C) They are watching television.
　　　　　　　　(D) The shop is closed for repair.

Statement (A), "The men are all smiling," best describes what you see in the picture. Therefore, you should choose answer (A).

Part II: Question-Response

Directions: On the compact disc, you will hear a question and three possible answers. Choose the answer that most closely answers the question and fill in the corresponding oval on your answer sheet.

SAMPLE QUESTIONS

Question 1

You will hear: 1. Have you ever been to Jakarta before?
　　　　　　　　(A) Yes, there are four of them.
　　　　　　　　(B) Only once.
　　　　　　　　(C) No, they don't have it.

The best response to the question "Have you ever been to Jakarta before?" is choice (B), "Only once." Therefore, you should choose answer (B).

Question 2

You will hear: 2. How can I get to the airport from here?
　　　　　　　　(A) Take a taxi. It's just a short ride.
　　　　　　　　(B) No, I don't.
　　　　　　　　(C) You can get on easily.

The best response to the question "How can I get to the airport from here?" is choice (A), "Take a taxi. It's just a short ride." Therefore, you should choose answer (A).

OVERVIEW—PARTS I, II, III, AND IV **13**

Part III: Short Conversations

Directions: On the compact disc, you will hear a short conversation. In your test book, you will see a question and four possible answers. Choose the best answer to the question and fill in the corresponding oval on your answer sheet.

SAMPLE QUESTIONS

Question 1

You will hear: Man: We'll need to resurface this whole stretch.
              Woman: Is that really necessary? We paved this section last year.
              Man: I know. The heavy trucking has ruined it in no time at all.

You will read: Who is likely talking?
               (A) Truck drivers.
               (B) Road engineers.   Ⓐ ● Ⓒ Ⓓ
               (C) Mechanics.
               (D) Accountants.

The best response to the question "Who is talking?" is choice (B), "Road engineers." Therefore, you should choose answer (B).

Question 2

You will hear: Man: We'll need your medical history so take this form and fill it out, please.
              Woman: Will there be a long wait for my appointment?
              Man: No, the doctor is seeing patients on schedule.

You will read: Where are the speakers?
               (A) At a sidewalk cafe.
               (B) In a history class.
               (C) At an airport check-in counter.
               (D) In a physician's office.

The best response to the question "Where are the speakers?" is choice (D), "In a physician's office." Therefore, you should choose answer (D).

Part IV: Short Talks

Directions: On the compact disc, you will hear a short talk. In your test book, you will see several questions on the talk and four possible answers. Choose the best answer to the question and fill in the corresponding oval on your answer sheet.

SAMPLE QUESTIONS

Questions 1–2 are based on the following talk:

You will hear: In five minutes, for one hour only, women's coats and hats go on sale in our fifth-floor Better Fashions department. All merchandise is reduced by twenty-five to forty percent. Not all styles in all sizes, but an outstanding selection nonetheless.

You will hear: Now read question 1 in your test book and answer it.

You will read:
1. When does the sale begin?
    (A) In five minutes.
    (B) In one hour.
    (C) At 2:45.
    (D) Tomorrow.

● Ⓑ Ⓒ Ⓓ

The best response to the question "When does the sale begin?" is choice (A), "In five minutes." Therefore, you should choose answer (A).

You will hear: Now read question 2 in your test book and answer it.

You will read:
2. What is going on sale?
    (A) Men's coats.
    (B) Women's hats.
    (C) Cosmetics.
    (D) Old merchandise.

Ⓐ ● Ⓒ Ⓓ

The best response to the question "What is going on sale?" is choice (B), "Women's hats." Therefore, you should choose answer (B).

TYPES OF PROBLEMS IN THE LISTENING COMPREHENSION SECTION

To prepare for the four parts of the Listening Comprehension section, you must develop certain skills:

Skills Needed	Part I	Part II	Part III	Part IV
Analyzing pictures	■			
Analyzing answer choices	■	■	■	■
Analyzing question types		■	■	■
Analyzing language functions		■	■	■

For Part I, you will need skills in analyzing both pictures and answer choices. For Parts II, III, and IV, you will need to develop skills in analyzing answer choices, questions types, and language functions. Improving your skills in these areas will improve your TOEIC score.

Problems Analyzing Pictures

1. Making Assumptions
2. Identifying People
3. Identifying Things
4. Identifying Actions
5. Identifying General Locations
6. Identifying Specific Locations

Problems Analyzing Answer Choices

7. Similar Sounds
8. Related Words
9. Homonyms
10. Same Sound and Same Spelling But Different Meaning
11. Time
12. Negation
13. Word Order
14. Comparisons
15. Modals
16. *Used to*

Problems Analyzing Question Types

17. Questions Asking About People
18. Questions Asking About Someone's Occupation
19. Questions Asking About the Speakers' Relationship
20. Questions Asking About a Location
21. Questions Asking About Time
22. Questions Asking About an Activity
23. Questions Asking About an Event or Fact
24. Questions Asking About an Emotion
25. Questions Asking About a Reason
26. Questions Asking About Measurement
27. Questions Asking About an Opinion
28. Questions Asking About the Main Topic

Problems Analyzing Language Functions

29. Conditionals
30. Identifying Suggestions
31. Identifying Offers
32. Identifying Requests
33. Identifying Restatements

Problems Analyzing Pictures

1 Making Assumptions

You may have to *make assumptions* when you listen to the TOEIC test. These assumptions will be based on what you actually see in the picture. You will have to determine which of the four statements you hear is true or might be true. One statement (answer choice) will be true or will most likely be true. That choice will be the correct answer.

PROBLEM: The answer choices may all seem true.
SOLUTION: Listen carefully to the whole sentence and determine which one choice best matches the picture.

EXAMPLE

These statements are true.

This is a laboratory.
There are bottles on the shelves.
There is equipment on the counter.

The people are wearing protective clothing.
There are at least four people in the lab.
Wires run from the equipment.

These statements are probably true, but you can't tell for sure.

The people are lab technicians.	*They look like technicians, but they could be pharmacists.*
The people are students with a teacher.	*A teacher may be working with a class, or they may all be employees.*
The technicians are doing experiments.	*They might be doing experiments, or they might be producing some chemical compound.*

 Listen to Track 2 of compact disc 1 to hear the statements for Problems 1 through 7 of the Problems Analyzing Pictures section. The answers to these questions are on page 467. The transcript begins on page 573.

EXERCISE

Part I: Picture

Choose the statement that best describes what you see in the picture.

For more practice, look at the other pictures in this book and try to make assumptions about what you see.

18 LISTENING COMPREHENSION REVIEW

Identifying People

You may have to *identify the people* in a picture. You may identify them by number, gender, location, description, activity, or occupation.

PROBLEM: The people may be incorrectly identified.
SOLUTION: Determine the number, gender, location, description, activity, and occupation of the people as best you can.

Example

 Number: There are four people in the picture.
 Gender: There are two men and two women in the picture.
 Location: On the left, there are two men.
 On the right, there are two women.
Description: One of the men is wearing glasses.
 The woman on the right is shorter than the other woman.
 Activity: The group is looking at a map.
 One woman is pointing to the map.
 All four people are leaning on the table.
Occupation: Their profession is unknown. They are looking at and discussing a map. We can assume they are planners of some sort.

You may not be able to answer all questions. You may not know their occupation, for example. However, the more assumptions you can make, the easier it will be to answer the questions.

Exercise

Part I: Picture

Choose the statement that best describes what you see in the picture.

Ⓐ Ⓑ Ⓒ Ⓓ

For more practice, look at the other pictures in this book and try to identify the people you see in the pictures.

When you look at a picture, analyze the people. Determine their number, gender, location, occupation, etc. Be careful about statements that are not totally true.

20 LISTENING COMPREHENSION REVIEW

Identifying Things

You may have to *identify things* in a picture. When you look at a picture, try to name everything you see. On the TOEIC, you will NOT have to know words, expressions, or idioms that are specific to one particular occupation. For example, in a picture of a man working in a plastics factory, you should know the general word "machine." You do not have to know the occupation-specific term "extruder."

PROBLEM: You may not know the words needed to identify the things in the picture.
SOLUTION: Use the context of the picture to help you identify the things.

EXAMPLE

Find the following items in the picture. Keep in mind the context of the picture: It is a family scene, at home, in a living room or family room.

Words to Find			
mother	woman	painting	wall
father	parents	plant	door
son	curtains	sweater	door knob
daughter	TV	toys	skirt
boy	video recorder	hair	pants
girl	piano	eyes	TV stand
man	sheet music	carpet	chair

EXERCISE

Part I: Picture

Choose the statement that best describes what you see in the picture.

For more vocabulary practice, look at the other pictures in this book and try to name as many things as you can.

22 LISTENING COMPREHENSION REVIEW

Identifying Actions

You may have to *identify the actions* in a picture. When you look at a picture, analyze the time sequence of the actions. This will help you understand what is happening *now*.

PROBLEM: You may not understand what is happening in the picture.
SOLUTION: Use the context of the picture to help you make assumptions about what happened before, during, and after the action.

EXAMPLE

Past: The workers removed the earth.
Present: They are laying a pipe.
Future: They will cover the pipe with earth.

You know only what you see—the workers are laying a piece of pipe in a trench. Of course, they must have dug the trench, but you didn't see it. You can only assume it. They will probably cover the pipe with earth, but you won't see it. You can only assume it.

The more assumptions you can make, the easier it will be for you to answer the questions.

EXERCISE

Part I: Picture

Choose the statement that best describes what you see in the picture.

For more practice, look at the other pictures in this book and identify past, present, and future actions.

24 LISTENING COMPREHENSION REVIEW

5 Identifying General Locations

You may have to *identify the general location* of a picture. When you look at a picture, analyze the clues to determine a location. If you see a car, a mechanic, some tools, and a customer in a picture, you can assume the location is an automobile repair shop. If you see men and women working at desks with computers, you can assume the location is an office. A picture is full of clues to help you identify the general location.

PROBLEM: You may not understand where the action is taking place.
SOLUTION: Use the context of the picture to help you make assumptions about the general location.

EXAMPLE

The following is a list of context clues in the picture. You may hear these words or variations of these words in Part I. Pay attention—the words may differ on the actual test.

Context Clues	
Security checkpoint	Security officers
Departure information	Man with portable radiophone
Gate sign	Airline names
People with baggage	Names of destinations
Porter with luggage cart	Sign about X-ray
Security personnel	Uniformed personnel

EXERCISE

Part I: Picture

Choose the statement that best describes what you see in the picture.

   Ⓐ Ⓑ Ⓒ Ⓓ

For more practice, look at the other pictures in this book and find the clues that will help you identify the general location.

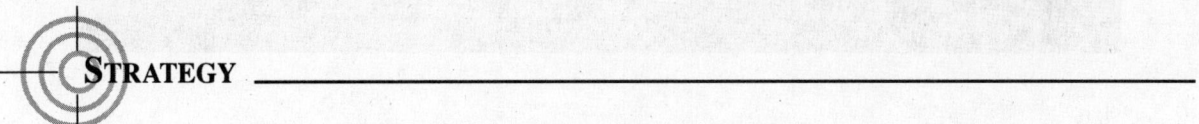

Use context clues to determine where the action is taking place.

26 LISTENING COMPREHENSION REVIEW

6 Identifying Specific Locations

You may have to *identify the specific location* of people and things in a picture. When you look at a picture, analyze the relationship of the people and things.

PROBLEM: The wrong preposition may be used to identify a location.
SOLUTION: Listen for the correct preposition.

EXAMPLES

Prepositions and Phrases of Location				
above	beneath	far from	near to	over
across	beside	in	next to	to the left of
around	between	in back of	on	to the right of
at	by	in front of	on top of	under
below	close to	inside	outside	underneath

EXERCISE

Part I: Picture

Choose the statement that best describes what you see in the picture.

Ⓐ Ⓑ Ⓒ Ⓓ

For more practice, look at the other pictures in this book and identify the specific location of each person or thing. You should also study the section on Prepositions in Chapter 3, Reading Review.

STRATEGY

Strategies for Analyzing Pictures

- When you look at a picture, analyze the people. Determine their number, gender, location, occupation, etc.
- Look for context clues in the picture.
- Listen for the meaning of the *whole sentence* to determine which choice best matches the picture.

Problems Analyzing Answer Choices

Problem 7: Similar Sounds

On the TOEIC, you may have to distinguish between words with *similar sounds*. When you hear the answer choices, pay attention to the meaning. There will be context clues that help you understand the meaning. Do not be confused by words with similar sounds.

PROBLEM: The answer choices contain words with similar sounds.
SOLUTION: Listen carefully to the *meaning* of the statement or question and determine which answer choice really answers the question.

EXAMPLES

Here are examples of similar sounds:

Different Vowel Sounds			
bass	car	deep	gun
base	core	dip	gone
boots	cart	fall	grass
boats	court	full	grease
bus	drug	fun	letter
boss	drag	phone	later

Different Initial Consonant Sounds			
back	core	race	hair
pack	tore	case	fair
rack	sore	place	tear

Different Final Consonant Sounds			
cab	little	nab	think
cap	litter	nap	thing

Two or More Words That Sound Like One Word			
mark it	sent her	letter	in tents
market	center	let her	intense

Words That Have Sounds That Are Part of a Longer Word			
nation	mind	give	intention
imagination	remind	forgive	unintentional

EXERCISES

Part I: Picture

Choose the statement that best describes what you see in the picture.

Ⓐ Ⓑ Ⓒ Ⓓ

Part II: Question-Response

Choose the best response to the question.

Ⓐ Ⓑ Ⓒ

Part III: Short Conversations

Choose the best answer to the question.

What does the woman enjoy?
(A) Wearing her new boots.
(B) Talking on the phone.
(C) Selling a new house.
(D) Sailing her boat.

Ⓐ Ⓑ Ⓒ Ⓓ

30 LISTENING COMPREHENSION REVIEW

Part IV: Short Talks

Choose the best answer to the question.

What does the man want people to do?   Ⓐ Ⓑ Ⓒ Ⓓ
(A) Mark all answers.
(B) Change clothes.
(C) Leave the store.
(D) Buy some plant seed.

Problem 8 Related Words

On the TOEIC, you may have to distinguish between *related words*. When you hear the answer choices, pay attention to the meaning. Be careful of words from the same word family or words with associated meanings.

Sometimes these related words may not be written down or spoken. They may be suggested by the picture. For example, a picture of someone putting on snow skis may make you think of the related word *mountain*, even if a mountain is not in the picture.

PROBLEM: The answer choices may contain words that are related to the context.
SOLUTION: Listen and look for the choice that completely answers the question or exactly matches the picture.

PROBLEMS ANALYZING ANSWER CHOICES / PROBLEM 8   31

EXAMPLES

These are some related words:

Airline				
ticket	pilot	reservation	baggage claim	check-in
seatbelt	flight attendant	ticket counter	crew	turbulence

Plants				
bud	seed	stem	flower	branch
root	leaf	blossom	bush	tree

Nature				
river	rural	mountain	country	field
stream	farm	brook	hill	lake

Weather				
sunny	cool	rain	drizzle	wind
cold	sleet	rainstorm	mist	breeze
freezing	warm	hot	cloudy	blizzard
snow	humid	smoggy	thunder	tornado
chilly	humidity	fog	lightning	hurricane

Energy				
oil	electricity	solar power	atomic energy	hydroelectric power
coal	gas	windmill	oil well	nuclear energy

STRATEGY

Listen and look for the *meaning* of the statement, question, and answer choices. Do not be confused by related words.

32 LISTENING COMPREHENSION REVIEW

EXERCISES

Part I: Picture

Listen to Track 3 of compact disc 1 to hear the statements for Problems 8 to 16.

Choose the statement that best describes what you see in the picture.

Ⓐ Ⓑ Ⓒ Ⓓ

Part II: Question-Response

Choose the best response to the question.

Ⓐ Ⓑ Ⓒ

Part III: Short Conversations

Choose the best answer to the question.

Where are the speakers?   Ⓐ Ⓑ Ⓒ Ⓓ
(A) In a car.
(B) In a plane.
(C) At sea.
(D) On a bus.

Part IV: Short Talks

Choose the best answer to the question.

What does this announcement concern?   Ⓐ Ⓑ Ⓒ Ⓓ
(A) Sporting events.
(B) Auto repair garages.
(C) Garden center hours.
(D) The weekend weather.

For more practice with related words, study Problem 1, Word Families, in Chapter 3, Reading Review.

Problem 9 Homonyms

On the TOEIC, you may have to determine whether the answer choices contain a word that is a *homonym*. Homonyms are words that are pronounced the same, but have different meanings and different spellings.

PROBLEM: A homonym may be used.
SOLUTION: Listen and look for the meaning of the word in the context of the picture, sentence, or conversation.

EXAMPLES

Homonyms				
week	for	male	seen	sowing
weak	four	mail	scene	sewing
wait	bear	sail	morning	steak
weight	bare	sale	mourning	stake
flour	steel	fare	threw	bough
flower	steal	fair	through	bow
plane	tale	rite	flew	due
plain	tail	right	flu	dew
too	feet	light	pale	sight
two	feat	lite	pail	site
to				

EXERCISES
Part I: Picture

Choose the statement that best describes what you see in the picture.

Ⓐ Ⓑ Ⓒ Ⓓ

Part II: Question-Response

Choose the best response to the question.

      (A) No, he's going tomorrow.
      (B) Yes, he's very weak.
      (C) The leaves are turning yellow.

Ⓐ Ⓑ Ⓒ

Part III: Short Conversations

Choose the best answer to the question.

Why can't the other man help?
    (A) The field is too wet to sow.
    (B) He's out of thyme.
    (C) He's too busy.
    (D) There are only four buttons.

Ⓐ Ⓑ Ⓒ Ⓓ

Part IV: Short Talks

Choose the best answer to the question.

What is the man talking about?
    (A) Whether to buy two storm windows.
    (B) The weather.
    (C) His son.
    (D) The reign of the king.

Ⓐ Ⓑ Ⓒ Ⓓ

Problem 10: Same Sound and Same Spelling But Different Meaning

On the TOEIC, you may have to distinguish between *words that have the same sound and same spelling but have a different meaning*. When you hear the answer choices, pay attention to the meaning. Be careful of words with the same sounds and same spellings, but with different meanings.

PROBLEM: A word that sounds like the correct word may be used.
SOLUTION: Listen and look at the context for the word that answers the question.

EXAMPLES

Different Meanings for the Same Word				
Call:	Animal or bird noise		*File:*	Folder
	Shout			Row
	Telephone call			Tool
Class:	Social position		*Hard:*	Difficult
	Group of students			Tough
	Level of quality			Firm
Court:	Tennis court		*Note:*	Musical note
	Court of law			Short letter
	Royal court			Currency
Date:	Type of fruit		*Seat:*	A chair
	Meeting with someone			Location of power
	Particular day			Membership in a club

PROBLEMS ANALYZING ANSWER CHOICES / PROBLEM 10   37

EXERCISES

Part I: Picture

Choose the statement that best describes what you see in the picture.

Ⓐ Ⓑ Ⓒ Ⓓ

Part II: Question-Response

Choose the best response to the question.

Ⓐ Ⓑ Ⓒ Ⓓ

Part III: Short Conversations

Choose the best answer to the question.

What will the man do?   Ⓐ Ⓑ Ⓒ Ⓓ
   (A) Call the woman on the phone.
   (B) Give her an engagement ring.
   (C) Take a summer vacation.
   (D) Call the woman names.

38 LISTENING COMPREHENSION REVIEW

Part IV: Short Talks

Choose the best answer to the question.

What does the man suggest people do?   Ⓐ Ⓑ Ⓒ Ⓓ
- (A) Get married at Forest Lawn.
- (B) See a tennis game.
- (C) Go to a night club.
- (D) Not use the last match.

Problem 11 Time

On the TOEIC, you may have to determine the sequence of time. When you hear the answer choices, pay attention to the meaning. Listen for time markers, which will help you determine the order of events.

PROBLEM: You may not hear or see a time marker.
SOLUTION: Listen and look for the time marker.

EXAMPLES

The following chart shows sequence time markers. The sentences below the chart illustrate sequences of events.

Happened before	Happened close to the same time	Happened after
before prior to until preceding no later than already	when while during as soon as as	after once then afterwards following and

The manager <u>cleared his desk</u> <u>before he left</u>.

             1st   2nd
What happened first?   He cleared his desk.
What happened next?   He left.
What happened before he left?   He cleared his desk.

The <u>mail was sorted</u> <u>as soon as it arrived</u>.

             2nd   1st
What happened first?   The mail arrived.
What happened next?   It was sorted.
What happened as the mail arrived? It was sorted.

PROBLEMS ANALYZING ANSWER CHOICES / PROBLEM 11   39

EXERCISES

Part I: Picture

Choose the statement that best describes what you see in the picture.

Ⓐ Ⓑ Ⓒ Ⓓ

Part II: Question-Response

Choose the best response to the question.

Ⓐ Ⓑ Ⓒ

40 LISTENING COMPREHENSION REVIEW

Part III: Short Conversations

Choose the best answer to the question.

When did the man decide? Ⓐ Ⓑ Ⓒ Ⓓ
(A) Before he heard about the competition.
(B) Long after he heard about the competition.
(C) As soon as he heard about the competition.
(D) Shortly after he heard about the competition.

Part IV: Short Talks

Choose the best answer to the question.

How long has Mr. Saleh been Chairman? Ⓐ Ⓑ Ⓒ Ⓓ
(A) Until next quarter.
(B) About twenty years.
(C) For five years.
(D) Since his retirement.

Problem 12 Negation

On the TOEIC, you may have to determine whether a statement is positive or *negative*. When you hear the answer choices, pay attention to the meaning. Listen for "negative markers" which will help you determine if the sense of the statement is positive or negative. Look for negative markers in the answer choices.

Remember that a negative prefix contradicts the word it joins. This usually results in a negative meaning. For example, *unfriendly* contradicts *friendly* and has the negative meaning *not friendly*. But when a negative prefix is added to a negative word, the resulting meaning can be positive. For example, *unselfish* contradicts *selfish* and has the positive meaning *not selfish*.

PROBLEM: You cannot tell whether a statement is positive or negative.
SOLUTION: Listen and look for a negative marker.

EXAMPLES

The following table lists common negative markers.

Before verbs/clauses	Before nouns/phrases	Negative prefixes	Positive meaning from negative prefixes
not isn't/can't/ doesn't/won't shouldn't/couldn't/hasn't mustn't rarely/only rarely hardly scarcely seldom never barely not since not until and neither . . .	no nowhere nothing at no time not at this time in no case by no means	un- undone im- impossible il- illegal in- definite non- nonsense	unlimited unparalleled invaluable nonrestrictive nonviolence

Remember: Having two negative expressions in a sentence makes the sentence positive. For example, *This is not illegal* means *This is legal*.

42 LISTENING COMPREHENSION REVIEW

EXERCISES

Part I: Picture

Choose the statement that best describes what you see in the picture.

Ⓐ Ⓑ Ⓒ Ⓓ

Part II: Question-Response

Choose the best response to the question.

Ⓐ Ⓑ Ⓒ

Part III: Short Conversations

Choose the best answer to the question.

What does the man advise the woman?   Ⓐ Ⓑ Ⓒ Ⓓ
(A) Take more than she needs.
(B) Take less than she needs.
(C) Buy what she needs later.
(D) Take only what she needs.

Part IV: Short Talks

Choose the best answer to the question.

What word or phrase describes this report? Ⓐ Ⓑ Ⓒ Ⓓ
- (A) Extremely positive.
- (B) Extremely negative.
- (C) Unenthusiastic.
- (D) Mediocre.

Problem 13 Word Order

On the TOEIC, you may need to pay attention to the *word order* to determine whether a sentence is a question or a statement, or is positive or negative. When you hear the answer choices, pay attention to the word order. Note the placement of the subject and the auxiliary verb.

PROBLEM: You may not be able to tell whether the sentence is a question or a statement or is positive or negative.

SOLUTION: Listen and look for the word order.

EXAMPLES

What a big boy you are!	means	*You are a very big boy.*
Never has this room been so crowded.	means	*This room has never been so crowded.* and *There are a lot of people in this room.*

44 LISTENING COMPREHENSION REVIEW

EXERCISES

Part I: Picture

Choose the statement that best describes what you see in the picture.

Ⓐ Ⓑ Ⓒ Ⓓ

Part II: Question-Response

Choose the best response to the question.

Ⓐ Ⓑ Ⓒ

Part III: Short Conversations

Choose the best answer to the question.

What does the woman think about the trip?
(A) It will be long.
(B) It will be exciting.
(C) She doesn't envy the man.
(D) It will not be as great as he thinks.

Part IV: Short Talks

Choose the best answer to the question.

What describes the weather this morning?
(A) Unchanged.
(B) Hot.
(C) Still.
(D) Very windy.

Problem 14 Comparisons

On the TOEIC, you may need to determine whether words are being *compared*. It is important to know the relationship between two things or actions.

PROBLEM: You cannot determine the relationship between things being compared.
SOLUTION: Look for "comparison markers."

EXAMPLES

The following table shows three types of comparison markers.

COMPARISON MARKERS Three degrees of comparison	EXAMPLES
Positive tall expensive *Comparative* taller more expensive *Superlative* tallest most expensive	This brand of fax paper is expensive. The fax paper is more expensive. This third brand is the most expensive.
Comparisons of equals	
as ... as	Your office is as large as mine.
not as ... as	This window is not as dirty as that one.
not as many ... as ... not as much ... as ...	There are not as many seats as we need.
Double comparative	
The + (comparative) ... the + (comparative)	The less you work, the less you will earn. The more you travel, the less time you will have at home.

PROBLEMS ANALYZING ANSWER CHOICES / PROBLEM 14   47

EXERCISES
Part I: Picture

Choose the statement that best describes what you see in the picture.

Ⓐ Ⓑ Ⓒ Ⓓ

Part II: Question-Response

Choose the best response to the question.

Ⓐ Ⓑ Ⓒ

48 LISTENING COMPREHENSION REVIEW

Part III: Short Conversations

Choose the best answer to the question.

What do they think about the meeting?   Ⓐ Ⓑ Ⓒ Ⓓ
- (A) It's not long enough.
- (B) It will begin soon.
- (C) It's not very interesting.
- (D) It will end soon.

Part IV: Short Talks

Choose the best answer to the question.

What is said about roads and cars?   Ⓐ Ⓑ Ⓒ Ⓓ
- (A) Fewer people drive nowadays.
- (B) The number of cars will increase as roads improve.
- (C) There will be less cars on the roads in the future.
- (D) There are fewer good roads today.

Problem 15 Modals

On the TOEIC, you may need to determine how *modals* affect the meaning of the statement, conversation, or talk.

PROBLEM: You may not hear the modal.
SOLUTION: Listen carefully for the modal.

EXAMPLES

The following charts show modals, their meanings, and specific sentences using them.

Modal	Meaning	Examples
can	present ability permission (informal) possibility	She can use the new phone system. They can leave when they want. The machine can be on. *(continued)*

Modal	Meaning	Examples
could	past ability	They could not understand how to send a fax until they were trained.
	permission (polite)	Could you come in, please?
	possibility	The train could be late.
may/might	permission	May I interrupt, please?
	possibility	They may/might sign the contract.
should	advisability	He should work harder.
	logical conclusion	It should be cooler in the refrigerated room.
must	necessity	Everyone must register at the door.
	probability	Here's a reply to my fax; she must have sent it immediately.
	authority/requirement	
have to/ have got to	necessity	We have to pick up the files before the meeting.
ought to	obligation (spoken English) generally	They ought to be more positive in their response.
will	future	I will deliver this for you tonight.
	polite request	Will you reserve a table for two at 8:00?
	polite refusal	I will not be able to accept your invitation.
would	past habit	She would park in the same location every day.
	polite request	Would you be available for a meeting at 2:00?
	polite refusal	They would not agree to our terms.
had better	advisability	Your presentation is in ten minutes. You had better get ready.
had rather	preference	He'd rather memorize his speech than use notes.

Past form of modal	Meaning	Examples
may/might have + (past participle)	past possibility (action may not have occurred)	She may have sent the package by regular mail. We aren't sure.
should have + (past participle)	advisable action (action did not occur)	He should have signed for the shipment.
ought to have + (past participle)	advisable action (action did not occur)	We ought to have made a reservation.

(continued)

50 LISTENING COMPREHENSION REVIEW

Past form of modal	Meaning	Examples
must have + (past participle)	probability	We cannot wait any longer; he must have missed the train.
would have + (past participle)	past intention (unfulfilled)	They would have ordered more supplies.
could have + (past participle)	past possibility (action may or may not have occurred)	The designer could have used color photographs in the annual report, but it would have cost more.

EXERCISES

Part I: Picture

Choose the statement that best describes what you see in the picture.

Ⓐ Ⓑ Ⓒ Ⓓ

Part II: Question-Response

Choose the best response to the question.

Ⓐ Ⓑ Ⓒ

Part III: Short Conversations

Choose the best answer to the question.

Did the woman go to the reception? Ⓐ Ⓑ Ⓒ Ⓓ
   (A) She didn't go, because she was busy.
   (B) She went because she had nothing else to do.
   (C) She went because there was no charge.
   (D) She didn't go, because there was an admission fee.

Part IV: Short Talks

Choose the best answer to the question.

How does this critique describe the presentation? Ⓐ Ⓑ Ⓒ Ⓓ
   (A) Interesting.
   (B) Confusing.
   (C) Visually exciting.
   (D) Colorful.

Problem 16 *Used to*

On the TOEIC, you may have to determine from context which meaning of *used to* is correct. One form means habitual action and the other means to be accustomed to something.

PROBLEM: You don't know which meaning of *used to* is correct.
SOLUTION: Listen for a form of the verb *be*. If a form of *be* appears, the meaning is *accustomed to*.

52 LISTENING COMPREHENSION REVIEW

EXAMPLES

Modal form	Meaning	Examples
used to	habitual action	We used to have a staff meeting every Friday.
be used to *be* used to ... -ing	be accustomed to be accustomed to	They are used to long flights. She is used to working without lunch.

EXERCISES

Part I: Picture

Choose the statement that best describes what you see in the picture.

Ⓐ Ⓑ Ⓒ Ⓓ

Part II: Question-Response

Choose the best response to the question.

Ⓐ Ⓑ Ⓒ

Part III: Short Conversations

Choose the best answer to the question.

What does the man say about himself? (A) (B) (C) (D)
   (A) He recently started giving more speeches.
   (B) He often gave presentations at conferences.
   (C) He never speaks in public.
   (D) He can't think of anything people want to hear.

Part IV: Short Talks

Choose the best answer to the question.

What changes did the photocopier bring about? (A) (B) (C) (D)
   (A) People no longer use carbon paper.
   (B) People don't write as much.
   (C) People don't type as well.
   (D) People are not yet used to making many copies.

STRATEGY

Strategies for Analyzing Answer Choices

- Listen and look for context clues.
- Listen and look for the *meaning* of the statement, question, and answer choices. Do not be confused by similar sounds, homonyms, related words, etc.
- Listen and look for sequence time markers, negative markers, and comparison markers.
- Pay attention to word order.
- Listen and look for modals and determine how the modal affects the meaning.

Problems Analyzing Question Types

Problem 17: Questions Asking About People

Most questions about people begin with *who* or *what*. These questions are generally answered by a person's title, occupation, or relationship to another person.

In Parts III and IV, the speakers are identified most frequently by their occupational titles or their relationship to one another. This will be discussed more completely in the following sections.

PROBLEM: The question asks about people.

SOLUTION: Look for names or group terms (*class*, *family*, *tourists*) in the answer choices BEFORE you hear the audio.

EXAMPLES

If you see or hear these question types, look or listen for answers about people.

Common Questions	
Questions with *what*	Questions with *who*
What is your name?	Who is taking part in this conversation?
What is her title?	Who is the man?
	Who is the woman?
	Who are the speakers?

If you see or hear these answers, the question may be about people.

Common Answers		
Proper names	Identification by activity or role	Identification by group
Mr. Tanza	A tourist	Business people
Mrs. Green	A passenger	Family members
Ms. Hu	A driver	College students
Dr. Shapiro	A jogger	

Listen to Track 4 of compact disc 1 to hear the statements for Problems 17 to 24.

EXERCISES

Part II: Question-Response

Choose the best response to the question.

Ⓐ Ⓑ Ⓒ

Part III: Short Conversations

Choose the best answer to the question.

        Who are the speakers?   Ⓐ Ⓑ Ⓒ Ⓓ
        (A) Lifeguards at the beach.
        (B) Painters.
        (C) Salespeople selling coats.
        (D) Bartenders.

Part IV: Short Talks

Choose the best answer to the question.

        Who is listening to this announcement?   Ⓐ Ⓑ Ⓒ Ⓓ
        (A) Migrant workers.
        (B) Airline passengers.
        (C) Gas station attendants.
        (D) Customs officers.

Problem 18: Questions Asking About Someone's Occupation

Questions about a person's occupation are commonly asked on the TOEIC. You should first look at the answer choices to see what four occupations are given. Then you should try to think of words related to those occupations. These words will be clues.

It is important to listen for occupational clues in the conversations and short talks. If a person is an auto mechanic, you might hear references to engines, cars, oil, brakes, gas stations, etc. If you hear those words, it is likely that the correct answer is *auto mechanic*.

56 LISTENING COMPREHENSION REVIEW

PROBLEM: The question asks about a speaker's occupation.
SOLUTION: Look for types of occupations in the answer choices BEFORE you hear the audio. Make assumptions about those occupations and listen for the clues.

EXAMPLES

If you see or hear these question types, look or listen for answers about someone's occupation.

Common Questions
What kind of job does the man have?   What is Mr. Smith's present position?
What type of work does the woman do?   How does this man earn a living?
What is the man's job?   What kind of job is available?
What is the woman's occupation?   Who can benefit from seeing this memo?
What is the man's profession?   Who was interviewed?
What does this woman do?   Who would most likely use the conference hall?

The answers to those questions are usually job titles. If you see or hear answers like these, look or listen for questions about someone's occupation.

Common Answers
Architect   Psychologist   Telephone installer
Housekeeper   Operator   Receptionist
Secretary   Travel agent   Teacher
Political advisor   Information clerk   Office manager
Chemist   Railroad conductor   Reporter
Driving instructor   Manager   Accountant
Theater employee   Personnel director   Chairman of the Board
Police officer   Sales representative   Branch manager
Sign painter   Technician   Professor of Mathematics
Reporter   Hotel clerk   Senior Vice-President
Novelist   Telegraph agent
Pilot   Flight attendant

EXERCISES

Part II: Question-Response

Choose the best response to the question.

Ⓐ Ⓑ Ⓒ

Part III: Short Conversations

Choose the best answer to the question.

What is the woman's occupation?   Ⓐ Ⓑ Ⓒ Ⓓ
- (A) Running coach.
- (B) Baseball player.
- (C) Telephone operator.
- (D) Telephone installer.

Part IV: Short Talks

Choose the best answer to the question.

Who will listen to this announcement?   Ⓐ Ⓑ Ⓒ Ⓓ
- (A) Chefs.
- (B) Restaurant patrons.
- (C) School children in a cafeteria.
- (D) Guests at a dinner party.

Problem 19: Questions Asking About the Speakers' Relationship

Questions about the speakers' relationship are also commonly asked on the TOEIC. You should first look at the answer choices to see what four relationships are given. Then you should try to think of words related to those relationships. These words will be clues.

It is important to listen for relationship clues in the conversations and short talks. If a person is a family member, you might hear references to *mother*, *father*, *aunt*, etc. If you hear those words, it is likely that the correct answer is *family member*.

PROBLEM: The question asks about the speakers' relationship.
SOLUTION: Look for types of relationships in the answer choices BEFORE you hear the audio. Make assumptions about those relationships and listen for the clues.

EXAMPLES

If you see or hear these question types, look or listen for answers about the speakers' relationship.

Common Questions
What is the relationship between the speakers?
What is the relationship between the man and the woman?
What is the relationship of the man to the woman?
What is the relationship of the woman to the man?

The answers to those questions usually indicate a professional or personal relationship. If you see or hear answers like these, look or listen for questions about the speakers' relationship.

Common Answers	
Professional relationship	Personal relationship
Employer and employee	Brother
Professor and pupil	Uncle
Doctor and patient	Father
Lawyer and client	Cousin
Waiter and customer	Sister
Bank manager and customer	Aunt
Librarian and patron	Mother
Teacher and student	Husband
Salesperson and customer	Wife
Colleagues	Friend

EXERCISES

Part II: Question-Response

Choose the best response to the question.

Ⓐ Ⓑ Ⓒ

Part III: Short Conversations

Choose the best answer to the question.

What is the relationship of the speakers?
 (A) Banker and client.
 (B) Accountant and cashier.
 (C) Waiter and customer.
 (D) Coffee grower and bean picker.

Ⓐ Ⓑ Ⓒ Ⓓ

Part IV: Short Talks

Choose the best answer to the question.

What two people might pay attention to this message? (A) (B) (C) (D)
(A) Librarian and patron.
(B) Author and publisher.
(C) Police officer and speeder.
(D) Bookseller and customer.

Problem 20: Questions Asking About a Location

Most questions about location begin with *where*. These questions are generally answered by locations preceded by *in*, *on*, or *at*.

PROBLEM: The question asks about location.
SOLUTION: Look for prepositions of location (such as *in*, *on*, or *at*) in the answers BEFORE you hear the audio. Listen carefully for those prepositions in the audio.

EXAMPLES

If you see or hear these question types, look or listen for answers about the speakers' location. Note the questions will begin with *where*.

Common Questions	
Where did the conversation probably take place? Where did the conversation likely occur?	Where has the man/woman been? Where does the man/woman want to go? Where did the man/woman come from?
Where is the man? Where is the woman? Where is the speaker?	Where are they going? Where did the man think the woman was?
Where are the man and woman? Where are the speakers?	Where should he call?

The answers to those questions usually indicate a location. The location can be identified either with or without a preposition. If you see or hear answers like these, look or listen for questions about the speakers' location.

Common Answers		
Without prepositions The train station. The store. The office. The house.	With prepositions On the bus. At the movies. In Union Station. In a city office building.	On a tennis court. In an architect's office. In a banker's office. In a lawyer's office.

EXERCISES

Part II: Question-Response

Choose the best response to the question.

Ⓐ Ⓑ Ⓒ

Part III: Short Conversations

Choose the best answer to the question.

Where did he put the letter? Ⓐ Ⓑ Ⓒ Ⓓ
(A) On the shelf.
(B) Under the books.
(C) On top of the books on the desk.
(D) In the drawer.

Part IV: Short Talks

Choose the best answer to the question.

Where should you put your initials? Ⓐ Ⓑ Ⓒ Ⓓ
(A) At the bottom of the communication.
(B) Next to your name.
(C) Under your name.
(D) On every list.

PROBLEM 21: Questions Asking About Time

Most questions about time begin with *when* or *how long*. These questions are generally answered by time of day, days of the week, seasons, and dates. The answers give a specific time or a duration. Some answers are in adverbial clauses:

When can I have breakfast?

You can have breakfast
{ whenever you want.
  when you get up.
  as soon as the coffee is ready. }

PROBLEM: The question asks about time.

SOLUTION: Look for clues on time in the answer choices BEFORE you hear the audio. Listen carefully for those clues in the audio.

EXAMPLES

If you see or hear these question types, look or listen for answers about time. Note the questions begin with *when* and *how*.

Common Questions	
Questions with *When*	**Questions with *How***
When did the conversation take place?	How long will the manager live in Tokyo?
When is the man's birthday?	How long will it take to arrive?
When is the woman's vacation date?	How often is the magazine published?
When is the restaurant open?	How many weeks were most people away each year?
When was the meeting?	
When will the increase go into effect?	
When did he join the firm?	

The answers to those questions usually indicate a time. The time can be identified either with or without a preposition. It can be a specific moment or a duration. It can be a time, a day, a date, a season, a year. If you see or hear answers like these, look or listen for questions about time.

Common Answers			
11:00 A.M.	In January.	1946.	This week.
Noon.	In February.	1964.	This month.
3:00 P.M.	January 3.	1914.	Next week.
Midnight.	February 14.	1916.	Next month.
At 6:00.	January 3 of this year.	In the summer.	On weekday evenings.
Before 5:30.	January 30 of next year.	In the fall.	Any evening from 6:30 to 8:30.
After 8:00.		In the spring.	
Sunday.	On January 3rd.	Tomorrow.	
Monday.	On February 14th.	Yesterday.	
Tuesday.			

STRATEGY

Remember that questions about time generally begin with *when, how often, how many days,* or *how long.*

EXERCISES

Part II: Question-Response

Choose the best response to the question.

(A) (B) (C)

Part III: Short Conversations

Choose the best answer to the question.

How much longer will the man stay? (A) (B) (C) (D)
- (A) 10 minutes.
- (B) 15 minutes.
- (C) 30 minutes.
- (D) 60 minutes.

Note that the times are listed in ascending order, with the smallest number first. This will help you find the number you are looking for faster.

Part IV: Short Talks

Choose the best answer to the question.

How often has it snowed? (A) (B) (C) (D)
- (A) Every hour.
- (B) Daily.
- (C) Only once last week.
- (D) Twice a month.

Problem 22: Questions Asking About an Activity

Most questions about activities begin with *what*. Some questions can begin with *how*. These questions are generally answered by short phrases or complete sentences. You should first look at the answer choices to see what four activities are given. Then you should try to think of words related to those activities. These words will be activity clues.

It is important to listen for activity clues in the conversations and short talks. For example, the activity playing golf might have words such as *golf club*, *bag*, *course*, *fairway*, *hole*, and *green* in the audio.

PROBLEM: The question asks about activities.
SOLUTION: Look for types of activities in the answer choices BEFORE you hear the audio. Make assumptions about those activities and listen for the clues.

EXAMPLES

If you see or hear these question types, look or listen for answers about an activity. Note the questions begin with *what* and *how*.

Common Questions	
Questions with *to Do*	Questions about an event or occurrence
What will the man do?	What happened?
What did the woman do?	What occurred?
What has the customer decided to do?	What took place?
What are they planning to do?	What happened to the woman?
What does the woman have to do?	What will happen next?
What is the man going to do?	
What is Mrs. Park supposed to do?	Questions with *How*
What are they doing?	How can the package be sent?
	How will the room be changed?

The answers to those questions usually indicate an activity. The activity can be identified either in a phrase or a complete sentence. It can be a specific event or represent a method. If you see or hear answers like these, look or listen for questions about an activity.

64 LISTENING COMPREHENSION REVIEW

Common Answers	
Activities in phrases See a movie. Go out for lunch. Take a Spanish course. Play golf. Attend tonight's lecture. Finish the proposal. Take the day off. Read the fax. **Activities in complete sentences** They will go out for dinner. He will send a fax. She should call her office.	**Events or occurrences** The car stopped. The conference let out early. The chemical tanker arrived on schedule. She was late for the meeting. The phone lines were out of service. **Method or manner** By overnight mail. By express mail. By messenger. By courier. By moving the desk. By painting the walls. By covering the windows. By adding more light.

EXERCISES

Part II: Question-Response

Choose the best response to the question.

Ⓐ Ⓑ Ⓒ

Part III: Short Conversations

Choose the best answer to the question.

What are they doing?
(A) Taking a walk.
(B) Taking a nap.
(C) Buying a map.
(D) Driving a car.

Ⓐ Ⓑ Ⓒ Ⓓ

Part IV: Short Talks

Choose the best answer to the question.

What will happen if it rains?
(A) The picnic will be rescheduled.
(B) The office cafeteria will be closed.
(C) The mail will not be delivered.
(D) The picnic will be held inside.

Ⓐ Ⓑ Ⓒ Ⓓ

Problem 23: Questions Asking About an Event or Fact

Most questions about events begin with *what*. These questions are generally answered by phrases or complete sentences. The strategy for these questions is similar to the strategies for the previous questions. Read the answer choices, make some assumptions about the events listed, and listen for the relevant clues.

PROBLEM: The question asks about events.
SOLUTION: Look for clues on events or facts in the answer choices BEFORE you hear the audio. Listen carefully for those clues in the audio.

EXAMPLES

If you see or hear these question types, look or listen for answers about an event or fact. Note that the questions begin with *what*.

Common Questions	
What is the conversation about?	What happens if they don't like the movie?
What are they talking about?	What is unusual about this event?
What are they discussing?	What was the outcome of the meeting?

The answers to those questions are usually events or facts. They can be in phrases or short sentences. If you see or hear answers like these, look or listen for questions about an event or fact.

Common Answers	
Phrases	Sentences
Cost of insurance.	It's free.
Shipping fees.	They can leave.
Overdue accounts.	The companies decided not to merge.
Methods of delivery.	

EXERCISES

Part II: Question-Response

Choose the best response to the question.

Ⓐ Ⓑ Ⓒ

Part III: Short Conversations

Choose the best answer to the question.

🔘 What will happen if the goods don't clear customs?   Ⓐ Ⓑ Ⓒ Ⓓ
(A) Production will be postponed.
(B) The advertisers will complain.
(C) More customs duty will be paid.
(D) They will wait until Friday.

Part IV: Short Talks

Choose the best answer to the question.

🔘 What is unusual about this past week?   Ⓐ Ⓑ Ⓒ Ⓓ
(A) The earthquakes in all regions.
(B) The absence of disasters.
(C) The large number of disasters.
(D) The blizzard in the South.

Problem 24 — Questions Asking About an Emotion

Most questions about an emotion begin with *what* or *how*. These questions are generally answered by single words or phrases.

PROBLEM: The question asks about emotions.
SOLUTION: Look for clues on emotions in the answer choices BEFORE you hear the audio. Listen carefully for those clues.

EXAMPLES

If you see or hear these question types, look or listen for answers about an emotion. Note that the questions begin with *what* or *how*.

Common Questions
What is the man's mood?
What is the woman angry about?
How does the speaker feel?

The answers to those questions are usually emotions or feelings. Usually single words answer the questions about moods and feelings, and short phrases answer the questions about the cause of the emotion. If you see or hear answers like these, look or listen for questions about an emotion.

Common Answers		
Emotion or feeling	Frustrated.	Shocked.
Afraid.	Full.	Sick.
Angry.	Happy.	Sleepy.
Annoyed.	Hot.	Surprised.
Ashamed.	Hungry.	Thirsty.
Bored.	Ill.	Unhappy.
Cold.	Jealous.	Upset.
Confused.	Mad.	Worried.
Disappointed.	Miserable.	
Disgusted.	Nervous.	Cause of emotion or feeling
Ecstatic.	Pleased.	His job.
Embarrassed.	Proud.	Leaving home.
Exhausted.	Sad.	Being alone.

STRATEGY

Read the answer choices, make assumptions about the emotions listed, and listen for the relevant choices.

EXERCISES

Part II: Question-Response

Choose the best response to the question.

Ⓐ Ⓑ Ⓒ

Part III: Short Conversations

Choose the best answer to the question.

How do the speakers feel? Ⓐ Ⓑ Ⓒ Ⓓ
(A) Hungry.
(B) Worried.
(C) Angry.
(D) Lost.

68 LISTENING COMPREHENSION REVIEW

Part IV: Short Talks

Choose the best answer to the question.

Why are the neighbors upset?   Ⓐ Ⓑ Ⓒ Ⓓ
(A) There is no parking for them.
(B) Cars are parked on their property.
(C) Employees leave early.
(D) No one waters the lawns.

Problem 25: Questions Asking About a Reason

Most questions about reasons begin with *why*. Sometimes the question can begin with *what*. These questions are generally answered by complete sentences, but sometimes by short phrases. Use the same strategies that you have been using for the other question types.

PROBLEM: The question asks about a reason.
SOLUTION: Look for clues on reasons in the answer choices BEFORE you hear the audio. Listen carefully for those clues.

EXAMPLES

If you see or hear these question types, look or listen for answers about a reason. Note that most of the questions begin with *why*.

Common Questions	
Why did the man come?	Why is she going by taxi?
Why did the woman come?	Why is he going by train?
Why did the man leave?	Why is she going by car?
Why did the woman leave?	What does the man say about the delay?
Why does he need a typewriter?	What did she request?
Why does she need a map?	

The answers to these questions are usually in complete sentences, but are sometimes in short phrases. If you see or hear answers like these, look or listen for questions about a reason.

Common Answers
He wanted to take a tour. A taxi is faster than the train. She wanted to pick up the package. The train goes directly to New York. He didn't have a reservation. It will be only ten more minutes. He needs to write a letter. More justification for expenses. She needs directions to the conference.

Listen to Track 5 of compact disc 1 to hear the statements for Problems 25 to 33.

EXERCISES

Part II: Question-Response

Choose the best response to the question.

Ⓐ Ⓑ Ⓒ

Part III: Short Conversations

Choose the best answer to the question.

Why don't they travel by car? Ⓐ Ⓑ Ⓒ Ⓓ
  (A) It's being repaired.
  (B) They like to read while traveling.
  (C) The train is cheaper.
  (D) They need to get to work faster.

Part IV: Short Talks

Choose the best answer to the question.

Why is there a delay? Ⓐ Ⓑ Ⓒ Ⓓ
  (A) Workers are staging a work action.
  (B) Bad weather.
  (C) Flight control problems.
  (D) Passengers are boarding slowly.

Problem 26: Questions Asking About Measurement

The way things are measured in American English may be different than the way things are measured in British, Canadian, or Australian English. Since the TOEIC is an international test, it is important to understand the different measurement systems that might be encountered on the TOEIC.

PROBLEM: The question asks about measurement.
SOLUTION: Listen carefully for numbers and words that indicate a mathematical calculation.

EXAMPLES

Look at these words that express measurements and their equivalents:

Common Measurements	
Temperature	
Fahrenheit	Centigrade
32 degrees	0 degrees
212 degrees (water boils)	100 degrees (water boils)
Distance	
Foot	Meter
1 inch	2.54 centimeters
1 yard	0.9144 meter
1 mile	1.609 kilometers
12 inches	1 foot
3 feet	1 yard
Quantity	
1 dozen	12 units
1 baker's dozen	13 units
1 half dozen	6 units
1 ounce	28.350 grams
1 pound	453.59237 grams
1 US ton = 2000 pounds	0.907 metric ton of 907 kilograms
1 British ton = 2240 pounds	0.1016 metric ton or 1016 kilograms
1 cup	8 ounces
2 cups	1 pint
4 cups	1 quart
8 cups	1/2 gallon
16 cups	1 gallon

(continued)

Common Measurements

Fluid measurement

1 ounce	29.573 milliliters
1 pint	0.473 liter
1 quart	0.946 liter
1 gallon	3.785 liters
1 imperial gallon	4.55 liters

Dry measurement

pint	0.551 liter
quart	8.810 liter

Money

penny	1 cent
nickel	5 cents
dime	10 cents
quarter	25 cents
half dollar	50 cents
dollar	100 cents

100 pennies	dollar
20 nickels	dollar
10 dimes	dollar
4 quarters	dollar
2 half dollars	dollar

Time

60 seconds	minute
60 minutes	1 hour
24 hours	1 day
noon	12:00 midday
midnight	24:00 in the night

Morning: 6 A.M. to Noon
Afternoon: Noon to 6 P.M.
Evening: 6 P.M. to 10 P.M.
Night: 10 P.M. to 6 A.M.

Average seasonal weather in the United States

Spring	March 21 to June 20 (temperate)
Summer	June 21 to September 20 (hot)
Autumn (fall)	September 21 to December 20 (cool)
Winter	December 21 to March 20 (cold)

LISTENING COMPREHENSION REVIEW

Look at these words that indicate a mathematical calculation.

Common Mathematical Calculations	
twice	100 becomes 200
three times	100 becomes 300
half as much	100 becomes 50
twice as much	100 becomes 200
half as much again	100 becomes 150
half off	100 becomes 50
third off	100 becomes 66.66
10% off	100 becomes 90
per hour	$100 for 6 hours becomes $600
per day	$100 for 3 days becomes $300

STRATEGY

Although you are not tested on your mathematical ability, you may have to perform simple math calculations. Listen carefully for words that indicate division, multiplication, addition, or subtraction.

You hear: Bob bought a half-dozen eggs.
Question: How many eggs did he buy?
Answer: 6

You hear: The door is 30 inches wide and the window is twice as wide as the door.
Question: How wide is the window?
Answer: 60 inches wide (5 feet wide)

These two examples test your understanding of the words *half*, *dozen*, and *twice*.

EXERCISES

Part II: Question-Response

Choose the best response to the question.

Ⓐ Ⓑ Ⓒ

Part III: Short Conversations

Choose the best answer to the question.

What do they think about the weather? Ⓐ Ⓑ Ⓒ Ⓓ
(A) It's cool.
(B) It's very warm.
(C) It's really cold.
(D) It's hot.

Part IV: Short Talks

Choose the best answer to the question.

What is the potential discount on an order of $200? Ⓐ Ⓑ Ⓒ Ⓓ
(A) $10
(B) $15
(C) $20
(D) $25

Problem 27: Questions Asking About an Opinion

Most questions about opinions begin with *what*. These questions are generally answered by complete sentences that begin with *it* or clauses that begin with *that*. Some opinion questions begin with an auxiliary. These *yes/no* questions are answered with *yes* or *no*. Use the same strategies that you have been using for the other question types.

PROBLEM: The question asks about opinions.
SOLUTION: Look for clues on opinions in the answers BEFORE you hear the audio. Listen carefully for those clues.

EXAMPLES

If you see or hear these question types, look or listen for answers about an opinion.

Common Questions	
What questions What did the man think about the play? What did the speaker think about the talk? What did the woman say about the presentation? What was the matter with the conference? What do you think about the new manager?	*Yes/No* questions Did you like the movie? Does she like her new job?

The answers to those questions are usually opinions. If you see or hear answers like these, look or listen for questions that ask about an opinion.

Common Answers	
To *what* questions It was too long. It was boring. That she is qualified.	To *yes/no* questions Yes, I did. Yes, she does.

EXERCISES

Part II: Question-Response

Choose the best response to the question.

Ⓐ Ⓑ Ⓒ

Part III: Short Conversations

Choose the best answer to the question.

What did they like about the speaker?   Ⓐ Ⓑ Ⓒ Ⓓ
(A) His short presentation.
(B) His humor.
(C) His clothes.
(D) His folks.

Part IV: Short Talks

Choose the best answer to the question.

What kind of a movie is it?   Ⓐ Ⓑ Ⓒ Ⓓ
(A) A short one.
(B) One with four stars.
(C) One without credits.
(D) A sad one.

Problem 28: Questions Asking About the Main Topic

Answers to questions are often details, but sometimes they are about larger ideas. On the TOEIC, questions about the main topic concern the overall purpose of the conversation or small talk.

PROBLEM: No specific answer is evident.
SOLUTION: Look for the overall subject.

EXAMPLES

If you see or hear these question types, look or listen for answers about the main topic. When you see or hear these types of questions, you should look in the answer choices for the overall subject of what you heard. Sometimes the question might ask for the purpose or the speaker of the passage: it might be a safety warning from a firefighter or instructions from the boss.

76 LISTENING COMPREHENSION REVIEW

Common Questions	
Who is listening to this information?	What is the subject of the discussion?
Where does this conversation take place?	What problem must be solved?

The answers to those questions are usually about topic, purpose, and speaker. When you see or hear these types of answers, you should look for the overall subject in the answer choices. The answer will not be a detail answer.

Common Answers	
General categories:	Specific examples:
A role, job title, or group	A client. A ticket clerk. The woman's colleagues. Airline passengers.
A kind of place or a situation	In an office. At a convention. During a banquet. At an airport.
Any subject	The new machinery. Politics. Environmental responsibility. An advertising campaign.
A summary or implication	The supervisor doesn't agree with the idea. They need more time to finish the project. A change in the regulations. Consumers' confidence in the product.

EXERCISES

Part II: Question-Response

Choose the best response to the question.

Ⓐ Ⓑ Ⓒ

Part III: Short Conversations

Choose the best answer to the question.

What does the man mean?
(A) He is a generous person.
(B) The woman has no shame.
(C) He needs a loan.
(D) The woman's clothes are too small.

Ⓐ Ⓑ Ⓒ Ⓓ

Part IV: Short Talks

Choose the best answer to the question.

What changes are taking place in the company?
(A) The Board of Directors resigned.
(B) The Managing Director was fired.
(C) The workers went on strike.
(D) All letters will be sent by computer.

Ⓐ Ⓑ Ⓒ Ⓓ

STRATEGY

Strategies for Analyzing Question Types

- Learn to recognize types of questions. Study the common questions and common answers presented in this chapter. Remember that questions about people generally begin with *who* or *what*, questions about location generally begin with *where*, questions about time generally begin with *when* or *how long*, etc.
- Read the answer choices, make assumptions about the items listed, and listen for relevant clues.

Problems Analyzing Language Functions

Problem 29: Conditionals

On the TOEIC, you may need to pay attention to *conditional* clauses. There are two kinds of conditional clauses; (1) real condition *if* clauses, and (2) unreal condition *if* clauses. They both contain the marker *if*. The verb in the independent clause will contain a modal.

PROBLEM: You may not be able to tell if the statement is actually true or conditionally true.
SOLUTION: Listen and look for the word *if* and modals such as *will, should, would,* etc.

EXAMPLES

Real Conditions
If we start by ten, we finish by noon.
If we start by ten, we will finish by noon.
If we start by ten, we will be finished by noon.

Unreal Conditions (Present)
If we started by ten, we would finish by noon. (but we can't start by ten)

Unreal Conditions (Past)
If we had started by ten, we would have finished by noon.

EXERCISES

Part II: Question-Response

Choose the best response to the question.

Ⓐ Ⓑ Ⓒ

Part III: Short Conversations

Choose the best answer to the question.

🔘 What should the speakers have done? Ⓐ Ⓑ Ⓒ Ⓓ
    (A) Submitted a budget.
    (B) Asked for more money.
    (C) Asked for less money.
    (D) Completed the project anyway.

Part IV: Short Talks

Choose the best answer to the question.

🔘 What will investors do if stock prices decrease? Ⓐ Ⓑ Ⓒ Ⓓ
    (A) Jump from buildings.
    (B) Sell immediately.
    (C) Change brokers.
    (D) Buy at the lowest point.

For more practice with conditional statements, study the section entitled "Conditional Sentences" in Chapter 3, Reading Review.

STRATEGY

Learn to recognize conditional clauses. Look for *if* and a modal.

Problem 30 Identifying Suggestions

On the TOEIC, we usually find answers in the statements. But sometimes the key to the answer is in the question.

PROBLEM: The answer is not in the statements.
SOLUTION: Look for an answer in the suggestion question itself.

EXAMPLES

If you see or hear these question types, look or listen for answers about suggestions.

Common Suggestions		
Shall we Why don't we Perhaps we should You could always Let's Why not You may/might want to Maybe we should What if you Shouldn't you You should If I were you, I'd If I were in your shoes, I'd } leave	How about What about Have you ever thought of Try } leaving	

The answers to those questions are usually responses to a suggestion. The responses can be positive (*let's go*) or negative (*let's not*). If you see or hear answers like these, look or listen for questions that are suggestions.

Common Answers	
Yes, let's. That's a good idea. Why not? Suits me.	What a brilliant idea! No, I haven't yet. OK. Good idea.

EXERCISES

Part II: Question-Response

Choose the best response to the question.

Ⓐ Ⓑ Ⓒ

Part III: Short Conversations

Choose the best answer to the question.

What does the man suggest the woman do?
(A) Go last.
(B) Go first.
(C) Have something to drink.
(D) Save money.

Ⓐ Ⓑ Ⓒ Ⓓ

Part IV: Short Talks

Choose the best answer to the question.

What does the man suggest?
(A) We get a new job.
(B) We move homes.
(C) We help the needy.
(D) We stop caring.

Ⓐ Ⓑ Ⓒ Ⓓ

Problem 31: Identifying Offers

When the answer is not in a statement, sometimes it is in an offer. Learn to recognize "offer markers."

PROBLEM: The answer is not in the statement.
SOLUTION: Look for an offer marker in the question.

EXAMPLES

If you see or hear these question types, which begin with these common offer markers, look or listen to see what is being offered.

Common Offers
Let me   Allow me to   Can I   Shall I   Do you want me to   Would you like me to } carry your books

82 LISTENING COMPREHENSION REVIEW

The answers to those questions are usually polite responses that accept or decline an offer. If you see or hear answers like these, look or listen for questions that make an offer.

Common Answers
Thank you.
That's very kind of you.
I'd appreciate that.
You're too kind.
No, thanks. I can manage.

EXERCISES

Part II: Question-Response

Choose the best response to the question.

Ⓐ Ⓑ Ⓒ

Part III: Short Conversations

Choose the best answer to the question.

How will they get warm?
    (A) Have some hot coffee.
    (B) Get on the train.
    (C) Go back home.
    (D) Walk on the platform.

Ⓐ Ⓑ Ⓒ Ⓓ

Part IV: Short Talks

Choose the best answer to the question.

What is being offered?
    (A) First class upgrades.
    (B) Frequent Flyer cards.
    (C) Early boarding.
    (D) Infant travel seats.

Ⓐ Ⓑ Ⓒ Ⓓ

Problem 32

Identifying Requests

A request is a polite way of asking someone to do something. Learn to recognize requests and the information in them.

PROBLEM: The answer is not in the statements.
SOLUTION: Look for a request marker in the question.

EXAMPLES

If you see or hear these question types, which begin with these common request markers, look or listen to see what is being requested.

Common Requests		
Can you May I Would you Could you Do you think you could } speak louder?	How about Would you mind } speaking louder?

The answers to those questions are usually polite responses that acknowledge a request. If you see or hear answers like these, look or listen for questions that make a request.

Common Answers
Of course.   I'm sorry. I can't. Is this OK?   Regretfully, no. No problem.   Not at all. I'd be glad to.

EXERCISES

Part II: Question-Response

Choose the best response to the question.

Ⓐ Ⓑ Ⓒ

Part III: Short Conversations

Choose the best answer to the question.

What did the man ask the woman to do?   Ⓐ Ⓑ Ⓒ Ⓓ
- (A) Mail a letter.
- (B) Go to the bank.
- (C) Stay home.
- (D) Finish a novel.

Part IV: Short Talks

Choose the best answer to the question.

What does the speaker request the audience do?   Ⓐ Ⓑ Ⓒ Ⓓ
- (A) Stop smoking.
- (B) Stop talking.
- (C) Applaud enthusiastically.
- (D) Be seated.

Problem 33 Identifying Restatements

The answer of a question is often a restatement of what you hear in a conversation. Usually the answer restates what you heard in the second or third line of the short conversation in Part III. You will not hear restatement in Part I or Part II.

PROBLEM: The question asks for a restatement.
SOLUTION: Pay attention to synonyms and similar phrases that restate the meaning of a statement.

EXAMPLES

Most questions that ask for restatement ask you for an interpretation: *What does the man mean? What does the woman mean? What is the purpose of the letter?*

When you hear these questions, look for a restatement.

Look at these restatements.

Statement: She would rather live in a warm, dry climate.
Restatement: She prefers arid conditions.

Statement: Unlike me, most people don't like to commute by car.
Restatement: I like to drive to work.

Statement: This is the oldest building in the neighborhood and it was built just 2 years ago.
Restatement: The community is relatively new.

Part III: Short Conversations

Choose the best answer to the question.

What does the woman imply? Ⓐ Ⓑ Ⓒ Ⓓ
 (A) She'll leave if he is not punctual.
 (B) She'd been waiting a long time.
 (C) She never gets angry.
 (D) She doesn't believe his excuses.

Part IV: Short Talks

Choose the best answer to the question.

What is the purpose of the form? Ⓐ Ⓑ Ⓒ Ⓓ
 (A) To make a complaint.
 (B) To borrow money.
 (C) To apply for a job.
 (D) To get a license.

STRATEGY

Strategies for Analyzing Language Functions

- Learn to recognize conditional clauses. Look for *if* and a modal.
- Look for suggestions, offer markers, and request markers in the question. Remember that when the answer is not in the statement, it may be in the question.

86 LISTENING COMPREHENSION REVIEW

Mini-Test for Listening Comprehension
Parts I, II, III, and IV

General directions: Follow the instructions for each part below and use the answer sheet on page 673. When you have finished all four parts, check your answers using the Answer Key on page 467 and see the Explanatory Answers on page 488. The transcript begins on page 587.

Listen to Track 6 of compact disc 1 to hear the statements for Part I.

SECTION I: LISTENING COMPREHENSION
Part I: Picture

Directions: In your test book, you will see a picture. On the compact disc you will hear four statements. Choose the statement that most closely matches the picture and fill in the corresponding oval on your answer sheet.

1.

MINI-TEST FOR LISTENING COMPREHENSION PARTS I, II, III, AND IV 87

2.

3.

GO ON TO THE NEXT PAGE

88 LISTENING COMPREHENSION REVIEW

4.

5.

MINI-TEST FOR LISTENING COMPREHENSION PARTS I, II, III, AND IV 89

6.

7.

GO ON TO THE NEXT PAGE

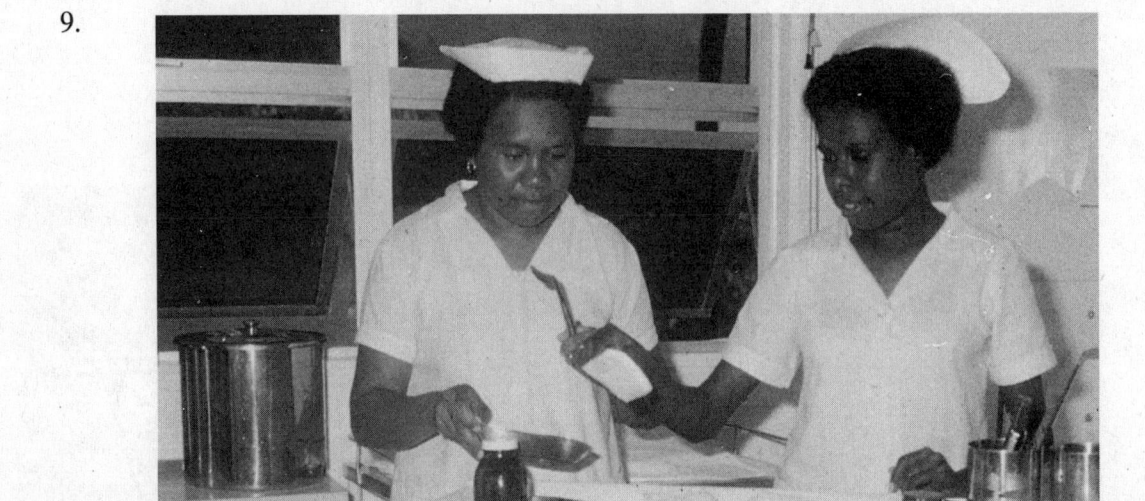

8.

9.

10.

Listen to Track 7 of compact disc 1 to hear the statements for Part II.

Part II: Question-Response

Directions: On the compact disc, you will hear a question and three possible answers. Choose the answer that most closely answers the question and fill in the corresponding oval on your answer sheet.

---

11. Mark your answer on your answer sheet.

12. Mark your answer on your answer sheet.

13. Mark your answer on your answer sheet.

14. Mark your answer on your answer sheet.

15. Mark your answer on your answer sheet.

16. Mark your answer on your answer sheet.

17. Mark your answer on your answer sheet.

18. Mark your answer on your answer sheet.

19. Mark your answer on your answer sheet.

20. Mark your answer on your answer sheet.

21. Mark your answer on your answer sheet.

22. Mark your answer on your answer sheet.

23. Mark your answer on your answer sheet.

24. Mark your answer on your answer sheet.

25. Mark your answer on your answer sheet.

Listen to Track 8 of compact disc 1 to hear the conversations for Part III.

Part III: Short Conversations

Directions: On the compact disc, you will hear a short conversation. In your test book, you will see a question and four possible answers. Choose the best answer to the question and fill in the corresponding oval on your answer sheet.

26. What are they going to do?
    (A) Make a phone call.
    (B) Play tennis.
    (C) Go to the theater.
    (D) See a movie.

27. Who are the speakers?
    (A) A doctor and patient.
    (B) A carpenter and foreman.
    (C) A mother and son.
    (D) A bus driver and a rider.

28. Why does the woman want to wait?
    (A) She doesn't want to be early.
    (B) There is too much traffic.
    (C) She is sick.
    (D) She prefers to be late.

29. What does the man want to do?
    (A) Play in the snow.
    (B) Go skiing.
    (C) Play golf.
    (D) Go away for the weekend.

30. Where does this conversation take place?
    (A) On the street.
    (B) In an office.
    (C) On a bus.
    (D) At home.

31. When will they get together?
    (A) The week after next.
    (B) On Friday afternoon.
    (C) Next week.
    (D) On Wednesday morning.

32. What percentage was spent on advertising?
    (A) 5%.
    (B) 13%.
    (C) 15%.
    (D) 30%.

33. How do the speakers feel?
    (A) Tired.
    (B) Sad.
    (C) Poor.
    (D) Ecstatic.

34. What are the speakers doing?
    (A) Signing letters.
    (B) Buying a new pen.
    (C) Making a sign.
    (D) Finishing a book.

35. Where does this conversation take place?
    (A) At the stock exchange.
    (B) At a restaurant.
    (C) At a train station.
    (D) At a clothing store.

36. What is the relationship of the speakers?
    (A) Singer and conductor.
    (B) Banker and customer.
    (C) Accountant and client.
    (D) Computer buyer and clerk.

GO ON TO THE NEXT PAGE

37. What does the man suggest the woman do?
    (A) Go to warmer place.
    (B) Stay home.
    (C) Visit Paris.
    (D) Move to New York.

38. What does the woman offer to do?
    (A) Fix the printer.
    (B) Type a letter.
    (C) Mail the letters.
    (D) Buy some jam.

39. What did the man decide to do?
    (A) Take another bus.
    (B) Walk to 75th Street.
    (C) Turn at 57th Street.
    (D) Wait for his friend.

40. What did the man see?
    (A) Someone with the flu.
    (B) A fast-flying bird.
    (C) A kind person.
    (D) Someone from his past.

Listen to Track 9 of compact disc 1 to hear the short talks for Part IV.

Part IV: Short Talks

Directions: On the compact disc, you will hear a short talk. In your test book, you will see several questions on the talk and four possible answers. Choose the best answer to the question and fill in the corresponding oval on your answer sheet.

41. Where was this announcement made?
    (A) On a train.
    (B) At an intersection.
    (C) On an escalator.
    (D) In a grain elevator.

42. What kind of service is provided?
    (A) Express—no stops.
    (B) Local—all stops.
    (C) Limited—some stops.
    (D) Out-of-service.

43. What should people take to work in the morning?
    (A) Snow boots.
    (B) Luggage.
    (C) Briefcases.
    (D) Umbrellas.

44. When will the weather clear up?
    (A) By 6:00 A.M.
    (B) By noon.
    (C) By late afternoon.
    (D) By early evening.

45. Why is power being turned off?
    (A) To reduce total demand.
    (B) To save money.
    (C) To make it cooler.
    (D) To make the city pay its bill.

46. How long will power be off?
    (A) Longer than two hours.
    (B) Less than two hours.
    (C) For one day.
    (D) Until the weather changes.

47. Where does this announcement take place?
    (A) On a tour bus.
    (B) At the shore.
    (C) In a cocktail lounge.
    (D) On a ship.

48. What is required for the first excursion?
    (A) A hearty breakfast.
    (B) Some beautiful clothes.
    (C) A ticket.
    (D) A health report.

49. What is being offered?
    (A) A television.
    (B) A radio.
    (C) A video recorder.
    (D) A remote control device.

50. How can a consumer learn more?
    (A) Have a salesperson call at home.
    (B) Visit their office.
    (C) Call a toll-free number.
    (D) Read an electronic magazine.

STRATEGY

Strategies to Improve Your Listening Comprehension Score

The following strategies are a review of those presented in this Listening Comprehension Review. Using these strategies will improve your score on the TOEIC.

Problems Analyzing Pictures

- When you look at the picture, analyze the people. Determine their number, gender, location, occupation, etc.
- Look for context clues in the picture.
- Listen for the meaning of the *whole sentence* to determine which choice best matches the picture.

Problems Analyzing Answer Choices

- Listen and look for context clues.
- Listen and look for the *meaning* of the statement, question, and answer choices. Do not be confused by similar sounds, homonyms, related words, etc.
- Listen and look for sequence time markers, negative markers, and comparison markers.
- Pay attention to word order.
- Listen and look for modals and determine how the modal affects the meaning.

Problems Analyzing Question Types

- Learn to recognize types of questions. Study the common questions and common answers presented in this chapter. Remember that questions about people generally begin with *who* or *what*, questions about location generally begin with *where*, questions about time generally begin with *when* or *how long*, etc.
- Read the answer choices, make assumptions about the items listed, and listen for relevant clues.

Problems Analyzing Language Functions

- Learn to recognize conditional clauses. Look for *if* and a modal.
- Look for suggestions, offer markers, and request markers in the question. Remember that when the answer is not in the statement, it may be in the question.

3

READING REVIEW

WHAT TO LOOK FOR IN THIS CHAPTER
- Directions for the Reading Section, Parts V, VI, and VII
- Examples of TOEIC Reading Exercises
- Types of Problems in the Reading Section
  - Problems analyzing vocabulary
  - Problems analyzing grammar
  - Problems analyzing reading passages
- Mini-Test for Reading Parts V and VI
- Strategies to Improve Your Reading Score
- Mini-Test for Reading Part VII

OVERVIEW—PARTS V, VI, AND VII

There are three parts to the Reading section of the TOEIC test. You will have approximately 75 minutes to complete this section.

Part V:	Incomplete Sentences	40 questions
Part VI:	Error Recognition	20 questions
Part VII:	Reading Comprehension	40 questions

TOEIC Sample Questions

This section will show you the kind of questions you will have to answer on Parts V–VII. You should familiarize yourself with the actual directions used on the TOEIC before you take the exam. You can find these directions in the Model TOEIC test and the TOEIC Bulletin. You can get these publications from the TOEIC offices list on page 5.

SECTION II—READING
Part V: Incomplete Sentences

Directions: In your test book, you will see a sentence with a missing word. Four possible answers follow the sentence. Choose the best answer to the question and fill in the corresponding oval on your answer sheet.

Part VI: Error Recognition

Directions: In your test book, you will see a sentence with four words or phrases underlined. Choose the word or phrase that is incorrect and fill in the corresponding oval on your answer sheet.

Part VII: Reading Comprehension

Directions: In your test book, you will see a reading passage followed by several questions. Each question has four answer choices. Choose the best answer to the question and fill in the corresponding oval on your answer sheet.

READING REVIEW

TYPES OF PROBLEMS IN THE READING SECTION

Problems like those in this Reading Review frequently appear on Parts V, VI, and VII of the Reading section of the TOEIC. If you study these sections carefully and review the strategies at the end of this chapter, you will improve your score on the TOEIC exam.

Problems Analyzing Vocabulary

1. Prefixes
2. Suffixes
3. Word Families
4. Similar Words

Problems Analyzing Grammar

Count and Non-count Nouns

5. Non-count Nouns and Plural Verbs
6. Differences in Meaning Between Count and Non-count Nouns

Articles

7. Specified Noun with Incorrect Article
8. Unspecified Noun with *the*
9. Wrong Article with Generic Count Noun
10. Article with Generic Non-count Noun
11. Wrong Form of *a* or *an*

Subject-Verb Agreement

12. Subject and Verb May Not Agree
13. *You* as Subject
14. Nouns and Pronouns: Singular or Plural

Prepositions

15. Incorrect Preposition
16. Prepositional Phrase and Verb Agreement

Coordinating Conjunctions

17. Wrong Coordinating Conjunctions
18. Joined Items Not Parallel

Subordinating Conjunctions

19. Misplaced Subordinating Conjunctions
20. Incorrect Subordinating Conjunctions

Comparisons with Adjectives and Adverbs

21. Use of *as - as*
22. *More/-er* or *Than* Omitted
23. *The* or *Most/-est* Omitted

Adverbs of Frequency

24. Misplaced Adverbs of Definite Frequency
25. Misplaced Adverbs of Indefinite Frequency
26. Adverbs of Indefinite Frequency with *Be*
27. Adverbs of Indefinite Frequency with Auxiliaries
28. Meanings of Adverbs of Frequency

Causative Verbs

29. Causative Verb + Simple Form
30. Causative Verb + Infinitive
31. Causative Verb + Past Participle

Conditional Sentences

32. Real Condition *if* Clause Not in Present Tense
33. Unreal Condition *if* Clause Not in Appropriate Tense

34 Unreal Condition *if* Clause + *Were*

Verb Tenses and Stative Verbs

35 Verb Tenses
36 Stative Verbs in the Progressive Form

Relative Clauses

37 Relative Clause: Repeated Subject
38 Relative Clause: No Relative Pronoun
39 Relative Clause: *That* ≠ *Who*

Gerunds and Infinitives

40 Verb + Gerund or Infinitive

Participles

41 Incorrect Participles

Problems Analyzing Reading Passages

42 Questions on Advertisements
43 Questions on Forms
44 Questions on Reports
45 Questions on Letters
46 Questions on Faxes
47 Questions on Memos
48 Questions on Tables
49 Questions on Indexes
50 Questions on Charts
51 Questions on Graphs
52 Questions on Announcements
53 Questions on Notices
54 Questions on Newspaper Articles
55 Questions on Magazine Articles
56 Questions on Schedules
57 Questions on Calendars

Grammar and Vocabulary Terms

Parts of Speech

In the "Problems Analyzing Vocabulary" and "Problems Analyzing Grammar" sections that follow, words such as *noun*, *adjective*, *verb*, and *adverb* are used. These words are called parts of speech, and each one has a different use. If you understand how a word is used in a sentence, you will be able to understand when it is used incorrectly. Studying the parts of speech and their functions will help you analyze a sentence.

These are the eight parts of speech and their abbreviations:

Part of Speech (Abbreviation)	
noun (n)	adverb (adv)
pronoun (pron)	preposition (prep)
adjective (adj)	conjunction (conj)
verb (v)	interjection (interj)

Other important grammar terms to know are auxiliary verb (aux) and article (art).

Look at the following analysis of the parts of speech in these statements.

EXAMPLES

pron	adv	v	n	prep	art	n
We	usually	have	coffee	in	the	morning,

conj	pron	aux + adv	v	adv	adj	n
but	we	cannot	find	any	clean	cups.

interj	adv	v	art	n
Hey!	Where	are	the	cups?

Parts of speech can make up phrases.

EXAMPLES

noun phrase		
adv	adj	n
any	clean	cups

prepositional phrase		
prep	art	n
in	the	morning,

verb phrase	
aux + adv	v
cannot	find

Parts of speech can also be referred to by their function:

EXAMPLE

subject	modifier	verb	indirect object	direct object	prep	modifier	object of prep
We	usually	make	them	coffee	in	the	morning.

Parts of a Sentence

The parts of a sentence can also be classified. A sentence is usually made up of an independent clause: a subject and verb that can stand on its own and make sense. An independent clause is also referred to as a main clause.

EXAMPLE

main clause
We all have coffee in the morning.

Another main clause can be added and joined to the first with a coordinate conjunction:

EXAMPLE

main clause	coordinate conj	main clause
I bring the pastries,	and	we all have coffee in the morning.

A clause that cannot stand alone and is joined to a main clause is called a subordinate clause (or a dependent clause). A subordinate clause is preceded by a subordinate conjunction. A subordinate clause can come before or after the main clause.

EXAMPLES

adverbial clause	
subordinate clause	main clause
Before we start working,	we usually have coffee.

noun clause	
main clause	subordinate clause as direct object
Everyone knows	that we usually have coffee in the morning.

adjective clause	
main clause	subordinate clause
We like coffee	that is very strong.

Again, note that in some grammar books, a main clause is called an independent clause and a subordinate clause is called a dependent clause.

These terms will help you as you study the "Problems Analyzing Vocabulary" and the "Problems Analyzing Grammar" sections.

Problems Analyzing Vocabulary

It is difficult to learn vocabulary by studying long lists of words. Studies have shown that it is important to learn new words in context, that is, to learn what words mean in a sentence, what the sentence means in a paragraph, and what the paragraph means to the whole reading passage.

In the "Study Plan" section on page 6, you were advised to start your own vocabulary notebook. In this notebook, you should write down the new words you learn. You should also write down the sentences in which you found them. If you also create your own sentence using the word, you will increase your chances of remembering the word. The more often you use a word and the more ways you use it, the more likely you will not forget its meaning.

In this section, you will study about word families. When you learn a new word, look it up in the dictionary and find other members of the same word family. Write these words in your vocabulary notebook, too.

In a dictionary, you may also find the synonyms and antonyms of a word. Write these words down, too. But be careful. Not all synonyms can be interchanged. Study Problem 4, "Similar Words," on page 115.

Problem 1 Prefixes

A prefix is a syllable added to the beginning of the root of a word. The prefix can change the meaning of the root word.

Look at these words and their meanings:

Word	Meaning
deduce	to reason
induce	to cause to happen
introduce	to make known
produce	to make
reduce	to make smaller

The root *duce* comes from the Latin *ducere*, which means *to lead*. By adding the prefix, you can change the meaning of the word.

Prefix	Meaning	Word	Abstract Meaning
de-	from	deduce	to lead from
in-	in	induce	to lead into
intro-	together	introduce	to lead together
pro-	forward	produce	to lead forward
re-	back	reduce	to lead back

Memorizing the prefixes will not always help you understand the meaning of the word. A prefix added to a word changes the meaning very subtly. It will be better for you to learn the word in context.

Here are some common prefixes and their meanings. Note how the abstract meaning of the prefix and the root is subtly different from the actual meaning of the combined word.

Common Prefixes			
Prefix	Meaning	Word	Abstract Meaning	Actual Meaning
a-	without	apolitical	without a policy; without a city	without an interest in politics
a-	toward	aboard	to ship	on a boat, plane, etc.; as a new member of a group
ab-	away from	abhor	to tremble from	to have an extreme dislike for
abs-	away from	abstain	to keep away from	to hold oneself back; to refrain from
ac-	toward	accurate	with care	free from error; precise
ad-	toward	adjust	toward what is right	to regulate or correct
ag-	toward	aggregate	brought together	combined total

(continued)

Common Prefixes

Prefix	Meaning	Word	Abstract Meaning	Actual Meaning
al-	toward	allude	to play beside	to refer indirectly to
an-	without	anarchy	without a leader	disorder due to a lack of government
an-	to	annotate	to mark	to make explanatory notes
ambi-	both	ambiguous	leading both ways	having two meanings
amphi-	on both sides	amphibious	both sides of life	living on land and in water
ante-	before	anteroom	before the room	waiting room
anti-	against	anti-war	against war	pacifist
bi-	two, twice	bicoastal	having two coasts	on the East Coast and the West Coast of the United States
bio-	life	biography	writing of a life	an account of a person's life
circum-	around	circumscribe	to write around	to limit
co-	together	cochair	two authorities	shared chairmanship
col-	together	collate	bring together	put pages in order
com-	together	compassion	feel sorrow together	to feel deep sympathy for
con-	together	confide	trust together	to discuss private matters
cor-	together	corrupt	broken apart	dishonest; lacking integrity
contra-	opposing	contradict	speak against	assert opposite information or opinion
counter-	opposing	counterattack	an opposite attack	an attack designed to reply to another attack
de-	from	detract	draw away from	reduce in value or quality
de-	removal of something	debug	remove the virus	get the mistakes out (usually a computer program)
de-	reduction	degrade	reduce the scale	reduce status
de-	disparage	demean	make smaller	debase
di-	two	digress	go in two directions	leave the main point
dif-	apart	differ	to carry apart	to be unlike
dis-	apart	disabuse	to stop the abuse of	to correct a deception or a misperception
e-	from	emit	to send forth	to give off
en-	cause to be	encourage	to give courage	to give emotional support to
em-	cause to be	empower	give power to	give authority to
ex-	from	expedite	to disengage	to speed up a process
extra-	beyond	extraordinary	beyond the ordinary	unusual
extro-	beyond	extrovert	turn out	an outgoing person
fore-	before	foremost	before all others	first in rank or knowledge
in-	not	invaluable	not valuable	priceless; cannot have a monetary value placed on it
in-	in	inbound	coming in	headed toward a city, port, etc.
im-	not	impartial	not partial	unbiased; fair
im-	in	impress	to press in	to affect or influence
ir-	not	irregular	not regular	without symmetry or pattern *(continued)*

Common Prefixes

Prefix	Meaning	Word	Abstract Meaning	Actual Meaning
inter-	between	interview	to see face to face	a meeting in which one person asks questions of another
intra-	within	intramural	within the walls	consisting of students from the same school
intro-	together	introduce	to lead together	to make one person or thing known to another
macro-	big	macroeconomy	a big economy	general aspects of an economy
mal-	wrong	malfunction	wrong function	failure to function correctly
mega-	big	megacorporation	a big company	a large company formed by acquisition of smaller ones
meta-	beyond	metalanguage	beyond language	language used to discuss characteristics of a language
micro-	small	microeconomy	a small economy	particular aspects of an economy
mid-	middle	midstream	middle of a stream	halfway across a stream
mini-	small	miniskirt	a small skirt	a short skirt
mis-	wrong	misgivings	offered wrongly	doubts or apprehension
mono-	one	monotonous	having one tone	lacking variety
multi-	many	multimedia	different media	use of several media in combination
non-	not	nonprofessional	not professional	not trained in a particular profession; an amateur
ob-	toward	obtain	to hold	to acquire
oc-	to	occupy	to take	to use up time or space
of-	to	offer	bring to	to present or suggest
op-	to	opportunity	access to	a chance
over-	more than necessary	overpass	go too far	a bridge or elevated walkway
para-	beside	parameter	to a boundary	within specified limits
per-	completely	pervade	to go	to spread throughout
poly-	many	polyphasic	having multiple phases	doing several things at the same time
post-	after	postpone	to put after	to defer or delay
pre-	before	prevent	to come before	to keep from happening
pre-	already	prearranged	already arranged	arranged in advance
pre-	preliminary work	preschool	work before school	classes before elementary grades
pro-	supportive	pro-business	supportive of business	biased towards business
pseudo-	false	pseudonym	false name	pen name; alternative name used by a writer
re-	again	recite	to say again	to quote a literary passage
re-	restore	replace	restore to placement	put back
re-	backward	retract	take back	withdraw
retro-	backward	retrofit	to fit backwards	to modify older equipment with newly available parts

(continued)

Common Prefixes

Prefix	Meaning	Word	Abstract Meaning	Actual Meaning
semi-	half, part	semiannual	part of a year	twice a year
sub-	under	subclass	under a class	a division of a class
super-	over	supersede	to sit above	to replace in authority
sur-	over	surpass	to pass over	to exceed
syn-	together	syntax	arranged together	sentence structure
sym-	together	symposium	drink together	a conference
trans-	across	transfer	to carry across	to change from one person or place to another
ultra-	extremely	ultraclean	extremely clean	germ-free
un-	not	unfocused	not clear	lacking direction or purpose

The most commonly used prefixes are negative prefixes. They all mean *not*.

Negative Prefixes

Prefix	Word	Meaning
dis-	disloyal	not loyal
in-	incapable	not capable
im-	impatient	not patient
ir-	irregular	not regular
mis-	misplace	not placed correctly
non-	nonresident	not a resident
un-	unable	not able

PROBLEM: The prefix or root does not match the context.
SOLUTION: Choose the appropriate prefix and root.

EXAMPLES

Incorrect: Gina *refers* using a computer to a typewriter.
Correct: Gina *prefers* using a computer to a typewriter

noun	verb	gerund	noun phrase	prep phrase
Gina	prefers	using	a computer	to a typewriter.

Explanation: *Refer* (back–to carry: to carry back) means to direct someone to someone or something. *I referred John to you because I thought you could help him.* *Prefer* (before–carry; to carry in front) means to choose someone or something more than something else. Gina would rather use a computer than a typewriter.

Incorrect: The audience left early because they were *immobile*.
Correct: The audience left early because they were *impatient*.

noun phrase	verb	adv	conj.	pron.	verb	adj.
The audience	left	early	because	they	were	impatient.

Explanation: The prefix *im-* means not. *Immobile* means not mobile. If the audience was immobile, they could not move and, therefore, could not leave early. They left early because they had exhausted their patience.

EXERCISES

Part V: Incomplete Sentences

Choose the one word or phrase that best completes the sentence.

Even though he usually tells the truth, this story was _____. Ⓐ Ⓑ Ⓒ Ⓓ
- (A) unbelievable
- (B) unavailable
- (C) uncomfortable
- (D) unsuccessful

Part VI: Error Recognition

Identify the one underlined word or phrase that should be corrected or rewritten. Then, write the correct sentence.

NOTE: On the TOEIC test, you will NOT have to rewrite the correct sentence. This, however, is an excellent study technique and good practice.

The <u>annual</u> <u>conference</u> to which I'm a <u>delegate</u> <u>occurs</u> every other year. Ⓐ Ⓑ Ⓒ Ⓓ
    A   B   C   D

Problem 2: Suffixes

A suffix is a syllable added to the end of the root of a word. The suffix can change the grammatical structure of the root word.

Look at these suffixes and their meanings:

Suffix	Added to	Forms	Meaning	Example
-ability	adjective	noun	state of the adjective	capability
-able	verb	adjective	describe affect	lovable
-age	noun, verb, adjective	noun	state	marriage
-al	noun	adjective	relationship	national
-al	verb	noun	action	burial
-ance	verb	noun	action	attendance
-ant	verb	noun	occupation	accountant
-ant	verb	noun	effect	pollutant
-arian	noun	noun	association	vegetarian
-ary	noun, verb	adjective	describe characteristics	momentary
-ary	noun	noun	occupation	notary
-cy	adjective, noun	noun	describe quality	consistency

(continued)

Suffix	Added to	Forms	Meaning	Example
-cy	noun	noun	occupation	consultancy
-ee	verb	noun	occupation	trainee
-en	noun, adjective	verb	process	darken
-en	noun	adjective	describe characteristic	wooden
-ence	verb	noun	action	existence
-ence	adjective	noun	quality	confidence
-ent	verb	adjective, noun	person, process	student
-er	verb	noun	person	walker
-er	verb	noun	thing	computer
-ery	verb	noun	action	robbery
-ery	adjective, noun	noun	behavior	bravery
-ery	verb, noun	noun	place	bakery
-ess	noun	noun	person	waitress
-ful	noun	noun	amount	handful
-ful	noun	adjective	characteristic	beautiful
-hood	noun	noun	states	childhood
-ian	noun, adjective	noun	job	physician
-ibility	adjective	noun	state	feasibility
-ible	verb	adjective	characteristic	accessible
-ic	noun	adjective	characteristic	idiotic
-fy	(root)	verb	process	amplify
-ion	verb	noun	state	decision
-ish	adjective	adjective	small characteristic	largish
-ish	noun	adjective	characteristic	childish
-ism	noun, adjective	adjective	concepts	consumerism
-ist	noun, adjective	noun	person	capitalist
-ist	noun	noun	field	scientist
-ity	adjective	noun	condition	equality
-ize	noun	verb	action	criticize
-ize	noun, adjective	verb	process	colonize
-less	noun	adjective	without	flawless
-less	noun, verb	adjective	cannot be measured	countless
-let	noun	noun	smaller example	booklet
-ly	adjective	adverb	manner	clearly
-ly	noun, adjective	adjective	characteristic	costly
-ly	noun	adjective	frequency	monthly
-ment	verb	noun	result of process	assignment
-ness	adjective	noun	quality	illness
-or	verb	noun	person	editor
-ous	(root)	adjective	quality	curious
-some	noun, verb	adjective	characteristic	lonesome
-ular	noun	adjective	characteristic	angular
-ure	verb	noun	action	enclosure
-y	noun	adjective	characteristic	dirty

Memorizing the suffixes will not always help you understand the meaning of the word. It will be better for you to learn the word in context. Knowing the suffixes will help you determine the word's part of speech in a sentence. See the related information in Problem 3, "Word Families," on page 112.

PROBLEM: The suffix does not match the required part of speech or the meaning of the root does not match the context.

SOLUTION: Choose the appropriate suffix and root.

EXAMPLES

Incorrect: Check the schedule to see how *frequency* the trains run.
Correct: Check the schedule to see how *frequently* the trains run.

understood subject	verb	noun phrase	infinitive	conj	adv	noun
(You)	check	the schedule	to see	how	frequently	the

phrase	verb
trains	run.

Explanation: *Frequency* is a noun formed by adding *-cy* to the adjective *frequent*. The sentence requires an adverb. Adding *-ly* to the adjective *frequent* gives us the adverb *frequently*.

Incorrect: The accountant was terminated because of her *effectiveness*.
Correct: The accountant was terminated because of her *carelessness*.

noun phrase	passive verb	prep	noun	phrase
The accountant	was terminated	because of	her	carelessness.

Explanation: You need a noun to be the object of the preposition *of*. *Carelessness* is a noun formed by adding *-ness* to the adjective *careless*. *Effectiveness* is also a noun formed by adding *-ness* to the adjective *effective;* however, an accountant would not be fired because she was too effective. *Effectiveness* does not match the context.

EXERCISES

Part V: Incomplete Sentences

Choose the one word or phrase that best completes the sentence.   Ⓐ Ⓑ Ⓒ Ⓓ

The _____ for the job filled out the wrong form.
- (A) defendant
- (B) applicant
- (C) occupant
- (D) assistant

Part VI: Error Recognition

Identify the one underlined word or phrase that should be corrected or rewritten. Then, write the correct sentence.

The manager's inform, issued weekly, was helpful   Ⓐ Ⓑ Ⓒ Ⓓ
     A   B   C   D

Problem 3: Word Families

Word families are created by adding endings to a word. These endings will change the word into a noun, verb, adjective, or adverb.

Common Word Endings			
noun	v	adj	adv
-ance -ancy -ence -ation -ian -ism -ist -ment -ness -ship -or -er	-en -ify -ize	-able -ible -al -ful -ish -ive -ous	-ly -ward -wise

Common Word Families

noun		v	adj	adv
thing	person			
application	applicant	apply	applicable	
competition	competitor	compete	competitive	competitively
criticism	critic	criticize	critical	critically
decision		decide	decisive	decisively
economy	economist	economize	economical	economically
finale	finalist	finalize	final	finally
interpretation	interpreter	interpret	interpretive	
maintenance	maintainer	maintain	maintainable	
management	manager	manage	managerial	
mechanism	mechanic	mechanize	mechanical	mechanically
nation	nationalist	nationalize	national	nationally
negotiation	negotiator	negotiate	negotiable	
politics	politician	politicize	political	politically
production	producer	produce	productive	productively
prosperity		prosper	prosperous	prosperously
repetition	repeater	repeat	repetitious	repetitively
simplification		simplify	simple	simply
theory	theoretician	theorize	theoretical	theoretically

PROBLEM: The word may be the wrong member of the word family.
SOLUTION: Check the ending of the word for the correct member of the word family.

EXAMPLES

Incorrect: The manager read the report *careful*.
Correct: The manager read the report *carefully*.

Explanation: *Careful* is an adjective. Adverbs modify verbs. *How* did the manager read the report? Change the adjective *careful* to the adverb *carefully* to modify the verb *read*.

noun phrase	v	noun phrase	adv
The manager	read	the report	carefully.

Incorrect: That process is not *economize* in the factory.
Correct: That process is not *economical* in the factory.

Explanation: *Economize* is a verb. The sentence requires an adjective to modify *process*. Change the verb *economize* to the adjective *economical* to modify *process*.

noun phrase	v	adj	prep phrase
That process	is not	economical	in the factory.

EXERCISES

Part V: Incomplete Sentences

Choose the one word or phrase that best completes the sentence.

The director of purchasing can _____ the best price.
(A) negotiable
(B) negotiate
(C) negotiator
(D) negotiation

Ⓐ Ⓑ Ⓒ Ⓓ

Part VI: Error Recognition

Identify the one underlined word or phrase that should be corrected or rewritten. Then, write the correct sentence.

Management decided to distribution the product nationally.
   A   B   C   D

Ⓐ Ⓑ Ⓒ Ⓓ

Problem 4 — Similar Words

It is easy to confuse words that have similar meanings or similar spellings. However, these words CANNOT be interchanged.

Common Similar Words			
accept	except	accede	expect
advise	advice	advisory	advisable
affect	effect	affection	effective
borrow	lend	loan	lease
develop	expand	elaborate	enhance
lose	loose	loss	lost
money	cash	currency	coin
obtain	earn	win	achieve
raise	rise	elevate	ascend
say	tell	speak	talk
travel	commute	go	journey

PROBLEM: The word may not have the correct meaning.
SOLUTION: Pay attention to both the meaning and the spelling of the word.

EXAMPLES

Incorrect: Mr. Chang *said* his secretary to schedule a meeting.
Correct: Mr. Chang *told* his secretary to schedule a meeting.

Explanation: *Say* is followed by a direct object. *Tell* is followed by an indirect object. Use *say* when you just say something. (Mr. Chang *said* to schedule a meeting.) Use *tell* when you say something *to someone else*. (Mr. Chang *told his secretary* to schedule a meeting.)

noun phrase	verb	direct object
Mr. Chang	said	to schedule a meeting.

noun phrase	verb	noun phrase: indirect object	direct object
Mr. Chang	told	his secretary	to schedule a meeting.

Incorrect: The vice-president will *commute* to Tahiti on her vacation.
Correct: The vice-president will *travel* to Tahiti on her vacation.

Explanation: *Commute* means to travel to and from work every day. It cannot be used for other trips. Change *commute* to *travel*, which can be used for vacations and other trips.

noun phrase	v	prep phrase	prep phrase
The vice-president	will travel	to Tahiti	on her vacation.

Incorrect: My typewriter ribbon is *lose*.
Correct: My typewriter ribbon is *loose*.

Explanation: The spelling of a word can change it into a different word. To *lose* something means that you cannot find it. Check the spelling; *lose* should probably be *loose*, which means not tight.

noun phrase	v	adj
My typewriter ribbon	is	loose.

EXERCISES

Part V: Incomplete Sentences

Choose the one word or phrase that best completes the sentence.

New employees _____ only a small salary during the first six months.
(A) win
(B) achieve
(C) obtain
(D) earn

Ⓐ Ⓑ Ⓒ Ⓓ

Part VI: Error Recognition

Identify the one underlined word or phrase that should be corrected or rewritten. Then, write the correct sentence.

The personnel manager gives good advise about problems at work.
     A   B   C   D

Ⓐ Ⓑ Ⓒ Ⓓ

CUMULATIVE REVIEW EXERCISES:
Prefixes, Suffixes, Word Families, and Similar Words

Part V: Incomplete Sentences

In sentences 1–5, decide which part of speech is necessary in the sentence. Then, choose the <u>one</u> word or phrase that best completes the sentence. In sentences 6–10, choose the <u>one</u> word or phrase that best completes the sentence.

Sentences 1–5

1. The manager should _____ the procedure to reduce errors.
    - (A) noun
    - (B) verb
    - (C) adjective
    - (D) adverb
    - (E) simple
    - (F) simplify
    - (G) simplicity
    - (H) simplification

2. Arguing over the use of the copy machine is very _____ .
    - (A) noun
    - (B) verb
    - (C) adjective
    - (D) adverb
    - (E) fool
    - (F) fooled
    - (G) foolish
    - (H) foolishly

3. We could print newspaper ads to _____ our new restaurant.
    - (A) noun
    - (B) verb
    - (C) adjective
    - (D) adverb
    - (E) publicity
    - (F) publicize
    - (G) public
    - (H) publication

4. The _____ will be announced on Friday.
    - (A) noun
    - (B) verb
    - (C) adjective
    - (D) adverb
    - (E) decision
    - (F) decide
    - (G) decisive
    - (H) decisively

5. Our research facility is the better _____ to manage this project.
    (A) noun
    (B) verb
    (C) adjective
    (D) adverb
    (E) qualify
    (F) qualification
    (G) quality
    (H) qualified

Sentences 6–10

6. The project was separated into _____ parts.
    (A) equal
    (B) same
    (C) match
    (D) likable

7. He was _____ pleased by the results of the team effort.
    (A) specially
    (B) especially
    (C) specialty
    (D) special

8. Everyone left the building _____ the security guard.
    (A) except
    (B) excess
    (C) access
    (D) accept

9. Airline ticket prices _____ when the cost of fuel increases.
    (A) ascend
    (B) grow
    (C) rise
    (D) elevate

10. Mr. Arnold can _____ a pen from Ms. Lee.
    (A) lend
    (B) give
    (C) offer
    (D) borrow

Part VI: Error Recognition

Identify the one underlined word or phrase that should be corrected or rewritten. Then, write the correct sentence.

1. The client's <u>criticize</u> of his work <u>made</u> the secretary try <u>harder</u>.
   A   B   C   D
   Ⓐ Ⓑ Ⓒ Ⓓ

2. The <u>board of directors</u> must choose <u>the most</u> <u>economically</u> plan <u>for the</u> company.
        A   B   C   D
   Ⓐ Ⓑ Ⓒ Ⓓ

3. <u>Applications</u> for the seminar on <u>manager</u> techniques <u>are due</u> on <u>Friday</u>.
      A   B   C   D
   Ⓐ Ⓑ Ⓒ Ⓓ

4. It is Mr. Sloan's <u>responsibility</u> to <u>maintenance</u> all computer <u>files</u> on <u>current</u> projects.
                  A   B   C   D
   Ⓐ Ⓑ Ⓒ Ⓓ

5. Ms. Chin is a <u>partner</u> in a <u>national</u> known firm of <u>marketing</u> <u>consultants</u>.
            A   B   C   D
   Ⓐ Ⓑ Ⓒ Ⓓ

6. The <u>company</u> does not have <u>enough</u> <u>currency</u> to build a new <u>headquarters</u>.
        A   B   C   D
   Ⓐ Ⓑ Ⓒ Ⓓ

7. <u>Our</u> investments <u>obtained</u> more money <u>this</u> year <u>than</u> last year.
     A   B   C   D
   Ⓐ Ⓑ Ⓒ Ⓓ

8. The <u>affect</u> of the new <u>manufacturing</u> process on the <u>environment</u> is not <u>known</u>.
       A   B   C   D
   Ⓐ Ⓑ Ⓒ Ⓓ

9. The department of <u>human resources</u> will <u>elaborate</u> the insurance benefits <u>to include</u> new <u>employees</u>.
                       A   B   C   D
   Ⓐ Ⓑ Ⓒ Ⓓ

10. Mr. Sung can <u>lend</u> a <u>typewriter</u> from Ms. Wilson, <u>because</u> his typewriter is <u>broken</u>.
                  A   B   C   D
    Ⓐ Ⓑ Ⓒ Ⓓ

STRATEGY

Strategies for Analyzing Vocabulary

There is, as you know, no vocabulary section on the TOEIC, but you must know the meaning of words in order to be able to comprehend the reading passages and the grammar exercises. The best way to learn words is by using them. If you read a new word, try to use it in another way. Write it down; say it in a sentence. Listen for others to use it. Notice how the word is used when you read it.

Strategies for learning vocabulary can be summarized as follows:
- Read as much as you can in English.
- Keep a notebook of the words you learn.
- Learn words in context—not from word lists.

Problems Analyzing Grammar

GENERALIZATIONS: COUNT AND NON-COUNT NOUNS

Count nouns are nouns that can be counted. Count nouns can be either singular or plural, and they can use either singular or plural verbs.

	count noun	v	pron	
Singular	The client	has	his	invitation.
Plural	The clients	have	their	invitations.

Non-count nouns are nouns that cannot be counted. Non-count nouns do not have plural forms and therefore cannot use plural verbs.

	n	v	pron	
Singular	Quality	is	our	goal.
Plural	*No plural*			

Non-count nouns are often (1) nouns that are "whole" and made up of smaller parts (*cash, furniture*); (2) nouns about food (*coffee, fruit*); (3) *some* nouns about weather (*wind, rain*); and (4) abstract nouns (*efficiency, progress*).

Common Count and Non-count Nouns	
Whole (non-count)	**Parts (count)**
cash	dimes, nickels, pennies, dollar bills
furniture	chairs, tables, desks, lamps
Weather (non-count)	**Weather (count)**
(some) weather	one storm, two storms...
(some) rain	one shower, two showers...
(some) sunshine	one ray of sunshine, two rays of sunshine...
Food (non-count)	**Foods (count)**
(some) fruit	one apple, two apples...
(some) coffee	one cup, two cups...
Abstract (non-count)	
(some) efficiency	
(some) progress	
	Irregular plural (count)
	one fish, two fish...
	one child, two children...
	one foot, two feet...

Problem 5: Non-count Nouns and Plural Verbs

Non-count nouns use singular verbs.

PROBLEM: A non-count noun has a plural verb.
SOLUTION: Use a singular verb with the non-count noun, or add a countable quantity.

EXAMPLES

Incorrect: *Confidence are* reassuring to clients.
Correct: *Confidence is* reassuring to clients.

Explanation: *Confidence* is a non-count noun. It never has a plural form, and always uses a singular verb. Change the verb to *is*.

	n	v	adj	prep phrase
Non-count	Confidence	is	reassuring	to clients.

Incorrect: The new *furnitures look* good in the lobby.
Correct: The new *furniture looks* good in the lobby.
Correct: The new *pieces of furniture look* good in the lobby.

Explanation: *Furniture* is a non-count noun. It never has a plural form, and always uses a singular verb. Change the verb to *looks*.

Use a countable quantity with the non-count noun. You cannot count *furniture*, but you can count *pieces*. Because *pieces* is plural, use a plural verb.

	noun phrase	v	adv	prep phrase
Non-count	The new furniture	looks	good	in the lobby.
Count	The new pieces of furniture	look	good	in the lobby.

EXERCISES

Part V: Incomplete Sentences

Choose the one word or phrase that best completes the sentence.

The employees collected several _____ to give to the poor.
(A) clothes
(B) some clothes
(C) bags of clothes
(D) bag of clothes

Ⓐ Ⓑ Ⓒ Ⓓ

Part VI: Error Recognition

Identify the <u>one</u> underlined word or phrase that should be corrected or rewritten. Then, write the correct sentence.

The food, including the <u>fruits</u> and <u>vegetables,</u> <u>were</u> on the <u>table</u>.   Ⓐ Ⓑ Ⓒ Ⓓ
　　　　　　　　　　　　A　　　　　B　　　　C　　　　D

See the Cumulative Review Exercises on count and non-count nouns after Problem 6.

Problem 6: Differences in Meaning Between Count and Non-count Nouns

PROBLEM: Some nouns have different count and non-count meanings.
SOLUTION: Pay attention to the meanings of the noun.

EXAMPLES

　Incorrect: *Fish* is swimming in the office pond.
　　Correct: Ten *fish* are swimming in the office pond. *(count)*
　　Correct: *Fish* makes a healthy dinner. *(non-count)*

Explanation: *Ten fish* is countable because it means ten individual living things. *Fish* for dinner is a non-count noun like *food*. Nouns, such as *light* or *hair*, change meanings depending on whether they are count or non-count nouns. For example:

Non-count: There's not enough light to read from.
　　Count: The street lights go on at dusk.

	noun phrase	v	noun phrase	prep phrase
Non-count	Fish	makes	a healthy dinner.	
Count	Ten fish	are swimming		in the office pond.

　Incorrect: The shop sells many different *wool*.
　　Correct: The shop sells many different *wools*. *(count)*
　　Correct: The shop sells many different kinds of *wool*. *(non-count)*

Explanation: The non-count noun *wool* can be a plural count noun when it refers to different varieties of *wool*. The non-count noun *wool* can be used with a countable quantity *kinds of*.

	noun phrase	v	adv	adj	n	prep	n
Non-count	The shop	sells	many	different	kinds	of	wool.
Count	The shop	sells	many	different	wools.		

EXERCISES

Part V: Incomplete Sentences

Choose the one word or phrase that best completes the sentence.

We need more _____ on this shelf.
(A) room
(B) rooms
(C) places of room
(D) places of rooms

Ⓐ Ⓑ Ⓒ Ⓓ

Part VI: Error Recognition

Identify the one underlined word or phrase that should be corrected or rewritten. Then, write the correct sentence.

Please open the curtains and let more lights into the room.
      A   B   C   D

Ⓐ Ⓑ Ⓒ Ⓓ

CUMULATIVE REVIEW EXERCISES:
Count and Non-count Nouns

Part V: Incomplete Sentences

Choose the one word or phrase that best completes the sentence. (Note: There are only two answer options in this practice section, unlike the actual TOEIC test, which has four.)

1. New employees _____ asked to attend orientation.
   (A) is
   (B) are

   Ⓐ Ⓑ

2. The secretary ordered two _____ for the meeting.
   (A) trays of food
   (B) foods

   Ⓐ Ⓑ

3. A reporter _____ interviewing witnesses.
   (A) is
   (B) are

   Ⓐ Ⓑ

4. Production _____ increased since Mr. Garcia revised the plan.
   (A) has
   (B) have

   Ⓐ Ⓑ

5. The plane cannot take off until the rain _____ .
   (A) stop
   (B) stops

   Ⓐ Ⓑ

Part VI: Error Recognition

Identify the one underlined word or phrase that should be corrected or rewritten. Then, write the correct sentence.

1. <u>Traffic</u> <u>are</u> always bad <u>during</u> rush <u>hour</u>.
    A   B   C   D   Ⓐ Ⓑ Ⓒ Ⓓ

2. Toothpaste for <u>hotel</u> <u>guests</u> <u>are</u> available at the front <u>desk</u>.
                          A   B   C   D   Ⓐ Ⓑ Ⓒ Ⓓ

3. Lunch <u>are</u> provided <u>on</u> Tuesday for conference <u>attendees</u>.
            A   B   C   D   Ⓐ Ⓑ Ⓒ Ⓓ

4. <u>Several</u> baskets of <u>fruits</u> were <u>delivered</u> to the <u>ambassador's</u> room.
         A   B   C   D   Ⓐ Ⓑ Ⓒ Ⓓ

5. <u>Sunshine</u> <u>are</u> expected <u>for</u> the next two <u>days</u>.
          A   B   C   D   Ⓐ Ⓑ Ⓒ Ⓓ

GENERALIZATIONS: ARTICLES

Nouns are usually preceded by the articles *a*, *an*, or *the*. Articles indicate whether a noun is specified (you are identifying which one you are talking about), unspecified (you are not identifying which one you are talking about) or generic (you are talking about something in general).

Common Use of Articles			
N	Specified	Unspecified	Generic
Singular (count)	the	a (an)	a (an)
Plural (count)	the	some (many, etc.)	————
Non-count	the	some (a lot of, etc.)	————

Specified Nouns

Use *the* when you are specifying a noun (you are identifying which thing you are talking about). *The* is used with all nouns (singular and plural count nouns and non-count nouns).

Count (singular)	*The book* is on the table.
Count (plural)	*The books* are on the table.
Non-count	*The stuff* is on the table.

Unspecified Nouns

Use *a* or *an* when you are talking about a singular noun that is unspecified (you are not identifying which one you are talking about). Using *a* or *an* is a way of saying *one*. Consequently, neither *a* nor *an* can be used with plural nouns or non-count nouns. You can use a quantity word (e.g., *some* or *lots*) for plural and non-count nouns.

Count (singular)	I read *a book* that was very good.
Count (plural)	I read *some books* that were very good.
Non-count	I read *some literature* that was very good.

Remember: If you identify (specify) the noun, use *the*.
Unspecified nouns can become specified nouns.

Count (singular)	I read *a book* that was very good. The title of *the* book was...
Count (plural)	I read *some books* that were very good. The author of *the* books was...
Non-count	I read *some literature* that was very good. The theme of *the* literature was...

Note: *A* vs. *an*

The word *an* is a form of *a* that is used before vowel sounds (*a, e, i, o, u*). This makes pronunciation easier.

Consonant Sounds	Vowel Sounds
a table a university a job a quick errand	an office an update an errand an easy job

Generic Nouns

Sometimes you talk about something in general and do not need to identify which particular "thing." Therefore, you do not need to use an article.

You do not need to use an article with most generic plural nouns and non-count nouns. But singular nouns must always use an article. Use *a* or *an*.

Remember: you cannot use *the* because you are not identifying which specific noun.

Count (singular)	I always take *a book* on vacation.
Count (plural)	I always take *books* on vacation.
Non-count	I always take *stuff* to read on vacation.

Problem 7: Specified Noun with Incorrect Article

If a noun is specified, it can be preceded by *the*. *A* or *an* is not used with specified nouns.

PROBLEM: A specified noun may be used without *the*.
SOLUTION: Replace the article used with *the*.

EXAMPLES

Incorrect: The name of *a company* is Swiss Marketing Associates.
Correct: The name of *the company* is Swiss Marketing Associates.

Explanation: You know which company you are talking about. Use *the*.

	noun phrase	prep phrase	v	noun phrase
Specified	The name	of the company	is	Swiss Marketing Associates.

Incorrect: Please answer *questions* on this form.
Correct: Please answer *the questions* on this form.

Explanation: You know which questions you are talking about. Use *the*.

	verb phrase	art	n	prep phrase
Specified	Please answer	the	questions	on this form.

EXERCISES

Part V: Incomplete Sentences

Choose the one word or phrase that best completes the sentence.

_____ of the entire department made the project a success.
(A) An effort
(B) A effort
(C) Effort
(D) The effort

Ⓐ Ⓑ Ⓒ Ⓓ

128 READING REVIEW

Part VI: Error Recognition

Identify the <u>one</u> underlined word or phrase that should be corrected or rewritten. Then, write the correct sentence.

The topic of a seminar is teamwork among managers and employees.   Ⓐ Ⓑ Ⓒ Ⓓ
  A   B   C   D

See the Cumulative Review Exercises on articles after Problem 11.

Problem 8: Unspecified Noun with *the*

If a noun is not specified, it can be preceded by *a* or *an*. *The* is not used with unspecified nouns.

PROBLEM: *The* may be used with an unspecified singular count noun.
SOLUTION: Replace *the* with *a* or *an*.

EXAMPLES

Incorrect: Mr. Jackson needs to hire *the* new secretary.
Correct: Mr. Jackson needs to hire *a* new secretary.

Explanation: *Secretary* is unspecified. Mr. Jackson needs to hire one new secretary. Use *a*.

	noun phrase	verb phrase	art	unspecified noun phrase
Unspecified	Mr. Jackson	needs to hire	a	new secretary.

EXAMPLES

Incorrect: Please bring *the* notepads to the meeting.
Correct: Please bring *notepads* to the meeting.

Explanation: *Notepads* is unspecified; you are talking about any notepad that you can use for taking notes. Do not use an article for an unspecified plural noun.

	verb phrase	unspecified noun
Unspecified	Please bring	notepads.

EXERCISES

Part V: Incomplete Sentences

Choose the one word or phrase that best completes the sentence.

_____ always interrupts your work during the day.
(A) Long meeting
(B) The long meeting
(C) A long meeting
(D) The meeting

Ⓐ Ⓑ Ⓒ Ⓓ

Part VI: Error Recognition

Identify the one underlined word or phrase that should be corrected or rewritten. Then, write the correct sentence.

I need the good book to read in the mornings on the subway.
      A   B   C   D

Ⓐ Ⓑ Ⓒ Ⓓ

See the Cumulative Review Exercises on articles after Problem 11.

Problem 9: Wrong Article with Generic Count Noun

An article should precede a count noun in the generic sense unless the noun is plural.

PROBLEM: The wrong article, or no article, may be used with a count noun in the generic sense.
SOLUTION: Remove the article if the noun is plural. Change the article to *a* or *an* if the noun is a singular count noun.

EXAMPLES

Incorrect: *Computer* processes information quickly.
Correct: *A computer* processes information quickly.
Correct: *Computers* process information quickly.

Explanation: *Computer* is a count noun used in a generic sense. Use *a* with the singular form (*a computer*) or no article with the plural form (*computers*).

	count noun	v	n	adv
Generic	Computers	process	information	quickly.

130 READING REVIEW

Incorrect: *The pictures* add color to an office.
Correct: *Pictures* add color to an office.

Explanation: *Picture* is a count noun used here in a generic sense. Use no article with the plural form (*pictures*).

	count noun	v	n	prep phrase
Generic	Pictures	add	color	to an office.

EXERCISES

Part V: Incomplete Sentences

Choose the one word or phrase that best completes the sentence.

_____ keeps an office running smoothly.
(A) The schedule
(B) Schedule
(C) A schedule
(D) Schedules

Ⓐ Ⓑ Ⓒ Ⓓ

Part VI: Error Recognition

Identify the one underlined word or phrase that should be corrected or rewritten. Then, write the correct sentence.

Package should always have a label with a clearly written address.
   A   B   C   D

Ⓐ Ⓑ Ⓒ Ⓓ

See the Cumulative Review Exercises on articles after Problem 11.

Problem 10 — Article with Generic Non-count Noun

An article should NOT precede a non-count noun in the generic sense.

PROBLEM: An article may be used with a generic non-count noun.
SOLUTION: Remove the article if the noun is non-count.

EXAMPLES

Incorrect: *A software* processes information in many ways.
Correct: *Software* processes information in many ways.

Explanation: *Software* is a non-count noun used in a generic sense. Do not use an article.

	non-count noun	v	n	prep phrase
Generic	Software	processes	information	in many ways.

Incorrect: A faster copier would increase *the efficiency*.
Correct: A faster copier would increase *efficiency*.

Explanation: *Efficiency* is a non-count noun used in a generic sense. Do not use an article.

	noun phrase	v	non-count noun
Generic	A faster copier	would increase	efficiency.

EXERCISES

Part V: Incomplete Sentences

Choose the one word or phrase that best completes the sentence.

Employees with high production rates will receive _____ at the banquet.
(A) recognition
(B) a recognition
(C) the recognition
(D) several recognition

Ⓐ Ⓑ Ⓒ Ⓓ

Part VI: Error Recognition

Identify the one underlined word or phrase that should be corrected or rewritten. Then, write the correct sentence.

Some employees like to listen to a music during the day while they work.
     A   B   C   D

Ⓐ Ⓑ Ⓒ Ⓓ

See the Cumulative Review Exercises on articles after Problem 11.

Problem 11   Wrong Form of *a* or *an*

The use of *a* or *an* depends on the initial sound of the noun. If the word begins with a vowel sound, *an* is used. If the word begins with a consonant sound, *a* is used. This is not often tested on the TOEIC test.

PROBLEM: The wrong form of *a* or *an* may be used.
SOLUTION: Pay attention to the beginning sound of the word after *a* or *an*.

132 READING REVIEW

EXAMPLES

Incorrect: Ms. Rolf received *a* interesting job offer.
Correct: Ms. Rolf received *an* interesting job offer.

Explanation: The word *interesting* begins with a vowel sound. Use *an*.

	noun phrase	v	art	noun phrase
Vowel sound	Ms. Rolf	received	an	interesting job offer.
No vowel sound	Ms. Rolf	received	a	job offer.

Incorrect: The power company sends us *an* utility bill every month.
Correct: The power company sends us *a* utility bill every month.

Explanation: The word *utility* begins with the consonant sound *y* (although it starts with *u*). Use *a*.

	noun phrase	verb phrase	art	noun phrase
Vowel sound	The power company	charges us	an	increase every year.
No vowel sound	The power company	sends us	a	utility bill every month.

EXERCISES

Part V: Incomplete Sentences

Choose the one word or phrase that best completes the sentence.

Mr. Sohasky was eager to make _____ announcement about the new project.
(A) an
(B) a
(C) those
(D) these

Ⓐ Ⓑ Ⓒ Ⓓ

Part VI: Error Recognition

Identify the one underlined word or phrase that should be corrected or rewritten. Then, write the correct sentence.

Every waiter must wear an uniform that is neat and clean, and a black
   A   B   C   D
bow tie.

Ⓐ Ⓑ Ⓒ Ⓓ

CUMULATIVE REVIEW EXERCISES: Articles

Part V: Incomplete Sentences

Choose the one word or phrase that best completes the sentence.

1. _____ are expected to attend the seminar.
   - (A) Manager
   - (B) A manager
   - (C) Managers
   - (D) The manager

2. _____ sent three packages this morning.
   - (A) The shipper
   - (B) A shipper
   - (C) Shipper
   - (D) Shippers

3. _____ of human resources is interviewing applicants.
   - (A) Director
   - (B) The director
   - (C) A director
   - (D) Directors

4. The new computer has improved _____ in the office.
   - (A) efficiency
   - (B) the efficiency
   - (C) an efficiency
   - (D) efficiencies

5. If we do not see _____ soon, we will cancel the project.
   - (A) one progress
   - (B) a progress
   - (C) the progress
   - (D) some progress

Part VI: Error Recognition

Identify the one underlined word or phrase that should be corrected or rewritten. Then, write the correct sentence.

1. It <u>is</u> difficult to <u>achieve</u> <u>the success</u> in a <u>competitive</u> market.
      A   B   C   D

2. Ms. Le Blanc is <u>a excellent</u> secretary <u>who</u> has worked <u>in</u> our office <u>for</u>
                   A   B   C   D

   five years.

3. <u>Report</u> was <u>delivered</u> to <u>the</u> vice-president's office <u>at</u> 11:00 this morning.
      A   B   C   D

4. A <u>manager</u> needs <u>the</u> good staff <u>to make</u> a department operate <u>smoothly</u>.   Ⓐ Ⓑ Ⓒ Ⓓ
      A   B   C   D

5. <u>The</u> task will be finished <u>more</u> quickly <u>if</u> we show <u>a</u> teamwork.   Ⓐ Ⓑ Ⓒ Ⓓ
    A   B   C   D

GENERALIZATIONS: SUBJECT-VERB AGREEMENT

The subject and the verb of a sentence must match in person (*I*, *you*, *he/she/it*) and in number (singular or plural). If the subject is singular, the verb must be singular; if the subject is plural, the verb must be plural.

Singular	The *service desk is* always busy.
Plural	The *service desks are* always busy.

Phrases and clauses that come between the subject and the verb do not affect subject-verb agreement.

For example, a relative clause (adjective clause) that comes between the subject and the verb does not affect the verb. In the example below, *Pacific Ocean* is singular, but *islands* is plural. The verb must be plural (*are*).

noun phrase	adj clause	v	prep phrase
The islands,	which are in the Pacific Ocean,	are	below the equator.

The pronoun *you* always takes a plural verb, even when it refers to one person.

	subj	v	noun phrase
Singular	You	have	your coat.
Plural	You all	have	your coats.

Some nouns and pronouns are always singular and others are always plural. Names of countries and companies that end in a plural word are singular.

Nouns that Are Always Singular
the United States National Autos Cables, Inc.

Nouns that Are Always Plural
people police

Problem 12: Subject and Verb May Not Agree

PROBLEM: The verb may not match the subject.
SOLUTION: Change the verb to match the subject.

EXAMPLES

Incorrect: The *suppliers* in the Southeast Asian region *is* very prompt.
Correct: The *suppliers* in the Southeast Asian region *are* very prompt.

Explanation: The subject of the sentence is *suppliers*. It requires a plural verb (*are*).

plural noun as subject	prep phrase	v	adjective phrase
The suppliers	in the Southeast Asian region	are	very prompt.

Incorrect: The *schedule* for the June meetings *have changed*.
Correct: The *schedule* for the June meetings *has changed*.

Explanation: The subject of the sentence is *schedule*. It requires a singular verb (*has changed*).

singular noun as subject	prep phrase	v
The schedule	for the June meetings	has changed.

EXERCISES

Part V: Incomplete Sentences

Choose the one word or phrase that best completes the sentence.

The officers of the company _____ today at 1:00.
(A) is meeting
(B) meets
(C) has met
(D) are meeting

Ⓐ Ⓑ Ⓒ Ⓓ

Part VI: Error Recognition

Identify the one underlined word or phrase that should be corrected or rewritten. Then, write the correct sentence.

The head of the regional <u>divisions</u> <u>have submitted</u> <u>the</u> latest productivity
　　　　　　　　　　　　　A　　　　　B　　　　　　　C

<u>report</u>.
D

Ⓐ Ⓑ Ⓒ Ⓓ

READING REVIEW

See the Cumulative Review Exercises on subject-verb agreement after Problem 14.

STRATEGY

Ask Yourself..... What is the subject of this sentence?
What is the number of the subject?
How do I change this verb to match the subject?

Problem 13

You as Subject

PROBLEM: *You* may be used with a singular verb.
SOLUTION: Use a plural verb.

EXAMPLES

Incorrect: You *is* offered the position of purchasing clerk.
Correct: You *are* offered the position of purchasing clerk.

Explanation: Even though *you* refers to one person in this sentence, use a plural verb (*are*).

	subj	verb phrase	noun phrase	prep phrase
Singular	You	are offered	the position	of purchasing clerk.
Plural	You	are offered	the positions	of purchasing clerks.

Incorrect: You *has* a message on your machine.
Correct: You *have* a message on your machine.

Explanation: Even though *you* refers to one person in this sentence, use a plural verb (*have*).

	subj	v	noun phrase	prep phrase
Singular	You	have	a message	on your machine.
Plural	You	have	messages	on your machine.

EXERCISES

Part V: Incomplete Sentences

Choose the <u>one</u> word or phrase that best completes the sentence.

You _____ the only person who can do this job.
(A) is
(B) are
(C) was
(D) has

Ⓐ Ⓑ Ⓒ Ⓓ

Part VI: Error Recognition

Identify the <u>one</u> underlined word or phrase that should be corrected or rewritten. Then, write the correct sentence.

Even though you <u>be</u> busy, we <u>hope</u> you <u>are</u> happy.
          A   B   C   D

Ⓐ Ⓑ Ⓒ Ⓓ

See the Cumulative Review Exercises on subject-verb agreement after Problem 14.

Problem 14: Nouns and Pronouns: Singular or Plural

PROBLEM: The verb may not match the subject.
SOLUTION: Know whether the subject is considered singular or plural.

EXAMPLES

Incorrect: *People likes* comfortable desk chairs.
Correct: *People like* comfortable desk chairs.

Explanation: *People* is a plural subject. Use a plural verb (*like*).

	subj	v	noun phrase
Plural	People	like	comfortable desk chairs.
Singular	Each employee	likes	a comfortable desk chair.

Incorrect: *National Autos own* this factory.
Correct: *National Autos owns* this factory.

Explanation: Even though the name *National Autos* ends in a plural word (*Autos*), it is one company. It is singular. Use a singular verb (*owns*).

	subj	v	noun phrase
Plural	Mr. Ho and his partner	own	this factory.
Singular	National Autos	owns	this factory.

138 READING REVIEW

EXERCISES

Part V: Incomplete Sentences

Choose the one word or phrase that best completes the sentence.

The police _____ very conscientious about parking violations.
(A) is
(B) are
(C) was
(D) has

Ⓐ Ⓑ Ⓒ Ⓓ

Part VI: Error Recognition

Identify the one underlined word or phrase that should be corrected or rewritten. Then, write the correct sentence.

Western Industries are the nation's largest manufacturer of heavy equipment.
               A   B   C   D

Ⓐ Ⓑ Ⓒ Ⓓ

CUMULATIVE REVIEW EXERCISES:
Subject-Verb Agreement

Part V: Incomplete Sentences

Choose the one word or phrase that best completes the sentence.

1. The manager from headquarters _____ us this afternoon.
   (A) visit
   (B) visits
   (C) to visit
   (D) visiting

   Ⓐ Ⓑ Ⓒ Ⓓ

2. You _____ assigned to the programming team.
   (A) be
   (B) is
   (C) are
   (D) will

   Ⓐ Ⓑ Ⓒ Ⓓ

3. The police _____ when the alarm goes off.
   (A) arrive quickly
   (B) is arriving
   (C) arrives quickly
   (D) has arrived

   Ⓐ Ⓑ Ⓒ Ⓓ

4. International Communications _____ merging with ERI. Ⓐ Ⓑ Ⓒ Ⓓ
   (A) is
   (B) are
   (C) has been
   (D) have been

5. Every employee _____ his own desk. Ⓐ Ⓑ Ⓒ Ⓓ
   (A) get
   (B) gotten
   (C) getting
   (D) gets

Part VI: Error Recognition

Identify the one underlined word or phrase that should be corrected or rewritten. Then, write the correct sentence.

1. The accountants is writing specifications for the clerks to follow. Ⓐ Ⓑ Ⓒ Ⓓ
      A   B   C   D

2. The chairman of the board are going to retire this spring. Ⓐ Ⓑ Ⓒ Ⓓ
        A   B   C   D

3. A team of the company's best writers produce the annual report. Ⓐ Ⓑ Ⓒ Ⓓ
        A   B   C   D

4. Each of the entrances to company headquarters have a security guard. Ⓐ Ⓑ Ⓒ Ⓓ
            A   B   C   D

5. All employees is taught how to get out of the building in case of fire. Ⓐ Ⓑ Ⓒ Ⓓ
          A   B   C   D

GENERALIZATIONS: PREPOSITIONS

Prepositions show the relationships between nouns or pronouns and other words. A prepositional phrase begins with a preposition and ends with a noun.

Common Prepositions					
about	as	between	in	out	toward(s)
above	at	beyond	inside	outside	under
across	before	by	into	over	until
after	behind	down	like	past	up
against	below	during	near	since	upon
along	beneath	except	of	through	with
among	beside	for	off	till	within
around	besides	from	on	to	without

Problem 15: Incorrect Preposition

PROBLEM: The wrong preposition may be used.
SOLUTION: Pay attention to the meaning and use of the preposition.

EXAMPLES

Incorrect: The meeting is *on* 3:00.
Correct: The meeting is *at* 3:00.

Explanation: *On* is used with days of the week. (*The meeting is on Wednesday.*) *At* is used with specific time.

	noun phrase	v	prep	object of prep
Days of week	The meeting	is	on	Monday.
Specific time	The meeting	is	at	3:00.

Incorrect: Edit the report *by* a pencil.
Correct: Edit the report *with* a pencil.

Explanation: *By* is used for deadlines (*by 3:00*) and for how something was transmitted (*by fax; by telephone*). *With* indicates the instrument used (*wrote with a pen; cut with a knife*).

v	noun phrase	prep	object of prep
Edit	the report	with	a pencil.

EXERCISES

Part V: Incomplete Sentences

Choose the <u>one</u> word or phrase that best completes the sentence.

Just leave the report _____ my desk before you go to lunch.
(A) in
(B) on
(C) at
(D) for

Ⓐ Ⓑ Ⓒ Ⓓ

Part VI: Error Recognition

Identify the <u>one</u> underlined word or phrase that should be corrected or rewritten. Then, write the correct sentence.

I have to catch a flight with Seoul at 2:00 this afternoon.   Ⓐ Ⓑ Ⓒ Ⓓ
       A   B   C   D

See the Cumulative Review Exercises on prepositions after Problem 16.

Problem 16: Prepositional Phrase and Verb Agreement

A prepositional phrase between the subject and the verb does not change the pattern of subject-verb agreement.

PROBLEM: The verb may match the prepositional phrase instead of the subject.
SOLUTION: Pay attention to the number of the subject.

EXAMPLES

Incorrect: The *order* for office supplies *were* on my desk.
Correct: The *order* for office supplies *was* on my desk.

Explanation: The subject of the sentence is *order*. It requires a singular verb (*was*).

	noun phrase	prep phrase	v	prep phrase
Singular subject	The order	for office supplies	was	on my desk.
Plural subject	Duplicate orders	for office supplies	were	on my desk.

EXERCISES

Part V: Incomplete Sentences

Choose the <u>one</u> word or phrase that best completes the sentence.

The award for the best office manager _____ to Ms. Ajai.
(A) is
(B) go
(C) goes
(D) are

Ⓐ Ⓑ Ⓒ Ⓓ

Part VI: Error Recognition

Identify the <u>one</u> underlined word or phrase that should be corrected or rewritten. Then, write the correct sentence.

The sales representatives <u>in</u> the northeastern region <u>is having</u> problems Ⓐ Ⓑ Ⓒ Ⓓ
                            A   B

<u>because</u> the weather <u>is</u> so bad.
    C   D

STRATEGY

Learn to recognize the eight parts of speech.

CUMULATIVE REVIEW EXERCISES: Prepositions

Part V: Incomplete Sentences

Choose the <u>one</u> word or phrase that best completes the sentence.

1. The messenger left the package _____ the receptionist's desk.
   - (A) at
   - (B) to
   - (C) until
   - (D) by

   Ⓐ Ⓑ Ⓒ Ⓓ

2. The convention will be held _____ Stuttgart.
   - (A) at
   - (B) from
   - (C) for
   - (D) in

   Ⓐ Ⓑ Ⓒ Ⓓ

3. There is a meeting _____ Friday.
   - (A) by
   - (B) on
   - (C) in
   - (D) at

   Ⓐ Ⓑ Ⓒ Ⓓ

4. The banquet starts _____ 7:00 p.m. in the Terrengauv Room.
   - (A) on
   - (B) at
   - (C) in
   - (D) for

   Ⓐ Ⓑ Ⓒ Ⓓ

5. Mr. Kim will not know the results of the negotiations _____ tomorrow.
   (A) on
   (B) from
   (C) until
   (D) at

Part VI: Error Recognition

Identify the <u>one</u> underlined word or phrase that should be corrected or rewritten. Then, write the correct sentence.

1. <u>The session on time management</u> <u>is</u> at 2:00 <u>for</u> the Lincoln Room.
       A   B C   D

2. Ms. Bisutti has <u>to arrange</u> <u>for</u> a representative <u>to meet</u> the guests <u>with</u>
                    A   B   C   D
   the airport.

3. Mr. Pang <u>will leave</u> <u>off</u> Toronto <u>at</u> 4:00 <u>on</u> Tuesday.
              A   B   C   D

4. Dr. Cole will be <u>on</u> a meeting <u>from</u> 2:00 <u>this</u> afternoon <u>until</u> 6:00 tonight.
                    A   B   C   D

5. <u>The</u> personnel office is the second office <u>through</u> the right <u>past</u> the water
      A   B   C   D
   fountain.

GENERALIZATIONS: COORDINATING CONJUNCTIONS

Coordinating conjunctions are used to join words, phrases, and clauses of equal importance and whose functions are grammatically similar.

Coordinating Conjunctions	Paired Coordinating Conjunctions
and nor so but for or yet	either ... or neither ... nor not only ... but also both ... and

Conjunction Joining Two Adjectives			
noun phrase	v	adj	conj	adj
The conference	was	long,	but	interesting.

Conjunction Joining Two Prepositional Phrases				
noun phrase	v	prep phrase	conj	prep phrase
The keys	are	on the desk	or	in a drawer.

Conjunction Joining Two Clauses			
verb phrase	noun clause	conj	noun clause
He told us	what he did	and	what he plans to do next.

Problem 17 — Wrong Coordinating Conjunctions

PROBLEM: The wrong coordinating conjunction may be used.
SOLUTION: Pay attention to the meaning of the conjunction.

EXAMPLES

Incorrect: The meeting was interesting *or* productive.
Correct: The meeting was interesting *and* productive.

Explanation: *Or* indicates a choice. *The meeting was interesting* or *The meeting was productive* but not both. *And* indicates both: *The meeting was interesting; it was also productive.*

Meaning	noun phrase	v	conj	adj	conj	adj
Positive	The meeting	was	both	interesting	and	productive.
Positive	The meeting	was		interesting	and	productive.
Negative	The meeting	was	neither	interesting	nor	productive.

Incorrect: Would you like a window seat *and* an aisle seat?
Correct: Would you like a window seat *or* an aisle seat?

Explanation: *And* indicates *both*. The question should use *or* to indicate choice.

Meaning	subj	v	noun phrase	conj	noun phrase
Choice	Would you	like	a window seat	or	an aisle seat?

EXERCISES

Part V: Incomplete Sentences

Choose the one word or phrase that best completes the sentence.

Ms. Sam's work is both creative _____ accurate.
(A) but
(B) or
(C) and
(D) nor

Ⓐ Ⓑ Ⓒ Ⓓ

Part VI: Error Recognition

Identify the one underlined word or phrase that should be corrected or rewritten. Then, write the correct sentence.

You can take a <u>non-stop</u> <u>flight</u> at 10:00 <u>and</u> a direct flight <u>at</u> 2:00.
     A   B   C   D

Ⓐ Ⓑ Ⓒ Ⓓ

See the Cumulative Review Exercises on subordinating conjunctions after Problem 18.

Problem 18 — Joined Items Not Parallel

The two words, phrases, or clauses joined by a coordinating conjunction must be alike: two noun forms, two verb forms, two gerunds, etc.

PROBLEM: The joined items may not be alike.
SOLUTION: Make them alike.

EXAMPLES

Incorrect: The boss likes *to type* and *proofreading* her own letters.
Correct: The boss likes *to type* and *to proofread* her own letters.
     The boss likes *typing* and *proofreading* her own letters.

Explanation: *To type* is an infinitive; *proofreading* is a gerund. You cannot use a coordinating conjunction to join two different forms. Make them both infinitives (*to type* and *to proofread*) or both gerunds (*typing* and *proofreading*).

	noun phrase	v	verbal	conj	verbal	noun phrase
Infinitive	The boss	likes	to type	and	to proofread	her own letters.
Gerund	The boss	likes	typing	and	proofreading	her own letters.

Incorrect: *The manager* or *assisting her* made the request.
Correct: *The manager* or *her assistant* made the request.

Explanation: *The manager* is a noun phrase; *assisting her* is a verb phrase. Because *the manager* is the subject of the sentence, make both of the joined items noun phrases (*the manager* or *her assistant*).

noun phrase	conj	noun phrase	v	noun phrase
The manager	or	her assistant	made	the request.

Incorrect: *The president issued the memo* but *written by her secretary*.
Correct: *The president issued the memo* but *her secretary wrote it*.

Explanation: *The president issued the memo* is a sentence; *written by her secretary* is a sentence fragment. Add a subject and verb to the fragment to make it a complete sentence (*her secretary wrote it*).

sentence			conj	sentence		
noun phrase	v	noun phrase	conj	noun phrase	verb	pron
The president	issued	the memo,	but	her secretary	wrote	it.

Incorrect: Mr. Lee types *quickly* and is *accurate*.
Correct: Mr. Lee types *quickly* and *accurately*.

Explanation: *Quickly* is an adverb; *accurate* is an adjective. Make them both adverbs (*quickly* and *accurately*) to modify the verb *types*.

noun phrase	v	adv	conj	adv
Mr. Lee	types	quickly	and	accurately.

Incorrect: This report is *long* and it *bores* me.
Correct: This report is *long* and *boring*.

Explanation: *Long* is an adjective; *bores* is a verb. Make them both adjectives (*long* and *boring*) to modify the noun *report*.

noun phrase	v	adj	conj	adj
This report	is	long	and	boring.

EXERCISES

Part V: Incomplete Sentences

Choose the one word or phrase that best completes the sentence.

Mr. Medeiros likes to arrive early or _____ to get his work done.
(A) is staying late
(B) stays late
(C) stay late
(D) staying late

Ⓐ Ⓑ Ⓒ Ⓓ

Part VI: Error Recognition

Identify the one underlined word or phrase that should be corrected or rewritten. Then, write the correct sentence.

The <u>company</u> is <u>dedicated</u> to <u>product</u> quality and customer <u>satisfied</u>.
    A   B   C   D

Ⓐ Ⓑ Ⓒ Ⓓ

STRATEGY

Recognize the correct grammatical form: Learn to distinguish gerunds from infinitives, noun phrases from verb phrases, adjectives from adverbs, etc.

CUMULATIVE REVIEW EXERCISES:
Coordinating Conjunctions

Part V: Incomplete Sentences

Choose the one word or phrase that best completes the sentence.

1. Would you like a room overlooking the park _____ the river?
   (A) but
   (B) so
   (C) or
   (D) that

Ⓐ Ⓑ Ⓒ Ⓓ

2. My letters _____ my phone calls have not been answered.
   (A) or
   (B) and
   (C) but
   (D) so

Ⓐ Ⓑ Ⓒ Ⓓ

3. Mr. Dairova will work the morning shift, _____ he prefers to work in the evenings.
   (A) but
   (B) or
   (C) when
   (D) and

4. Our hotel is located between the business district _____ the historical district.
   (A) or
   (B) if
   (C) but
   (D) and

5. Dr. Corso can see you at 10:00 _____ at 10:30.
   (A) or
   (B) and
   (C) but
   (D) though

Part VI: Error Recognition

Identify the one underlined word or phrase that should be corrected or rewritten. Then, write the correct sentence.

1. Ms. Ngai <u>could not see</u> <u>the</u> speaker, <u>or</u> she could hear him <u>clearly</u>.
                A   B   C   D

2. Students enjoy <u>to see</u> our facility <u>and</u> learning <u>how</u> computer games are <u>designed</u>.
                  A   B   C   D

3. <u>Tourist</u> <u>maps but</u> guidebooks are <u>available</u> <u>at</u> the corner newsstand.
      A   B   C   D

4. You <u>have</u> your choice <u>of</u> a morning <u>and</u> <u>an</u> evening flight.
         A   B   C D

5. Mr. Tao <u>is</u> available <u>for</u> a meeting at 1:00, <u>or</u> Ms. Kelsey is not <u>available until</u> 3:00.
          A   B   C
       D

GENERALIZATIONS: SUBORDINATING CONJUNCTIONS

Subordinating conjunctions are used to join clauses (not words or phrases) that have grammatically different functions.

Common Subordinating Conjunctions			
after	before	that	when
although	if	though	where
as	once	until	while
because	since		

The subordinating conjunction must be the first word in the subordinate clause for the sentence to make sense. The subordinate clause can be before or after the main clause.

Problem 19: Misplaced Subordinating Conjunctions

PROBLEM: The subordinating conjunction may be in the wrong clause.
SOLUTION: Put the subordinating conjunction at the beginning of the subordinate clause.

EXAMPLES

Incorrect: The mail arrived *after* the clerk sorted it.
Correct: *After* the mail arrived, the clerk sorted it.
Incorrect: *After* the clerk sorted it, the mail arrived.
Correct: The clerk sorted the mail *after* it arrived.

Explanation: *The clerk sorted the mail* is the main clause; subordinate conjunctions cannot start main clauses. Move *after* to the subordinate clause (*after the mail arrived*).

main clause			subordinate clause		
noun phrase	first verb	noun phrase	conj	pron	second verb
The clerk	sorted	the mail	after	it	arrived.

Incorrect: *While* the copier broke, we were typing the report.
Correct: The copier broke *while* we were typing the report.
Incorrect: We were typing the report *while* the copier broke.
Correct: *While* we were typing the report, the copier broke.

Explanation: *The copier broke* is the main clause; subordinate conjunctions cannot start main clauses. Move *while* to the subordinate clause (*while we were typing the report*).

main clause		subordinate clause			
noun phrase	first verb	conj	pron	second verb	noun phrase
The copier	broke	while	we	were typing	the report.

150 READING REVIEW

EXERCISES

Part V: Incomplete Sentences

Choose the one word or phrase that best completes the sentence.

The project has moved faster _____ .
  (A) the computers arrived since
  (B) the computers since arrived
  (C) since arrived the computers
  (D) since the computers arrived

Ⓐ Ⓑ Ⓒ Ⓓ

Part VI: Error Recognition

Identify the one underlined word or phrase that should be corrected or rewritten. Then, write the correct sentence.

The secretary hid the key to his desk before he locked the confidential papers
 A   B   C
in it.
 D

Ⓐ Ⓑ Ⓒ Ⓓ

See the Cumulative Review Exercises on subordinating conjunctions after Problem 20.

Problem 20: Incorrect Subordinating Conjunctions

PROBLEM: The wrong subordinating conjunction may be used.
SOLUTION: Pay attention to the meaning of the conjunction.

EXAMPLES

Incorrect: *Because* Ms. Do worked very hard, she did not receive a promotion.
Correct: *Although* Ms. Do worked very hard, she did not receive a promotion.

Explanation: *Because* indicates cause and effect. It is not likely that working hard would cause someone to lose a promotion. Therefore, *because* has the wrong meaning for the sentence. *Although* indicates that one thing happens in spite of another (*she did not receive a promotion in spite of her hard work*). This makes sense, so *although* can be used in this sentence.

conj	noun phrase	verb phrase	pron	verb phrase	noun phrase
Although	Mrs. Do	worked hard,	she	did not receive	a promotion.
Because	Mrs. Do	worked hard,	she	received	a promotion.

Incorrect: The secretary will mail the letter *though* his manager signs it.
Correct: The secretary will mail the letter *when* his manager signs it.

Explanation: *Though* indicates unexpected actions. This sentence reflects the expected actions (the manager will sign the letter; the secretary will mail the letter). Therefore, *though* has the wrong meaning for the sentence. *When* indicates a logical time relationship between the events, so it can be used in this sentence.

noun phrase	verb phrase	noun phrase	conj	noun phrase	verb phrase
The secretary	will mail	the letter	when	his manager	signs it.

EXERCISES

Part V: Incomplete Sentences

Choose the one word or phrase that best completes the sentence.

The usher allowed Ms. Sello into the concert hall _____ she was late.
(A) because
(B) yet
(C) even though
(D) before

Ⓐ Ⓑ Ⓒ Ⓓ

Part VI: Error Recognition

Identify the one underlined word or phrase that should be corrected or rewritten. Then, write the correct sentence.

The secretary began to type the report when Ms. Bartos was still writing it.
              A   B   C   D

Ⓐ Ⓑ Ⓒ Ⓓ

CUMULATIVE REVIEW EXERCISES:
Subordinating Conjunctions

Part V: Incomplete Sentences

Choose the one word or phrase that best completes the sentence.

1. _____ the team worked very hard, their proposal was not accepted.
   (A) Because
   (B) Although
   (C) Before
   (D) Where

Ⓐ Ⓑ Ⓒ Ⓓ

152 READING REVIEW

2. Mr. Atari started his company in the town _____ he grew up.
   - (A) although
   - (B) that
   - (C) where
   - (D) if

3. _____ Mr. Lafer joined our company, he had worked for our competitor.
   - (A) After
   - (B) During
   - (C) Before
   - (D) While

4. Please sign for the package _____ it arrives.
   - (A) because
   - (B) until
   - (C) although
   - (D) when

5. _____ Ms. Belazi missed her connection, she had to take a later flight.
   - (A) Although
   - (B) Because
   - (C) If
   - (D) Where

Part VI: Error Recognition

Identify the one underlined word or phrase that should be corrected or rewritten. Then, write the correct sentence.

1. The secretary could not make copies of the report although the copier was broken.
   A   B   C   D

2. Because the new equipment is expensive, it will increase production.
   A   B   C   D

3. The plane is on time, if Mr. Yung will attend the meeting.
                 A   B   C   D

4. Visitors may walk in the gardens where it is time to tour the house.
             A   B   C   D

5. She was promoted, since Ms. Lawrence has been much happier.
       A   B   C   D

Generalizations: Comparisons with Adjectives and Adverbs

Adjectives and adverbs can be used to show the similarities and differences among people, places, things, and actions. There are three degrees of comparison: (1) positive; (2) comparative (*-er* and *more* forms); and (3) superlative (*-est* and *most* forms).

Adjectives and adverbs that have the *-er -est* forms:

Adjectives		
Positive	Comparative	Superlative
pretty	prettier	prettiest
thick	thicker	thickest
narrow	narrower	narrowest

Adverbs		
Positive	Comparative	Superlative
far	farther	farthest
soon	sooner	soonest
lively	livelier	liveliest

Adjectives and adverbs that have the *more-most* forms:

Adjectives		
Positive	Comparative	Superlative
beautiful	more beautiful	most beautiful
popular	more popular	most popular
competent	more competent	most competent

Adverbs		
Positive	Comparative	Superlative
politely	more politely	most politely
efficiently	more efficiently	most efficiently
quickly	more quickly	most quickly

Some adjectives and adverbs are irregular. They do not form their comparative and superlative degrees by using *-er/more* or *-est/most*.

Adjectives		
Positive	Comparative	Superlative
good	better	best
bad	worse	worst

Adverbs		
Positive	Comparative	Superlative
well	better	best
little	less	least

There are two kinds of comparisons: (1) equal comparisons and (2) unequal comparisons.
Use the positive form with *as - as* to make an equal comparison.
Equal comparison between two things:

Adverb	My computer retrieves information *as quickly* as yours does.
Adjective	My chair is *as comfortable* as yours.

Unequal comparison between two things:
Use the comparative form to make an unequal comparison between two things. Use *than*.

Adverb	My computer processes information *faster than* yours.
Adjective	My chair is *more comfortable than* your chair.

Unequal comparison between three or more things:
Use the superlative form to make an unequal comparison among three or more things. Use *the*.

Adverb	My computer runs *the fastest*.
Adjective	My chair is *the most comfortable* chair in the office.

Problem 21: Use of *as - as*

An equal comparison can be made using the positive form of an adjective or adverb with *as - as*.

PROBLEM: *As* may be used only once.
SOLUTION: Make sure you use *as* on both sides of the adjective or adverb.

EXAMPLES

Incorrect: Her work is *accurate as* his.
Incorrect: Her work is *as accurate* his.
  Correct: Her work is *as accurate as* his.

Explanation: *As* must be used twice before the comparison is complete.

			Comparison		
noun phrase	verb		adj		pron
Her work	is	as	accurate	as	his.

Incorrect: That printer operates *quietly as* the computer.
Incorrect: That printer operates *as quietly* the computer.
  Correct: That printer operates *as quietly as* the computer.

Explanation: *As* must be used twice before the comparison is complete.

			Comparison		
noun phrase	verb		adv		noun phrase
That printer	operates	as	quietly	as	the computer.

EXERCISES

Part V: Incomplete Sentences

Choose the one word or phrase that best completes the sentence.

The new employee would like to be _____ his predecessor.
  (A) popular as
  (B) as popular as
  (C) as popular
  (D) popular than

Ⓐ Ⓑ Ⓒ Ⓓ

Part VI: Error Recognition

Identify the one underlined word or phrase that should be corrected or rewritten. Then, write the correct sentence.

Unfortunately, our competitor's latest product is good as our own.   Ⓐ Ⓑ Ⓒ Ⓓ
     A   B   C   D

See the Cumulative Review Exercises on comparisons after Problem 23.

Problem 22: *More/-er* or *Than* Omitted

An unequal comparison between two things uses the positive form with *more* and *than* or *-er* and *than*.

PROBLEM: *More/-er* or *than* may be left out.
SOLUTION: Make sure you use a *more/-er* form of the adjective or adverb. Use *than* after the adjective or adverb.

EXAMPLES

Incorrect: Her work is *more accurate* his.
Incorrect: Her work is *accurate than* his.
  Correct: Her work is *more accurate than* his.

Explanation: *More/-er* and *than* must be used before the comparison is complete.

noun phrase	v	Comparison adj		pron
Her work	is	more accurate	than	his.

Incorrect: His work is *neater* hers.
Incorrect: His work is *neat than* hers.
  Correct: His work is *neater than* hers.

Explanation: *More/-er* and *than* must be used before the comparison is complete.

noun phrase	v	Comparison adj		pron
His work	is	neater	than	hers.

Incorrect: He acts *friendlier* his father.
Incorrect: He acts *friendly than* his father.
Correct: He acts *friendlier than* his father

Explanation: *More/-er* and *than* must be used before the comparison is complete.

		Comparison		
pron	v	adv		noun phrase
He	acts	friendlier	than	his father.

Incorrect: That printer operates *more quietly* the computer.
Incorrect: That printer operates *quietly than* the computer.
Correct: That printer operates *more quietly than* the computer.

Explanation: *More/-er* and *than* must be used before the comparison is complete.

		Comparison		
noun phrase	v	adv		noun phrase
That printer	operates	more quietly	than	the computer.

EXERCISES

Part V: Incomplete Sentences

Choose the one word or phrase that best completes the sentence.

The view from your office is _____ from mine.
(A) better than
(B) better
(C) the better
(D) the better of

Ⓐ Ⓑ Ⓒ Ⓓ

Part VI: Error Recognition

Identify the one underlined word or phrase that should be corrected or rewritten. Then, write the correct sentence.

The office furniture you have requested is more expensive the
          A   B   C
budget allows.
       D

Ⓐ Ⓑ Ⓒ Ⓓ

See the Cumulative Review Exercises on comparisons after Problem 23.

Problem 23: *The* or *Most/-est* Omitted

An unequal comparison among three or more things can be made using the positive form with: (1) *the* and *most* or (2) *the* and *-est*.

PROBLEM: *The* or *most /-est* may be left out.
SOLUTION: Make sure you use *the* and the superlative form of the adjective or adverb.

EXAMPLES

Incorrect: Her work is *most accurate* of all.
Incorrect: Her work is *the accurate* of all.
Correct: Her work is *the most accurate* of all.

Explanation: *The* and *most/-est* must be used before the comparison is complete.

		Comparison		
noun phrase	v	art	adj	prep phrase
Her work	is	the	most accurate	of all.

Incorrect: Her work is *the neat* of all.
Incorrect: Her work is *neatest* of all.
Correct: Her work is *the neatest* of all.

Explanation: *The* and *most/-est* must be used before the comparison is complete.

		Comparison		
noun phrase	v	art	adj	prep phrase
Her work	is	the	neatest	of all.

Incorrect: He commutes *farthest* of anyone in the office.
Incorrect: He commutes *the far* of anyone in the office.
Correct: He commutes *the farthest* of anyone in the office.

Explanation: *The* and *most/-est* must be used before the comparison is complete.

		Comparison		
noun phrase	v	art	adv	prep phrases
He	commutes	the	farthest	of anyone in the office.

Incorrect: That printer operates *most quietly* of all the equipment.
Incorrect: That printer operates *the quietly* of all the equipment.
 Correct: That printer operates *the most quietly* of all the equipment.

Explanation: *The* and *most/-est* must be used before the comparison is complete.

		Comparison		
noun phrase	v	art	adv	prep phrase
That printer	operates	the	most quietly	of all the equipment.

EXERCISES

Part V: Incomplete Sentences

Choose the one word or phrase that best completes the sentence.

Johnson's Delivery is _____ messenger service in town.
 (A) the faster than
 (B) faster
 (C) fastest
 (D) the fastest

Ⓐ Ⓑ Ⓒ Ⓓ

Part VI: Error Recognition

Identify the one underlined word or phrase that should be corrected or rewritten. Then, write the correct sentence.

In our office, June is most popular month for taking vacations.
　A　　　　　　　B　　　　　　　C　　　D

Ⓐ Ⓑ Ⓒ Ⓓ

CUMULATIVE REVIEW EXERCISES:
Comparisons with Adjectives and Adverbs

Part V: Incomplete Sentences

Choose the one word or phrase that best completes the sentence.

1. The controller has the _____ office on this floor.
    (A) most spacious
    (B) more spacious
    (C) spacious
    (D) space

Ⓐ Ⓑ Ⓒ Ⓓ

2. Ms. Voss types _____ than Mr. Prince.
   - (A) accurately
   - (B) most accurately
   - (C) more accurately
   - (D) the accurately

3. Their prices have always been _____ than ours.
   - (A) highest
   - (B) the higher
   - (C) the highest
   - (D) higher

4. This idea is _____ the previous one.
   - (A) good as
   - (B) as good as
   - (C) better as
   - (D) best as

5. It is _____ to call than to write.
   - (A) quickest
   - (B) quickly as
   - (C) quicker
   - (D) quicker than

Part VI: Error Recognition

Identify the one underlined word or phrase that should be corrected or rewritten. Then, write the correct sentence.

1. Our competitor is <u>large</u>, <u>but</u> we <u>are</u> more <u>profitable</u>.
       A   B   C   D

2. The manager <u>works</u> <u>much</u> overtime as <u>his</u> staff <u>does</u>.
              A   B   C   D

3. <u>This</u> is the <u>better</u> <u>advertising</u> campaign in <u>several</u> years.
   A   B   C   D

4. Mr. Owens <u>is</u> the <u>more</u> admired <u>employee</u> in the <u>company</u>.
             A   B   C   D

5. We seem <u>to work</u> <u>long</u> hours <u>in</u> the winter <u>than</u> in the summer.
           A   B   C   D

GENERALIZATIONS: ADVERBS OF FREQUENCY

Adverbs of frequency tell *when* or *how often* something is done. There are two kinds: adverbs of definite frequency and adverbs of indefinite frequency.

Common Adverbs of Definite Frequency	
every day	once a month
twice a week	every other year

Adverbs of definite frequency occur at the beginning or at the end of a sentence.

	Adverb of Definite Frequency			
	pron	v	prep phrase	adverb of definite frequency
	I	study	for the TOEIC	every day.
Every day	I	study	for the TOEIC.	

Common Adverbs of Indefinite Frequency		
always	seldom	often
rarely	usually	occasionally
never	sometimes	

Adverbs of indefinite frequency occur in the middle of the sentence. They occur:
1. after the auxiliary verb;
2. before any main verb except *be*; or
3. after *be* if it is the main verb.

	pron	aux	adv and verb	prep
After the auxiliary	They	can	always work	until six.
Before main verb	They		usually start	at eight.
After *be* (main verb)	They		are never	on time.

Problem 24: Misplaced Adverbs of Definite Frequency

PROBLEM: An adverb of definite frequency may be in the middle of the sentence.
SOLUTION: Move the adverb to the beginning or end.

EXAMPLES

Incorrect: The manager *twice a week* arrives early.
Correct: The manager arrives early *twice a week*.
Correct: *Twice a week*, the manager arrives early.

Explanation: *Twice a week* cannot occur in the middle of a sentence. Move it to the beginning or the end of the sentence.

adverb of definite frequency	noun phrase	verb phrase	adverb of definite frequency
	The manager	arrives early	twice a week.
Twice a week,	the manager	arrives early.	

Incorrect: The editor *every day* eats lunch in the park.
Correct: The editor eats lunch in the park *every day*.
Correct: *Every day*, the editor eats lunch in the park.

Explanation: *Every day* cannot occur in the middle of a sentence. Move it to the beginning or the end of the sentence.

adverb of definite frequency	noun phrase	verb phrase	adverb of definite frequency
	The editor	eats lunch in the park	every day.
Every day,	the editor	eats lunch in the park.	

EXERCISES

Part V: Incomplete Sentences

Choose the <u>one</u> word or phrase that best completes the sentence.

_____ with each of his employees.
 (A) The manager once a month talks
 (B) The manager once talks a month
 (C) Once a month the manager talks
 (D) Once the manager talks a month

Ⓐ Ⓑ Ⓒ Ⓓ

Part VI: Error Recognition

Identify the <u>one</u> underlined word or phrase that should be corrected or rewritten. Then, write the correct sentence.

<u>The</u> marketing department <u>once a quarter</u> compiles <u>an</u> <u>advertising</u> report.   Ⓐ Ⓑ Ⓒ Ⓓ
 A   B   C   D

See the Cumulative Review Exercises on adverbs of frequency after Problem 28.

STRATEGY

Recognize the correct word order.

Problem 25: Misplaced Adverbs of Indefinite Frequency

PROBLEM: The adverb of indefinite frequency may come after the main verb.
SOLUTION: Move the adverb before the main verb.

EXAMPLES

Incorrect: The crew takes *usually* a break at 11:00.
Correct: The crew *usually* takes a break at 11:00.

Explanation: The adverb should come before the main verb.

noun phrase	adverb of indefinite frequency	v	noun phrase	prep phrase
The crew	usually	takes	a break	at 11:00.

Incorrect: The president holds *occasionally* meetings in her office.
Correct: The president *occasionally* holds meetings in her office.

Explanation: The adverb should come before the main verb.

noun phrase	adverb of indefinite frequency	v	n	prep phrase
The president	occasionally	holds	meetings	in her office.

EXERCISES

Part V: Incomplete Sentences

Choose the one word or phrase that best completes the sentence.

Before I go to work, I _____ .
(A) always have breakfast and read the paper
(B) have breakfast always and read the paper
(C) have breakfast and read the paper always
(D) have breakfast and read always the paper

(A) (B) (C) (D)

Part VI: Error Recognition

Identify the one underlined word or phrase that should be corrected or rewritten. Then, write the correct sentence.

The phone rings always when I'm taking a shower in the morning.
 A   B   C   D

(A) (B) (C) (D)

See the Cumulative Review Exercises on adverbs of frequency after Problem 28.

Problem 26: Adverbs of Indefinite Frequency with *Be*

PROBLEM: The adverb of indefinite frequency may come before the main verb *be*.
SOLUTION: Move the adverb after the main verb *be*.

EXAMPLES

Incorrect: *Seldom* the manager is late.
Incorrect: The manager is late *seldom*.
  Correct: The manager is *seldom* late.

Explanation: The main verb is a form of *be*. There is no auxiliary verb. The adverb of indefinite frequency must occur after *be (is)*.

noun phrase	v	adverb of indefinite frequency	adv
The manager	is	seldom	late.

Incorrect: *Rarely* the client is unreasonable.
Incorrect: The client is unreasonable *rarely*.
  Correct: The client is *rarely* unreasonable.

Explanation: The main verb is a form of *be*. There is no auxiliary verb. The adverb of indefinite frequency must occur after a form of *be (is)*.

noun phrase	v	adverb of indefinite frequency	adv
The client	is	rarely	unreasonable.

EXERCISES

Part V: Incomplete Sentences

Choose the one word or phrase that best completes the sentence.

_____ when I arrive.
(A) On my desk is usually my mail
(B) Usually my mail on my desk is
(C) My mail is usually on my desk
(D) On my desk is my mail usually

Ⓐ Ⓑ Ⓒ Ⓓ

Part VI: Error Recognition

Identify the one underlined word or phrase that should be corrected or rewritten. Then, write the correct sentence.

The waiters are friendly and helpful always at that restaurant.
    A   B   C   D

Ⓐ Ⓑ Ⓒ Ⓓ

See the Cumulative Review Exercises on adverbs of frequency after Problem 28.

Problem 27: Adverbs of Indefinite Frequency with Auxiliaries

PROBLEM: The adverb of indefinite frequency may come before the auxiliary or after the main verb.

SOLUTION: Move the adverb so it comes between the auxiliary and the main verb.

EXAMPLES

Incorrect: *Seldom* the manager has been late.
Incorrect: The manager has been late *seldom*.
Correct: The manager has *seldom* been late.

Explanation: The main verb is a form of *be*, but there is also an auxiliary verb. The adverb of indefinite frequency must occur between the auxiliary verb and the main verb (has *seldom* been).

noun phrase	aux verb	adverb of indefinite frequency	main verb	adv
The manager	has	seldom	been	late.

166 READING REVIEW

Incorrect: *Often* the assistant has worked overtime.
Incorrect: The assistant has worked overtime *often*.
Correct: The assistant has *often* worked overtime.

Explanation: The main verb is a form of *work*, the auxiliary verb is *have* (*has*). The adverb of indefinite frequency must occur between the auxiliary verb and the main verb (has *often* worked).

noun phrase	aux	adverb of indefinite frequency	main verb	object
The assistant	has	often	worked	overtime.

EXERCISES

Part V: Incomplete Sentences

Choose the one word or phrase that best completes the sentence.

The personnel manager _____ the employee's best advocate.
(A) has been always
(B) has always been
(C) has been once
(D) once been

Ⓐ Ⓑ Ⓒ Ⓓ

Part VI: Error Recognition

Identify the one underlined word or phrase that should be corrected or rewritten. Then, write the correct sentence.

<u>Never</u> the company has forgotten <u>to acknowledge</u> the most
  A   B   C

<u>outstanding</u> employees.
    D

Ⓐ Ⓑ Ⓒ Ⓓ

See the Cumulative Review Exercises on adverbs of frequency after Problem 28.

Problem 28 — Meanings of Adverbs of Frequency

PROBLEM: The wrong adverb may be used.
SOLUTION: Change to an adverb with the correct meaning.

EXAMPLES

Incorrect: Since the manager hates to be late, he *never* arrives on time.
Correct: Since the manager hates to be late, he *always* arrives on time.

Explanation: *Never* means the manager does *not* arrive on time. This does not make sense if the manager hates to be late. Use an adverb that means the manager does arrive on time (*always*).

subordinate clause	pron	adverb of indefinite frequency	v	adv
Since the manager hates to be late,	he	always	arrives	on time.

Incorrect: Because our printer is slow, we *rarely* have to wait.
Correct: Because our printer is slow, we *frequently* have to wait.

Explanation: *Rarely* means they almost never have to wait. This does not make sense if the printer is slow. Use an adverb that means they have to wait a lot (*frequently*).

subordinate clause	pron	adverb of indefinite frequency	v
Because our printer is slow,	we	frequently	have to wait.

Exercises

Part V: Incomplete Sentences

Choose the one word or phrase that best completes the sentence.

The new secretary _____ does her work or helps anyone else.
(A) frequently
(B) occasionally
(C) never
(D) always

Ⓐ Ⓑ Ⓒ Ⓓ

Part VI: Error Recognition

Identify the one underlined word or phrase that should be corrected or rewritten. Then, write the correct sentence.

The company accountant is never neat and hates sloppy work.
  A   B   C   D

Ⓐ Ⓑ Ⓒ Ⓓ

CUMULATIVE REVIEW EXERCISES:
Adverbs of Frequency

Part V: Incomplete Sentences

Choose the one word or phrase that best completes the sentence.

1. Ms. Lee brings her lunch to work _____.
   (A) never
   (B) every day
   (C) always
   (D) yet

Ⓐ Ⓑ Ⓒ Ⓓ

2. You _____ to listen carefully.
   (A) try always should
   (B) should always try
   (C) should every day try
   (D) every day should try

3. Our department is _____ not as efficient as it should be.
   (A) still
   (B) never
   (C) twice a week
   (D) always

4. Mr. Kent _____ asked to speak in public.
   (A) has been rarely
   (B) has every day been
   (C) every day has been
   (D) has rarely been

5. Our chairman gives a party for our department _____.
   (A) never
   (B) always
   (C) still
   (D) every year

Part VI: Error Recognition

Identify the one underlined word or phrase that should be corrected or rewritten. Then, write the correct sentence.

1. The mail is distributed seldom before 2:00 in the afternoon.
       A   B   C   D

2. Interest that is compounded daily will every quarter be calculated.
            A   B   C   D

3. Always the president of the company enjoys meeting each new employee.
      A   B   C   D

4. The housekeeping staff services twice a day the rooms.
     A   B   C   D

5. The department of human resources every six months prints a new
    A   B

   directory of employee telephone numbers.
           C   D

GENERALIZATIONS: CAUSATIVE VERBS

Causative verbs show that one person makes another person do something. They also show that one person makes something happen. A causative verb is followed by another verb in (1) the simple form, (2) the infinitive form, or (3) the past participle form. The causative verb can be in any tense.

When the causative verb shows that one person makes another person do something, the causative verb is followed by either the simple form or the infinitive form of another verb.

	Common Causative Verbs that Require the Simple Form				
	noun phrase	causative verb	noun (person)	verb (simple form)	noun phrase
make have let	The manager	made will have could have let	Mr. Smith	demonstrate	the product.

	Common Causative Verbs that Are Followed by the Infinitive				
	noun phrase	causative verb	noun (person)	verb (infinitive form)	noun phrase
get want order permit allow	The manager	got wants can order will permit should have allowed	Mr. Cox	to demonstrate	the product.

When the causative verb shows that one person makes something happen, the causative verb is followed by the past participle form.

	Common Causative Verbs that Are Followed by the Past Participle				
	pron	causative verb	noun phrase	verb (past participle form)	prep phrase
had got	I	had will get	the documents	prepared	in two languages.

Problem 29 Causative Verb + Simple Form

PROBLEM: The verb after the causative verb is not in the simple form.
SOLUTION: Change the verb to the simple form.

170 READING REVIEW

EXAMPLES

Incorrect: Ms. Carter *had* Mr. Yung *reviewed* the report.
Correct: Ms. Carter *had* Mr. Yung *review* the report.

Explanation: The verb after the causative *had* must be in the simple form. Change *reviewed* to the simple form (*review*). One person causes another person to do something.

noun phrase	v (past tense)	n (person)	causative verb (simple form)	noun phrase
Ms. Carter	had	Mr. Yung	review	the report.

Incorrect: The manager *let* his assistant *gives* the presentation.
Correct: The manager *let* his assistant *give* the presentation.

Explanation: The verb after the causative *let* must be in the simple form. Change *gives* to the simple form (*give*). One person causes another person to do something.

noun phrase	v (past tense)	n (person)	causative verb (simple form)	noun phrase
The manager	let	his assistant	give	the presentation.

EXCERISES

Part V: Incomplete Sentences

Choose the one word or phrase that best completes the sentence.

The human resources assistant makes all job applicants _____ a typing test.
(A) take
(B) takes
(C) to take
(D) had taken

Ⓐ Ⓑ Ⓒ Ⓓ

Part VI: Error Recognition

Identify the one underlined word or phrase that should be corrected or rewritten. Then, write the correct sentence.

The hotel requests that guests left their keys at the front desk when
                        A   B   C
checking out.
D

Ⓐ Ⓑ Ⓒ Ⓓ

See the Cumulative Review Exercises on causative verbs after Problem 31.

Problem 30: Causative Verb + Infinitive

PROBLEM: The verb after the causative verb is not the infinitive.
SOLUTION: Change the verb to the infinitive.

EXAMPLES

Incorrect: Mr. Chin *will allow* Mr. Baur *will attend* the meeting.
Correct: Mr. Chin *will allow* Mr. Baur *to attend* the meeting.

Explanation: The verb after the causative *allow* must be an infinitive. Change *attend* to the infinitive *to attend*. One person causes another person to do something.

noun phrase	causative verb	n (person)	v (infinitive form)	noun phrase
Mr. Chin	will allow	Ms. Davis	to attend	the meeting.

Incorrect: The president *got* Dr. Carrino *speak* at the seminar.
Correct: The president *got* Dr. Carrino *to speak* at the seminar.

Explanation: The verb after the causative *get* must be an infinitive. Change *speak* to the infinitive *to speak*. One person causes another person to do something.

noun phrase	causative verb	n (person)	v (infinitive form)	prep phrase
The president	got	Dr. Carrino	to speak	at the seminar.

EXERCISES

Part V: Incomplete Sentences

Choose the one word or phrase that best completes the sentence.

The company has never permitted employees _____ public statements.
(A) making
(B) to make
(C) make
(D) made

Ⓐ Ⓑ Ⓒ Ⓓ

Part VI: Error Recognition

Identify the one underlined word or phrase that should be corrected or rewritten. Then, write the correct sentence.

Because of the new project, the director wants all employees work
      A   B   C   D
this weekend.

Ⓐ Ⓑ Ⓒ Ⓓ

See the Cumulative Review Exercises on causative verbs after Problem 31.

Problem 31: Causative Verb + Past Participle

PROBLEM: The noun after the causative verb is a "thing," but the verb after the causative verb is not the past participle.

SOLUTION: Change the verb to the past participle.

EXAMPLES

Incorrect: The new director *had* the office *was painted*.
Correct: The new director *had* the office *painted*.

Explanation: The verb after the causative *had* must be the past participle when something happens (*the office was painted*). Change *was painted* to the past participle (*painted*). One person causes something to happen.

noun phrase	causative verb	n (thing)	v (past participle form)
The new director	had	the office	painted.

Incorrect: The manager *can get* the projector *fix* before the meeting.
Correct: *The manager* can get *the projector* fixed *before the meeting*.

Explanation: The verb after the causative *can get* must be the past participle when something will happen (*the projector will be fixed*). Change *fix* to the past participle (*fixed*). One person causes something to happen.

noun phrase	causative verb	n (thing)	v (past participle form)	prep phrase
The manager	can get	the projector	fixed	before the meeting.

EXERCISES

Part V: Incomplete Sentences

Choose the <u>one</u> word or phrase that best completes the sentence.

The owner of the hotel had the rooms _____ .
(A) redecorated
(B) redecorate
(C) redecorating
(D) to redecorate

Ⓐ Ⓑ Ⓒ Ⓓ

Part VI: Error Recognition

Identify the one underlined word or phrase that should be corrected or rewritten. Then, write the correct sentence.

Mr. Fong <u>had</u> to get his car <u>repairing</u> before he <u>could</u> drive <u>to work</u>.   Ⓐ Ⓑ Ⓒ Ⓓ
      A   B   C   D

STRATEGY

Recognize the correct grammatical form. Learn to distinguish verb forms and to recognize the past participle.

CUMULATIVE REVIEW EXERCISES: Causative Verbs

Part V: Incomplete Sentences

Choose the one word or phrase that best completes the sentence.

1. The personnel director made the applicant _____ half an hour.
   - (A) wait
   - (B) waited
   - (C) waiting
   - (D) waits

   Ⓐ Ⓑ Ⓒ Ⓓ

2. Mr. Wang can't have the package _____ until Monday.
   - (A) deliver
   - (B) will deliver
   - (C) delivering
   - (D) delivered

   Ⓐ Ⓑ Ⓒ Ⓓ

3. Our company wants its clients _____ with our work.
   - (A) satisfying
   - (B) satisfy
   - (C) satisfied
   - (D) satisfaction

   Ⓐ Ⓑ Ⓒ Ⓓ

4. I'll have my assistant _____ for an appointment.
   - (A) called
   - (B) calling
   - (C) will call
   - (D) call

   Ⓐ Ⓑ Ⓒ Ⓓ

174 READING REVIEW

5. The owner had the store _____ for the holiday.
   (A) close
   (B) closing
   (C) closed
   (D) will close

Part VI: Error Recognition

Identify the one underlined word or phrase that should be corrected or rewritten. Then, write the correct sentence.

1. The laboratory technician had a sample took from the water in the pond.
         A   B   C   D

2. Mr. Gazek should get Ms. Ward helping with the closing inventory.
               A   B   C   D

3. The operations manager permitted his assistant leave the meeting early.
                   A   B   C   D

4. The supervisor let the new clerk asking as many questions as she wanted.
    A   B   C   D

5. The travel agent had the reservation change to a later time.
        A   B   C   D

GENERALIZATIONS: CONDITIONAL SENTENCES

Conditional sentences can express two kinds of conditions: real and unreal.

Real Conditions

Real conditions express what is possible. The *if* clause is in the present tense. The other clause expresses habitual action, future action, or a command. The *if* clause can occur in any position in the sentence.

	if clause (real condition)	main clause
Habit	If it rains,	I drive.
Future	If it rains,	I will drive.
Command	If it rains,	drive.

Unreal Conditions

Unreal conditions express something that is not true or is not possible. The *if* clause is in the past (for a situation in the present) or in the past perfect (for a situation in the past). The main clause uses *would* or *would have*.

	if clause (unreal condition)	main clause
Present	If I owned the company,	I would accept the project.
Past	If I had owned the company,	I would have accepted the project.

The verb *be* is always *were* in an unreal condition, even if the subject is singular.

subject	*if* clause (unreal condition)	main clause
I	If I were the boss,	I would take a vacation.
He (she, it)	If he were the boss,	he would take a vacation.

Problem 32: Real Condition *if* Clause Not in Present Tense

PROBLEM: The *if* clause of a real condition may not be in the present tense.
SOLUTION: Change the verb in the *if* clause to the present tense.

EXAMPLES

Incorrect: I will call *if* the plane *will be* late.
Correct: *I* will call *if* the plane *is* late.
Correct: *If* the plane *is* late, I *will* call.

Explanation: This is a real condition (it is possible for planes to be late). The verb in the *if* clause must be in the present tense. Change the verb in the *if* clause to *is*.

if clause (real condition)	main clause
If the plane is late,	I will call.

Incorrect: We cannot send the fax if the phone lines *will be damaged*.
Correct: We cannot send the fax *if* the phone lines are damaged.
Correct: *If* the phone lines *are damaged*, we cannot send the fax.

Explanation: This is a real condition (it is possible for lines to be damaged). The verb in the *if* clause must be in the present tense. Change the verb in the *if* clause to *are damaged*.

if clause (real condition)	main clause
If the phone lines are damaged,	we cannot send the fax.

EXERCISES

Part V: Incomplete Sentences

Choose the one word or phrase that best completes the sentence.

If I _____ this report before 2:00, my secretary will type it.
- (A) finish
- (B) finished
- (C) has finished
- (D) will finish

Ⓐ Ⓑ Ⓒ Ⓓ

Part VI: Error Recognition

Identify the one underlined word or phrase that should be corrected or rewritten. Then, write the correct sentence.

Sign out with the security guard if you will leave after the building closes.
　　　　　　　　　　　　　　　A　　B　　　C　　　　　　　　D

Ⓐ Ⓑ Ⓒ Ⓓ

See the Cumulative Review Exercises on conditional sentences after Problem 34.

Problem 33 — Unreal Condition *if* Clause Not in Appropriate Tense

PROBLEM: The verb in the *if* clause is not in the past or past perfect.
SOLUTION: Change the tense of the verb in the *if* clause. Pay attention to the form of *would* in the other clause.

EXAMPLES

Incorrect: *If I supervise the department, I would hire an assistant.*
Correct: *If I supervised the department, I would hire an assistant.*
Correct: *I would hire an assistant if I supervised the department.*

Explanation: This is an unreal condition (I do not supervise the department). The verb in the *if* clause must be in the past tense (*supervised*).

main clause			if clause (unreal condition)		
pron	v (past conditional)	noun phrase	conj	pron	v (past tense)	noun phrase
I	would hire	an assistant	if	I	supervised	the department.

Incorrect: *If I had written the letter, I would sign it.*
Correct: *If I had written the letter, I would have signed it.*
Correct: *I would have signed the letter if I had written it.*

Explanation: This is an unreal condition in the past tense (I did not write the letter). The other clause requires *would have*. Change the verb in the *if* clause to *would have signed*.

if clause (unreal condition)				main clause		
conj	pron	v (past perfect)	noun phrase	pron	v (past conditional)	pron
If	I	had written	the letter,	I	would have signed	it.

EXERCISES

Part V: Incomplete Sentences

Choose the one word or phrase that best completes the sentence.

If I _____ the promotion, I would have bought a new car.
 (A) received
 (B) had received
 (C) will receive
 (D) would receive

Ⓐ Ⓑ Ⓒ Ⓓ

Part VI: Error Recognition

Identify the one underlined word or phrase that should be corrected or rewritten. Then, write the correct sentence.

I would give you a lift to the airport if I drive a car.
          A   B   C   D

Ⓐ Ⓑ Ⓒ Ⓓ

See the Cumulative Review Exercises on conditional sentences after Problem 34.

Problem 34 Unreal Condition *if* Clause + *Were*

PROBLEM: *Were* is not used.
SOLUTION: Change the verb to *were*.

EXAMPLES

Incorrect: If I *am* you, I would give the speech.
Correct: If I *were* you, I would give the speech.

Explanation: This is an unreal condition (*I* am NOT *you*). Change the verb to were.

if clause (unreal condition)					main clause		
conj	pron	verb *to be*	pron	v pron	v (future conditional)	noun phrase	
If	I	were	you,	I	would give	the speech.	

Incorrect: If he *was* the boss, he would fire everyone.
Correct: If he *were* the boss, he would fire everyone.

Explanation: This is an unreal condition (he is NOT the boss). Change the verb *was* to *were*.

if clause (unreal condition)					main clause		
conj	pron	verb *to be*	noun phrase	v pron	v (future conditional)	pron	
If	he	were	the boss,	he	would fire	everyone.	

EXERCISES

Part V: Incomplete Sentences

Choose the <u>one</u> word or phrase that best completes the sentence.

I would never take a job if the salary _____ too low.
(A) were
(B) was
(C) is
(D) are

Ⓐ Ⓑ Ⓒ Ⓓ

Part VI: Error Recognition

Identify the <u>one</u> underlined word or phrase that should be corrected or rewritten. Then, write the correct sentence.

If I <u>was</u> the boss, I would <u>let</u> everyone <u>leave</u> early <u>in</u> the summer.
     A   B   C   D

Ⓐ Ⓑ Ⓒ Ⓓ

CUMULATIVE REVIEW EXERCISES:
Conditional Sentences

Part V: Incomplete Sentences

Choose the one word or phrase that best completes the sentence.

1. If the speaker _____ her presentation, she will have more confidence.
   - (A) prepared
   - (B) prepares
   - (C) had prepared
   - (D) were preparing

2. If Mr. Musso _____ the answer, he would have told you.
   - (A) would know
   - (B) had known
   - (C) knew
   - (D) knows

3. Ask me for help if you _____ the questionnaire.
   - (A) do not understand
   - (B) would not understand
   - (C) did not understand
   - (D) had not understood

4. If I _____ you, I would accept the position.
   - (A) was
   - (B) were
   - (C) would be
   - (D) could be

5. _____ a message if you can't transfer the telephone call.
   - (A) Take
   - (B) Will take
   - (C) Taken
   - (D) Would take

Part VI: Error Recognition

Identify the one underlined word or phrase that should be corrected or rewritten. Then, write the correct sentence.

1. <u>If</u> I <u>was</u> you, I would <u>work hard</u> <u>for a promotion</u>.
     A   B   C   D

2. Ms. Lieu will <u>call</u> you if <u>the package</u> <u>arrive</u> <u>today</u>.
               A   B   C   D

3. If I <u>live</u> <u>near</u> the office, <u>I</u> would walk <u>to</u> work.
       A   B   C   D

4. If the product have been successful, the company would have made   Ⓐ Ⓑ Ⓒ Ⓓ
       A   B   C

a large profit.
   D

5. Notify the customer right away if the order be late.   Ⓐ Ⓑ Ⓒ Ⓓ
         A   B   C D

GENERALIZATIONS: VERB TENSES

The tense of a verb tells when something happens. There are three tenses in English: present, past, and future. All tenses have four forms: simple, progressive, perfect, and perfect progressive.

	Simple	Progressive	Perfect	Perfect Progressive
Present	call	am calling	have called	have been calling
Past	called	was calling	had called	had been calling
Future	will call	will be calling	will have called	will have been calling

Use the simple tenses to show habit or occurrence.

pron	verb phrase (simple tense)	n	time marker
I	usually write	letters	in the afternoon.
I	wrote	letters	this morning.
I	will write	some letters	tomorrow.

Use the progressive tenses to show action in progress.

pron	verb phrase (progressive tense)	n	time marker
I	am writing	letters	right now.
I	was writing	letters	when someone telephoned.
I	will be writing	letters	all afternoon.

Use the perfect tenses to show a time relationship between occurrence of an action and the present, past, or future.

pron	verb phrase (perfect tense)	noun phrase	time marker
I	have written	three letters	so far.
I	had written	two letters	before I went to the meeting.
I	will have written	one more letter	before I go home.

Use the perfect progressive to show a relationship between the duration of an action and the present, past, or future.

pron	verb phrase (perfect progressive tense)	noun phrase	time marker
I	have been writing	letters	for three hours.
I	had been writing	letters	all morning when the telephone rang.
I	will have been writing	letters	all day by the time I leave tonight.

Pay attention to the tenses of all the verbs in the sentence. The tenses must make sense together.

Problem 35 Verb Tenses

PROBLEM: The tenses may not be logical together.
SOLUTION: Change the tenses so that they make sense together.

EXAMPLES

Incorrect: I *will be working* on the project when Mr. Dubois *arrived*.
Correct: I *was working* on the project when Mr. Dubois *arrived*.

Explanation: *Will be working* is future; *arrived* is past. If Mr. Dubois arrived (past tense), you know if you *were working* when he arrived. Change *work* to a past tense form (*was working* is past progressive).

main clause			subordinate/adverbial clause		
pron	v (past progressive)	prep phrase	conj	noun phrase	v (past tense)
I	was working	on the project	when	Mr. Dubois	arrived.

Incorrect: The manager *left* for her vacation after she *gives* her speech.
Correct: The manager *will leave* for her vacation after she *gives* her speech.

Explanation: *Left* is past; *gives* is present. If she has not given her speech yet, she cannot have left for her vacation. Change *left* to a present or future tense form.

main clause			subordinate/adverbial clause		
pron	v (future)	prep phrase	conj	n + v	noun phrase
The manager	will leave	for her vacation	after	she gives	her speech.

EXERCISES

Part V: Incomplete Sentences

Choose the one word or phrase that best completes the sentence.

I _____ all members by tomorrow night.
   (A) contacted
   (B) contacts
   (C) has contacted
   (D) will have contacted

Ⓐ Ⓑ Ⓒ Ⓓ

Part VI: Error Recognition

Identify the one underlined word or phrase that should be corrected or rewritten. Then, write the correct sentence.

I had <u>been</u> waiting <u>an</u> hour <u>when</u> the bus finally <u>had arrived</u>.
      A   B   C   D

Ⓐ Ⓑ Ⓒ Ⓓ

See the Cumulative Review Exercise on verb tenses after Problem 36.

GENERALIZATIONS: STATIVE VERBS

Stative verbs are verbs of a "state" of being: a state of sensory perception, of mental perception, of emotion, of measurement, or of relationship. Stative verbs are rarely used in the progressive.

Common Stative Verbs	
appreciate	We *appreciate* your coming.
believe	He *believes* in what he is doing.
belong	I *belong* to many clubs.
care	The citizens *care* about their community.
dislike	We *dislike* unpleasant chores.
doubt	They *doubt* they can come.
forget	Don't *forget* to leave your number.
hate	I've *hated* to get out of bed all my life.
imagine	I *imagined* I would succeed, and I did.
know	They have *known* the secret for some time.
like	We would *like* to go to.
love	The children *love* ice cream.
mean	They *meant* to start earlier.
mind	Would you *mind* shutting the door?
need	They *need* all the help they can get.
own	I *own* an old model car.
prefer	She would have *preferred* to go alone.
possess	Whatever *possessed* you?
realize	They *realized* their mistake too late.

(*continued*)

Common Stative Verbs	
recognize	Do you *recognize* me?
remember	I *remember* when you first came to the office.
seem	They *seemed* to enjoy themselves.
suppose	I *suppose* you are wondering who I am.
understand	We *understand* what you say, but not what you mean.
want	We've *wanted* to quit since the day we started.

Problem 36: Stative Verbs in the Progressive Form

PROBLEM: A stative verb is used in the progressive.
SOLUTION: Change the verb to a form that is not progressive.

EXAMPLES

Incorrect: *I was knowing about the merger before I saw the paper.*
Correct: *I knew about the merger before I saw the paper.*

Explanation: *Know* is not often used in the progressive. Change to the simple past (*knew*).

main clause			subordinate clause (adverbial clause)			
pron	stative verb	prep phrase	conj	pron	v	noun phrase
I	knew	about the merger	before	I	saw	the paper.

Incorrect: *I will be remembering him when I meet him.*
Correct: *I will remember him when I meet him.*

Explanation: *Remember* is not often used in the progressive. Change to the future (*will remember*).

main clause			subordinate clause (adverbial clause)			
pron	stative verb	pron	conj	pron	v	pron
I	will remember	him	when	I	meet	him.

EXERCISES

Part V: Incomplete Sentences

Choose the one word or phrase that best completes the sentence.

I _____ the job very much now that I understand the work.
- (A) will like
- (B) like
- (C) would be liking
- (D) liking

Part VI: Error Recognition

Identify the one underlined word or phrase that should be corrected or rewritten. Then, write the correct sentence.

Mr. Chen's <u>realtor</u> told him how <u>much</u> she <u>was appreciating</u> his help <u>on</u>
            A   B   C   D
the contract.

CUMULATIVE REVIEW EXERCISES:
Verb Tenses and Stative Verbs

Part V: Incomplete Sentences

Choose the one word or phrase that best completes the sentence.

1. When my visitor _____, will you please call me?
   - (A) will arrive
   - (B) arrives
   - (C) arrived
   - (D) is arriving

2. Mr. Santo's assistant _____ more relaxed since his promotion.
   - (A) has become
   - (B) has been becoming
   - (C) becomes
   - (D) had become

3. Mr. Sanchez _____ his first job with us twenty-five years ago.
   - (A) accepts
   - (B) was accepting
   - (C) has accepted
   - (D) accepted

4. The president _____ the reports in her speech this afternoon.
   - (A) was discussing
   - (B) will discuss
   - (C) discussed
   - (D) has discussed

5. My parents know that I _____ next year.
   (A) would graduate
   (B) graduated
   (C) will graduate
   (D) have graduated

Part VI: Error Recognition

Identify the one underlined word or phrase that should be corrected or rewritten. Then, write the correct sentence.

1. Mr. Feldman has left on his vacation before Ms. Hoik returned
                A   B   C
   from her trip.
       D

2. The computer program was running when Mr. Yu finds a mistake
         A   B   C
   in the data.
      D

3. The broker is making telephone calls in the mornings and attends
                A   B   C
   meetings in the afternoons.
           D

4. I am recognizing the president of the company from his picture.
         A   B   C   D

5. The clerk checks the figures right now so the report will be ready
           A   B   C
   by 5:00.
   D

GENERALIZATIONS: RELATIVE CLAUSES

A relative clause combines two sentences. The second sentence describes a noun in the first sentence. A relative clause uses a special pronoun to replace the noun. This pronoun is called a relative pronoun.

Relative pronouns	
that	Pronoun for things (used only in restrictive clauses)
which	Pronoun for things
who	Subject pronoun for people
whom	Object pronoun for people
whose	Possessive pronoun

There are two kinds of relative clauses: restrictive and nonrestrictive. Note in the example below that *clerk* is the subject of both sentences.

A restrictive clause identifies a noun.

	noun phrase	verb phrase	v	prep phrase
Sentence 1	A clerk		will start	on Monday.
Sentence 2	The clerk	was just hired.		
Combined	The clerk	who was just hired	will start	on Monday.
	noun phrase	relative clause	v	prep phrase

A nonrestrictive clause gives information about a noun (but does not identify the noun). A nonrestrictive clause has a comma at each end. *That* is not used in nonrestrictive clauses.

	noun phrase	verb phrase	v	adj phrase
Sentence 1	My secretary		is	very efficient.
Sentence 2	She	has worked for me for ten years.		
Combined	My secretary,	who has worked for me for ten years,	is	very efficient.
	noun phrase	relative clause	v	adj phrase

Notice that you have already identified which secretary by saying *my secretary*. The nonrestrictive clause merely adds the information that she has worked for you for ten years.

Problem 37 Relative Clause: Repeated Subject

PROBLEM: The noun (or a pronoun) may be repeated in the relative clause.
SOLUTION: Delete the noun (or its pronoun).

EXAMPLES

Incorrect: The report that we sent *it* last week was returned.
Correct: The report that we sent last week was returned.

Explanation: There is already a relative pronoun (*that*) in the sentence. The relative pronoun substitutes for the noun (*that = the report*). You do not need to repeat a noun or pronoun. Delete the pronoun *it*.

subj	relative clause		v
noun phrase	relative pron		verb phrase
The report	that	we sent last week	was returned.

Incorrect: The manager *who he* hired an assistant is still overworked.
Correct: The manager *who* hired an assistant is still overworked.

Explanation: There is already a relative pronoun in the sentence (*who*). The relative pronoun substitutes for the noun (*who = he*). You do not need to repeat a noun or pronoun. Delete the pronoun *he*.

subj	relative clause		v
noun phrase	relative pron		verb phrase
The manager	who	hired an assistant	is still overworked.

EXERCISES

Part V: Incomplete Sentences

Choose the one word or phrase that best completes the sentence.

The wallet _____ was found in the hall has been claimed.
(A) that it
(B) it
(C) that
(D) whose it

Ⓐ Ⓑ Ⓒ Ⓓ

Part VI: Error Recognition

Identify the one underlined word or phrase that should be corrected or rewritten. Then, write the correct sentence.

The woman who she applied last week is the best candidate for the job.
  A   B   C   D

Ⓐ Ⓑ Ⓒ Ⓓ

See the Cumulative Review Exercises for relative clauses after Problem 39.

STRATEGY

Be aware of whether or not there is more than one subject in a sentence. Consider which subject goes with which verb.

Problem 38: Relative Clause: No Relative Pronoun

PROBLEM: A wrong pronoun may be used. It may not be a relative pronoun.
SOLUTION: Use a relative pronoun. Pay attention to the meaning of the pronoun.

EXAMPLES

Incorrect: Mr. Zabel, *his* mother owns the company, works very hard.
Correct: Mr. Zabel, *whose* mother owns the company, works very hard.

Explanation: *His* is not a relative pronoun. A relative clause must begin with a relative pronoun. Start with the possessive relative pronoun *whose*.

subj	relative clause			v
noun phrase	relative pron	noun	verb phrase	verb phrase
Mr. Zabel,	whose	mother	owns the company,	works very hard.

Incorrect: This report, *it* was published last week, is not accurate.
Correct: This report, *which* was published last week, is not accurate.

Explanation: *It* is not a relative pronoun. A relative clause must begin with a relative pronoun. Start with the relative pronoun *which*.

subj	relative clause		v
noun phrase	relative pron	verb phrase	verb phrase
This report,	which	was published last week,	is not accurate.

EXERCISES

Part V: Incomplete Sentences

Choose the one word or phrase that best completes the sentence.

The man _____ shares this office is very good with computers.
(A) who
(B) he
(C) whose
(D) his

Ⓐ Ⓑ Ⓒ Ⓓ

Part VI: Error Recognition

Identify the one underlined word or phrase that should be corrected or rewritten. Then, write the correct sentence.

The author, he prefers to remain anonymous, has written an excellent book.
         A   B   C   D

Ⓐ Ⓑ Ⓒ Ⓓ

See the Cumulative Review Exercises for relative clauses after Problem 39.

Problem 39: Relative Clause: *That* ≠ *Who*

PROBLEM: *That* or *who* may be used incorrectly.
SOLUTION: Pay attention to the modified word.

Incorrect: The package *who* we were expecting finally arrived.
Correct: The package *that* we were expecting finally arrived.

Explanation: *Who* is a relative pronoun, but it is used only for people. A package is a thing. Use *that*.

subj	relative clause			v
noun phrase	relative pron	pron	verb phrase	verb phrase
The package	that	we	were expecting	finally arrived.

Incorrect: The sales representative *which* started made several large sales.
Correct: The sales representative *who* started made several large sales.

Explanation: *Which* is a relative pronoun, but it is used only for things. A sales representative is a person. Use *who*.

subj	relative clause		v
noun phrase	relative pron	v	verb phrase
The sales representative	who	started	made several large sales.

EXERCISES

Part V: Incomplete Sentences

Choose the one word or phrase that best completes the sentence.

Mr. Maurice, _____ has worked here for many years, is retiring.
(A) which
(B) he
(C) that
(D) who

Ⓐ Ⓑ Ⓒ Ⓓ

Part VI: Error Recognition

Identify the one underlined word or phrase that should be corrected or rewritten. Then, write the correct sentence.

The letter <u>who</u> was <u>mailed</u> a month ago <u>has never been</u> <u>received</u>.
       A   B   C   D

Ⓐ Ⓑ Ⓒ Ⓓ

CUMULATIVE REVIEW EXERCISES:
Relative Clauses

Part V: Incomplete Sentences

Choose the one word or phrase that best completes the sentence.

1. Ms. Caras, _____ is quite well-known, is arriving at 3:00.
   (A) when
   (B) whom
   (C) that
   (D) who

   Ⓐ Ⓑ Ⓒ Ⓓ

2. A letter _____ is not properly typed is hard to read.
   (A) which it
   (B) it
   (C) that it
   (D) that

   Ⓐ Ⓑ Ⓒ Ⓓ

3. Mr. La Porte, _____ starts tomorrow, has already left.
   (A) whose vacation
   (B) his vacation
   (C) the vacation
   (D) its vacation

   Ⓐ Ⓑ Ⓒ Ⓓ

4. The report _____ this process is in the library.
   (A) it explains
   (B) explains
   (C) who explains
   (D) that explains

   Ⓐ Ⓑ Ⓒ Ⓓ

5. A machine _____ could monitor efficiency would be very useful.
   (A) whom
   (B) that
   (C) it
   (D) when

   Ⓐ Ⓑ Ⓒ Ⓓ

Part VI: Error Recognition

Identify the one underlined word or phrase that should be corrected or rewritten. Then, write the correct sentence.

1. A manager which can motivate his staff is a valuable employee.
     A   B   C   D

   Ⓐ Ⓑ Ⓒ Ⓓ

2. This chair, that has been broken for weeks, must be repaired.
           A   B   C   D

   Ⓐ Ⓑ Ⓒ Ⓓ

3. The person who she has this information is Jane Fenimore.
      A   B C   D

   Ⓐ Ⓑ Ⓒ Ⓓ

4. The company who pays attention to its customers will be successful.
           A   B   C   D

   Ⓐ Ⓑ Ⓒ Ⓓ

5. That building, its architect is unknown, is a popular tourist attraction.
        A   B   C   D

   Ⓐ Ⓑ Ⓒ Ⓓ

GENERALIZATIONS: GERUNDS AND INFINITIVES

The main verb can be followed immediately by a second verb. This second verb can be a gerund (-ing form) or an infinitive (to + verb). The main verb usually determines which form is used.

Common Verbs Followed by a Gerund	
appreciate	I *appreciate* having the opportunity to speak.
avoid	They *avoided* looking us in the eye.
consider	We *considered* staying longer.
delay	We *delayed* writing you until we had more information.
discuss	Have you *discussed* working together on this project?
enjoy	We *enjoyed* having you for dinner.
finish	They will *finish* correcting the report soon.
mind	She *minded* using our toothbrush.

(continued)

Common Verbs Followed by a Gerund

miss	We *miss* going to the movies with you.
postpone	Could we *postpone* leaving?
quit	He wants to *quit* smoking.
risk	They *risked* losing everything.
suggest	We *suggest* leaving on time.

Common Verbs Followed by an Infinitive

agree	He *agreed* to complete the project.
attempt	They *attempted* to climb Mt. Fuji.
claim	She *claims* to be an expert.
decide	We *decided* to hire her anyway.
demand	He *demanded* to know what we were doing.
fail	We *failed* to give a satisfactory answer.
hesitate	I *hesitated* to tell the truth.
hope	We *hope* to leave before dawn.
intend	She *intends* to start her own club.
learn	They will *learn* to swim at camp.
need	She *needs* to stop smoking.
offer	They *offered* to take us home.
plan	We *plan* to accept their offer.
prepare	She *prepared* to leave.
refuse	He *refused* to come with us.
seem	She *seemed* to be annoyed.
try	I *tried* to convince him to come.
want	He didn't *want* to leave.

Problem 40 — Verb + Gerund or Infinitive

PROBLEM: The wrong form may be used.
SOLUTION: Pay attention to the main verb to determine the form needed.

EXAMPLES

Incorrect: Ms. Utz *enjoys to program* computers.
Correct: Ms. Utz *enjoys programming* computers.

Explanation: *Enjoys* must be followed by a gerund. Use the gerund *programming*.

noun phrase	v	gerund	n
Ms. Utz	enjoys	programming	computers.

Incorrect: The clerk finished *to verify* the orders.
Correct: The clerk finished *verifying* the orders.

Explanation: *Finish* must be followed by a gerund. Use the gerund *verifying*.

noun phrase	v	gerund	noun phrase
The clerk	finished	verifying	the orders.

Incorrect: Mr. White offered *helping* the children.
Correct: Mr. White offered *to help* the children.

Explanation: *Offered* must be followed by an infinitive. Use the infinitive *to help*.

noun phrase	v	infinitive	noun phrase
Ms. White	offered	to help	the children.

Incorrect: The computer failed *running* the program.
Correct: The computer failed *to run* the program.

Explanation: *Fail* must be followed by an infinitive. Use the infinitive *to run*.

noun phrase	v	infinitive	noun phrase
The computer	failed	to run	the program.

EXERCISES

Part V: Incomplete Sentences

Choose the one word or phrase that best completes the sentence.

The clerk intends _____ her supervisor's job in a few years.
(A) having
(B) to have
(C) have
(D) will have

Ⓐ Ⓑ Ⓒ Ⓓ

Part VI: Error Recognition

Identify the one underlined word or phrase that should be corrected or rewritten. Then, write the correct sentence.

The chairman always minds to answer his phone when the secretary is out.
                A   B   C   D

Ⓐ Ⓑ Ⓒ Ⓓ

CUMULATIVE REVIEW EXERCISES: Gerunds and Infinitives

Part V: Incomplete Sentences

Choose the one word or phrase that best completes the sentence.

1. Mr. Ingles is preparing _____ his speech.
   (A) give
   (B) giving
   (C) given
   (D) to give

2. We did not want _____ the meeting.
   (A) to delay
   (B) delaying
   (C) delayed
   (D) delay

3. The committee postponed _____ until tomorrow.
   (A) to vote
   (B) voted
   (C) vote
   (D) voting

4. The president considered _____ a train instead of a plane.
   (A) taking
   (B) will take
   (C) taken
   (D) to take

5. The company failed _____ a profit last year.
   (A) make
   (B) made
   (C) making
   (D) to make

Part VI: Error Recognition

Identify the one underlined word or phrase that should be corrected or rewritten. Then, write the correct sentence.

1. Ms. Helm refuses planning the banquet for the convention next month.
                               A   B   C   D

2. Although Mr. Ozel could not attend, he appreciated to receive an invitation.
       A   B   C   D

3. Ms. Wu intends <u>taking</u> her <u>vacation</u> in September <u>after</u> the project <u>is</u> Ⓐ Ⓑ Ⓒ Ⓓ
   　　　　　　　　　 A　　　　　　 B　　　　　　　　　　　C　　　　　　　　 D
   completed.

4. Mr. Madhava suggested <u>to illustrate</u> the <u>presentation</u> <u>with</u> charts <u>and</u> graphs. Ⓐ Ⓑ Ⓒ Ⓓ
   　　　　　　　　　　　　　　A　　　　　　　　　　B　　　　　C　　　　　　 D

5. <u>When</u> the president hesitated <u>signing</u> the <u>contract</u>, the company <u>lost</u> the Ⓐ Ⓑ Ⓒ Ⓓ
   　　A　　　　　　　　　　　　　　 B　　　　　　 C　　　　　　　　　　　　　 D
   project.

GENERALIZATIONS: PARTICIPLES

Participles are verb forms that are used like adjectives. Participles describe nouns. There are two kinds: (1) present participles and (2) past participles. Present participles end in *-ing*. Past participles can end in *-ed*, *-en*, *-d*, *-t*, or *-n*. Their meanings are different.

v	present participle	past participle
bore	boring	bored
excite	exciting	excited
confuse	confusing	confused
sort	sorting	sorted
surprise	surprising	surprised
enclose	enclosing	enclosed
include	including	included
suggest	suggesting	suggested

Use a present participle to describe a noun when the noun causes the action.

	Causes Action			
			noun phrase	
pron	v	art	present participle	noun
That	is	an	exciting	announcement.

Use a past participle to describe a noun when the noun is affected by the action.

	Receives Action			
	noun phrase			
art	past participle	n	v	noun phrase
The	excited	workers	had heard	the announcement.

Problem 41: Incorrect Participles

PROBLEM: The wrong type of participle may be used.
SOLUTION: Pay attention to the noun you want to describe.

EXAMPLES

Incorrect: The *confused* memo created problems for the staff.
Correct: The *confusing* memo created problems for the staff.

Explanation: The memo caused the confusion. Use the present participle *confusing*.

noun phrase			
art	present participle	n	verb phrase
The	confusing	memo	created problems for the staff.

Incorrect: The *bored* speech made everyone fall asleep.
Correct: The *boring* speech made everyone fall asleep

Explanation: The speech caused the boredom. Use the present participle *boring*.

noun phrase			
art	present participle	noun	verb phrase
The	boring	speech	caused everyone to fall asleep.

Incorrect: The *confusing* staff did not understand the memo.
Correct: The *confused* staff did not understand the memo.

Explanation: The staff did not cause the confusion. The staff received the confusion. Use the past participle *confused*.

noun phrase			
art	past participle	noun	verb phrase
The	confused	staff	did not understand the memo.

Incorrect: The *boring* audience fell asleep during the speech.
Correct: The *bored* audience fell asleep during the speech.

Explanation: The audience did not cause the boredom. The audience received the boredom. Use the past participle *bored*.

	noun phrase		
art	past participle	noun	verb phrase
The	bored	audience	fell asleep during the speech.

EXERCISES

Part V: Incomplete Sentences

Choose the one word or phrase that best completes the sentence.

The _____ report gave the team the information they needed.
(A) enclosing
(B) enclosed
(C) to enclose
(D) has been enclosed

Part VI: Error Recognition

Identify the one underlined word or phrase that should be corrected or rewritten. Then, write the correct sentence.

The surprised message about the salary cuts made everyone very unhappy.
  A   B   C   D

CUMULATIVE REVIEW EXERCISES: Participles

Part V: Incomplete Sentences

Choose the one word or phrase that best completes the sentence.

1. The _____ employees did not like their jobs.
   (A) boring
   (B) bored
   (C) bores
   (D) bore

2. The office boy will distribute the _____ mail.
   (A) sorted
   (B) sort
   (C) sort of
   (D) sorting

3. The _____ application was delivered with the job offer.
   (A) approval
   (B) approves
   (C) approved
   (D) approving

4. It is difficult to work in these _____ offices.
   (A) crowding
   (B) crowded
   (C) crowds
   (D) crowd

5. The _____ audience enjoyed the speaker.
   (A) laugh
   (B) laughter
   (C) laughed
   (D) laughing

Part VI: Error Recognition

Identify the one underlined word or phrase that should be corrected or rewritten. Then, write the correct sentence.

1. The <u>typing</u> letters <u>were placed</u> <u>on</u> the <u>manager's</u> desk.
      A   B   C   D

2. <u>In the front office</u>, a <u>smiled</u> receptionist <u>greets</u> <u>visitors</u>.
        A   B   C   D

3. The <u>interesting</u> crowd <u>listened</u> <u>carefully</u> to <u>the</u> speech.
           A   B   C   D

4. Everyone's work <u>was delayed</u> <u>by</u> the <u>breaking</u> copy machine.
       A   B   C   D

5. The <u>tiring</u> engineers <u>were glad</u> <u>to finish</u> <u>their</u> work.
          A   B   C   D

STRATEGY

Strategies for Analyzing Grammar

The many grammar rules and solutions to potential problems that you learned in this section can be summarized in the following strategies. If you can learn to recognize these components and how they work together, you will score well on Parts V and VI.
- Recognize the parts of speech.
- Recognize agreement of person, number, and tense.
- Recognize the correct grammatical form.
- Recognize correct usage.
- Recognize the correct word order.
- Recognize potentially wrong answers.

Mini-Test for Reading Parts V and VI

General directions: Follow the instructions for each part below and use the answer sheet on page 673. When you have finished both parts, check your answers using the Answer Key on page 471 and see the Explanatory Answers on page 501.

Part IV: Incomplete Sentences

Directions: In your test book, you will see a sentence with a missing word. Four possible answers follow the sentence. Choose the best answer to the question and fill in the corresponding oval on your answer sheet.

1. The fax machine and the telephone _____ on separate lines.
   (A) am
   (B) is
   (C) are
   (D) be

2. Attach this cable _____ the computer.
   (A) with
   (B) into
   (C) in
   (D) to

3. Tomorrow we _____ submit the budget.
   (A) will
   (B) has
   (C) did
   (D) are

4. The _____ was concise and effective.
   (A) presenting
   (B) presented
   (C) present
   (D) presentation

5. Salaries must be _____ if we are to remain competitive.
   (A) ascended
   (B) increased
   (C) escalated
   (D) risen

6. We drove to the site in an open jeep _____ it was raining.
   (A) although
   (B) since
   (C) because
   (D) with

7. The meeting was scheduled to begin _____ noon.
   (A) on
   (B) to
   (C) in
   (D) at

8. This letter was _____ by overnight mail.
   (A) send
   (B) been sent
   (C) sent
   (D) sending

9. The staff _____ after 5:00 if there is work to finish.
   (A) will usually stay
   (B) will usually stays
   (C) will stay usually
   (D) usually will stay

10. Our office is _____ the post office and the bank.
    (A) among
    (B) outside
    (C) between
    (D) through

11. If you need to order supplies, _____ a purchase order form.
    (A) complete
    (B) completely
    (C) completion
    (D) to complete

12. The oil rig is located _____ shore.
    (A) over
    (B) under
    (C) off
    (D) beside

13. _____ exports have increased, the trade deficit has become smaller.
    (A) Although
    (B) During
    (C) Since
    (D) While

14. Immigration forms must _____ be stamped before leaving the customs area.
    (A) never
    (B) always
    (C) sometimes
    (D) rarely

15. Neither lunch _____ dinner was served at the hotel.
    (A) or
    (B) and
    (C) but
    (D) nor

16. The consultant recommended that more support staff _____ hired.
    (A) are
    (B) have
    (C) be
    (D) do

17. If you _____ how to use a computer, consult the manual.
    (A) won't understand
    (B) don't understand
    (C) understood
    (D) not understanding

18. Before the Foreign Minister arrived, the police had the conference center _____.
    (A) clear
    (B) cleared
    (C) clearing
    (D) be clear

19. The Bangkok branch of our bank _____ ten years ago this month.
    (A) opens
    (B) has opened
    (C) opened
    (D) was opening

20. All visitors must _____ their coats and packages before entering the museum.
    (A) checked
    (B) checking
    (C) checks
    (D) check

Part IV: Error Recognition

Directions: In your test book, you will see a sentence with four words or phrases underlined. Choose the word or phrase that is incorrect and fill in the corresponding oval on your answer sheet.

21. At the end of year, bonuses are distributed
    A   B   C
    to the employees.
           D

22. The international association of
    A
    petrochemical industries have come under
                            B   C
    attack from environmentalists.
                D

23. The catering staff has scheduled a meeting
                      A   B
    in the same room where us are holding a
        C   D
    meeting.

24. The legislature would have pass the trade
        A   B
    agreement if the labor unions had not been
       C
    so opposed to it.
              D

25. The interest rates are more higher this year
        A   B
    than they were last.
         C   D

26. While ten weeks, Ms. Tanaka has been
    A
    traveling to our international offices and
    B   C
    meeting with our sales
            D
    representatives.

27. The dollar has never been as lower as it is
        A   B   C   D
    now.

28. For immediately service, please fax us your
    A   B   C   D
    order.

29. In the morning, there will be a ten-minutes
        A   B   C
    coffee break between speeches.
                D

30. I thought this letter of recommendation
        A   B
    had been mailed last week before.
        C   D

Reading Comprehension Tips

Types of Questions Found on the TOEIC

There are three types of questions found on the Reading Comprehension part of the TOEIC. The most common question type is the one that begins with a "wh" word.

1. Questions that begin with "wh" words: *How, what, when, where, which, who, why.*

    Who completed the form?
    - (A) The hotel clerk
    - (B) The manager
    - (C) The client
    - (D) The travel agent

2. Questions that begin with "if" and "wh" words.

    If the form is incomplete, what will happen?
    - (A) It will be returned.
    - (B) It will be destroyed.
    - (C) It will be rewritten.
    - (D) It will be filed.

3. Open questions.

    This form must be completed at
    - (A) a hotel.
    - (B) an airport.
    - (C) a police station.
    - (D) a car rental agency.

Study the examples given in the chart on pages 203–204. Look for these kinds of questions in the "Problems Analyzing Reading Passages" section beginning on page 206.

Types of Information Sought on the TOEIC

The three question types are looking for six different types of information. The most frequently asked question is the one looking for *factual information*.

Most commonly asked questions:

1. Positive factual questions
2. Negative factual questions
3. Inference questions

Less commonly asked questions:

4. Main idea questions
5. Viewpoint questions
6. Computation questions

Study the examples given in the chart on pages 203–204. These examples show how those questions commonly asked match the information sought. Look for these types of questions in the "Problems Analyzing Reading Passages" section beginning on page 206.

READING COMPREHENSION TIPS

Common Questions	Common Words or Phrases
Positive Factual Which of the following would be included? How do people plan to raise money? Who made the phone calls? Why was the call made? At what time was the call received? What is one problem with the management? When can visitors see the exhibit? When is the fare the lowest? How much will it cost to produce the product? What is the base charge for one kilowatt hour of electricity?	How What When Where Which Who Why
If expenses are $50, how much does the company earn? If no directions are given, the workers will...	If
According to the table, which city had the least rainfall? Of the following, which would apply?	According to the author... According to the bulletin... Of the following...
The division had to decide whether or not to... One of the factors that was included was... One of the articles listed is...	
Part-time workers are MOST likely to have...	MOST
Negative Factual EXCEPT for (besides) Sundays, the offices are open... Which of the following would NOT be part of the plan? All of the following are essential EXCEPT... Students are the LEAST likely to...	NOT EXCEPT LEAST
Inference Why are there fewer computers? Why was this graph produced? Why is he writing this letter?	Why likely probably
Where is this announcement likely to be found?	
It can be inferred from the chart that 19__ was... This type of form must be filled out at...	It can be inferred that The author implies that...
Main Idea What is the purpose of this letter? Why was this letter written?	main point mainly discuss main idea
The main idea of the article is... The main topic of the article is...	main purpose main topic *(continued)*

204 READING REVIEW

Common Questions	Common words or phrases
Viewpoint (not commonly asked) The authors of the article believe that... The tone of this letter is... The author describes capitalism as...	The authors believe... The general tone of... The writer's attitude... The author's purpose... feel
Computation (not commonly asked) How much does the total package cost? How much more does it cost for four than one?	How much cost total

The PSRA Strategy

An important strategy for reading comprehension is learning to approach a passage in an organized way. First make a *Prediction* about the passage, then *Scan* it; next *Read* it, and finally *Answer* the questions. We can abbreviate this strategy to **PSRA**.

Prediction

Learning how to make predictions about what you are going to read BEFORE you read will help you establish a context for understanding the passage. This will improve your reading score.

Before you begin to read one of the reading passages, you should first look at the question introduction line. This line looks like this:

Questions 161–163 refer to the following office memo.

In the question introduction line, you will learn how many questions there are and what kind of reading passage it is (in this case an office memo). The look of the reading passage will also give you a clue: a fax will look like a fax; a phone message like a phone message, a graph like a graph, etc. This will help you PREDICT what the passage is about.

There are generally two or three questions for every reading passage. Look at the questions and the four answer options. This will give you a clue what to look for. These clues will help you PREDICT what the passage is about.

According to the memo, which equipment has multiple uses?
(A) Computers
(B) Fax machines
(C) Answering machines
(D) CD-players

Scan

We can predict that the memo has something to do with electronics. When we *Scan* the passage, we look for the Key Words. You may not find the exact words, but you might find words with similar meanings. Try to think of words that have meanings similar to those in the Key Words. The Key Words for this question are:

READING COMPREHENSION TIPS 205

Questions		Answer Options
Key words equipment multiple uses	Similar meanings electronic tools; hardware useful in a variety of settings	computers fax machines answering machines CD-players

Look first for the Key Words from the question; then look around the Question Key Words for the Key Words from the answer options. When you find the Answer Option Key Words, see if the words answer the question. Try to answer the question (in your head, NOT on the answer sheet). Here's a sample:

MEMORANDUM

To: Lafite, Pierre
 Purchasing Department

From: Clement, Marie France
 Personnel

We need **computers** for use in the office, **answering machines** for our consultants, **fax machines** for the shipping department, and **CD-players** for everyone. This **last piece of hardware** can be **used in a variety** of ways.

According to the memo, which equipment has multiple uses?
 (A) Computers
 (B) Fax machines
 (C) Answering machines
 (D) CD-players

The correct answer is (D). A CD-player is the **last** piece of hardware mentioned. *This last piece of hardware can be used in a variety of ways.*

Note how much different the answer would be if the last sentence were:

This **first piece of hardware** can be **used in a variety** of ways.

The word "first" changes the answer completely from (D) CD-players to (A) Computers. This is why you must NOT rely on Prediction and Scanning alone.

Read

You must READ the passage as well. But when you read, read quickly. Read to confirm your predictions.

You should not make any mark on your answer sheet until you have made a PREDICTION based on all of the questions, SCANNED the passage looking for key words, answered the questions in your head, and READ the passage to confirm your answer choices. The answer to the first question is found in the first part of the reading passage. The answer to the second question is found in the next part and so on. The questions follow the sequence of the passage.

Answer

Now you are ready to mark your answer sheet. ANSWER the easy questions first. If you don't know an answer, scan the passage again, look for the key words, read parts of the passage. If you still don't know, GUESS. Do NOT leave any answer blank.

These strategies are easy to remember; just memorize PSRA: Predict, Scan, Read, and Answer.

STRATEGY

Strategies for Reading Comprehension

Predict.
Look at the introduction line.
Look at the question and answer options.

Scan the passage.
Look for Key Words from the question.
Look for Key Words from the answer options.
Answer questions (in your head, NOT on answer sheet).

Read the passage.
Read quickly, but carefully. Don't stop if you don't know a word.
Confirm your predictions.

Answer the questions on the answer sheet.
Answer the easy questions first.
Guess if you don't know.

Now practice the PSRA strategy with the following reading passages. There are more questions on each reading passage in this book than on the TOEIC test. This will give you more practice.

For each reading passage, you should circle the Key Words; answer the questions in your head; time yourself as you read; and finally answer the questions.

Try to finish quickly. You should not spend more than one minute on each question. At the most, you will have only three minutes to read the passage and answer all the questions. Try to do each passage in less than two minutes.

Problems Analyzing Reading Passages

The reading passages on the TOEIC test can be anything that is written in English. The most likely types of reading passages on the TOEIC test are:
- Advertisements
- Forms
- Reports

- Letters, Faxes, and Memos
- Tables and Indexes
- Charts and Graphs
- Announcements and Notices
- Newspaper and Magazine Articles
- Schedules and Calendars

Examples of each type follow. Do the exercises for each Reading Comprehension problem. Check your answers using the Answer Key on page 471 and the Explanatory Answers on page 503.

Problem 42 — Questions on Advertisements

Advertisements on the TOEIC are similar to those found in magazines or newspapers. You can find other examples in English-language newspapers and magazines and ask yourself questions about the products being advertised.

EXERCISE

Part VII: Reading Comprehension

Choose the one best answer to each question.

Questions 1–2 refer to the following advertisement.

ATTENTION MANUFACTURERS!

We introduce and distribute your products to 125,000 distributors in 155 countries, FREE!

For a FREE information kit call:

Tel: (310) 553-4434 Ext. 105 • Fax (310) 553-5555

GRAND TECHNOLOGIES LIMITED

---

1. Who is the advertisement written for?
   (A) Distributors
   (B) Sales representatives
   (C) Manufacturers
   (D) Information specialists

208 READING REVIEW

2. How many countries are mentioned?
   (A) 125
   (B) 155
   (C) 310
   (D) 501

   (A) (B) (C) (D)

Problem 43 Questions on Forms

A form is a template: a standard form that an individual adds information to. These could include magazine subscription forms, purchase orders, immigration forms, hotel check-in forms, telephone message blanks, etc.

EXERCISES

Part VII: Reading Comprehension

Choose the one best answer to each question.

Questions 1–4 refer to the following form.

Special Subscription Offer

Subscribe to the journal that recently received the Editorial Excellence Award from the Society of Industrial Designers

☑ **YES!** send me INTERNATIONAL INDUSTRY for 1 year (12 issues) at just $48, a savings of 20% off the full cover price of $5.00.

☐ Payment enclosed   ☑ Bill me.

Name: _____Anne Kwok_____
Title: _____Design Specialist_____
Company: _Pharmaceutical Supply Co._____
Address: ___Tong Chong Street_____
           ___Quarry Bay Hong Kong_____

Please allow four weeks for first issue.

1. Why did Anne Kwok complete this form?
   - (A) To win an award
   - (B) To apply for a design job
   - (C) To enroll in design school
   - (D) To receive a journal

   Ⓐ Ⓑ Ⓒ Ⓓ

2. How much is the full cover price per issue?
   - (A) $4
   - (B) $5
   - (C) $12
   - (D) $48

   Ⓐ Ⓑ Ⓒ Ⓓ

3. How long will it take for the first issue to arrive?
   - (A) One week
   - (B) One month
   - (C) One year
   - (D) Unknown

   Ⓐ Ⓑ Ⓒ Ⓓ

4. The magazine comes
   - (A) daily.
   - (B) weekly.
   - (C) monthly.
   - (D) once a year.

   Ⓐ Ⓑ Ⓒ Ⓓ

Problem 44: Questions on Reports

A report is a short paragraph containing the kind of information that might be included in a capsule summary. A report could appear in a newspaper; it could be part of a larger document such as annual report; it could be most any kind of descriptive or narrative prose.

EXERCISES

Part VII: Reading Comprehension

Choose the one best answer to each question.

Questions 1–3 refer to the following report.

> In October, Markel On-Line acquired Peptel Visual of Berlin, one of Europe's leading educational software companies. The deal calls for Markel (a $49 million Toronto-based company) to pay $5 million up front for Peptel and as much as $5 million more over the next few years, depending on the German company's performance. Peptel posted $4.2 million in sales last year.

1. If Peptel performs well, what is the largest total price Markel will have to pay?
   (A) $4.2 million
   (B) $5 million
   (C) $10 million
   (D) $49 million

2. Peptel is based in
   (A) Canada.
   (B) the United States.
   (C) Great Britain.
   (D) Germany.

3. What field are these companies in?
   (A) Computer software
   (B) Postal service
   (C) Visual arts
   (D) Toy manufacturing

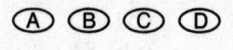

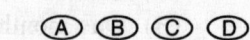

Problem 45 Questions on Letters

The TOEIC will generally always have one letter on the test. The important information is generally contained in the body of the letter—the part between the greeting (*Dear ...*) and the closing (*Sincerely yours*).

EXERCISES

Part VII: Reading Comprehension

Choose the one best answer to each question.

Questions 1–3 refer to the following letter.

EUTECH, s.r.o.
Zborovská 23,150 00 Praha 5
Czech Republic
Tel: (02) 513.2343 Fax: (02) 513.2334

December 3, 19___

Post Comptoir
43 Griffith Road
Dinsdale, Hamilton
North Island, New Zealand

Dear Sir or Madam:

We are interested in becoming distributors for your software products in the Czech Republic. Would you please send us your latest catalogs, descriptive brochures, and terms?

We are a hardware company that would like to add software to our sales offerings. Our annual report is enclosed.

We look forward to hearing from you soon.

Sincerely yours,

Peter Zavel
Peter Zavel
Chairman

---

1. Which was NOT requested?
    (A) Catalogs
    (B) Brochures
    (C) Samples
    (D) Pricing information

2. What does EUTECH sell now?
    (A) Software
    (B) Computers
    (C) Financial reports
    (D) Printing services

3. EUTECH wants to
    (A) distribute software.
    (B) manufacture computers.
    (C) purchase hardware.
    (D) receive an annual report.

Problem 46: Questions on Faxes

A fax (facsimile) is like a letter except it is delivered electronically on a fax machine. The main difference in format is the additional piece of information that tells how many pages were sent as part of a fax.

EXERCISES

Part VII: Reading Comprehension

Choose the <u>one</u> best answer to each question.

Questions 1–4 refer to the following fax.

FAX COVER SHEET

ARS TECH
Avenida Diagonal 673–683
08028 Barcelona
Spain
Tel: (3) 318-4300
Fax: (3) 318-4308

To: All Board Members
From: Fernando Murillo
Accounting Department
Date: October 23, 19__
Pages: This +10
Ref: 19__ Budget

Message:

Please review the attached budget before the meeting tomorrow. The meeting will begin Tuesday, October 24 at 10:00 a.m. in room 42 in Building B. It will last through Thursday and will finish at 5:00 p.m. There will be a reception at the Sofitel Hotel Thursday evening.

---

1. Where will the meeting be held?
   (A) In Room 24
   (B) In Building B
   (C) Next door
   (D) At the Sofitel Hotel

2. How many days will the meeting last?
    (A) Two
    (B) Three
    (C) Four
    (D) Five

    Ⓐ Ⓑ Ⓒ Ⓓ

3. What day was the fax written?
    (A) Monday
    (B) Tuesday
    (C) Thursday
    (D) Friday

    Ⓐ Ⓑ Ⓒ Ⓓ

4. How many pages are in the whole fax?
    (A) One
    (B) Two
    (C) Ten
    (D) Eleven

    Ⓐ Ⓑ Ⓒ Ⓓ

Problem 47 Questions on Memos

A memorandum (memo) is an internal form of communication that is sent from one member of a company to a member of the same company. Today these memos (memoranda) are often sent by computer. Computer mail is referred to as e-mail, short for electronic mail.

EXERCISES

Part VII: Reading Comprehension

Choose the one best answer to each question.

Questions 1–4 refer to the following memorandum.

MEMORANDUM

To: All Personnel

From: Simon Gonzales
      Personnel Officer

Date: May 15, 19__

Sub: Company Travel

Effective June 1 all personnel traveling on company business must use the most economical means possible. No flights under five hours can be booked in Business Class. No flights regardless of duration can be booked in First Class or on the Concorde.

214 READING REVIEW

1. If a flight is over five hours, what class can be booked?
   (A) Economy
   (B) Business
   (C) First
   (D) Concorde

2. When will this rule go into effect?
   (A) In about two weeks
   (B) At the end of the summer
   (C) At the first of the year
   (D) In five months

3. Why was this memo written?
   (A) To save time
   (B) To save money
   (C) To reward the employees
   (D) To increase company travel

4. Who is affected by this memo?
   (A) Only the Board of Directors
   (B) Only frequent travelers
   (C) Only the personnel department
   (D) All personnel

Problem 48 Questions on Tables

The TOEIC will often have a table on the exam. A table is a compilation of data that is useful for quick comparison. Tables could be on most any subject. Look for tables in English-language newspapers or magazines or also material printed in your own language.

EXERCISE

Part VII: Reading Comprehension

Choose the one best answer to each question.

Questions 1–4 refer to the following table.

WORLD TEMPERATURES
January 5

	Hi C/F	Lo C/F	Weather
Amsterdam	5/41	3/37	c
Athens	13/55	8/46	sh
Bangkok	32/90	27/80	sh
Beijing	12/53	1/34	pc
Brussels	4/39	1/34	sh
Budapest	3/37	0/32	r
Frankfurt	3/37	1/34	r
Jakarta	29/84	24/75	sh
Kuala Lampur	31/88	24/75	t
Madrid	9/48	1/34	sh
Manila	33/91	21/70	pc
Seoul	9/48	-2/29	s
Taipei	21/70	14/57	c
Tokyo	9/48	-2/29	pc

Weather: s-sunny; pc-partly cloudy; c-cloudy; sh-showers; t-thunderstorms; r-rain

1. Which two cities were cloudy on January 5?
    (A) Amsterdam and Taipei
    (B) Beijing and Manila
    (C) Athens and Tokyo
    (D) Bangkok and Seoul

    Ⓐ Ⓑ Ⓒ Ⓓ

2. Which city had the highest temperature?
    (A) Athens
    (B) Bangkok
    (C) Jakarta
    (D) Manila

    Ⓐ Ⓑ Ⓒ Ⓓ

3. Which city had the closest spread between high and low temperature?
    (A) Brussels
    (B) Frankfurt
    (C) Seoul
    (D) Tokyo

    Ⓐ Ⓑ Ⓒ Ⓓ

4. Kuala Lampur had
    (A) sun.
    (B) thunderstorms.
    (C) rain.
    (D) showers.

    Ⓐ Ⓑ Ⓒ Ⓓ

Problem 49: Questions on Indexes

An index is a compilation of information that people can use to find additional information. A telephone book is an example of an index.

EXERCISES

Part VII: Reading Comprehension

Choose the one best answer to each question.

Questions 1–2 refer to the following index.

Company Index
This index lists businesses mentioned in this issue of Global Economy

Acme Power and Light	44
Allied Steel	53
Best Iron Ore Supply	56
Canadian Rail Service	83
Chemical Times	15
Consumer's Electric	41
Ford Gas	4
Health, Inc.	12
International Oil	16
Liberty Funds	46
Network Travel	52
Pride Hotels	76
TNT Air	34

1. This index is most likely found in
   (A) a magazine.
   (B) an interoffice memo.
   (C) a newsletter.
   (D) a book.

2. What type of industries are NOT represented?
   (A) Travel
   (B) Computer
   (C) Heavy industries
   (D) Utilities industries

Problem 50: Questions on Charts

A chart can be either a table or a graph. Charts are found in most printed materials.

EXERCISE

Part VII: Reading Comprehension

Choose the one best answer to each question.

Questions 1–2 refer to the following chart.

Top Ten Companies in Total Sales

Company	Sales (in billion)
Sankyu, Inc.	$2,890
Executive Jet	$1,450
InterCon	$1,400
Continental, Ltd.	$1,380
Hospital Supply	$1,370
Tislak Leasing	$1,300
Leber Bank	$1,250
Euro Data	$1,250
InterAccess	$1,220
TeleVide	$1,200

1. What does this chart show?
    (A) Selling price of companies
    (B) Corporate salaries
    (C) Relative positions of successful companies
    (D) Numbers of investors

2. What can be said about Sankyu, Inc.?
    (A) It performed better last year.
    (B) Its sales are almost double the next ranking company.
    (C) Its sales are half as much as TeleVide.
    (D) Its earnings equaled that of Executive Jet.

Problem 51: Questions on Graphs

A graph is a drawing that shows the relationship between variables. On the TOEIC test there can be line graphs, bar graphs, or pie graphs.

EXERCISES

Part VII: Reading Comprehension

Choose the <u>one</u> best answer to each question.

Questions 1–2 refer to the following graph.

Hotel Chain Market Share

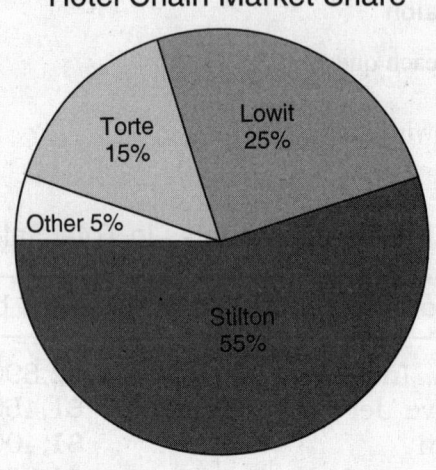

- Lowit 25%
- Torte 15%
- Other 5%
- Stilton 55%

1. Who would be most interested in reading this graph?
    (A) Tourists
    (B) Competing hotels
    (C) Landscape architects
    (D) Job hunters

2. According to this graph, Lowit
    (A) is the top-ranking hotel chain.
    (B) is only in Latin America.
    (C) has less of a share than Torte.
    (D) has one-quarter of the market.

Problem 52 Questions on Announcements

An announcement is similar to a report except it has more immediate information. There is usually an announcement on the TOEIC test.

EXERCISES

Part VII: Reading Comprehension

Choose the <u>one</u> best answer to each question.

Questions 1–4 refer to the following announcement.

> The Omnicable Company representatives said yesterday that John A. Kaspar, its president and chief operating officer, would resign on April 30. The announcement added to speculation that the world's third-largest cable television system could be bought within a few weeks. Mr. Kaspar, 62, said he was leaving after more than 22 years for "personal reasons."

1. What is the company's world ranking?
    (A) 3
    (B) 22
    (C) 30
    (D) 62

    Ⓐ Ⓑ Ⓒ Ⓓ

2. What might happen to the company?
    (A) It may be bought.
    (B) It may expand.
    (C) It may diversify.
    (D) It may become international.

    Ⓐ Ⓑ Ⓒ Ⓓ

3. How long has Mr. Kaspar worked for Omnicable?
    (A) For a few weeks
    (B) Since April 30
    (C) Since he was 40
    (D) 62 years

    Ⓐ Ⓑ Ⓒ Ⓓ

4. What kind of business is Omnicable?
    (A) Communications
    (B) Computer
    (C) Manufacturing
    (D) Service

    Ⓐ Ⓑ Ⓒ Ⓓ

Problem 53 Questions on Notices

A notice is information that the writer feels the general public or specific product users must be made aware of. There are often notices attached to walls and public buildings or enclosed with product literature.

EXERCISES

Part VII: Reading Comprehension

Choose the one best answer to each question.

Questions 1–2 refer to the following notice.

> **Corporate Policy Change**
>
> Moving Expenses. You can be reimbursed for your expenses of moving to a new home only if your new home is at least 50 miles away from your former home. In addition, expenses are limited to the costs of moving your household goods and personal effects from your former home to your new home. Meals, pre-move house-hunting expenses, and temporary-quarters expenses are no longer reimbursable.

1. Who would be most affected by this notice?
   - (A) Hotel chains
   - (B) Furniture rental companies
   - (C) Real estate agents
   - (D) New employees moving from another city

2. Which of the following will be reimbursed?
   - (A) Lunch for the movers
   - (B) Shipping household goods
   - (C) Gas used looking for a house
   - (D) Hotel expenses

Problem 54: Questions on Newspaper Articles

A newspaper article is a passage written by a journalist for a newspaper. Usually the topic is very current, but there are many kinds of newspapers: some come out daily, others weekly. Even companies may have their own internal newspaper which, because of their small size, are often called newsletters.

EXERCISES

Part VII: Reading Comprehension

Choose the one best answer to each question.

Questions 1–3 refer to the following newspaper article.

> Before the fall of the Berlin Wall, East Berlin was like the rest of East Germany — drab and depressed. Today it is a different story. There are over 40 major construction projects underway and investments in new construction are expected to exceed $20 billion. Part of this boom can be attributed to the fact that the national government of Germany will move to Berlin. The city will once again be Germany's leading city and a gateway to the expanding markets in Poland, the Czech Republic, and other countries east of the German border.

1. According to the article, what caused the change in East Berlin?
   (A) Expanding markets in Poland
   (B) Border changes east of Germany
   (C) The completion of 40 construction projects
   (D) The collapse of the Berlin Wall

2. Which is NOT given as a reason for increased prosperity?
   (A) The location of Berlin
   (B) The destruction of the Berlin Wall
   (C) The move of the national government
   (D) The drab character of East Berlin

3. A sum of at least $20 billion will be invested in
   (A) moving the government.
   (B) new construction.
   (C) expanding markets.
   (D) border control.

Problem 55 Questions on Magazine Articles

Like a newspaper article, a magazine article is written by a journalist. The topic could be any subject.

EXERCISE

Part VII: Reading Comprehension

Choose the one best answer to each question.

Questions 1–3 refer to the following magazine article.

> The Information Highway is the road that links computer users to an infinite number of on-line services using communication technology like the telephone, cable lines, and satellite links. On the Information Highway a person sitting in front of his or her computer can have access to news, electronic mail, public forums, and software, to mention a few services. The lower prices of computers have put more computers in the home and set the stage for the information revolution. In 1994 only 4 million households used on-line services, but by 2000 that number should exceed 30 million. The growth potential in this market is enormous.

1. What is this article about?
    (A) The information revolution
    (B) Cheaper computers
    (C) Traveling by highway in the 1990s
    (D) The importance of news

2. What is described as enormous?
    (A) The Information Highway
    (B) The cable system
    (C) The market potential
    (D) The on-line services

3. According to the article, what has put more computers in homes?
    (A) Increased services
    (B) Better software
    (C) Lower costs
    (D) The information revolution

Problem 56 Questions on Schedules

A schedule is a printed form with lists of information: stock prices, train departure times, payment schedules, etc.

EXERCISES

Part VII: Reading Comprehension

Choose the one best answer to each question.

Questions 1–4 refer to the following schedule.

Airline Schedule
All Flights From: Mexico City
Reservations: 202-1308

Lv	Ar	Flt(s)	Stp(s)	Miles/Frequency
Amsterdam				5729
11:10	7:20 †	238/44	C	Daily
Honolulu				3796
8:00	**2:25**	345/234	C	Daily
Los Angeles				1552
8:00	9:59	345	0	Daily
5:10	**6:53**	57	0	Daily
6:55	**8:56**	377	0	x,67
Moscow				6653
10:10	10:30 †	782/34	C	x,27
11:10	**5:45**	339/40	C	3
Zurich				6021
11:10	9:55 †	339/40	C	3

Key:

x – except

boldface - PM

† – next day

1 – Monday; 2 – Tuesday; 3 – Wednesday; 4 – Thursday; 5 – Friday; 6 – Saturday; 7 – Sunday

1. Passengers change planes in Los Angeles en route to
    (A) Amsterdam.
    (B) Honolulu.
    (C) Moscow.
    (D) New York.

2. Flight 40 makes a stop in
    (A) Mexico City.
    (B) Honolulu.
    (C) Los Angeles.
    (D) Zurich.

3. It can be inferred that
    (A) Flight 339 stops in Los Angeles.
    (B) the Moscow flights operate daily.
    (C) Flight 40 operates only on Wednesday.
    (D) Flight 44 originates in Los Angeles.

224 READING REVIEW

4. The flights to Los Angeles
   - (A) do not operate on Wednesdays.
   - (B) make one stop.
   - (C) are the longest in miles.
   - (D) are the shortest in miles.

   Ⓐ Ⓑ Ⓒ Ⓓ

Problem 57 Questions on Calendars

A calendar is a form for keeping track of future events or activities. The calendar could be personal, like a daily diary, or professional, like a timeline for completion of a project.

EXERCISE

Part VII: Reading Comprehension

Choose the one best answer to each question.

Questions 1–4 refer to the following calendar.

January

	1 Holiday Golf w/JR	2 10:00 Mtg w/ Travel Agent Assoc.	3 11:00 Fly to Rio	4 Hotel Copa	5 Brkfst mtg with hotel refs 12:00 City tour	6 AM: Mtg with tour guides 5:00 P.M. flight home
7 Golf w/JR at club	8 6 P.M. Company dinner	9 7 A.M. Brkfst mtg with airline agents	10 3 P.M. Meeting w/ editor of travel mag	11 6:00 A.M. train to NY 8 P.M. Return	12 4 P.M. Dr's Appointment	13 10 A.M. Golf at club

1. What field is this person probably in?
   - (A) Tourism
   - (B) Medicine
   - (C) Education
   - (D) Sports

   Ⓐ Ⓑ Ⓒ Ⓓ

2. How many out-of-town trips are planned?
   - (A) One
   - (B) Two
   - (C) Three
   - (D) Four

   Ⓐ Ⓑ Ⓒ Ⓓ

3. How many nights will the person be away?
    (A) One
    (B) Two
    (C) Three
    (D) Four

    Ⓐ Ⓑ Ⓒ Ⓓ

4. For recreation this person probably
    (A) plays golf.
    (B) dances.
    (C) cooks.
    (D) learns Portuguese.

    Ⓐ Ⓑ Ⓒ Ⓓ

Mini-Test for Reading Part VII

General directions: Read the passages below and choose the one best answer (A), (B), (C), or (D), to each question. Answer all questions following the passage based on what is *stated* or *implied* in that passage. Check your answers using the Answer Key on page 471 and the Explanatory Answers on page 506. Use the answer sheet on page 673.

Questions 1–2 refer to the following advertisement.

ARABIC TO ZULU
225 languages

**The Only
Full Service**
International Book Supplier
in North America

Global Publishing Services
One World Trade Center
Suite 3007
Renaissance Plaza
Detroit, Michigan

Phone   Fax
313-555-9808   313-555-9800

1. What is being offered?
   - (A) Translation services
   - (B) Office supplies
   - (C) Vacations to Africa
   - (D) Books in many languages

2. What feature of the company is mentioned in this advertisement?
   - (A) Its multilingual staff
   - (B) Its complete service
   - (C) Its fax number
   - (D) Its price

Questions 3–6 refer to the following purchase order.

PURCHASE ORDER
Ship Prepaid • Add all delivery charges on invoice

TECH 2000
44 Sankey Street
Warrington, Cheshire
WA 1 1SG ENGLAND

Tel: 0925 412 555
Fax: 0925 412 559

Vendor:
Comtex
65-67 Lowgate Hull
HU 1 1HP
England
Tel: 482-593-678
Fax: 482-593-689

Ship To: Marc Greenspan
Purchasing Department
Address above

Reference: P.O. 03-687-47X
Date: 12 June 19__

Invoice To: Marcia Goodall
Accounting Department
Address above

Delivery Date: ASAP

Item	Model Number	Quantity	Unit Cost	Total Cost
C180 Hard drive	M4569A	10	£675.00	£6750.00
C-52 Serial cable	C323	20	£ 12.50	£ 250.00
SE-Ethernet card	NET 0422	10	£ 50.00	£ 500.00

Sub-total   £7500.00
Shipping/Handling 10%   £ 750.00
TOTAL   £8250.00

Prepared by: ___Marc Greenspan_____
Date: _12 June 19_____

cc: Accounting Department; Purchasing Department; Receiving Department

3. Who will be billed for the purchase?
   (A) The Purchasing Department, TECH 2000
   (B) The Accounting Department, TECH 2000
   (C) The Purchasing Department, Comtex
   (D) The Shipping Department, Comtex

4. Who sells hard drives and serial cables?
   (A) Comtex
   (B) TECH 2000
   (C) Marc Greenspan
   (D) Marcia Goodall

5. If the Ethernet cards were NOT ordered, what would be the subtotal?
   (A) £7000
   (B) £7500
   (C) £7700
   (D) £8250

6. Which department does NOT get a copy of the purchase order?
   (A) Accounting
   (B) Purchasing
   (C) Receiving
   (D) Personnel

Questions 7–8 refer to the following report.

> Midsize companies that want to increase their sales in international markets cannot rely on exporting their goods—not if they want to grow substantially. Customers want to be close to their suppliers. They want to provide input on design, engineering, and quality control. Also, local governments want jobs created for their citizens. This means that international companies will have to establish a manufacturing operation near their customers.

7. If international companies want to grow, they will need to
   (A) improve quality control.
   (B) export more goods.
   (C) build factories close to their customers.
   (D) design better products.

8. Who wants to provide input on design?
   (A) Design consultants
   (B) Customers
   (C) Suppliers
   (D) Engineers

Questions 9–10 refer to the following letter.

HAMBURG PAPER COMPANY
Postfach 806010
Rungerdamm 2
2050 Hamburg 80
Germany

March 10, 19__

Mr. Frank Knockaert
Crestco Inc.
26 Avenue Marnix
B-1000 Brussels
Belgium

Dear Mr. Knockaert:

In response to your letter of February 23, we apologize for the error in your shipment. We are sending immediately the additional 1000 cases of facsimile paper, model P-345X, that were not included in the shipment.

We value our relationship with your company, and we regret the inconvenience the incomplete shipment may have caused you. You can be assured that this will not happen in the future.

Sincerely yours,

Gertrude Rombach
Gertrude Rombach
Manager, Order Department

---

9. What is the purpose of this letter?
   (A) To complain
   (B) To place an order
   (C) To apologize
   (D) To introduce services

10. The first shipment
    (A) was not complete.
    (B) arrived late.
    (C) was damaged.
    (D) was sent to the wrong address.

Questions 11–13 refer to the following fax.

```
International Cargo                    FAX TRANSMISSION
Place de la Concorde
45040 Orleans Cedex 1
France
Tel:    (33) - 387-87445
Fax:    (33) - 387-87454

To:     Markus Tarasov
        P.O. Box 10382 Manama, Bahrain
        Fax: 973 - 213324
        Tel: 973 - 213300

From:   Marie Martin
        Sales Representative

Date:   April 18, 19__

Pages:  This

Ref:    Your fax of April 18, 19__
Messages:

Your order was received this morning and is being
processed. You should expect delivery by the end of the
week or at the very latest on Monday. We will fax exact
time of arrival before Friday.
```

11. When was the order received?
    (A) The end of the week
    (B) Yesterday
    (C) Today
    (D) Friday

12. How will Ms. Martin communicate the delivery time?
    (A) By phone
    (B) By fax
    (C) By letter
    (D) By messenger

13. If the order does NOT arrive by Friday, when will it arrive?
    (A) At the end of the week
    (B) At the first of the month
    (C) On Monday
    (D) On the following Friday

Questions 14–17 refer to the following memorandum.

MEMORANDUM

To: J. Wilson
      Engineering Department
From: Marcello Palombo

Date: October 23, 19__

Sub: Elena Kuzikov, Ukrainian engineer

Dr. Elena Kuzikov will be visiting our company on Tuesday, March 23rd. I would like you to prepare a program for her. She will arrive in the morning before noon. Please start with lunch in the cafeteria and then show her your department. Like you, she has done research on the effects of earthquakes on bridge construction.

---

14. What kind of engineer is the Ukrainian?
    (A) Electrical
    (B) Nuclear
    (C) Mechanical
    (D) Railroad

15. Who will be the visitor's guide?
    (A) J. Wilson
    (B) Elena Kuzikov
    (C) Marcello Palombo
    (D) No one

16. When will she arrive?
    (A) Before 12:00
    (B) At noon
    (C) After lunch
    (D) In the evening

17. What is her chief area of interest?
    (A) Designing bridges
    (B) Eating lunch
    (C) Touring the department
    (D) Visiting

232 READING REVIEW

Questions 18–20 refer to the following index.

Newspaper Index

Amex Stocks	B-11
Arts	C-1
Bond Data	B-16
Commodities	B-4
World Stock Index	B-15
Economy	A-5
Editorials	A-10
Film	C-3
Foreign Exchange	B-17
International News	A-1
Legal Issues	A-6
Technology	C-4
World Markets	B-1

18. What type of features would more likely be found in the B section?
    (A) Sports scores
    (B) Movie reviews
    (C) Market forecasts
    (D) Obituaries

19. The editor's opinions are found on
    (A) A-1.
    (B) B-4.
    (C) C-1.
    (D) A-10.

20. Movie reviews would be found on
    (A) B-11.
    (B) C-1.
    (C) C-3.
    (D) A-6.

Questions 21–23 refer to the following chart.

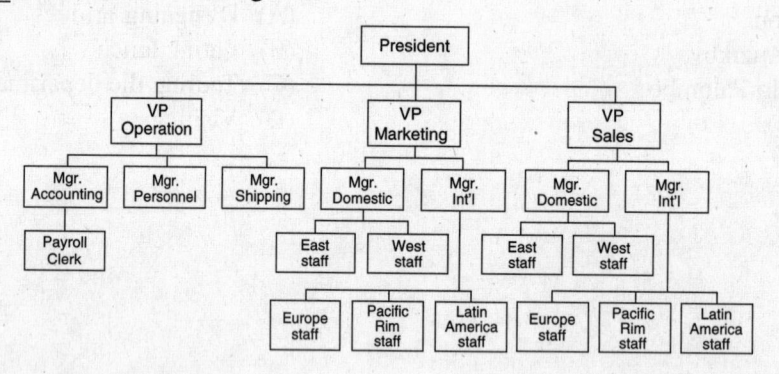

```
                              President
            ┌────────────────────┼────────────────────┐
           VP                   VP                   VP
        Operation            Marketing              Sales
    ┌─────┼─────┐           ┌─────┐            ┌─────┐
   Mgr.  Mgr.  Mgr.       Mgr.   Mgr.        Mgr.   Mgr.
 Accounting Personnel Shipping Domestic Int'l  Domestic Int'l
    │                      ┌────┴────┐        ┌────┴────┐
  Payroll                 East      West     East      West
   Clerk                  staff     staff    staff     staff
                          ┌──┼──┐           ┌──┼──┐
                       Europe Pacific Latin  Europe Pacific Latin
                        staff  Rim  America  staff  Rim  America
                              staff  staff         staff  staff
```

21. The payroll clerk reports directly to
    (A) the Manager of Personnel.
    (B) the Vice-President of Operations.
    (C) the Manager of Accounting.
    (D) the President.

22. Which divisions have similar staffing patterns?
    (A) Accounting and Personnel.
    (B) Operations and Marketing.
    (C) Marketing and Sales.
    (D) Sales and Shipping.

23. The Vice-President of Sales supervises
    (A) the International Manager for Sales.
    (B) the President.
    (C) the Personnel Manager.
    (D) the Accounting Manager.

Questions 24–25 refer to the following graph.

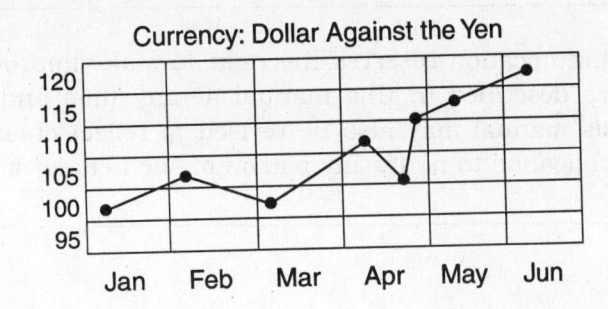

Currency: Dollar Against the Yen

24. This graph shows
    (A) a six-month comparison of dollar-yen conversion rates.
    (B) the price of Japanese commodities.
    (C) the value of the dollar against all currencies.
    (D) an annual highlight of currency rates.

25. In what month were there several fluctuations?
    (A) January
    (B) February
    (C) April
    (D) June

Questions 26–27 refer to the following announcement.

Advanced Communication Systems, Inc., of San Francisco, California, won a $250,000 contract from the Space and Navel Warfare Systems Group, Washington, D.C., for technical and management support services. The three-month contract will begin in June.

---

26. Where is the contractor located?
    (A) Washington, D.C.
    (B) San Francisco, California
    (C) On the sea
    (D) In space

27. About when will the contract end?
    (A) January
    (B) June
    (C) September
    (D) December

Questions 28–29 refer to the following notice in a computer manual.

> International Communication reserves the right to make improvements in the hardware and software described in this manual at any time and without notice. The information in this manual may also be revised to reflect changes in the described product without obligation to notify any person of such changes.

28. This notice gives the company the right
    (A) to make changes without notice.
    (B) to request a refund.
    (C) to return software that doesn't work.
    (D) to start a new company.

29. Where would this notice most likely be found?
    (A) On an appliance warranty card
    (B) In a computer manual
    (C) On an airline ticket
    (D) In a stock offering prospectus

Questions 30–34 refer to the following newspaper article.

> September 1, Zurich: RADD, A.G., the Swiss chemical company purchased the European polypropylene business of Royal Chemical Industries, P.L.C., of Britain. No price was disclosed, but RCI said the deal represented 1 to 2 percent of its net assets and would be paid in cash. Based on net assets, the price would be between $100 million and $160 million. The acquisition includes RCI production plants in England, Denmark, Norway, and Poland. The plants alone are valued at $60 million to $80 million. Polypropylene, a tough, flexible plastic, has uses that range from rope fibers to bottles.

30. RADD is probably located in
    (A) England.
    (B) Switzerland.
    (C) Denmark.
    (D) Poland.

31. According to the article, what is used to make rope fibers?
    (A) Hemp
    (B) Cotton
    (C) Steel
    (D) Polypropylene

32. How much will RADD pay for RCI?
    (A) $80 million
    (B) $100 million
    (C) Between $100 and $160 million
    (D) Between $60 and $80 million

33. Where is RCI's head office?
    (A) Norway
    (B) Denmark
    (C) Britain
    (D) Poland

34. What are the terms of the deal?
    (A) Payment in cash
    (B) Payment in stock
    (C) 2% of gross assets
    (D) 1% down payment

Questions 35–36 refer to the following magazine article.

> Hollywood is no longer just in California. Today the entertainment industry is finding new homes in Europe, Latin America, and Asia. The American media and communications industries are looking all over the globe for new opportunities. Although many companies are investing in the fast-growing European media industry, many industry executives believe the biggest long-term opportunity is in China and other countries in Southeast Asia. The potential market is huge—over 310 million people in the European community, but over 650 million in the Pacific Rim.

35. Which of the following is the main purpose of the article?
    (A) The media industry is changing its center.
    (B) China is a big market today.
    (C) New homes are being built in Europe.
    (D) There are many opportunities in Hollywood.

36. According to the article, what does "Hollywood" represent?
    (A) All executives
    (B) American enterprise
    (C) The media industry
    (D) Big markets

Questions 37–38 refer to the following schedule.

Meeting: Conference Room C

8:30	Coffee
9:00	Opening Remarks
9:15	Introductions
9:30	Presentations
	Accounting
	Personnel
	Marketing
10:30	**BREAK**
10:45	Presentations
	CEO
	Chairman of the Board
11:30	Questions and Answers
12:00	Adjourn

37. Why was this schedule prepared?
    (A) To make everyone pay attention
    (B) To limit the number of coffee breaks
    (C) To introduce the speakers
    (D) To establish an agenda for the meeting

38. What immediately follows the presentations by the senior officers?
    (A) A break
    (B) Introductions
    (C) A question-and-answer period
    (D) Lunch

Questions 39–40 refer to the following timeline.

	Jan	Feb	Mar	Apr	May	June	July	Aug	Sept
Review budget	■								
Submit project proposal		■							
Develop prototype			■	■					
Test prototype					■	■			
Develop marketing plan						■	■	■	
Start production								■	
Ship to distributors									■

39. This timeline shows
    (A) the number of man-hours involved in a project.
    (B) the stages in developing a product.
    (C) how long it takes to make money.
    (D) the changes in the seasons.

40. It can be inferred that
    (A) the cost will be too high.
    (B) the marketing plan will be more important than testing.
    (C) the project will be approved in February.
    (D) testing will slow down production.

STRATEGY

Strategies to Improve Your Reading Score

The following strategies are a review of those presented in this Reading Review chapter. The more strategies you can use while reading English, the more you will be able to understand what you read.

Analyzing vocabulary
- Read as much as you can in English.
- Keep a notebook of the words you learn.
- Learn words in context—not from word lists.

Analyzing grammar
- Recognize the parts of speech.
- Recognize agreement of person, number, and tense.
- Recognize the correct grammatical forms.
- Recognize the correct usage.
- Recognize the correct word order.
- Recognize potentially wrong answers.

Analyze reading passages
- Know the types of questions found on the TOEIC.
- Know the types of information sought on the TOEIC.
- Know how to use PSRA:
    Predict what the passage will be about.
    Scan the passage and answer options for key words.
    Read the passage quickly.
    Answer the questions.
    Use the PSRA whenever you read.

4

TOEIC MODEL TESTS

WHAT TO LOOK FOR IN THIS CHAPTER
- TOEIC Model Tests 1–6 with Answer Sheets

MODEL TEST 1—ANSWER SHEET

Listening Section

1. Ⓐ Ⓑ Ⓒ Ⓓ
2. Ⓐ Ⓑ Ⓒ Ⓓ
3. Ⓐ Ⓑ Ⓒ Ⓓ
4. Ⓐ Ⓑ Ⓒ Ⓓ
5. Ⓐ Ⓑ Ⓒ Ⓓ
6. Ⓐ Ⓑ Ⓒ Ⓓ
7. Ⓐ Ⓑ Ⓒ Ⓓ
8. Ⓐ Ⓑ Ⓒ Ⓓ
9. Ⓐ Ⓑ Ⓒ Ⓓ
10. Ⓐ Ⓑ Ⓒ Ⓓ
11. Ⓐ Ⓑ Ⓒ Ⓓ
12. Ⓐ Ⓑ Ⓒ Ⓓ
13. Ⓐ Ⓑ Ⓒ Ⓓ
14. Ⓐ Ⓑ Ⓒ Ⓓ
15. Ⓐ Ⓑ Ⓒ Ⓓ
16. Ⓐ Ⓑ Ⓒ Ⓓ
17. Ⓐ Ⓑ Ⓒ Ⓓ
18. Ⓐ Ⓑ Ⓒ Ⓓ
19. Ⓐ Ⓑ Ⓒ Ⓓ
20. Ⓐ Ⓑ Ⓒ Ⓓ
21. Ⓐ Ⓑ Ⓒ
22. Ⓐ Ⓑ Ⓒ
23. Ⓐ Ⓑ Ⓒ
24. Ⓐ Ⓑ Ⓒ
25. Ⓐ Ⓑ Ⓒ
26. Ⓐ Ⓑ Ⓒ
27. Ⓐ Ⓑ Ⓒ
28. Ⓐ Ⓑ Ⓒ
29. Ⓐ Ⓑ Ⓒ
30. Ⓐ Ⓑ Ⓒ
31. Ⓐ Ⓑ Ⓒ
32. Ⓐ Ⓑ Ⓒ
33. Ⓐ Ⓑ Ⓒ
34. Ⓐ Ⓑ Ⓒ
35. Ⓐ Ⓑ Ⓒ
36. Ⓐ Ⓑ Ⓒ
37. Ⓐ Ⓑ Ⓒ
38. Ⓐ Ⓑ Ⓒ
39. Ⓐ Ⓑ Ⓒ
40. Ⓐ Ⓑ Ⓒ
41. Ⓐ Ⓑ Ⓒ
42. Ⓐ Ⓑ Ⓒ
43. Ⓐ Ⓑ Ⓒ
44. Ⓐ Ⓑ Ⓒ
45. Ⓐ Ⓑ Ⓒ
46. Ⓐ Ⓑ Ⓒ
47. Ⓐ Ⓑ Ⓒ
48. Ⓐ Ⓑ Ⓒ
49. Ⓐ Ⓑ Ⓒ
50. Ⓐ Ⓑ Ⓒ
51. Ⓐ Ⓑ Ⓒ Ⓓ
52. Ⓐ Ⓑ Ⓒ Ⓓ
53. Ⓐ Ⓑ Ⓒ Ⓓ
54. Ⓐ Ⓑ Ⓒ Ⓓ
55. Ⓐ Ⓑ Ⓒ Ⓓ
56. Ⓐ Ⓑ Ⓒ Ⓓ
57. Ⓐ Ⓑ Ⓒ Ⓓ
58. Ⓐ Ⓑ Ⓒ Ⓓ
59. Ⓐ Ⓑ Ⓒ Ⓓ
60. Ⓐ Ⓑ Ⓒ Ⓓ
61. Ⓐ Ⓑ Ⓒ Ⓓ
62. Ⓐ Ⓑ Ⓒ Ⓓ
63. Ⓐ Ⓑ Ⓒ Ⓓ
64. Ⓐ Ⓑ Ⓒ Ⓓ
65. Ⓐ Ⓑ Ⓒ Ⓓ
66. Ⓐ Ⓑ Ⓒ Ⓓ
67. Ⓐ Ⓑ Ⓒ Ⓓ
68. Ⓐ Ⓑ Ⓒ Ⓓ
69. Ⓐ Ⓑ Ⓒ Ⓓ
70. Ⓐ Ⓑ Ⓒ Ⓓ
71. Ⓐ Ⓑ Ⓒ Ⓓ
72. Ⓐ Ⓑ Ⓒ Ⓓ
73. Ⓐ Ⓑ Ⓒ Ⓓ
74. Ⓐ Ⓑ Ⓒ Ⓓ
75. Ⓐ Ⓑ Ⓒ Ⓓ
76. Ⓐ Ⓑ Ⓒ Ⓓ
77. Ⓐ Ⓑ Ⓒ Ⓓ
78. Ⓐ Ⓑ Ⓒ Ⓓ
79. Ⓐ Ⓑ Ⓒ Ⓓ
80. Ⓐ Ⓑ Ⓒ Ⓓ
81. Ⓐ Ⓑ Ⓒ Ⓓ
82. Ⓐ Ⓑ Ⓒ Ⓓ
83. Ⓐ Ⓑ Ⓒ Ⓓ
84. Ⓐ Ⓑ Ⓒ Ⓓ
85. Ⓐ Ⓑ Ⓒ Ⓓ
86. Ⓐ Ⓑ Ⓒ Ⓓ
87. Ⓐ Ⓑ Ⓒ Ⓓ
88. Ⓐ Ⓑ Ⓒ Ⓓ
89. Ⓐ Ⓑ Ⓒ Ⓓ
90. Ⓐ Ⓑ Ⓒ Ⓓ
91. Ⓐ Ⓑ Ⓒ Ⓓ
92. Ⓐ Ⓑ Ⓒ Ⓓ
93. Ⓐ Ⓑ Ⓒ Ⓓ
94. Ⓐ Ⓑ Ⓒ Ⓓ
95. Ⓐ Ⓑ Ⓒ Ⓓ
96. Ⓐ Ⓑ Ⓒ Ⓓ
97. Ⓐ Ⓑ Ⓒ Ⓓ
98. Ⓐ Ⓑ Ⓒ Ⓓ
99. Ⓐ Ⓑ Ⓒ Ⓓ
100. Ⓐ Ⓑ Ⓒ Ⓓ

Reading Section

101. Ⓐ Ⓑ Ⓒ Ⓓ
102. Ⓐ Ⓑ Ⓒ Ⓓ
103. Ⓐ Ⓑ Ⓒ Ⓓ
104. Ⓐ Ⓑ Ⓒ Ⓓ
105. Ⓐ Ⓑ Ⓒ Ⓓ
106. Ⓐ Ⓑ Ⓒ Ⓓ
107. Ⓐ Ⓑ Ⓒ Ⓓ
108. Ⓐ Ⓑ Ⓒ Ⓓ
109. Ⓐ Ⓑ Ⓒ Ⓓ
110. Ⓐ Ⓑ Ⓒ Ⓓ
111. Ⓐ Ⓑ Ⓒ Ⓓ
112. Ⓐ Ⓑ Ⓒ Ⓓ
113. Ⓐ Ⓑ Ⓒ Ⓓ
114. Ⓐ Ⓑ Ⓒ Ⓓ
115. Ⓐ Ⓑ Ⓒ Ⓓ
116. Ⓐ Ⓑ Ⓒ Ⓓ
117. Ⓐ Ⓑ Ⓒ Ⓓ
118. Ⓐ Ⓑ Ⓒ Ⓓ
119. Ⓐ Ⓑ Ⓒ Ⓓ
120. Ⓐ Ⓑ Ⓒ Ⓓ
121. Ⓐ Ⓑ Ⓒ Ⓓ
122. Ⓐ Ⓑ Ⓒ Ⓓ
123. Ⓐ Ⓑ Ⓒ Ⓓ
124. Ⓐ Ⓑ Ⓒ Ⓓ
125. Ⓐ Ⓑ Ⓒ Ⓓ
126. Ⓐ Ⓑ Ⓒ Ⓓ
127. Ⓐ Ⓑ Ⓒ Ⓓ
128. Ⓐ Ⓑ Ⓒ Ⓓ
129. Ⓐ Ⓑ Ⓒ Ⓓ
130. Ⓐ Ⓑ Ⓒ Ⓓ
131. Ⓐ Ⓑ Ⓒ Ⓓ
132. Ⓐ Ⓑ Ⓒ Ⓓ
133. Ⓐ Ⓑ Ⓒ Ⓓ
134. Ⓐ Ⓑ Ⓒ Ⓓ
135. Ⓐ Ⓑ Ⓒ Ⓓ
136. Ⓐ Ⓑ Ⓒ Ⓓ
137. Ⓐ Ⓑ Ⓒ Ⓓ
138. Ⓐ Ⓑ Ⓒ Ⓓ
139. Ⓐ Ⓑ Ⓒ Ⓓ
140. Ⓐ Ⓑ Ⓒ Ⓓ
141. Ⓐ Ⓑ Ⓒ Ⓓ
142. Ⓐ Ⓑ Ⓒ Ⓓ
143. Ⓐ Ⓑ Ⓒ Ⓓ
144. Ⓐ Ⓑ Ⓒ Ⓓ
145. Ⓐ Ⓑ Ⓒ Ⓓ
146. Ⓐ Ⓑ Ⓒ Ⓓ
147. Ⓐ Ⓑ Ⓒ Ⓓ
148. Ⓐ Ⓑ Ⓒ Ⓓ
149. Ⓐ Ⓑ Ⓒ Ⓓ
150. Ⓐ Ⓑ Ⓒ Ⓓ
151. Ⓐ Ⓑ Ⓒ Ⓓ
152. Ⓐ Ⓑ Ⓒ Ⓓ
153. Ⓐ Ⓑ Ⓒ Ⓓ
154. Ⓐ Ⓑ Ⓒ Ⓓ
155. Ⓐ Ⓑ Ⓒ Ⓓ
156. Ⓐ Ⓑ Ⓒ Ⓓ
157. Ⓐ Ⓑ Ⓒ Ⓓ
158. Ⓐ Ⓑ Ⓒ Ⓓ
159. Ⓐ Ⓑ Ⓒ Ⓓ
160. Ⓐ Ⓑ Ⓒ Ⓓ
161. Ⓐ Ⓑ Ⓒ Ⓓ
162. Ⓐ Ⓑ Ⓒ Ⓓ
163. Ⓐ Ⓑ Ⓒ Ⓓ
164. Ⓐ Ⓑ Ⓒ Ⓓ
165. Ⓐ Ⓑ Ⓒ Ⓓ
166. Ⓐ Ⓑ Ⓒ Ⓓ
167. Ⓐ Ⓑ Ⓒ Ⓓ
168. Ⓐ Ⓑ Ⓒ Ⓓ
169. Ⓐ Ⓑ Ⓒ Ⓓ
170. Ⓐ Ⓑ Ⓒ Ⓓ
171. Ⓐ Ⓑ Ⓒ Ⓓ
172. Ⓐ Ⓑ Ⓒ Ⓓ
173. Ⓐ Ⓑ Ⓒ Ⓓ
174. Ⓐ Ⓑ Ⓒ Ⓓ
175. Ⓐ Ⓑ Ⓒ Ⓓ
176. Ⓐ Ⓑ Ⓒ Ⓓ
177. Ⓐ Ⓑ Ⓒ Ⓓ
178. Ⓐ Ⓑ Ⓒ Ⓓ
179. Ⓐ Ⓑ Ⓒ Ⓓ
180. Ⓐ Ⓑ Ⓒ Ⓓ
181. Ⓐ Ⓑ Ⓒ Ⓓ
182. Ⓐ Ⓑ Ⓒ Ⓓ
183. Ⓐ Ⓑ Ⓒ Ⓓ
184. Ⓐ Ⓑ Ⓒ Ⓓ
185. Ⓐ Ⓑ Ⓒ Ⓓ
186. Ⓐ Ⓑ Ⓒ Ⓓ
187. Ⓐ Ⓑ Ⓒ Ⓓ
188. Ⓐ Ⓑ Ⓒ Ⓓ
189. Ⓐ Ⓑ Ⓒ Ⓓ
190. Ⓐ Ⓑ Ⓒ Ⓓ
191. Ⓐ Ⓑ Ⓒ Ⓓ
192. Ⓐ Ⓑ Ⓒ Ⓓ
193. Ⓐ Ⓑ Ⓒ Ⓓ
194. Ⓐ Ⓑ Ⓒ Ⓓ
195. Ⓐ Ⓑ Ⓒ Ⓓ
196. Ⓐ Ⓑ Ⓒ Ⓓ
197. Ⓐ Ⓑ Ⓒ Ⓓ
198. Ⓐ Ⓑ Ⓒ Ⓓ
199. Ⓐ Ⓑ Ⓒ Ⓓ
200. Ⓐ Ⓑ Ⓒ Ⓓ

Remove answer sheet by cutting on dotted line

MODEL TEST 1
LISTENING COMPREHENSION

In this section of the test, you will have the chance to show how well you understand spoken English. There are four parts to this section, with special directions for each part. You will find the Answer Sheet for Model Test 1 on page 241. Detach it from the book and use it to record your answers. Check your answers using the Answer Key on page 471 and see the Explanatory Answers on page 508.

Listen to Track 1 of compact disc 2 to hear the statements for Part I of Model Test 1.

Part I: Picture

Directions: In your test book, you will see a picture. On the compact disc, you will find four statements. Choose the statement that most closely matches the picture and fill in the corresponding oval on your answer sheet.

244 TOEIC MODEL TESTS

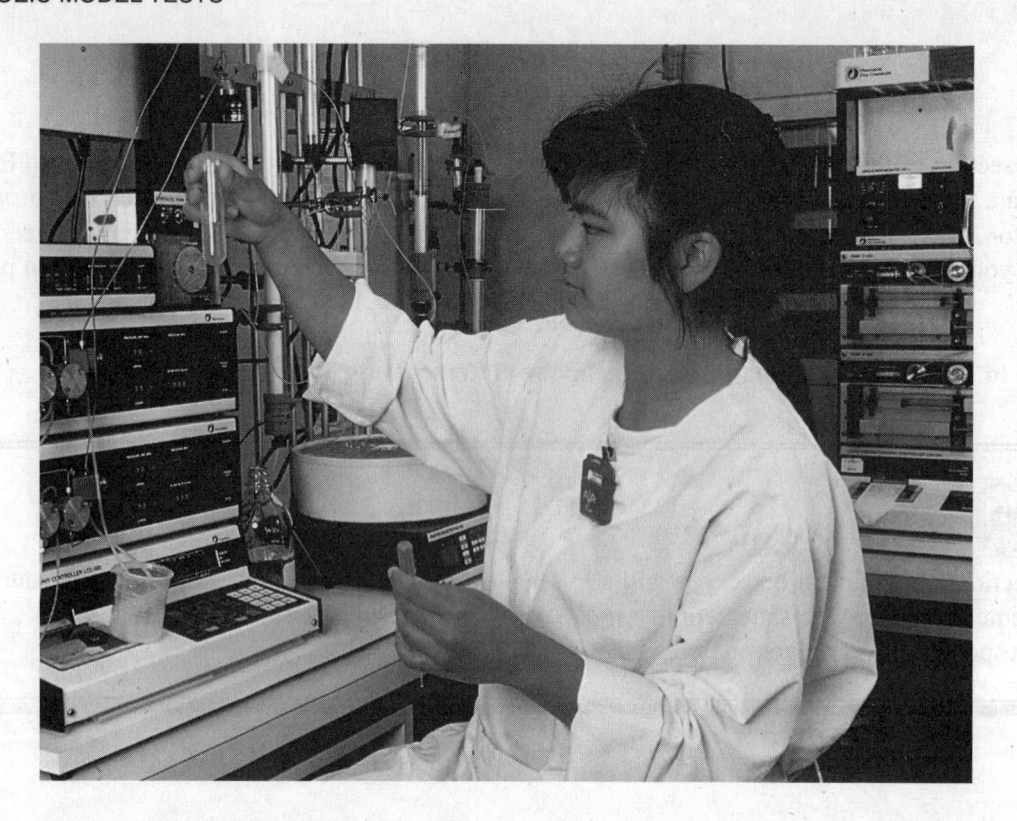

1.

2.

3.

4.

246 TOEIC MODEL TESTS

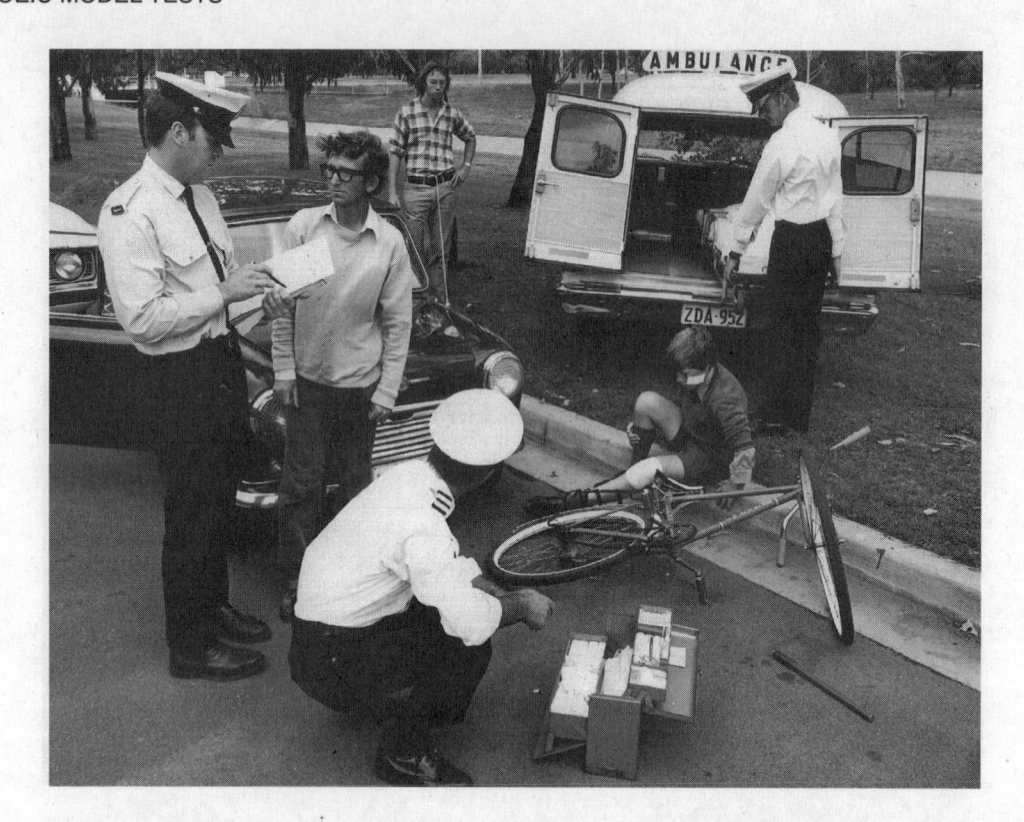

5.

6.

7.

8.

GO ON TO THE NEXT PAGE

248 TOEIC MODEL TESTS

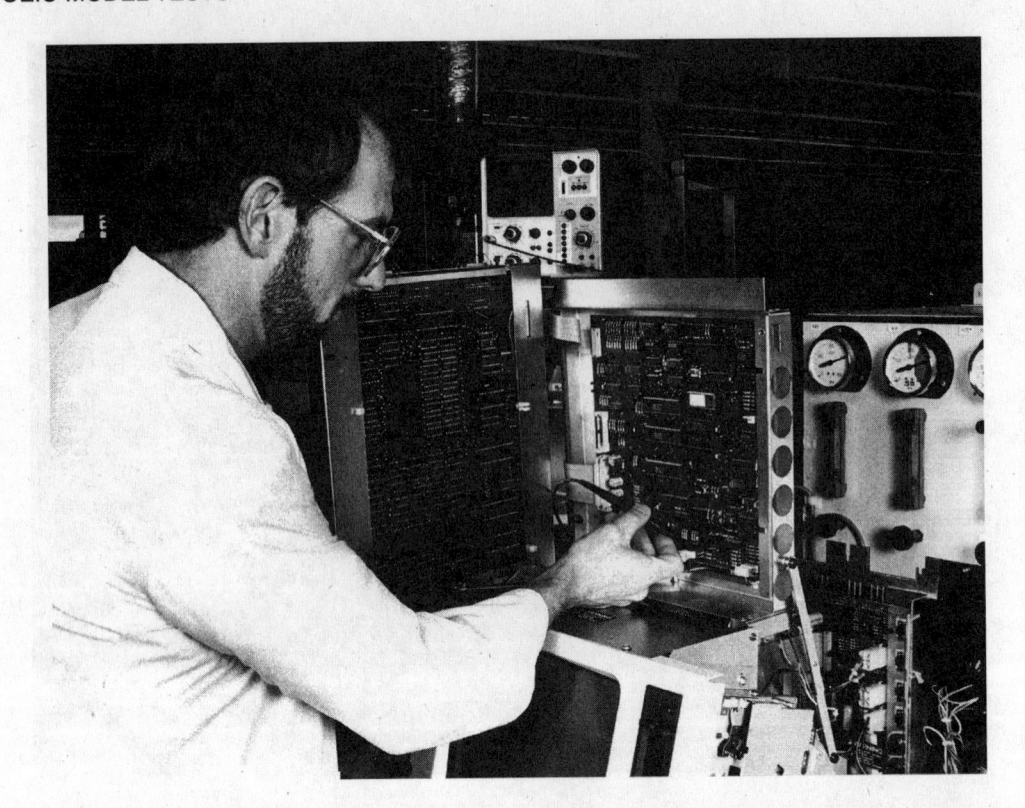

9.

10.

11.

12.

GO ON TO THE NEXT PAGE

250 TOEIC MODEL TESTS

13.

14.

15.

16.

252 TOEIC MODEL TESTS

17.

18.

19.

20.

Listen to Track 2 of compact disc 2 to hear the statements for Part II of Model Test 1.

Part II: Question-Response

Directions: On the compact disc, you will hear a question and three possible answers. Choose the answer that most closely answers the question and fill in the corresponding oval on your answer sheet.

21. Mark your answer on your answer sheet.
22. Mark your answer on your answer sheet.
23. Mark your answer on your answer sheet.
24. Mark your answer on your answer sheet.
25. Mark your answer on your answer sheet.
26. Mark your answer on your answer sheet.
27. Mark your answer on your answer sheet.
28. Mark your answer on your answer sheet.
29. Mark your answer on your answer sheet.
30. Mark your answer on your answer sheet.
31. Mark your answer on your answer sheet.
32. Mark your answer on your answer sheet.
33. Mark your answer on your answer sheet.
34. Mark your answer on your answer sheet.
35. Mark your answer on your answer sheet.
36. Mark your answer on your answer sheet.

37. Mark your answer on your answer sheet.
38. Mark your answer on your answer sheet.
39. Mark your answer on your answer sheet.
40. Mark your answer on your answer sheet.
41. Mark your answer on your answer sheet.
42. Mark your answer on your answer sheet.
43. Mark your answer on your answer sheet.
44. Mark your answer on your answer sheet.
45. Mark your answer on your answer sheet.
46. Mark your answer on your answer sheet.
47. Mark your answer on your answer sheet.
48. Mark your answer on your answer sheet.
49. Mark your answer on your answer sheet.
50. Mark your answer on your answer sheet.

GO ON TO THE NEXT PAGE

256 TOEIC MODEL TESTS

Listen to Track 3 of compact disc 2 to hear the conversations for Part III of Model Test 1.

Part III: Short Conversations

Directions: On the compact disc, you will hear a short conversation. In your test book, you will see a question and four possible answers. Choose the best answer to the question and fill in the corresponding oval on your answer sheet.

51. When can they meet?
    (A) At 3:00.
    (B) At 4:00.
    (C) At 5:00.
    (D) At 10:00.

52. Who is the man talking to?
    (A) A teller.
    (B) A conductor.
    (C) A ranch hand.
    (D) An accountant.

53. Where will they go after visiting the museum?
    (A) To a shrine.
    (B) To some stores.
    (C) To a famous street.
    (D) To the government buildings.

54. What would the woman prefer?
    (A) To take a direct flight.
    (B) To change planes in Denver.
    (C) To exchange her money.
    (D) To go by car.

55. What does the man want?
    (A) A new apartment.
    (B) Better hotel service.
    (C) Towels and soap.
    (D) A different room.

56. What does the man want to do?
    (A) Stand on the corner.
    (B) Get a taxi.
    (C) Find his way.
    (D) Pay his taxes.

57. Who is the woman talking to?
    (A) Her boss.
    (B) Her doctor.
    (C) A waiter.
    (D) A maid.

58. What did the woman want to know about?
    (A) His experience.
    (B) His appearance.
    (C) His attitude.
    (D) His appetite.

59. When must the man's copies be done?
    (A) By 12:00.
    (B) By 1:00.
    (C) By 2:00.
    (D) By 2:30.

60. Where will the man finish the report?
    (A) At the office.
    (B) At home.
    (C) On a plane.
    (D) In a meeting.

61. What does the man ask about?
    (A) The view.
    (B) His room.
    (C) The city.
    (D) His luggage.

62. What should the man do when it rains?
    (A) Leave earlier.
    (B) Take an umbrella.
    (C) Drive his own car.
    (D) Stay at home.

63. Who is the man waiting for?
    (A) A sales clerk.
    (B) His children.
    (C) A waitress.
    (D) His wife.

64. What are they discussing?
    (A) Staying overnight.
    (B) Sending a package.
    (C) Specializing in deliveries.
    (D) Getting mail.

65. What was wrong with the convention?
    (A) It was too serious.
    (B) It was too conventional.
    (C) It was too crowded.
    (D) It was too big.

66. Why is the man taking a train?
    (A) Flying is shorter.
    (B) It's going to rain.
    (C) Brussels is far away.
    (D) The train station is in the city.

67. What will the woman do next?
    (A) Address the brochures.
    (B) Write the brochures.
    (C) Print the brochures.
    (D) Copy the brochures.

68. Where does this conversation take place?
    (A) In a bus.
    (B) In a taxi.
    (C) In a store.
    (D) In an office.

69. What is the woman doing?
    (A) Turning off a machine.
    (B) Answering a call.
    (C) Taking a message.
    (D) Making a phone call.

70. What is the man's job?
    (A) Travel agent.
    (B) Bank teller.
    (C) Sales representative.
    (D) Tour guide.

71. Where does the woman want to go?
    (A) To a fast food restaurant.
    (B) To the bank.
    (C) To the park.
    (D) To the parking lot.

72. What might solve the problem?
    (A) Using fewer printers.
    (B) Starting a sign-up sheet.
    (C) Making people wait.
    (D) Buying more printers.

73. Why can't the man play golf tomorrow?
    (A) He's getting sick.
    (B) He's tired.
    (C) It's going to rain.
    (D) He'll play at ten.

74. When should the woman call?
    (A) After 1:00.
    (B) After 2:00.
    (C) After 4:00.
    (D) After 10:00.

75. What is the woman happy about?
    (A) She got the job.
    (B) She made an offer.
    (C) She found some resources.
    (D) She accepted some help.

76. What will the man get from the supply room?
    (A) Paper clips.
    (B) Boxes.
    (C) Pens and stationery.
    (D) Stationery, pens, and paper clips.

77. Why is the man uncomfortable?
    (A) He needs a different keyboard.
    (B) He needs a different chair.
    (C) He needs new shoes.
    (D) He should sit up straight.

GO ON TO THE NEXT PAGE

78. What was wrong with the woman's phone?
    (A) It was broken.
    (B) It was being used.
    (C) It was off the hook.
    (D) It was tied up with important calls.

79. What will the woman do?
    (A) Borrow the report from Mr. Smith.
    (B) Lend the report to Mr. Smith.
    (C) Take out a loan.
    (D) Go to the bank.

80. What is happening?
    (A) The windows need cleaning.
    (B) There is a fire.
    (C) There is a traffic accident.
    (D) Someone is smoking.

Listen to Track 4 of compact disc 2 to hear the conversations for Part IV of Model Test 1.

Part IV: Short Talks

Directions: On the compact disc, you will hear a short talk. In your test book, you will see several questions on the talk and four possible answers. Choose the best answer to the question and fill in the corresponding oval on your answer sheet.

81. Where is this train probably located?
    (A) In an airport.
    (B) In a city.
    (C) Along the coast.
    (D) At an amusement park.

82. Where should you stand when in a train car?
    (A) By the doors.
    (B) By the windows.
    (C) In the center.
    (D) At either end.

83. When can you visit the museum on Sundays?
    (A) In the morning.
    (B) In the afternoon.
    (C) In the evening.
    (D) All day.

84. If you would like information about lectures, what should you do?
    (A) Go to the museum.
    (B) Write a letter.
    (C) Call another number.
    (D) Stay on the line.

85. What is the first step in getting organized?
    (A) Start working on something.
    (B) Get clutter out of your life.
    (C) Get the boss to tell you what to do.
    (D) Make a list of things to be done.

86. What should you do next?
    (A) Rank the tasks by their importance.
    (B) Do a little work on every task.
    (C) Start working on the first task.
    (D) Eliminate items and rewrite the list.

87. What does the advertisement encourage you to do?
    (A) Take a holiday.
    (B) Redecorate your office.
    (C) Look at your office again.
    (D) Save some money.

88. Which items does the ad mention?
    (A) Decorations.
    (B) Carpeting.
    (C) Wallpaper.
    (D) Furniture.

89. What is this announcement for?
    (A) Schoolteachers.
    (B) Schoolchildren.
    (C) Volunteer tutors.
    (D) Businesspeople.

90. How much time does it take to participate?
    (A) A minimum of 2 hours a week.
    (B) A maximum of 2 hours a week.
    (C) One week a year.
    (D) One day a week.

GO ON TO THE NEXT PAGE

91. What is the approximate temperature for today?
    (A) About 15 degrees.
    (B) About 60 degrees.
    (C) About 65 degrees.
    (D) About 90 degrees.

92. What does the weather forecaster suggest that people do?
    (A) Stay inside.
    (B) Go outdoors.
    (C) Take sunglasses.
    (D) Wear a sweater.

93. What is included in the cost of the lodge?
    (A) Breakfast and dinner.
    (B) Ski equipment.
    (C) Ski lift tickets.
    (D) Lunch on the ski slopes.

94. What does the hotel offer if you don't know how to ski?
    (A) A beautiful view.
    (B) Ski instruction.
    (C) Low prices.
    (D) A rental shop.

95. How long are the delays?
    (A) 5 minutes.
    (B) 15 minutes.
    (C) 45 minutes.
    (D) 4 hours.

96. What is causing the delays?
    (A) Weather.
    (B) Engine trouble.
    (C) Power problems.
    (D) Damage to the tracks.

97. What are they doing to help people commute quickly?
    (A) Providing bus service.
    (B) Asking commuters to wait.
    (C) Trying to fix the trains.
    (D) Using extra trains.

98. What happened at Central and Main?
    (A) An explosion.
    (B) An infection.
    (C) An exception.
    (D) An irritation.

99. What was probably the cause of the problem?
    (A) An electric wire.
    (B) A water pipe.
    (C) A hole in the street.
    (D) A gas leak.

100. What happened to nearby office workers?
    (A) They were injured.
    (B) They were removed.
    (C) They were reported.
    (D) They were suspected.

**This is the end of the Listening Comprehension portion of the test.
Turn to Part V in your test book.**

READING

In this section of the test, you will have the chance to show how well you understand written English. There are three parts to this section, with special directions for each part.

YOU WILL HAVE ONE HOUR AND FIFTEEN MINUTES TO COMPLETE PARTS V, VI, AND VII OF THE TEST.

Part V: Incomplete Sentences

Directions: In your test book, you will see a sentence with a missing word. Four possible answers follow the sentence. Choose the best answer to the question and fill in the corresponding oval on your answer sheet.

101. If the customer _____ not satisfied, please have him call the manager.
    (A) am
    (B) is
    (C) are
    (D) be

102. Our goal is to turn _____ into success.
    (A) failing
    (B) fail
    (C) failed
    (D) failure

103. The plane will be landing _____ Chicago in twenty minutes.
    (A) with
    (B) into
    (C) in
    (D) for

104. The seminar was canceled because the invitations were not _____ in time.
    (A) printer
    (B) printed
    (C) printing
    (D) print

105. If the waiter cannot handle your request, the captain _____ assist you.
    (A) will
    (B) has
    (C) did
    (D) is

GO ON TO THE NEXT PAGE

106. We depend on Mr. Wong for his knowledge and _____.
    (A) leading
    (B) lead
    (C) leadership
    (D) leader

107. Ms. Guida expects costs to _____ 5 percent this year.
    (A) ascend
    (B) increase
    (C) escalate
    (D) raise

108. _____ is the key to efficiency.
    (A) Organized
    (B) Organizing
    (C) Organizer
    (D) Organization

109. The meeting is postponed _____ Mr. Tan's plane was late.
    (A) although
    (B) while
    (C) because
    (D) with

110. The training session has been changed from 8:30 _____ 9:00.
    (A) at
    (B) to
    (C) in
    (D) by

111. The head of sales _____ to San Diego for the annual sales convention.
    (A) went
    (B) gone
    (C) go
    (D) going

112. Because Ms. Kimura has a long _____, she will always leave work at 5:30.
    (A) commute
    (B) commune
    (C) community
    (D) compost

113. The fax machine is _____ the postage meter and the copy machine.
    (A) among
    (B) outside
    (C) between
    (D) through

114. Mr. Maxwell will interview _____ applicants from 9:00 until 11:00 today.
    (A) job
    (B) occupation
    (C) chore
    (D) career

115. When you need supplies, _____ a request with the office manager.
    (A) filling
    (B) fell
    (C) fallen
    (D) file

116. All cabin attendants must lock the cabin door _____ leaving the room.
    (A) afterwards
    (B) after
    (C) later than
    (D) late

117. _____ it was Mr. Guiton's birthday, his staff took him to lunch.
    (A) Although
    (B) During
    (C) Because
    (D) While

118. Hotel employees are _____ to knock before entering the rooms.
    (A) requited
    (B) required
    (C) requisite
    (D) repulsed

119. The billing clerk was not able to find the invoice _____ the order.
    (A) or
    (B) and
    (C) but
    (D) though

120. This product _____ our most popular item.
    (A) always has considered been
    (B) has been always considered
    (C) has been considered always
    (D) has always been considered

121. Is the annual report _____ yet?
    (A) avail
    (B) available
    (C) availability
    (D) availing

122. The bell captain suggested that more porters _____ hired.
    (A) are
    (B) have
    (C) be
    (D) do

123. The office requires that all employees park in their _____ spaces.
    (A) signed
    (B) assignment
    (C) assigned
    (D) significant

124. These addresses should be listed in _____ order.
    (A) alphabet
    (B) alphabetize
    (C) alphabetically
    (D) alphabetical

125. The purchasing department is located _____ the reception desk.
    (A) across
    (B) between
    (C) behind
    (D) from

126. The guard must _____ your identification at the gate.
    (A) checked
    (B) checking
    (C) checks
    (D) check

127. Employees dislike tasks that are too _____.
    (A) repeat
    (B) repetitive
    (C) repetition
    (D) repetitively

128. Visitors are reminded _____ name tags at all times.
    (A) to wear
    (B) wear
    (C) be worn
    (D) is wearing

129. At the end of the year, the company puts _____ a picnic for the employees.
    (A) for
    (B) by
    (C) up
    (D) on

130. Clients are _____ allowed to see the research department.
    (A) every day
    (B) weekly
    (C) never
    (D) no time

131. If we had started earlier, we _____ the deadline.
    (A) would meet
    (B) would have met
    (C) will meet
    (D) will have met

132. Mr. Nolde called to cancel his _____.
    (A) schedule
    (B) calendar
    (C) appointment
    (D) time

GO ON TO THE NEXT PAGE

133. If Ms. Kamano leaves at 2:00, she _____ at the station on time.
    (A) arrives
    (B) will arrive
    (C) arrived
    (D) would arrive

134. A letter for Mr. Carn was left _____ Mr. Britto's desk.
    (A) in
    (B) on
    (C) for
    (D) of

135. The last train to Hamburg _____ at 10:30.
    (A) depart
    (B) departs
    (C) to depart
    (D) departing

136. _____ the meeting, Ms. Tran missed several important phone calls.
    (A) Although
    (B) In spite of
    (C) Because
    (D) During

137. Because his finger was broken, the secretary could not type _____.
    (A) efficiently
    (B) carefully
    (C) slowly
    (D) gradually

138. The CD-player was damaged when it _____.
    (A) was delivered
    (B) has delivered
    (C) was delivering
    (D) had delivered

139. Mr. Hatori was very _____ when he got a promotion.
    (A) excite
    (B) exciting
    (C) excited
    (D) excites

140. The restaurant is open on weekends, _____ not on holidays.
    (A) either
    (B) or
    (C) so
    (D) but

Part VI: Error Recognition

Directions: In your test book, you will see a sentence with four words or phrases underlined. Choose the word or phrase that is incorrect and fill in the corresponding oval on your answer sheet.

141. Our biggest problem <u>are</u> <u>that</u> the supplies
          A   B
    <u>are not</u> readily <u>available</u>.
       C   D

142. Guests <u>who</u> may be <u>delayed</u> are asked
            A   B   C
    <u>registering</u> for late arrival.
         D

143. The director hired a new <u>salesperson</u> who
                                   A
    <u>he</u> had worked <u>for</u> our <u>largest</u> competitor.
      B   C   D

144. Ms. Haufman wants <u>to look</u> for <u>another</u>
                          A   B
    job <u>because</u> she likes <u>the work</u>.
           C   D

145. Awards <u>given</u> <u>to</u> the company <u>is displayed</u>
               A   B   C
    <u>in the lobby</u>.
         D

146. Ms. Giambi ran the department <u>for</u> Mr.
                                     A
    Kim <u>during</u> he was <u>in</u> the hospital <u>with</u>
           B   C   D
    the flu.

147. <u>The manager</u> is <u>hoping</u> to buy <u>new</u>
          A   B   C
    software <u>to tracking</u> all the company's
                 D
    deliveries.

148. Ms. Minor drinks <u>her</u> tea <u>with</u> <u>the lemon</u>
                       A   B   C
    and <u>a little</u> sugar.
           D

149. All <u>of the</u> bad news <u>about</u> <u>the</u> new contract
            A   B   C
    <u>have finally been</u> confirmed.
         D

150. A good waiter should be knowing about
     A   B
     local tourist attractions.
     C   D

151. Mr. Guzman wanted spending more
                      A   B
     money on advertising after consulting a
                          C   D
     marketing expert.

152. The project manager suggested that the
     A   B
     team worked closely together.
          C   D

153. The accountants explained that the new
                     A   B
     software is more faster than the old
                 C   D
     software.

154. Mr. Gilden's friends thoroughly enjoyed
         A   B
     to plan his retirement party.
     C   D

155. The manager researched many companies,
         A   B
     and decided that TruAtom, Inc., had the
         C
     good development program.
     D

156. Ms. Jenkins knew she will have to go
                         A
     as soon as possible if she wanted to catch
     B   C
     the last flight.
     D

157. Mr. Sarosdy considered to stay at another
                            A   B
     hotel which had better service.
           C   D

158. Their lawyer helped them choose the
     A   B
     more easy way to solve the problem.
     C   D

159. The secretary waited all morning for the
                        A   B   C
     fax which never comes.
         D

160. The factory it was built on Dock Street
                 A   B
     near the river in 1969.
     C   D

Part VII: Reading Comprehension

Directions: In your test book, you will see a reading passage followed by several questions. Each question has four answer choices. Choose the best answer to the question and fill in the corresponding oval on your answer sheet.

Questions 161–162 refer to the following message.

```
To:    Helga Kloss
Date:  11/5      Time:   10:05  (AM)  PM
```

WHILE YOU WERE OUT

Mr. Denby

of The Holiday Shop

Phone: 909-243-7078

☑ TELEPHONED   ☐ PLEASE CALL
☐ CALLED TO SEE YOU ☐ WILL CALL AGAIN
☐ WANTS TO SEE YOU ☐ RETURNED YOUR CALL
☑ RUSH

Message: Needs a duplicate order of models—double the last order

Operator Dieter Stein

161. Who does the caller want to talk to?
  (A) Mr. Denby
  (B) Mr. Stein
  (C) Mr. Holiday
  (D) Ms. Kloss

162. What was the call about?
  (A) A repeat order
  (B) Delayed shipment
  (C) Scheduling a delivery
  (D) Correcting a mistake

GO ON TO THE NEXT PAGE →

Questions 163–167 refer to the following newspaper article.

> Job trends for the future emphasize careers in sales and marketing. Most of the growth will come in those areas which can take advantage of modern technology, such as electronic marketing and computerized inventory management. Advertising and market research will show significant growth as the electronic exchange of information becomes common.
>
> As worldwide competition accelerates, the successful marketers must find new avenues to increase consumer awareness of their products. The sales and marketing personnel of the future will have to be familiar with marketing resources available in computer networks and be able to use them effectively. The marketers of the future will also have to be inventive. They must be able to devise new strategies to reach the consumer as the technology continues to change.

163. Which kinds of careers show promise for the future?
    (A) Research and development
    (B) Sales and marketing
    (C) Finance and accounting
    (D) Distribution and service

164. Why are these careers increasing in importance?
    (A) There are more people in the world.
    (B) They pay well.
    (C) They can use modern technology.
    (D) They are easy to learn.

165. According to the article, how will consumers learn about products in the future?
    (A) From door-to-door sales personnel
    (B) From computer networks
    (C) From direct mail campaigns
    (D) From personal experience

166. The author believes that the marketer of the future must be
    (A) knowledgeable about world politics.
    (B) better paid.
    (C) well-trained.
    (D) creative.

167. What strategies will the marketer of the future employ?
    (A) Innovative ones
    (B) Traditional ones
    (C) Country-specific ones
    (D) Consumer-generated ones

Questions 168–170 refer to the following announcement.

> In order to expand into the lucrative entertainment market,
>
> ## ARC Computer Company
>
> is pleased to announce the formation of an entertainment division,
>
> ## Interactive Films Company.
>
> ARC shareholders of record as of August 30, 19__, will be issued one share of Interactive Films Company common stock for every five ARC shares held. No action is required on the part of shareholders to receive Interactive Films shares.

168. Why is ARC going into the entertainment business?
    (A) It is popular.
    (B) It is profitable.
    (C) It is productive.
    (D) It is powerful.

169. If a person owns 5 shares of ARC, how many shares of Interactive Films will he receive?
    (A) 1
    (B) 5
    (C) 10
    (D) 25

170. What do ARC shareholders need to do to receive stock in Interactive Films?
    (A) Verify ownership
    (B) Fund another division
    (C) Reply by August 30
    (D) Nothing

Questions 171–172 refer to the following announcement.

> We are announcing today that we are bringing the Milestone and Ever Green brands even closer together. Effective December 5, 199_, our official name will be:
>
> ## GREEN MILES WEST
>
> The substitution of "West" in our name—replacing "California"—is the result of an agreement we reached with the California Gardening Association, following a protest over the original use of "California" in our name.
>
> We hope this does not create any confusion among our loyal consumers. While this represents a change from our initial name introduction, it does not change the quality of products we offer our customers.

171. What was the original name of the merged companies?
    (A) Milestone
    (B) Green Miles California
    (C) Green Miles West
    (D) Milestone California

172. According to the announcement, why was the name changed?
    (A) The corporate offices were relocated.
    (B) There was a conflict with another organization.
    (C) They did not like the initial choice.
    (D) Loyal consumers were confused.

Questions 173–177 refer to the following magazine article.

Hotels are changing their wasteful habits and getting involved in the move to save the environment. At major hotels throughout the world, guests are being greeted by shampoo and mouthwash in glass dispensers instead of elaborate plastic bottles. They are discovering recycling bins in their rooms, and are encouraged to use towels more than once before they are washed.

This green movement is becoming increasingly popular among tourists who look for service providers with an environmental conscience. The business of eco-tours is increasing rapidly. Travel agents are booking clients on "Save the Rainforest" expeditions and similar trips where the emphasis is on protecting the world.

The tourists on these trips are given lectures on the effects of the loss of our planet's natural wonders and what they can do to reverse the trend. They do not need much convincing. The travelers on these excursions are already committed to environmental protection. In fact, a two-year study of litter in Antarctica found that the entire collection of litter left by visitors to the continent could be put in one small sandwich bag. Compare that amount of litter with what the average traveler finds strewn on the streets around a hotel, even an environmentally sensitive hotel.

173. What trend is currently affecting hotels and their guests?
  (A) Larger rooms
  (B) Better amenities
  (C) Lighter foods
  (D) Protecting the earth

174. What does the article imply about glass dispensers and re-using towels?
  (A) It's a marketing gimmick.
  (B) It's only effective on eco-tours.
  (C) It's a wise choice environmentally.
  (D) Hotels can set consumer trends.

175. Which group defines the green movement?
  (A) Fashion designers
  (B) First-time visitors
  (C) Environmentally conscious travelers
  (D) Golf course owners

176. According to the article, eco-travelers should expect
  (A) to find litter.
  (B) to hear lectures on the environment.
  (C) to pay more than other travelers.
  (D) to carry their own food.

177. "Eco" in this sense most likely means
  (A) economy.
  (B) ecology.
  (C) Ecuador.
  (D) echo.

GO ON TO THE NEXT PAGE

Questions 178–180 refer to the following press release.

VAL D' **O**R CATERING **S**UPPLY
Von-Gablenz Straße 3-7
D-50679 Köln
Germany
Telephone: (02 21) 8 25 22 00
Telefax (02 21) 8 25 22 06

FOR IMMEDIATE RELEASE

By fax

To: All Business Editors
Fm: Johann Heger
     Public Relations Officer

Val D'Or is pleased to announce its purchase of Gourmet Galore, a company that specializes in specialty food products, cookware, and kitchen accessories. Gourmet Galore has profited from the customers' revived interest in cooking. There are plans to expand and open five more stores across Europe. Ten of their sixteen stores were remodeled last year, and similar plans are being made for the remaining six.

The company will also open a new line of cooking schools focusing on healthful foods. Regional specialties will be included and guest cooks from all over Europe will participate in the one-week classes.

Please call us for more information.

178. What sort of products does Gourmet Galore sell?
(A) Fabric and furniture
(B) Food and cooking supplies
(C) Washing machines and dryers
(D) Clothes and shoes

179. What will Val D'Or do to six of Gourmet's stores?
(A) Remodel them
(B) Buy them
(C) Sell them
(D) Relocate them

180. What will be the emphasis in the cooking classes?
(A) Healthful regional foods
(B) Recipes from one region
(C) New cooking techniques
(D) Using the latest equipment

Questions 181–183 refer to the following advertisement.

SALES MANAGER

Multinational company seeks business manager for its office products division. Candidate must have 10 years experience in sales development and management in the field and have demonstrated the ability to motivate and train incoming sales staff. Good salary and benefits package. Qualified candidates should send their resumes to: The Daily News, Box 8552, 1627 Elm Street, Adelaide, Australia

181. Which segment of the business is looking for a sales manager?
    (A) The office products division
    (B) The multinational company
    (C) The personnel division
    (D) The overseas staff

182. What experience is required for the job?
    (A) Product development
    (B) Teaching new salespeople
    (C) Ten years in office management
    (D) Research in the field

183. Where should applicants send their resumes?
    (A) To the company
    (B) To the division manager
    (C) To the vice-president of sales
    (D) To the newspaper

Questions 184–186 refer to the following notice.

> The company provides a benefit pension plan covering all employees. Benefits are based on years of service and on the employee's highest salary. Both the company and the employee make contributions to the plan according to government regulations. Employees eligible to receive pension funds are paid monthly through the plan.

184. What determines the rules of contribution?
 (A) Years at the company and salary
 (B) Bonuses
 (C) Starting wage
 (D) Company profits

185. Who determines the rules of contribution?
 (A) Managers of the benefit pension plan
 (B) Anyone who is eligible to receive funds
 (C) The company and the employee
 (D) The government

186. How often do eligible employees receive payments from the plan?
 (A) Every week
 (B) Every two weeks
 (C) Once a month
 (D) Once a year

Questions 187–189 refer to the following letter.

> Dear Member,
>
> The goal of Regents is to be the premier name in health care.
>
> Since merging Royal Medical Green Shield and Jason County Medical Bureau in April, we have been working with our customers and business partners to provide, over the long term, more innovative health benefit plans and services, wider provider networks, and enhanced access to health care coverage.
>
> We've been pleased to receive your suggestions for these service improvements, and we look forward to receiving your further thoughts or suggestions. Our suggestion line is open 24 hours a day at 800-998-3445.
>
> We appreciate your patronage.
>
> Sincerely,
>
> Rick Nelson
> President

187. What is the purpose of this note?
 (A) To explain a merger
 (B) To talk about Regents' plans
 (C) To give a new toll-free number
 (D) To describe expanded health coverage

188. What is one goal of Regents?
 (A) To increase availability of health care
 (B) To publish a primer for new members
 (C) To reduce costs to members
 (D) To work with customers and business partners

189. What does Regents request of members?
 (A) To inform new potential clients of its innovations
 (B) To plan for health over the long term
 (C) To learn about services on the Internet
 (D) To submit idea to the company

GO ON TO THE NEXT PAGE

276 TOEIC MODEL TESTS

Questions 190–192 refer to the following invoice.

```
Cooper & Allen, Architects        April 5, 19__
149 Bridge Street, Suite 107      INVOICE NUMBER  3892
Harrisville, Colorado 76521       PROJECT NAME   Headquarters—Final Design
                                  PROJECT NUMBER 925639

The Williams Corporation
5110 Falls Avenue
Thomaston, Colorado 76520

The following amounts for the period ending March 30 are due the end of
this month.

                          Current period fees      $8,200.00
                          Unpaid prior balance       $362.00
                          Total due at this time   $8,562.00

Thank you very much for the opportunity to service you. Your prompt payment
is greatly appreciated.
```

190. Who sent this invoice?
 (A) The Williams Corporation
 (B) Cooper & Allen, Architects
 (C) Headquarters—Final Design
 (D) A collection agency

191. When is the payment due?
 (A) March 1
 (B) March 30
 (C) April 5
 (D) April 30

192. What is owed in addition to current fees?
 (A) Prepayment on the next project
 (B) Taxes on the current fees
 (C) Service charges on current fees
 (D) Money not paid on a previous invoice

Questions 193–196 refer to the following memo.

> # FCC
> ## FISCHER COMMUNICATIONS COMPANY
>
> Interoffice Memorandum
>
> To: All Department Supervisors
> Fm: J. Reinhardt
>   Personnel Officer
>
> Sub: Summary of 3/24 training session on improving job performance.
>
> Date: April 1, 19__
>
> Employees work best if they are happy. As a supervisor, there are things you can do to increase employees' job satisfaction. Make sure your employees understand what they have to do. Give them proper and thorough training so they can do it well, and give them opportunities to bring that training up to date. Make sure that employees have freedom to exercise their own judgment, to offer their suggestions, and to point out problems. Most of all, make sure that you tell them they are doing a good job, not only during special assignments but when they maintain a high standard of routine work.

193. When do employees do their best work?
  (A) When they are challenged
  (B) When they are happy
  (C) When they are busy
  (D) When they are pressured

194. Once you have trained an employee, what should you do?
  (A) Provide ways to update training
  (B) Make the employee train others
  (C) Move the employee to a different job
  (D) Control his or her chance to practice

195. What is NOT mentioned as a freedom employees should have?
  (A) Exercise their own judgment
  (B) Offer suggestions
  (C) Make changes
  (D) Point out problems

196. What should a boss praise employees for?
  (A) Exercising their freedom
  (B) Staying happy
  (C) Accepting special assignments
  (D) Doing consistently good work

Questions 197–200 refer to the following magazine article.

> Busy people don't want their vacations to be a hassle. That's why all-inclusive resorts are becoming popular. At these resorts, one price includes all meals, drinks, lodging, and sightseeing. Golf, tennis, and swimming are available for free. Other sports, such as scuba diving, deep sea fishing, and rock climbing, may require separate fees for equipment rental but instruction and excursions are included. Many resorts also include children's activities as part of the package. Check with a travel agent to find an all-inclusive resort with activities you would enjoy.

197. What does it mean to be an "all-inclusive" resort?
 (A) Anyone can stay there.
 (B) One price includes food, lodging, and activities.
 (C) They take care of your children for you.
 (D) Room price and airfare are included.

198. Why are all-inclusive resorts popular?
 (A) They are not as much trouble.
 (B) They are cheaper.
 (C) They have more facilities.
 (D) Travel agents handle all of the planning.

199. What might cost extra at these resorts?
 (A) Excursions and instruction
 (B) Transportation for sightseeing
 (C) Hotel maid service
 (D) Sports equipment rental

200. What is the best way to find an all-inclusive resort?
 (A) Ask a friend.
 (B) Read in a travel guide.
 (C) Consult a travel agent.
 (D) Call some hotels.

STOP!
This is the end of the test. If you finish before time is called, you may go back to Parts V, VI, and VII and check your work.

MODEL TEST 2—ANSWER SHEET

Listening Section

1. Ⓐ Ⓑ Ⓒ Ⓓ
2. Ⓐ Ⓑ Ⓒ Ⓓ
3. Ⓐ Ⓑ Ⓒ Ⓓ
4. Ⓐ Ⓑ Ⓒ Ⓓ
5. Ⓐ Ⓑ Ⓒ Ⓓ
6. Ⓐ Ⓑ Ⓒ Ⓓ
7. Ⓐ Ⓑ Ⓒ Ⓓ
8. Ⓐ Ⓑ Ⓒ Ⓓ
9. Ⓐ Ⓑ Ⓒ Ⓓ
10. Ⓐ Ⓑ Ⓒ Ⓓ
11. Ⓐ Ⓑ Ⓒ Ⓓ
12. Ⓐ Ⓑ Ⓒ Ⓓ
13. Ⓐ Ⓑ Ⓒ Ⓓ
14. Ⓐ Ⓑ Ⓒ Ⓓ
15. Ⓐ Ⓑ Ⓒ Ⓓ
16. Ⓐ Ⓑ Ⓒ Ⓓ
17. Ⓐ Ⓑ Ⓒ Ⓓ
18. Ⓐ Ⓑ Ⓒ Ⓓ
19. Ⓐ Ⓑ Ⓒ Ⓓ
20. Ⓐ Ⓑ Ⓒ Ⓓ
21. Ⓐ Ⓑ Ⓒ
22. Ⓐ Ⓑ Ⓒ
23. Ⓐ Ⓑ Ⓒ
24. Ⓐ Ⓑ Ⓒ
25. Ⓐ Ⓑ Ⓒ
26. Ⓐ Ⓑ Ⓒ
27. Ⓐ Ⓑ Ⓒ
28. Ⓐ Ⓑ Ⓒ
29. Ⓐ Ⓑ Ⓒ
30. Ⓐ Ⓑ Ⓒ
31. Ⓐ Ⓑ Ⓒ
32. Ⓐ Ⓑ Ⓒ
33. Ⓐ Ⓑ Ⓒ
34. Ⓐ Ⓑ Ⓒ
35. Ⓐ Ⓑ Ⓒ
36. Ⓐ Ⓑ Ⓒ
37. Ⓐ Ⓑ Ⓒ
38. Ⓐ Ⓑ Ⓒ
39. Ⓐ Ⓑ Ⓒ
40. Ⓐ Ⓑ Ⓒ
41. Ⓐ Ⓑ Ⓒ
42. Ⓐ Ⓑ Ⓒ
43. Ⓐ Ⓑ Ⓒ
44. Ⓐ Ⓑ Ⓒ
45. Ⓐ Ⓑ Ⓒ
46. Ⓐ Ⓑ Ⓒ
47. Ⓐ Ⓑ Ⓒ
48. Ⓐ Ⓑ Ⓒ
49. Ⓐ Ⓑ Ⓒ
50. Ⓐ Ⓑ Ⓒ
51. Ⓐ Ⓑ Ⓒ Ⓓ
52. Ⓐ Ⓑ Ⓒ Ⓓ
53. Ⓐ Ⓑ Ⓒ Ⓓ
54. Ⓐ Ⓑ Ⓒ Ⓓ
55. Ⓐ Ⓑ Ⓒ Ⓓ
56. Ⓐ Ⓑ Ⓒ Ⓓ
57. Ⓐ Ⓑ Ⓒ Ⓓ
58. Ⓐ Ⓑ Ⓒ Ⓓ
59. Ⓐ Ⓑ Ⓒ Ⓓ
60. Ⓐ Ⓑ Ⓒ Ⓓ
61. Ⓐ Ⓑ Ⓒ Ⓓ
62. Ⓐ Ⓑ Ⓒ Ⓓ
63. Ⓐ Ⓑ Ⓒ Ⓓ
64. Ⓐ Ⓑ Ⓒ Ⓓ
65. Ⓐ Ⓑ Ⓒ Ⓓ
66. Ⓐ Ⓑ Ⓒ Ⓓ
67. Ⓐ Ⓑ Ⓒ Ⓓ
68. Ⓐ Ⓑ Ⓒ Ⓓ
69. Ⓐ Ⓑ Ⓒ Ⓓ
70. Ⓐ Ⓑ Ⓒ Ⓓ
71. Ⓐ Ⓑ Ⓒ Ⓓ
72. Ⓐ Ⓑ Ⓒ Ⓓ
73. Ⓐ Ⓑ Ⓒ Ⓓ
74. Ⓐ Ⓑ Ⓒ Ⓓ
75. Ⓐ Ⓑ Ⓒ Ⓓ
76. Ⓐ Ⓑ Ⓒ Ⓓ
77. Ⓐ Ⓑ Ⓒ Ⓓ
78. Ⓐ Ⓑ Ⓒ Ⓓ
79. Ⓐ Ⓑ Ⓒ Ⓓ
80. Ⓐ Ⓑ Ⓒ Ⓓ
81. Ⓐ Ⓑ Ⓒ Ⓓ
82. Ⓐ Ⓑ Ⓒ Ⓓ
83. Ⓐ Ⓑ Ⓒ Ⓓ
84. Ⓐ Ⓑ Ⓒ Ⓓ
85. Ⓐ Ⓑ Ⓒ Ⓓ
86. Ⓐ Ⓑ Ⓒ Ⓓ
87. Ⓐ Ⓑ Ⓒ Ⓓ
88. Ⓐ Ⓑ Ⓒ Ⓓ
89. Ⓐ Ⓑ Ⓒ Ⓓ
90. Ⓐ Ⓑ Ⓒ Ⓓ
91. Ⓐ Ⓑ Ⓒ Ⓓ
92. Ⓐ Ⓑ Ⓒ Ⓓ
93. Ⓐ Ⓑ Ⓒ Ⓓ
94. Ⓐ Ⓑ Ⓒ Ⓓ
95. Ⓐ Ⓑ Ⓒ Ⓓ
96. Ⓐ Ⓑ Ⓒ Ⓓ
97. Ⓐ Ⓑ Ⓒ Ⓓ
98. Ⓐ Ⓑ Ⓒ Ⓓ
99. Ⓐ Ⓑ Ⓒ Ⓓ
100. Ⓐ Ⓑ Ⓒ Ⓓ

Reading Section

101. Ⓐ Ⓑ Ⓒ Ⓓ
102. Ⓐ Ⓑ Ⓒ Ⓓ
103. Ⓐ Ⓑ Ⓒ Ⓓ
104. Ⓐ Ⓑ Ⓒ Ⓓ
105. Ⓐ Ⓑ Ⓒ Ⓓ
106. Ⓐ Ⓑ Ⓒ Ⓓ
107. Ⓐ Ⓑ Ⓒ Ⓓ
108. Ⓐ Ⓑ Ⓒ Ⓓ
109. Ⓐ Ⓑ Ⓒ Ⓓ
110. Ⓐ Ⓑ Ⓒ Ⓓ
111. Ⓐ Ⓑ Ⓒ Ⓓ
112. Ⓐ Ⓑ Ⓒ Ⓓ
113. Ⓐ Ⓑ Ⓒ Ⓓ
114. Ⓐ Ⓑ Ⓒ Ⓓ
115. Ⓐ Ⓑ Ⓒ Ⓓ
116. Ⓐ Ⓑ Ⓒ Ⓓ
117. Ⓐ Ⓑ Ⓒ Ⓓ
118. Ⓐ Ⓑ Ⓒ Ⓓ
119. Ⓐ Ⓑ Ⓒ Ⓓ
120. Ⓐ Ⓑ Ⓒ Ⓓ
121. Ⓐ Ⓑ Ⓒ Ⓓ
122. Ⓐ Ⓑ Ⓒ Ⓓ
123. Ⓐ Ⓑ Ⓒ Ⓓ
124. Ⓐ Ⓑ Ⓒ Ⓓ
125. Ⓐ Ⓑ Ⓒ Ⓓ
126. Ⓐ Ⓑ Ⓒ Ⓓ
127. Ⓐ Ⓑ Ⓒ Ⓓ
128. Ⓐ Ⓑ Ⓒ Ⓓ
129. Ⓐ Ⓑ Ⓒ Ⓓ
130. Ⓐ Ⓑ Ⓒ Ⓓ
131. Ⓐ Ⓑ Ⓒ Ⓓ
132. Ⓐ Ⓑ Ⓒ Ⓓ
133. Ⓐ Ⓑ Ⓒ Ⓓ
134. Ⓐ Ⓑ Ⓒ Ⓓ
135. Ⓐ Ⓑ Ⓒ Ⓓ
136. Ⓐ Ⓑ Ⓒ Ⓓ
137. Ⓐ Ⓑ Ⓒ Ⓓ
138. Ⓐ Ⓑ Ⓒ Ⓓ
139. Ⓐ Ⓑ Ⓒ Ⓓ
140. Ⓐ Ⓑ Ⓒ Ⓓ
141. Ⓐ Ⓑ Ⓒ Ⓓ
142. Ⓐ Ⓑ Ⓒ Ⓓ
143. Ⓐ Ⓑ Ⓒ Ⓓ
144. Ⓐ Ⓑ Ⓒ Ⓓ
145. Ⓐ Ⓑ Ⓒ Ⓓ
146. Ⓐ Ⓑ Ⓒ Ⓓ
147. Ⓐ Ⓑ Ⓒ Ⓓ
148. Ⓐ Ⓑ Ⓒ Ⓓ
149. Ⓐ Ⓑ Ⓒ Ⓓ
150. Ⓐ Ⓑ Ⓒ Ⓓ
151. Ⓐ Ⓑ Ⓒ Ⓓ
152. Ⓐ Ⓑ Ⓒ Ⓓ
153. Ⓐ Ⓑ Ⓒ Ⓓ
154. Ⓐ Ⓑ Ⓒ Ⓓ
155. Ⓐ Ⓑ Ⓒ Ⓓ
156. Ⓐ Ⓑ Ⓒ Ⓓ
157. Ⓐ Ⓑ Ⓒ Ⓓ
158. Ⓐ Ⓑ Ⓒ Ⓓ
159. Ⓐ Ⓑ Ⓒ Ⓓ
160. Ⓐ Ⓑ Ⓒ Ⓓ
161. Ⓐ Ⓑ Ⓒ Ⓓ
162. Ⓐ Ⓑ Ⓒ Ⓓ
163. Ⓐ Ⓑ Ⓒ Ⓓ
164. Ⓐ Ⓑ Ⓒ Ⓓ
165. Ⓐ Ⓑ Ⓒ Ⓓ
166. Ⓐ Ⓑ Ⓒ Ⓓ
167. Ⓐ Ⓑ Ⓒ Ⓓ
168. Ⓐ Ⓑ Ⓒ Ⓓ
169. Ⓐ Ⓑ Ⓒ Ⓓ
170. Ⓐ Ⓑ Ⓒ Ⓓ
171. Ⓐ Ⓑ Ⓒ Ⓓ
172. Ⓐ Ⓑ Ⓒ Ⓓ
173. Ⓐ Ⓑ Ⓒ Ⓓ
174. Ⓐ Ⓑ Ⓒ Ⓓ
175. Ⓐ Ⓑ Ⓒ Ⓓ
176. Ⓐ Ⓑ Ⓒ Ⓓ
177. Ⓐ Ⓑ Ⓒ Ⓓ
178. Ⓐ Ⓑ Ⓒ Ⓓ
179. Ⓐ Ⓑ Ⓒ Ⓓ
180. Ⓐ Ⓑ Ⓒ Ⓓ
181. Ⓐ Ⓑ Ⓒ Ⓓ
182. Ⓐ Ⓑ Ⓒ Ⓓ
183. Ⓐ Ⓑ Ⓒ Ⓓ
184. Ⓐ Ⓑ Ⓒ Ⓓ
185. Ⓐ Ⓑ Ⓒ Ⓓ
186. Ⓐ Ⓑ Ⓒ Ⓓ
187. Ⓐ Ⓑ Ⓒ Ⓓ
188. Ⓐ Ⓑ Ⓒ Ⓓ
189. Ⓐ Ⓑ Ⓒ Ⓓ
190. Ⓐ Ⓑ Ⓒ Ⓓ
191. Ⓐ Ⓑ Ⓒ Ⓓ
192. Ⓐ Ⓑ Ⓒ Ⓓ
193. Ⓐ Ⓑ Ⓒ Ⓓ
194. Ⓐ Ⓑ Ⓒ Ⓓ
195. Ⓐ Ⓑ Ⓒ Ⓓ
196. Ⓐ Ⓑ Ⓒ Ⓓ
197. Ⓐ Ⓑ Ⓒ Ⓓ
198. Ⓐ Ⓑ Ⓒ Ⓓ
199. Ⓐ Ⓑ Ⓒ Ⓓ
200. Ⓐ Ⓑ Ⓒ Ⓓ

Remove answer sheet by cutting on dotted line

MODEL TEST 2
LISTENING COMPREHENSION

In this section of the test, you will have the chance to show how well you understand spoken English. There are four parts to this section, with special directions for each part. You will find the Answer Sheet for Model Test 2 on page 279. Detach it from the book and use it to record your answers. Check your answers using the Answer Key on page 473 and see the Explanatory Answers on page 519. Turn on the compact disc when you are ready to begin.

Listen to Track 5 of compact disc 2 to hear the statements for Part I of Model Test 2.

Part I: Picture

Directions: In your test book, you will see a picture. On the compact disc, you will hear four statements. Choose the statement that most closely matches the picture and fill in the corresponding oval on your answer sheet.

GO ON TO THE NEXT PAGE

282 TOEIC MODEL TESTS

1.

2.

3.

4.

284 TOEIC MODEL TESTS

5.

6.

7.

8.

9.

10.

11.

12.

288 TOEIC MODEL TESTS

13.

14.

15.

16.

17.

18.

19.

20.

Listen to Track 6 of compact disc 2 to hear the statements for Part II of Model Test 2.

Part II: Question-Response

Directions: On the compact disc, you will hear a question and three possible answers. Choose the answer that most closely answers the question and fill in the corresponding oval on your answer sheet.

21. Mark your answer on your answer sheet.
22. Mark your answer on your answer sheet.
23. Mark your answer on your answer sheet.
24. Mark your answer on your answer sheet.
25. Mark your answer on your answer sheet.
26. Mark your answer on your answer sheet.
27. Mark your answer on your answer sheet.
28. Mark your answer on your answer sheet.
29. Mark your answer on your answer sheet.
30. Mark your answer on your answer sheet.
31. Mark your answer on your answer sheet.
32. Mark your answer on your answer sheet.
33. Mark your answer on your answer sheet.
34. Mark your answer on your answer sheet.
35. Mark your answer on your answer sheet.
36. Mark your answer on your answer sheet.

37. Mark your answer on your answer sheet.
38. Mark your answer on your answer sheet.
39. Mark your answer on your answer sheet.
40. Mark your answer on your answer sheet.
41. Mark your answer on your answer sheet.
42. Mark your answer on your answer sheet.
43. Mark your answer on your answer sheet.
44. Mark your answer on your answer sheet.
45. Mark your answer on your answer sheet.
46. Mark your answer on your answer sheet.
47. Mark your answer on your answer sheet.
48. Mark your answer on your answer sheet.
49. Mark your answer on your answer sheet.
50. Mark your answer on your answer sheet.

GO ON TO THE NEXT PAGE

Listen to Track 7 of compact disc 2 to hear the conversations for Part III of Model Test 2.

Part III: Short Conversations

Directions: On the compact disc, you will hear a short conversation. In your test book, you will see a question and four possible answers. Choose the best answer to the question and fill in the corresponding oval on your answer sheet.

51. Why does the man eat at noon?
    (A) The afternoon seems shorter.
    (B) He is hungry.
    (C) He is diabetic.
    (D) He doesn't want to be late.

52. What did the man agree to do?
    (A) Leave the receptionist.
    (B) Mail a package.
    (C) Take a package to the receptionist.
    (D) Save packages in the lobby.

53. Where did this conversation take place?
    (A) In a classroom.
    (B) In a store.
    (C) In an office.
    (D) In the post office.

54. What does the woman want to buy?
    (A) A carved box.
    (B) A clock.
    (C) A souvenir.
    (D) Some local beer.

55. What will the woman do tonight?
    (A) Eat in her room.
    (B) Attend the evening session.
    (C) Go to the evening church service.
    (D) Meet the speaker.

56. What did the waiter do?
    (A) Cook a specialty.
    (B) Try some fish.
    (C) Suggest a dish.
    (D) Get a room.

57. What did the woman give the man?
    (A) A business card.
    (B) A credit card.
    (C) A check.
    (D) Cash.

58. What are the man and woman doing?
    (A) Saying good-bye.
    (B) Greeting each other.
    (C) Issuing invitations.
    (D) Introducing each other.

59. Who is the man probably talking to?
    (A) The janitor.
    (B) The company nurse.
    (C) The vice-president.
    (D) The receptionist.

60. What went wrong?
    (A) The woman didn't get the report.
    (B) The man didn't copy the report.
    (C) The man didn't write the report.
    (D) The woman doesn't want the report.

61. Why are they happy?
    (A) The proposal was successful.
    (B) The woman made a good contact.
    (C) Pollution has decreased.
    (D) The man has just proposed.

62. What did the woman decide?
    (A) To make coffee.
    (B) To get a replacement.
    (C) To buy a coffeemaker.
    (D) To get her money back.

63. What sport do the man and woman have in common?
    (A) Golf.
    (B) Tennis.
    (C) Bowling.
    (D) Skiing.

64. What will they do next time?
    (A) Fly to Atlanta.
    (B) Book an earlier flight.
    (C) Call the airport before they leave.
    (D) Leave the airport.

65. What did the man want to do?
    (A) Find the computer.
    (B) Switch computers.
    (C) Start the computer.
    (D) Give the computer back.

66. How will the man get to his hotel?
    (A) By hotel bus.
    (B) By subway.
    (C) By taxi.
    (D) By phone.

67. When will they meet for dinner?
    (A) 3:00.
    (B) 6:00.
    (C) 6:30.
    (D) 7:00.

68. What did the man ask the desk clerk to do?
    (A) Take him to his meeting.
    (B) Wake him up.
    (C) Call his home.
    (D) Set his clock.

69. What happened to the man?
    (A) He took a pay-cut.
    (B) He needs a better watch.
    (C) He didn't get the job.
    (D) His application got lost.

70. Why do the meetings run late?
    (A) There is too much to discuss.
    (B) Everyone wants to wait.
    (C) People arrive late.
    (D) Time escapes them.

71. How late can the man check in?
    (A) 3:00.
    (B) 5:00.
    (C) 7:00.
    (D) 9:00.

72. What is the woman's job?
    (A) Flight attendant.
    (B) Tour guide.
    (C) Newsstand owner.
    (D) Waiter.

73. Why can't the woman meet tomorrow?
    (A) She's tired.
    (B) She doesn't want to discuss it.
    (C) She has to pay a fine.
    (D) She's busy.

74. Why will the man call?
    (A) To get his money back.
    (B) To hurry the cab.
    (C) To report his lost briefcase.
    (D) To pay his tab.

75. Why is the man upset?
    (A) His earnings are incomplete.
    (B) He can't watch his program.
    (C) He can't stand up.
    (D) He can't use the software.

76. What does the man want the woman to do?
    (A) Work on a project.
    (B) Congratulate her coworkers.
    (C) Take his credit card.
    (D) Work with a team.

77. What is the woman's advice?
    (A) Get a job.
    (B) Have confidence in yourself.
    (C) Know what you can do well.
    (D) Start on a trip.

78. What will the woman do?
    (A) Go on a date.
    (B) Fix the date.
    (C) Sign the letter.
    (D) Leave right away.

GO ON TO THE NEXT PAGE

79. Why does the man let the woman go first?
    (A) Her copies are due earlier.
    (B) He only needs to make four.
    (C) She has no copies to make.
    (D) He has to go by noon.

80. What are they discussing?
    (A) How to get some sunlight.
    (B) Where to have lunch.
    (C) Where the cafe is located.
    (D) How to keep a good mood.

Listen to Track 8 of compact disc 2 to hear the short talks for Part IV of Model Test 2.

Part IV: Short Talks

Directions: On the compact disc, you will hear a short talk. In your test book, you will see several questions on the talk and four possible answers. Choose the best answer to the question and fill in the corresponding oval on your answer sheet.

81. Who is the audience for this advertisement?
    - (A) Airline pilots.
    - (B) Businesspeople.
    - (C) Tourists.
    - (D) Students.

82. Why is this computer useful away from the office?
    - (A) It's portable.
    - (B) It can be rented.
    - (C) It has a long-life battery pack.
    - (D) It's easy to use.

83. What best describes the weather conditions the area is facing?
    - (A) Cold.
    - (B) Fog.
    - (C) Snow and ice.
    - (D) Wind and rain.

84. What problems will this weather cause tomorrow?
    - (A) People will have trouble getting to work.
    - (B) People won't have enough heat.
    - (C) Flights will be cancelled.
    - (D) People should buy plenty of food.

85. According to the study, who is expected to be less fit?
    - (A) A mail carrier.
    - (B) A construction worker.
    - (C) An oil rigger.
    - (D) An accountant.

86. Which is mentioned as a way to get more exercise?
    - (A) Doing aerobics after work.
    - (B) Riding a stationary bicycle during breaks.
    - (C) Walking during lunch.
    - (D) Stretching.

87. Where would you be likely to hear this message?
    - (A) At a government agency.
    - (B) On a personal phone.
    - (C) At a recording studio.
    - (D) On an intercom.

88. What type of message should you leave?
    - (A) Confidential.
    - (B) Clear.
    - (C) Detailed.
    - (D) Short.

89. What can this company do for you?
    - (A) Prepare your taxes.
    - (B) Claim your return.
    - (C) Write your financial records.
    - (D) Staff your accounting department.

90. How does the company determine its fees?
    - (A) By a flat rate.
    - (B) With a single price.
    - (C) By a prorated amount.
    - (D) By an hourly rate.

GO ON TO THE NEXT PAGE

91. What did the airlines do to increase sales?
    (A) Reduce ticket prices.
    (B) Provide more polite service.
    (C) Guarantee the arrival of your bags.
    (D) Serve better meals.

92. Why have these airlines lost customers?
    (A) Fewer people are flying.
    (B) The planes were always late.
    (C) Regional airlines are competing.
    (D) It's off-season.

93. Who would be likely to call this number?
    (A) A salesperson.
    (B) A computer user.
    (C) A customer service representative.
    (D) An accountant.

94. What should you do if you want information not listed?
    (A) Dial 10.
    (B) Hang up and call again.
    (C) Go to a local store.
    (D) Stay on the line.

95. What is the destination for this flight?
    (A) Dallas.
    (B) Houston.
    (C) Madison.
    (D) Wilmington.

96. When will the flight land?
    (A) 4:00.
    (B) 4:47.
    (C) 7:00.
    (D) 7:44.

97. What is the weather like there?
    (A) Humid.
    (B) Rainy.
    (C) Breezy.
    (D) Sunny.

98. What kind of problem does the area have?
    (A) There was an accident on the freeway.
    (B) The area is flooded.
    (C) There was a fire.
    (D) There was an earthquake.

99. Why are local relief centers running low on food?
    (A) Flood victims have filled the shelters.
    (B) Food spoiled because of moisture.
    (C) There was too much rain to grow food.
    (D) They cannot deliver the food.

100. If you want to donate food, where should you take it?
    (A) To the public.
    (B) The relief center.
    (C) The radio station.
    (D) A food collection center.

**This is the end of the Listening Comprehension portion of the test.
Turn to Part V in your test book.**

READING

In this section of the test, you will have the chance to show how well you understand written English. There are three parts to this section, with special directions for each part.

YOU WILL HAVE ONE HOUR AND FIFTEEN MINUTES TO COMPLETE PARTS V, VI, AND VII OF THE TEST.

Part V: Incomplete Sentences

Directions: In your test book, you will see a sentence with a missing word. Four possible answers follow the sentence. Choose the best answer to the question and fill in the corresponding oval on your answer sheet.

101. Inter Coast Airlines flight _____ Seoul has been delayed.
    (A) to
    (B) in
    (C) by
    (D) at

102. An _____ training period will be instituted in July.
    (A) extend
    (B) extended
    (C) extension
    (D) extent

103. _____ she left the ship, the purser signed out.
    (A) Because
    (B) Since
    (C) And
    (D) Before

104. Many subscribers have requested that we _____ the journals to their offices.
    (A) mails
    (B) mailed
    (C) mail
    (D) mailing

105. The clerk found the typographical error after the messenger _____ the proposal.
    (A) delivered
    (B) delivers
    (C) has delivered
    (D) is delivering

GO ON TO THE NEXT PAGE

106. Ms. Franklin directed a very _____ project.
    (A) successfully
    (B) successive
    (C) success
    (D) successful

107. You should register for the seminar _____ you attend.
    (A) while
    (B) before
    (C) nor
    (D) and

108. The speaker has _____ his speech by two minutes.
    (A) short
    (B) shortening
    (C) shortened
    (D) shortage

109. The vice-president will be seated _____ the chairman at the banquet.
    (A) as
    (B) by
    (C) to
    (D) from

110. The new waiter has not made any _____ mistakes.
    (A) foolish
    (B) fool
    (C) foolishness
    (D) fooled

111. By Friday, twenty-five applications had been submitted _____ the desk clerk.
    (A) at
    (B) on
    (C) for
    (D) by

112. The ship provisions officer _____ his supplies in large quantities.
    (A) buy
    (B) buys
    (C) buying
    (D) to buy

113. Mr. Cruz needs someone to _____ him with the conference display.
    (A) assume
    (B) assign
    (C) assent
    (D) assist

114. Budget meetings are held _____ in the conference room.
    (A) rarely
    (B) every week
    (C) always
    (D) sometimes

115. At midnight, the second shift of security guards _____ on duty.
    (A) coming
    (B) to come
    (C) comes
    (D) come

116. The final purchase price was higher than the investors _____.
    (A) had expected
    (B) expect
    (C) are expecting
    (D) will expect

117. A manager _____ new things from his or her staff.
    (A) can sometimes learn
    (B) learning sometimes can
    (C) sometimes learn can
    (D) sometimes can learning

118. The new insurance plan is especially _____ with employees who have families.
    (A) popularized
    (B) popular
    (C) populated
    (D) popularity

119. The finance committee will meet again _____ the eighth of May.
    (A) for
    (B) to
    (C) from
    (D) on

120. The airline will refund the money _____ you cancel the reservation.
    (A) during
    (B) soon
    (C) when
    (D) until

121. Did Mr. Fisk _____ the reference guide from the company library?
    (A) loan
    (B) borrow
    (C) lend
    (D) sent

122. _____ they were ordered, the brochures and business cards were never printed.
    (A) Although
    (B) Even
    (C) However
    (D) Despite

123. The operator does not remember receiving a fax from the Madrid office _____ from the Paris office.
    (A) or
    (B) and
    (C) either
    (D) but

124. Have you ever used this type of copy machine _____?
    (A) before
    (B) prior
    (C) advance
    (D) previous

125. If our ship _____ fewer passengers, the crew would not have to share rooms.
    (A) had
    (B) have
    (C) will have
    (D) would have

126. You should check your messages _____.
    (A) as soon as
    (B) twice a day
    (C) seldom
    (D) rarely

127. The receptionist receives packages and _____ them until the proper department is notified.
    (A) is holding
    (B) held
    (C) hold
    (D) holds

128. The purpose of our conference is to help employees _____ our policies.
    (A) understood
    (B) understanding
    (C) understand
    (D) is understanding

129. _____ none of us were familiar with the city, Mr. Gutman drove us to the meeting.
    (A) Although
    (B) Because
    (C) Therefore
    (D) However

130. The auditor discovered that the accountant had not been _____ the checks into the correct account.
    (A) deposited
    (B) deposits
    (C) deposit
    (D) depositing

131. If this report is sent by overnight delivery, it _____ Milan by noon tomorrow.
    (A) reaches
    (B) will reach
    (C) is reaching
    (D) has reached

132. Most employees drive to work and _____ the building from the parking lot.
    (A) enter
    (B) entered
    (C) entering
    (D) entrance

GO ON TO THE NEXT PAGE

133. Employees who _____ attending the conference can get a discount on travel arrangements.
    (A) have going
    (B) are going
    (C) will
    (D) will be

134. Mr. Vasco worked hard to develop his _____ in electronics.
    (A) expertly
    (B) expert
    (C) expertise
    (D) expectant

135. The _____ rates change daily.
    (A) money
    (B) bills
    (C) coins
    (D) currency

136. The head housekeeper is going to ask Ms. Chang how much time she _____ available.
    (A) will have had
    (B) is having
    (C) have
    (D) has

137. The hotel marketing director is quite _____ about advertising in Europe.
    (A) knowing
    (B) knowledge
    (C) knowledgeable
    (D) knows

138. Mr. Ni _____ in charge of the research division for two years.
    (A) has
    (B) has been
    (C) is
    (D) had

139. The operator _____ Mr. Smith if she knew where to reach him.
    (A) will call
    (B) had called
    (C) called
    (D) would call

140. The trainers for the seminar had the crew _____ their equipment to the conference center.
    (A) move
    (B) moving
    (C) mover
    (D) moved

Part VI: Error Recognition

Directions: In your test book, you will see a sentence with four words or phrases underlined. Choose the word or phrase that is incorrect and fill in the corresponding oval on your answer sheet.

141. The secretary had her manager signed the
     ___A___   ___B___
letter before he left the office.
      ___C__ __D__

142. The managers worked hard on the
                  ___A__
presentation, and is pleased to learn that
              ___B___   ___C___
they won the award.
     ___D__

143. Ms. Wang, who is transferring
                  __A__
to this branch, she is an experienced teller.
___B___   ___C__ ___D___

144. The proposing topic for the seminar does
         ____A____   ___B___
not meet our company's needs.
___C__   ____D____

145. The shipping department always handles
                          ___A___
lots of packages, but today they have
___B___   ___C__
handle more than usual.
___D__

146. Ms. Gramm wants to know where we
                     ___A__
will be staying in case she need to call us
___B___   ___C___
during our trip.
___D__

147. Could you get a report you told me about
                  ___A___   ___B__
that explains the latest environmental
     ___C___   ___D___
regulations?

GO ON TO THE NEXT PAGE

148. Mr. Miliken is worried(A) that he would be(B) stuck in traffic on his way(C) home this afternoon.(D)

149. The desk clerk does not know(A) how many(B) rooms to reserve(C) for guests who is attending(D) the conference.

150. The buyer realized that(A) he should have verified(B) the delivery date when(C) he makes the purchase.(D)

151. The company headquarters is(A) much closest(B) to your office than(C) to mine.(D)

152. Ms. Kent will return from(A) her business trip before(B) her secretary had to leave(C) for her vacation.(D)

153. Have you thought(A) about to look(B) for a new job that offers(C) opportunities for advancement and(D) a better salary?

154. The passengers, which(A) were frustrated by(B) the delays, crowded in front of(C) the ticket counter to change(D) their flights.

155. Riding(A) a bicycle to work is not fast as(B) driving a car,(C) but it is healthier.(D)

156. Office policy(A) requires smokers smoking(B) cigarettes and(C) cigars outside the(D) building.

157. The personnel director decided(A) to give the applicant a(B) chance to show(C) where she(D) knew about business.

158. Though(A) the clerks needed to track the(B) shipment, they did not take their(C) coffee break on time.(D)

159. Mr. Lee is concerned(A) because there has been(B) no response from client(C) about the changes made(D) in the contract.

160. Visitors(A) must be accompanied by a employee(B) when(C) they are in the(D) building.

Part VII: Reading Comprehension

Directions: In your test book, you will see a reading passage followed by several questions. Each question has four answer choices. Choose the best answer to the question and fill in the corresponding oval on your answer sheet.

Questions 161–162 refer to the following announcement.

> As our company plans new products and processes, health, safety and environmental considerations are a priority. We are committed to operating our manufacturing plants and research facilities in a manner that protects the environment and safeguards the health and safety of all people. We will continue to allocate money to improve existing facilities as new safety information is brought to light.

161. What is this statement intended to do?
 (A) Announce an expansion
 (B) Tell about a merger
 (C) Reassure the public about safety
 (D) Give a new policy

162. What will the company do with existing facilities?
 (A) Continue to make them safe
 (B) Tear them down
 (C) Have them inspected
 (D) Operate them

GO ON TO THE NEXT PAGE

Questions 163–165 refer to the following form.

NewsEvents

Subscribe Now

Receive NewsEvents magazine for as little as $1.00 per copy. That's less than half of the $2.25 newsstand price! Just fill in your name and address below to get great savings.

Name Mr. Ms._____
Street_____
City-State-Zip_____

Check one:
Check enclosed _____
Bill me in full _____
Bill me in installments _____

163. What is this form for?
 (A) Subscribing to a magazine
 (B) Buying a newspaper
 (C) Entering a contest
 (D) Registering for class

164. How much does NewsEvents cost at a store?
 (A) $.50
 (B) $1.00
 (C) $2.00
 (D) $2.25

165. What is NOT listed as an acceptable method of payment?
 (A) A bill
 (B) Bills for installments
 (C) A check
 (D) Cash

Questions 166–168 refer to the following report.

> The profits for the Wu Company more than doubled in the fourth quarter over profit levels of a year ago. This is due in part to lower operating and administrative expenses. The electronics store chain earned $42.6 million, compared with $21.1 million in the fourth quarter of last year. Total profits for the year are $122.8 million, compared with $48.5 million last year.

166. How do fourth quarter profits for this year compare to those of last year?
    (A) Stayed the same
    (B) Increased by twice as much
    (C) Increased by more than twice as much
    (D) Decreased by half

167. What contributed to the change?
    (A) Reduction of operating costs
    (B) Higher number of customers
    (C) New and better products
    (D) More expensive products

168. What kind of business is the Wu Company?
    (A) Business supplies
    (B) Manufacturing
    (C) Storage and shipping
    (D) Retail electronics

Questions 169–170 refer to the following advertisement.

> **Data Entry/Clerk** Insurance firm seeks reliable person for operations division. Must be good with details and computer-literate. Responsibilities include data entry, filing, and word processing. Good salary and benefits. Pleasant atmosphere. Room to advance.

169. What is one responsibility of this job?
    (A) Answering the phone
    (B) Data entry
    (C) Selling insurance
    (D) Operating a division

170. What is one benefit of the position?
    (A) They'll give you your own office later.
    (B) You can work toward promotions.
    (C) The air is clean.
    (D) You can earn commissions.

GO ON TO THE NEXT PAGE

Questions 171–172 refer to the following magazine article.

When you are looking for a new job, you must talk to as many people as you can who work in your field or in related fields. This is called networking. Networking allows you to learn about new areas to pursue and to find out which companies may need someone with your skills. Networking is a fun and easy way to find out about new opportunities. And when your new job comes along, you will already know some of your colleagues.

171. What is networking?
(A) Learning your job well
(B) Meeting people in related fields
(C) Studying lots of companies
(D) Getting along with your colleagues

172. What is NOT mentioned as something you can learn from networking?
(A) New career areas
(B) Your colleagues and what they do
(C) Which companies may need you
(D) What the companies pay

Questions 173–175 refer to the following memo.

MEMORANDUM

To: All employees
Fm: Donetta Muscillo
    Safety Coordinator
Date: June 5, 19__

Sub: Fire doors.

Employees are reminded that doors designated as fire doors must stay closed at all times. The purpose of fire doors is to help direct smoke away from areas where people are working in case of a fire in the building. Even though the weather is hot and the repairs to the company's air conditioner are not complete, keeping the fire doors open is dangerous and is not allowed.

173. What kind of memo is this?
(A) A notice about new policy
(B) A safety warning
(C) A personnel memo
(D) A reception invitation

174. What is the purpose of fire doors?
(A) To keep smoke away from people
(B) To provide escape routes
(C) To keep fire from spreading
(D) To contain heat

175. Why were employees probably keeping the fire doors open?
(A) To get to a higher floor
(B) To look at the view
(C) To go from office to office
(D) To let in cool air

Questions 176–178 refer to the following calendar.

FEBRUARY	MARCH	APRIL	MAY
February 4–February 24 Bonn, Germany International Jewelry Trade Fair	March 11–April 15 Budapest, Hungary International Furniture Fair March 12–March 20 Milan, Italy Automobile Show March 15–March 18 Guangzhou, China International Shoe Fair March 20–March 25 Moscow, Russia International Textile Fair	April 16–April 24 Hannover, Germany Art and Antiques Fair April 14–April 21 Basel, Switzerland European Watch Fair	May 27–June 12 Bath, England International Computer Exhibit

176. What does this calendar list?
    (A) Trade shows
    (B) Musical events
    (C) Sport competitions
    (D) Tour itinerary

177. Which event is NOT in Europe?
    (A) Automobile Show
    (B) International Shoe Fair
    (C) Art and Antiques Fair
    (D) International Jewelry Trade Fair

178. If you bought cloth for a dress manufacturer, where should you go in March?
    (A) Budapest
    (B) Bonn
    (C) Moscow
    (D) Hannover

GO ON TO THE NEXT PAGE

Questions 179–181 refer to the following announcement.

ESTATE AUCTION

An auction for the estate of
Raul Diega
has been set for

Saturday, October 3, at 11:00 A.M.
(preview starts at 10:00 A.M.)

Location: 5667 North Hedge Lane

Some of the items to be auctioned
* 1994 Porsche
* China and crystal
* Oriental rugs
* Jewelry

Questions? Please call Estate Planners at 778-0099 between noon and 5 P.M.

179. What is being announced?
   (A) A show
   (B) A sale
   (C) A store opening
   (D) A fund-raiser

180. What might you find at this event?
   (A) Chinese antiques
   (B) Porch furniture
   (C) Bracelets
   (D) Wall-to-wall carpeting

181. When can you start to look at things?
   (A) October 3, 11:00 A.M.
   (B) By appointment after calling 778-0099
   (C) An day from noon to five
   (D) October 3, 10:00 A.M.

Questions 182–184 refer to the following magazine article.

> Historically, the businessperson has wanted his or her company to grow. Larger companies meant greater success and greater profits. Larger companies also meant more jobs for people in the community. But some companies have become so large that they are no longer profitable or practical to run. When this happens, the company may downsize, or deliberately reduce growth. This corporate downsizing is no longer unusual. Major corporations have either already downsized or have announced plans to do so. But the decision to downsize is not always popular with the community, because it means loss of jobs.

182. What has been the trend for businesses in the past?
 (A) To grow larger
 (B) To get smaller
 (C) To be less successful
 (D) To downsize

183. What current tendency contrasts with this past trend?
 (A) Profit-making
 (B) Downsizing
 (C) Energy-boosting
 (D) Cooperating

184. Why may the community dislike the decision to downsize?
 (A) Area residents may lose their jobs
 (B) The company will probably move
 (C) The company's products will get more expensive
 (D) The company will lose profits

GO ON TO THE NEXT PAGE

Questions 185–187 refer to the following notice.

Lecture Series

by Chin Fong

International Trade in the Global Community

Sponsor: The School of Business
Beaumont University

Date and Time: March 18, 19, and 20 at 7:30 p.m.
Location: Sims Lecture Hall of the Carmichael Building

To register, please call the
Center for Professional Development
953-2703

---

185. What is the purpose of this notice?
 (A) To announce a lecture series
 (B) To advertise the university
 (C) To announce a trade fair
 (D) To recruit students

186. Where will the event be held?
 (A) At the School of Business
 (B) In Sims Lecture Hall
 (C) In the Center for Professional Development
 (D) In the Global Community Center

187. What should you do to sign up?
 (A) Contact Beaumont University
 (B) Contact Chin Fong
 (C) Contact the School of Business
 (D) Contact the Center for Professional Development

Questions 188–191 refer to the following advertisement.

This new and unusual building in the downtown business district offers unique opportunities for small to midsized tenants to occupy an entire floor

OFFICE SUITES

from 1,600 to 6,000 square feet are available for immediate occupancy.

Commuting is easy, with the subway stop only one block away. It's convenient to shops, restaurants, hotels, and business services.

For leasing information call **303-572-5947**

188. What is this advertisement for?
 (A) Renting office space
 (B) Buying a building
 (C) Starting a business
 (D) Staying at a hotel

189. Why does this building present a rare opportunity for smaller firms?
 (A) It's a new building.
 (B) They don't have to share a floor.
 (C) Smaller firms are better tenants.
 (D) They get lower rates.

190. How soon are the suites available?
 (A) When the building is finished
 (B) Next month
 (C) Right now
 (D) In six weeks

191. What is NOT mentioned as being close to the building?
 (A) Parks
 (B) Shopping
 (C) Hotels
 (D) Restaurants

GO ON TO THE NEXT PAGE

Questions 192–196 refer to the following article.

Meetings

Meetings can waste a great deal of time. But you can make your meeting run more smoothly by following a few simple rules. First, have an agenda. This will help keep you focused on what is important. Next, decide who needs to be involved. More people mean less efficient discussion. Finally, keep the discussion moving. Thank each speaker as he or she finishes and move on to the next speaker. This encourages people to make their remarks brief.

The problem with meetings, of course, is that no one likes them, no one wants them, and no one needs them. Yet, everyone has them. Meetings are the corporate world's response to primitive socializing behaviors. People feel more comfortable in making decisions in groups. They can then share blame if a decision turns out to be the wrong decision. Sharing credit for a correct decision is not often found in groups. Then individuals tend to remind people of how persuasive they were in the meeting when the "right" decision was made.

What happens after a meeting is more important than what happens during the meeting. The skills used then are more professional and less procedural. So no matter how well you run a meeting, it is the work that gets done after the meeting that is important.

192. What is one way to run a meeting well?
    (A) Watch how your manager runs meetings.
    (B) Minimize the number of participants.
    (C) Let the group make decisions.
    (D) Let everyone speak.

193. What is the purpose of a meeting agenda?
    (A) To keep the speakers organized
    (B) To allow free discussion
    (C) To send to others in advance
    (D) To keep focused on important items

194. How should you receive other people's comments at a meeting?
    (A) Try to keep others from talking.
    (B) Thank them and move on.
    (C) Give them as much time as they want.
    (D) Criticize them in public.

195. The author feels that meetings
    (A) give people an opportunity to socialize
    (B) are an effective tool
    (C) are cost-efficient
    (D) are well-attended

196. In conclusion the author feels
    (A) meetings should be held more frequently
    (B) all meetings should be in the morning
    (C) no one should receive credit for their work
    (D) real work is left to the professional

Questions 197–200 refer to the following announcement.

> **H** **The Hesseltine Corporation**
> is moving 60 technical and management-level employees to their new manufacturing plant in the western United States. A big part of the process is to prepare the employees for the cultural changes they will encounter when moving from urban Europe to a small town in the American West. The employees and their families are attending special seminars on the habits of Americans. They learn about the regional vocabulary and the daily life. Without this training, even small cultural differences could cause big misunderstandings.

197. Where is the new manufacturing plant?
  (A) In an urban area
  (B) In Western Europe
  (C) In the western United States
  (D) In a large town

198. What important part of the moving process is discussed?
  (A) Completing the plant
  (B) Getting the office furnishings
  (C) Arranging airline tickets
  (D) Teaching cultural differences

199. Who is attending the seminars with the employees?
  (A) Their secretaries
  (B) Their families
  (C) Their supervisors
  (D) Their staffs

200. What are they learning about?
  (A) Travel plans
  (B) Management methods
  (C) American culture
  (D) Manufacturing techniques

STOP!

This is the end of the test. If you finish before time is called, you may go back to Parts V, VI, and VII and check your work.

MODEL TEST 3—ANSWER SHEET

Listening Section

1. Ⓐ Ⓑ Ⓒ Ⓓ
2. Ⓐ Ⓑ Ⓒ Ⓓ
3. Ⓐ Ⓑ Ⓒ Ⓓ
4. Ⓐ Ⓑ Ⓒ Ⓓ
5. Ⓐ Ⓑ Ⓒ Ⓓ
6. Ⓐ Ⓑ Ⓒ Ⓓ
7. Ⓐ Ⓑ Ⓒ Ⓓ
8. Ⓐ Ⓑ Ⓒ Ⓓ
9. Ⓐ Ⓑ Ⓒ Ⓓ
10. Ⓐ Ⓑ Ⓒ Ⓓ
11. Ⓐ Ⓑ Ⓒ Ⓓ
12. Ⓐ Ⓑ Ⓒ Ⓓ
13. Ⓐ Ⓑ Ⓒ Ⓓ
14. Ⓐ Ⓑ Ⓒ Ⓓ
15. Ⓐ Ⓑ Ⓒ Ⓓ
16. Ⓐ Ⓑ Ⓒ Ⓓ
17. Ⓐ Ⓑ Ⓒ Ⓓ
18. Ⓐ Ⓑ Ⓒ Ⓓ
19. Ⓐ Ⓑ Ⓒ Ⓓ
20. Ⓐ Ⓑ Ⓒ Ⓓ
21. Ⓐ Ⓑ Ⓒ
22. Ⓐ Ⓑ Ⓒ
23. Ⓐ Ⓑ Ⓒ
24. Ⓐ Ⓑ Ⓒ
25. Ⓐ Ⓑ Ⓒ
26. Ⓐ Ⓑ Ⓒ
27. Ⓐ Ⓑ Ⓒ
28. Ⓐ Ⓑ Ⓒ
29. Ⓐ Ⓑ Ⓒ
30. Ⓐ Ⓑ Ⓒ
31. Ⓐ Ⓑ Ⓒ
32. Ⓐ Ⓑ Ⓒ
33. Ⓐ Ⓑ Ⓒ
34. Ⓐ Ⓑ Ⓒ
35. Ⓐ Ⓑ Ⓒ
36. Ⓐ Ⓑ Ⓒ
37. Ⓐ Ⓑ Ⓒ
38. Ⓐ Ⓑ Ⓒ
39. Ⓐ Ⓑ Ⓒ
40. Ⓐ Ⓑ Ⓒ
41. Ⓐ Ⓑ Ⓒ
42. Ⓐ Ⓑ Ⓒ
43. Ⓐ Ⓑ Ⓒ
44. Ⓐ Ⓑ Ⓒ
45. Ⓐ Ⓑ Ⓒ
46. Ⓐ Ⓑ Ⓒ
47. Ⓐ Ⓑ Ⓒ
48. Ⓐ Ⓑ Ⓒ
49. Ⓐ Ⓑ Ⓒ
50. Ⓐ Ⓑ Ⓒ
51. Ⓐ Ⓑ Ⓒ Ⓓ
52. Ⓐ Ⓑ Ⓒ Ⓓ
53. Ⓐ Ⓑ Ⓒ Ⓓ
54. Ⓐ Ⓑ Ⓒ Ⓓ
55. Ⓐ Ⓑ Ⓒ Ⓓ
56. Ⓐ Ⓑ Ⓒ Ⓓ
57. Ⓐ Ⓑ Ⓒ Ⓓ
58. Ⓐ Ⓑ Ⓒ Ⓓ
59. Ⓐ Ⓑ Ⓒ Ⓓ
60. Ⓐ Ⓑ Ⓒ Ⓓ
61. Ⓐ Ⓑ Ⓒ Ⓓ
62. Ⓐ Ⓑ Ⓒ Ⓓ
63. Ⓐ Ⓑ Ⓒ Ⓓ
64. Ⓐ Ⓑ Ⓒ Ⓓ
65. Ⓐ Ⓑ Ⓒ Ⓓ
66. Ⓐ Ⓑ Ⓒ Ⓓ
67. Ⓐ Ⓑ Ⓒ Ⓓ
68. Ⓐ Ⓑ Ⓒ Ⓓ
69. Ⓐ Ⓑ Ⓒ Ⓓ
70. Ⓐ Ⓑ Ⓒ Ⓓ
71. Ⓐ Ⓑ Ⓒ Ⓓ
72. Ⓐ Ⓑ Ⓒ Ⓓ
73. Ⓐ Ⓑ Ⓒ Ⓓ
74. Ⓐ Ⓑ Ⓒ Ⓓ
75. Ⓐ Ⓑ Ⓒ Ⓓ
76. Ⓐ Ⓑ Ⓒ Ⓓ
77. Ⓐ Ⓑ Ⓒ Ⓓ
78. Ⓐ Ⓑ Ⓒ Ⓓ
79. Ⓐ Ⓑ Ⓒ Ⓓ
80. Ⓐ Ⓑ Ⓒ Ⓓ
81. Ⓐ Ⓑ Ⓒ Ⓓ
82. Ⓐ Ⓑ Ⓒ Ⓓ
83. Ⓐ Ⓑ Ⓒ Ⓓ
84. Ⓐ Ⓑ Ⓒ Ⓓ
85. Ⓐ Ⓑ Ⓒ Ⓓ
86. Ⓐ Ⓑ Ⓒ Ⓓ
87. Ⓐ Ⓑ Ⓒ Ⓓ
88. Ⓐ Ⓑ Ⓒ Ⓓ
89. Ⓐ Ⓑ Ⓒ Ⓓ
90. Ⓐ Ⓑ Ⓒ Ⓓ
91. Ⓐ Ⓑ Ⓒ Ⓓ
92. Ⓐ Ⓑ Ⓒ Ⓓ
93. Ⓐ Ⓑ Ⓒ Ⓓ
94. Ⓐ Ⓑ Ⓒ Ⓓ
95. Ⓐ Ⓑ Ⓒ Ⓓ
96. Ⓐ Ⓑ Ⓒ Ⓓ
97. Ⓐ Ⓑ Ⓒ Ⓓ
98. Ⓐ Ⓑ Ⓒ Ⓓ
99. Ⓐ Ⓑ Ⓒ Ⓓ
100. Ⓐ Ⓑ Ⓒ Ⓓ

Reading Section

101. Ⓐ Ⓑ Ⓒ Ⓓ
102. Ⓐ Ⓑ Ⓒ Ⓓ
103. Ⓐ Ⓑ Ⓒ Ⓓ
104. Ⓐ Ⓑ Ⓒ Ⓓ
105. Ⓐ Ⓑ Ⓒ Ⓓ
106. Ⓐ Ⓑ Ⓒ Ⓓ
107. Ⓐ Ⓑ Ⓒ Ⓓ
108. Ⓐ Ⓑ Ⓒ Ⓓ
109. Ⓐ Ⓑ Ⓒ Ⓓ
110. Ⓐ Ⓑ Ⓒ Ⓓ
111. Ⓐ Ⓑ Ⓒ Ⓓ
112. Ⓐ Ⓑ Ⓒ Ⓓ
113. Ⓐ Ⓑ Ⓒ Ⓓ
114. Ⓐ Ⓑ Ⓒ Ⓓ
115. Ⓐ Ⓑ Ⓒ Ⓓ
116. Ⓐ Ⓑ Ⓒ Ⓓ
117. Ⓐ Ⓑ Ⓒ Ⓓ
118. Ⓐ Ⓑ Ⓒ Ⓓ
119. Ⓐ Ⓑ Ⓒ Ⓓ
120. Ⓐ Ⓑ Ⓒ Ⓓ
121. Ⓐ Ⓑ Ⓒ Ⓓ
122. Ⓐ Ⓑ Ⓒ Ⓓ
123. Ⓐ Ⓑ Ⓒ Ⓓ
124. Ⓐ Ⓑ Ⓒ Ⓓ
125. Ⓐ Ⓑ Ⓒ Ⓓ
126. Ⓐ Ⓑ Ⓒ Ⓓ
127. Ⓐ Ⓑ Ⓒ Ⓓ
128. Ⓐ Ⓑ Ⓒ Ⓓ
129. Ⓐ Ⓑ Ⓒ Ⓓ
130. Ⓐ Ⓑ Ⓒ Ⓓ
131. Ⓐ Ⓑ Ⓒ Ⓓ
132. Ⓐ Ⓑ Ⓒ Ⓓ
133. Ⓐ Ⓑ Ⓒ Ⓓ
134. Ⓐ Ⓑ Ⓒ Ⓓ
135. Ⓐ Ⓑ Ⓒ Ⓓ
136. Ⓐ Ⓑ Ⓒ Ⓓ
137. Ⓐ Ⓑ Ⓒ Ⓓ
138. Ⓐ Ⓑ Ⓒ Ⓓ
139. Ⓐ Ⓑ Ⓒ Ⓓ
140. Ⓐ Ⓑ Ⓒ Ⓓ
141. Ⓐ Ⓑ Ⓒ Ⓓ
142. Ⓐ Ⓑ Ⓒ Ⓓ
143. Ⓐ Ⓑ Ⓒ Ⓓ
144. Ⓐ Ⓑ Ⓒ Ⓓ
145. Ⓐ Ⓑ Ⓒ Ⓓ
146. Ⓐ Ⓑ Ⓒ Ⓓ
147. Ⓐ Ⓑ Ⓒ Ⓓ
148. Ⓐ Ⓑ Ⓒ Ⓓ
149. Ⓐ Ⓑ Ⓒ Ⓓ
150. Ⓐ Ⓑ Ⓒ Ⓓ
151. Ⓐ Ⓑ Ⓒ Ⓓ
152. Ⓐ Ⓑ Ⓒ Ⓓ
153. Ⓐ Ⓑ Ⓒ Ⓓ
154. Ⓐ Ⓑ Ⓒ Ⓓ
155. Ⓐ Ⓑ Ⓒ Ⓓ
156. Ⓐ Ⓑ Ⓒ Ⓓ
157. Ⓐ Ⓑ Ⓒ Ⓓ
158. Ⓐ Ⓑ Ⓒ Ⓓ
159. Ⓐ Ⓑ Ⓒ Ⓓ
160. Ⓐ Ⓑ Ⓒ Ⓓ
161. Ⓐ Ⓑ Ⓒ Ⓓ
162. Ⓐ Ⓑ Ⓒ Ⓓ
163. Ⓐ Ⓑ Ⓒ Ⓓ
164. Ⓐ Ⓑ Ⓒ Ⓓ
165. Ⓐ Ⓑ Ⓒ Ⓓ
166. Ⓐ Ⓑ Ⓒ Ⓓ
167. Ⓐ Ⓑ Ⓒ Ⓓ
168. Ⓐ Ⓑ Ⓒ Ⓓ
169. Ⓐ Ⓑ Ⓒ Ⓓ
170. Ⓐ Ⓑ Ⓒ Ⓓ
171. Ⓐ Ⓑ Ⓒ Ⓓ
172. Ⓐ Ⓑ Ⓒ Ⓓ
173. Ⓐ Ⓑ Ⓒ Ⓓ
174. Ⓐ Ⓑ Ⓒ Ⓓ
175. Ⓐ Ⓑ Ⓒ Ⓓ
176. Ⓐ Ⓑ Ⓒ Ⓓ
177. Ⓐ Ⓑ Ⓒ Ⓓ
178. Ⓐ Ⓑ Ⓒ Ⓓ
179. Ⓐ Ⓑ Ⓒ Ⓓ
180. Ⓐ Ⓑ Ⓒ Ⓓ
181. Ⓐ Ⓑ Ⓒ Ⓓ
182. Ⓐ Ⓑ Ⓒ Ⓓ
183. Ⓐ Ⓑ Ⓒ Ⓓ
184. Ⓐ Ⓑ Ⓒ Ⓓ
185. Ⓐ Ⓑ Ⓒ Ⓓ
186. Ⓐ Ⓑ Ⓒ Ⓓ
187. Ⓐ Ⓑ Ⓒ Ⓓ
188. Ⓐ Ⓑ Ⓒ Ⓓ
189. Ⓐ Ⓑ Ⓒ Ⓓ
190. Ⓐ Ⓑ Ⓒ Ⓓ
191. Ⓐ Ⓑ Ⓒ Ⓓ
192. Ⓐ Ⓑ Ⓒ Ⓓ
193. Ⓐ Ⓑ Ⓒ Ⓓ
194. Ⓐ Ⓑ Ⓒ Ⓓ
195. Ⓐ Ⓑ Ⓒ Ⓓ
196. Ⓐ Ⓑ Ⓒ Ⓓ
197. Ⓐ Ⓑ Ⓒ Ⓓ
198. Ⓐ Ⓑ Ⓒ Ⓓ
199. Ⓐ Ⓑ Ⓒ Ⓓ
200. Ⓐ Ⓑ Ⓒ Ⓓ

Remove answer sheet by cutting on dotted line

MODEL TEST 3
LISTENING COMPREHENSION

In this section of the test, you will have the chance to show how well you understand spoken English. There are four parts to this section, with special directions for each part. You will find the Answer Sheet for Model Test 3 on page 317. Detach it from the book and use it to record your answers. Check your answers using the Answer Key on page 474 and see the Explanatory Answers on page 529. Turn on the compact disc when you are ready to begin.

Listen to Track 1 of compact disc 3 to hear the statements for Part I of Model Test 3.

Part I: Picture

Directions: In your test book, you will see a picture. On the compact disc, you will hear four statements. Choose the statement that most closely matches the picture and fill in the corresponding oval on your answer sheet.

GO ON TO THE NEXT PAGE

320 TOEIC MODEL TESTS

1.

2.

3.

4.

5.

6.

7.

8.

324 TOEIC MODEL TESTS

9.

10.

11.

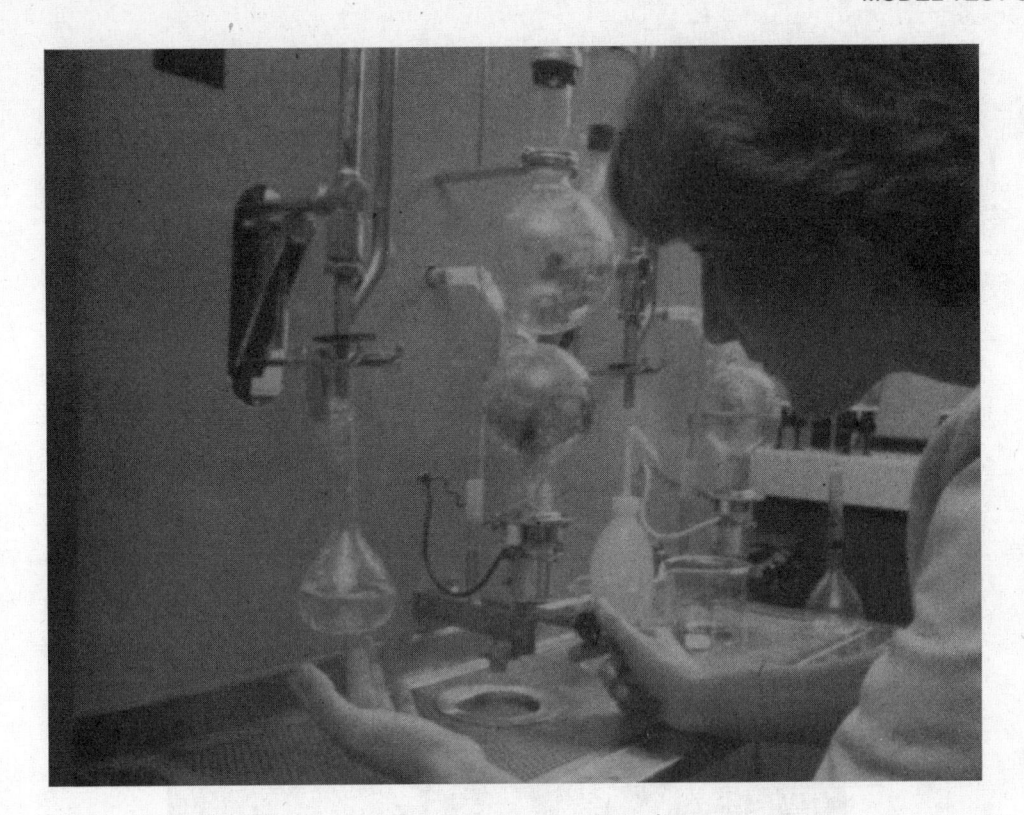

12.

326 TOEIC MODEL TESTS

13.

14.

15.

16.

GO ON TO THE NEXT PAGE

328 TOEIC MODEL TESTS

17.

18.

19.

20.

GO ON TO THE NEXT PAGE

Part II: Question-Response

Directions: On the compact disc, you will hear a question and three possible answers. Choose the answer that most closely answers the question and fill in the corresponding oval on your answer sheet.

21. Mark your answer on your answer sheet.
22. Mark your answer on your answer sheet.
23. Mark your answer on your answer sheet.
24. Mark your answer on your answer sheet.
25. Mark your answer on your answer sheet.
26. Mark your answer on your answer sheet.
27. Mark your answer on your answer sheet.
28. Mark your answer on your answer sheet.
29. Mark your answer on your answer sheet.
30. Mark your answer on your answer sheet.
31. Mark your answer on your answer sheet.
32. Mark your answer on your answer sheet.
33. Mark your answer on your answer sheet.
34. Mark your answer on your answer sheet.
35. Mark your answer on your answer sheet.
36. Mark your answer on your answer sheet.

37. Mark your answer on your answer sheet.
38. Mark your answer on your answer sheet.
39. Mark your answer on your answer sheet.
40. Mark your answer on your answer sheet.
41. Mark your answer on your answer sheet.
42. Mark your answer on your answer sheet.
43. Mark your answer on your answer sheet.
44. Mark your answer on your answer sheet.
45. Mark your answer on your answer sheet.
46. Mark your answer on your answer sheet.
47. Mark your answer on your answer sheet.
48. Mark your answer on your answer sheet.
49. Mark your answer on your answer sheet.
50. Mark your answer on your answer sheet.

GO ON TO THE NEXT PAGE

Part III: Short Conversations

Directions: On the compact disc, you will hear a short conversation. In your test book, you will see a question and four possible answers. Choose the best answer to the question and fill in the corresponding oval on your answer sheet.

51. Why can't they go after work?
    (A) It's dark.
    (B) It's in the park.
    (C) It's going to rain.
    (D) They don't have warm clothes.

52. What does the woman want to do?
    (A) Get a magazine.
    (B) Leave the bank.
    (C) Buy some traveler's checks.
    (D) Look for a desk.

53. What should people do if they get lost?
    (A) Stay with the tour.
    (B) Find the bus.
    (C) Go to the market.
    (D) Take a bus on Main Street.

54. What should the woman do?
    (A) Cash a check.
    (B) Get a roll of quarters.
    (C) Change buses.
    (D) Check her coins.

55. What is the man going to do?
    (A) Figure sales.
    (B) Illustrate programs.
    (C) Sell computers.
    (D) Make graphs and charts.

56. Where does this conversation take place?
    (A) In a movie theater.
    (B) On a plane.
    (C) On a bus.
    (D) In an auditorium.

57. When should the housekeeper clean the room?
    (A) Before 11:00.
    (B) After 11:00.
    (C) At the scheduled time.
    (D) At 2:35.

58. What is the appointment for?
    (A) A medical checkup.
    (B) A sales meeting.
    (C) A possible presentation.
    (D) A job interview.

59. What might solve the problem?
    (A) Mopping it up.
    (B) Fixing the leak.
    (C) Building a stand.
    (D) Keeping it wetter.

60. When will the television set be ready?
    (A) Today.
    (B) One week.
    (C) Two weeks.
    (D) Three weeks.

61. What is the man going to do?
    (A) Manage the director.
    (B) Wear glasses.
    (C) Meet the director.
    (D) Introduce the director.

62. What should the woman expect tomorrow?
    (A) A newspaper.
    (B) Some stationery.
    (C) More room.
    (D) A directory.

63. Why do they need Mr. Chung?
    (A) To address some letters.
    (B) To speak at a meeting.
    (C) To show the film.
    (D) To announce the date.

64. How will the man pay for the sweater?
    (A) Charge it.
    (B) With a check.
    (C) With a credit card.
    (D) Pay cash.

65. Where does the man want to go?
    (A) The park.
    (B) The capitol building.
    (C) The train station.
    (D) The history museum.

66. What does the man do during his lunch hour?
    (A) Takes a walk.
    (B) Exercises.
    (C) Eats lunch.
    (D) Tries to work.

67. Why was the letter returned?
    (A) It didn't contain a check.
    (B) The street didn't exist.
    (C) The company sent it back.
    (D) The man didn't mail it.

68. What was wrong with the lobby before?
    (A) It was too light.
    (B) It was out of style.
    (C) It was too white.
    (D) It was too dark.

69. What are the man and woman doing?
    (A) Working hard.
    (B) Scheduling a meeting.
    (C) Introducing themselves.
    (D) Leaving a party.

70. Where does the man want the desk?
    (A) By the door.
    (B) Under the light.
    (C) In the entrance.
    (D) By the window.

71. What does the project need?
    (A) A different schedule.
    (B) Fewer people.
    (C) A special assignment.
    (D) Some temporary workers.

72. What is the man's problem?
    (A) He's meeting too many people.
    (B) There's no place to have the meeting.
    (C) There's no schedule for Tuesday.
    (D) No one is attending the conference.

73. Why can't the woman take her suitcase with her?
    (A) They have to examine it.
    (B) It's too heavy.
    (C) It's too large.
    (D) She doesn't have any bags.

74. Why didn't the man get an answer?
    (A) They're taking a break.
    (B) They're out on a lake.
    (C) They've broken a plane.
    (D) They're out in the rain.

75. Where did this conversation probably take place?
    (A) At a convention.
    (B) During a performance.
    (C) At a meeting.
    (D) On a tour.

76. Why don't they call a repair person?
    (A) The printer is working.
    (B) The printer is too old.
    (C) The printer is guaranteed.
    (D) The printer is still good.

77. What is the woman's profession?
    (A) Ticket agent.
    (B) Flight attendant.
    (C) Baggage handler.
    (D) Caterer.

GO ON TO THE NEXT PAGE

78. Why does the man want a gas station?
    (A) He's out of gas.
    (B) He's tired.
    (C) He's on a long road.
    (D) He has a flat.

79. How does the man feel?
    (A) Rested.
    (B) Sleepy.
    (C) Motion sick.
    (D) Unstable.

80. What does the woman need to do first?
    (A) Read the report.
    (B) Comment on the report.
    (C) Recommend the report.
    (D) Think about the report.

Listen to Track 4 of compact disc 3 to hear the short talks for Part IV of Model Test 3.

Part IV: Short Talks

Directions: On the compact disc, you will hear a short talk. In your test book, you will see several questions on the talk and four possible answers. Choose the best answer to the question and fill in the corresponding oval on your answer sheet.

81. What is wrong with the number dialed?
    (A) It is the wrong number.
    (B) It is not working.
    (C) It has an answering machine.
    (D) It has a busy signal.

82. Who will help you if you stay on the line?
    (A) A repair person.
    (B) An operator.
    (C) A customer service representative.
    (D) A telephone executive.

83. What is wrong with the water supply?
    (A) There is no more water.
    (B) The water tastes bad.
    (C) The water is contaminated.
    (D) The water is rusted.

84. How can residents make the water safe?
    (A) Boil it.
    (B) Freeze it.
    (C) Put tablets in it.
    (D) Let sediment settle before drinking.

85. What kind of training does this school provide?
    (A) Computer training.
    (B) Business management.
    (C) Personnel training.
    (D) Teacher training.

86. How long will the training take?
    (A) Three months.
    (B) Six months.
    (C) Nine months.
    (D) One year.

87. Where is this train going?
    (A) New York and Baltimore.
    (B) New York and Wilmington.
    (C) New York and Philadelphia.
    (D) New York and Boston.

88. Where should New York passengers board the train?
    (A) At the front.
    (B) At the back.
    (C) In the middle.
    (D) Anywhere.

89. When should you call back?
    (A) In the evenings.
    (B) On Saturdays.
    (C) During business hours.
    (D) Early in the mornings.

90. If you can't call back, how can you contact the company?
    (A) Via e-mail.
    (B) Write them a letter.
    (C) Send them a fax.
    (D) Go to their office.

91. How should you apply for these jobs?
    (A) Send a resume.
    (B) Go to the hotel.
    (C) Write a letter.
    (D) Make a phone call.

GO ON TO THE NEXT PAGE

92. What do the jobs offer, besides a good wage?
    (A) Benefits.
    (B) Free food.
    (C) Good hours.
    (D) Possible promotions.

93. What does this advertisement want you to buy?
    (A) A high-tech computer.
    (B) An electronic mail system.
    (C) A document duplication system.
    (D) A distribution service.

94. How does the ad suggest you will save money?
    (A) With low prices on the system.
    (B) Fewer workers are required.
    (C) Lower printer and paper costs.
    (D) Eliminates interoffice mail.

95. What problem can the city expect?
    (A) An epidemic.
    (B) Extremely hot weather.
    (C) Flooding.
    (D) Infestation of insects.

96. How high are the temperatures expected to be?
    (A) In the seventies.
    (B) In the eighties.
    (C) In the nineties.
    (D) In the hundreds.

97. How can citizens protect themselves?
    (A) Wear dark clothing.
    (B) Exercise frequently.
    (C) Drink lots of water.
    (D) Swim.

98. What advice is given for busy executives?
    (A) Delegate tasks to others.
    (B) Keep your secretary busy.
    (C) Work overtime.
    (D) Establish a quiet hour.

99. How can you keep others from disturbing you?
    (A) Stay away from your office.
    (B) Close your office door.
    (C) Display a DO NOT DISTURB sign.
    (D) Refuse to handle emergencies.

100. What should you do during this time?
    (A) Work on difficult tasks.
    (B) Return phone calls.
    (C) Complete projects that are overdue.
    (D) Work closely with staff.

**This is the end of the Listening Comprehension portion of the test.
Turn to Part V in your test book.**

READING

In this section of the test, you will have the chance to show how well you understand written English. There are three parts to this section, with special directions for each part.

YOU WILL HAVE ONE HOUR AND FIFTEEN MINUTES TO COMPLETE PARTS V, VI, AND VII OF THE TEST.

Part V: Incomplete Sentences

Directions: In your test book, you will see a sentence with a missing word. Four possible answers follow the sentence. Choose the best answer to the question and fill in the corresponding oval on your answer sheet.

101. When the contracts _____ ready, have them sent to the purchaser.
    (A) am
    (B) is
    (C) are
    (D) be

102. The _____ of the new building will start next month.
    (A) constructive
    (B) construction
    (C) construct
    (D) constructed

103. The stapler is _____ the desk.
    (A) on
    (B) through
    (C) into
    (D) without

104. Mr. Selvas delivered the _____ bid to the client.
    (A) seals
    (B) seal
    (C) sealing
    (D) sealed

105. If your flight is delayed, _____ me from the airport.
    (A) calling
    (B) will call
    (C) call
    (D) called

GO ON TO THE NEXT PAGE

106. The airport taxes are _____ in the ticket price.
    (A) including
    (B) include
    (C) been included
    (D) included

107. Ms. Najar wants to _____ the costs by tonight.
    (A) final
    (B) finalize
    (C) finally
    (D) finality

108. A computer is _____ than a typewriter.
    (A) more efficient
    (B) most efficient
    (C) the most efficient
    (D) the more efficient

109. Mr. Flynn is the person _____ orders office supplies.
    (A) which
    (B) whose
    (C) who
    (D) whom

110. The budget analysis is due _____ Friday.
    (A) at
    (B) from
    (C) until
    (D) on

111. New paint _____ pictures will make the office look better.
    (A) but
    (B) and
    (C) as
    (D) though

112. Everyone is _____ that Ms. Howard seldom leaves before 6:30.
    (A) aware
    (B) await
    (C) awaken
    (D) awed

113. The itinerary _____ with the cruise list.
    (A) be filing
    (B) is filed
    (C) be filed
    (D) is filing

114. Passengers can check in for the charter flight _____ 8:00 and 12:00 tomorrow.
    (A) between
    (B) with
    (C) through
    (D) from

115. The president had her travel agent _____ the reservations.
    (A) made
    (B) has made
    (C) make
    (D) makes

116. _____ way to transfer a document is by fax.
    (A) The quicker
    (B) The faster
    (C) The quickest than
    (D) The quickest

117. Mr. Dietze typed the speech, _____ Ms. Lang prepared the charts.
    (A) or
    (B) and
    (C) where
    (D) during

118. The head of the porters _____ guests with their luggage.
    (A) assist
    (B) is assisting
    (C) assists
    (D) are assisting

119. Ask the accounts receivable clerk _____ the invoice.
    (A) to send
    (B) sending
    (C) will send
    (D) sends

120. _____ administrative assistant keeps an office running smoothly.
 (A) One
 (B) A
 (C) The
 (D) An

121. Each passenger's name _____ with his or her cabin number.
 (A) is list
 (B) listing
 (C) is listed
 (D) is listing

122. The manager got his staff _____ last weekend.
 (A) to work
 (B) was working
 (C) work
 (D) worked

123. The variety of insurance benefits _____ very broad under this policy.
 (A) are
 (B) is
 (C) being
 (D) be

124. The directory lists each passenger's name _____ address.
 (A) and
 (B) or
 (C) but
 (D) nor

125. Please leave your luggage _____ the bus for loading.
 (A) among
 (B) between
 (C) from
 (D) beside

126. Mr. Cain will return your call _____ he arrives.
 (A) soon
 (B) as soon
 (C) as soon as
 (D) soon than

127. If the product were not safe, we _____ it.
 (A) would sell
 (B) don't sell
 (C) will sell
 (D) would not sell

128. The cruise handbook _____ all ship policies.
 (A) explains
 (B) is explaining
 (C) explain
 (D) explaining

129. _____ costs make profits smaller.
 (A) Raise
 (B) Risen
 (C) Rising
 (D) Raised

130. Mr. Larsen _____ for meetings.
 (A) late is always
 (B) is always late
 (C) always late is
 (D) is late always

131. _____ we had checked the figures, the supervisor found a mistake.
 (A) Unless
 (B) However
 (C) Since
 (D) Even though

132. Mr. Lazer wants to make _____ .
 (A) a meeting
 (B) an hour
 (C) an appointment
 (D) a time

133. The financial team _____ that the offer was rejected.
 (A) was disappointed
 (B) were disappointed
 (C) was disappointing
 (D) were disappointing

GO ON TO THE NEXT PAGE

134. A record of complaints _____ kept in the purser's office.
    (A) are
    (B) is
    (C) were
    (D) has

135. The only difference _____ the two flights is time of departure.
    (A) with
    (B) then
    (C) between
    (D) among

136. _____ Ms. Butrus was late, she did not miss the performance.
    (A) During
    (B) Because
    (C) In spite of
    (D) Although

137. Mr. Dekar was responsible for collecting and _____ the data.
    (A) organization
    (B) organizing
    (C) organized
    (D) organize

138. The company _____ spouses of employees in the invitation to the banquet.
    (A) are included
    (B) have included
    (C) is including
    (D) has including

139. Ms. Yu has suggested _____ more reservation clerks.
    (A) hire
    (B) hiring
    (C) hired
    (D) to hire

140. The meeting will be held _____ Thursday.
    (A) of
    (B) in
    (C) for
    (D) on

Part VI: Error Recognition

Directions: In your test book, you will see a sentence with four words or phrases underlined. Choose the word or phrase that is incorrect and fill in the corresponding oval on your answer sheet.

141. Copies of the new personnel policy has
          A   B   C
been distributed to everyone.
     D

142. If the product were unsatisfactory, please
     A   B
return it to the manufacturer immediately.
                                 C
for a replacement.
    D

143. Both the shipping charges but the
              A   B
handling charges are included in the price.
         C   D

144. This excited advertisement should make
          A   B
people pay attention to our product.
       C   D

145. The research assistant submitted
         A
a interesting report on consumer preference.
B   C   D

146. But Mr. Gueri's desk is very neat, he can
     A   B
never find anything.
  C   D

147. The visitor his car is in front of the
             A   B
entrance did not read the parking signs.
          C   D

148. The chairman of the board has sitting in
     A   B
meetings all morning and all afternoon.
         C   D

149. The employees have been happier during
         A   B   C
their offices were redecorated.
              D

GO ON TO THE NEXT PAGE

150. The travel agent advised to go in the
                              A   B
    winter when the prices are lower.
              C   D

151. The building who wins the award for
        A   B   C
    architecture will become famous.
                      D

152. Ms. Guillermo will has been absent for six
                       A   B
    weeks by the time she recovers from her
          C   D
    accident.

153. Progress must be careful controlled
        A   B
    so that the company will not grow too fast.
       C   D

154. Using a word processor is more easier
       A   B
    than using a typewriter.
     C   D

155. I allowed Mr. Cooper take his vacation
     A   B
    during our busiest period.
      C   D

156. The letter that you typed it had many
                  A   B   C
    careless mistakes.
       D

157. We will not release the report while the
          A   B   C
    test results are verified.
                        D

158. Although Ms. Daudier is the president's
        A   B
    daughter, the other employees
    do not treat her different.
       C   D

159. Consolidated Pharmaceuticals are the
                                   A
    largest and most successful company
      B   C
    in the city.
     D

160. The company president once a week eats
           A   B
    lunch in the cafeteria with the other
      C   D
    employees.

Part VII: Reading Comprehension

Directions: In your test book, you will see a reading passage followed by several questions. Each question has four answer choices. Choose the best answer to the question and fill in the corresponding oval on your answer sheet.

Questions 161–163 refer to the following paragraph and table.

The research division has four priorities: (1) improving the quality of our products through advancements in manufacturing technology; (2) lowering the costs by improving manufacturing processes; (3) exploring research possibilities to develop new products; and (4) doing all of this in an environmentally responsible manner.

Research Division Priorities	
What	How
1. Improve product quality	By using better technology
2. Lower cost	By improving the manufacturing process
3. Develop research	By increasing research
4. Be globally responsible	By being sensitive to the environment

161. What is the purpose of technology for the research division?
    (A) It lowers costs.
    (B) It is used in research.
    (C) It follows consumer trends.
    (D) It increases product quality.

162. What is NOT mentioned as a priority?
    (A) Improving quality
    (B) Being environmentally responsible
    (C) Developing new products
    (D) Hiring good engineers

163. How does this division try to lower costs?
    (A) By conserving energy
    (B) By improving manufacturing processes
    (C) By working fewer hours
    (D) By limiting exploration

GO ON TO THE NEXT PAGE

Questions 164–166 refer to the following advertisement.

WHY WAIT FOR A BETTER JOB?

Get a great job now!

National Air is hiring full-time representatives for Sales & Reservations. Talk to our employees and discover why we're the best thing in the air.

OPEN HOUSE
National Air Headquarters
Southeast Regional Airport

Thursday, June 15 7:30 p.m.

164. What is the purpose of this ad?
 (A) To meet new people
 (B) To sell tickets
 (C) To find job applicants
 (D) To show off the new headquarters

165. Where will the event be held?
 (A) At their headquarters
 (B) At the owner's house
 (C) On a plane
 (D) At the regional office

166. What jobs does the airline have available?
 (A) Baggage handlers
 (B) Pilots and co-pilots
 (C) Reservations and sales
 (D) Operations and management

Questions 167–170 refer to the following form letter.

> Northeast Electric Company
> Account # 0725 6880 243 9379
>
> The due date on your bill has passed and we have not received your payment. Unless we receive a payment of £53.30 by 7-10, we must interrupt your service. If interrrupted, you will be charged £14.00 for reconnection. Service will be restored within 24 hours. We will also request an additional deposit. If we do not receive payment within ten days after interruption, we will discontinue your service. If you decide to resume service later, a reinstallation charge of £42.50 will apply. If you have any questions concerning your bill or this notice, please call us.

167. What kind of service is this form letter discussing?
    (A) Telephone service
    (B) Electrical service
    (C) Water service
    (D) Sanitation service

168. What must they receive by July 10?
    (A) A deposit
    (B) Payment
    (C) Statement of service
    (D) Electrical fixtures

169. If payment is not received by July 10, what will they do?
    (A) Discontinue service
    (B) Reinstall service
    (C) Interrupt service
    (D) Restore service

170. What is the purpose of this letter?
    (A) Apologize for interrupted service
    (B) Offer improved services
    (C) Announce rate change
    (D) Request payment of delinquent charges

GO ON TO THE NEXT PAGE

Questions 171–175 refer to the following fax.

FAX TRANSMISSION   FAX TRANSMISSION   FAX TRANSMISSION

InterGulf Export
P.O. Box 23145
Sharjah, UAE

To: F. Omoboriowo
Head of Marketing
P.O. Box 19133
Nairobi, Kenya

Fm: Ravi Niazi *RN*
Trade Consultant

Date: 18 October, 19__
Sub: Your marketing question of October 17, 19__

We were very pleased to receive your fax of October 17. We have sent under separate cover information regarding our company and its services. This should arrive in your offices tomorrow.

In the meantime, the following will answer your immediate question:

The company sells products through a worldwide marketing network. This network operates 36 sales offices in 21 countries. Approximately 75% of company sales are direct, and 25% are through other channels. Purchased products are shipped to customers through company distribution centers, by the method of shipment preferred by the customer when possible.

If you need any more information, please contact me.

---

171. What did the fax respond to?
 (A) A newspaper ad
 (B) A personal visit
 (C) A telephone inquiry
 (D) A faxed question

172. How does the company sell its products?
 (A) In stores
 (B) By phone
 (C) From the office
 (D) Through a network

173. What percentage of sales are not direct?
 (A) 25%
 (B) 50%
 (C) 75%
 (D) 100%

174. Who is responsible for shipping purchased goods?
 (A) The customer
 (B) The airlines
 (C) Company distribution centers
 (D) Company headquarters

175. What was probably Omoboriowo's question?
 (A) How large is your company?
 (B) How are your goods distributed?
 (C) When was your company founded?
 (D) What is your marketing plan for next year?

Questions 176–179 refer to the following notice.

ETIQUETTE FOR RIDERS OF CITY BUSES

- Pay the exact fare when boarding the bus. Drivers cannot make change for fares.

- Upon boarding the bus, move toward the rear of the bus. Stand in the passenger area, not in the doorways or beside the driver.

- Allow the senior citizens and disabled riders to use the priority seating area at the front of the bus.

- Passengers must not play radios or other electronic devices without using earphones.

- Eating, drinking, and smoking are not allowed on the bus.

---

176. What does this passage discuss?
 (A) Rules for riding buses
 (B) Safety concerns
 (C) Bus routes and fares
 (D) Problems of the bus service

177. Why should passengers pay the exact fare?
 (A) Passengers will know what they paid.
 (B) The money is easier to count.
 (C) The fare buys a ticket.
 (D) Drivers cannot make change.

178. Who is entitled to use the priority seating area?
 (A) Mothers and children
 (B) Elderly and handicapped people
 (C) Bus company employees
 (D) Riders who pay extra

179. Which activity is prohibited on a bus?
 (A) Chewing gum
 (B) Talking loudly
 (C) Smoking
 (D) Using earphones

GO ON TO THE NEXT PAGE

Questions 180–183 refer to the following chart.

Results of Study on Time Distribution of Tasks for Sales Managers	
Training new sales personnel	15%
Identifying possible clients	10%
Reviewing monthly sales records	25%
Taking care of customer problems	5%
Making sales assignments	22%
Interacting with technical staff	10%
Administrative duties	5%
Miscellaneous	8%

180. What did this study try to find out?
    (A) What sales managers should do
    (B) How sales managers spend their time
    (C) How many sales managers make assignments
    (D) How long it takes for sales managers to do their jobs

181. What task do sales managers spend the most time on?
    (A) Training salespeople
    (B) Performing administrative tasks
    (C) Reviewing sales records
    (D) Making sales assignments

182. How much of their time do sales managers spend with the technical staff?
    (A) 5%
    (B) 8%
    (C) 10%
    (D) 15%

183. It can be assumed that
    (A) there are few customer problems.
    (B) sales are a low priority.
    (C) little time is spent on training.
    (D) no time is spent on finding new customers.

Questions 184–187 refer to the following advertisement.

**Summer is a great time to return to school!
If you need better business skills, let us help.**

Each summer Claybourne University School of Business Administration offers special courses for experienced managers who want to sharpen their existing business skills or learn new ones. You will study with your peers in a week-long intensive session that simulates the world of international commerce. You will learn new theories and study the way business is conducted around the world. Students in previous sessions have reported that what they learned was immediately applicable to their own work situations.

Only one person from a company is accepted into this special program. All applications require three letters of recommendation and proof of employment.

For more information, call the

Summer Education Center
School of Business Administration
Claybourne University
903-477-6768 Fax: 903-477-6777

---

184. What does this ad suggest that you do this summer?
  (A) Take a vacation
  (B) Go to school
  (C) Get a new job
  (D) Consider a career in business

185. Who attends this center?
  (A) Professional managers
  (B) College professors changing careers
  (C) Undergraduate students in business
  (D) Office staff

186. What is required for admission?
  (A) The name of your manager
  (B) A copy of your grades
  (C) Your job title and duties
  (D) Letters of recommendation

187. How long is the course?
  (A) All summer long
  (B) One week
  (C) Three evenings a month
  (D) Two years

Questions 188–191 refer to the following announcement.

$$$$$$$$$$$$$$$$$$$$$$$$$$$$$$$$$$$$$$$

OUR STORE GUARANTEE

We have the lowest prices in town. For every item we sell, we'll beat any legitimate price from any other store. Plus, if you find a lower price within 30 days of your date of purchase, we'll refund the difference. This offer is good even on our own sale prices. The item must be the same brand and style as the original purchase and be in its original factory-sealed box. Our low price guarantee does not apply to limited quantity offers.

$$$$$$$$$$$$$$$$$$$$$$$$$$$$$$$$$$$$$$$

188. What does this statement guarantee?
 (A) The lowest price
 (B) The best service
 (C) The most convenient location
 (D) The most helpful salesclerks

189. What will the store do if you find the identical item for less money at another store?
 (A) Call the other store
 (B) Charge you more
 (C) Reduce the price
 (D) Send it back

190. If you buy an item and find it for a lower price within 30 days, what will the store do?
 (A) Give you a second item.
 (B) Pay you the difference in price.
 (C) Buy the item from you.
 (D) Refund your money.

191. What kind of offers are not covered by this guarantee?
 (A) In-store items
 (B) New items
 (C) Clearance sales
 (D) Limited quantity offers

Questions 192–195 refer to the following memo.

> **MEMO**
>
> To: All employees
> From: K. Osafo
> Director, Personnel
>
> Date: November 23, 19__
> Subject: Charitable Leave
>
> The corporation is pleased to announce a new policy which will allow employees to take paid time off for volunteer activities. Employees may take up to eight hours of paid leave per month to volunteer for charity organizations. Employees are eligible for this program if they are full-time and have been employed here for at least one year. Charitable leave must be requested in advance; otherwise, employees will not be paid for that time. Charitable leave must also be approved by the employee's supervisor.

192. What does the new policy allow employees to do?
    (A) Take paid leave during pregnancy
    (B) Have more holidays
    (C) Get paid for volunteer work
    (D) Go home early

193. How much time may an employee take under this program?
    (A) One hour per week
    (B) Three hours per week
    (C) Six hours per month
    (D) Eight hours per month

194. Which employees may participate in this program?
    (A) All employees whose supervisors let them
    (B) Part-time employees who have worked for six months
    (C) Full-time employees who have worked for one year
    (D) Employees who donate money to charitable organizations

195. What must an employee do to get paid time off?
    (A) Get the permission of the charity
    (B) Leave work for one day
    (C) Fill out an absence form
    (D) Ask his or her supervisor in advance

GO ON TO THE NEXT PAGE

Questions 196–200 refer to the following magazine article.

Many offices now use large computer networks to communicate with buyers, suppliers, clients, and other divisions of the company. While this is efficient, it can also lead to security problems. Users are supposed to enter these systems by using a private password. But sometimes these passwords do not stay private. If a "computer thief" discovers a password, he or she can gain illegal access to the system. Once this happens, the thief can open private computer files and destroy, change, or copy them. To help prevent this problem, users should change their passwords often.

Computer thieves are becoming increasingly common. Passwords will slow them down, but will not prevent the serious, determined thief from gaining access to your records. Real computer criminals are not as big a problem as young adults who try to get into your computer system just for the fun of it. Once there they can leave small messages or create havoc with your data. Once your privacy has been broken, you will feel as if your home has just been robbed. Time to change your password again.

196. What is one kind of problem with computer networks?
(A) Cost
(B) Security
(C) Ease of use
(D) Efficiency

197. How do users typically enter the system?
(A) They ask an operator.
(B) They buy the software.
(C) They use a password.
(D) They attend a computer class.

198. What has to happen before a "computer thief" can harm someone's files?
(A) The thief has to learn the password.
(B) The thief has to know the system.
(C) The thief has to read the files.
(D) The thief has to get a job in the company.

199. What should users do to help prevent this?
(A) Have conversations on the telephone
(B) Use another computer system
(C) Keep secret files at home
(D) Change passwords often

200. According to the author, who presents the greatest danger to our computer security?
(A) Mischievous young adults
(B) Professional computer thieves
(C) Inexperienced users
(D) People who don't change their passwords

STOP!

This is the end of the test. If you finish before time is called, you may go back to Parts V, VI, and VII and check your work.

MODEL TEST 4—ANSWER SHEET

Listening Section

1 A B C D	51 A B C D
2 A B C D	52 A B C D
3 A B C D	53 A B C D
4 A B C D	54 A B C D
5 A B C D	55 A B C D
6 A B C D	56 A B C D
7 A B C D	57 A B C D
8 A B C D	58 A B C D
9 A B C D	59 A B C D
10 A B C D	60 A B C D
11 A B C D	61 A B C D
12 A B C D	62 A B C D
13 A B C D	63 A B C D
14 A B C D	64 A B C D
15 A B C D	65 A B C D
16 A B C D	66 A B C D
17 A B C D	67 A B C D
18 A B C D	68 A B C D
19 A B C D	69 A B C D
20 A B C D	70 A B C D
21 A B C	71 A B C D
22 A B C	72 A B C D
23 A B C	73 A B C D
24 A B C	74 A B C D
25 A B C	75 A B C D
26 A B C	76 A B C D
27 A B C	77 A B C D
28 A B C	78 A B C D
29 A B C	79 A B C D
30 A B C	80 A B C D
31 A B C	81 A B C D
32 A B C	82 A B C D
33 A B C	83 A B C D
34 A B C	84 A B C D
35 A B C	85 A B C D
36 A B C	86 A B C D
37 A B C	87 A B C D
38 A B C	88 A B C D
39 A B C	89 A B C D
40 A B C	90 A B C D
41 A B C	91 A B C D
42 A B C	92 A B C D
43 A B C	93 A B C D
44 A B C	94 A B C D
45 A B C	95 A B C D
46 A B C	96 A B C D
47 A B C	97 A B C D
48 A B C	98 A B C D
49 A B C	99 A B C D
50 A B C	100 A B C D

Reading Section

101 A B C D	151 A B C D
102 A B C D	152 A B C D
103 A B C D	153 A B C D
104 A B C D	154 A B C D
105 A B C D	155 A B C D
106 A B C D	156 A B C D
107 A B C D	157 A B C D
108 A B C D	158 A B C D
109 A B C D	159 A B C D
110 A B C D	160 A B C D
111 A B C D	161 A B C D
112 A B C D	162 A B C D
113 A B C D	163 A B C D
114 A B C D	164 A B C D
115 A B C D	165 A B C D
116 A B C D	166 A B C D
117 A B C D	167 A B C D
118 A B C D	168 A B C D
119 A B C D	169 A B C D
120 A B C D	170 A B C D
121 A B C D	171 A B C D
122 A B C D	172 A B C D
123 A B C D	173 A B C D
124 A B C D	174 A B C D
125 A B C D	175 A B C D
126 A B C D	176 A B C D
127 A B C D	177 A B C D
128 A B C D	178 A B C D
129 A B C D	179 A B C D
130 A B C D	180 A B C D
131 A B C D	181 A B C D
132 A B C D	182 A B C D
133 A B C D	183 A B C D
134 A B C D	184 A B C D
135 A B C D	185 A B C D
136 A B C D	186 A B C D
137 A B C D	187 A B C D
138 A B C D	188 A B C D
139 A B C D	189 A B C D
140 A B C D	190 A B C D
141 A B C D	191 A B C D
142 A B C D	192 A B C D
143 A B C D	193 A B C D
144 A B C D	194 A B C D
145 A B C D	195 A B C D
146 A B C D	196 A B C D
147 A B C D	197 A B C D
148 A B C D	198 A B C D
149 A B C D	199 A B C D
150 A B C D	200 A B C D

Remove answer sheet by cutting on dotted line

MODEL TEST 4
LISTENING COMPREHENSION

In this section of the test, you will have the chance to show how well you understand spoken English. There are four parts to this section, with special directions for each part. You will find the Answer Sheet for Model Test 4 on page 353. Detach it from the book and use it to record your answers. Check your answers using the Answer Key on page 475 and see the Explanatory Answers on page 539. Turn on the compact disc when you are ready to begin.

Listen to Track 5 of compact disc 3 to hear the statements for Part I of Model Test 4.

Part I: Picture

Directions: In your test book, you will see a picture. On the compact disc, you will hear four statements. Choose the statement that most clearly matches the picture and fill in the corresponding oval on your answer sheet.

GO ON TO THE NEXT PAGE

356 TOEIC MODEL TESTS

1.

2.

3.

4.

GO ON TO THE NEXT PAGE

358 TOEIC MODEL TESTS

5.

6.

7.

8.

GO ON TO THE NEXT PAGE

360 TOEIC MODEL TESTS

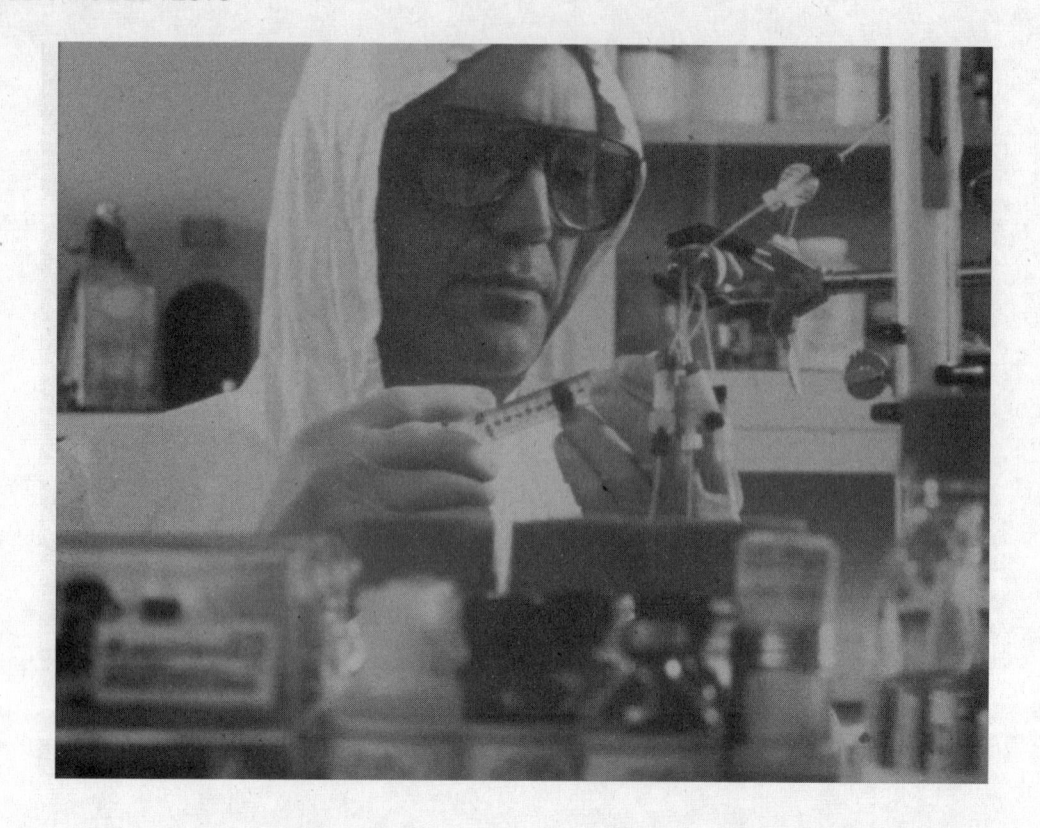

9.

10.

11.

12.

362 TOEIC MODEL TESTS

13.

14.

15.

16.

364 TOEIC MODEL TESTS

17.

18.

19.

20.

GO ON TO THE NEXT PAGE

Listen to Track 6 of compact disc 3 to hear the statements for Part II of Model Test 4.

> **Part II: Question-Response**
>
> Directions: On the compact disc, you will hear a question and three possible answers. Choose the answer that most closely answers the question and fill in the corresponding oval on your answer sheet.

21. Mark your answer on your answer sheet.
22. Mark your answer on your answer sheet.
23. Mark your answer on your answer sheet.
24. Mark your answer on your answer sheet.
25. Mark your answer on your answer sheet.
26. Mark your answer on your answer sheet.
27. Mark your answer on your answer sheet.
28. Mark your answer on your answer sheet.
29. Mark your answer on your answer sheet.
30. Mark your answer on your answer sheet.
31. Mark your answer on your answer sheet.
32. Mark your answer on your answer sheet.
33. Mark your answer on your answer sheet.
34. Mark your answer on your answer sheet.
35. Mark your answer on your answer sheet.
36. Mark your answer on your answer sheet.

37. Mark your answer on your answer sheet.
38. Mark your answer on your answer sheet.
39. Mark your answer on your answer sheet.
40. Mark your answer on your answer sheet.
41. Mark your answer on your answer sheet.
42. Mark your answer on your answer sheet.
43. Mark your answer on your answer sheet.
44. Mark your answer on your answer sheet.
45. Mark your answer on your answer sheet.
46. Mark your answer on your answer sheet.
47. Mark your answer on your answer sheet.
48. Mark your answer on your answer sheet.
49. Mark your answer on your answer sheet.
50. Mark your answer on your answer sheet.

GO ON TO THE NEXT PAGE

368 TOEIC MODEL TESTS

Listen to Track 7 of compact disc 3 to hear the conversations for Part III of Model Test 4.

Part III: Short Conversations

Directions: On the compact disc, you will hear a short conversation. In your test book, you will see a question and four possible answers. Choose the best answer to the question and fill in the corresponding oval on your answer sheet.

51. Which day does the store open early?
    (A) Monday.
    (B) Friday.
    (C) Saturday.
    (D) Sunday.

52. What happened to the woman's shoes?
    (A) She got them wet.
    (B) She left them on the train.
    (C) She dropped them at the corner.
    (D) She left them in the car.

53. Why didn't the woman get the call?
    (A) She wasn't home.
    (B) She didn't know how to answer.
    (C) She didn't check the answering machine.
    (D) She didn't hear the phone.

54. Why is the woman glad?
    (A) They didn't pay extra.
    (B) They didn't take a plane.
    (C) They're leaving the country.
    (D) They're staying inside.

55. Why is the woman worried?
    (A) The supervisor canceled their meeting.
    (B) She wants to see his office.
    (C) She thinks she made a mistake.
    (D) She hasn't done anything right.

56. What kind of room does the woman want?
    (A) Small.
    (B) Quiet.
    (C) Large.
    (D) Noisy.

57. Where did this conversation take place?
    (A) In an office.
    (B) In an airplane.
    (C) In a park.
    (D) In a restaurant.

58. What was wrong with the credit card?
    (A) It was out of date.
    (B) It was out of place.
    (C) It hadn't been signed.
    (D) The store doesn't accept credit cards.

59. When can they meet?
    (A) For lunch.
    (B) On Tuesday.
    (C) For dinner.
    (D) For breakfast.

60. How many towels are missing?
    (A) One.
    (B) Two.
    (C) Three.
    (D) Four.

61. What is the man's profession?
    (A) Hotel clerk.
    (B) Travel agent.
    (C) Airline pilot.
    (D) Ticket clerk.

62. Why does the man want to take the next train?
    (A) It's an express.
    (B) He wants to buy a paper.
    (C) He wants to sit down.
    (D) He wants to ride downtown.

63. What is the man going to do?
    (A) Make some coffee.
    (B) Make some tea.
    (C) Get ice water.
    (D) Serve some fish.

64. Who is the woman talking to?
    (A) The receptionist.
    (B) The shipping clerk.
    (C) The librarian.
    (D) The personnel director.

65. Why does the man want to leave at three-thirty?
    (A) He likes to arrive early.
    (B) He's afraid he'll miss the plane.
    (C) He doesn't like to hurry.
    (D) He thinks traffic will get bad.

66. Where should the man put the plant?
    (A) On his desk.
    (B) In artificial light.
    (C) By the window.
    (D) In the hall.

67. What kind of ticket did the woman get?
    (A) Round-trip.
    (B) One-way.
    (C) Discounted.
    (D) Full-fare.

68. How long will Mr. Tan be away from work?
    (A) One night.
    (B) One week.
    (C) Three weeks.
    (D) Four weeks.

69. What is the woman's solution to the problem?
    (A) Buy a new ribbon.
    (B) Get a different typewriter.
    (C) Learn to use a computer.
    (D) Get another job.

70. What is the woman going to do?
    (A) Postpone the meeting.
    (B) Be late to work.
    (C) Cancel the meeting.
    (D) Wonder whether it's a good idea.

71. What did the man ask the woman to do?
    (A) Turn the radio around.
    (B) Practice her music.
    (C) Try to work harder.
    (D) Lower the volume on her radio.

72. What did the man suggest that the woman do?
    (A) Take another tour.
    (B) Hurry up.
    (C) Go back to the museum alone.
    (D) Get a painting of her own.

73. Why is the man late?
    (A) He lost his map.
    (B) His map is old.
    (C) He forgot the restaurant's name.
    (D) He got lost.

74. When is the report due?
    (A) This afternoon.
    (B) At 7:00.
    (C) At 10:00.
    (D) Tomorrow.

75. Why does the woman take the subway?
    (A) Driving is too expensive.
    (B) She sometimes needs her car.
    (C) She likes to drive.
    (D) She doesn't like to park.

76. Why doesn't the man leave a message?
    (A) He doesn't know Ms. Kim.
    (B) He won't have a telephone with him.
    (C) He won't talk to the receptionist.
    (D) He's calling long-distance.

77. Where will they put the display?
    (A) By the door.
    (B) By the window.
    (C) Along the wall.
    (D) In the mall.

GO ON TO THE NEXT PAGE

78. What does the man need to do?
    (A) Call the nurse.
    (B) Help her walk.
    (C) Lift the chairs.
    (D) Buy her some new shoes.

79. Why is the man disappointed?
    (A) The post office isn't close.
    (B) The post office is closed.
    (C) The post office isn't round.
    (D) The post office is on the bus route.

80. When are the paychecks due?
    (A) Once a week.
    (B) Once a month.
    (C) Twice a month.
    (D) By two o'clock.

Listen to Track 8 of compact disc 3 to hear the short talks for Part IV of Model Test 4.

Part IV: Short Talks

Directions: On the compact disc, you will hear a short talk. In your test book, you will see several questions on the talk and four possible answers. Choose the best answer to the question and fill in the corresponding oval on your answer sheet.

81. Who should get on the plane during priority boarding?
    (A) Students.
    (B) Large groups.
    (C) Elderly people.
    (D) Airline personnel.

82. If someone needs help, who should they ask?
    (A) The security office.
    (B) A flight attendant.
    (C) The pilot.
    (D) The ticket agent.

83. What kind of books does this store carry?
    (A) Novels.
    (B) Children's books.
    (C) Professional books.
    (D) Textbooks.

84. If they don't have the book you want, what will they do?
    (A) Refer you to another store.
    (B) Look it up in the master list.
    (C) Give you a different book at a discount.
    (D) Order it.

85. When can we expect it to get cloudy?
    (A) In the morning.
    (B) In the afternoon.
    (C) In the evening.
    (D) At night.

86. How long will the rain last?
    (A) All weekend.
    (B) All day.
    (C) All afternoon.
    (D) All morning.

87. How long do most colds last?
    (A) 1 day.
    (B) 1–2 days.
    (C) 3 days.
    (D) 3–5 days.

88. How can you speed recovery?
    (A) Stay warm.
    (B) Drink fluids.
    (C) Take medication.
    (D) Avoid caffeine.

89. Who should hear this advertisement?
    (A) Homemakers.
    (B) Business people.
    (C) Mail clerks.
    (D) Receptionists.

90. What does this company provide?
    (A) Conference planning.
    (B) Furniture rentals.
    (C) Food for business occasions.
    (D) Maid service.

GO ON TO THE NEXT PAGE

91. Where is this train going?
    (A) Into the city.
    (B) To the hospital.
    (C) To the business district.
    (D) To the shopping mall.

92. Which subway line goes to the airport?
    (A) The gray line.
    (B) The green line.
    (C) The red line.
    (D) The blue line.

93. Why are these closings taking place?
    (A) It's Sunday.
    (B) There is no transportation.
    (C) It's a federal holiday.
    (D) The weather is bad.

94. What service is the transportation system eliminating for the day?
    (A) Rush hour service.
    (B) Weekend service.
    (C) Service into the city.
    (D) Service to recreation areas.

95. Who participated in this survey?
    (A) Hotel owners.
    (B) Secretaries.
    (C) Housekeepers.
    (D) Business travelers.

96. Where would travelers prefer to have hotels located?
    (A) In the business district.
    (B) Close to parks and museums.
    (C) Near shopping and entertainment.
    (D) Beside the airport.

97. What additional service should the hotels provide at night?
    (A) Access to exercise and recreation rooms.
    (B) Movies in the rooms.
    (C) Light snacks in the lobby.
    (D) Transportation services.

98. What does this service do?
    (A) Provide visitors with maps.
    (B) Tell you which buses and subways to take.
    (C) Sell you tickets for transportation.
    (D) Tell you what you should see.

99. What information is necessary to get help?
    (A) Your ticket number.
    (B) Your budget.
    (C) How you would like to get there.
    (D) The day and time of travel.

100. What should you have ready by the phone?
    (A) An address book.
    (B) A list of tourist attractions.
    (C) A pencil and some paper.
    (D) A guidebook.

**This is the end of the Listening Comprehension portion of the test.
Turn to Part V in your test book.**

READING

In this section of the test, you will have the chance to show how well you understand written English. There are three parts to this section, with special directions for each part.

YOU WILL HAVE ONE HOUR AND FIFTEEN MINUTES TO COMPLETE PARTS V, VI, AND VII OF THE TEST.

Part V: Incomplete Sentences

<u>Directions</u>: In your test book, you will see a sentence with a missing word. Four possible answers follow the sentence. Choose the best answer to the question and fill in the corresponding oval on your answer sheet.

101. If the delivery is late, we _____ the shipping charges.
    (A) paid
    (B) will pay
    (C) have paid
    (D) are paying

102. We cannot process the order _____ we get a copy of the purchase order.
    (A) because
    (B) that
    (C) until
    (D) when

103. The visitors will be arriving _____ the office in twenty minutes.
    (A) at
    (B) with
    (C) into
    (D) for

104. Please use the _____ envelope for your reply.
    (A) is enclosed
    (B) enclose
    (C) enclosing
    (D) enclosed

GO ON TO THE NEXT PAGE

105. Mr. Mura depends on his assistant for _____ .
    (A) advise
    (B) adverse
    (C) advice
    (D) adversity

106. The package should arrive _____ Tuesday.
    (A) in
    (B) on
    (C) over
    (D) at

107. The newspaper expects circulation _____ next year.
    (A) to ascend
    (B) to increase
    (C) to escalate
    (D) to raise

108. Using a checklist is an _____ way to make plans.
    (A) effective
    (B) effect
    (C) effectiveness
    (D) effectively

109. The food has been ordered, _____ it has not arrived.
    (A) or
    (B) since
    (C) because
    (D) but

110. The bus will leave promptly _____ 8:30.
    (A) until
    (B) to
    (C) at
    (D) for

111. The head of operations _____ to the management convention.
    (A) going
    (B) are going
    (C) go
    (D) is going

112. A customer service representative _____ at our catalogue number.
    (A) always is available
    (B) is always available
    (C) is available always
    (D) being always available

113. The telephone directory is _____ the telephone.
    (A) among
    (B) to
    (C) under
    (D) between

114. Our company stands for quality _____ design.
    (A) or
    (B) and
    (C) but
    (D) neither

115. The supervisor had Ms. Balla _____ her job responsibilities.
    (A) writing
    (B) wrote
    (C) written
    (D) write

116. Mr. Camelio promises _____ the error right away.
    (A) will correct
    (B) correcting
    (C) to correct
    (D) corrects

117. _____ it was late, Ms. Glaser stayed to finish her work.
    (A) Although
    (B) During
    (C) Since
    (D) While

118. The _____ about our recycling plans will reassure consumers.
    (A) public
    (B) publish
    (C) publishing
    (D) publicity

119. The travel agent persuaded us _____ an evening flight.
    (A) to take
    (B) taking
    (C) took
    (D) taken

120. This model has seldom been brought in for _____.
    (A) despair
    (B) compares
    (C) impairs
    (D) repairs

121. Can you meet with us _____ 11:00?
    (A) on
    (B) for
    (C) at
    (D) in

122. The manager suggested _____ a research team.
    (A) organized
    (B) organizing
    (C) organizes
    (D) to organize

123. Mr. Benito received the notice _____ January 5.
    (A) on
    (B) in
    (C) at
    (D) to

124. This list of contributors is more _____ that one.
    (A) current
    (B) currently
    (C) current than
    (D) current as

125. The fax was not received _____ the fax number was wrong.
    (A) until
    (B) because
    (C) although
    (D) once

126. The ship's captain requests that all passengers _____ emergency procedures.
    (A) reviewing
    (B) reviews
    (C) review
    (D) to review

127. The person _____ lost a briefcase may claim it in the lobby.
    (A) whose
    (B) which
    (C) whom
    (D) who

128. This memo is _____ the previous one.
    (A) as confusing
    (B) confusing as
    (C) as confusing as
    (D) as confused as

129. Ms. Friel _____ about her promotion before it was announced.
    (A) knew
    (B) known
    (C) is knowing
    (D) has known

130. Please _____ me any time if I can help you.
    (A) are calling
    (B) call
    (C) calls
    (D) will call

131. The ship's restaurant is located _____ the sun deck.
    (A) on
    (B) under
    (C) in
    (D) over

132. What _____ will the delay have on the contract?
    (A) affect
    (B) affection
    (C) effect
    (D) effective

GO ON TO THE NEXT PAGE

133. Mr. Dimitri has a _____ for the Palace Hotel.
    (A) rumination
    (B) reservation
    (C) trepidation
    (D) motivation

134. Our latest advertising package includes videos _____ brochures.
    (A) but
    (B) or
    (C) and
    (D) either

135. The merger, _____ will be announced today, should be extremely profitable.
    (A) when
    (B) whose
    (C) it
    (D) which

136. The receptionist _____ a message if you do not answer your phone.
    (A) takes
    (B) took
    (C) take
    (D) taken

137. The secretary _____ a letter when the typewriter broke.
    (A) typed
    (B) is typing
    (C) was typing
    (D) types

138. Tomorrow we _____ the letter by overnight mail.
    (A) will send
    (B) sent
    (C) had sent
    (D) is sending

139. My cousin was very _____ when he got the job.
    (A) surprise
    (B) surprised
    (C) surprising
    (D) surprises

140. The computer operators work at night _____ on weekends.
    (A) nor
    (B) but
    (C) neither
    (D) and

Part VI: Error Recognition

Directions: In your test book, you will see a sentence with four words or phrases underlined. Choose the word or phrase that is incorrect and fill in the corresponding oval on your answer sheet.

141. If the <u>service</u> is not <u>prompt</u>, the customer
           A   B
   <u>would have gone</u> to <u>another</u> restaurant.
         C   D

142. <u>Good</u> salesperson <u>always</u> <u>meets</u> the <u>needs</u>
      A   B   C   D
   of the customer.

143. I asked <u>Mr. Lee give</u> the client a
               A
   tour <u>of the office</u> and a demonstration <u>of</u>
        B   C
   the <u>latest</u> product.
        D

144. New employees <u>twice a week</u> are required
           A   B
   <u>to attend</u> company <u>training</u> sessions.
      C   D

145. The <u>fax</u> <u>that</u> Mr. Gerard sent <u>it</u> <u>from</u>
          A   B C
   Toronto is <u>incomplete</u>.
      C   D

146. The company <u>expects</u> sales to decrease
                  A
   <u>during</u> the summer <u>and</u> <u>increasing</u> again in
      B   C   D
   the fall.

147. An <u>attractive</u> display <u>is</u> one thing that
         A   B
   encourages customers <u>buy</u> our <u>product</u>.
                        C   D

148. A <u>charge</u> <u>for</u> labor is <u>including</u> in the
        A   B   C
   repair <u>estimate</u>.
        D

GO ON TO THE NEXT PAGE

149. The staff meeting lasts more than 30
    A   B   C
    minutes rarely.
            D

150. The items on this invoice has incorrect
              A   B
    stock identification numbers.
         C   D

151. Ms. Harrison had written already the
                   A
    proposal when the office lights went out.
            B   C   D

152. If Mr. Goa is away from his desk, Ms.
    A   B
    Carter is answering his telephone for him.
           C   D

153. Ms. Belko insists her staff written weekly
                    A   B   C
    updates on each project.
              D

154. The clerks in the accounting department
                A   B
    needs two days to process a check.
     C   D

155. Mr. Kent would hire another manager if
                   A   B   C
    the company allows it.
                  D

156. Until that item is currently out of stock,
    A   B   C
    we can order it for you.
        D

157. Ms. Uri's argument was so convinced that
                       A   B   C
    the committee voted to accept the
                         D
    proposal.

158. A person he forgets names will not make
             A   B   C
    many friends.
     D

159. Ms. Griffin will go to England when she
                 A   B   C
    took her vacation last summer.
                      D

160. The director of the publications
         A   B
    department works hard as his staff does.
                       C   D

Part VII: Reading Comprehension

Directions: In your test book, you will see a reading passage followed by several questions. Each question has four answer choices. Choose the best answer to the question and fill in the corresponding oval on your answer sheet.

Questions 161–163 refer to the following letter.

CD Consolidated Data
C. so Buenos Aires 45
20124 Milan, Italy

Mr. Arnold Jiggit   October 12, 19__
Avenue Louis 358
B - 1050 Brussels, Belgium

Dear Mr. Jiggit:

Your resume is very impressive, but we are no longer hiring full-time workers. Like many companies, we are trying to operate with a minimum staff, hiring temporary office workers. When the workload increases, or when we need people for a specific project, we look for part-time workers.

Should such a need arise, we will contact you.

With every good wish.

Sincerely yours,

Sa Osheroff
Employment Clearing House

161. What employment practice does this company share with others?
   (A) Hiring a maximum staff
   (B) Training its own workers
   (C) Hiring temporary workers
   (D) Asking retirees to return

162. When are these workers usually hired?
   (A) When the workload increases
   (B) When employees are ill
   (C) When costs are high
   (D) When business is bad

163. Mr. Jiggit probably wrote to the company
   (A) to inquire about a part-time job.
   (B) to ask about company benefits.
   (C) to seek full-time employment.
   (D) to look for temporary office workers.

GO ON TO THE NEXT PAGE

Questions 164–166 refer to the following coupon.

BOARDING PASS

Name of Passenger: Monica Colandern
009322778395
From: New York LaGuardia
To: Los Angeles

Carrier	Flight	Class	Date	Time	Gate	Seat	Smoke
TU	740	V	8 May	11:30	67	12A	NO

---

164. What is this coupon?
 (A) Ticket for a concert
 (B) Boarding pass for an airline flight
 (C) Registration form for classes
 (D) Job application

165. Where is Monica going?
 (A) New York
 (B) Los Angeles
 (C) La Guardia High School
 (D) To an interview

166. Where will she sit?
 (A) Seat 8C
 (B) Seat 11B
 (C) Seat 12A
 (D) Seat 67E

Questions 167–169 refer to the following notice.

Invoices are due upon receipt. All accounts unpaid as of the last day of the current month shall accrue interest at the Consumers Bank lending rate plus 1–12% per annum.

---

167. When are invoices due?
 (A) The last day of the month
 (B) The first day of the month
 (C) At the date on the invoice
 (D) When they are received

168. If your account is unpaid, what will happen?
 (A) You will owe interest.
 (B) You will have to close your account.
 (C) You will pay twice as much.
 (D) You will have to borrow money.

169. What is the role of the Consumers Bank?
 (A) It will assist with loans.
 (B) It acts as a collections agent.
 (C) It receives payment on all accounts.
 (D) It sets a base interest rate.

Questions 170–172 refer to the following invitation

> Trust Line cordially invites you to attend a morning seminar to learn how you can predict the trends that will assist your clients with the success of their investments.
>
> To reserve a seat, fill out the attached card and mail it with your registration fee.
>
> Don't miss this chance to learn about the sources that drive successful fiduciary service management firms.
>
> For further information, please call 676-9980.

170. Who would be likely to attend the seminar?
    (A) A private investor
    (B) A manager in a not-for-profit organization
    (C) A stockbroker
    (D) A newspaper publisher

171. What will be discussed at the seminar?
    (A) Building client relationships
    (B) Fiduciary service management firms
    (C) How to foresee good investments
    (D) How to get rid of poor investments

172. How can you join the seminar?
    (A) Present this letter.
    (B) Send a short from and payment.
    (C) Send your business card and request.
    (D) Call 676-9980.

GO ON TO THE NEXT PAGE

Questions 173–177 refer to the following magazine article.

NewTech Equipment Company announced it expects to cut 4,000 jobs within the next six months in Brazil as part of its strategy to reorganize its money-losing business. NewTech has been struggling to make a profit after two years of losses worldwide.

The reduction in labor comes as a surprise to business analysts, who had been impressed with the performance of the company in recent months. Although its revenues have not matched those of its first two years of business, they had been increasing steadily since June.

New competition was blamed for this loss of revenue, but sources close to the company place the blame on the lack of direction from the chairman of the company, Pierre Reinartz. Mr. Reinartz has been with the company for only a year, and he will probably resign soon.

It is expected that Elizabeth Strube will succeed him. Ms. Strube was responsible for opening the international offices, which have been more cost-effective than those in Brazil. NewTech employs about 25,000 people in Brazil, another 20,000 in Asia, and 10,000 in Europe. The international offices will not be affected by the staff reductions.

173. Why will NewTech cut jobs?
    (A) To be more profitable
    (B) Because it is moving overseas
    (C) Because labor costs have gone up
    (D) Because Chairman Reinartz directed it

174. Where will these jobs be cut?
    (A) Asia
    (B) Brazil
    (C) the United States
    (D) Europe

175. How long has NewTech been losing money?
    (A) Six months
    (B) One year
    (C) A year and a half
    (D) Two years

176. What surprised analysts?
    (A) The recent growth of income
    (B) The resignation of the chairman
    (C) The decision to reduce employees
    (D) The opening of an international branch

177. What describes the international branch of NewTech?
    (A) It is more cost-effective.
    (B) It loses more money than the Brazilian branch.
    (C) It is older than the Brazilian branch.
    (D) It will be closed.

Questions 178–180 refer to the following schedule.

BUS FARES

		Peak	Off Peak
Effective March 1	Any one zone	1.00	.75
Peak hours,	Between zones 1 and 2	1.35	1.00
Weekdays 5:30–9:30 A.M.	zones 1 and 3	1.70	1.35
and 3:00–7:00 P.M.	zones 2 and 3	1.35	1.00

178. When do these bus fares take effect?
 (A) Immediately
 (B) On March 1
 (C) On February 28
 (D) Next week

179. Which time is off-peak?
 (A) 7:00 A.M. Monday
 (B) 9:00 A.M. Wednesday
 (C) 8:00 P.M. Thursday
 (D) 5:00 P.M. Friday

180. What is the peak fare between zones 1 and 3?
 (A) $.75
 (B) $1.00
 (C) $1.35
 (D) $1.70

Questions 181–183 refer to the following advertisement.

Leading TV-Advertising company with broadcast interests worldwide seeks a Specialist in Audience Research. The Specialist will design studies to determine consumer preferences and write reports for use within the company. Candidates must have a college degree with courses in research. Must also have experience in advertising. Outstanding oral, written, and computer skills are necessary. Downtown location. Excellent benefits.

181. What does this job involve?
 (A) Making TV commercials
 (B) Discovering what consumers like
 (C) Advertising products
 (D) Testing products

182. Who will use the reports the Specialist writes?
 (A) The consumer
 (B) The television station
 (C) The manufacturers
 (D) The TV-advertising company

183. What qualifications should the candidate have?
 (A) Education in research and experience in advertising
 (B) Experience in television audiences
 (C) Ability in accounting
 (D) A degree in broadcasting

GO ON TO THE NEXT PAGE

Questions 184–185 refer to the following calendar.

14	
8:00 –8:45	Brkfst. meeting with accountants
8:30	Prepare for sales meeting
9:00	Greet sales staff/coffee
9:30	Meeting starts
10:00	
10:30	
11:00	Break
11:30	Meeting
12:00	
12:30	
1:00	Lunch

184. What is a feature of this person's day?
    (A) Breakfast with the sales staff
    (B) Lunch at noon
    (C) The day off
    (D) A full morning

185. How is this calendar arranged?
    (A) By the minute
    (B) By the half-hour
    (C) By the hour
    (D) By the month

Questions 186–190 refer to the following report.

Peru is reforming its maritime transportation system. New regulations designed to reduce port costs and increase efficiency have already had encouraging results. As a result of these reforms, Peru has established itself as the gateway for exports to the booming Pacific Rim markets. These reforms have been in three areas: labor, regulations, and custom clearances.

High labor costs had sabotaged Peru's import and export businesses. Where once 80% of all goods had been transported by ship, ports in recent years had been moving only half of their capacity. Shipping companies had taken their business to Chilean ports where costs were a sixth what they were in Peru. Reform in this area was needed quickly. Consequently, agreements with port workers now allow shippers and receivers to make their prices competitive with other ports in Latin America. The port workers benefit as well, since many have formed limited partnerships or cooperatives.

Prior to the reforms, 60% of all exports had to be shipped on Peruvian flag-carriers. That regulation has been abolished and has opened the ports to ships from around the world. This increase in traffic meant that dock procedures had to be streamlined. Accordingly, customs regulations were made more efficient and commercial processing is accomplished more quickly.

186. Why were reforms necessary?
    (A) The industry was outdated.
    (B) Corruption was the norm.
    (C) Labor regulations were being violated.
    (D) The shipping industry was inefficient and costly.

187. What are Peruvian shippers most interested in?
    (A) North America
    (B) The Pacific Rim
    (C) Europe
    (D) Chile

188. Prior to the reforms, at what percentage capacity did the ports operate?
    (A) 20%
    (B) 50%
    (C) 60%
    (D) 80%

189. What do Peruvian ships now do?
    (A) Carry all cargo.
    (B) Carry 60% of all cargo.
    (C) Compete with non-Peruvian ships.
    (D) Display their flag.

190. According to the report, why were dock procedures streamlined?
    (A) To make them easier to read
    (B) To handle increased traffic
    (C) To reduce labor costs
    (D) To satisfy the dock workers

GO ON TO THE NEXT PAGE

Questions 191–194 refer to the following fax.

Starling Brothers Investment Firm
145 East 45th Street
New York NY 10019

To: All airline investors
Fm: Alfonso O'Reilly
  Broker

BY FAX
Pages: This only

Stock Alert   Stock Alert   Stock Alert   Stock Alert

Southern Regional Airlines earned $9.8 million in the fourth quarter, compared with a loss of $584.1 million the previous year. The profit was due to reduced costs and an increase in profitable routes. This year, the airline lost $112.4 million in total, compared with a loss of $1 billion last year.

If the present management does not change, we assume that the cost-reduction measures and their choice of routes will continue to have a positive effect on earnings. By eliminating even more routes across the Atlantic, the airline should be able to focus on the short-haul markets where it built its strong base.

We suggest keeping Southern Regional stock at this time. If there is any change in this forecast, we will advise you.

---

191. What is the purpose of this notice?
 (A) To warn investors of poor stock performance
 (B) To suggest a change in management
 (C) To explain recent success to investors
 (D) To encourage investors to hold on to their stock

192. To what is this profit due?
 (A) New marketing strategies
 (B) Lower cost and more profitable routes
 (C) Greater ticket sales
 (D) Changes in the competition

193. How much did the airline lose this year?
 (A) $1 million
 (B) $9.8 million
 (C) $112.4 million
 (D) $1 billion

194. What is the core of the airlines' business?
 (A) Shipping
 (B) Transatlantic routes
 (C) Short-haul routes
 (D) Charter flights

Questions 195–196 refer to the following notice.

> ## The Griffith Hotel
> Charleston, South Carolina
> 803-349-7204
>
> Reservations will be held until 4:00 p.m. unless guaranteed by advance deposit or credit card.
>
> $
>
> Cancellations must be made 24 hours prior to scheduled arrival in order to avoid the first night's room charge.

195. Why would you guarantee your reservation by credit card?
 (A) So you can cancel your room
 (B) So you can arrive after 4:00
 (C) So you can arrive before 4:00
 (D) So you don't have to check in

196. What happens if you do not cancel 24 hours in advance?
 (A) You must pay for one night.
 (B) You get first choice of rooms.
 (C) You can schedule your arrival.
 (D) You can get an advance deposit.

Questions 197–200 refer to the following memo.

> **MEMO**
>
> from the desk of Mazola Sawarani
>
> To: All Employees
>
> Sub: Vacation
>
> Supervisors must approve any and all vacation periods longer than one week. Approval is not automatic. If (1) your absence would create a heavy workload for your team, or cause your team to miss deadlines; (2) you fail to give at least one week's advance notice; (3) there are problems with your job performance; or (4) you have had other frequent absences, your request could be denied. In that case, please contact the Personnel Review Board.

197. What is this memo about?
 (A) Work shortage
 (B) Vacation time
 (C) Sick leave
 (D) Starting hours

198. Which of the following vacation periods requires a supervisor's approval?
 (A) One hour
 (B) One day
 (C) One week
 (D) One month

199. What might influence a supervisor's decision?
 (A) You are a new employee.
 (B) You are poorly paid.
 (C) You are a team leader.
 (D) You often miss work.

200. If approval is not given, the employee can
 (A) Ask another supervisor
 (B) Stay at work
 (C) Take a different vacation
 (D) Ask the Personnel Review Board

STOP!

This is the end of the test. If you finish before time is called, you may go back to Parts V, VI, and VII and check your work.

MODEL TEST 5—ANSWER SHEET

Listening Section

1. Ⓐ Ⓑ Ⓒ Ⓓ
2. Ⓐ Ⓑ Ⓒ Ⓓ
3. Ⓐ Ⓑ Ⓒ Ⓓ
4. Ⓐ Ⓑ Ⓒ Ⓓ
5. Ⓐ Ⓑ Ⓒ Ⓓ
6. Ⓐ Ⓑ Ⓒ Ⓓ
7. Ⓐ Ⓑ Ⓒ Ⓓ
8. Ⓐ Ⓑ Ⓒ Ⓓ
9. Ⓐ Ⓑ Ⓒ Ⓓ
10. Ⓐ Ⓑ Ⓒ Ⓓ
11. Ⓐ Ⓑ Ⓒ Ⓓ
12. Ⓐ Ⓑ Ⓒ Ⓓ
13. Ⓐ Ⓑ Ⓒ Ⓓ
14. Ⓐ Ⓑ Ⓒ Ⓓ
15. Ⓐ Ⓑ Ⓒ Ⓓ
16. Ⓐ Ⓑ Ⓒ Ⓓ
17. Ⓐ Ⓑ Ⓒ Ⓓ
18. Ⓐ Ⓑ Ⓒ Ⓓ
19. Ⓐ Ⓑ Ⓒ Ⓓ
20. Ⓐ Ⓑ Ⓒ Ⓓ
21. Ⓐ Ⓑ Ⓒ
22. Ⓐ Ⓑ Ⓒ
23. Ⓐ Ⓑ Ⓒ
24. Ⓐ Ⓑ Ⓒ
25. Ⓐ Ⓑ Ⓒ
26. Ⓐ Ⓑ Ⓒ
27. Ⓐ Ⓑ Ⓒ
28. Ⓐ Ⓑ Ⓒ
29. Ⓐ Ⓑ Ⓒ
30. Ⓐ Ⓑ Ⓒ
31. Ⓐ Ⓑ Ⓒ
32. Ⓐ Ⓑ Ⓒ
33. Ⓐ Ⓑ Ⓒ
34. Ⓐ Ⓑ Ⓒ
35. Ⓐ Ⓑ Ⓒ
36. Ⓐ Ⓑ Ⓒ
37. Ⓐ Ⓑ Ⓒ
38. Ⓐ Ⓑ Ⓒ
39. Ⓐ Ⓑ Ⓒ
40. Ⓐ Ⓑ Ⓒ
41. Ⓐ Ⓑ Ⓒ
42. Ⓐ Ⓑ Ⓒ
43. Ⓐ Ⓑ Ⓒ
44. Ⓐ Ⓑ Ⓒ
45. Ⓐ Ⓑ Ⓒ
46. Ⓐ Ⓑ Ⓒ
47. Ⓐ Ⓑ Ⓒ
48. Ⓐ Ⓑ Ⓒ
49. Ⓐ Ⓑ Ⓒ
50. Ⓐ Ⓑ Ⓒ
51. Ⓐ Ⓑ Ⓒ Ⓓ
52. Ⓐ Ⓑ Ⓒ Ⓓ
53. Ⓐ Ⓑ Ⓒ Ⓓ
54. Ⓐ Ⓑ Ⓒ Ⓓ
55. Ⓐ Ⓑ Ⓒ Ⓓ
56. Ⓐ Ⓑ Ⓒ Ⓓ
57. Ⓐ Ⓑ Ⓒ Ⓓ
58. Ⓐ Ⓑ Ⓒ Ⓓ
59. Ⓐ Ⓑ Ⓒ Ⓓ
60. Ⓐ Ⓑ Ⓒ Ⓓ
61. Ⓐ Ⓑ Ⓒ Ⓓ
62. Ⓐ Ⓑ Ⓒ Ⓓ
63. Ⓐ Ⓑ Ⓒ Ⓓ
64. Ⓐ Ⓑ Ⓒ Ⓓ
65. Ⓐ Ⓑ Ⓒ Ⓓ
66. Ⓐ Ⓑ Ⓒ Ⓓ
67. Ⓐ Ⓑ Ⓒ Ⓓ
68. Ⓐ Ⓑ Ⓒ Ⓓ
69. Ⓐ Ⓑ Ⓒ Ⓓ
70. Ⓐ Ⓑ Ⓒ Ⓓ
71. Ⓐ Ⓑ Ⓒ Ⓓ
72. Ⓐ Ⓑ Ⓒ Ⓓ
73. Ⓐ Ⓑ Ⓒ Ⓓ
74. Ⓐ Ⓑ Ⓒ Ⓓ
75. Ⓐ Ⓑ Ⓒ Ⓓ
76. Ⓐ Ⓑ Ⓒ Ⓓ
77. Ⓐ Ⓑ Ⓒ Ⓓ
78. Ⓐ Ⓑ Ⓒ Ⓓ
79. Ⓐ Ⓑ Ⓒ Ⓓ
80. Ⓐ Ⓑ Ⓒ Ⓓ
81. Ⓐ Ⓑ Ⓒ Ⓓ
82. Ⓐ Ⓑ Ⓒ Ⓓ
83. Ⓐ Ⓑ Ⓒ Ⓓ
84. Ⓐ Ⓑ Ⓒ Ⓓ
85. Ⓐ Ⓑ Ⓒ Ⓓ
86. Ⓐ Ⓑ Ⓒ Ⓓ
87. Ⓐ Ⓑ Ⓒ Ⓓ
88. Ⓐ Ⓑ Ⓒ Ⓓ
89. Ⓐ Ⓑ Ⓒ Ⓓ
90. Ⓐ Ⓑ Ⓒ Ⓓ
91. Ⓐ Ⓑ Ⓒ Ⓓ
92. Ⓐ Ⓑ Ⓒ Ⓓ
93. Ⓐ Ⓑ Ⓒ Ⓓ
94. Ⓐ Ⓑ Ⓒ Ⓓ
95. Ⓐ Ⓑ Ⓒ Ⓓ
96. Ⓐ Ⓑ Ⓒ Ⓓ
97. Ⓐ Ⓑ Ⓒ Ⓓ
98. Ⓐ Ⓑ Ⓒ Ⓓ
99. Ⓐ Ⓑ Ⓒ Ⓓ
100. Ⓐ Ⓑ Ⓒ Ⓓ

Reading Section

101. Ⓐ Ⓑ Ⓒ Ⓓ
102. Ⓐ Ⓑ Ⓒ Ⓓ
103. Ⓐ Ⓑ Ⓒ Ⓓ
104. Ⓐ Ⓑ Ⓒ Ⓓ
105. Ⓐ Ⓑ Ⓒ Ⓓ
106. Ⓐ Ⓑ Ⓒ Ⓓ
107. Ⓐ Ⓑ Ⓒ Ⓓ
108. Ⓐ Ⓑ Ⓒ Ⓓ
109. Ⓐ Ⓑ Ⓒ Ⓓ
110. Ⓐ Ⓑ Ⓒ Ⓓ
111. Ⓐ Ⓑ Ⓒ Ⓓ
112. Ⓐ Ⓑ Ⓒ Ⓓ
113. Ⓐ Ⓑ Ⓒ Ⓓ
114. Ⓐ Ⓑ Ⓒ Ⓓ
115. Ⓐ Ⓑ Ⓒ Ⓓ
116. Ⓐ Ⓑ Ⓒ Ⓓ
117. Ⓐ Ⓑ Ⓒ Ⓓ
118. Ⓐ Ⓑ Ⓒ Ⓓ
119. Ⓐ Ⓑ Ⓒ Ⓓ
120. Ⓐ Ⓑ Ⓒ Ⓓ
121. Ⓐ Ⓑ Ⓒ Ⓓ
122. Ⓐ Ⓑ Ⓒ Ⓓ
123. Ⓐ Ⓑ Ⓒ Ⓓ
124. Ⓐ Ⓑ Ⓒ Ⓓ
125. Ⓐ Ⓑ Ⓒ Ⓓ
126. Ⓐ Ⓑ Ⓒ Ⓓ
127. Ⓐ Ⓑ Ⓒ Ⓓ
128. Ⓐ Ⓑ Ⓒ Ⓓ
129. Ⓐ Ⓑ Ⓒ Ⓓ
130. Ⓐ Ⓑ Ⓒ Ⓓ
131. Ⓐ Ⓑ Ⓒ Ⓓ
132. Ⓐ Ⓑ Ⓒ Ⓓ
133. Ⓐ Ⓑ Ⓒ Ⓓ
134. Ⓐ Ⓑ Ⓒ Ⓓ
135. Ⓐ Ⓑ Ⓒ Ⓓ
136. Ⓐ Ⓑ Ⓒ Ⓓ
137. Ⓐ Ⓑ Ⓒ Ⓓ
138. Ⓐ Ⓑ Ⓒ Ⓓ
139. Ⓐ Ⓑ Ⓒ Ⓓ
140. Ⓐ Ⓑ Ⓒ Ⓓ
141. Ⓐ Ⓑ Ⓒ Ⓓ
142. Ⓐ Ⓑ Ⓒ Ⓓ
143. Ⓐ Ⓑ Ⓒ Ⓓ
144. Ⓐ Ⓑ Ⓒ Ⓓ
145. Ⓐ Ⓑ Ⓒ Ⓓ
146. Ⓐ Ⓑ Ⓒ Ⓓ
147. Ⓐ Ⓑ Ⓒ Ⓓ
148. Ⓐ Ⓑ Ⓒ Ⓓ
149. Ⓐ Ⓑ Ⓒ Ⓓ
150. Ⓐ Ⓑ Ⓒ Ⓓ
151. Ⓐ Ⓑ Ⓒ Ⓓ
152. Ⓐ Ⓑ Ⓒ Ⓓ
153. Ⓐ Ⓑ Ⓒ Ⓓ
154. Ⓐ Ⓑ Ⓒ Ⓓ
155. Ⓐ Ⓑ Ⓒ Ⓓ
156. Ⓐ Ⓑ Ⓒ Ⓓ
157. Ⓐ Ⓑ Ⓒ Ⓓ
158. Ⓐ Ⓑ Ⓒ Ⓓ
159. Ⓐ Ⓑ Ⓒ Ⓓ
160. Ⓐ Ⓑ Ⓒ Ⓓ
161. Ⓐ Ⓑ Ⓒ Ⓓ
162. Ⓐ Ⓑ Ⓒ Ⓓ
163. Ⓐ Ⓑ Ⓒ Ⓓ
164. Ⓐ Ⓑ Ⓒ Ⓓ
165. Ⓐ Ⓑ Ⓒ Ⓓ
166. Ⓐ Ⓑ Ⓒ Ⓓ
167. Ⓐ Ⓑ Ⓒ Ⓓ
168. Ⓐ Ⓑ Ⓒ Ⓓ
169. Ⓐ Ⓑ Ⓒ Ⓓ
170. Ⓐ Ⓑ Ⓒ Ⓓ
171. Ⓐ Ⓑ Ⓒ Ⓓ
172. Ⓐ Ⓑ Ⓒ Ⓓ
173. Ⓐ Ⓑ Ⓒ Ⓓ
174. Ⓐ Ⓑ Ⓒ Ⓓ
175. Ⓐ Ⓑ Ⓒ Ⓓ
176. Ⓐ Ⓑ Ⓒ Ⓓ
177. Ⓐ Ⓑ Ⓒ Ⓓ
178. Ⓐ Ⓑ Ⓒ Ⓓ
179. Ⓐ Ⓑ Ⓒ Ⓓ
180. Ⓐ Ⓑ Ⓒ Ⓓ
181. Ⓐ Ⓑ Ⓒ Ⓓ
182. Ⓐ Ⓑ Ⓒ Ⓓ
183. Ⓐ Ⓑ Ⓒ Ⓓ
184. Ⓐ Ⓑ Ⓒ Ⓓ
185. Ⓐ Ⓑ Ⓒ Ⓓ
186. Ⓐ Ⓑ Ⓒ Ⓓ
187. Ⓐ Ⓑ Ⓒ Ⓓ
188. Ⓐ Ⓑ Ⓒ Ⓓ
189. Ⓐ Ⓑ Ⓒ Ⓓ
190. Ⓐ Ⓑ Ⓒ Ⓓ
191. Ⓐ Ⓑ Ⓒ Ⓓ
192. Ⓐ Ⓑ Ⓒ Ⓓ
193. Ⓐ Ⓑ Ⓒ Ⓓ
194. Ⓐ Ⓑ Ⓒ Ⓓ
195. Ⓐ Ⓑ Ⓒ Ⓓ
196. Ⓐ Ⓑ Ⓒ Ⓓ
197. Ⓐ Ⓑ Ⓒ Ⓓ
198. Ⓐ Ⓑ Ⓒ Ⓓ
199. Ⓐ Ⓑ Ⓒ Ⓓ
200. Ⓐ Ⓑ Ⓒ Ⓓ

Remove answer sheet by cutting on dotted line

MODEL TEST 5
LISTENING COMPREHENSION

In this section of the test, you will have the chance to show how well you understand spoken English. There are four parts to this section, with special directions for each part. You will find the Answer Sheet for Model Test 5 on page 389. Detach it from the book and use it to record your answers. Check your answers using the Answer Key on page 476 and see the Explanatory Answers on page 549. Turn on the compact disc for when you are ready to begin.

Listen to Track 1 of compact disc 4 to hear the statements for Part I of Model Test 5.

Part I: Picture

Directions: In your test book, you will see a picture. On the compact disc, you will hear four statements. Choose the statement that more closely matches the picture and fill in the corresponding oval on your answer sheet.

GO ON TO THE NEXT PAGE

392 TOEIC MODEL TESTS

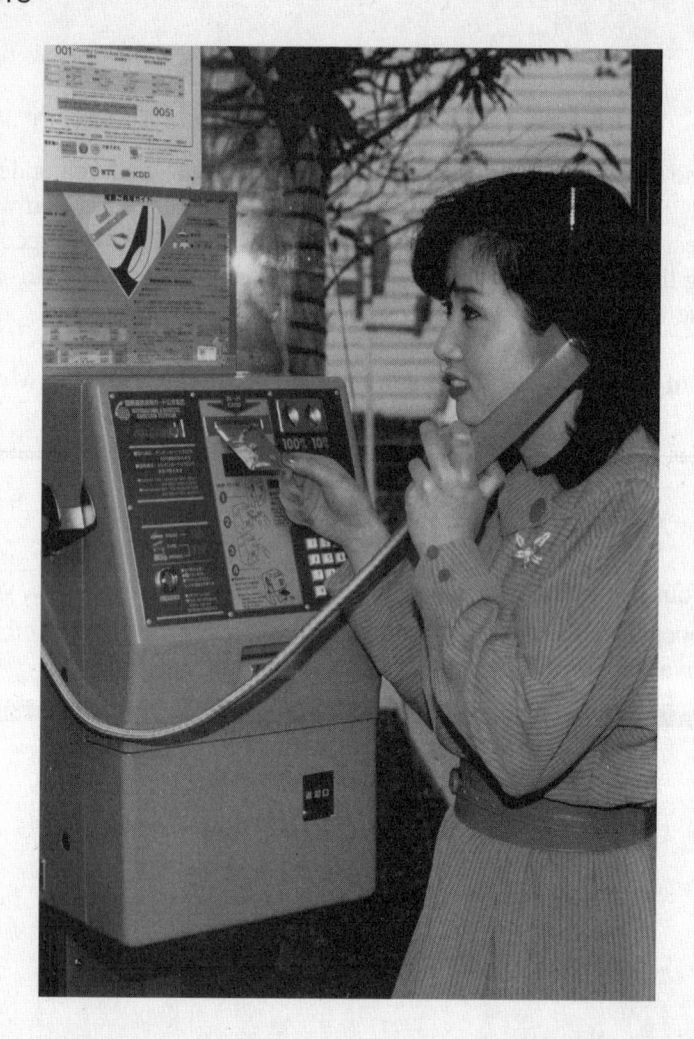

1.

2.

3.

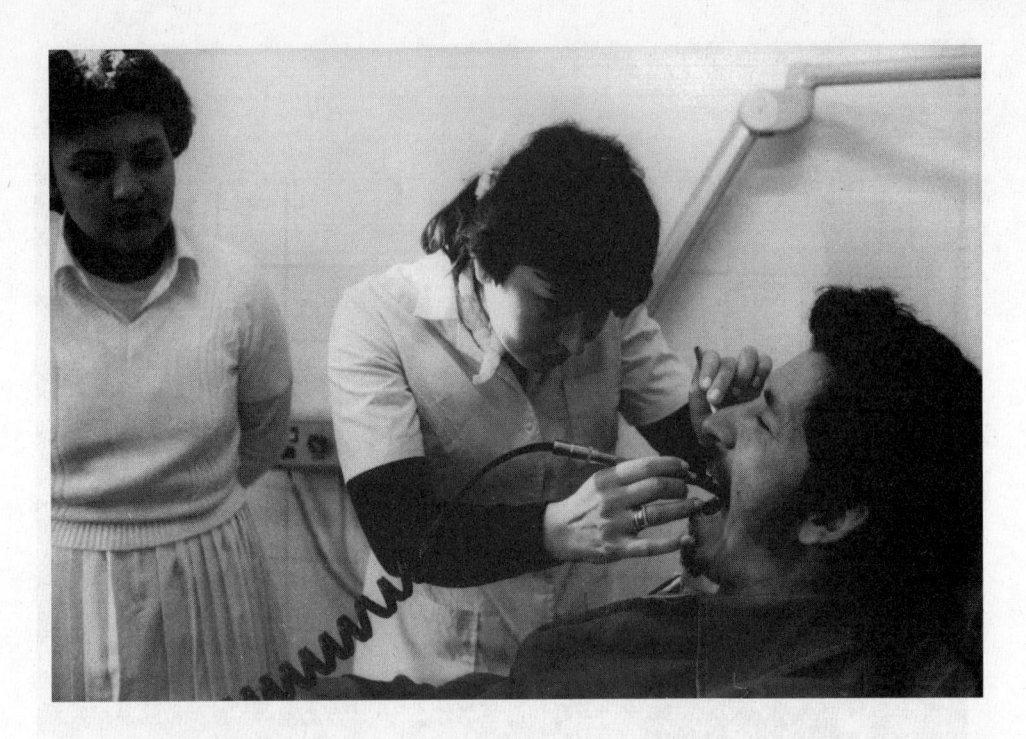

4.

GO ON TO THE NEXT PAGE

394 TOEIC MODEL TESTS

5.

6.

7.

8.

396 TOEIC MODEL TESTS

9.

10.

11.

12.

GO ON TO THE NEXT PAGE →

398 TOEIC MODEL TESTS

13.

14.

15.

16.

400 TOEIC MODEL TESTS

17.

18.

19.

20.

GO ON TO THE NEXT PAGE

402 TOEIC MODEL TESTS

Listen to Track 2 of compact disc 4 to hear the statements for Part II of Model Test 5.

Part II: Question-Response

Directions: On the compact disc, you will hear a question and three possible answers. Choose the answer that most closely answers the question and fill in the corresponding oval on your answer sheet.

21. Mark your answer on your answer sheet.

22. Mark your answer on your answer sheet.

23. Mark your answer on your answer sheet.

24. Mark your answer on your answer sheet.

25. Mark your answer on your answer sheet.

26. Mark your answer on your answer sheet.

27. Mark your answer on your answer sheet.

28. Mark your answer on your answer sheet.

29. Mark your answer on your answer sheet.

30. Mark your answer on your answer sheet.

31. Mark your answer on your answer sheet.

32. Mark your answer on your answer sheet.

33. Mark your answer on your answer sheet.

34. Mark your answer on your answer sheet.

35. Mark your answer on your answer sheet.

36. Mark your answer on your answer sheet.

37. Mark your answer on your answer sheet.
38. Mark your answer on your answer sheet.
39. Mark your answer on your answer sheet.
40. Mark your answer on your answer sheet.
41. Mark your answer on your answer sheet.
42. Mark your answer on your answer sheet.
43. Mark your answer on your answer sheet.
44. Mark your answer on your answer sheet.
45. Mark your answer on your answer sheet.
46. Mark your answer on your answer sheet.
47. Mark your answer on your answer sheet.
48. Mark your answer on your answer sheet.
49. Mark your answer on your answer sheet.
50. Mark your answer on your answer sheet.

GO ON TO THE NEXT PAGE

Listen to Track 3 of compact disc 4 to hear the conversations for Part III of Model Test 5.

Part III: Short Conversations

Directions: On the compact disc, you will hear a short conversation. In your test book, you will see a question and four possible answers. Choose the best answer to the question and fill in the corresponding oval on your answer sheet.

51. What is the woman's solution to the problem?
    (A) Move into a larger place.
    (B) Throw away old magazines.
    (C) Buy another bookcase.
    (D) Sell the books.

52. What does the man mean?
    (A) He wants his eggs fried.
    (B) He had a bad dream.
    (C) He wants coffee the most.
    (D) He doesn't put anything in his coffee.

53. What seems to be the problem?
    (A) A headlight is out.
    (B) The mechanic is unavailable.
    (C) The brakes are bad.
    (D) The engine is broken.

54. What does the woman do while she waits for the train?
    (A) Reads the paper.
    (B) Files her nails.
    (C) Stays out of the rain.
    (D) Thinks and rests.

55. What will the desk clerk do?
    (A) Bring a new TV.
    (B) Get someone to fix the TV.
    (C) Take the TV away.
    (D) Put the TV in the right room.

56. Why do they need sandwiches?
    (A) The meeting will continue past lunchtime.
    (B) The meeting is scheduled at noon.
    (C) They'll need to work hard at the meeting.
    (D) They'll need snacks.

57. How many nights did the woman stay?
    (A) One.
    (B) Two.
    (C) Three.
    (D) Four.

58. How does the woman suggest cooling the room?
    (A) Close the window.
    (B) Pull the drapes.
    (C) Turn off the heater.
    (D) Get an air-conditioner.

59. What does the man want to do?
    (A) Clean the coffee pot.
    (B) Change his shirt.
    (C) Watch the kitchen.
    (D) Sweep the floor.

60. Why is the man annoyed?
    (A) They can't get a taxi.
    (B) They can't find his bags.
    (C) They have to wait for her luggage.
    (D) They're stuck in the city.

61. What does the man need?
    (A) The phone number.
    (B) The fax number.
    (C) A check.
    (D) A dial.

62. Where are they going to eat lunch?
    (A) On the sidewalk.
    (B) In the park.
    (C) At a cafe.
    (D) At home.

63. What does the man need?
    (A) The dictionary.
    (B) The directory.
    (C) The phone log.
    (D) The new number.

64. What's the matter with the woman's camera?
    (A) It's not very good.
    (B) It's at the hotel.
    (C) It was stolen.
    (D) It can be used in a moment.

65. What topic might the man and woman have in common?
    (A) Food.
    (B) Golf.
    (C) Free time.
    (D) Books.

66. What should the woman do with the paper?
    (A) Throw it away.
    (B) Circulate it.
    (C) Separate it according to color.
    (D) Label the boxes.

67. Where did this conversation take place?
    (A) In a library.
    (B) In a bookstore.
    (C) In a bank.
    (D) In a post office.

68. Why didn't the woman take the man's paper?
    (A) He hadn't read it.
    (B) She doesn't want a paper.
    (C) She wanted to buy her own copy.
    (D) She wanted a different one.

69. How does the man pay for the meal?
    (A) Leaves the money on the table.
    (B) Takes the money to the cash register.
    (C) Gives the money to the waitress.
    (D) Writes a check for the tip.

70. What does the woman have?
    (A) A view of the park.
    (B) A view of the parking lot.
    (C) A beautiful desk.
    (D) An overlooked office.

71. What kind of statement might the woman prefer?
    (A) Combined statement.
    (B) Savings account statement.
    (C) Checking account statement.
    (D) Activity statement.

72. What was wrong with the man's room?
    (A) It was too big.
    (B) It was too dirty.
    (C) It had the wrong bed.
    (D) It wasn't reserved.

73. Where did this conversation probably take place?
    (A) At a store.
    (B) In a film store.
    (C) At home.
    (D) In an office.

74. What must the man remember to do?
    (A) Get a rental car.
    (B) Get tickets for the flight.
    (C) Drive to the conference.
    (D) Reserve a place at the conference.

75. Why do they need extra help?
    (A) To clean the rooms.
    (B) To get ready for the banquet.
    (C) To talk to the housekeeping staff.
    (D) To wait on tables.

GO ON TO THE NEXT PAGE

76. What is the woman doing?
    (A) Introducing herself.
    (B) Interviewing a job applicant.
    (C) Testing a student.
    (D) Mailing a package.

77. Why are the man and woman upset?
    (A) They can't catch their train.
    (B) They can't make copies.
    (C) They can't start on time.
    (D) They can't find the film.

78. Why do the man's feet hurt?
    (A) It's hot weather.
    (B) His shoes hurt his feet.
    (C) He's walked a lot.
    (D) He didn't wear socks.

79. Which flight does the man have tickets for?
    (A) The 2:00.
    (B) The 4:00.
    (C) The 5:00.
    (D) The 7:00.

80. What is the woman's job?
    (A) Tour guide.
    (B) Desk clerk.
    (C) Housekeeper.
    (D) Waitress.

Listen to Track 4 of compact disc 4 to hear the short talks for Part IV of Model Test 5.

Part IV: Short Talks

Directions: On the compact disc, you will hear a short talk. In your test book, you will see several questions on the talk and four possible answers. Choose the best answer to the question and fill in the corresponding oval on your answer sheet.

81. Where would you hear this message?
    (A) On the telephone.
    (B) At a reception desk.
    (C) In an elevator.
    (D) On the radio.

82. What should you do if you want to talk to an advisor?
    (A) Call during business hours.
    (B) Visit their office in person.
    (C) Dial until you get someone.
    (D) Stay on the line.

83. What kind of subway station is Downtown Central?
    (A) A suburban station.
    (B) A transfer station.
    (C) A through station.
    (D) A rural station.

84. Where do passengers catch the East-West line?
    (A) On the lower level platform.
    (B) On the upper level platform.
    (C) On the same platform.
    (D) On the outside platform.

85. What will the weather be like today?
    (A) Stormy.
    (B) Partly sunny.
    (C) Rainy.
    (D) Cold.

86. What will increase during the afternoon?
    (A) Stormy.
    (B) Rain.
    (C) Wind.
    (D) Snow.

87. What new service is being offered?
    (A) Payment of handling charges.
    (B) Two-day delivery.
    (C) Quality service.
    (D) Telephone orders.

88. What is different about the service for customers in Alaska?
    (A) They have to pay more.
    (B) They get delivery in three days.
    (C) The service isn't offered there.
    (D) They must ship with another company.

89. What is the purpose of this hotline?
    (A) To tell about special events.
    (B) To give sports news.
    (C) To give weather updates.
    (D) To suggest restaurants.

90. What additional information does the hotline provide?
    (A) Information about new city ordinances.
    (B) Public transportation information.
    (C) Breaking news.
    (D) Movie reviews.

91. What is the first thing the receptionist should do for a visitor?
    (A) Say hello.
    (B) Ask his name.
    (C) Have him sign the book.
    (D) Call the person he is visiting.

GO ON TO THE NEXT PAGE

92. Where should the visitor wait while you are calling?
    (A) By the desk.
    (B) Outside.
    (C) In the office.
    (D) In the lobby.

93. What change is planned for buses on this route?
    (A) They will leave four minutes sooner.
    (B) They will arrive four minutes later.
    (C) They will make fewer trips.
    (D) They will make more trips.

94. When will this change take place?
    (A) Immediately.
    (B) Currently.
    (C) On June 5.
    (D) On June 21.

95. What is the largest group that the conference center can handle?
    (A) Ten.
    (B) Twenty.
    (C) One hundred.
    (D) Two hundred.

96. Where do participants stay while attending the conference?
    (A) At a nearby hotel.
    (B) At their own homes.
    (C) In the center's guest rooms.
    (D) In town.

97. Where is the conference center probably located?
    (A) In the country.
    (B) In the city.
    (C) In the suburbs.
    (D) In a park.

98. What problem is occurring?
    (A) There is a power failure.
    (B) There is a water problem.
    (C) There is a gas shortage.
    (D) There is flooding.

99. What has caused the problem?
    (A) An accident.
    (B) A snowstorm.
    (C) A thunderstorm.
    (D) A fire.

100. What are residents asked to do?
    (A) Stay indoors.
    (B) Light candles.
    (C) Call for help.
    (D) Turn off electrical appliances.

**This is the end of the Listening Comprehension portion of the test.
Turn to Part V in your test book.**

READING

In this section of the test, you will have the chance to show how well you understand written English. There are three parts to this section, with special directions for each part.

YOU WILL HAVE ONE HOUR AND FIFTEEN MINUTES TO COMPLETE PARTS V, VI, AND VII OF THE TEST.

Part V: Incomplete Sentences

Directions: In your test book, you will see a sentence with a missing word. Four possible answers follow the sentence. Choose the best answer to the question and fill in the corresponding oval on your answer sheet.

101. If your meal is unsatisfactory, we _____ it without question.
    (A) will replace
    (B) replaces
    (C) are replacing
    (D) replaced

102. _____ the manager's suggestions were reasonable, the supervisor agreed with them.
    (A) Until
    (B) Although
    (C) Because
    (D) Even though

103. The proposal is due at the client's office _____ Thursday.
    (A) with
    (B) on
    (C) at
    (D) for

104. The results of the traveler preference survey are _____.
    (A) surprised
    (B) surprises
    (C) surprise
    (D) surprising

GO ON TO THE NEXT PAGE

105. We cannot ship the order now because our _____ is low.
 (A) invitation
 (B) inventory
 (C) invention
 (D) invoice

106. The train from Madrid arrives _____ noon.
 (A) in
 (B) on
 (C) over
 (D) at

107. The company has quit _____ in that magazine.
 (A) to advertise
 (B) advertise
 (C) advertising
 (D) advertisement

108. Western Components, Inc., is _____ than Consolidated Electronics Company.
 (A) as reliable
 (B) most reliable
 (C) the reliable
 (D) more reliable

109. The project has been completed, _____ the final report is not ready yet.
 (A) because
 (B) but
 (C) or
 (D) since

110. Most cruise passengers will board the ship _____ 4:00 and 5:00.
 (A) between
 (B) at
 (C) until
 (D) with

111. The technicians in the research division _____ the process confidential.
 (A) is keeping
 (B) are keeping
 (C) to keep
 (D) has kept

112. A good waiter _____ to explain the menu.
 (A) is never too busy
 (B) never too busy is
 (C) is too busy never
 (D) being never too busy

113. The laundry bag is _____ the cabinet.
 (A) within
 (B) among
 (C) inside
 (D) between

114. The name of our company symbolizes tradition _____ experience.
 (A) nor
 (B) but
 (C) or
 (D) and

115. Mr. Fong had the client _____ her questions in writing.
 (A) submit
 (B) submitted
 (C) submitting
 (D) submits

116. Ms. Ripola is _____ an accountant when totaling the receipts.
 (A) careful as
 (B) as careful
 (C) as careful as
 (D) careful than

117. _____ the seminar, the audience had trouble hearing the speaker.
 (A) Since
 (B) During
 (C) Although
 (D) While

118. Reductions in the budget require us _____ our costs for international travel.
 (A) limits
 (B) to limit
 (C) limiting
 (D) limit

119. Hiring temporary workers can be very _____.
    (A) economize
    (B) economically
    (C) economy
    (D) economical

120. Marketing costs are _____ the department predicted.
    (A) higher than
    (B) high as
    (C) highest
    (D) highest than

121. The housekeeping staff comes on duty _____ 2:00.
    (A) in
    (B) on
    (C) at
    (D) with

122. We missed the deadline _____ our computer malfunctioned.
    (A) until
    (B) because
    (C) if
    (D) though

123. Our representative will meet you _____ Rome.
    (A) on
    (B) for
    (C) in
    (D) to

124. Computer software is a _____ market.
    (A) competitor
    (B) competitive
    (C) competition
    (D) competitively

125. We will not send the payment _____ the invoice is corrected.
    (A) until
    (B) because
    (C) although
    (D) once

126. Most of the employees _____ in the company cafeteria.
    (A) eating
    (B) eats
    (C) eat
    (D) to eat

127. Salespeople _____ attract new clients receive a bonus.
    (A) whose
    (B) which
    (C) whom
    (D) who

128. The new instructions are _____ the old ones.
    (A) more difficult
    (B) difficult as
    (C) difficult than
    (D) more difficult than

129. Mr. Meisel _____ to get to work early.
    (A) is liking
    (B) likes
    (C) would be liking
    (D) like

130. The ticketholders may be _____ about the change in date.
    (A) confusing
    (B) confuse
    (C) confused
    (D) confuses

131. The corporate office is located _____ the Jamieson Building.
    (A) on
    (B) under
    (C) in
    (D) over

132. Our service technicians receive _____ training available.
    (A) better
    (B) as good
    (C) best
    (D) the best

GO ON TO THE NEXT PAGE

133. Your room has been reserved _____ two nights.
    (A) in
    (B) for
    (C) with
    (D) at

134. The price of the equipment is low, _____ the maintenance costs can be high.
    (A) or
    (B) but
    (C) and
    (D) either

135. The conference _____ was scheduled for next week has been postponed.
    (A) that
    (B) whose
    (C) it
    (D) who

136. Mr. Ho's assistant _____ his mail while he was away.
    (A) will answer
    (B) answered
    (C) answers
    (D) answering

137. The reception clerk _____ on the telephone when the phone went dead.
    (A) talked
    (B) is talking
    (C) was talking
    (D) would talk

138. Overnight mail is _____ way to send a package.
    (A) faster
    (B) the fastest
    (C) faster than
    (D) as fast as

139. A list of compatible software _____ with your new computer.
    (A) includes
    (B) is included
    (C) is including
    (D) included

140. The hotel offers guests a continental breakfast in the lobby _____ a full breakfast in the restaurant.
    (A) with
    (B) since
    (C) either
    (D) or

Part VI: Error Recognition

Directions: In the test book, you will see a sentence with four words or phrases underlined. Choose the word or phrase that is incorrect and fill in the corresponding oval on your answer sheet.

141. Ms. Furtado would <u>help</u> with the program
                              A
     testing <u>if</u> she <u>is not</u> supervising the
           B   C
     <u>inventory</u> project.
        D

142. <u>Because</u> we <u>need</u> more space, the
        A   B
     company cannot <u>afford</u> <u>larger</u> premises.
                    C   D

143. We <u>will have</u> one <u>staff meeting</u> on
          A   B
     Tuesday <u>or</u> another <u>by</u> Friday.
            C   D

144. <u>Employees</u> are required <u>often</u> <u>to work</u>
        A   B   C
     overtime <u>during</u> our busy season.
          D

145. The <u>attaching</u> brochure <u>describes</u> the tours
           A   B
     <u>that</u> are <u>available</u>.
      C   D

146. The marketing department <u>has designed</u> a
                                   A
     package <u>that</u> <u>is</u> both attractive and
             B   C
     <u>economizes</u>.
        D

147. <u>An</u> helpful receptionist <u>makes</u> <u>visitors</u> feel
      A   B   C
     <u>relaxed</u> and welcome.
       D

148. The advertisement <u>which</u> <u>it</u> <u>appeared in</u>
                         A B   C
     today's newspaper is very <u>clever</u>.
                            D

GO ON TO THE NEXT PAGE

149. Housekeepers they have received good
              A   B
    performance reviews will get pay raises.
                        C   D

150. The engineer was leaving the office when
      A   B   C
    the security alarm rings.
                         D

151. Mr. Kam had another salesperson making
                  A   B
    his sales calls while he was sick.
                   C   D

152. Ms. Gabor every day takes a long walk
                A   B   C
    during her lunch hour.
      D

153. This report that the accountant reviewed
                 A
    it is filled with numerical errors.
    B   C   D

154. Our word processing program is the more
    A   B   C
    efficient of any program on the market.
                             D

155. A software that uses the most current
    A   B
    technology is always expensive.
               C   D

156. We will ship the merchandise by
         A   B
    overnight mail soon as we receive the
                   C   D
    order.

157. The information provided in the enclosing
                    A   B
    report answers your questions about the
           C   D
    safety of the product.

158. In order for us to be successful in the
                            A   B
    computer field, our prices must be
                    C
    competitively.
       D

159. The regional manager makes a speech at
                         A
    the banquet that was held on Saturday
      A   B   C
    night.

160. Our competitor's product, available in all
         A
    countries, are made poorly and sold
               B   C
    inexpensively.
         D

Part VII: Reading Comprehension

Directions: In your test book, you will see a reading passage followed by several questions. Each questions has four answer choices. Choose the best answer to the question and fill in the corresponding oval on your answer sheet.

Questions 161–163 refer to the following report.

Over the past two years the company has spent $6 million, about half per year, on environmental improvements for plants and facilities. The company estimates that such expenditures will increase by approximately $2 million per year for the next two years. Future expenditures will be dependent to some extent upon pending environmental regulations.

161. About how much did the company spend on the environment this year?
 (A) $3 million
 (B) $5 million
 (C) $6 million
 (D) $8 million

162. How much do they expect to spend next year?
 (A) $3 million
 (B) $5 million
 (C) $6 million
 (D) $8 million

163. On what does future spending depend?
 (A) Availability of funds
 (B) Quality of the environment
 (C) Possible rules
 (D) State of facilities

GO ON TO THE NEXT PAGE

Questions 164–166 refer to the following advertisement.

The advantages that made us #1 in Asia
YES! Please send me your student travel catalog.

Experience
We have the most experience in overseas student travel: 47 years of discovering the best sights and events, the best hotels and restaurants, the best staff here and abroad.

Popularity
More students choose our Out to Asia trips than any other.

References
We stand by our reputation. We'll give you the names of past participants so you can get a firsthand impression.

Savings
We can pass on greater volume discounts, so your dollars will buy you more.

Member, Association of World Travel Organizations.

164. Why should someone choose Out to Asia?
 (A) It offers varied travel packages.
 (B) It has a good safety record.
 (C) Its packages are all-inclusive.
 (D) Other people like it.

165. How can you do grassroots research into Out to Asia?
 (A) Talk to a former Out to Asia traveler.
 (B) Call the Association of World Travel Organizations.
 (C) Order its catalog.
 (D) Contemplate its experience.

166. What describes the cost of Out to Asia tours?
 (A) They're very expensive because they include study opportunities.
 (B) They're quite expensive, but everything's the best.
 (C) They're cheap because they're planned for big numbers.
 (D) They're in middle price range.

Questions 167–169 refer to the following table.

Low Airfares

New York	Berlin	$249
New York	San Francisco	$139
New York	Bombay	$438
Washington	Rome	$279
San Francisco	Paris	$356

All flights make at least one stop with a change of aircraft. Tickets must be purchased two weeks in advance. Once ticketed any alteration will cost $25.00. No refunds.

167. If you go from New York to Berlin, what happens?
   (A) You can get a refund.
   (B) You change planes.
   (C) You must pay an alteration fee.
   (D) You pay $139.

168. How early do you have to purchase your ticket in order to get the lowest fare?
   (A) One day
   (B) One week
   (C) Ten days
   (D) Fourteen days

169. If you want to change your ticket, what do you have to do?
   (A) Trade tickets at the airport
   (B) Buy a new ticket
   (C) Pay a $25 charge
   (D) Fly with another airline

GO ON TO THE NEXT PAGE

Questions 170–173 refer to the following announcement.

> To save you time on your phone calls, our concert and theater complex has installed an automated phone system. Special phone lines now link you directly with a trained representative for each of our services.
>
> After calling our main number,
>   dial 1 to purchase individual tickets;
>   dial 2 to purchase tickets for groups and organizations;
>   dial 3 to request a schedule of events; and
>   dial 4 to inquire about special services for the disabled.
>
> Line 5 is available for other information not covered by these categories.

170. What is the purpose of this announcement?
 (A) To encourage concert-goers to make calls during intermission
 (B) To inform patrons of a new phone system
 (C) To complain about past phone problems
 (D) To propose installation of an automated phone system

171. Why was the automated phone system installed?
 (A) It is cheaper.
 (B) It is more private.
 (C) It is friendlier.
 (D) It is faster.

172. Which service does dialing 2 connect you to?
 (A) Requesting a schedule
 (B) Services for the disabled
 (C) Purchasing group tickets
 (D) Purchasing individual tickets

173. If your inquiry is not in these categories, what can you do?
 (A) Dial 5
 (B) Stay on the line
 (C) Call the main number again
 (D) Ask for the call to be transferred

Questions 174–176 refer to the following notice.

> Delicious Foods Corporation said it will raise prices an average of three percent for 19 different brands of jams and jellies. This is the second increase in eight months. The company attributes this recent rise to higher prices for the fruits and vegetables, due to the dry weather last spring.

174. On what foods have prices risen?
 (A) Gelatin
 (B) Cakes and sweets
 (C) Condiments
 (D) Seafood

175. How many increases has the company recently made?
 (A) One increase in six months
 (B) Two increases in eight months
 (C) One increase in twelve months
 (D) Two increases in eighteen months

176. Why has the price of fruits and vegetables risen?
 (A) The farmers want more money.
 (B) There were floods last summer.
 (C) The weather last spring was dry.
 (D) They can't ship the food.

GO ON TO THE NEXT PAGE

Questions 177–179 refer to the following advertisement.

Careers in HOTEL & RESTAURANT MANAGEMENT

Learn professional hospitality at our training institute!

- 6–12 month certificate programs
- Classes days, nights, or weekends
- Job placement assistance upon completion

Classes begin April 1. Call the school for further information.

177. How long will you have to study at this school?
 (A) 1–2 weeks
 (B) 4–6 weeks
 (C) 2–6 months
 (D) 6–12 months

178. When will the school help you get a job?
 (A) When you enroll
 (B) While you are studying
 (C) When you have finished the course
 (D) After you have found work

179. What should you do if you want to know more?
 (A) Visit classes
 (B) Meet some graduates
 (C) Talk to employers
 (D) Call the school

Questions 180–182 refer to the following memo.

Welcome

Enclosed in your Welcome packet are two documents which provide information concerning our company's Total Compensation Plan. Please give these documents your full attention, since they contain important information on salary and benefits. A summary of each document's contents is listed on page two.

We are glad you have decided to join our company and we look forward to a long and mutually beneficial relationship.

180. What is in the packet?
 (A) Checks
 (B) Invoices
 (C) Documents
 (D) Bills

181. Who would be likely to receive the welcome packet?
 (A) Retirees
 (B) New employees
 (C) Health insurance salespeople
 (D) Visitors

182. What should you do with this packet?
 (A) Go to Human Resources
 (B) Read it carefully
 (C) Fill out all the forms
 (D) Decide about your options

GO ON TO THE NEXT PAGE

Questions 183–184 refer to the following letter.

CDS..**Carlyle Department Store**
2000 River Oak Mall
Los Angeles, CA 90024

May 30, 19__

Dear Customer:

We would like to thank you.

Our company has maintained a steady profit margin during the recent recession because of you, our satisfied customers. We have more than 14,000 customers across the city who visit us every week, sometimes twice a week. And to thank you, we would like to give the first 100 customers who spend $1,000 in a ten-day period a 10% discount on their next purchase over $100.

Again thanks, and I look forward to seeing you soon.

Sincerely yours,

Marsden Hartley

Marsden Hartley
President and Founder

---

183. What is the status of the economy?
   (A) It is weak.
   (B) It is strong.
   (C) It fluctuates frequently.
   (D) It is steady.

184. What is being offered?
   (A) A free gift
   (B) A price reduction
   (C) $100 cash
   (D) A rebate

Questions 185–187 refer to the following index.

Customer Service Numbers
Please call 684-5555 and at the tone press your option.

Change billing address	1
Dispute fees	2
General fee information	3
How to make payments	4
Have not received monthly bill	5

185. What is this index designed to show?
 (A) Number of calls received
 (B) Customer call records
 (C) Information available
 (D) Amount of customer bill

186. What type of service is provided by the most lines?
 (A) Information about addresses
 (B) Areas of dispute
 (C) Updates on service options
 (D) Information about money and bills

187. Who would most likely use Option 1?
 (A) New customers
 (B) People with a complaint
 (C) People who have moved
 (D) Customers with poor credit ratings

GO ON TO THE NEXT PAGE

Questions 188–192 refer to the following magazine article.

> **If** you want to advance in your career, you will have to make some careful decisions about which jobs you take. Evaluate a job offer for the value it has to your career. It may mean sacrifices at first. You may have to move to a different region or a different country to get a job that is right for you. You may have to work late hours, at least temporarily. You might even have to take a lower salary for a job that offers you the experience that you need. But you should never accept a job if it is not related to your career goals.
>
> Accepting a job that is not within your career path will not give you the training or experience you need or want. You will find yourself frustrated in such a position and consequently will not perform your best. This will have an effect on the people around you, who will not feel as if you are being part of the team. The best advice is to think carefully before accepting any position and make sure the job is one you want to have.

188. What is the most significant factor in evaluating a job?
 (A) Location
 (B) Salary
 (C) Value to your career
 (D) How much you will like it

189. What is NOT mentioned as a sacrifice for a valuable job?
 (A) Moving
 (B) No benefits
 (C) Bad hours
 (D) Low salary

190. What kind of job should you never accept?
 (A) One not related to your career goals
 (B) One that requires a long commute
 (C) One that has a negative effect on people around you
 (D) One that makes you work hard

191. What is wrong with taking a job outside your career path?
 (A) You will earn less.
 (B) You won't perform as well.
 (C) People will give you advice.
 (D) You will be part of a team.

192. What is the author's best advice?
 (A) Take the first job offered.
 (B) Consider changing careers.
 (C) Don't work with other people.
 (D) Think before accepting a job.

Questions 193–195 refer to the following form.

The Palmer Hotel

Room Type and Daily Rate (tax not included)
Double $86.00 per night

Arrival Date   4-25
Departure Date   4-28
Guest   2
Arrival Time   4:00p.m.

Number of Rooms   1
Confirmation Number   24-0726

Check-in time is 3:00 p.m.
Check-out time is 1:00 p.m.

Guest Name: Mr. & Mrs. R. Wolf

193. Why is this card used?
 (A) To register at a hotel
 (B) To reserve space at a convention
 (C) To receive messages
 (D) To check out

194. What kind of room has been requested?
 (A) A single room
 (B) A double room
 (C) A comfortable room
 (D) A quiet room

195. What is added to the daily room rate?
 (A) A service fee
 (B) A reservation charge
 (C) Tips for the maid
 (D) Tax

GO ON TO THE NEXT PAGE

Questions 196–200 refer to the following memorandum.

> **MEMORANDUM**
>
> **To:** All office personnel being transferred to the Paris office
>
> **Fm:** A. Scheider
>
> **Re:** Suggestions to prepare for move
>
> Each day my E-Mail is full of messages concerning this move. Rather than responding to each of you individually I am forwarding this memo to all of you. Please follow the instructions below carefully. Do not omit any steps and please do not ask me these questions again.
>
> - √ Pack all of the items in or on your desk in boxes.
> - √ Retrieve and delete all messages in your telephone to clear it for the person who will occupy your desk.
> - √ Change the outgoing message on your answering machine so callers can get your new office number.
> - √ Make sure the movers pack your computer equipment safely.
> - √ Provide the administrator for the computer system with your old password and computer identification number.
> - √ Remember to label all boxes clearly to make unpacking easier.
> - √ Notify clients in writing of your new location and phone number.

196. Why was this memo written?
  (A) To respond to several queries regarding the move
  (B) To train the staff in Paris
  (C) To suggest ways to use the computer
  (D) To propose procedures for answering the telephone

197. What should you pack yourself?
  (A) Items in your files
  (B) Items on your desk
  (C) Your computer equipment
  (D) Your phone system

198. What should you do for the person who will occupy your desk?
  (A) Clear old messages from your phone
  (B) Get a new computer password
  (C) Move boxes to the edge of the room
  (D) Notify clients of your replacement

199. What do you need to give to the computer system administrator?
  (A) Your computer equipment
  (B) Your computer files
  (C) Your password and ID number
  (D) Your computer

200. What will make the unpacking easier?
  (A) Clear labels on the boxes
  (B) Caution with computers
  (C) Advance shipping
  (D) An empty desk

STOP!

This is the end of the test. If you finish before time is called, you may go back to Parts V, VI, and VII and check your work.

MODEL TEST 6—ANSWER SHEET

Listening Section

1. Ⓐ Ⓑ Ⓒ Ⓓ
2. Ⓐ Ⓑ Ⓒ Ⓓ
3. Ⓐ Ⓑ Ⓒ Ⓓ
4. Ⓐ Ⓑ Ⓒ Ⓓ
5. Ⓐ Ⓑ Ⓒ Ⓓ
6. Ⓐ Ⓑ Ⓒ Ⓓ
7. Ⓐ Ⓑ Ⓒ Ⓓ
8. Ⓐ Ⓑ Ⓒ Ⓓ
9. Ⓐ Ⓑ Ⓒ Ⓓ
10. Ⓐ Ⓑ Ⓒ Ⓓ
11. Ⓐ Ⓑ Ⓒ Ⓓ
12. Ⓐ Ⓑ Ⓒ Ⓓ
13. Ⓐ Ⓑ Ⓒ Ⓓ
14. Ⓐ Ⓑ Ⓒ Ⓓ
15. Ⓐ Ⓑ Ⓒ Ⓓ
16. Ⓐ Ⓑ Ⓒ Ⓓ
17. Ⓐ Ⓑ Ⓒ Ⓓ
18. Ⓐ Ⓑ Ⓒ Ⓓ
19. Ⓐ Ⓑ Ⓒ Ⓓ
20. Ⓐ Ⓑ Ⓒ Ⓓ
21. Ⓐ Ⓑ Ⓒ
22. Ⓐ Ⓑ Ⓒ
23. Ⓐ Ⓑ Ⓒ
24. Ⓐ Ⓑ Ⓒ
25. Ⓐ Ⓑ Ⓒ
26. Ⓐ Ⓑ Ⓒ
27. Ⓐ Ⓑ Ⓒ
28. Ⓐ Ⓑ Ⓒ
29. Ⓐ Ⓑ Ⓒ
30. Ⓐ Ⓑ Ⓒ
31. Ⓐ Ⓑ Ⓒ
32. Ⓐ Ⓑ Ⓒ
33. Ⓐ Ⓑ Ⓒ
34. Ⓐ Ⓑ Ⓒ
35. Ⓐ Ⓑ Ⓒ
36. Ⓐ Ⓑ Ⓒ
37. Ⓐ Ⓑ Ⓒ
38. Ⓐ Ⓑ Ⓒ
39. Ⓐ Ⓑ Ⓒ
40. Ⓐ Ⓑ Ⓒ
41. Ⓐ Ⓑ Ⓒ
42. Ⓐ Ⓑ Ⓒ
43. Ⓐ Ⓑ Ⓒ
44. Ⓐ Ⓑ Ⓒ
45. Ⓐ Ⓑ Ⓒ
46. Ⓐ Ⓑ Ⓒ
47. Ⓐ Ⓑ Ⓒ
48. Ⓐ Ⓑ Ⓒ
49. Ⓐ Ⓑ Ⓒ
50. Ⓐ Ⓑ Ⓒ
51. Ⓐ Ⓑ Ⓒ Ⓓ
52. Ⓐ Ⓑ Ⓒ Ⓓ
53. Ⓐ Ⓑ Ⓒ Ⓓ
54. Ⓐ Ⓑ Ⓒ Ⓓ
55. Ⓐ Ⓑ Ⓒ Ⓓ
56. Ⓐ Ⓑ Ⓒ Ⓓ
57. Ⓐ Ⓑ Ⓒ Ⓓ
58. Ⓐ Ⓑ Ⓒ Ⓓ
59. Ⓐ Ⓑ Ⓒ Ⓓ
60. Ⓐ Ⓑ Ⓒ Ⓓ
61. Ⓐ Ⓑ Ⓒ Ⓓ
62. Ⓐ Ⓑ Ⓒ Ⓓ
63. Ⓐ Ⓑ Ⓒ Ⓓ
64. Ⓐ Ⓑ Ⓒ Ⓓ
65. Ⓐ Ⓑ Ⓒ Ⓓ
66. Ⓐ Ⓑ Ⓒ Ⓓ
67. Ⓐ Ⓑ Ⓒ Ⓓ
68. Ⓐ Ⓑ Ⓒ Ⓓ
69. Ⓐ Ⓑ Ⓒ Ⓓ
70. Ⓐ Ⓑ Ⓒ Ⓓ
71. Ⓐ Ⓑ Ⓒ Ⓓ
72. Ⓐ Ⓑ Ⓒ Ⓓ
73. Ⓐ Ⓑ Ⓒ Ⓓ
74. Ⓐ Ⓑ Ⓒ Ⓓ
75. Ⓐ Ⓑ Ⓒ Ⓓ
76. Ⓐ Ⓑ Ⓒ Ⓓ
77. Ⓐ Ⓑ Ⓒ Ⓓ
78. Ⓐ Ⓑ Ⓒ Ⓓ
79. Ⓐ Ⓑ Ⓒ Ⓓ
80. Ⓐ Ⓑ Ⓒ Ⓓ
81. Ⓐ Ⓑ Ⓒ Ⓓ
82. Ⓐ Ⓑ Ⓒ Ⓓ
83. Ⓐ Ⓑ Ⓒ Ⓓ
84. Ⓐ Ⓑ Ⓒ Ⓓ
85. Ⓐ Ⓑ Ⓒ Ⓓ
86. Ⓐ Ⓑ Ⓒ Ⓓ
87. Ⓐ Ⓑ Ⓒ Ⓓ
88. Ⓐ Ⓑ Ⓒ Ⓓ
89. Ⓐ Ⓑ Ⓒ Ⓓ
90. Ⓐ Ⓑ Ⓒ Ⓓ
91. Ⓐ Ⓑ Ⓒ Ⓓ
92. Ⓐ Ⓑ Ⓒ Ⓓ
93. Ⓐ Ⓑ Ⓒ Ⓓ
94. Ⓐ Ⓑ Ⓒ Ⓓ
95. Ⓐ Ⓑ Ⓒ Ⓓ
96. Ⓐ Ⓑ Ⓒ Ⓓ
97. Ⓐ Ⓑ Ⓒ Ⓓ
98. Ⓐ Ⓑ Ⓒ Ⓓ
99. Ⓐ Ⓑ Ⓒ Ⓓ
100. Ⓐ Ⓑ Ⓒ Ⓓ

Reading Section

101. Ⓐ Ⓑ Ⓒ Ⓓ
102. Ⓐ Ⓑ Ⓒ Ⓓ
103. Ⓐ Ⓑ Ⓒ Ⓓ
104. Ⓐ Ⓑ Ⓒ Ⓓ
105. Ⓐ Ⓑ Ⓒ Ⓓ
106. Ⓐ Ⓑ Ⓒ Ⓓ
107. Ⓐ Ⓑ Ⓒ Ⓓ
108. Ⓐ Ⓑ Ⓒ Ⓓ
109. Ⓐ Ⓑ Ⓒ Ⓓ
110. Ⓐ Ⓑ Ⓒ Ⓓ
111. Ⓐ Ⓑ Ⓒ Ⓓ
112. Ⓐ Ⓑ Ⓒ Ⓓ
113. Ⓐ Ⓑ Ⓒ Ⓓ
114. Ⓐ Ⓑ Ⓒ Ⓓ
115. Ⓐ Ⓑ Ⓒ Ⓓ
116. Ⓐ Ⓑ Ⓒ Ⓓ
117. Ⓐ Ⓑ Ⓒ Ⓓ
118. Ⓐ Ⓑ Ⓒ Ⓓ
119. Ⓐ Ⓑ Ⓒ Ⓓ
120. Ⓐ Ⓑ Ⓒ Ⓓ
121. Ⓐ Ⓑ Ⓒ Ⓓ
122. Ⓐ Ⓑ Ⓒ Ⓓ
123. Ⓐ Ⓑ Ⓒ Ⓓ
124. Ⓐ Ⓑ Ⓒ Ⓓ
125. Ⓐ Ⓑ Ⓒ Ⓓ
126. Ⓐ Ⓑ Ⓒ Ⓓ
127. Ⓐ Ⓑ Ⓒ Ⓓ
128. Ⓐ Ⓑ Ⓒ Ⓓ
129. Ⓐ Ⓑ Ⓒ Ⓓ
130. Ⓐ Ⓑ Ⓒ Ⓓ
131. Ⓐ Ⓑ Ⓒ Ⓓ
132. Ⓐ Ⓑ Ⓒ Ⓓ
133. Ⓐ Ⓑ Ⓒ Ⓓ
134. Ⓐ Ⓑ Ⓒ Ⓓ
135. Ⓐ Ⓑ Ⓒ Ⓓ
136. Ⓐ Ⓑ Ⓒ Ⓓ
137. Ⓐ Ⓑ Ⓒ Ⓓ
138. Ⓐ Ⓑ Ⓒ Ⓓ
139. Ⓐ Ⓑ Ⓒ Ⓓ
140. Ⓐ Ⓑ Ⓒ Ⓓ
141. Ⓐ Ⓑ Ⓒ Ⓓ
142. Ⓐ Ⓑ Ⓒ Ⓓ
143. Ⓐ Ⓑ Ⓒ Ⓓ
144. Ⓐ Ⓑ Ⓒ Ⓓ
145. Ⓐ Ⓑ Ⓒ Ⓓ
146. Ⓐ Ⓑ Ⓒ Ⓓ
147. Ⓐ Ⓑ Ⓒ Ⓓ
148. Ⓐ Ⓑ Ⓒ Ⓓ
149. Ⓐ Ⓑ Ⓒ Ⓓ
150. Ⓐ Ⓑ Ⓒ Ⓓ
151. Ⓐ Ⓑ Ⓒ Ⓓ
152. Ⓐ Ⓑ Ⓒ Ⓓ
153. Ⓐ Ⓑ Ⓒ Ⓓ
154. Ⓐ Ⓑ Ⓒ Ⓓ
155. Ⓐ Ⓑ Ⓒ Ⓓ
156. Ⓐ Ⓑ Ⓒ Ⓓ
157. Ⓐ Ⓑ Ⓒ Ⓓ
158. Ⓐ Ⓑ Ⓒ Ⓓ
159. Ⓐ Ⓑ Ⓒ Ⓓ
160. Ⓐ Ⓑ Ⓒ Ⓓ
161. Ⓐ Ⓑ Ⓒ Ⓓ
162. Ⓐ Ⓑ Ⓒ Ⓓ
163. Ⓐ Ⓑ Ⓒ Ⓓ
164. Ⓐ Ⓑ Ⓒ Ⓓ
165. Ⓐ Ⓑ Ⓒ Ⓓ
166. Ⓐ Ⓑ Ⓒ Ⓓ
167. Ⓐ Ⓑ Ⓒ Ⓓ
168. Ⓐ Ⓑ Ⓒ Ⓓ
169. Ⓐ Ⓑ Ⓒ Ⓓ
170. Ⓐ Ⓑ Ⓒ Ⓓ
171. Ⓐ Ⓑ Ⓒ Ⓓ
172. Ⓐ Ⓑ Ⓒ Ⓓ
173. Ⓐ Ⓑ Ⓒ Ⓓ
174. Ⓐ Ⓑ Ⓒ Ⓓ
175. Ⓐ Ⓑ Ⓒ Ⓓ
176. Ⓐ Ⓑ Ⓒ Ⓓ
177. Ⓐ Ⓑ Ⓒ Ⓓ
178. Ⓐ Ⓑ Ⓒ Ⓓ
179. Ⓐ Ⓑ Ⓒ Ⓓ
180. Ⓐ Ⓑ Ⓒ Ⓓ
181. Ⓐ Ⓑ Ⓒ Ⓓ
182. Ⓐ Ⓑ Ⓒ Ⓓ
183. Ⓐ Ⓑ Ⓒ Ⓓ
184. Ⓐ Ⓑ Ⓒ Ⓓ
185. Ⓐ Ⓑ Ⓒ Ⓓ
186. Ⓐ Ⓑ Ⓒ Ⓓ
187. Ⓐ Ⓑ Ⓒ Ⓓ
188. Ⓐ Ⓑ Ⓒ Ⓓ
189. Ⓐ Ⓑ Ⓒ Ⓓ
190. Ⓐ Ⓑ Ⓒ Ⓓ
191. Ⓐ Ⓑ Ⓒ Ⓓ
192. Ⓐ Ⓑ Ⓒ Ⓓ
193. Ⓐ Ⓑ Ⓒ Ⓓ
194. Ⓐ Ⓑ Ⓒ Ⓓ
195. Ⓐ Ⓑ Ⓒ Ⓓ
196. Ⓐ Ⓑ Ⓒ Ⓓ
197. Ⓐ Ⓑ Ⓒ Ⓓ
198. Ⓐ Ⓑ Ⓒ Ⓓ
199. Ⓐ Ⓑ Ⓒ Ⓓ
200. Ⓐ Ⓑ Ⓒ Ⓓ

Remove answer sheet by cutting on dotted line

MODEL TEST 6
LISTENING COMPREHENSION

In this section of the test, you will have the chance to show how well you understand spoken English. There are four parts to this section, with special directions for each part. You will find the Answer Sheet for Model Test 6 on page 427. Detach it from the book and use it to record your answers. Check your answers using the Answer Key on page 477 and see the Explanatory Answers on page 559. Turn on the compact disc when you are ready to begin.

Listen to Track 5 of compact disc 4 to hear the statements for Part I of Model Test 6.

Part I: Picture

Directions: In your test book, you will see a picture. On the compact disc, you will hear four statements. Choose the statement that most closely matches the picture and fill in the corresponding oval on your answer sheet.

GO ON TO THE NEXT PAGE

430 TOEIC MODEL TESTS

1.

2.

3.

4.

5.

6.

MODEL TEST 6   433

7.

8.

GO ON TO THE NEXT PAGE

434 TOEIC MODEL TESTS

9.

10.

11.

12.

GO ON TO THE NEXT PAGE

436 TOEIC MODEL TESTS

13.

14.

15.

16.

438 TOEIC MODEL TESTS

17.

18.

19.

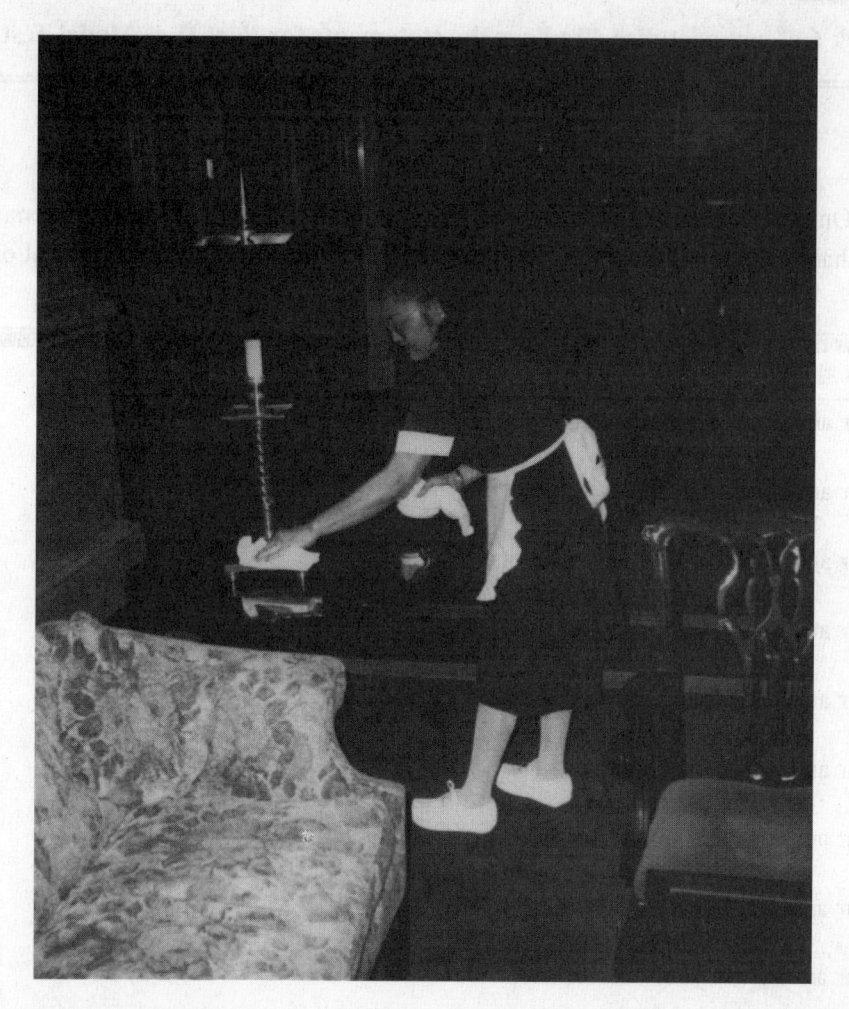

20.

GO ON TO THE NEXT PAGE

Listen to Track 6 of compact disc 4 to hear the statements for Part II of Model Test 6.

Part II: Question-Response

Directions: On the compact disc, you will hear a question and three possible answers. Choose the answer that most closely answers the question and fill in the corresponding oval on your answer sheet.

21. Mark your answer on your answer sheet.

22. Mark your answer on your answer sheet.

23. Mark your answer on your answer sheet.

24. Mark your answer on your answer sheet.

25. Mark your answer on your answer sheet.

26. Mark your answer on your answer sheet.

27. Mark your answer on your answer sheet.

28. Mark your answer on your answer sheet.

29. Mark your answer on your answer sheet.

30. Mark your answer on your answer sheet.

31. Mark your answer on your answer sheet.

32. Mark your answer on your answer sheet.

33. Mark your answer on your answer sheet.

34. Mark your answer on your answer sheet.

35. Mark your answer on your answer sheet.

36. Mark your answer on your answer sheet.

37. Mark your answer on your answer sheet.
38. Mark your answer on your answer sheet.
39. Mark your answer on your answer sheet.
40. Mark your answer on your answer sheet.
41. Mark your answer on your answer sheet.
42. Mark your answer on your answer sheet.
43. Mark your answer on your answer sheet.
44. Mark your answer on your answer sheet.
45. Mark your answer on your answer sheet.
46. Mark your answer on your answer sheet.
47. Mark your answer on your answer sheet.
48. Mark your answer on your answer sheet.
49. Mark your answer on your answer sheet.
50. Mark your answer on your answer sheet.

GO ON TO THE NEXT PAGE

Listen to Track 7 of compact disc 4 to hear the conversations for Part III of Model Test 6.

Part III: Short Conversations

Directions: On the compact disc, you will hear a short conversation. In your test book, you will see a question and four possible answers. Choose the best answer to the question and fill in the corresponding oval on your answer sheet.

51. When will they have dinner?
    (A) At 4:00.
    (B) At 4:30.
    (C) At 6:00.
    (D) At 8:00.

52. What does the man want to do?
    (A) Buy a car.
    (B) Cash a check.
    (C) Open an account.
    (D) Introduce himself.

53. Why can't they see the houses?
    (A) They'll spend all their time in the museum.
    (B) They're too crowded with the public.
    (C) Sightseers aren't allowed.
    (D) The plaza is too large.

54. What did the woman ask about?
    (A) Meal service.
    (B) Launching times.
    (C) Arrival times.
    (D) Departure dates.

55. What does the man want?
    (A) Dinner.
    (B) Maid service.
    (C) A larger room.
    (D) A movie.

56. What does the woman want to know?
    (A) When her flight leaves.
    (B) Which signs to follow.
    (C) How to get to the gate.
    (D) Whether she is departing.

57. Where will they put the printer?
    (A) In his office.
    (B) In her office.
    (C) In another room.
    (D) In the hall.

58. Where does the man need more light?
    (A) On his desk.
    (B) By the file cabinet.
    (C) On a dark ramp.
    (D) By his reading chair.

59. What kind of paper will the woman buy?
    (A) A local paper.
    (B) A morning paper.
    (C) An evening paper.
    (D) A national paper.

60. Why are they going to be late?
    (A) They're tired.
    (B) They have a flat tire.
    (C) They tried to fix it.
    (D) They took too long to fix it.

61. What did the man give the woman?
    (A) A brochure.
    (B) A tour.
    (C) A guide.
    (D) An exhibit.

62. How does the clerk suggest sending the package?
    (A) One-day service.
    (B) Today's mail.
    (C) Two-day mail.
    (D) Regular delivery.

63. What does the woman want to discuss at the meeting?
    (A) Making new contacts.
    (B) The contract deadline.
    (C) Installing new phone lines.
    (D) The project timeline.

64. What should the man do when the client arrives?
    (A) Send him up.
    (B) Meet him.
    (C) Come downstairs.
    (D) Call the woman.

65. What are they discussing?
    (A) Their hobbies.
    (B) Their computers.
    (C) Their colleagues.
    (D) Their jobs.

66. What will the man take for his sales appointment?
    (A) Sample products.
    (B) A car.
    (C) A raincoat.
    (D) A videocassette.

67. What does the woman want to do?
    (A) Go to an exhibit.
    (B) Hear a concert.
    (C) Eat at a new restaurant.
    (D) Work overtime.

68. What is the problem?
    (A) The supplies haven't arrived.
    (B) The supplies were never ordered.
    (C) The supplies are always late.
    (D) The supplies weren't paid for.

69. What are people forgetting to do?
    (A) Use the dictionaries.
    (B) Borrow the dictionaries.
    (C) Lend the dictionaries.
    (D) Return the dictionaries.

70. What should the man do differently?
    (A) Be happy.
    (B) Get organized.
    (C) Learn to write a letter.
    (D) Make time for some fun.

71. When should job status reports be submitted?
    (A) On Mondays.
    (B) On Fridays.
    (C) As soon as they're ready.
    (D) Twice a week.

72. What are the speakers discussing?
    (A) Transportation cost.
    (B) Efficiency.
    (C) Transportation preferences.
    (D) Weather.

73. What mistake was made?
    (A) The sales figures are too low.
    (B) The total was wrong.
    (C) The check was for the wrong amount.
    (D) The figures should be faxed.

74. What are the speakers doing?
    (A) Preparing an exhibit.
    (B) Putting on a play.
    (C) Unlocking doors.
    (D) Having lunch.

75. What are the man and woman discussing?
    (A) The company.
    (B) The health club.
    (C) Her old office.
    (D) Her new office.

76. Why isn't the woman going to the cafeteria?
    (A) She's not having lunch.
    (B) She'll have dinner at 5:00.
    (C) She's got too much work to do.
    (D) She's going out for a sandwich.

77. What did the woman offer to do for the man?
    (A) Mail a letter.
    (B) Attend a meeting.
    (C) Take him home.
    (D) Type three letters.

GO ON TO THE NEXT PAGE

78. Why are the man and woman upset?
    (A) The restaurant is bad.
    (B) They can't come back to the restaurant.
    (C) They want to talk to the waiter.
    (D) They had to wait to get in.

79. What did the man forget?
    (A) His hat.
    (B) His son.
    (C) His eyeglasses.
    (D) His sunglasses.

80. Who is the man talking to?
    (A) A kitchen repair person.
    (B) A service station attendant.
    (C) A parking lot attendant.
    (D) A housekeeper.

Listen to Track 8 of compact disc 4 to hear the short talks for Part IV of Model Test 6.

Part IV: Short Talks

Directions: On the compact disc, you will hear a short talk. In your test book, you will see several questions on the talk and four possible answers. Choose the best answer to the question and fill in the corresponding oval on your answer sheet.

81. What does this service offer?
    (A) Categories.
    (B) News.
    (C) Codes.
    (D) Lists.

82. What do you do if you do not know the category code number?
    (A) Stay on the line.
    (B) Dial the operator.
    (C) Make up a number.
    (D) Press 1000.

83. What has this study found?
    (A) Secretaries are more efficient than managers.
    (B) Managers are more efficient than secretaries.
    (C) Secretaries ask managers for help.
    (D) Secretaries do too much work.

84. What do managers say?
    (A) Their secretaries are hard-working.
    (B) Secretaries take more time off.
    (C) Secretaries ease a manager's workload.
    (D) Secretaries have more work.

85. What is the fastest way to order over the phone?
    (A) Look through the catalogue.
    (B) Fill out the order form.
    (C) Give the item number.
    (D) Give them the page number.

86. What else should you have to complete the order?
    (A) A money order.
    (B) A check.
    (C) Cash.
    (D) A credit card.

87. What is this ad announcing?
    (A) Job openings.
    (B) Food service.
    (C) A new phone number.
    (D) A new restaurant.

88. What sort of experience should applicants have?
    (A) Experience with the public.
    (B) Sales experience.
    (C) Experience in food service.
    (D) Grocery store experience.

89. What weather condition will develop by noon?
    (A) Rain.
    (B) Snow.
    (C) Sleet.
    (D) Ice.

90. What problem can drivers expect tonight?
    (A) Icy roads.
    (B) Wet roads.
    (C) Low visibility.
    (D) Frozen engines.

GO ON TO THE NEXT PAGE

446   TOEIC MODEL TESTS

91. Where would you hear this announcement?
    (A) On an airplane.
    (B) On a bus.
    (C) On a train.
    (D) On a ship.

92. What should passengers do to prepare?
    (A) Pack their bags.
    (B) Secure their luggage.
    (C) Change their seats.
    (D) Get out their tickets.

93. Why should you go to this store?
    (A) The prices are low.
    (B) The quality is high.
    (C) The store is nearby.
    (D) They're having a sale.

94. What can you do if you need help?
    (A) Wait in line.
    (B) Consult their design specialist.
    (C) Go to another store.
    (D) Ask your boss.

95. What is wrong at the station?
    (A) The elevator is broken.
    (B) The escalator isn't working.
    (C) The stairway is closed.
    (D) The exits are blocked.

96. How has the problem been solved for passengers in need?
    (A) They can get a wheelchair.
    (B) They can take a taxi.
    (C) They can take a bus.
    (D) They can get a refund.

97. What does the announcer do at the end of the statement?
    (A) Thanks the passengers.
    (B) Apologizes to the passengers.
    (C) Warns the passengers.
    (D) Advises the passengers.

98. Why is there a higher demand than usual?
    (A) The weather is hot.
    (B) The weather is cold.
    (C) New equipment uses more energy.
    (D) High use of private autos in the city.

99. What is the public asked to do?
    (A) Use less power.
    (B) Take food to the poor.
    (C) Take people to the hospital.
    (D) Take public transportation.

100. What is the purpose of the announcement?
    (A) To warn.
    (B) To inform.
    (C) To chastise.
    (D) To request.

**This is the end of the Listening Comprehension portion of the test.
Turn to Part V in your test book.**

READING

In this section of the test, you will have the chance to show how well you understand written English. There are three parts to this section, with special directions for each part.

YOU WILL HAVE ONE HOUR AND FIFTEEN MINUTES TO COMPLETE PARTS V, VI, AND VII OF THE TEST.

Part V: Incomplete Sentences

<u>Directions</u>: In your test book, you will see a sentence with a missing word. Four possible answers follow the sentence. Choose the best answer to the question and fill in the corresponding oval on your answer sheet.

---

101. The price of all cruises _____ airfare and all transfers.
    (A) to include
    (B) includes
    (C) including
    (D) include

102. Mr. Brett missed the plane _____ he was working late.
    (A) after
    (B) until
    (C) because
    (D) and

103. Many customers have requested that they _____ notice of our sales.
    (A) receive
    (B) receives
    (C) received
    (D) receiving

104. The workers were loading the truck when the boxes _____.
    (A) has fallen
    (B) falls
    (C) fell
    (D) is falling

105. The new manager, _____ was just hired, will start tomorrow.
    (A) she
    (B) he
    (C) which
    (D) who

GO ON TO THE NEXT PAGE

106. Mr. Kumar _____ if he had been delayed.
    (A) would call
    (B) would have called
    (C) will be calling
    (D) will calling

107. Our _____ are trying to hire our best employees.
    (A) competition
    (B) competitive
    (C) competitors
    (D) competitively

108. Of all tour ships, this is our _____.
    (A) more bigger
    (B) big
    (C) bigger
    (D) biggest

109. The purser got his assistant _____ the passenger orientation.
    (A) conducting
    (B) to conduct
    (C) conducted
    (D) conducts

110. All travel arrangements must be completed _____ December 5.
    (A) with
    (B) in
    (C) for
    (D) by

111. The bookcase is _____ the door.
    (A) beside
    (B) among
    (C) between
    (D) across

112. Ms. Mosley is _____ member of our advertising team.
    (A) creative
    (B) most creative
    (C) more creative
    (D) the most creative

113. Meetings are scheduled _____ in the first floor auditorium.
    (A) always
    (B) sometimes
    (C) rarely
    (D) every month

114. _____ 5:00, the subway becomes very crowded.
    (A) When
    (B) After
    (C) Since
    (D) Until

115. The airport was _____ Mr. Debionne had expected.
    (A) the busiest
    (B) busier than
    (C) busy as
    (D) as busy

116. A good chef is always ready to _____ recipes.
    (A) adapt
    (B) adoption
    (C) adept
    (D) adjourn

117. The personnel director screened the job applicants _____ arranging interviews.
    (A) because
    (B) until
    (C) since
    (D) before

118. The board of directors will meet _____ October 10.
    (A) for
    (B) to
    (C) on
    (D) in

119. Ms. Nyen was giving her speech when the microphone _____.
    (A) is failing
    (B) fails
    (C) had failed
    (D) failed

120. The clerk _____ the computer manual from the secretary.
    (A) lent
    (B) to loan
    (C) loaned
    (D) borrowed

121. The status report _____ the financial projections were both late.
    (A) or
    (B) and
    (C) but
    (D) nor

122. A firm will not _____ if its employees are unhappy.
    (A) prosper
    (B) prosperous
    (C) prosperity
    (D) prospering

123. The intern _____ a fax machine before.
    (A) had used never
    (B) had never used
    (C) never had used
    (D) used had never

124. If there _____ some restaurants near the hotel, the tourist would not have to take taxis.
    (A) were
    (B) was
    (C) will be
    (D) would be

125. Mid America Airlines's flight _____ Phoenix arrives at Gate 9.
    (A) from
    (B) in
    (C) by
    (D) on

126. In the mornings the kitchen staff turns on the ovens and _____ coffee.
    (A) brewing
    (B) brew
    (C) brews
    (D) brewed

127. The _____ speech made the audience restless.
    (A) boring
    (B) bored
    (C) bores
    (D) bore

128. This year the annual meeting takes place _____ Toronto.
    (A) on
    (B) for
    (C) by
    (D) in

129. _____ we were late, we could not enter the conference hall.
    (A) Although
    (B) Because
    (C) Therefore
    (D) However

130. If the traffic is bad, _____ a bus.
    (A) take
    (B) takes
    (C) taking
    (D) will take

131. If I _____ you, I would send the contract by courier.
    (A) am
    (B) is
    (C) was
    (D) were

132. Please use the parking spaces _____ for visitors.
    (A) be designating
    (B) are designating
    (C) were designated
    (D) designated

133. Participants _____ fly to the convention can get a group rate.
    (A) they
    (B) who
    (C) which
    (D) whom

134. The department requires someone with computer _____ .
    (A) exploration
    (B) experience
    (C) explanatory
    (D) expectant

GO ON TO THE NEXT PAGE

135. If the smoke alarm rings, _____ the building quickly.
    (A) leaves
    (B) will leave
    (C) is leaving
    (D) leave

136. Pens and stationery _____ kept in the top drawer.
    (A) are
    (B) is
    (C) was
    (D) am

137. The chief engineer is knowledgeable and _____.
    (A) industrious
    (B) industry
    (C) industrial
    (D) industries

138. Ms. Neil _____ the general manager of the hotel since 1994.
    (A) has
    (B) has been
    (C) had been
    (D) had

139. The message is _____ Mr. Moriwaki's answering machine.
    (A) in
    (B) of
    (C) on
    (D) to

140. Mr. Ross got the graphics department _____ the charts.
    (A) to prepare
    (B) preparing
    (C) prepare
    (D) prepared

Part VI: Error Recognition

Directions: In your test book, you will see a sentence with four words or phrases underlined. Choose the word or phrase that is incorrect and fill in the corresponding oval on your answer sheet.

141. Our company is <u>most responsible</u> than
                        A
 theirs in <u>providing</u> additional services
             B
 <u>after</u> <u>making</u> a sale.
    C   D

142. The person <u>whom</u> lost <u>a</u> briefcase may
                   A   B
 claim <u>it</u> <u>at</u> the registration desk.
        C D

143. <u>The new employee</u> is <u>as eager</u> her boss
        A   B
 <u>to be part</u> <u>of</u> the development project.
      C   D

144. <u>When</u> the client finally <u>arrived</u>, Mr.
      A   B
 Speroni <u>has been</u> waiting <u>for</u> two hours.
           C   D

145. <u>Many</u> subscribers request <u>that</u> the orders
       A   B
 <u>are</u> sent to their <u>business address</u>.
    C   D

146. The <u>enclosing</u> card <u>gives</u> details <u>about</u>
          A   B   C
 room rates and <u>services</u>.
              D

147. The Nall Corporation <u>has been</u> a <u>valued</u>
                      A   B
 client <u>of</u> our law firm <u>in many years</u>.
       C   D

148. The construction crew <u>prepared</u> to start
                      A
 work <u>on Monday</u> <u>when</u> the building
       B   C
 project was <u>canceled</u>.
             D

149. <u>If</u> Ms. Weiss has missed the <u>last flight</u>, she
    A   B
 <u>could not</u> get another <u>until</u> tomorrow
      C   D
 morning.

GO ON TO THE NEXT PAGE

150. The standing committee suggested to hire an
    A   B
    outside consultant as advisor to the
                      C   D
    project.

151. Mr. Burks did not accept the job offer
                 A   B
    from Consolidated Mechanical although
                                 C
    the salary was too low.
                   D

152. A small service fee but monthly monitoring
     A   B   C
    charge will be added to your account.
                    D

153. Mr. Wang reviews once a week the
              A   B
    progress of the long-range planning
             C   D
    committee.

154. The sales representative suggested
    to leave early so they could avoid rush-
    A   B   C
    hour traffic altogether.
                 D

155. The report that you are looking for it is
                A   B
    on top of the file cabinet in the corner.
    C   D

156. Seldom Ms. Ericson leaves work before
     A   B
    all members of her staff are gone
                              C
    for the day.
    D

157. Give your name nor the name of the
                    A   B
    person you are seeing to the receptionist
                         C
    at the front desk.
    D

158. A printed brochure makes a good
       A   B
    impression than a brochure that is merely
               C   D
    typed.

159. The stockholders' meeting will take place
    on Tuesday in Atlanta at 9:00 of the
    A   B   C   D
    morning.

160. The board members discussed to delay
                A   B
    construction of the main office until the
                                   C
    highway is completed.
            D

Part VII: Reading Comprehension

Directions: In your test book, you will see a reading passage followed by several questions. Each question has four answer choices. Choose the best answer to the question and fill in the corresponding oval on your answer sheet.

Questions 161–163 refer to the following magazine article.

Hints for the Business Traveler

If you do a lot of business traveling, sooner or later you will need ground transportation. For trips that are too short for a rental car and too long for a taxi, it makes sense to hire a car service. Such services are often called limousine services. They operate in large cities and in small ones, and even in rural areas where there are few airports or major transportation centers.

161. Why would you want to hire a car service?
 (A) You need ground transportation.
 (B) You can't take a taxi or rental car.
 (C) It's less expensive.
 (D) You are in a large city.

162. What is another name for a car service?
 (A) Ground transportation service
 (B) Taxicab service
 (C) Limousine service
 (D) Airport service

163. According to this notice, who should hire a car service?
 (A) People whose flights are late
 (B) People whose flights are early
 (C) People on leisure trips
 (D) People on business trips

GO ON TO THE NEXT PAGE

Questions 164–165 refer to the following form.

IMMEDIATELY

Fill out this card and mail it to the businesses and publications who send you mail.

Your Name: John Carpenter

Old address: 268 Monroe Highway (Number and Street)
Salem, (City) South Carolina (State) 29702 (Zip Code)

New address: 764 Alston Street (Number and Street)
Columbia, (City) South Carolina (State) 29805 (Zip Code)

New address effective immediately

Signature: John Carpenter

164. Why would you send this card to a business?
 (A) To get their new address
 (B) To give them your new address
 (C) To find out where they are located
 (D) To send mail to someone else

165. When should the business start sending mail to the new address?
 (A) When they receive further notice
 (B) When they get the card
 (C) When the subscription starts
 (D) At the end of the year

Questions 166–167 refer to the following report.

> Tarstan, Inc., earned $8 million in the fourth quarter, after a significant loss the previous year. This verifies an impressive comeback for the country's oldest home-appliance manufacturer. For all of this year, Tarstan earned $24.7 million, compared with a loss of $4.2 million last year.

166. During what period did Trastan earn $8 million?
    (A) Last year
    (B) This year
    (C) The first half of the year
    (D) The last quarter of the year

167. Compared to last year, how did Trastan perform this year?
    (A) Poorly
    (B) Comparably
    (C) Somewhat better
    (D) Impressively

Questions 168–169 refer to the following advertisement.

> Now, When You Purchase A Wizard Foreign Language Program, We'll Send You
> **A FREE GIFT!**
>
> Order a full Wizard Language Program and we'll send you a portable stereo cassette player *absolutely free*. A great way to learn a new language and a fully portable way to take your lessons wherever you go.
>
> What a great way to enjoy your new language! So, order now. (Retail value $29.95)
>
> **Call 1-800-555-4980**

168. What is being offered?
    (A) A foreign language textbook
    (B) Language tapes
    (C) A cassette player
    (D) Trial materials

169. How can you get the promotional item?
    (A) Pay $29.95.
    (B) Send in a card.
    (C) Take a class.
    (D) Buy a language program.

GO ON TO THE NEXT PAGE

Questions 170–172 refer to the following advertisement.

> The City Convention Center is looking for an assistant convention coordinator. Duties include organizing exhibit and meeting space for upcoming conventions, overseeing exhibit set-up, and coordinating audio-visual requests of participants. If you are good with details, enjoy people, and don't want to sit behind a desk, this job is for you. Come by City Hall, Room 203, for an application.

170. What is NOT mentioned as the duties of the assistant?
    (A) Arranging travel
    (B) Organizing exhibit space
    (C) Supervising set-up
    (D) Handling audio-visual requests

171. What kind of person would like this job?
    (A) Someone who prefers to work alone
    (B) Someone who works well with people
    (C) Someone who likes a quiet atmosphere
    (D) Someone who hates details

172. How would you apply for this job?
    (A) Write a letter
    (B) Submit a resume
    (C) Get an application at City Hall
    (D) Call the Convention Center

Questions 173–175 refer to the following announcement.

LEGAL EDUCATION SEMINARS PRESENTS . . .

WORKERS' COMPENSATION:
Issues & Strategies

Thursday, February 1, 1999
The Platinum Hotel
Oklahoma, Nebraska

Our experienced faculty will

- alert you to key changes in legislation, regulations, and case law
- take you from the basics through advanced areas of Workers' Compensation law
- show you how to anticipate new trends in defense
- give you many practical strategies

---

173. Who would be likely to attend this seminar?
    (A) Workers
    (B) Legislators
    (C) Lawyers
    (D) Doctors

174. What will be taught?
    (A) Information about payment to injured workers
    (B) How employment and hiring laws are made
    (C) How to strategize to keep employees healthy
    (D) Ways to communicate with employees

175. What else can you learn?
    (A) Arguments being used by the defense
    (B) How to influence the law
    (C) How to advance your career
    (D) Where to practice your new skills

Questions 176–178 refer to the following advertisement.

The Office Writer's Handbook

is a necessary reference work for anyone who has to write for business purposes. It states the rules of English grammar accurately and clearly, and shows you how to apply them to your writing. It also gives approved formats for business letters, reports, and even charts. A special section covers the most common writing mistakes and how to avoid them.

176. Who would likely NOT use this book?
 (A) Students
 (B) Reservation agents
 (C) Hotel managers
 (D) Airline executives

177. How does this book describe the rules of English grammar?
 (A) Clearly and correctly
 (B) Slowly and carefully
 (C) Quickly and easily
 (D) In great detail

178. What material is covered in the special section?
 (A) Sample charts
 (B) Writing formats
 (C) Sample business letters
 (D) Common mistakes

Questions 179–181 refer to the following letter.

Gardens by Hok
PO Box 687
1103 Lisbon, Portugal
September 8, 19___

Guy Williams
Landscape Design Magazine
Ottho Heldringstraat 2
1066 AZ Amsterdam
The Netherlands

Dear Mr. Williams:

Thank you for sending the advertising information. We have decided not to place an ad in the December issue, but we will consider placing one in the next issue in March.
We will be in touch. Again thank you for your assistance.

Sincerely yours,

Sov Hok
Landscape Architect

179. What is Sov Hok's business?
    (A) Designing skyscrapers
    (B) Designing gardens
    (C) Selling advertising
    (D) Marketing

180. Why did Mr. Hok write this letter?
    (A) To ask Mr. Williams for a subscription
    (B) To get a job
    (C) To place an ad in December
    (D) To say he wasn't interested in placing an ad now

181. How often does the magazine come out?
    (A) Weekly
    (B) Monthly
    (C) Bi-monthly
    (D) Quarterly

Questions 182–184 refer to the following report.

Food products account for the largest portion of our agricultural exports, although it is traditionally thought that pesticides and other agricultural chemicals are in the lead. The value of food product exports has increased in recent years with the increased interest among consumers in more exotic food products. Our growers have responded to the demand and we have established one million hectares as a special development region for these products. Our low night-time temperatures, combined with the fact that we have little rain and plenty of sun in the daytime, gives us a competitive edge over growers in other regions.

Our exports of native tropical fruits and root vegetables have increased from less than 2% to more than 5% of total agricultural exports in the past two years, and growth is expected to continue. But we continue to anticipate new food trends and will be ready to respond as the market changes.

182. What is exported the most?
 (A) Pesticides
 (B) Fibers
 (C) Foods
 (D) Chemicals

183. Why has the value of their food product exports increased?
 (A) Increased interest in unfamiliar foods
 (B) Drought in other countries
 (C) Higher prices
 (D) Consumers who are willing to spend more

184. What trend do they expect to continue?
 (A) Regulations on agricultural exports
 (B) High demand for exotic fruits and root vegetables
 (C) High prices for foods
 (D) Desire to produce more

Questions 185–187 refer to the following form.

ARRIVAL FORM

Family Name: Manov
Given Name: Krasemir
Country of Citizenship: Bulgaria
Passport Number: 749 27156301
Country Where You Live: Bulgaria

Birth Date: 6-19-53
Sex: Male
Airline and Flight: Atlantic Airlines 651
Where Boarded: Sofia
Purpose of Travel: Pleasure

185. What country is Manov a citizen of?
   (A) Bosnia
   (B) Bulgaria
   (C) Hungary
   (D) Bolivia

186. What is his first name?
   (A) Krasemir
   (B) Manov
   (C) Sofia
   (D) Pleasure

187. Why is he traveling?
   (A) He is on a business trip.
   (B) He is visiting relatives.
   (C) He is studying the country.
   (D) He is on vacation.

GO ON TO THE NEXT PAGE

Questions 188–192 refer to the following magazine article.

Business travelers usually find they have little time to exercise, especially when their schedules are suddenly changed by late meetings or late flights. But everyone should get some exercise. There are ways to make exercise part of your day, even when you cannot make it to the hotel's exercise room. Experts suggest stretching your neck, arms, back, and shoulders while sitting in your airplane seat. At your hotel, you can stretch your legs and abdominal muscles. Then, you can run in place for a good aerobic workout.

Exercise is not just for your body; it is for your mind as well. The mind-body connection has long been established by professional medical associations. People who exercise regularly perform more efficiently at work and perform more effectively than their colleagues who don't exercise. So to get ahead of everyone else, try to exercise every day, even when traveling.

188. Who would be likely to read this article?
(A) Overweight people
(B) Frequent vacation-goers
(C) Businesspeople who take trips
(D) Pilots and flight attendants

189. Why is it difficult for travelers to get exercise?
(A) Their schedules may change unexpectedly.
(B) They work too hard.
(C) There are no places to exercise.
(D) They don't want to exercise.

190. Where can you exercise if you can't go to the exercise room?
(A) In your meetings
(B) In your airplane seat
(C) In your car
(D) On the bus

191. How can you get aerobic exercise in the hotel?
(A) Take the stairs.
(B) Work your abdomen.
(C) Stretch your arms.
(D) Run in place.

192. According to the report, why should one exercise?
(A) To perform better at work
(B) To lose weight
(C) To feel younger
(D) To be better at sports

Questions 193–195 refer to the following introduction.

> Darla K. Wise received her B.A. degree from Arizona State University in 1980 and her Doctorate of Jurisprudence from Harvard University in 1987.
>
> She represented self-insured employers in Central New York for five years before joining the law firm of Corman, Hagan, Wallis and White, where she has been a principal since 1990. Her practice emphasizes the representation of corporate interests in libel suits.
>
> Ms. Wise is a member of the New York Bar Association and the New York Trial Lawyers Association.
>
> This continuing education foundation of the New York Bar Association is pleased to have Ms. Wise speak to us today.

193. What does Darla do for a living?
    (A) She's a lawyer.
    (B) She's a professor.
    (C) She's an employee of the New York Bar Association.
    (D) She's a bar and restaurant manager.

194. What is her highest educational achievement?
    (A) A bachelor's degree
    (B) A master's degree
    (C) A certificate from the New York Trial Lawyers Association
    (D) A doctorate

195. What is her main focus in her work?
    (A) Personal injury
    (B) Corporate defense
    (C) Divorce
    (D) Education

GO ON TO THE NEXT PAGE

Questions 196–200 refer to the following fax.

```
Fax Transmission

KleanIt
Bravo Murillo, 320
Portal 4-2,
28020 Madrid
Spain

Dear fellow computer user:

A word of advice—It's time to clean out your computer. If you're
like me, you do not remove documents that are no longer necessary
from your computer. You never know when you may need a file so you
don't throw it away, right? Electronic mail messages pile up, too,
creating a huge warehouse of obscure file names.

I found that a simple software package called KleanIt gets rid of
everything I don't need and keeps the things I do. I was so
impressed with this package that I decided to share it with others.

No longer do those bothersome extra messages and computer files
waste processing time and cause my computer to perform
inefficiently. KleanIt makes sure that the only files in my
computer are files that relate to my current projects or routine
tasks.

Why don't you try it? I'll send you a trial copy and if you aren't
satisfied, send it back. If you are, and you will be, send your
check for $32.50 at your earliest convenience.

Have a nice day.

Robert Horstma
Robert Horstma
CEO
```

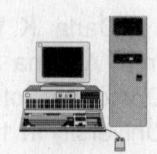

196. According to the fax, what prompted Mr. Horsta to sell KleanIt?
    (A) His e-mail responses
    (B) His poor computer skills
    (C) His need for money
    (D) His satisfaction with the product

197. What suggestion is made in this letter?
    (A) To buy new computers
    (B) To send less mail
    (C) To print out documents
    (D) To purchase new software

198. Besides documents, what else clutters memory on most computers?
    (A) Operating instructions
    (B) Help files
    (C) Electronic mail messages
    (D) Directories

199. What effect does clutter have on a computer?
    (A) The computer operates slowly.
    (B) The computer runs out of space.
    (C) The computer stops working.
    (D) The computer erases files.

200. Which documents should be in your computer?
    (A) Duplicate files
    (B) Current and routine files
    (C) Files from last year
    (D) Files others have sent you

STOP!

This is the end of the test. If you finish before time is called, you may go back to Parts V, VI, VII and check your work.

5

ANSWER KEYS FOR THE TOEIC REVIEW EXERCISES, MINI-TESTS, AND MODEL TESTS

WHAT TO LOOK FOR IN THIS CHAPTER
- Answer Key for Listening Comprehension Review
- Answer Key for Reading Review
- Answer Key for Model Tests 1–6

Answer Key for Listening Comprehension Review

PROBLEMS ANALYZING PICTURES

Problem	Part I
Problem 1 Making Assumptions	(B)
Problem 2 Identifying People	(A)
Problem 3 Identifying Things	(A)
Problem 4 Identifying Actions	(D)
Problem 5	(B)
Problem 6	(A)

PROBLEMS ANALYZING ANSWER CHOICES

Problem	Part I	Part II	Part III	Part IV
Problem 7 Similar Sounds	(D)	(A)	(D)	(C)
Problem 8 Related Words	(B)	(A)	(B)	(D)
Problem 9 Homonyms	(A)	(A)	(C)	(B)
Problem 10 Same Sound and Same Spelling But Different Meaning	(B)	(B)	(A)	(B)
Problem 11 Time	(A)	(A)	(A)	(C)
Problem 12 Negation	(C)	(A)	(A)	(A)
Problem 13 Word Order	(C)	(C)	(B)	(D)
Problem 14 Comparisons	(A)	(A)	(C)	(B)
Problem 15 Modals	(D)	(A)	(A)	(B)
Problem 16 Used to	(A)	(A)	(B)	(A)

PROBLEMS ANALYZING QUESTION TYPES

Problem	Part II	Part III	Part IV
Problem 17 Questions Asking About People	(A)	(B)	(B)
Problem 18 Questions Asking About Someone's Occupation	(A)	(D)	(A)
Problem 19 Questions Asking About the Speakers' Relationship	(B)	(C)	(A)
Problem 20 Questions Asking About a Location	(A)	(C)	(B)
Problem 21 Questions Asking About Time	(A)	(C)	(B)
Problem 22 Questions Asking About an Activity	(B)	(D)	(D)
Problem 23 Questions Asking About an Event or Fact	(A)	(A)	(C)
Problem 24 Questions Asking About an Emotion	(A)	(A)	(B)
Problem 25 Questions Asking About a Reason	(B)	(B)	(A)
Problem 26 Questions Asking About Measurement	(A)	(C)	(C)
Problem 27 Questions Asking About an Opinion	(A)	(B)	(D)
Problem 28 Asking About the Main Topic	(B)	(C)	(B)

PROBLEMS ANALYZING LANGUAGE FUNCTIONS

Problem	Part II	Part III	Part IV
Problem 29 Conditionals	(A)	(C)	(D)
Problem 30 Identifying Suggestions	(C)	(B)	(C)
Problem 31 Identifying Offers	(B)	(A)	(C)
Problem 32 Identifying Requests	(A)	(A)	(D)
Problem 33 Identifying Restatements		(A)	(B)

Answer Key for Mini-Test for Listening Comprehension Parts I, II, III, and IV

1. (A)
2. (C)
3. (D)
4. (A)
5. (A)
6. (D)
7. (A)
8. (B)
9. (D)
10. (A)

PART II: QUESTION-RESPONSE

11. (B)	14. (C)	17. (A)	20. (C)	23. (A)
12. (A)	15. (A)	18. (C)	21. (A)	24. (B)
13. (C)	16. (B)	19. (A)	22. (C)	25. (A)

PART III: SHORT CONVERSATIONS

26. (C)	29. (C)	32. (C)	35. (D)	38. (A)
27. (A)	30. (B)	33. (A)	36. (C)	39. (B)
28. (B)	31. (A)	34. (A)	37. (B)	40. (B)

PART IV: SHORT TALKS

41. (A)	43. (D)	45. (A)	47. (D)	49. (D)
42. (B)	44. (B)	46. (B)	48. (C)	50. (C)

Answer Key for Reading Review

PROBLEMS ANALYZING VOCABULARY

Prefixes and Suffixes

Problem	Part V	Part VI
Problem 1	(A)	(A)
Problem 2	(B)	(B)

Word Families and Similar Words

Problem	Part V	Part VI
Problem 3	(B)	(C) distribute
Problem 4	(D)	(C) advice

Cumulative Review Exercises

Part V	Part VI
1. (B) and (F)	1. (B) criticism
2. (C) and (G)	2. (C) economical
3. (B) and (F)	3. (B) managerial
4. (A) and (E)	4. (B) maintain
5. (C) and (H)	5. (B) nationally
6. (A)	6. (C) money
7. (B)	7. (B) earned
8. (A)	8. (A) effect
9. (C)	9. (B) extend, revise, or change
10. (D)	10. (A) borrow

PROBLEMS ANALYZING GRAMMAR

Count and Non-count Nouns

Problem	Part V	Part VI
Problem 5	(C)	(C) was
Problem 6	(A)	(C) light

Cumulative Review Exercises

Part V	Part VI
1. (B)	1. (B) is
2. (A)	2. (C) is
3. (A)	3. (A) is
4. (A)	4. (B) fruit
5. (B)	5. (B) is

Articles

Problem	Part V	Part VI
Problem 7	(D)	(B) the
Problem 8	(C)	(A) a
Problem 9	(C)	(A) Add A
Problem 10	(A)	(B) Delete a
Problem 11	(A)	(B) a uniform

Cumulative Review Exercises

Part V	Part VI
1. (C)	(C) Delete the
2. (A)	(A) an excellent
3. (B)	(A) The report
4. (A)	(B) a
5. (D)	(D) Delete a

Subject Verb Agreement

Problem	Part V	Part VI
Problem 12	(D)	(B) has
Problem 13	(B)	(B) are
Problem 14	(B)	(A) is

READING REVIEW 469

Cumulative Review Exercises

Part V	Part VI
1. (B)	(B) *are*
2. (C)	(B) *is going*
3. (A)	(D) *produces*
4. (A)	(C) *has*
5. (D)	(A) *are*

Prepositions

Problem	Part V	Part VI
Problem 15	(B)	(B) *to*
Problem 16	(C)	(B) *are having*

Cumulative Review Exercises

Part V	Part VI
1. (A)	(D) *in*
2. (D)	(D) *at*
3. (B)	(B) *from* or *for*
4. (B)	(A) *in*
5. (C)	(C) *on*

Coordinating Conjunctions

Problem	Part V	Part VI
Problem 17	(C)	(C) *or*
Problem 18	(C)	(D) *satisfaction*

Cumulative Review Exercises

Part V	Part VI
1. (C)	(C) *but*
2. (B)	(A) *seeing*
3. (A)	(B) *and*
4. (D)	(C) *or*
5. (A)	(C) *but*

Subordinating Conjunctions

Problem	Part V	Part VI
Problem 19	(D)	(B) *after*
Problem 20	(C)	(C) *even though* or *although*

Cumulative Review Exercises

Part V	Part VI
1. (B)	(C) *because* or *since*
2. (C)	(A) *although*
3. (C)	(B) *so*
4. (D)	(C) *until*
5. (B)	(B) Move *since* to the beginning of the subordinate clause.

Comparisons with Adjectives and Adverbs

Problem	Part V	Part VI
Problem 21	(B)	(C) *as good as*
Problem 22	(A)	(C) *more expensive than*
Problem 23	(D)	(B) *the most popular*

Cumulative Review Exercises

Part V	Part VI
1. (A)	(A) *larger*
2. (C)	(B) *as much as*
3. (D)	(B) *best*
4. (B)	(B) *most*
5. (C)	(B) *longer*

Adverbs of Frequency

Problem	Part V	Part VI
Problem 24	(C)	(B) Move *once a quarter* to the beginning or end of the sentence.
Problem 25	(A)	(B) Move *always* before *rings*.
Problem 26	(C)	(C) Move *always* after *are*.
Problem 27	(B)	(A) Move *never* after *has*.
Problem 28	(C)	(C) *always*

Cumulative Review Exercises

Part V	Part VI
1. (B)	(B) *is seldom distributed*
2. (B)	(D) Move *every quarter* to the beginning or end of the sentence.
3. (A)	(A) Move *always* to before *enjoys*.
4. (D)	(B) Move *twice a day* to the beginning or end of the sentence.
5. (D)	(B) Move *every six months* to the beginning or end of the sentence.

ANSWER KEY

Causative Verbs

Problem	Part V	Part VI
Problem 29	(A)	(B) *leave*
Problem 30	(B)	(D) *to work*
Problem 31	(A)	(B) *repaired*

Cumulative Review Exercises

Part V	Part VI
1. (A)	(B) *taken*
2. (D)	(B) *to help*
3. (C)	(C) *to leave*
4. (D)	(C) *ask*
5. (C)	(C) *changed*

Conditional Sentences

Problem	Part V	Part VI
Problem 32	(A)	(B) *leave*
Problem 33	(B)	(C) *drove*
Problem 34	(A)	(A) *were*

Cumulative Review Exercises

Part V	Part VI
1. (B)	(B) *were*
2. (B)	(C) *arrives*
3. (A)	(A) *lived*
4. (B)	(B) *had*
5. (A)	(C) *is*

Verb Tenses and Stative Verbs

Problem	Part V	Part VI
Problem 35	(D)	(D) *arrived*
Problem 36	(B)	(C) *appreciated*

Cumulative Review Exercises

Part V	Part VI
1. (B)	(A) *left*
2. (A)	(C) *found*
3. (D)	(A) *makes*
4. (B)	(A) *recognize*
5. (C)	(A) *is checking*

Relative Clauses

Problem	Part V	Part VI
Problem 37	(C)	(B) Omit *she*.
Problem 38	(A)	(A) *who*
Problem 39	(D)	(A) *that*

Cumulative Review Exercises

Part V	Part VI
1. (D)	(B) *who*
2. (D)	(A) *which*
3. (A)	(C) Omit *she*.
4. (D)	(A) *that*
5. (B)	(A) *whose*

Gerunds and Infinitives

Problem	Part V	Part VI
Problem 40	(B)	(B) *answering*

Cumulative Review Exercises

Part V	Part VI
1. (D)	(A) *to plan*
2. (A)	(C) *receiving*
3. (D)	(A) *to take*
4. (A)	(A) *illustrating*
5. (D)	(B) *to sign*

Participles

Problem	Part V	Part VI
Problem 41	(B)	(A) *surprising*

Cumulative Review Exercises

Part V	Part VI
1. (B)	(A) *typed*
2. (A)	(C) *smiling*
3. (C)	(A) *interested*
4. (B)	(D) *broken*
5. (D)	(A) *tired*

Answer Key for Mini-Test for Reading Parts V and VI

PART V

1. (C)	5. (B)	9. (A)	13. (C)	17. (B)
2. (D)	6. (A)	10. (C)	14. (B)	18. (B)
3. (A)	7. (D)	11. (A)	15. (D)	19. (C)
4. (D)	8. (C)	12. (C)	16. (C)	20. (D)

PART VI

21. (B)	23. (D)	25. (B)	27. (C)	29. (C)
22. (B)	24. (B)	26. (A)	28. (B)	30. (D)

PROBLEMS ANALYZING READING PASSAGES

Problem	Part VII			
Problem 42	1. (C)	2. (B)		
Problem 43	1. (D)	2. (B)	3. (B)	4. (C)
Problem 44	1. (C)	2. (D)	3. (A)	
Problem 45	1. (C)	2. (B)	3. (A)	
Problem 46	1. (B)	2. (B)	3. (A)	4. (D)
Problem 47	1. (B)	2. (A)	3. (B)	4. (D)
Problem 48	1. (A)	2. (D)	3. (B)	4. (B)
Problem 49	1. (A)	2. (B)		
Problem 50	1. (C)	2. (B)		
Problem 51	1. (B)	2. (D)		
Problem 52	1. (A)	2. (A)	3. (C)	4. (A)
Problem 53	1. (D)	2. (B)		
Problem 54	1. (D)	2. (D)	3. (B)	
Problem 55	1. (A)	2. (C)	3. (C)	
Problem 56	1. (B)	2. (D)	3. (C)	4. (D)
Problem 57	1. (A)	2. (B)	3. (C)	4. (A)

Answer Key for Mini-Test for Reading Part VII

PART VII

1. (D)	9. (C)	17. (A)	25. (C)	33. (C)
2. (B)	10. (A)	18. (C)	26. (B)	34. (A)
3. (B)	11. (C)	19. (D)	27. (C)	35. (A)
4. (A)	12. (B)	20. (C)	28. (A)	36. (C)
5. (A)	13. (C)	21. (C)	29. (B)	37. (D)
6. (D)	14. (C)	22. (C)	30. (B)	38. (C)
7. (C)	15. (A)	23. (A)	31. (D)	39. (B)
8. (B)	16. (A)	24. (A)	32. (C)	40. (C)

Answer Key for TOEIC Model Tests

MODEL TEST 1

Listening Comprehension

Part I: Picture

1. (B)	5. (B)	9. (D)	13. (C)	17. (C)
2. (C)	6. (C)	10. (C)	14. (A)	18. (B)
3. (A)	7. (D)	11. (A)	15. (B)	19. (A)
4. (D)	8. (A)	12. (C)	16. (D)	20. (D)

472 ANSWER KEY

PART II: QUESTION-RESPONSE
21. (B)
22. (A)
23. (B)
24. (C)
25. (A)
26. (A)
27. (A)
28. (C)
29. (A)
30. (C)
31. (B)
32. (A)
33. (C)
34. (B)
35. (C)
36. (A)
37. (C)
38. (B)
39. (B)
40. (C)
41. (B)
42. (A)
43. (C)
44. (B)
45. (A)
46. (C)
47. (A)
48. (B)
49. (C)
50. (A)

PART III: SHORT CONVERSATIONS
51. (C)
52. (A)
53. (D)
54. (A)
55. (C)
56. (B)
57. (C)
58. (A)
59. (B)
60. (C)
61. (D)
62. (A)
63. (D)
64. (B)
65. (C)
66. (D)
67. (A)
68. (B)
69. (D)
70. (A)
71. (B)
72. (D)
73. (C)
74. (C)
75. (A)
76. (D)
77. (B)
78. (C)
79. (A)
80. (B)

PART IV: SHORT TALKS
81. (A)
82. (C)
83. (B)
84. (C)
85. (D)
86. (A)
87. (B)
88. (D)
89. (C)
90. (A)
91. (C)
92. (B)
93. (A)
94. (B)
95. (C)
96. (D)
97. (A)
98. (A)
99. (D)
100. (B)

Reading

PART V: INCOMPLETE SENTENCES
101. (B)
102. (D)
103. (C)
104. (B)
105. (A)
106. (C)
107. (B)
108. (D)
109. (C)
110. (B)
111. (A)
112. (A)
113. (C)
114. (A)
115. (D)
116. (B)
117. (C)
118. (B)
119. (A)
120. (D)
121. (B)
122. (C)
123. (C)
124. (D)
125. (C)
126. (D)
127. (B)
128. (A)
129. (D)
130. (C)
131. (B)
132. (C)
133. (B)
134. (B)
135. (B)
136. (D)
137. (A)
138. (A)
139. (C)
140. (D)

PART VI: ERROR RECOGNITION
141. (A)
142. (D)
143. (B)
144. (C)
145. (C)
146. (B)
147. (D)
148. (C)
149. (D)
150. (B)
151. (A)
152. (C)
153. (C)
154. (C)
155. (D)
156. (A)
157. (A)
158. (C)
159. (D)
160. (A)

PART VII: READING COMPREHENSION
161. (D)
162. (A)
163. (B)
164. (C)
165. (B)
166. (D)
167. (A)
168. (B)
169. (A)
170. (D)
171. (B)
172. (B)
173. (D)
174. (C)
175. (C)
176. (B)
177. (B)
178. (B)
179. (A)
180. (A)
181. (A)
182. (B)
183. (D)
184. (A)
185. (D)
186. (C)
187. (B)
188. (A)
189. (D)
190. (B)
191. (D)
192. (D)
193. (B)
194. (A)
195. (C)
196. (D)
197. (B)
198. (A)
199. (D)
200. (C)

MODEL TEST 2

Listening Comprehension

Part I: Picture
1. (B)
2. (D)
3. (B)
4. (A)
5. (C)
6. (D)
7. (A)
8. (C)
9. (B)
10. (C)
11. (B)
12. (B)
13. (A)
14. (D)
15. (C)
16. (D)
17. (A)
18. (B)
19. (C)
20. (A)

Part II: Question-Response
21. (A)
22. (C)
23. (A)
24. (B)
25. (A)
26. (A)
27. (C)
28. (A)
29. (B)
30. (C)
31. (A)
32. (B)
33. (A)
34. (C)
35. (A)
36. (B)
37. (B)
38. (A)
39. (C)
40. (B)
41. (A)
42. (B)
43. (C)
44. (A)
45. (C)
46. (B)
47. (C)
48. (A)
49. (B)
50. (A)

Part III: Short Conversations
51. (B)
52. (C)
53. (C)
54. (C)
55. (A)
56. (C)
57. (B)
58. (A)
59. (D)
60. (A)
61. (A)
62. (D)
63. (B)
64. (C)
65. (C)
66. (A)
67. (D)
68. (B)
69. (C)
70. (C)
71. (D)
72. (B)
73. (D)
74. (C)
75. (D)
76. (B)
77. (C)
78. (B)
79. (A)
80. (B)

Part IV: Short Talks
81. (B)
82. (A)
83. (C)
84. (A)
85. (D)
86. (C)
87. (B)
88. (D)
89. (A)
90. (D)
91. (A)
92. (C)
93. (B)
94. (D)
95. (B)
96. (B)
97. (D)
98. (B)
99. (A)
100. (D)

Reading

Part V: Incomplete Sentences
101. (A)
102. (B)
103. (D)
104. (C)
105. (A)
106. (D)
107. (B)
108. (C)
109. (B)
110. (A)
111. (C)
112. (B)
113. (D)
114. (B)
115. (C)
116. (A)
117. (A)
118. (B)
119. (D)
120. (C)
121. (B)
122. (C)
123. (A)
124. (D)
125. (A)
126. (B)
127. (D)
128. (C)
129. (B)
130. (D)
131. (B)
132. (A)
133. (D)
134. (C)
135. (D)
136. (D)
137. (C)
138. (B)
139. (D)
140. (A)

Part VI: Error Recognition
141. (B)
142. (B)
143. (C)
144. (A)
145. (D)
146. (C)
147. (A)
148. (B)
149. (D)
150. (D)
151. (B)
152. (C)
153. (B)
154. (A)
155. (B)
156. (B)
157. (D)
158. (A)
159. (C)
160. (B)

Part VII: Reading Comprehension

161. (C)	169. (B)	177. (B)	185. (A)	193. (D)
162. (A)	170. (B)	178. (C)	186. (B)	194. (B)
163. (A)	171. (B)	179. (B)	187. (D)	195. (A)
164. (D)	172. (D)	180. (C)	188. (A)	196. (D)
165. (D)	173. (B)	181. (D)	189. (B)	197. (C)
166. (C)	174. (A)	182. (A)	190. (C)	198. (D)
167. (A)	175. (D)	183. (B)	191. (A)	199. (B)
168. (D)	176. (A)	184. (A)	192. (B)	200. (C)

MODEL TEST 3

Listening Comprehension

Part I: Picture
1. (C)	5. (B)	9. (C)	13. (B)	17. (B)
2. (D)	6. (C)	10. (B)	14. (B)	18. (C)
3. (D)	7. (D)	11. (D)	15. (A)	19. (A)
4. (A)	8. (A)	12. (A)	16. (A)	20. (A)

Part II: Question-Response
21. (A)	27. (A)	33. (B)	39. (A)	45. (B)
22. (C)	28. (C)	34. (A)	40. (A)	46. (A)
23. (B)	29. (A)	35. (C)	41. (C)	47. (B)
24. (B)	30. (C)	36. (B)	42. (B)	48. (C)
25. (A)	31. (C)	37. (C)	43. (A)	49. (A)
26. (C)	32. (A)	38. (A)	44. (C)	50. (A)

Part III: Short Conversations
51. (A)	57. (A)	63. (B)	69. (C)	75. (D)
52. (C)	58. (D)	64. (B)	70. (D)	76. (C)
53. (B)	59. (B)	65. (D)	71. (D)	77. (B)
54. (B)	60. (D)	66. (C)	72. (B)	78. (D)
55. (D)	61. (C)	67. (B)	73. (C)	79. (B)
56. (B)	62. (A)	68. (D)	74. (A)	80. (A)

Part IV: Short Talks
81. (B)	85. (A)	89. (C)	93. (B)	97. (C)
82. (C)	86. (B)	90. (B)	94. (C)	98. (D)
83. (C)	87. (D)	91. (B)	95. (B)	99. (B)
84. (A)	88. (A)	92. (D)	96. (D)	100. (A)

Reading

Part V: Incomplete Sentences
101. (C)	109. (C)	117. (B)	125. (D)	133. (A)
102. (B)	110. (D)	118. (C)	126. (C)	134. (B)
103. (A)	111. (B)	119. (A)	127. (D)	135. (C)
104. (D)	112. (A)	120. (D)	128. (A)	136. (D)
105. (C)	113. (B)	121. (C)	129. (C)	137. (B)
106. (D)	114. (A)	122. (A)	130. (B)	138. (C)
107. (B)	115. (C)	123. (B)	131. (D)	139. (B)
108. (A)	116. (D)	124. (A)	132. (C)	140. (D)

Part VI: Error Recognition

141. (C)	145. (B)	149. (C)	153. (B)	157. (C)
142. (B)	146. (A)	150. (A)	154. (B)	158. (D)
143. (B)	147. (A)	151. (B)	155. (B)	159. (A)
144. (A)	148. (B)	152. (A)	156. (B)	160. (B)

Part VII: Reading Comprehension

161. (D)	169. (C)	177. (D)	185. (A)	193. (D)
162. (D)	170. (D)	178. (B)	186. (D)	194. (C)
163. (B)	171. (D)	179. (C)	187. (B)	195. (D)
164. (C)	172. (D)	180. (B)	188. (A)	196. (B)
165. (A)	173. (A)	181. (C)	189. (C)	197. (C)
166. (C)	174. (C)	182. (C)	190. (B)	198. (A)
167. (B)	175. (B)	183. (A)	191. (D)	199. (D)
168. (B)	176. (A)	184. (B)	192. (C)	200. (A)

MODEL TEST 4

Listening Comprehension

Part I: Picture

1. (A)	5. (D)	9. (B)	13. (A)	17. (B)
2. (C)	6. (C)	10. (A)	14. (A)	18. (C)
3. (B)	7. (A)	11. (C)	15. (C)	19. (B)
4. (B)	8. (C)	12. (D)	16. (C)	20. (A)

Part II: Question-Response

21. (C)	27. (A)	33. (A)	39. (B)	45. (A)
22. (B)	28. (C)	34. (B)	40. (A)	46. (C)
23. (A)	29. (C)	35. (A)	41. (C)	47. (B)
24. (A)	30. (A)	36. (B)	42. (B)	48. (A)
25. (B)	31. (B)	37. (A)	43. (A)	49. (A)
26. (B)	32. (B)	38. (C)	44. (B)	50. (C)

Part III: Short Conversations

51. (C)	57. (D)	63. (B)	69. (C)	75. (D)
52. (A)	58. (A)	64. (A)	70. (A)	76. (B)
53. (D)	59. (D)	65. (D)	71. (D)	77. (C)
54. (B)	60. (C)	66. (C)	72. (C)	78. (A)
55. (C)	61. (B)	67. (A)	73. (D)	79. (A)
56. (B)	62. (C)	68. (D)	74. (D)	80. (C)

Part IV: Short Talks

81. (C)	85. (B)	89. (B)	93. (C)	97. (A)
82. (B)	86. (A)	90. (C)	94. (A)	98. (B)
83. (C)	87. (D)	91. (D)	95. (D)	99. (D)
84. (D)	88. (B)	92. (A)	96. (C)	100. (C)

Reading

Part V: Incomplete Sentences

101. (B)	109. (D)	117. (A)	125. (B)	133. (B)
102. (C)	110. (C)	118. (D)	126. (C)	134. (C)
103. (A)	111. (D)	119. (A)	127. (D)	135. (D)
104. (D)	112. (B)	120. (D)	128. (C)	136. (A)
105. (C)	113. (C)	121. (C)	129. (A)	137. (C)
106. (B)	114. (B)	122. (B)	130. (B)	138. (A)
107. (B)	115. (D)	123. (A)	131. (A)	139. (B)
108. (A)	116. (C)	124. (C)	132. (C)	140. (D)

Part VI: Error Recognition

141. (B)	145. (B)	149. (D)	153. (B)	157. (B)
142. (A)	146. (D)	150. (B)	154. (C)	158. (A)
143. (A)	147. (C)	151. (A)	155. (D)	159. (A)
144. (B)	148. (C)	152. (C)	156. (A)	160. (C)

Part VII: Reading Comprehension

161. (C)	169. (D)	177. (A)	185. (B)	193. (C)
162. (A)	170. (C)	178. (B)	186. (D)	194. (C)
163. (C)	171. (C)	179. (C)	187. (B)	195. (B)
164. (B)	172. (B)	180. (D)	188. (B)	196. (A)
165. (B)	173. (A)	181. (B)	189. (C)	197. (B)
166. (C)	174. (B)	182. (D)	190. (B)	198. (D)
167. (D)	175. (D)	183. (A)	191. (D)	199. (D)
168. (A)	176. (C)	184. (D)	192. (B)	200. (D)

MODEL TEST 5

Listening Comprehension

Part I: Picture

1. (C)	5. (A)	9. (C)	13. (A)	17. (B)
2. (A)	6. (D)	10. (C)	14. (C)	18. (A)
3. (B)	7. (B)	11. (B)	15. (D)	19. (C)
4. (D)	8. (A)	12. (D)	16. (A)	20. (A)

Part II: Question-Response

21. (A)	27. (B)	33. (A)	39. (A)	45. (C)
22. (B)	28. (C)	34. (A)	40. (A)	46. (B)
23. (B)	29. (C)	35. (B)	41. (B)	47. (A)
24. (A)	30. (A)	36. (C)	42. (C)	48. (B)
25. (B)	31. (B)	37. (A)	43. (B)	49. (A)
26. (C)	32. (C)	38. (B)	44. (A)	50. (B)

Part III: Short Conversations

51. (B)	57. (A)	63. (D)	69. (B)	75. (B)
52. (D)	58. (D)	64. (B)	70. (B)	76. (B)
53. (C)	59. (A)	65. (A)	71. (A)	77. (D)
54. (A)	60. (C)	66. (C)	72. (C)	78. (C)
55. (B)	61. (B)	67. (A)	73. (D)	79. (C)
56. (A)	62. (B)	68. (D)	74. (A)	80. (A)

Part IV: Short Talks

81. (A)	85. (B)	89. (A)	93. (B)	97. (A)
82. (D)	86. (C)	90. (B)	94. (C)	98. (A)
83. (B)	87. (B)	91. (A)	95. (D)	99. (C)
84. (A)	88. (A)	92. (D)	96. (C)	100. (D)

Reading

Part V: Incomplete Sentences

101. (A)	109. (B)	117. (B)	125. (A)	133. (B)
102. (C)	110. (A)	118. (B)	126. (C)	134. (B)
103. (B)	111. (B)	119. (D)	127. (D)	135. (A)
104. (D)	112. (A)	120. (A)	128. (D)	136. (B)
105. (B)	113. (C)	121. (C)	129. (B)	137. (C)
106. (D)	114. (D)	122. (B)	130. (C)	138. (B)
107. (C)	115. (A)	123. (C)	131. (C)	139. (B)
108. (D)	116. (C)	124. (B)	132. (D)	140. (D)

Part VI: Error Recognition

141. (C)	145. (A)	149. (A)	153. (B)	157. (B)
142. (A)	146. (D)	150. (D)	154. (C)	158. (D)
143. (C)	147. (A)	151. (B)	155. (A)	159. (A)
144. (B)	148. (B)	152. (A)	156. (C)	160. (B)

Part VII: Reading Comprehension

161. (A)	169. (C)	177. (D)	185. (C)	193. (A)
162. (B)	170. (B)	178. (C)	186. (D)	194. (B)
163. (C)	171. (D)	179. (D)	187. (C)	195. (D)
164. (D)	172. (C)	180. (C)	188. (C)	196. (A)
165. (A)	173. (A)	181. (B)	189. (B)	197. (B)
166. (C)	174. (A)	182. (B)	190. (A)	198. (A)
167. (B)	175. (B)	183. (A)	191. (B)	199. (C)
168. (D)	176. (C)	184. (B)	192. (D)	200. (A)

MODEL TEST 6

Listening Comprehension

Part I: Picture

1. (A)	5. (D)	9. (D)	13. (A)	17. (C)
2. (C)	6. (A)	10. (B)	14. (A)	18. (A)
3. (A)	7. (A)	11. (A)	15. (D)	19. (B)
4. (B)	8. (C)	12. (C)	16. (B)	20. (D)

Part II: Question-Response

21. (A)	27. (A)	33. (C)	39. (C)	45. (B)
22. (C)	28. (A)	34. (A)	40. (C)	46. (A)
23. (A)	29. (B)	35. (A)	41. (A)	47. (C)
24. (B)	30. (C)	36. (B)	42. (B)	48. (A)
25. (C)	31. (B)	37. (C)	43. (A)	49. (B)
26. (B)	32. (C)	38. (B)	44. (C)	50. (C)

Part III: Short Conversations

51. (D)	57. (D)	63. (B)	69. (D)	75. (D)
52. (B)	58. (B)	64. (D)	70. (B)	76. (C)
53. (C)	59. (D)	65. (D)	71. (A)	77. (A)
54. (A)	60. (B)	66. (C)	72. (C)	78. (A)
55. (A)	61. (A)	67. (B)	73. (B)	79. (D)
56. (C)	62. (C)	68. (A)	74. (A)	80. (B)

Part IV: Short Talks

81. (B)	85. (B)	89. (B)	93. (A)	97. (B)
82. (D)	86. (D)	90. (C)	94. (B)	98. (B)
83. (A)	87. (A)	91. (A)	95. (A)	99. (A)
84. (C)	88. (C)	92. (B)	96. (C)	100. (D)

Reading

Part V: Incomplete Sentences

101. (B)	109. (B)	117. (D)	125. (A)	133. (B)
102. (C)	110. (D)	118. (C)	126. (C)	134. (B)
103. (A)	111. (A)	119. (D)	127. (A)	135. (D)
104. (C)	112. (D)	120. (D)	128. (D)	136. (A)
105. (D)	113. (D)	121. (B)	129. (B)	137. (A)
106. (B)	114. (B)	122. (A)	130. (A)	138. (B)
107. (C)	115. (B)	123. (B)	131. (D)	139. (C)
108. (D)	116. (A)	124. (A)	132. (D)	140. (A)

Part VI: Error Recognition

141. (A)	145. (C)	149. (C)	153. (B)	157. (A)
142. (A)	146. (A)	150. (B)	154. (A)	158. (B)
143. (B)	147. (D)	151. (C)	155. (B)	159. (D)
144. (C)	148. (A)	152. (B)	156. (A)	160. (B)

Part VII: Reading Comprehension

161. (B)	169. (D)	177. (A)	185. (B)	193. (A)
162. (C)	170. (A)	178. (D)	186. (A)	194. (D)
163. (D)	171. (B)	179. (B)	187. (D)	195. (B)
164. (B)	172. (C)	180. (D)	188. (C)	196. (D)
165. (B)	173. (C)	181. (D)	189. (A)	197. (D)
166. (D)	174. (A)	182. (C)	190. (B)	198. (C)
167. (D)	175. (A)	183. (A)	191. (D)	199. (A)
168. (C)	176. (A)	184. (B)	192. (A)	200. (B)

6

EXPLANATORY ANSWERS FOR THE TOEIC REVIEW EXERCISES, MINI-TESTS, AND MODEL TESTS

WHAT TO LOOK FOR IN THIS CHAPTER
- Explanatory Answers for Listening Comprehension Review
- Explanatory Answers for Reading Review
- Explanatory Answers for Model Tests 1–6

Explanatory Answers for Listening Comprehension Review

Problems Analyzing Pictures

Making Assumptions
Problem 1
(B) In Choice (B) you can assume from the context that the people in white laboratory coats are technicians and that they could be doing experiments. Choice (A) is incorrect because the picture shows several people who could be pharmacists but none who could be customers. Choice (C) is incorrect because there are no laboratory animals pictured. Choice (D) is incorrect because the shelves contain bottles, jars and supplies.

Identifying People
Problem 2
(A) Choice (A) correctly identifies the number and activity of the people. Choice (B) is incorrect because the men are in shirt sleeves. Choice (C) is incorrect because one woman is not as tall as the men. Choice (D) is incorrect because one of the women is pointing to the map.

Identifying Things
Problem 3
(A) Choice (A) correctly identifies the location of the people (the floor), who they are (the children), and their activity (playing). Choice (B) is incorrect because the television is on. Choice (C) is incorrect because the mother is playing the piano. Choice (D) is incorrect because the curtains are shut.

Identifying Actions
Problem 4
(D) Choice (D) correctly describes what the people (workers) are doing (laying pipeline). Choice (A) is incorrect because the men are *laying pipe*, not *smoking pipes*. Choice (B) identifies an incorrect action. Choice (C) identifies a *previous* action.

Identifying General Locations
Problem 5
(B) Choice (B) assumes that the people are passengers and are passing through a security checkpoint. Choice (A) incorrectly identifies the scene as a store. Choice (C) incorrectly identifies the scene as a bank. Choice (D) takes place on the plane, not at airport security.

Identifying Specific Locations
Problem 6
(A) Choice (A) correctly identifies the specific location of the waiters. Choice (B) incorrectly identifies the location of the man; he is *across* from the woman. Choice (C) incorrectly identifies the location of the bottle; it's *on* the table. Choice (D) incorrectly identifies the location of the other table; it's *behind* the first table, so the people are also *behind* the first table.

Problems Analyzing Answer Choices

Similar Sounds
Problem 7

I **(D)** Choice (D) is correct because the other choices do not match the picture. Choice (A) has similar sounds: *fair/air* and *night/flight*. Choice (B) has similar sounds: *plane/train*. Choice (C) has similar sounds: *car door/cargo*. Listen for the meaning of the whole sentence; note the context clues in the picture.

II **(A)** Choice (A) answers the *yes/no* question with *Yes*. Choice (B) has related words: *delivery/truck* and similar sounds: *letter/ladder, delivered/delivery*. Choice (C) has similar sounds: *today/Tuesday*; *Was the/was he*. Listen for the whole meaning; note the grammar clue such as a *yes/no* question that begins with the auxiliary *was*.

III **(D)** *Sailing her boat* in Choice (D) matches the second line of the conversation: The woman is really having fun sailing her boat. Choice (A) has similar sounds: *boat/boots*. Choice (B) has similar sounds: *fun/phone*. Choice (C) has similar sounds: *selling/sailing*. Listen for the meaning of the whole conversation; note the context clues such as *boat* and *sailing*.

IV **(C)** Before shoppers leave the store, they must pass through the check-out counters to pay for their purchases. Choice (A) has similar sounds: *market/mark all*. Choice (B) has similar sounds: *closing/clothes*. Choice

(D) has similar sounds: *proceed/plant seed*. Listen for the meaning of the whole talk; note the context clues such as *shoppers*, *market*, *check-out*.

Related Words
Problem 8

I **(B)** The context clues in the picture indicate the people are engaged in skiing on a mountain. Choice (A) has the related words: *shoveling snow/snow*. Choice (C) has the related words: *iceberg/ice, cold*. Choice (D) has similar sounds: *skiers' poles/polls*. Listen for the meaning of the whole sentence; note the context clues in the picture.

II **(A)** Listen for the whole meaning; note the grammar clue: *How long* and the verb *married* suggests a length of time. Choice (A) gives the appropriate answer (ten years) to *how long*. Choice (B) has the related words: *long/five feet*, but the question refers to time, not distance. Choice (C) has the related words: *married/bride*.

III **(B)** Listen for the meaning of the whole conversation; note the context clues such as *seatbelt, to land*; and *in the air*. These words suggest air travel. Choice (A), a car, also has *seat belts*, but it does not agree with the context. Choice (C) has similar sounds: *seat* and *sea* and related words: *land* (v)/*land* (n). Choice (D) has the related word *bus* but does not fit the context.

IV **(D)** The correct answer is given in the first few words of the talk. Note the context clues such as *weather, weekend*, and *temperature*. Choice (A) has the related word *sporting*, but only *golf* is mentioned briefly. Choice (B) has related words: *chores/repairs*. Choice (C) has related words: *gardening/garden center*.

Homonyms
Problem 9

I **(A)** The location of the people and their movement suggests they are commuters, people who travel from home to work. We can assume they're in a hurry and rushing. Choice (B) has similar sounds: *train/trained*. Choice (C) has homonyms: *boarding* windows/*boarding* train. Choice (D) has homonyms: *stare/stairs*. Listen for the meaning of the whole sentence; note the context clues in the picture.

II **(A)** The tag question *doesn't he?* requires a *yes/no* answer. Choice (A) answers the question and tells when he will leave. Choice (B) has homonyms: *week/weak*. Choice (C) has homonyms: *leaves* (v)/*leaves* (n).

III **(C)** Listen for the meaning of the whole conversation; note the context clues such as *sew, button,* and *don't have time*. Choice (C) means the same as the man's excuse: *I don't have time now*. Choice (A) has homonyms *sew/sow* and similar sounds *to wait/too wet*. Choice (B) has homonyms: *time/thyme*. Choice (D) has homonyms: *for/four*.

IV **(B)** Listen for the meaning of the whole talk; note the context clues such as *sun, rain,* and *spring weather*. These clues indicate the weather. Choice (A) has homonyms: *weather/whether; by/buy; too/two* and similar sounds: *winds, too/windows*. Choice (C) has homonyms: *sun/son*. Choice (D) has homonyms: *rain/reign* and similar sounds *spring/king*.

Same Sound and Same Spelling But Different Meaning
Problem 10

I **(B)** The correct answer is (B), which describes a first-class airline cabin. In Choice (A) *class* means *instructional period*. In Choice (C) *class* means *socioeconomic level*. In Choice (D) *classified* means *restricted*.

II **(B)** The phrase in (B) *Not for me* is a *no* answer to the *yes/no* question. It means, *No, the bed is not too hard for me*. A *hard* bed is a *firm* bed. Choice (A) incorrectly interprets *hard* to mean *difficult*. In Choice (C) *bed* means *a place for flowers*.

III **(A)** The correct answer is (A). *To ring* someone is *to call* them on the phone. In Choice (B) *ring* means *jewelry*. The related word here *engagement* comes from the incorrect assumption that a *bachelor* may be getting engaged or married. Choice (C) has related words: *summer vacation*. Choice (D) repeats the word *call*, but does not fit the context of the conversation.

IV **(B)** The word *tennis* is the first word in the talk. There are other context clues such as *final match* and *championship match*. Choice (A) interprets *match* to mean *marriage* and suggests similar sounds: *Churchill/church*. Choice (C) confuses *dance club* with *golf club*. Choice (D) interprets *match* to mean *a light for a cigarette*.

Time
Problem 11
I **(A)** Choice (A) is the only sequence that makes sense. The sequence time marker in Choice (B) indicates the firefighters arrived first, and the fire started second. In Choice (C) the marker indicates they put away hoses first, and put the fire out second. In Choice (D) the marker indicates that the firefighters rested at the same time that the fire burned.

II **(A)** Only Choice (A) matches the tense of the question. The question is in the past tense. Choice (B) indicates future action. Choice (C) indicates action happening at the same time.

III **(A)** The decision was made *prior to their announcement*; only *before* means the same as *prior to*. Choice (B) indicates a time after. Choice (C) indicates a concurrent time. Choice (D) indicates a time after.

IV **(C)** The company merged with Rotel five years ago. At that time, Mr. Saleh became Chairman. Choice (A) confuses *retiring at the end of next* quarter with duration of office and does not use an appropriate time marker. Choice (B) indicates time with the company, not time as Chairman. Choice (D) indicates future action (happening at the same time as a future retirement).

Negation
Problem 12
I **(C)** Only Choice (C) matches the picture. The negative expressions in the other choices make the statements false. Choice (A) is incorrect because the seats *are* occupied. Choice (B) is incorrect because the men *are* sitting down. Choice (D) is incorrect because one person is wearing glasses.

II **(A)** A law-abiding citizen does not do anything illegal. Everything they do is legal because they obey the law. Choice (B) has negative/positive related words: *illegal/legal*. Choice (C) has negative terms with similar sounds: *illegal/illegible*.

III **(A)** In Choice (A), *You can never take too much* means *you should take a lot*. Choices (B) and (D) are contradicted by *I even have what I don't need*. Choice (C) is incorrect because she is *taking* what she needs, not *buying* it.

IV **(A)** All of the adjectives in the report are very positive. Choice (B) is incorrect because the adjectives in the report are positive, not negative. Choice (C) is incorrect because the report is *enthusiastic*, not *unenthusiastic*. Choice (D) is incorrect because the report is *positive*, not *mediocre*.

Word Order
Problem 13
I **(C)** Only Choice (C) matches the picture. Choice (A) reverses the subject and the verb, but there are no brochures in the picture. Choice (B) does not describe the picture. Choice (D) is contradicted by the picture.

II **(C)** *Nobody does as much as you* means *You do more than anybody else*. Choice (A) is almost a paraphrase, not a response. Choice (B) is not an appropriate response to a compliment.

III **(B)** *Isn't that great* means *that is really GREAT!* Choice (A) is incorrect because the speakers don't mention the length of the trip. Choice (C) is contradicted by *How I envy you!* Choice (D) is contradicted by *Isn't that great!*

IV **(D)** *It has never been so windy* means *it is very windy*. Choice (A) is contradicted by *How the weather changes!* Choice (B) is contradicted by *The temperature has fallen*. Choice (C) is contradicted by *It has never been so windy*.

Comparisons
Problem 14
I **(A)** The man on the right is trying on clothes to wear in extremely cold weather. Choice (B) is incorrect because only one man is wearing glasses. Choice (C) is incorrect because both have beards. Choice (D) is incorrect because one pair of pants is a dark shade and the other is a light shade.

484 EXPLANATORY ANSWERS

II **(A)** Choice (A) repeats the superlative *fastest* and provides an answer *a train*. Choice (B) has related words: *fastest/plane* and similar sounds: *home/Rome*, but does not answer the question. Choice (C) has similar sounds: *fastest/farther*, but does not answer the question.

III **(C)** The meeting was *the longest* and *the most boring*. Choice (A) is contradicted by *will never end, is longer than yesterday's,* and for being *the longest*. Choice (B) is incorrect because *the lecture has begun*. Choice (D) is contradicted by *will never end*.

IV **(B)** The better the roads, the more drivers there are. More drivers means more cars. Choice (A) is contradicted by *there never used to be as many cars* and *more people want to drive*. Choice (C) is contradicted by *the more cars there will be*. Choice (D) is contradicted by *as we improve the roads*.

Modals
Problem 15

I **(D)** We can assume that the people standing in line are waiting to check in. They *will* check in; they have not already checked in. Choice (A) is possible but it is not <u>directly</u> related to the picture and is not as accurate as (D). Choice (B) has the related phrase *check bags* but incorrectly places the action in the past. Choice (C) has the related word: *plane* but we cannot determine from the picture whether the plane is on time or not.

II **(A)** *I'd rather go* is a contraction for *I would rather go*. Therefore the answer *I would too* is correct. Choice (B) has similar sounds: *first class/first time*, but does not answer the question. Choice (C) has similar sounds: *economy/money*, but is not logical.

III **(A)** She was busy; she was NOT free (*if I had been free*). The reasons given in Choices (B), (C), and (D) are incorrect because the woman had other plans and was not free to attend the reception. Choice (C) has related words: *free/charge*. Choice (D) has similar sounds *free/fee*.

IV **(B)** The listeners felt *lost* during the presentation; they felt confused. Choice (A) is contradicted by *could have been more interesting*. Choice (C) is contradicted by *if the speakers had used some visuals*. Choice (D) is contradicted by *Colorful visuals...would have made it easier*.

Used to
Problem 16

I **(A)** We can assume that a professional kitchen is hot. People who work in such kitchens are chefs; they must be accustomed to the heat. Choice (B) has a related word, *cook*, but does not describe the picture. Choice (C) has related words: *pans* and *mix* but they refer to paint, not food. Choice (D) has the related word *food*, but does not describe the picture.

II **(A)** Since the person works at night, we assume he is accustomed to not sleeping much in the evening. Choice (B) suggests the speakers said *I used to work at night*. Choice (C) has the related words: *used to/used* and *night/days* but does not answer the question.

III **(B)** A *frequent speaker* is one who often gives presentations at conferences. Choices (A) and (C) are contradicted by *used to be a frequent speaker at conferences*. Choice (D) is contradicted by *anything people wanted to hear*.

IV **(A)** People used carbon paper to make copies before the photocopier was invented. In Choice (B), *as much* suggests frequency of writing, which is not mentioned. In Choice (C), *as well* suggests quality of typing, which is not mentioned. Choice (D) is contradicted by *We are now used to making many copies*.

Problems Analyzing Question Types

Questions Asking About People
Problem 17

II **(A)** Marketing Director is her title. Choice (B) incorrectly answers how long has she worked here. Choice (C) has similar words: *say/talk* and confuses *title* and *book*.

III **(B)** Listen for the context clues such as *sand, wall, first coat of paint,* and *mix the color*. Choice (A) suggests a related word for lifeguard: *sand* at the beach as opposed to the verb *to sand* a wall. Choice (C) has a word with the same sound but a different meaning: *coat of paint* (layer) and *coat* (clothing). Choice (D) has a related expression *to mix paints* (painters) and *to mix drinks* (bartenders).

IV **(B)** The general category that includes everyone is *airline passengers*. Look for the context clues: *flight attendants*, *cabin,* and *before we land*. Choices (A), (C), and (D) name people who might listen to the announcement, but *only if* they were passengers on the plane.

Questions Asking About Someone's Occupation
Problem 18
II **(A)** A housekeeper is usually responsible for towels and linens in a room. The occupations listed in (B) and (C) would not concern themselves with towels and linens.

III **(D)** Look for the context clues such as *put one in each room*, *wires along the baseboard*, and *phone rings*. Choice (A) confuses the meanings of *run wires/running* as in jogging. Choice (B) has similar sounds: *baseboard/baseball*. Choice (C) has related words: *phone rings/telephone operator*.

IV **(A)** Although all of the choices are related to food and eating, only a chef is an employee. Choices (B), (C), and (D) have related words but do not describe employees.

Questions Asking About the Speakers' Relationship
Problem 19
II **(B)** Browsing is the only possible option. The context clues of *Son* and *Father* suggest the speaker may be a woman and perhaps the boy's mother. Choice (A) does not answer the question. There is the similar sound of *do son* and *innocent*. Choice (C) does not match the tense of the question.

III **(C)** Look for the context clues: the polite *Would you like...*; *the check*; *pay at the cashier*. Choice (A) is suggested by related words like the banking terms *check* and *cashier*, but coffee is not served at a bank. Choice (B) also confuses related words such as *check* and *cashier*. Choice (D) uses related words for coffee production, but the conversation takes place in a restaurant, not a coffee plantation.

IV **(A)** Notice the context clues: *library's representative*, *fine*, *borrowed book*, *borrowers*, *library*. Choice (B) uses the related word *book*, but the context of the talk is not publishing. Choice (C) suggests the related words *to collect a fine*, but the context of the talk is not a traffic violation. Choice (D) uses the related word *book*, but the context of the talk concerns lending and borrowing books, not selling and buying them.

Questions Asking About a Location
Problem 20
II **(A)** Listen for the context clue *where*. When you hear a *where* question, scan all the answer choices and listen for the correct location when you hear the dialogue. Choices (B) and (C) use prepositions of location, but a person could not conveniently wait *in an envelope* or *under a cushion*.

III **(C)** Listen for the context clue: *I left the letter*....Choice (A) is contradicted by *the stack on the desk*. Choices (B) and (D) are contradicted by *on top of these books*.

IV **(B)** Listen for the context clue: *Please initial the routing*....*Next to* is similar to *by*. Choices (A), (C), and (D) are contradicted by *initial the routing next to your name*.

Questions Asking About Time
Problem 21
II **(A)** Listen for the context clue *when*. Choice (B) answers *how*. Choice (C) answers *with whom*.

III **(C)** A half-hour is equal to 30 minutes. You may sometimes have to change hours to minutes: for example, one and a half hours is 90 minutes. Choice (A) indicates when the man had planned to leave. Choice (B) is not mentioned. Choice (D) indicates how long the woman asked him to stay.

IV **(B)** *Every day* means *daily*. Choice (A) confuses *sixty inches/sixty minutes (one hour)*. Choice (C) is contradicted by *every day now for the last week*. Choice (D) confuses *two months/twice a month*.

Questions Asking About an Activity
Problem 22
II **(B)** Look for the context clue *what are you doing?* The subject and the tense of the verb

match the question. Choice (A) has similar sounds: *report/sports*. Choice (C) answers *what are you doing* but not the intended meaning *why do you have the report?*

III **(D)** Look for the context clues *turn left*, *one-way street*, and *map*. Choice (A) is contradicted by *one-way street*. Choice (B) has similar sounds: *map/nap*. Choice (C) is contradicted by *should have bought a map*.

IV **(D)** Look for the context clues: *event of rain*, *not be postponed*, *held as scheduled*; and *take place in the cafeteria*. Choice (A) has similar sounds: *scheduled/rescheduled* and is contradicted by *the picnic will not be postponed*. Choice (B) is contradicted by *will take place in the office cafeteria*. Choice (C) confuses the related word *post* with *postponed/mail*.

Questions Asking About an Event or Fact
Problem 23

II **(A)** Look for the context clue: *What happened to you?* Only Choice (A) has an event. Choice (B) has similar sounds: *last night/last Friday*. Choice (C) gives a time, not an event.

III **(A)** Look at the second line of the conversation. *Production will be delayed if the shipment is not released from customs.* Choices (B), (C), and (D) might be further results of delayed production but are not mentioned.

IV **(C)** Be careful of the negative inversion: *Never have so many disasters happened at one time* means *There have been a lot of disasters*. Choice (A) is incorrect because only the West has had earthquakes. Choice (B) is contradicted by the list of disasters given. Choice (D) is incorrect because the blizzard was in the Northeast.

Questions Asking About an Emotion
Problem 24

II **(A)** Only Choice (A) answers the question. Choice (B) answers *who*. Choice (C) answers *where*.

III **(A)** Look for the context clues: *starving, stomach growling, haven't eaten, Let's eat.* Choice (B) is not mentioned. Choice (C) has related words: *growl/angry*. Choice (D) has related words: *find/lost*.

IV **(B)** The neighbors are not pleased; they are upset because cars are being parked on their lawns. Choice (A) has the repeated word *parking*. Choice (C) is incorrect because the employees' quitting time is not mentioned. Choice (D) is incorrect because nothing is said about neighbors watering their lawns. The word *lawn* is repeated here.

Questions Asking About a Reason
Problem 25

II **(B)** Black coffee is coffee without cream or milk. The speaker prefers coffee without cream or milk. Choice (A) has similar sounds: *coffee/cough*. Choice (C) has related words: *coffee/tea*.

III **(B)** Neither speaker can read in the car. But they can read on a train or plane. The reasons in Choices (A), (C), and (D) are not mentioned in the conversation.

IV **(A)** A work slowdown is a work action. A slowdown is like a strike except workers show up, but do not work at their normal speed. They work more slowly. Choices (B), (C), and (D) do not give the reason *why*.

Questions Asking About an Measurement
Problem 26

II **(A)** A half hour is thirty minutes (10 × 3). Choice (B) confuses the amount of work done and the amount of time it took. Choice (C) is contradicted by Tom having more time to finish.

III **(C)** A record low temperature means it's really cold. Choices (A), (B), and (D) are contradicted by *record low*.

IV **(C)** If your purchase more than $100 worth of pencils, the supplier will give you a 10 percent discount. Ten percent of $200 is $20 (200 − 10%).

Questions Asking About an Opinion
Problem 27

II **(A)** Choice (A) is the only reason given. Choice (B) answers how the speaker got the book. Choice (C) refers to habitual action.

III **(B)** The context clues all refer to humor: *funny, laughed, jokes*. Be careful: *I never laughed so hard* means *I laughed harder than ever before*. Choice (A) has the related words: *speaker/presentation*. Choice (C) is not mentioned. Choice (D) confuses similar sounds: *jokes/folks*.

IV (D) Look for the context clues: *handkerchiefs, four-hanky movie,* and *crying*. Choice (A) confuses *short/within ten minutes*. Choice (B) is incorrect because the actors are not mentioned. Choice (C) is contradicted by *opening credits*.

Questions Asking About the Main Topic
Problem 28
II (B) The other choices are not about a particular subject and do not answer the question. Choice (A) does not answer a question about talking. Choice (C) refers to the length of the program, not a topic of conversation.

III (C) The man is looking for a generous person, but the woman declares that she is not at all generous. The man's comment *I won't ask for your help*, then suggests he would have asked her for help (money) if she had been generous. Choice (A) may be true, but this does not answer the question. Choice (B) repeats the word *shame*. Choice (D) confuses the words *tight* and *small*.

IV (B) The phrases *asked me to submit my letter of resignation* and *told me to leave by the close of business today* both indicate that the Managing Director was *fired*. Choice (A) repeats the words *Board of Directors* and *resignation*. Choice (C) is not mentioned. Choice (D) repeats the word *letter*.

Problems Analyzing Language Functions

Conditionals
Problem 29
II (A) Only Choice (A) matches the tense of the suggestion. Choice (B) is the past tense. Choice (C) repeats the word *if* and does not answer the question.

III (C) Look for the context clue following the conditional clause: *If we had asked for less money....* Choice (A) is incorrect because they DID submit a budget. Choice (B) is incorrect because they asked for too much money and the budget was not approved. Choice (D) is incorrect because they cannot complete the project without money.

IV (D) Prices *continue to fall* means prices *decrease*. Choice (A) is not mentioned.

Choice (B) is incorrect because investors will buy when prices hit bottom (the lowest point.) Choice (C) has a related word *broker* but is not mentioned.

Identifying Suggestions
Problem 30
II (C) Choice (C) answers the *yes/no* suggestion with *Yes* and suggests a time to leave. Choice (A) has similar sounding and related word phrases: *leave more time/left my watch*. Choice (B) confuses similar sounds: *more/anymore*.

III (B) Look for the context clue with the suggestion marker *should*: *should start with your report*. Choice (A) is the woman's suggestion, not the man's. Choice (C) confuses *first* with *drink* (*thirst*). Choice (D) confuses *save mine/save money*.

IV (C) Look for the context clue with the suggestion marker *should*: *shouldn't we all try to help the needy*. Choice (A) has related words: *job/unemployment*. Choice (B) has related words: *homeless/home*. Choice (D) is contradicted by *Shouldn't we all try to help the needy*.

Identifying Offers
Problem 31
II (B) The other choices do not respond to the offer. Choice (A) is the past tense. Choice (C) confuses similar sounds: *need/knee*.

III (A) The man offered to get the woman some coffee. Choice (B) is incorrect because the train is late so they can't get on it. Choice (C) has similar sounds: *hot/home*. Choice (D) has similar sounds: *warm/platform* and related words: *train/platform*.

IV (C) The speaker offered the opportunity to board the aircraft early to several types of passengers. Choices (A) and (B) describe related items passengers can have to board early. Choice (D) confuses similar sounds: *infants/infant seats* and uses the related word *travel*.

Identifying Requests
Problem 32
II (A) The other choices do not respond to the request. Choice (B) has related words: *window/door*. Choice (C) has related words: *window/curtains*.

488 EXPLANATORY ANSWERS

III (A) The other activities were mentioned, but they were not part of the request to mail a letter. Choice (B) describes one thing the woman will do herself. Choices (C) and (D) describe what the man himself wants to do.

IV (D) The answer is part of the request for the audience to return to their seats. Choices (A) and (B) are appropriate in the lobby; people are not asked to stop. Choice (C) is an expression of thanks, not a request.

Identifying Restatements
Problem 33

III (A) The woman says this is the last time she'll wait, meaning that in the future she will leave if he's not on time. Choice (B) is incorrect because she's only been waiting for five minutes. Choice (C) is contradicted by the man asking her not to be mad. Choice (D) is not mentioned.

IV (B) The talk says the form is to track your loan application. Choices (A), (C), and (D) are not mentioned.

Mini-Test for Listening Comprehension Parts I, II, III, and IV

Part I: Picture

1. **(A)** Choice (A) identifies things: *plates on a tray*. Choice (B) shows negation: there are not guests in the picture. Choice (C) uses the related word *buffet* but describes an incorrect action. Choice (D) confuses similar sounds: *bus* with *busboy*.

2. **(C)** Choice (C) identifies location: *large hall*. Choice (A) incorrectly identifies the location as a bank. Choice (B) confuses similar sounds *floor* with *flower*. Choice (D) is incorrect because the passengers are *at the ticket counters*, not *on the plane*.

3. **(D)** Choice (D) identifies action: *boat leaving harbor*. Choice (A) confuses similar sounds: *sheep* with *ship*. Choice (B) confuses a related word: *water*. Choice (C) confuses similar sounds: *votes* with *boats*.

4. **(A)** Choice (A) makes an assumption: because the man is talking into a microphone, he is probably trying to enunciate clearly so listeners can understand him. Choice (B) is incorrect because there is no panel in the picture. Choice (C) is incorrect because the man is wearing, not holding, a headset. Choice (D) is incorrect because the flipchart is blank.

5. **(A)** Choice (A) identifies the occupation *operator* and the action *pushing a button*. Choice (B) describes an incorrect action. Choice (C) confuses different meanings for *button* (in clothing) and *button* (on machinery). Choice (D) has the related phrase *going up* but concerning stocks, not elevators.

6. **(D)** Choice (D) identifies engineers and location: *on the site*. Choice (A) is incorrect because: the crane is *on the ground*, not *on a truck*. Choice (B) describes an incorrect action. Choice (C) is incorrect because the men are *holding* the plans; the plans are not on a table.

7. **(A)** Choice (A) identifies a thing: *electrical wires*. Choice (B) confuses the related word *poles*. Choice (C) confuses the related phrase *light fixture*. Choice (D) confuses homonyms (*polls* with *poles*) and similar sounds (*election* with *electricity*).

8. **(B)** Choice (B) identifies the action: *works with her hands*. Choice (A) cannot be assumed from the picture. Choice (C) incorrectly identifies the occupation of the woman and her action. Choice (D) is incorrect because the woman is not holding a saw.

9. **(D)** Choice (D) identifies the location: *in front of a window*. Choice (A) describes an incorrect action. Choice (B) confuses similar sounds: *purse* with *nurse* and incorrectly describes the location. Choice (C) confuses *pharmacists* with *nurses*.

10. **(A)** Choice (A) identifies the action: *offering a newspaper*. Choice (B) confuses similar sounds: *reading with sleeping*; Choice (C) has the related word *tourists* but does not match the picture. Choice (D) confuses newsstand with a cart full of newspapers.

Part II: Question-Response

11. **(B)** Choice (B) is a logical response to a question about *location*. Choice (A) confuses similar sounds: *live* with *five*. Choice (C) confuses similar sounds *live* with *leave* and is not a logical response to a question about *location*.

12. **(A)** Choice (A) is a logical response to a question about *time*. Choice (B) confuses similar sounds: *late* with *ate*. Choice (C) confuses similar sounds: *late* with *later*.
13. **(C)** Choice (C) is a logical response to a question about *who*. Choice (A) confuses similar sounds: *wait* with *weight*. Choice (B) confuses similar sounds: *wait* and *way*.
14. **(C)** Choice (C) is a logical response to a question about *current activity*. Choice (A) is in the past tense and does not answer *going to do now* (present tense). Choice (B) is in the past tense and does not answer *going to do now* (present tense).
15. **(A)** Choice (A) is a logical response to a question about *possession*. Choice (B) confuses similar sounds: *chair* with *cheer*. Choice (C) confuses similar sounds: *chair* with *fair*.
16. **(B)** Choice (B) is a logical response to a question about *time*. Choice (A) has the related word *train* but answers *how*, not *when*. Choice (C) has related the word *mail* but is not a logical answer; people don't arrive by mail.
17. **(A)** Choice (A) is a logical response to a question about *duration*. Choice (B) has the related word *work* but answers *which day* not *how long*. Choice (C) confuses similar sounds: *here* with *hear*; *long* with *along*.
18. **(C)** Choice (C) is a logical response to a question about *location*. Choice (A) confuses similar sounds: *park* with *dark*. Choice (B) confuses different meanings: *park* (leave your car) and *park* (recreational area).
19. **(A)** Choice (A) is a logical response to a question about *activity*. Choice (B) confuses similar sounds: *should* with *wood*. In Choice (C), *were* (past tense) does not answer *should do now* (present tense).
20. **(C)** Choice (C) is a logical response to a question about *time*. Choice (A) confuses similar sounds: *meet* with *meat*. Choice (B) confuses related words: *start* (begin) with *start* (turn on, engine turn over).
21. **(A)** Choice (A) is a logical response to a question about *who*. Choice (B) confuses similar sounds: *letter* with *ladder*. Choice (C) confuses similar sounds: *let her*, *later* with *letter*; *deliver* with *let her leave*.
22. **(C)** Choice (C) is a logical response to a question about *size*. Choice (A) confuses similar sounds: *large* with *inches*. Choice (B) confuses similar sounds *com(pany)* with *penny*.
23. **(A)** Choice (A) is a logical response to a question about *where*. Choice (B) confuses similar sounds: *eat* with *heat*. Choice (C) confuses similar sounds: *eat* with *eight*.
24. **(B)** Choice (B) is a logical response to a question about *no electricity*. Choice (A) has the related word *gas* but does not answer the question. Choice (C) confuses similar sounds: *electricity* with *elections*.
25. **(A)** Choice (A) is a logical response to a question about *which*. Choice (B) confuses similar sounds: *build* with *built*. Choice (C) has the related word *construction* but does not answer the question *which*.

Part III: Short Conversations
26. **(C)** They will *go to the theater* to see a *play*. Choice (A) confuses similar sounds: *fun* with *phone*. Choice (B) confuses different meanings: *play* (a game) with *play* (performance). Choice (D) confuses *see a movie* with *see a play*.
27. **(A)** *Doctors* take *X-rays*. Choice (B) confuses similar sounds: *forearm* with *foreman*. Choice (C) confuses similar sounds: *matter* with *mother*. Choice (D) refers to the events before those in the conversation.
28. **(B)** There is always a lot of *traffic* during *rush hour*. Choice (A) confuses *be there at 6:00* with *be there early*. Choice (C) confuses similar sounds: *six* with *sick*. Choice (D) confuses *prefer to be late* with *if we are late*.
29. **(C)** The man could ski in the snow; he can't play golf in the snow. Choices (A) and (D) are not mentioned. Choice (B) is incorrect because *I wish my sport were skiing* means he doesn't ski.
30. **(B)** The context clues *any calls, messages on your desk, purchase order form* indicate an office. Choices (A), (C), and (D) are not logical locations for this conversation.
31. **(A)** *The following week* means *the week after next*. Choice (B) is suggested but rejected. Choice (C) is what is originally proposed but rejected. Choice (D) is incorrect because the woman cannot meet on Wednesday.

490 EXPLANATORY ANSWERS

32. **(C)** Half of 30% is 15%. Choice (A) is not half of 30%. Choice (B) confuses similar sounds: *thirty* and *thirteen*. Choice (D) is the *total advertising budget*.

33. **(A)** *Exhausted* means *tired*. Choice (B) is not mentioned or implied. Choice (C) confuses related words: *poor* and *bonus*. Choice (D) confuses similar sounds: *ecstatic* with *exhausted*.

34. **(A)** They are *signing letters*. Choice (B) confuses *buy a new pen* with *going to need a new pen*. Choice (C) confuses related words: *sign* (poster, label) with *sign* (write your name). Choice (D) repeats the word *finish* but *writing a book* is not mentioned in the conversation.

35. **(D)** Choice (D) is correct because clothing stores *sell shirts*. Choice (A) confuses similar sounds: *exchange shirt* with *stock exchange*. Choice (B) is not logical. Choice (C) is incorrect because trains are not mentioned.

36. **(C)** *Invoices, payroll, tax statement, this quarter, compute the taxes,* and *salary* indicate the speakers are accountant and client. Choice (A) is incorrect because music is not mentioned in the conversation. Choice (B) is incorrect because bankers and customers do not discuss invoices. Choice (D) is incorrect because computer terms are not mentioned.

37. **(B)** *Why don't you stay home* is a suggestion to *stay home*. Choice (A) is what the woman wants, not what the man suggests. Choice (C) is incorrect because the woman rejects Paris. Choice (D) is incorrect because the woman rejects New York; it also confuses *go to* (visit) with *move to* (live there).

38. **(A)** The woman offers to *fix the printer*. Choice (B) confuses *type letters* with *mail letters*. Choice (C) is incorrect because the man has to mail the letters. Choice (D) confuses different meanings: *jam* (clog) with *jam* (jelly).

39. **(B)** The man *thinks he'll just walk* to 75th Street. Choice (A) is contradicted by *I'll just walk*. Choice (C) confuses the bus turning at 57th Street with the man turning at 57th Street. Choice (D) is incorrect because he is waiting for a bus, not a friend.

40. **(B)** He saw a *fast bird*. Choice (A) confuses homonyms: *flew* with *flu*. Choice (C) confuses *what kind* with *a kind person*. Choice (D) confuses similar sounds: *past* with *fast*.

Part IV: Short Talks

41. **(A)** *This train* indicates the location of the announcement. Choice (B) is incorrect because an *intersection* is *a crossroads for cars*. Choice (C) confuses related words: *step* and *escalator*. Choice (D) confuses related words: *elevator* and *escalator*.

42. **(B)** The train *makes all stops* so it's *local*. Choice (A) is contradicted by the *express is across the station*. Choice (C) is contradicted by *makes all stops*. Choice (D) is not a logical answer.

43. **(D)** If there is *rain early in the morning* they should take *umbrellas*. Choice (A) is incorrect because snow is not predicted; the day will be *seasonably mild*. Choices (B) and (C), *luggage* and *briefcases*, are not related to weather.

44. **(B)** It says skies *clearing by noon*. Choice (A) is incorrect because *rain early in the morning* suggests rain at 6:00 A.M. Choices (C) and (D) are contradicted by *clearing by noon* and *winds developing in the evening*.

45. **(A)** It is being turned off to *reduce total demand*. Choice (B) is incorrect because it will save *power*, not *money*. Choice (C) confuses *make cooler* with *hot weather*. Choice (D) is not mentioned.

46. **(B)** *Power will not be out longer than two hours* means it will be out *less than two hours*. Choices (A), (C), and (D) are contradicted by *not longer than two hours*.

47. **(D)** *Cruise, at sea, ashore,* and *Main Deck* indicate the announcement is *on a ship*. Choice (A) is incorrect because tour buses are not found at sea. Choice (B) confuses *at the shore* with *ashore, shore excursion*. Choice (C) confuses *report to the lounge* (room with comfortable chairs) and *cocktail lounge*.

48. **(C)** People are requested to *report for a ticket*. Choice (A) is incorrect because *enjoy your breakfast* does not mean that breakfast is required. Choices (B) and (D) are incorrect because *clothing* and *health* are not mentioned.

49. **(D)** They advertise a *new remote control*. Choices (A), (B), and (C) are devices you can operate with the remote control.

50. **(C)** Choice (C) Consumers can *call our toll-free number for more information*. Choice (A) is contradicted by *no sales personnel will call*. Choices (B) and (D) are not mentioned.

Explanatory Answers for Reading Review

Problems Analyzing Vocabulary

Prefixes
Problem 1
V **(A)** *Unbelievable* means not believable. (B) *Unavailable* means not available. (C) *Uncomfortable* means not comfortable. (D) *Unsuccessful* means not successful.
VI **(A)** Change to *semi*annual or *bi*annual, which means two times a year. Choice (B) is a correct noun. Choice (C) is a correct noun. Choice (D) is a correct verb.

Suffixes
Problem 2
V **(B)** *Applicant* means person applying for a job. Choice (A) is someone who defends him/herself. Choice (C) is someone who occupies a position. Choice (D) is someone who assists someone else.
VI **(B)** Change *inform* to *information* to make the correct noun form. Choice (A) is a correct noun. Choice (C) is a correct adverb. Choice (D) is a correct adjective.

Vocabulary—Word Families
Problem 3
V **(B)** *negotiate*. (B) *Negotiate* is a verb; (A) is an adjective; (C) is a noun; (D) is also a noun.
VI **(C)** Change to *distribute*. (A) is a correct noun; (B) is a correct verb; (D) is a correct adverb.

Similar Words
Problem 4
V **(D)** *earn*, is often used with money terms (e.g., *earning a living*). (A) *win* means to be first in a competition. (B) *achieve* means to accomplish something. (C) *obtain* means to acquire something.
VI **(C)** Change to *advice*; *advise* is the verb form and *advice* is the noun. The other choices are correct. (A) is a correct adjective. (B) is a correct verb. (D) is a correct preposition.

Cumulative Review Exercises

Part V
1. **(B)** Verb
(F) is a verb. (E) is an adjective. (G) and (H) are nouns.
2. **(C)** Adjective
(G) is an adjective. (E) is a noun (person) or a verb. (F) is a verb. (H) is an adverb.
3. **(B)** Verb
(F) is a verb. (E) is a noun. (G) can be either an adjective or a noun. (H) is a noun (thing).
4. **(A)** Noun
(E) is a noun. (F) is a verb. (G) is an adjective. (H) is an adverb.
5. **(C)** Adjective
(H) is an adjective. (E) is a verb. (F) is a noun (thing). (G) is a noun (thing).
6. **(A)** *Equal* means the same quality or quantity. (B) means *identical*. (C) means *go together*. (D) means other people will like it.
7. **(B)** *Especially* means *very*. (A) is the adverb form of special. (C) means *special thing*. (D) describes something.
8. **(A)** *Except* means *with the exception of*. (B) means *too much*. (C) means *availability*. (D) means to *agree to*.
9. **(C)** *Rise* means to *go up*. (A) is not used with prices or money. (B) means to *mature*. (D) is not used with money.
10. **(D)** *Borrow from* means to *use temporarily*. (A) means to *give to someone temporarily*. (B) means *allow to have*. (C) means to *suggest*.

Part VI
1. **(B)** Change to the noun *criticism*. (A) is a correct article. (C) is a correct verb. (D) is a correct adverb.

2. **(C)** Change to the adjective *economical*. (A) is a correct noun. (B) is a correct superlative. (D) is a correct preposition.
3. **(B)** Change to the adjective *managerial*. (A) is a correct noun. (C) is a correct verb. (D) is a correct preposition.
4. **(B)** Change to the verb *maintain*. (A) is a correct noun. (C) is a correct noun. (D) is a correct adjective.
5. **(B)** Change to the adjective *nationally*. (A) is a correct noun. (C) is a correct adjective. (D) is a correct noun.
6. **(C)** Change to *money*. *Currency* is used for kinds of money (foreign currency). (A) is a correct noun. (B) is a correct adjective. (D) is a correct noun.
7. **(B)** Change to *earned*. *Obtained* is used for *get*. (A) is a correct pronoun. (C) is a correct pronoun. (D) is a correct comparative.
8. **(A)** Change to the noun *effect*. *Affect* is a verb. (B) is a correct adjective. (C) is a correct noun. (D) is a correct participle.
9. **(B)** Change to *extend*, *revise*, or *change*. *Elaborate* means *explain more*. (A) is a correct noun. (C) is a correct verb. (D) is a correct noun.
10. **(A)** Change to *borrow*. *Lend* is not used with *from*. (B) is a correct noun. (C) is a correct conjunction. (D) is a correct participle.

Problems Analyzing Grammar

Non-count Nouns and Plural Verbs
Problem 5
V **(C)** *Bags of clothes* is a plural, count noun; the modifier *several* is plural and is used with count nouns. (A), *clothes*, is a non-count noun and could be used with the modifier *some*: *some clothes*; (B) is incorrect because you can't have both *several* and *some* together; (D) is incorrect because you need a plural noun with *several*, not a singular noun like *bag*.

VI **(C)** Change to *was*. The non-count noun *food* uses a singular verb. Both (A), *fruits*, and (B), *vegetables*, are objects of the preposition *including*; they are not the subject of the sentence. (D), *table*, is a count noun and is correct.

Differences in Meaning Between Count and Non-count Nouns
Problem 6
V **(A)** *Room* here means space; it is an abstract non-count noun. (B) is a combination count-noun. (C) and (D) are inappropriate word combinations.

VI **(C)** Change to *light*; *light*, because of this context (*opening curtains to let the sun come in*), is an abstract non-count noun; it does not mean *light* as in a *light bulb* or *lamp*. (A) is a verb, not a noun; (B) is a count noun; and (D), because of this context, is a count noun.

Cumulative Review Exercises
Part V
1. **(B)** *Employees* is a plural word.
2. **(A)** *Two trays of food* is a non-count noun with a countable quantity.
3. **(A)** *Reporter* is singular.
4. **(A)** *Production* is a non-count noun and thus takes a singular verb.
5. **(B)** *Rain* is a non-count noun and thus takes a singular verb.

Part VI
1. **(B)** *Traffic* is a non-count noun and uses *is*. (A) is a correct noun. (C) is a correct preposition. (D) is a correct noun.
2. **(C)** *Toothpaste* is a non-count noun. It needs the singular verb *is*. (A) needs no article. (B) is a correct noun. (D) is a correct noun.
3. **(A)** *Lunch* is a non-count noun and uses *is*. (B) and (C) are correct prepositions. (D) is a correct noun.
4. **(B)** *Fruit* is a non-count noun and not plural. (A) is a correct adjective. (C) is a correct verb. (D) is a correct adjective.
5. **(B)** *Sunshine* is a non-count noun and uses *is*. (A) is a correct noun. (C) is a correct preposition. (D) is a correct noun.

Specified Noun with Incorrect Article
Problem 7
V **(D)** *The* is used because it is a specified *effort* that actually happened. (A) and (C) cannot be used with a specified noun. (B) *a* is not used with the initial vowel sound of *effort*.

VI **(B)** Change to *the*. The seminar is specified; it's the one with *the topic* about *teamwork*.

(A), *The*, is correct here because *topic* is specified; (C), *managers*, and (D), *employees*, are unspecified nouns so no articles are necessary.

Unspecified Noun with *the*

Problem 8

V (C) An unspecified meeting requires an unspecified article; (A) requires an article; (B) is a specific meeting, which is not the sense of the sentence; (D) also specifies a particular meeting.

VI (A) Change to *a*. No specific book is mentioned; any good book will do; (B) is a verb and requires no article; (C) and (D) both specify nouns: *mornings* and *subway*.

Wrong Article with Generic Count Noun

Problem 9

V (C) Use *a schedule* with *an office* (any schedule for any office); if the sentence had *the office* you would have chosen (A) *the schedule* (the particular schedule for the particular office). (B) requires an article; (D) doesn't agree with the verb.

VI (A) Add *a*. The other articles are all unspecified so the first choice should match. (B), is unspecified. (C) is an article and an adverb. (D) is an unspecified noun.

Wrong Article with Generic Non-count Noun

Problem 10

V (A) *Recognition* is a non-count generic noun. No article is necessary. (B), (C), and (D) all have articles or other modifiers.

VI (B) Delete the article *a*. *Music* is a non-count generic noun. (A) and (C) both contain correct modifiers and (D) is a verb.

Wrong Form of *a* or *an*

Problem 11

V (A) *Announcement* has an initial vowel sound. (B) cannot be used; (C) and (D) could be used in another context.

VI (B) Change to *a* for words that do not begin with an initial vowel sound (*uniform, university, universal*, etc.). (A) is an adjective. (C) is a conjunction. (D) is an article and an adjective.

Cumulative Review Exercises

Part V

1. (C) Plural count nouns do not need articles. (A) must use *a*. Choices (B) and (D) cannot use a plural verbs.
2. (A) Singular count nouns require an article. (B) If you know that one particular shipper sent three packages, you need to use the definite article. (C) Singular count nouns require an article. (D) If you know that one particular shipper sent three packages, you need to use the definite article.
3. (B) Human resources has one definite director. (A) Singular count nouns require an article. (C) Human resources has one definite director; the indefinite article is impossible. (D) A plural noun cannot be used with a singular verb.
4. (A) Non-count nouns do not require an article. (B) Non-count nouns can be used without an article. (C) *An* cannot be used with a non-count noun. (D) Non-count nouns do not have plural forms.
5. (D) Non-count nouns may use *some*. (A) Non-count nouns cannot be counted. (B) and (C) Non-count nouns can be used without an article.

Part VI

1. (C) Non-count nouns do not require an article. Choices (A) and (B) are correct verbs. (D) is a correct adjective.
2. (A) *A* cannot be used before vowel sounds. (B) is a correct pronoun. Choices (C) and (D) are correct prepositions.
3. (A) Singular count nouns require an article. (B) is a correct verb. (C) is a correct article. (D) is a correct preposition.
4. (B) An indefinite *staff* requires an indefinite article. (A) is a correct noun. (C) is a correct infinitive. (D) is a correct adverb.
5. (D) Non-count nouns do not use *a*. (A) is a correct article. (B) is a correct comparative. (C) is a correct connector.

Subject and Verb May Not Agree

Problem 12

V (D) The subject of the sentence, the noun *officers*, is plural. (A), (B), and (C) are used with singular subjects.

494 EXPLANATORY ANSWERS

VI (B) Change to *has*. The subject, *the head*, is singular. The verb must be singular. Choice (A) is not the subject. It is the object of the preposition *of*. (C) is a correct article. (D) is a correct noun.

You as Subject
Problem 13
V (B) *You* always takes a plural verb. The other choices are all singular.
VI (B) Change to *are*. *You* always takes a plural verb form. (A) *even though* is a correct subordinate conjunction. (C) and (D) are correct verbs.

Nouns and Pronouns: Singular or Plural
Problem 14
V (B) *Police* is a plural noun (a group of police officers); it takes a plural verb. The other choices are all singular.
VI (A) *Western Industries* is the name of a company; it takes a singular verb. (B) is a correct superlative adjective. (C) is a correct noun. (D) is a correct noun.

Cumulative Review Exercises
Part V
1. **(B)** Singular *manager* requires singular *visits*. (A) is a plural verb. (C) is the infinitive. (D) is the gerund.
2. **(C)** *You* requires plural *are*. (A) is the simple form. (B) is singular. (D) is future tense.
3. **(A)** *Police* requires a plural; *goes off* suggests present; use *arrive*. Choices (B) and (C) are singular; Choice (D) is the wrong tense and the wrong number.
4. **(A)** Names of businesses are singular; use *is*. (B) is plural. (C) is present perfect. (D) is plural.
5. **(D)** Singular *employee* uses singular *gets*. (A) is the simple form. (B) is the past participle. (C) is the gerund.

Part VI
1. **(B)** Plural *accountants* takes plural *are*. (A) is a correct article. (C) is a correct noun. (D) is a correct infinitive.
2. **(B)** Singular *chairman* requires singular *is going*. (A) is a correct noun. (C) is a correct infinitive. (D) is a correct noun.
3. **(D)** Singular *team* requires singular *produces*. (A) is a correct preposition. (B) and (C) are correct nouns.
4. **(C)** Singular *each* requires singular *has*. (A), (B), and (D) are a correct nouns.
5. **(A)** Plural *employees* requires plural *are*. (B) and (D) are correct connectors. (C) is a correct preposition.

Incorrect Preposition
Problem 15
V (B) *On* is the preposition used with this common expression: *on my desk*. Choice (A) could be used, but more likely would be used with *in my desk drawer*; Choice (C) would be used for a person standing *at my desk*; Choice (D) refers to purpose.
VI (B) Change to *to*. Choice (A) is an infinitive; (C) is correct, and (D) is a pronoun.

Prepositional Phrase and Verb Agreement
Problem 16
V (C) The subject of the sentence is *award*. Choice (A) could not be used in this sentence and (B) and (D) are both plural.
VI (B) Change to *are having*. The subject of the sentence is *sales representatives*. (A) is a correct preposition. (C) is a correct conjunction. (D) is a correct verb.

Cumulative Review Exercises
Part V
1. **(A)** *At* refers to locations. (B) refers to direction toward. (C) refers to time. (D) expresses manner.
2. **(D)** *In* refers to city locations. (A) At refers to locations. (B) refers to direction away. (C) refers to purpose.
3. **(B)** *On* refers to days of the week. (A) refers to deadlines. (C) refers to location inside. (D) refers to location.
4. **(B)** *At* refers to definite time. (A) refers to days of the week. (C) refers to location inside. (D) refers to purpose.
5. **(C)** *Until* means up to a point in time. (A) refers to days of the week. (B) refers to direction away. (D) refers to locations.

Part VI
1. **(D)** Change to *in* for location inside a room. (A) is a correct article. (B) is a correct verb. (C) is a correct preposition.
2. **(D)** Change to *at* for location. (A) and (C) are correct infinitives. (B) is a correct preposition.

3. **(B)** Change to *from* for direction away or *to for* direction toward (depending on your meaning). (A) is a correct verb; (C) and (D) are correct prepositions. In (D) the preposition could be *next*.
4. **(A)** Change to *in* with meeting. (B) and (D) are correct prepositions; (C) is a pronoun.
5. **(C)** Change to *on* to indicate position. (A) is a correct article. (B) is a correct verb. (D) is a correct preposition.

Wrong Coordinating Conjunctions
Problem 17
V **(C)** The conjunction *both* needs *and*. The other choices do not work with *both*.
VI **(C)** Change to *or*. You can take only one plane at a time—either a non-stop *or* a direct, not both. (A) is a correct article. (B) is a correct noun. (D) is the correct preposition for time of day.

Joined Items Not Parallel
Problem 18
V **(C)** *Or* joins an infinitive with an infinitive. *Stay late* is the simple form. Choice (A) is present progressive, (B) is present; (D) is a participle form.
VI **(D)** Change to *satisfaction*; the conjunction *and* joins two nouns *quality* and *satisfaction*. (A) is a correct article. (B) is a correct participle. (C) is a correct adjective.

Cumulative Review Exercises
Part V
1. **(C)** *Or* expresses a choice. (A) indicates a contrast. (B) indicates purpose. (D) is a relative pronoun that joins clauses, not phrases.
2. **(B)** *And* links items equally. (A) expresses a choice. (C) indicates a contrast. (D) indicates purpose.
3. **(A)** *But* indicates a contrast. (B) expresses a choice. (C) indicates time. (D) links items equally.
4. **(D)** *And* links items equally. (A) expresses a choice. (B) indicates a possibility. (C) indicates contrast.
5. **(A)** *Or* indicates a choice. (B) links items equally. (C) and (D) indicate contrast.

Part VI
1. **(C)** Change to *but* to indicate contrast. (A) is a correct negative. (B) is a correct article. (D) is a correct adverb.
2. **(A)** Match with *learning*; *seeing* and *learning*. (B) links items equally. (C) is a correct verb. (D) is a correct participle.
3. **(B)** Change to *and* to link items equally. (A) is a correct adjective. (C) is a correct verb. (D) is a correct preposition.
4. **(C)** Change to *or* to indicate choice. (A) is a correct verb. (B) is a correct preposition. (D) is a correct article.
5. **(C)** Change to *but* to indicate contrast. (A) is a correct verb. (B) is a correct preposition. (D) is a correct adjective. (available) and preposition (until).

Misplaced Subordinating Conjunctions
Problem 19
V **(D)** The subordinate conjunction introduces the clause and is followed by the subject and verb of the clause. In the other choices the word order is incorrect.
VI **(B)** Change to *after*. You cannot leave your office and then lock your desk. The sequence must be logical. (A) is a correct determiner. (C) is a correct verb. (D) is a correct preposition.

Incorrect Subordinating Conjunction
Problem 20
V **(C)** Usually people cannot enter a concert after it has started; an exception was made for Ms. Sello *even though she was late*. Choice (A), (B), and (D) are not logical.
VI **(C)** Change to *even though* or *although*. Usually two people would not duplicate one another's work. Therefore the conjunction *when* is not logical. (A) is a correct verb. (B) is a correct article. (D) is a correct adverb.

Cumulative Review Exercises
Part V
1. **(B)** *Although* shows a contrast. (A) indicates cause and effect. (C) indicates time prior. (D) indicates place.
2. **(C)** *Where* indicates place. (A) shows a contrast. (B) is not possible because it doesn't replace *town*. (D) indicates possibility.
3. **(C)** *Before* indicates time prior. (A) indicates time later. (B) indicates time while. (D) indicates during.
4. **(D)** *When* indicates a time relationship. (A) indicates cause and effect. (B) indicates time up to. (C) indicates contrast.

5. **(B)** *Because* indicates cause and effect. (A) indicates a contrast. (C) indicates possibility. (D) indicates place.

Part VI
1. **(C)** Change to *because* or *since* to express cause and effect. (A) is a correct article. (B) is a correct noun. (D) is a correct verb.
2. **(A)** Change to *although* to express contrast. (B) is a correct noun. (C) is a correct adjective. (D) is a correct verb.
3. **(B)** Change to *so* to express result. (A) is a correct preposition. (C) is a correct verb. (D) is a correct article.
4. **(C)** Change to *until* to express time up to. (A) is a correct auxiliary. (B) is a correct preposition. (D) is a correct infinitive.
5. **(B)** Move *since* to the cause clause to express cause and effect *Since she was promoted*. (A) and (C) are correct verbs. (D) is a correct comparative.

Use of *as - as*
Problem 21
V **(B)** Only choice (B) has *as* twice. *Employee* is being compared equally with *predecessors*. Choice (A) and (C) have only one *as*. In choice (D) *than* is not used with equal comparisons.
VI **(C)** Change to *as good as*. You need to surround the adjective with *as*. Choice (A) is a correct adverb. Choice (B) is a correct superlative. Choice (D) is a correct pronoun.

More/-er or *Than* Omitted
Problem 22
V **(A)** Don't be confused with the preposition *from*. The comparison of two views requires *than*. Choices (B), (C), and (D) would need to read *the better of the two* to be correct.
VI **(C)** Change to *more expensive than*. You need to add the comparison form *than*.

The or *Most/-est* Omitted
Problem 23
V **(D)** When making a superlative, use *the*. (A) and (B) compare two messenger services; here we are talking about all of the messenger services in town. (C) needs *the*.
VI **(B)** Change to *the most popular*. Use *the* with most.

Cumulative Review Exercises
Part V
1. **(A)** Superlative forms use *the most* and the positive form. (B) is the comparative form. (C) is the positive form. (D) is a noun.
2. **(C)** is the comparative form. (A) is the positive form. (D) is incorrect because the comparative form does not use *the*.
3. **(D)** is the correct comparative form. (A) is the superlative form but omits *the*. (B) is incorrect because the comparative form does not use *the*. (C) is incorrect because the superlative form does not compare two things.
4. **(B)** In an equal comparison, have *as* on both sides of the adjective. (A) omits *as* before the positive form. (C) is the comparative form of *good* and (D) is the superlative form of *good*; neither use *as* before or after the adjective.
5. **(C)** is the comparative form. (A) is the superlative form but omits *the*. (B) omits *as* before the adverb. (D) is incorrect because *than* already appears in the sentence.

Part VI
1. **(A)** Comparison between two things requires the comparative form *larger*. (B) is a correct conjunction. (C) is a correct verb. (D) is a correct adjective.
2. **(B)** Change to *as much as* to express an equal comparison. (A) is a correct verb. (C) is a correct pronoun. (D) is a correct verb.
3. **(B)** Comparison among many things requires the superlative form *best*. (A) is a correct determiner. (C) is a correct adjective. (D) is a correct adverb.
4. **(B)** Comparison among many things requires the superlative form *most*. (A) is a correct verb. (C) is a correct noun. (D) is a correct noun.
5. **(B)** Comparison between two things requires the comparative form *longer*. (A) is a correct infinitive. (C) is a correct preposition. (D) is a correct comparative.

Misplaced Adverbs of Definite Frequency
Problem 24
V **(C)** The adverb of definite frequency must be at the beginning or end of a sentence. The word order in the other choices is incorrect.

VI **(B)** Move the adverb of definite frequency to the beginning or end of the sentence. (A) and (C) are correct articles. (D) is a correct adjective.

Misplaced Adverbs of Indefinite Frequency
Problem 25
V **(A)** The adverb of indefinite frequency *always* should come before the compound main verbs *have breakfast* and *read*. The word order in the other options is not correct.

VI **(B)** Move *always* after *rings*. The adverb of indefinite frequency should come before the main verb. (A) is a correct determiner. (C) is a correct gerund. (D) is a correct noun.

Adverbs of Indefinite Frequency with *Be*
Problem 26
V **(C)** The adverb of frequency follows the verb *be* when there is no auxiliary. The word order in the other options is not correct.

VI **(C)** Move *to* after *are*. The adverb of frequency follows the verb *be* when there is no auxiliary. (A) is a correct noun. (B) is a correct conjunction. (D) is a correct noun.

Adverbs of Indefinite Frequency with Auxiliary
Problem 27
V **(B)** The adverb of frequency follows the auxiliary. The word order in the other options is not correct.

VI **(A)** Move *never* after *has*: *has never forgotten*. The adverb of frequency follows the auxiliary. (B) is a correct infinitive. (C) is a correct determiner. (D) is a correct adjective.

Meanings of Adverbs of Frequency
Problem 28
V **(C)** The conjunction *or* and the pronoun *anyone* have a negative sense. The only answer choice with a negative sense is *never*. The other choices have a positive sense and would be used with conjunctions such as *and*.

VI **(C)** Change to *always*. In this sentence, the accountant hates sloppy work. He must be a neat person. Therefore, the conjunction *and* suggests the adverb should have a positive sense, not negative like *never*. (A) is a correct article. (B) and (D) are correct nouns.

Cumulative Review Exercises
Part V
1. **(B)** *Every day* can appear at the end of a sentence. (A), (C), and (D) must appear in the middle of the sentence.
2. **(B)** *Always* comes between the auxiliary and the main verb. (A) places the main verb before the auxiliary. (C) and (D) place *every day* in the middle of the sentence instead of at the beginning or end.
3. **(A)** *Still* comes after a form of *be*. (A) and (D) cannot be used before negatives. (C) must appear at the beginning or the end of the sentence.
4. **(D)** *Rarely* comes between the auxiliary and the main verb. In (A) *rarely* appears after the main verb. (B) and (C) are incorrect because *every day* must come at the beginning or the end of the sentence.
5. **(D)** *Every year* can appear at the end of a sentence. (A), (C), and (D) must appear in the middle of the sentence.

Part VI
1. **(B)** Move *seldom* to come between the auxiliary and the main verb. (A) is a correct noun. (C) is a correct conjunction. (D) is a correct preposition.
2. **(D)** Move *every quarter* to the beginning or end of the sentence. (A) is a correct relative pronoun. (B) is a correct verb. (C) is a correct adjective.
3. **(A)** Move *always* to come before the main verb. (B) is a correct preposition. (C) and (D) are correct nouns.
4. **(B)** Move *twice a day* to the beginning or end of the sentence. (A) is a correct article. (B) is a correct adjective. (C) is a correct verb.
5. **(B)** Move *every six months* to the beginning or end of the sentence. (A) is a correct article. (C) is a correct preposition. (D) is a correct noun.

Causative Verb + Simple Form
Problem 29
V **(A)** The causative verb *makes* is followed by a verb in the simple form (*take*). The other choices are not in the simple form.

VI **(B)** Change to *leave*. The causative verb *request* is followed by a verb in the simple form (*leave*).

Causative Verb + Infinitive
Problem 30
V **(B)** The causative verb *permit* must be followed by an infinitive *to make*. The other choices are not infinitives.

VI **(D)** Change to *to work*. The causative verb *want* must be followed by an infinitive. (A) is a correct two-word preposition. (B) is a correct article. (C) is a correct adjective.

Causative Verb + Past Participle
Problem 31
V **(A)** The past form of the causative verb *have* must be followed by the past participle. The other choices are not the past participle form.

VI **(B)** Change to *repaired*. The past form of the causative verb *have* must be followed by the past participle.

Cumulative Review Exercises
Part V
1. **(A)** The causative *makes* must be followed by the simple form of the verb. (B) is the past participle. (C) is the gerund. (D) is the present tense.
2. **(D)** The causative *have* must be followed by the past participle. (A) is the simple form. (B) is the future tense. (C) is the gerund.
3. **(C)** The causative *wants* must be followed by the past participle. (A) is the gerund. (B) is the simple form. (D) is a noun.
4. **(D)** The causative *have* must be followed by the simple form of the verb. (A) is the past participle. (B) is the gerund. (C) is the future tense.
5. **(C)** The causative *had* must be followed by the past participle. (A) is the simple form. (B) is the gerund. (D) is the future form.

Part VI
1. **(B)** The causative *had* must be followed by the past participle *taken*. (A) is a correct noun. (C) is a correct article. (D) is a correct preposition.
2. **(B)** The causative *get* must be followed by the infinitive *to help*. (A) is a correct auxiliary. (C) is a correct preposition. (D) is a correct noun.
3. **(C)** The causative *permitted* must be followed by the infinitive *to leave*. (A) is a correct noun. (B) is a correct pronoun. (D) is a correct adverb.
4. **(C)** The causative *let* must be followed by the simple form *ask*. (A) is a correct article. (B) is a correct adjective. (D) is a correct verb.
5. **(C)** The causative *had* must be followed by the past participle *changed*. (A) is a correct noun. (B) is a correct article. (D) is a correct adjective.

Real Condition *if* Clause Not in Present Tense
Problem 32
V **(A)** The *if* clause must be in the present tense. Choice (B) is past, Choice (C) is past perfect; Choice (D) is future.

VI **(B)** Change to *leave*. The *if* clause must be in the present tense. (A) and (C) are correct subordinate conjunctions. (D) is a correct verb.

Unreal Condition *if* Clause Not in Appropriate Tense
Problem 33
V **(B)** This is an unreal condition (*I didn't get a promotion*). It must be in the past perfect tense if the main clause is in the past. The tenses in the other choices are incorrect.

VI **(C)** Change to *drove*. An unreal condition (*I don't drive*) must be in the past tense if the main clause is in the present conditional. (A) is a correct pronoun. (B) is a correct prepositional phrase. (D) is a correct article.

Unreal Condition *if* Clause + *Were*
Problem 34
V **(A)** The verb *be* is always *were* in an unreal condition *if* clause—even though the subject here (*the salary*) is singular. Choices (B) and (C) are singular and (B), (C), and (D) are all in the wrong tense.

VI **(A)** The verb *be* is always *were* in an unreal condition *if* clause—even though the subject here (*I*) is singular. (B) and (C) are correct verbs. (D) is a correct preposition.

Cumulative Review Exercises
Part V
1. **(B)** A real condition requires a present tense verb in the *if* clause. (A) is past tense. (C) is the past perfect. (D) is the past progressive.

2. **(B)** *Would have told* is an unreal condition requiring the past perfect in the *if* clause. (A) is present. (C) is past tense. (D) is the present.
3. **(A)** A real condition requires a present verb in the *if* clause. (B) is a conditional in the tense future. (C) is past tense. (D) is the past perfect.
4. **(B)** An unreal condition requires *were* as a form of *be* in the *if* clause. (A) is past tense. (C) is a conditional in the future tense. (D) is a conditional in the past tense.
5. **(A)** A real condition can use a command form. (B) is future tense. (C) is the past perfect. (D) is the future.

Part VI
1. **(B)** Change to *were* as the form of *be* for the *if* clause of unreal condition. (A) is a correct conjunction. (C) is a correct verb. (D) is a correct prepositional phrase.
2. **(C)** Change to the present form in the *if* clause of real condition. (A) is a correct verb. (B) is a correct article. (D) is a correct adverb.
3. **(A)** *Would* and the present tense require the past tense in the *if* clause of unreal condition. (B) is a correct preposition. (C) is a correct pronoun. (D) is a correct preposition.
4. **(B)** *Would* and the past participle require the past perfect in the *if* clause. (A) is a correct article. (C) is a correct verb. (D) is a correct adjective.
5. **(C)** Change to present tense in the *if* clause of a real condition. (A) is a correct article. (B) is a correct adverb. (D) is a correct adjective.

Verb Tenses
Problem 35
V **(D)** The future perfect shows the relationship between an action in progress (*I am contacting people now*) and a time marker (*by tomorrow night*). *I will have contacted them all by tomorrow night.* The other choices do not match the future time marker *by tomorrow night*.
VI **(D)** Change to *arrived*. The past progressive verb *had been waiting* shows an action in progress that finished when something else happened (*the bus arrived*). (A) is a correct verb form. (B) is a correct article. (C) is a correct subordinate conjunction.

Stative Verbs in the Progressive Tense
Problem 36
V **(B)** The stative verb *like* is not often used in the progressive tense. Choice (A) is the future tense; (C) is a form of the progressive tense; (D) is a participle form.
VI **(C)** Change to *appreciated*. You cannot use the progressive tense with the stative verb *appreciate*. You need the past tense because of the sequence of verbs: *told* in the main clause. (A) is a correct noun. (B) *how much* is a correct subordinate conjunction. (D) is a correct preposition.

Cumulative Review Exercises
Part V
1. **(B)** *Will call* is future; match with simple present to show action that will happen in the very near future. (A) is the present perfect. (C) is the past participle. (D) is the present progressive.
2. **(A)** Action that started in the past and continues into the future is expressed by the present perfect. (B) is the past perfect progressive. (C) is the present. (D) is the past perfect.
3. **(D)** Use the simple past to show action that happened in the past. (A) is the present tense. (B) is the past progressive. (C) is the present perfect.
4. **(B)** *A speech this afternoon* is future; use the future tense. (A) is past progressive. (C) is the past tense. (D) is the present perfect.
5. **(C)** *Next year* is future; use the future tense. (A) is conditional. (B) is the past tense. (D) is the present perfect.

Part VI
1. **(A)** Change to simple past to express a one-time past action; *left*. (B) is a correct pronoun. (C) is a correct conjunction. (D) is a correct prepositional phrase.
2. **(C)** Match *was running* with another past *found* to indicate two past actions. (A) is a correct noun. (B) is a correct verb. (D) is a correct preposition.
3. **(A)** Change to simple present *makes* to express habit (match *attends*). (B) is a correct noun. (C) is a correct conjunction. (D) is a correct article.

4. **(A)** The stative verb *recognize* is rarely used in the progressive; use simple present *recognize*. (B) and (C) are correct prepositions. (D) is a correct noun.
5. **(A)** *Now* indicates action is progress; use present progressive *is checking* or the future, *will check*. (B) is a correct conjunction. (C) is a correct verb. (D) is a correct preposition.

Relative Clause: Repeated Subject
Problem 37
V **(C)** The subject of the sentence is *wallet*; the subject of the clause is *that*. In choice (A) and (B) you do not need to repeat the subject with the pronoun *it*. In choice (D) the relative pronoun *whose* refers to people, not things such as wallet.

VI **(B)** Omit *she*. The subject of the sentence is *woman*; the subject of the clause is *who*. You do not need to repeat the subject with the pronoun *she*. (A) is a correct article. (C) is a correct verb. (D) is a correct preposition.

Relative Clause: No Relative Pronoun
Problem 38
V **(A)** You need a relative pronoun to introduce the clause (*who shares the office*) and be the subject of the clause. Choices (B) and (D) are not relative pronouns. Choice (C) is a possessive relative pronoun.

VI **(A)** Change to *who*. You need a relative pronoun to introduce the clause (*who prefers to remain anonymous*) and be the subject of the clause. Choices (B), (C), and (D) are not pronouns.

Relative Clause: *That* ≠ *Who*
Problem 39
V **(D)** You need a relative pronoun to introduce the clause (*who has worked here for many years*) and you need *who* because the clause refers to a person. Choice (A) is a relative pronoun, but it is not used with people; (B) is not a relative pronoun; and (C) is a relative pronoun, but is not used with people.

VI **(A)** Change to *that*. You need a relative pronoun to introduce the clause (*that was mailed a month ago*) and you need *that* because the clause refers to a thing (*letter*). (B) is a correct verb. (C) is a correct verb phrase. (D) is a correct verb.

Cumulative Review Exercises
Part V
1. **(D)** *Who* replaces *Ms. Caras*. (A) refers to time. (B) is the objective form. (C) refers to things, not people.
2. **(D)** *That* replaces *letter*. In choices (A), (B), and (C) *it* repeats the subject.
3. **(A)** *Whose* replaces *Mr. La Porte* in the possessive. (B) is incorrect because *his* repeats *Mr. La Porte*. (C) and (D) omit relative forms.
4. **(D)** *That* replaces *report*: (A) is incorrect because *it* repeats *report*. (B) omits the relative form. (C) refers to people.
5. **(B)** *That* replaces *machine*. (A) refers to people. (C) is not a relative form. (D) refers to time.

Part VI
1. **(B)** *Which* refers to things; use *who* for people. (A) is a correct article. (C) is a correct noun phrase. (D) is a correct adjective time.
2. **(A)** *That* cannot be used in nonrestrictive clauses; use *which*. (B) and (D) are correct past participles. (C) is a correct auxiliary.
3. **(C)** *She* repeats *person*; omit. (A) is a correct article. (B) is a correct relative form. (D) is a correct verb.
4. **(A)** *Who* refers to people; use *that* or *which* for things. This sentence requires *that*. (B) is a correct noun. (D) is a correct pronoun. (C) is a correct verb.
5. **(A)** *It* is not a relative form; use possessive *whose*. (B) and (C) are correct verbs. (D) is a correct noun.

Verb + Gerund or Infinitive
Problem 40
V **(B)** Change to an infinitive after the verb *intend*. The other choices are not in the infinitive form.

VI **(B)** Change to *answering*. Use the gerund form after the verb *mind*. The other choices are not in the gerund form.

Cumulative Review Exercises
Part V
1. **(D)** *Prepare* is followed by the infinitive. (A) is the simple form. (B) is the *-ing* form. (C) is the past participle.

2. **(A)** *Want* is followed by the infinitive. (B) is the *-ing* form. (C) is the past participle. (D) is the simple form.
3. **(D)** *Postponed* is followed by the gerund. (A) is the infinitive. (B) is the past participle. (C) is the simple form.
4. **(A)** *Considered* is followed by the gerund. (B) is the future tense. (C) is the past participle. (D) is the infinitive.
5. **(D)** *Failed* is followed by the infinitive. (A) is the simple form. (B) is the past tense. (C) is the *-ing* form.

Part VI
1. **(A)** *Refuses* is followed by the infinitive *to plan*. (B) is a correct preposition. (C) is a correct noun. (D) is a correct adjective.
2. **(C)** *Appreciated* is followed by the gerund *receiving*. (A) is a correct conjunction. (B) is a correct verb. (D) is a correct noun.
3. **(A)** *Intends* is followed by the infinitive *to take*. (B) is a correct noun. (C) is a correct conjunction. (D) is a correct verb.
4. **(A)** *Suggested* is followed by the gerund *illustrating*. (B) is a correct noun. (C) is a correct preposition. (D) is a correct conjunction.
5. **(B)** *Hesitated* is followed by the infinitive *to sign*. (A) is a correct conjunction. (C) is a correct noun. (D) is a correct verb.

Incorrect Participles
Problem 41
V **(B)** Someone put something in the envelope; the envelope received the action. The past participle *enclosed* is required. Choice (A) is the present participle; Choice (C) is an infinitive; Choice (D) is the present perfect tense.

VI **(A)** Change to *surprising*. The message is inanimate; it could not react to itself. The message caused others to be surprised. Use the present participle. None of the other choices are participles.

Cumulative Review Exercises
Part V
1. **(B)** The jobs cause the employees to feel boredom; use the past participle. (A) is the present participle. (C) is the present tense. (D) is the simple form.
2. **(A)** Someone else sorted the mail; use the past participle. (B) is the simple form. (C) confuses *sort* and *sort of*. (D) is the present participle.
3. **(C)** Someone else approved the application; use the past participle. (A) is the noun form. (B) is the present tense. (D) is the present participle.
4. **(B)** People crowded the offices; use the past participle. (A) is the present participle. (C) is the present tense. (D) is the simple form.
5. **(D)** The speaker causes the audience to laugh; use the present participle. (A) is the simple form. (B) is the noun form. (C) is the past tense.

Part VI
1. **(A)** Someone else typed the letters: use *typed*. (B) is a correct verb. (C) is a correct preposition. (D) is a correct noun.
2. **(C)** The receptionist is smiling; use *smiling*. (A) is a correct preposition. (B) is a correct noun. (D) is a correct verb.
3. **(A)** The speaker made the crowd interested; use *interested*. (B) is a correct verb. (C) is a correct adverb. (D) is a correct article.
4. **(D)** Someone else broke the machine; use *broken*. (A) is a correct pronoun. (B) is a correct verb. (C) is a correct preposition.
5. **(A)** Something else tired the engineers; use *tired*. (B) is a correct verb. (C) is a correct infinitive. (D) is a correct pronoun.

Mini-Test for Reading Parts V and VI
Part V
1. **(C)** A compound subject requires a plural verb. Choice (A) is first person present tense. Choice (B) is singular present. (D) is the simple form.
2. **(D)** *To* indicates the one-way direction of the cable. Choice (A) implies the computer is used as *a means* to attach the cable. Choices (B) and (C) would imply that the computer is opened up and the cables are "inside" the computer itself.
3. **(A)** The word *tomorrow* suggests a future tense; use *will*. Choice (B) is present tense of *have*. Choice (C) is past tense of *do*. Choice (D) should also have an *-ing* verb (*are submitting*).

502 EXPLANATORY ANSWERS

4. **(D)** *The* requires the noun *presentation*. Choice (A) is the gerund form which is inappropriate here. Choice (B) is the past tense form. Choice (C) is the simple form.

5. **(B)** *Increased* means to *go up*. Choices (A) and (C) are not used with money. Choice (D) confuses *rise* and *raise*.

6. **(A)** *Although* here means *in spite of* the rain, we drove in a jeep without a roof. Choices (B) and (C) indicate cause and effect. Choice (D) is a preposition, not a conjunction.

7. **(D)** *At* is used with specific indications of time. Choice (A) is used for placement. Choice (B) is for location. Choice (C) is used for location.

8. **(C)** *Was* is followed by the past participle *sent*. Choice (A) is the simple form. Choice (B) uses *has*, not *was*. Choice (D) is the gerund form.

9. **(A)** The adverb of indefinite frequency comes between the auxiliary and the main verb. Choice (B) is followed by the simple form of the verb. In Choice (C) the adverb follows the main verb. In Choice (D) the adverb precedes the auxiliary.

10. **(C)** Choice (C) indicates position with the post office on one side and the bank on the other side. Choice (A) is used when there are three or more reference points. Choice (B) is incorrect because an office would not normally be *outside*. Choice (D) would be possible only if all three (post office, bank and office) were in one building and you had to pass through both to get to the office.

11. **(A)** A real condition can use a command form in the *if* clause. Choice (B) is an adverb. Choice (C) is a noun. Choice (D) is an infinitive.

12. **(C)** *Off* is used for distance toward the ocean. Choice (A) is not logical. Choice (B) would mean it is located beneath the sand. Choice (D), *beside* the shore, would be possible, but the article *the* would have to be used.

13. **(C)** *Since*, here, shows a cause and effect relationship. Choices (A) and (D) imply contradictions. Choice (B) must have a noun object (*during the time that exports have increased...*).

14. **(B)** expresses the truth about what really happens in the world. Choices (A), (C) and (D) are grammatical but not logical.

15. **(D)** *Nor* is the conjunction paired with *neither*. Choices (A), (B), and (C) are not used with *neither*.

16. **(C)** The causative *recommend* requires the simple form of *be*. Choice (A) is the present tense plural form. Choice (B), *have hired*, is present perfect. Choice (D) is not used with past participles.

17. **(B)** The command form signals a real condition; use the present tense in the *if* clause. Choice (A) would be used in an unreal condition. Choice (C) is the past tense. Choice (D) is the *-ing* form.

18. **(B)** The causative *had* requires the past participle. Choice (A) is the simple form. Choice (C) is the *-ing* form. Choice (D) is the command form.

19. **(C)** Use simple past tense to express a one-time past action. Choice (A) is the present tense. Choice (B) is the present perfect. Choice (D) is past progressive.

20. **(D)** The simple form of a verb is used after *must*. Choice (A) is the past tense. Choice (B) is the gerund. Choice (C) is the present tense.

Part VI

21. **(B)** The article *the* needs to precede the singular count noun *year*: *of the year*. Choice (A) is a correct preposition for specific time reference. Choice (C) is a correct verb for *bonuses*. Choice (D) is a correct noun.

22. **(B)** The singular *association* requires the singular verb *has*. *Industries* is the object of *of*. The association has come under attack. Choice (A) is a correct article for *association*. Choice (C) is a correct preposition with *attack*. Choice (D) is a correct noun.

23. **(D)** The pronoun *us* is an object pronoun. This spot requires the subject pronoun *we*. Choice (A) is a correct verb. Choice (B) is a correct noun phrase. Choice (C) is a correct article.

24. **(B)** The correct verb form of this conditional statement is *would have passed*. Choice (A) is a correct article. Choice (C)

is a correct noun. Choice (D) is a correct prepositional phrase.
25. **(B)** Never use *more* and *-er* form together. Omit *more*. *The rates are higher this year.* Choice (A) is a correct noun. Choice (C) is a correct pronoun. Choice (D) is a correct verb for *they*.
26. **(A)** *While* is a conjunction. Here use a preposition, *For ten weeks*. Choice (B) is a correct verb. Choices (C) and (D) are correct prepositions.
27. **(C)** Equal comparative forms require *as...as* around the simple form of the adjective; *The dollar has never been as low as it is now*. Choice (A) is a correct article. Choice (B) is a correct verb for *dollar*. Choice (D) is a correct pronoun.
28. **(B)** *Immediately* is an adverb. Use the adjective *immediate* to modify *service*: *For immediate service*. Choice (A) is a correct preposition. Choice (C) is a correct pronoun. Choice (D) is a correct adjective.
29. **(C)** Compound adjectives are not plural: *a ten-minute coffee break*. Choice (A) is a correct article. Choice (B) is a correct verb. Choice (D) is a correct preposition.
30. **(D)** The preposition *before* cannot end a sentence. Omit it or change the word order *before last week*. Be careful of the change in meaning of the sentence: when was the letter mailed, last week or before last week? Choice (A) is a correct verb to express past tense. Choice (B) is a correct preposition. Choice (C) is a correct verb to express prior past action.

Problems Analyzing Reading Passages

Questions on Advertisements
Problem 42
Part VII
1. **(C)** *Attention Manufacturers* indicates that the writers want manufacturers to read the ad. Choice (A) confuses the writers of the ad with the readers. Choices (B) and (D) are not mentioned.
2. **(B)** It indicates they can distribute in 155 countries. Choice (A) is less than the number mentioned. Choices (C) and (D) are more than the number mentioned.

Questions on Forms
Problem 43
Part VII
1. **(D)** To *subscribe* means that you will start to receive a periodical. Choices (A), (B), and (C) are contradicted by the heading *Special Subscription Offer*.
2. **(B)** The full cover price is $5 an issue ($60 divided by 12 months). Choice (A) is less than the price. Choices (C) and (D) are more than the price.
3. **(B)** *Allow four weeks for first issue* means about *one month*. Choice (A) is shorter than a month. Choices (C) and (D) are not logical.
4. **(C)** If there are 12 issues in one year, the magazine comes monthly. Choices (A) and (B) are more often. Choice (D) is less often.

Questions on Reports
Problem 44
Part VII
1. **(C)** They could pay $10 million; *$5 million up front* plus *as much as $5 million more*. Choice (A) is the amount Peptel posted in sales last year. Choice (B) is the initial price. Choice (D) is what Markel is worth.
2. **(D)** *Of Berlin* means the company is based there. Choice (A) is where Markel is based. Choices (B) and (C) are not mentioned.
3. **(A)** If Peptel is in educational software, Markel is probably in software, too. Choices (B) and (D) are not mentioned. Choice (C) confuses *visual arts* with the company name *Peptel Visual*.

Questions on Letters
Problem 45
Part VII
1. **(C)** *Samples* are not requested. Choices (A), (B), and (D) are explicitly requested. (*Terms* means *pricing information*.)
2. **(B)** *Hardware* includes computers. Choice (A) is contradicted by the fact that they are *adding software to their sales offerings*. Choices (C) and (D) are not mentioned.
3. **(A)** *Add software to our sales offerings* means *distribute software*. Choice (B) is not mentioned. Choice (C) confuses *selling hardware* with *purchasing hardware*. Choice (D) confuses *sending* an annual report with *receiving* an annual report.

Questions on Faxes
Problem 46
Part VII
1. **(B)** The meeting will be held in *Building B*. Choice (A) confuses *Room 42* and *Room 24* and *Tuesday the 24th*. Choice (C) has no reference point. Choice (D) is incorrect because the reception, not the meeting, is at the hotel.
2. **(B)** A meeting that *begins on Tuesday and lasts though Thursday* lasts 3 days. Choice (A) confuses *2 days* with *Tuesday* and *Thursday*. Choice (C) confuses days the meeting will last with *24* and *42*. Choice (D) is the time the meeting will end on Thursday.
3. **(A)** If Tuesday is the 24th and it was written on the 23rd, it was written on Monday. Choice (B) is the day the meeting starts. Choice (C) is the day the meeting ends. Choice (D) is not mentioned.
4. **(D)** There are *this + 10* pages for 11 pages total. Choice (A) omits the *attached budget*. Choice (B) confuses two items (*this* and *10*) with the number of pages. Choice (C) omits *this* cover sheet.

Questions on Memos
Problem 47
Part VII
1. **(B)** *No flights under five hours can be booked in Business Class*, but flights over that can. Choice (A) *Economy* is probably the class where flights under five hours can be booked. Choices (C) and (D) are contradicted by *No flights...can be booked in First Class or on the Concorde*.
2. **(A)** If it is written *May 15* and goes into effect *June 1*, it goes into effect in *two weeks*. Choices (B) and (C) are contradicted by *June 1*. Choice (D) confuses *five hours* with *five months*.
3. **(B)** The memo is about saving money. Choices (A), (C), and (D) are not mentioned.
4. **(D)** The memo affects *all personnel*. Choices (A), (B), and (C) are contradicted by *all personnel*.

Questions on Tables
Problem 48
Part VII
1. **(A)** Amsterdam and Taipei are both coded *C* for cloudy. Choice (B) cities were partly cloudy. Choices (C) and (D) had different weather but were not cloudy.
2. **(D)** Manila had a high of *33/91*. Choices (A), (B), and (C) had lower temperatures.
3. **(B)** Frankfurt had a spread from *3/37* to *1/34*. Choices (A), (C), and (D) had wider spreads.
4. **(B)** Kuala Lampur is coded for *t* thunderstorms. Choices (A), (C), and (D) are not mentioned for this city.

Questions on Indexes
Problem 49
Part VII
1. **(A)** Magazines need *indexes* and come in *issues*. Choices (B) and (D) do not come in issues. Choice (C) probably does not have a large index.
2. **(B)** *Computer industries* are not listed. In choice (A) travel is represented by Canadian Rail Service, Network Travel Pride Hotels, and TNT Air. In Choice (C) heavy industries are represented by Allied Steel, Best Iron Ore, and Chemical Times. In Choice (D) utilities are represented by Acme Power and Light, Consumer's Electric, and Ford Gas.

Questions on Charts
Problem 50
Part VII
1. **(C)** It shows the relative positions of successful companies by allowing you to compare sales figures. Choice (A) is incorrect because the chart lists *total sales*, not *selling price*. Choices (B) and (D) are not indicated on the chart.
2. **(B)** Sankyu's sales are almost twice those of the second-ranked company. Choice (A) is incorrect because sales from other years are not compared. Choices (C) and (D) are contradicted by the fact that it is the first-ranked company.

Questions on Graphs
Problem 51
Part VII
1. **(B)** Competing hotels would be most interested in market share information. Choices (A), (C), and (D) are unlikely to be interested.
2. **(D)** Lowit has 25%, or one-quarter, of the market. Choice (A) is incorrect because Stilton is the top-ranking chain. Choice (B) is incorrect because location information is not given in the graph. Choice (C) is incorrect because Torte has only 15% of the market.

Questions on Announcements
Problem 52
Part VII
1. **(A)** The world's third-largest means it has a rank of 3. Choice (B) is the number of years Mr. Kasper has been with the company. Choice (C) confuses the rank with the date of resignation. Choice (D) is Mr. Kasper's age.
2. **(A)** The company *could be bought*. Choices (B), (C), and (D) are contradicted by *could be bought*.
3. **(C)** If he is 62 and has been there 22 years, he has been there since he was 40. Choice (A) is contradicted by *22 years*. Choice (B) confuses the resignation date and the time he has been there. Choice (D) is his age.
4. **(A)** *Cable television systems* are communications companies. Choices (B), (C), and (D) do not include cable companies.

Questions on Notices
Problem 53
1. **(D)** Employees moving from other cities are most affected. Choices (A), (B), and (C) are not affected by these changes.
2. **(B)** *Moving household items* is reimbursed. Choices (A), (C), and (D) are *no longer reimbursable*.

Questions on Newspaper Articles
Problem 54
Part VII
1. **(D)** The collapse of the Berlin Wall has caused the change. Choice (A) is mentioned but did not cause the change. Choice (B) is not mentioned. Choice (C) is incorrect because 40 construction projects are *underway* but not completed.
2. **(D)** The article discusses how the drab aspect is changing. Choices (A), (B), and (C) are explicitly mentioned as reasons for the improvements.
3. **(B)** It says that *investments in new construction are expected to exceed $120 billion*. Choices (A) and (C) do not have costs mentioned. Choice (D) is not mentioned.

Questions on Magazine Articles
Problem 55
Part VII
1. **(A)** It is about the information revolution. Choice (B) is part of the cause but not the subject of the article. Choice (C) confuses *highways for cars* with the *Information Highway*. Choice (D) is not the subject of the article.
2. **(C)** It says *the growth potential in the market is enormous*. Choices (A), (B), and (D) may also be enormous but are not described that way.
3. **(C)** It says *the lower prices of computers have put more computers in the home*. Choices (A), (B), and (D) are the result of increased computer use.

Questions on Schedules
Problem 56
Part VII
1. **(B)** Flight 345 arrives in Los Angeles at 9:59 and in Honolulu at 2:25. Choices (A) and (C) do not stop in Los Angeles. Choice (D) is not mentioned.
2. **(D)** Flight 40 stops in Zurich. Choices (A), (B), and (C) do not pass through Zurich.
3. **(C)** Flight 40 is coded *3* for *Wednesday*. Choice (A) is incorrect because Flight 339 does not stop in Los Angeles. Choice (B) is incorrect because flights to Moscow do not operate on Tuesdays or Sundays. Choice (D) is incorrect because Flight 44 originates in Amsterdam.
4. **(D)** Flights to Los Angeles are only 1552 miles. Choice (A) is incorrect because all flights operate Monday through Friday. Choice (B) is incorrect because the flights make no stops. Choice (C) is contradicted by the mileage given.

Questions on Calendars
Problem 57
Part VII

1. **(A)** Meeting with hotel representatives, tour guides, airline agents, and the editor of a travel magazine indicates someone who works in tourism. Choices (B), (C), and (D) would not have so many meetings within the travel industry.
2. **(B)** There is one trip to Rio and another to New York. Choices (A), (C), and (D) are contradicted by the trips listed.
3. **(C)** The nights of the 3rd, 4th, and 5th will be spent away from home, making three nights away. Choices (A), (B), and (D) are contradicted by the information given.
4. **(A)** Three golf games are listed. Choices (B), (C), and (D) are not mentioned.

Mini-Test for Reading Part VII

1. **(D)** The ad is for an *international book supplier* who has books in many languages. Choice (A) uses *225 languages* to incorrectly suggest translation services. Choice (B) is contradicted by *book supplier*. Choice (C) is incorrectly suggested by the reference to *Zulu*.
2. **(B)** The third line says it's *full service*. Choice (A) is probably true but not emphasized. Choice (C) is listed but is not a *feature of the company*. Choice (D) is not mentioned.
3. **(B)** The invoice goes to the *accounting department*, which pays the bill. Choice (A) receives the shipment. Choice (C) is the vendor's purchasing department. Choice (D) sent the shipment.
4. **(A)** *Vendor* means *seller*. Choice (B) bought the equipment. Choice (C) prepared the invoice. Choice (D) will get the invoice in the accounting department.
5. **(A)** Choice (A) is the subtotal without the cards. Choice (B) is the subtotal with the cards. Choice (C) is not given. Choice (D) is the total, with cards and shipping and handling.
6. **(D)** The personnel department does not get a copy of the purchase order. Choices (A), (B), and (C) are listed by *cc:* which means they get copies of the order.
7. **(C)** *Establish a manufacturing operation near their customers* means *build factories close to their customers*. Choices (A) and (D) are areas that customers would like to be involved in. Choice (B) is contradicted by *cannot simply export more goods*.
8. **(B)** It says customers want *to provide input on design*. Choices (A) and (D), design consultants and engineers, would already have design input. Choice (C) is incorrect because suppliers probably do not want design input and are not mentioned.
9. **(C)** The purpose is to apologize. Choice (A) is contradicted by *we apologize* and *we regret*. Choice (B) is incorrect because the writer is *filling* an order. Choice (D) is not mentioned.
10. **(A)** *Were not included in the first shipment* means that *the shipment was incomplete*. Choices (B), (C), and (D) are possible shipping problems but are not mentioned.
11. **(C)** The fax was received *this morning*. Choices (A), (B), and (D) are all contradicted by *this morning*.
12. **(B)** She will *fax exact time of delivery*. Choices (A), (C), and (D) are contradicted by *by fax*.
13. **(C)** It says *at the end of the week, or at the very latest on Monday*. Choices (A), (B), and (D) are all contradicted by *on Monday*.
14. **(C)** A guest of the *engineering department* who has *done research on the effects of earthquakes* is probably a mechanical engineer. Choices (A), (B), and (D) are not logical.
15. **(A)** Mr. Wilson will be the Ukrainian's guide, since the memo is to him. Choice (B) is the visitor. Choice (C) is the person who wrote the memo. Choice (D) is contradicted by the memo.
16. **(A)** She will arrive before noon. Choices (B), (C), and (D) are contradicted by *before noon*.
17. **(A)** She is interested in designing bridges. Choices (B), (C), and (D) may be interesting but are not areas of interest within a field.
18. **(C)** Section B has other business news, so it is a likely place for market forecasts. Choices (A), (B), and (D) are not likely to be found there.

19. **(D)** Editorials contain opinions and are found on A-10. Choice (A) contains international news. Choice (B) contains commodities. Choice (C) has information on the arts.
20. **(C)** Films (movies) are found on C-3. Choice (A) is incorrect because B-11 contains information on stocks, not movies. Choice (B), page C-1, covers arts, but this choice is not as specific as Choice (C). Choice (D) is incorrect because a page covering legal issues would not contain reviews of movies.
21. **(C)** The payroll clerk reports to the Manager of Accounting. Choice (A) is not concerned with the payroll. Choices (B) and (D) do not supervise clerks.
22. **(C)** Marketing and Sales have similar staffing patterns. Choices (A), (B), and (D) do not have similar patterns.
23. **(A)** The VP of Sales supervises both the Domestic Sales Managers and International Sales Managers. Choice (B) is incorrect because the President supervises only Vice-Presidents. Choices (C) and (D) are incorrect because they are not in the Sales Department.
24. **(A)** It shows a comparison of dollar-yen rates. Choices (B), (C), and (D) are not depicted by the graph.
25. **(C)** There were fluctuations in April. Choices (A), (B), and (D) did not show such fluctuations.
26. **(B)** The contractor is located in San Francisco. Choice (A) is the location of the group that awarded the contract. Choices (C) and (D) are not logical locations for a contractor.
27. **(C)** A *three-month contract beginning in June* will end sometime in September. Choices (A), (B), and (D) are contradicted by this information.
28. **(A)** *Without notice* and *without obligation to notify* mean they can change things without telling the customer. Choices (B), (C), and (D) are not the subject of the notice.
29. **(B)** *In this manual* indicates where the information is found. Choice (A) contains information about repairs and service. Choices (C) and (D) are not logical given the subject of the notice.
30. **(B)** A *Swiss chemical company* would probably be located in Switzerland. Choice (A) is the country where Royal Chemical is located. Choices (C) and (D) are places where Royal Chemical has production plants, not the place where RADD is located.
31. **(D)** *Uses that range from rope fibers to bottles* means that polypropylene is used to make ropes, bottles, and other things. Choice (A) is also used for rope but is not mentioned. Choice (B) is used for string. Choice (C) is used for cable.
32. **(C)** The price is *between $100 million and $160 million*. Choices (A) and (B) are lower than the purchase price given. Choice (D) gives the price for only the RCI plants.
33. **(C)** *Of Britain* means *located in Britain*. Choices (A), (B), and (D) are the locations of production plants.
34. **(A)** It says the deal *would be paid in cash*. Choice (B) is not mentioned. Choices (C) and (D) are confused with *1 to 2 percent of its net assets*.
35. **(A)** The article mentions many different places where the entertainment industry is expanding. Choice (B) is incorrect because China is a *potential market*; it is not a huge market now. Choice (C) confuses the meanings of *home* (house) and *home* (base of operations). Choice (D) is incorrect because the status of opportunities in Hollywood is not mentioned.
36. **(C)** *Hollywood* is used to mean *the media*. Choices (A) and (B) are incorrect because many executives and American enterprises are not part of entertainment or media. Choice (D) is incorrect because other industries also have big markets worldwide.
37. **(D)** A schedule for a meeting is an *agenda*. Choice (A) is incorrect: An agenda shows people what to expect but cannot make them pay attention. Choice (B) is a benefit of the agenda but not the purpose of it. Choice (C) is incorrect because an agenda does not introduce speakers.
38. **(C)** A question-and-answer period follows the presentations. Choice (A) comes before the presentations. Choice (B) comes after

opening remarks. Choice (D) probably follows the close of the meeting but is not part of the meeting and is not mentioned.
39. **(B)** The items listed are stages in developing a product. Choice (A) is incorrect because the time is shown in months, not man-hours. Choices (C) and (D) are not represented by the timeline.
40. **(C)** If the proposal is submitted in February and they start work in March, the proposal will probably be approved in February. Choice (A) is incorrect because cost is not mentioned. Choice (B) is incorrect because marketing and testing are shown for the same amount of time. Choice (D) is not likely: Time is allowed for testing, so it should not slow down production.

Explanatory Answers for TOEIC Model Tests

Model Test 1

Listening Comprehension
Part I: Picture

1. **(B)** Choice (B) identifies the *technician* and the location *in a laboratory*. Choice (A) is incorrect because the woman is alone, not with a patient. Choice (C) has the related word *chemist* but incorrectly describes the action. Choice (D) incorrectly describes the action.
2. **(C)** Choice (C) identifies a *conductor directing a symphony orchestra*. Choice (A) confuses similar sounds: *sympathy* with *symphony*. Choice (B) incorrectly describes the *audience's* actions. Choice (D) confuses similar sounds: *cancer* with *concert*.
3. **(A)** Choice (A) identifies *negotiators* and the location a *meeting*. Choice (B) confuses *glasses* on the table and *eyeglasses* on the participants. They are not being washed. Choice (C) describes a *banquet*, not a *meeting*. Choice (D) is contradicted by all the seats being filled.
4. **(D)** Choice (D) identifies *skiers* and the action *walking across the mountain*. Choice (A) confuses similar sounds: *show* with *snow*. Choice (B) describes an incorrect action. Choice (C) is incorrect because there is no camping gear in the picture.
5. **(B)** Choice (B) identifies the action *emergency crew at an accident*. Choice (A) mentions a *policeman* but confuses his action; he is taking a report, not writing a ticket. Choice (C) has related words, *victim* and *hospital,* but incorrectly describes the victim at the hospital (he may go later but it is not in the picture). Choice (D) incorrectly describes that the boy is riding his bicycle now (that came before but it is not in the picture).
6. **(C)** Choice (C) identifies the *worker* and the action *assembling a car in a factory*. Choice (A) is incorrect because the man is *installing* a fan, not *delivering* one. Choice (B) uses related words *plant* and *manufacturing,* but making cars is not light manufacturing. Choice (D) has the related word *car* but does not describe the picture.
7. **(D)** Choice (D) identifies *men* and the action *stacking fruit in a truck*. Choice (A) is incorrect because the men are wearing *cowboy hats* but are not *at a rodeo*. Choice (B) confuses *vines are full of fruit* and *boxes full of fruit*. Choice (C) confuses similar sounds: *straw is very* with *strawberry*.
8. **(A)** Choice (A) identifies *employees* and the action *working with their computers*. Choice (B) confuses similar sounds: *terminal* (bus) with *terminal* (computer). Choice (C) is incorrect because the workers are in one big, common office with many desks. Choice (D) is incorrect because each worker is working separately.
9. **(D)** Choice (D) identifies the *technician* and the action: *checking circuitry*. Choice (A) confuses similar sounds *signing* and *circuitry*. Choice (B) has the related word *electric* (as in *electric circuit*) but does not describe the picture. Choice (C) confuses the *ceiling beams* with *laser beams*.
10. **(C)** Choice (C) identifies the action *exercising* and the place *gym*. Choice (A) is incorrect because there are no racquet sports

being played in the picture. Choice (B) confuses similar sounds: *train* (locomotive) with *training* (exercising). Choice (D) is incorrect because the television monitors are not even on, and no one is looking at them.

11. **(A)** Choice (A) identifies the action *flags fly* and the location *from the roof*. Choice (B) confuses two meanings: *court (judicial)* with *court (yard)*. Choice (C) confuses related words: *ceiling* and *roof*. Choice (D) is incorrect because the yard is empty.

12. **(C)** Choice (C) identifies the person *conductor*. Choice (A) is incorrect because everyone, except the conductor, is seated, and there are plenty of empty seats available. Choice (B) confuses similar sounds: *fair* with *fare*; *trampled* with *tram*. Choice (D) incorrectly describes the action.

13. **(C)** Choice (C) identifies the *worker* and the action *recording data*. Choice (A) incorrectly mentions a *robot*. Choice (B) incorrectly describes an action *pulling a lever*. Choice (D) incorrectly describes the action.

14. **(A)** Choice (A) identifies the action *horses racing*. Choice (B) confuses *hoarse throat* with *horses* and *catch up* with *race*. Choice (C) has the related word *fast* but confuses similar sounds: *writer* with *rider*. Choice (D) has the related word *jockey* but confuses similar sounds *twin* with *to win*.

15. **(B)** Choice (B) identifies the *technician* and *patient* and the action *stands beside*. Choice (A) has the related word *medicine* but does not describe the picture. Choice (C) confuses *scanned the newspaper* with a *medical scan*. Choice (D) uses the related word *patient* but incorrectly describes the situation.

16. **(D)** Choice (D) makes assumptions: *the chairs on the street seem to be part of a cafe*. Choice (A) is not able to be determined by the picture. Choice B confuses similar sounds: *cart* with *car*, and shows negation (there is no street vendor). Choice (C) is incorrect because some of the women are wearing dresses, not carrying them.

17. **(C)** Choice (C) identifies the things *pipelines* and the location *crossing the field*. Choice (A) confuses similar sounds: *banks* with *tanks*. Choice (B) incorrectly identifies an action *plowed*. Choice (D) confuses similar sounds *pipeline* with *pale lime*.

18. **(B)** Choice (B) identifies the action *cleaning the floor*. Choice (A) incorrectly identifies the location. Choice (C) incorrectly identifies how he is cleaning the floor (he is vacuuming with a vacuum cleaner, not sweeping with a broom). Choice (D) is incorrect because the man is using the vacuum, so it cannot be stored.

19. **(A)** Choice (A) identifies the thing *boat* and the action *passes under the bridge*. Choice (B) is incorrect because the boat is passing through the water without any problem. Choice (C) confuses similar sounds *ridge* and *bridge*. Choice (D) confuses a *bridge over water* with a card game called *bridge*.

20. **(D)** Choice (D) identifies the action *newlyweds are posing*. Choice (A) confuses the associated word *gardeners* with *flowers*. Choice (B) incorrectly identifies the person; the *bride*, not the *bridegroom*, is in the middle. Choice (C) incorrectly identifies the person; the *wife*, not the *husband*, is waving.

Part II: Question-Response

21. **(B)** Choice (B) is a logical response to a question about *health*. Choice (A) confuses related words: *evening* and *bed*. Choice (C) confuses similar sounds: *good evening* with *Mr. Goode*.

22. **(A)** Choice (A) is a logical response to a question about *possession*. Choice (B) confuses similar sounds: *happen* with *your pen*; *I don't know* is not a common answer for possession. Choice (C) confuses similar sounds *European* with *your pen*; *pen* uses the pronoun *it* not *he*.

23. **(B)** Choice (B) is a logical response to a question about *being late*. Choice (A) answers how long did you wait and confuses similar sounds *late* and *wait*. Choice (C) confuses similar sounds *eight* and *late*.

24. **(C)** Choice (C) is a logical response to a question about *who*. Choice (A) confuses time: *came* (past) with *is coming* (present). Choice (B) confuses the action *combing* with *coming*.

25. **(A)** Choice (A) is a logical response to a question about *time*. Choice (B) confuses

similar sounds: *when does* with *windows*. Choice (C) confuses *meet* with *meeting*.

26. **(A)** Choice (A) is a logical response to a question about *food*. Choice (B) answers *Who's coming to dinner?* Choice (C) answers *When is dinner?*

27. **(A)** Choice (A) is a logical response to a question about *location*. Choice (B) confuses time: *this weekend* (present-future) and *last week* (past). Choice (C) confuses duration of time *will last a week* with past time *last week*.

28. **(C)** Choice (C) is a logical response to a question about *frequency*. Choice (A) confuses words with same sound and different meaning: *play* (verb) with *play* (performance). Choice (B) confuses similar sounds: and *often* and *get off*.

29. **(A)** Choice (A) is a logical response to a question about *which*. Choice (B) confuses similar sounds: *fast* with *last*; *horse* is related to the idea *fast*. Choice (C) confuses homonyms: *way* with *weigh*.

30. **(C)** Choice (C) is a logical response to a question about *messages*. Choice (A) confuses *massage* (rubbing muscles) with *message*. Choice (B) confuses similar sounds: *messages* with *any of us*.

31. **(B)** Choice (B) is a logical response to a question about a *purchase*. Choice (A) confuses similar sounds: *customer* with *customs officer*. Choice (C) confuses similar sounds *(custo)mer buy* with *nearby*.

32. **(A)** Choice (A) is a logical response to a question about *how much*. Choice (B) confuses a request for *how much* (quantity) with a request for *how much* (price) and confuses *paper* with *newspaper*. Choice (C) confuses similar sounds: *pay more* with *paper*.

33. **(C)** Choice (C) is a logical response to a question about *time*. Choice (A) identifies place (*airport*) but not time. Choice (B) has the related phrase *take off* but does not answer *when*.

34. **(B)** Choice (B) is a logical response to a question about *taking a break*. Choice (A) confuses *coffee break* with *broken (coffee) cup*. Choice (C) confuses *break* with *brakes* on a car and with *won't work* (broken).

35. **(C)** Choice (C) is a logical response to a question about *finishing eating*. Choice (A) confuses *finish* (eating) with *finish* (a report), and *she* is not a response for *have you?* Choice (B) has the related word *eggs* (*food*) but does not answer the question, and it confuses similar sounds: *finished eating* with *been beaten*.

36. **(A)** Choice (A) is a logical response to a question about *location*. Choice (B) gives the price of the rooms, not the location of the hotel. Choice (C) confuses similar sounds: *el(evator)* with *(ho)tel*.

37. **(C)** Choice (C) is a logical response to a question about the *artist*. Choice (A) confuses *paid* with *painted* and *picture* with *picture frame*. Choice (B) confuses related words: *picture-painter* with *picture-photographer*.

38. **(B)** Choice (B) is a logical response to a question about *which*. Choice (A) confuses similar sounds: *hours* with *ours*. Choice (C) has the related word *seat* but does not answer *which*.

39. **(B)** Choice (B) is a logical response to a question about *time*. Choice (A) confuses *join* and *company* with an invitation (contrast *alone*). Choice (C) confuses similar sounds: *join* with *joint*.

40. **(C)** Choice (C) is a logical response to a question about *location*. Choice (A) confuses similar sounds: *ear* with *here*. Choice (B) confuses *closed* with *near* (*close*).

41. **(B)** Choice (B) is a logical response to a question about *possession*. Choice (A) confuses similar sounds: *open* with *pen*. Choice (C) confuses similar sounds: *European* with *your pen*.

42. **(A)** Choice (A) is a logical response to a question about *what kind*. Choice (B) confuses similar sounds: *read* with *proceed* and *like* (v) with *like* (conj.). Choice (C) confuses similar sounds: *kind* with *find*.

43. **(C)** Choice (C) is a logical response to a question about *buying a house*. Choice (A) has the related word *room* but does not answer *why don't you buy?* Choice (B) confuses *sell* with *buy*.

44. **(B)** Choice (B) is a logical response to a question about *where*. Choice (A) confuses time: *lunch tomorrow* with *did have lunch*. Choice (C) answers *when* (at noon), not *where*.
45. **(A)** Choice (A) is a logical response to a question about *asking your father*. Choice (B) confuses similar sounds: *far* with *father*. Choice (C) confuses similar sounds: *ask* with *task*.
46. **(C)** Choice (C) is a logical response to a question about *who attended the conference*. Choice (A) confuses similar sounds: *conference* with *fence*. Choice (B) gives the day of the conference, not who attended.
47. **(A)** Choice (A) is a logical response to a question about *which shoes*. Choice (B) confuses similar sounds: *comfortable* with *table*. Choice (C) confuses *taking off* shoes with *wearing* shoes.
48. **(B)** Choice (B) is a logical response to a question about *location for a coat*. Choice (A) confuses similar sounds: *leave* with *live*. Choice (C) confuses *leave my coat* with *leave a note*.
49. **(C)** Choice (C) is a logical response to a question about an *order*. Choice (A) confuses similar sounds: *place* with *race*. Choice (B) confuses different meanings: *place* (submit) and *place* (location) and similar sounds: *order* with *door*.
50. **(A)** Choice (A) is a logical response to a question about *finishing*. Choice (B) confuses being *done* (finishing) with *well-done* (how meat is cooked). Choice (C) confuses similar sounds: *done* with *fun*.

Part III: Short Conversations

51. **(C)** *5:00* is a possible time for them both. Choices (A) and (B) are rejected by the woman. Choice (D) confuses the sounds *then* and *ten*.
52. **(A)** *Deposit, account, branch,* and *checking* all suggest *bank*. Choice (B) confuses *deposit* and *depot*. Choice (C) confuses *ranch* with *branch*. Choice (D) confuses *account* and *accounting*.
53. **(D)** The man states that *government buildings* are next on the tour. Choices (A) and (C) are the kinds of stops common on tours. Choice (B) is incorrect because although a *commercial district* would probably have *stores*, it's not next on the tour.
54. **(A)** The woman asks about a *direct flight*, so she would probably prefer one. Choice (B) is suggested, but we don't know if the woman agrees. Choice (C) confuses *change* with *exchange*. Choice (D) is unlikely if the woman is already purchasing tickets.
55. **(C)** The man requests *two towels*; then *soap*. Choice (A) is incorrect because he's in a *hotel*, not an *apartment*. Choices (B) and (D) are incorrect because he doesn't mention bad service or a different room.
56. **(B)** The man complains about *not finding a taxi*, then agrees to try the taxi *stand*. Choice (A) confuses *stand on the corner* with *taxi stand on the corner*. Choice (C) repeats *find*. Choice (D) confuses *taxi* and *taxes*.
57. **(C)** The person who *takes food orders* is a waiter. Choices (A) and (B) are also people who *recommend* things, but they don't take orders. Choice (D) may take a food order, but not in this manner.
58. **(A)** An applicant's *experience* is a common question at a job interview. Choice (B), sounds similar to *experience*. Choice (C) confuses *and* with *attitude*. Choice (D), *appetite*, evokes a food context, but does not fit the context of the conversation.
59. **(B)** *By 1:00* indicates a deadline. Choice (A) is not mentioned. Choices (C) and (D) are when the repairman is expected.
60. **(C)** The man can finish it *on the plane*. Choices (A) and (B) are stated as places the woman *can* work. Choice (D) is what they need the report for.
61. **(D)** The man asks about *bags,* another term for *luggage*. Choices (A), (B), and (C) are all mentioned by the woman.
62. **(A)** The woman advises the man to *leave earlier*. Choices (B), (C), and (D) are not mentioned.
63. **(D)** The man states he is *waiting for his wife*. Choice (A) confuses *shopping* with *sales clerk*. Choice (B) confuses *kids* with *children*. Choice (C) confuses *lunch* with *waitress*.
64. **(B)** *Package* is not mentioned, but *sending* is; *special delivery* and *overnight mail* are

both ways to send packages. Choice (A) confuses *staying overnight* (as at a hotel) with *overnight mail*. Choice (C) confuses *specializing in deliveries* with *special delivery*. Choice (D) confuses *getting* with *sending*.

65. **(C)** Speakers mention *too many people* and *overcrowded*. Choice (A) is not mentioned. Choice (B) confuses *conventional* (adjective meaning *traditional, expected*) with *convention* (noun, from *to convene*). Choice (D) confuses the ideas of a *big convention* and *bigger rooms*.

66. **(D)** The man says the train station is *downtown* and the airport is *too far away*. Choice (A) is true, but you still have to get from the airport to the city. Choice (B) confuses *rain* and *train*. Choice (C) is not mentioned.

67. **(A)** The woman states she will *address* and *mail* the brochures. Choices (B) and (C) are not logical; if the brochures are *back from the printer* they have been written and printed already. Choice (D) is not logical; if they are printed, they don't need to be *copied*.

68. **(B)** *Meter, bags,* and *driver* all suggest *taxi*. Choices (A), (C), and (D) are not places you pay a *driver*.

69. **(D)** *Dialing a number* and *leaving a message* on an *answering machine* are activities associated with making a phone call. Choice (A) is incorrect because the machine is *turning itself off*; the woman isn't turning it off. Choice (B) confuses *answering a call* and *making a call*. Choice (C) confuses *leaving a message* and *taking a message*.

70. **(A)** Questions about *window seats, dinner flights*, and mention of *movies* suggest the purchase of plane tickets; *travel agent* is the only profession mentioned that arranges ticket purchases. Choices (B), (C), and (D) do not handle ticket purchases.

71. **(B)** The man's directions end at a *bank;* the woman asks about a *drive-in window*. She is looking for a *bank*. Choice (A) confuses *drive-through window* of fast food restaurants with *drive-in window*. Choice (C) confuses *park, past the park,* and *parking lot*. Choice (D) assumes the *parking lot* is the final destination.

72. **(D)** The man proposes *buying more printers* as a way to solve the problem of people waiting to use printers. Choice (A) is not a good solution if the things really need to be printed. Choice (B) would not solve the problem. Choice (C) is the problem now.

73. **(C)** He can't play *golf* because it will probably *rain*. Choice (A) is a possible reason for not playing golf, but not true here. Choice (B) confuses *tired* with *tired of rain*. Choice (D) is not true; he will not play.

74. **(C)** If he is *in his office after 4:00*, she should call after 4:00. Choice (A) confuses *1:00* with the number of changes Mr. Green would like to make. Choice (B) confuses *2:00* with *to the proposal*. Choice (D) was when Mr. Green called, not when *the woman should call back*.

75. **(A)** *Offer you the position* means *give you the job*. Choice (B) confuses *made an offer* with *offer you the position*. Choice (C) confuses *resources* with *human resources assistant*. Choice (D) confuses *accept (the offer)* with the common expression *accept help*.

76. **(D)** He needs *stationery;* she needs *pens and paper clips;* he will probably bring all three. Choices (A), (B), and (C) do not mention all of the needed items.

77. **(B)** The man might be more comfortable in a chair designed for *his height*. Choice (A) is incorrect; a *keyboard* can be *uncomfortable,* but is not mentioned here. Choice (C) is not mentioned. Choice (D) is incorrect; he may want to *sit up straight*, but the *chair* won't let him.

78. **(C)** The woman states the phone was *off the hook*. Choice (A) is not mentioned. Choice (B) is not true; it can't be used if it is off the hook. Choice (D) confuses *tied up* with *important calls* with the man's statement that the woman might *miss important calls*.

79. **(A)** If Mr. Smith has the report, she can *borrow it from him*. Choice (B) confuses *borrow* and *lend*. Choice (C) associates *borrow, lend,* and *loan* with *take out a loan*. Choice (D) associates *loan* and *banking report* for a bank context.

80. **(B)** *Smoke* and the *fire department* suggest that there is a fire. Choice (A) will be true

after the fire but may not be true now. Choice (C) is a different reason to *move out of the street*. Choice (D) confuses a person *smoking (a cigarette)* with *smoke* from a fire.

Part IV: Short Talks

81. **(A)** *Arrival and departure gates, baggage claims,* and *ticketing areas* all suggest an airport. Choices (B) and (C) are not specific enough. Choice (D) is incorrect because an amusement park train would not lead to *baggage claims*.
82. **(C)** The instructions say you should be in the *center of the car*. Choice (A) is contradicted by *away from the doors*. Choice (B) is incorrect because *windows* are not mentioned. Choice (D) is contradicted by *in the center*.
83. **(B)** The museum is open from *one until five on Sundays*; this is afternoon. Choices (A) and (C) are not mentioned. Choice (D) contradicts the fact that the museum is open from *one until five on Sundays*.
84. **(C)** The announcement says that *lecture information can be obtained by calling our Education Office at 548-6251*. Choices (A), (B), and (D) are not mentioned.
85. **(D)** The passage says to *start the morning by making a list*. Choices (A), (B), and (C) are not mentioned.
86. **(A)** The passage says that you should *next, rank each task ...according to its importance*. Choice (B) is contradicted by *stay with (the task) until it is completed*. Choice (C) is contradicted by *work on the most important task first*. Choice (D) is not mentioned.
87. **(B)** Since the ad is for *office furniture* and *accessories, it encourages you to redecorate your office*. Choice (A) is not mentioned. Choices (C) and (D) are part of redecorating and purchasing their furniture.
88. **(D)** The ad mentions a sale on *furniture*. Choices (A), (B), and (C) are not mentioned.
89. **(C)** The ad states that you can help by *serving as a volunteer tutor*. Choice (A) is not mentioned but is associated with *schoolwork, child, learning,* and *school system*. Choice (B) *school children* are the people tutors will be helping. Choice (D) *businessmen* and *businesswomen* are reading the ad.
90. **(A)** You can help for *as little as two hours a week*. Choice (B) is contradicted by *as little as*. Choices (C) and (D) are not mentioned.
91. **(C)** If temperatures are in the *mid-sixties*, it's about *65 degrees*. Choice (A) is confused with *breezes of ten to fifteen miles per hour*. In Choice (B), *sixty* is the first part of *sixty-five*. Choice (D) is not mentioned.
92. **(B)** The weatherman says to *spend some time outdoors*. Choice (A) is contradicted by *spend some time outdoors*. Choices (C) and (D) are possible but not mentioned.
93. **(A)** Lodge costs include *continental breakfast and gourmet dinner*. Choice (B) is contradicted by *ski equipment is available...for a small additional fee*. Choice (C) is not mentioned. Choice (D) is not provided.
94. **(B)** The ad says that *certified ski instructors provide classes*. Choice (A) is not mentioned. Choice (C) applies to skiers and non-skiers. Choice (D) is not interesting if you don't know how to ski.
95. **(C)** The announcement says there are delays of *up to 45 minutes*. Choices (A) and (D) are not mentioned. Choice (B) is confused with *trains are currently running every fifteen minutes*.
96. **(D)** Delays are caused by *damage to the tracks*. Choices (A), (B), and (C) are not mentioned.
97. **(A)** They are providing *special buses to carry commuters around the damaged portions of the track*. Choice (B) will not help people commute quickly. Choice (C) does not address the problem; the trains are fine, the track *is broken*. Choice (D) is not logical; it is impossible to use any trains if the track is damaged.
98. **(A)** The problem is *an explosion*. Choices (B), (C), and (D) all confuse similar sounds.
99. **(D)** Though the cause is not known, they *suspect a leaking gas pipe*. Choices (A), (B), and (C) are possible problems but are not mentioned.

100. **(B)** *Evacuated* means *removed*. Choice (A) is contradicted *by no injuries were reported*. Choice (C) confuses *no injuries were reported* with *people being reported*. Choice (D) is incorrect because a *gas leak* was suspected; people were not suspected.

Reading

Part V: Incomplete Sentences

101. **(B)** *Customer* is singular, so it takes a singular verb; it is also third person, so it takes the third person form of *is*. Choice (A) is singular but first person. Choice (C) is plural. Choice (D) is the simple form of the verb.
102. **(D)** The direct object position must be filled by a noun; *failure* is the only noun listed. Choices (A), (B), and (C) are all verb forms.
103. **(C)** *In* is used with city locations. Choices (A) and (D) are not used with locations in this context. Choice (B) may be used only when a from/to contrast is stated or implied (e.g., *from the suburbs into the city*).
104. **(B)** *Were not* requires a past participle to complete the verb. Choice (A) is a noun. Choice (C) is in the progressive form. Choice (D) is the simple form.
105. **(A)** The present tense in the *if* clause can be matched with future tense in the second clause; *will* can also be used with *assist* to make a complete verb. Choices (B) and (C) are past tense. Choice (D) is present tense, and must be used with either the *past participle* or the progressive form.
106. **(C)** The noun *knowledge* followed by *and* should be joined to another noun. Choices (A) and (B) are verbs. Choice (D) is a noun, but refers to a person rather than a thing.
107. **(B)** *Increase* is the most common verb meaning *go up* used with *costs*. Choices (A), (C), and (D) mean *go up* but are not used for nouns related to percentages.
108. **(D)** The subject position requires a noun; there is no article so the noun must be non-count. Choices (A) and (B) are verbs. Choice (C) is a singular count noun.
109. **(C)** *Because* establishes a logical cause and effect relationship between the two events. Choice (A) indicates contrast; it is not logical unless the plane *was on time*. Choice (B) suggests a simultaneous relationship, not possible because of present tense *is* and past tense *was*. Choice (D) is a preposition and cannot be used to join clauses.
110. **(B)** *To* indicates a change in time. Choice (A) is used with one specific time. Choice (C) is used with a period of time (e.g., *in two hours*). Choice (D) is used with deadlines.
111. **(A)** *Went* is the only verb in the list that can be used. Choice (B) is a past participle and requires *have* (*has gone*). Choice (C) is the simple form. Choice (D) is the progressive form and requires a form of *be* (*is going*).
112. **(A)** *Commute* means to travel from home to work. Choices (B), (C), and (D) do not fit the context of the sentence.
113. **(C)** Indicates that one object has another object on each side. Choice (A) is most often used when one hard-to-count group is indicated (*among the paper clips, among the office equipment*). Choices (B) and (D) are not logical.
114. **(A)** *Job* is used here to refer to an individual position. Choices (B) and (D) imply professional standing greater than individual jobs. (*In his career (occupation) as an insurance investigator, he held jobs with several companies*). Choice (C) implies unpleasant work smaller than an individual job. (*I like my job as a secretary, but it's a chore to sort the boss's mail*).
115. **(D)** *File* has the same meaning here as *submit*. Choice (A) is a form of the verb *fill*. Choices (B) and (C) are forms of the verb *fall*.
116. **(B)** *After* establishes a logical time relationship between the two events. Choice (A) is an adverb, indicating a period of time after a specific event. Choice (C) indicates a comparison. (*His fax arrived later than mine*). Choice (D) is an adjective and cannot be used to join clauses.

117. **(C)** *Because* indicates a cause and effect relationship between the two events. Choice (A) implies contrast. Choice (B) *during* cannot be followed by a sentence. Choice (D) indicates a contrast.

118. **(B)** *Required* means to be obliged. Choices (A), (C), and (D) do not fit the context of the sentence.

119. **(A)** *Or* is logical and can join two nouns. Choice (B) is not usually used in a negative relationship. Choices (C) and (D) are not logical.

120. **(D)** *Always* comes between the auxiliary and *be* (if *be* occurs in the sentence). Choices (A), (B), and (C) do not place *always* between the auxiliary and *be*.

121. **(B)** The blank requires an adjective; *available* is the only one given. Choices (A) and (D) are verbs. Choice (C) is a noun.

122. **(C)** The causative *suggest* is followed by the simple form of the verb. Choice (A) is the plural form. Choices (B) and (D) are simple forms, but are not logical.

123. **(C)** *Spaces* must be modified by an adjective. Choices (A) and (D) are adjectives, but are not logical. Choice (B) is a noun.

124. **(D)** *Order* must be modified by an adjective. Choice (A) is a noun. Choice (B) is a verb. Choice (C) is an adverb.

125. **(C)** *Behind* is logical and does not need other words to complete the expression. Choice (A) requires *from* (*across from the reception desk*). Choice (B) requires a second location (*between the reception desk and the door*). Choice (D) is not logical.

126. **(D)** *Must* requires the simple form of the verb. Choice (A) is the past tense. Choice (B) is the progressive form. Choice (C) is the third-person singular form.

127. **(B)** *Tasks* must be modified by an adjective. Choice (A) is a verb. Choice (C) is a noun. Choice (D) is an adverb.

128. **(A)** *Reminded* requires the infinitive. Choice (B) is the simple form. Choice (C) is the past participle. Choice (D) is the progressive form.

129. **(D)** *Put on* is a two-word verb that in this context means *to produce*. The other prepositions in Choices (A), (B), and (C) do not fit the context of the sentence.

130. **(C)** *Never* can come between the auxiliary and the verb. Choices (A), (B), and (D) cannot.

131. **(B)** The *if* clause in the past perfect conditional matches with a past tense in the second clause. Choice (A) is the past conditional. Choice (C) is future tense. Choice (D) is future perfect.

132. **(C)** *Appointment* means a planned time. Choice (A), *schedule*, might be changed but not canceled. Choice (B), *calendar*, is the thing you plan schedules and appointments on. Choice (D), *time*, is used with appointment (*an appointment at a scheduled time*).

133. **(B)** Present tense in the *if* clause can be matched with future tense in the second clause. Choice (A) is present tense. Choice (C) is past tense. Choice (D) is present tense but indicates an unreal condition.

134. **(B)** *On* indicates *placed upon the surface of*. Choice (A) means *inside* or *within*. Choice (C) indicates the *recipient* of the letter. Choice (D) indicates *origin* of the letters.

135. **(B)** The sentence requires a present third person singular or past tense verb; only *departs* is given. Choice (A) is present tense, but not third person singular. Choice (C) is the infinitive. Choice (D) is an *-ing* form.

136. **(D)** *During* is logical and can immediately precede a noun phrase. Choice (A) is not logical and must be followed by a clause. Choice (B) is not logical. Choice (C) needs *of* (*because of the meeting*).

137. **(A)** *Efficiently* is logical. Choices (B), (C), and (D) are not logical; he probably does have to type more carefully, slowly, and gradually.

138. **(A)** *Was damaged* can be followed by the past tense. Choice (B) uses the present *has*. Choice (C) uses *was* but with the progressive form of *deliver*. Choice (D) is the past perfect.

139. **(C)** *Mr. Green* should be modified by the *-ed* form (something else caused Mr. Green to become excited). Choice (B)

isn't logical because it means that Mr. Green made someone else feel excited. Choices (A) and (D) are verbs, not adjective forms.

140. **(D)** Choice (D) is logical; it implies a contrast between *weekends* and *holidays*. Choice (A) is used with *or*. Choice (B) implies a choice between items. Choice (C) indicates cause and effect.

Part VI: Error Recognition

141. **(A)** (biggest problem is) The subject *problem* requires the singular verb *is*. Choice (B) correctly links two clauses. Choice (C) is plural to match *supplies*. Choice (D) is an adjective modifying *supplies*.

142. **(D)** (are asked to register) *Asked* requires the infinitive *are asked to register*. Choice (A) is plural countable so it does not require an article. Choice (B) correctly refers to *guests*. Choice (C) *delayed* is correct use of the past participle.

143. **(B)** (who had worked) *He* isn't necessary with *who*. Choice (A), *salesperson*, is correct with *a*. Choice (C) *for* indicates the source of the job. Choice (D) is a correct comparison.

144. **(C)** (even though; although) *Because* isn't logical; it should be something that indicates a contrast, such as *although*. Choice (A) is a correct infinitive after *wants*. Choice (B) is correct with *job*. Choice (D) is correct.

145. **(C)** (are) *Awards* is a plural noun and subject. The verb should be *are*. Choice (A) is a correct participle form. Choice (B) is the correct preposition. Choice (D) is the correct prepositional phrase.

146. **(B)** (while) *During* must be followed by a noun phrase (e.g., *during his hospital stay*). *While* should be used here because it can be followed by a clause. Choice (A), *for*, means *in place of*. Choice (C), *in*, is used with *hospital*. Choice (D) is a correct preposition; sick *with* expresses illness.

147. **(D)** (to track) *To* cannot be used with the *-ing* form of a verb; use the infinitive *to track*. Choice (A) is a correct match between *the* and a singular count noun. Choice (B) is correct with *is*. Choice (C) correctly modifies *software*.

148. **(C)** (lemon) *Lemon* is used here as a non-count noun and does not need *the*. Choice (A) is singular to match *Ms. Minor*. Choice (B) correctly refers to *Ms. Minor*. Choice (D) correctly indicates a quantity of the non-count noun *sugar*.

149. **(D)** (has finally been) *News* is a non-count subject and takes a singular verb *has*. Choice (A) *the* is a correct article for a non-count noun. Choice (B) *about* means *concerning*. Choice (C) *new* correctly modifies *contract*.

150. **(B)** (should know) *Know* is rarely used in a progressive tense (*is knowing*, *was knowing*, etc.) Choice (A) *a* is correct for a singular count noun. Choice (C) modifies *attractions*. Choice (D) is a correct plural.

151. **(A)** (wanted to spend) *Want* is followed by the infinitive *to spend*, not the gerund. Choice (B) correctly modifies *money*. Choice (C) establishes a logical time link between clauses. Choice (D) *a* is correct for the singular count noun *expert*.

152. **(C)** (suggested that the team work) The causative *suggest* is followed by the simple form of the verb. Choice (A) is correct for a specified noun. Choice (B) is a correct form of the verb. Choice (D) modifies how the team should *work*.

153. **(C)** (is faster than) Never use *more* with an *-er* form. Choice (A) is a correct verb form. Choice (B) modifies *software*. Choice (D) is a correct comparison with *faster* (*is faster than*).

154. **(C)** (enjoyed planning) *Enjoy* is followed by the gerund *planning*, not the infinitive. Choice (A) is a correct possessive. Choice (B) modifies how he *enjoyed* it. Choice (D) tells what kind of party.

155. **(D)** (the best development program) A comparison of many companies requires the superlative form *best*. Choice (A) is a correct noun subject with *the*. Choice (B) is a correct plural. Choice (C) is a correct verb form.

156. **(A)** (would) Future *will* does not match past tense *wanted* in the *if* clause; use

would. Choice (B) correctly indicates a time relationship. Choice (C) correctly links an event with a real condition. Choice (D) correctly modifies *flight.*

157. **(A)** (considered staying) *Considered* is followed by the gerund *staying.* Choice (B) correctly modifies *hotel.* Choice (C) is a correct relative pronoun. Choice (D) is a correct comparative.

158. **(C)** (the easier way) Choice (A) correctly modifies *lawyer.* Choice (B) correctly uses the simple form after *help.* Choice (D) is correct for a specified noun.

159. **(D)** (which never came) Present tense *comes* doesn't match past tense *waited.* Choice (A) is correct for a specified noun. Choice (B) tells how long the secretary waited. Choice (C) is a correct preposition.

160. **(A)** (The factory was built) *It* doubles the subject; *the factory was* or *it was* but not both. Choice (B) is the correct location preposition. Choice (C) is correct for a specified noun. Choice (D) is the correct time preposition.

Part VII: Reading Comprehension

161. **(D)** The message reads *To: Helga Kloss.* Choice (A) is the person who is leaving the message. Choice (B) is the person who is taking the message. Choice (C) is incorrect because *Holiday* is the name of the shop.

162. **(A)** *Duplicate* and *repeat* have the same meaning. Choices (B) and (D) are not mentioned. Choice (C) is incorrect because delivery can't be scheduled until the order is confirmed.

163. **(B)** Trends emphasize *careers in sales and marketing.* Choices (A), (C), and (D) are not mentioned.

164. **(C)** Growth is in *areas that take advantage of modern technology.* Choice (A) may be true but is not given as a reason. Choices (B) and (D) are not mentioned.

165. **(B)** People will learn about products through *resources available in computer networks.* The other options are not mentioned.

166. **(D)** The marketer of the future will *have to be inventive,* which is similar to *creative.* The other options are not mentioned.

167. **(A)** The marketer must *devise new strategies.* The author eschews traditional strategies and does not mention the other choices.

168. **(B)** *Lucrative* and *profitable* have the same meaning. Choices (A), (C), and (D) may be true but are not given as reasons.

169. **(A)** *One share of Interactive Films Company common stock for every 5 ARC shares.* Choice (B) is true for a five-to-one ratio. Choice (C) is true for a ten-to-one ratio. Choice (D) is true for a twenty-five-to-one ratio.

170. **(D)** *No action is required* means they don't have to do anything. Choices (A), (B), and (C) are all contradicted by *no action required.*

171. **(B)** The original name Green Miles California was changed. "California" was replaced by "West." Choice (A) is a brand name. Choice (C) is the new name. Choice (D) is a brand name combined with California.

172. **(B)** The California Gardening Association did not like the similarity of the corporations' names. Choice (A) confuses *offices* with *brands.* Choice (C) repeats the word *initial.* Choice (D) confuses the hope that they not be confused with the actual reason the names were changed.

173. **(D)** *Protecting the earth* is the same *as saving the environment.* Choices (A), (B), and (C) are probably true but are not the subject of the passage.

174. **(C)** Hotels are joining the movement to save the environment. Choice (A) identifies recycling as a gimmick, but it is a trend, not a gimmick. Choice (B) implies only hotels used by Eco-Tours practice sound environmental policies. Choice (D) is true, but is not mentioned in this passage.

175. **(C)** Although the other groups could all be concerned about the environment, they are not typical of the green movement.

176. **(B)** The passage talks about *lectures* and does not mention the other options.

177. **(B)** *Ecology* is the study of the earth's life systems which is the focus of the article. Choices (A), (C), and (D) are not mentioned.

518 EXPLANATORY ANSWERS

178. **(B)** It sells *specialty food products, cookware, and kitchen accessories*. Choices (A), (C), and (D) are not items related to the food industry.
179. **(A)** *Similar plans* refers to *remodeling*. Choices (B), (C), and (D) sound possible but are not mentioned. Val D'Or bought all sixteen stores so it would not buy only the remaining six.
180. **(A)** The article stresses that chefs will come from all over and that regional foods will be featured. Choice (B) contradicts the statement that chefs will come from all over Europe. Choices (C) and (D) are not mentioned.
181. **(A)** The office products division. Choice (B) is incorrect because the office products division is part of a multinational company. Choices (C) and (D) are not mentioned.
182. **(B)** *Teaching new salespeople* is the same as *training incoming sales staff*. Choices (A) and (D) are not mentioned. Choice (C) is incorrect because experience is needed in *sales* management not *office* management.
183. **(D)** The newspaper's address is given for resumes. Choices (A), (B), and (C), are not accepting resumes.
184. **(A)** *Years of service* means *years working for the company*. Choices (B) and (D) are not considered. Choice (C) is contradicted by *highest salary*.
185. **(D)** Contributions must be made according to government regulations. Choice (A) would have to follow the government's rules. Choices (B) and (C) can contribute to the plan but are still obligated to follow government regulations.
186. **(C)** Paid *monthly* means paid *once a month*. Choices (A), (B), and (D) are all contradicted by *monthly*.
187. **(B)** The note is about Regents' plans for improvements. Choices (A), (C), and (D) are mentioned, but they are not the main purpose of the letter.
188. **(A)** Regents has been working to provide enhanced access to health care coverage. Choice (B) confuses *primer* and *premier* and is not mentioned. Choice (C) is not mentioned. Choice (D) is already being done.
189. **(D)** Regents wants members to continue making suggestions. Choices (A), (B), and (C) are not mentioned.
190. **(B)** Cooper & Allen is the company on the return address. Choice (A) received the invoice. Choice (C) is the subject of the invoice. Choice (D) is contradicted by the name on the stationery.
191. **(D)** *At the end of this month* means April 30. Choice (A) is not mentioned. Choice (B) is the last day of the period covered by the invoice. Choice (C) is the date of the invoice.
192. **(D)** *Unpaid prior balance* means they owe money on the last invoice. Choice (A) is not mentioned. Choices (B) and (C) are incorrect because charges are not broken down into taxes and other charges.
193. **(B)** They *work best if they are happy*. Choice (A) is possible but not mentioned. Choices (C) and (D) are unlikely.
194. **(A)** *Bring up to date* has the same meaning as *update*. Choice (B) is unlikely. Choices (C) and (D) are not logical.
195. **(C)** It is not suggested that employees have the power to decide changes. Choices (A), (B), and (D) are explicitly mentioned.
196. **(D)** *Maintain a high standard of routine work* means *doing a consistently good job*. Choices (A), (B), and (C) are desired by an employer but not praised.
197. **(B)** *All-inclusive* means one price covers most costs. Choice (A) is not logical. Choice (C) is a service that might be provided. Choice (D) is incorrect because airfare is not mentioned.
198. **(A)** *Not a hassle* and *not trouble* have the same meaning. Choice (B) is incorrect because costs are not compared to other costs of resorts. Choices (C) and (D) are possible, but the article specifically says these resorts are popular because they are not a hassle.
199. **(D)** *Separate fees for equipment rental* means rental costs extra. Choices (A) and (B) are included at some resorts. Choice (C) is a service at all hotels.

200. **(C)** *Check with a travel agent* means to *consult a travel agent*. Choices (A), (B), and (D) are not mentioned.

Model Test 2

Part I: Picture

1. **(B)** Choice (B) makes an assumption about the *action:* They could be *signing their names*. Choice (A) describes an incorrect action; the men are not talking to each other. Choice (C) is incorrect because if negotiations had stopped, the men wouldn't be signing documents. Choice (D) is wrong because the man on the right wears *glasses*.
2. **(D)** Choice (D) identifies the *occupation* and the *action*. The kitchen and the uniforms imply they are *cooks* engaged in their occupation. Choice (A) is incorrect because in the photo there is a man pointing, not a sign. Choice (B) is incorrect because no one is chopping vegetables. Choice (C) is incorrect because there is no way to know this from the picture.
3. **(B)** Choice (B) identifies the action of a *technician pushing buttons*. Choice (A) is incorrect because the man is not in a plane, nor is he *turning a dial;* he is clearly *pushing a button*. Choice (C) confuses a *switchboard* with the panel shown in the picture. In addition, the man is not an operator, but an engineer. Choice (D) confuses the related word *panel* (of people) with *electric panel*.
4. **(A)** Choice (A) identifies the couples' action, viewing art. Choice (B) is incorrect because some paintings are smaller than others. Choice (C) is incorrect because in the picture the *pictures are on the wall*, not *stacked on the floor*. Choice (D) is incorrect because there are no sculptures in the picture and it confuses *stand out* and people *standing*.
5. **(C)** Choice (C) makes the assumption that the location is an *airport* and that the people waiting are *passengers*. Choice (A) is incorrect because most of the passengers are *males*, not *females*. Choice (B) is contradicted by *empty*; there are many people on the concourse. Choice (D) does not describe the location of the *bags*, which are on the *floor* not on a *truck*.
6. **(D)** Choice (D) identifies the action of a *football player* who is *carrying the ball*. Choice (A) confuses *puck* with *ball*. Choice (B) identifies the people as *athletes,* but they are not *resting*. Choice (C) is incorrect because if the tackle was a success, the player with the ball would be lying on the ground.
7. **(A)** Choice (A) identifies the action of a man who looks at the *monitors*. Choice (B) incorrectly describes the location of the chair. Choice (C) confuses *computer monitor* with *television monitor*. Choice (D) cannot be determined by looking at the picture.
8. **(C)** Choice (C) identifies the person and the action. Choice (A) identifies the *drill*, but it is not being used by a *dentist*. Choice (B) identifies the *car*, but this is a *factory* not a *showroom*. Choice (D) incorrectly describes what the worker is working on.
9. **(B)** Choice (B) identifies the specific locations of the *trains*. Choice (A) confuses the sound of *train* with *crane* and uses the related word to *bridge, water*. Choice (C) uses words related to *train (narrow* and *tunnel)* but does not describe the picture and confuses the sound of *cart* with *train car*. Choice (D) is incorrect because although the city looks cluttered, there are not many skyscrapers in the picture.
10. **(C)** Choice (C) identifies the location; people are seated in front of the hotel. Choice (A) associates *shade* with *umbrella*, but the guest rooms are most likely inside the hotel. Choice (B) is incorrect because the roof of the hotel is arched, but there is no arch over the passage. Choice (D) is incorrect because all of the windows have shutters.
11. **(B)** Choice (B) identifies the action. Choice (A) associates *takeoff* with airport but describes an incorrect action. Choices (C) and (D) incorrectly describe the location, which is an airline counter and waiting area.

12. **(B)** Choice (B) identifies the action. Choice (A) confuses the sound *ten of us* with *tennis*. Choice (C) has the related word *matches*. Choice (D) is incorrect because the tennis player may be struggling to hit the ball, but there's no sign of an injury.
13. **(A)** Choice (A) identifies the action and the people. Choice (B) confuses *train* (v) and *train* (n). Choice (C) is incorrect because no one is using the hanging straps. Choice (D) uses *is not true: NOT* everyone has to *stand*.
14. **(D)** Choice (D) identifies the thing and the action. Choice (A) uses a related word: *space*. Choice (B) confuses the sound of *rocking* with *rocket* and *chair* with *air*. Choice (C) uses related words: *fly* and *air*.
15. **(C)** Choice (C) identifies the location and the action. Choice (A) uses negation; the *auditorium is not crowded*. Choice (B) is incorrect because there is no panel, and the audience is not interacting, but watching. Choice (D) uses related words such as *chairs*.
16. **(D)** Choice (D) identifies the location of people. Choice (A) is incorrect because the men's suits are solid, not striped. Choice (B) uses negation; the men are not *reading*; nor are they *eating*—similar sound. Choice (C) uses negation; the men are *sitting down* not *standing*. The word *booth* implies a *convention* or *exhibit hall*; notice the men are wearing badges.
17. **(A)** Choice (A) identifies the object and its direction. Choice (B) uses the related word *dish*, but there are no aircraft in the picture. Choice (C) uses the related word *saucer*, but there is no technician in the picture. Choice (D) uses the related word *antennae*, but there is no truck in the picture.
18. **(B)** Choice (B) makes assumptions that the woman is *repairing a machine;* she has *tools in her hand;* maybe she is repairing the machine. Choice (A) is incorrect because she is *wearing gloves*, not *measuring them*. Choice (C) confuses the *machine* with *a robot*. Choice (D) confuses the similar sound *produce* (n) with *produce* (v).
19. **(C)** Choice (C) identifies the location of the *ship*. Choice (A) is incorrect because we cannot tell if the holds are full in this picture. Choice (B) incorrectly identifies the kind of ship; it is a *tanker* not a *cruise ship*. Choice (D) is incorrect because there are no crew in the picture.
20. **(A)** Choice (A) identifies the action and the occupation. Choice (B) confuses the related word *keys* with *keyboard*. Choice (C) uses negation; the man is *not wearing glasses*. Choice (D) cannot be seen in the picture.

Part II: Question-Response
21. **(A)** Choice (A) is a logical response to the *yes/no* question that begins with the auxiliary *Did*. Choice (B) uses the vacation month *August* to confuse you; Choice (C) repeats the word *good*.
22. **(C)** Choice (C) is a logical response to the question about *length of stay*. Choice (A) gives a time and a word with similar sounds: *stay* with *day*; and answers *How long is a day?* Choice (B) answers *where*.
23. **(A)** Choice (A) is a logical response to the question about *who wrote a letter*. Choice (B) confuses similar sounds: *letter* with *better*. Choice (C) confuses sounds: *rate* with *wrote*; and *letter* with *better*.
24. **(B)** Choice (B) is a logical response to the question about *color*. Choice (A) describes the type of *shirt*. Choice (C) confuses the similar sound of *wearing* with *where I am*.
25. **(A)** Choice (A) is a logical response to the question *when*. Choice (B) confuses similar words: *call* (v) and *call* (n); Choice (C) uses related words: *call* (telephone) and *call* (She *said* I was lazy).
26. **(A)** Choice (A) is a logical reason for *waiting inside*. Choice (B) confuses similar sounds: *waiting* and *way*. Choice (C) confuses similar sounds: *waiting* and *waiter*.
27. **(C)** Choice (C) is a logical response to the question about *family origins*. Choice (A) confuses similar sounds: *family* and *famous;* Choice (B) uses related words: *children* and an answer to a *where* question: *at school*.
28. **(A)** Choice (A) is a logical response to the question *how soon*. Choice (B) confuses

similar sounds: *soon* and *son*. Choice (C) confuses similar sounds: *ready* and *red*.
29. **(B)** Choice (B) is a logical response to the question about *a restaurant choice*. Choice (A) confuses similar sounds: *to* and *tonight* Choice (C) confuses similar sounds: *restaurant* and *restored* and *shall* and *hall*.
30. **(C)** Choice (C) is a logical response to the question about *a train departure*. Choice (A) uses the related word *stop* and the similar sound of *train* and *rain*; Choice (B) repeats the words *train* and *time*.
31. **(A)** Choice (A) is a logical response to the question. Only Choice (A) answers the telephone expression: *Will you hold?* Choice (B) repeats the word *busy*. Choice (C) has similar sounds: *old* and *hold*.
32. **(B)** Choice (B) is a logical response to the question. Choice (A) uses related words: *night* and *sleep*. Choice (C) uses the similar sounds of *late* and *eat* and the related words *after ten*.
33. **(A)** Choice (A) is a logical response to the question about *the date an invoice was sent*. Choice (B) confuses similar sounds: *invoice* and *voice*. Choice (C) confuses similar sounds: *sent* and *went*, and has a date (*when* ⨯ *in March*) but doesn't answer about the *invoice*.
34. **(C)** Choice (C) is a logical response to the question about *the number of times you have been to Asia*. Choice (A) uses related words like *Chinese* for *Asia* and *watch* for *times*. Choice (B) would answer *how long does it take*.
35. **(A)** Choice (A) is a logical response to the *invitation for tonight*. Choice (B) uses similar sounds: *tonight* and *tight*. Choice (C) also uses similar sounds: *tonight* and *light*.
36. **(B)** Choice (B) is a logical response to the question of *preference*. Choice (A) confuses *tea* and *team*. Choice (C) confuses (*favo*)*rite* and *right*, *team* and *seem*.
37. **(B)** Choice (B) is a logical response to the question of *introductions*; only (B) continues the idea of *meeting* with a self-introduction. Choice (A) repeats the word *new* and answers a *yes/no* question with *no*. Choice (C) uses similar sounds: *new* and *newspaper* and *met* and *wet*.
38. **(A)** Choice (A) is a logical response to the question of *location*. Choice (B) confuses *true facts* with *fax*. Choice (C) confuses the similar sounds *machine* and *magazine*. Choices (A) and (C) both answer the question *where* but (C) refers to a *magazine* not a *fax machine*.
39. **(C)** Choice (C) is a logical response to the question about *arrival day*. All of the choices answer *when*. Choice (A) answers *what day* but is in the past tense, not the future (*is she coming*). Choice (B) answers *what month*.
40. **(B)** Choice (B) is a logical response to the question about *reservations*. Choice (A) states the idea (that reservations are required) behind the question and uses similar words: *reservation* and *reserve*; Choice (C) uses another travel industry expression (*housekeeper*) and repeats the word *bed*.
41. **(A)** Choice (A) is a logical response to the question concerning *possession*. Choice (B) confuses the sounds of *pen* with *when*. Choice (C) confuses the sounds of *pen* with *open*. Choice (C) also uses related words: *to use* and *used to*, *to having* and *have to*. Only Choice (A) answers the *yes/no* question.
42. **(B)** Choice (B) is a logical response to the question concerning a *time limit*. Both Choices (A) and (B) have time markers, but only (B) answers the question. Choice (A) confuses similar sounds: *dead* with *died*. Choice (C) confuses similar sounds: *project* and *reject;* and uses related words: *project* and *bid*.
43. **(C)** Choice (C) is a logical response to the question concerning a person's *amusement*. Choice (A) confuses *laughing* with *staffing*. Choice (B) is the wrong tense and does not give a reason. Only Choice (C) gives a probable reason for *why*.
44. **(A)** Choice (A) is a logical response to the question *who*. Choice (B) repeats the word *window* and refers to a *plant* not a *person*. Choice (C) confuses *standing* with *sanding*.
45. **(C)** Choice (C) is a logical response to the question about the *location of an address book*. Choice (A) uses a similar word: *address* (v) for *address* (n/adj). Choice (B) answers *when*. Only Choice (C) answers the question *where*.

46. **(B)** Choice (B) is a logical response to the question about *laundry service*. Choice (A) confuses similar sounds: *pressed* and *depressed*. Choice (C) uses related words: *pants* and *pair*. Only Choice (B) provides a suggestion.

47. **(C)** Choice (C) is a logical response to the question about *time*. Choice (A) uses related words: *exercise* and *healthful*; Choice (B) confuses *exercises* (n) with *exercise* (v). Only Choice (C) answers the question *when*.

48. **(A)** Choice (A) is a logical answer to why you were *late*. Choice (B) uses the similar sound *keep* for *kept*. Choices (B) and (C) repeat related words: *so long*, *the long one* or *a long time*. Only Choice (A) provides a reason.

49. **(B)** Choice (B) is a logical response to the request to *summarize*. Choice (A) confuses *article* with *art* and *(summa)rize* with *size*. Choice (C) confuses *summarize* with *summer*. Only Choice (B) responds to the request.

50. **(A)** Choice (A) is a logical response to the question about *location*. Choice (B) repeats the word *go* and answers the question *when*. Choice (C) confuses *recommend* with *comment*; and *go* with *memo*. Only Choice (A) answers the question *where*.

Part III: Short Conversations

51. **(B)** The man states that he *eats early* because he is *hungry*. Choice (A) is the woman's reason for *eating at 1:00*. Choices (C) and (D) are not mentioned.

52. **(C)** The man agrees to the woman's request. Choice (A) confuses *leave the receptionist* and *leave this package with the receptionist*. Choice (B) confuses *leave the package* and *mail the package*. Choice (D) is what the receptionist will do with packages.

53. **(C)** An *office* is the most likely place for people to *type memos* for each other. Choice (A) is incorrect because in a *classroom*, each person would type his or her own memo. Choice (B) is not a place where people type memos. Choice (D) is where people *mail letters*, not type them.

54. **(C)** The woman wants a *souvenir* to *take home*. Choice (A) is what the clerk suggests to her. Choice (B) is not mentioned. Choice (D) rhymes with *souvenir*.

55. **(A)** Since the woman is too tired, she will order room service and eat in her room. Choice (B) is what the man will do. Choice (C) confuses *room service* and *church service*. Choice (D) is unlikely if she's not attending the session.

56. **(C)** The waiter made a suggestion about *what to order*. Choice (A) is incorrect because someone at the restaurant will cook a *specialty*, but it won't be the *waiter*. Choice (B) is what the waiter *suggests* that the woman do. Choice (D) confuses *room* with *mushrooms*.

57. **(B)** You give a *credit card* when you want to *charge* something. Choice (A), a *business card*, won't help you pay for something at a *store*. Choice (C) you give to a *friend* on his or her *birthday*. Choice (D) is incorrect because the woman did not pay with *cash*.

58. **(A)** The man wishes the woman a *good trip*; they refer to *meeting again in the future*. This a proper *good-bye*. Choice (B) is the opposite of what they are doing. Choice (C) is not mentioned. Choice (D) is not possible—they have been working together.

59. **(D)** The *receptionist* is the most likely person to take *messages*. Choice (A), the *janitor*, cleans the building. Choice (B), the *nurse*, takes care of people who hurt themselves at work. Choice (C), the *vice-president*, probably does not take anyone's messages.

60. **(A)** The man sent the report, but the woman didn't receive it. Choice (B) is probably true but is not something that *went wrong*. Choice (C) is incorrect because the author of the report is not mentioned. Choice (D) is incorrect because the woman says that she *would like to see* a copy of the report.

61. **(A)** If they got the proposal, it was successful. Choice (B) confuses *contact* with *contract*. Choice (C) is not mentioned. Choice (D) is incorrect because the man has not *proposed*, but is talking about a *proposal*.

62. **(D)** A *refund* means the store will return your *money*. Choice (A) is what the man wanted to do when he *purchased the coffeemaker*. Choice (B) is one of the choices the clerk offered him. Choice (C) is what the man did originally.
63. **(B)** Both the man and the woman play *tennis*. Choice (A), *golf*, is what the man would probably play, since he mentions it first. Choice (C) is what the woman plays in addition to tennis. Choice (D) is not mentioned.
64. **(C)** Because they are *upset at their long wait*, they will *call next time*. Choice (A) is not a solution to a long wait. Choice (B) will not make a difference if the flight is delayed. Choice (D) confuses *leave for the airport* and *before we leave the airport*.
65. **(C)** The man wanted to *start the computer*. Choice (A) is impossible—he has the computer already. Choice (B) confuses *on switch* with the verb *switch*, meaning *to change*. Choice (D), give the computer back, is confused with the switch is at the *back*.
66. **(A)** The easiest way is the *hotel shuttle bus*. Choices (B) and (C) are the woman's suggestions. Choice (D) will allow him to call the hotel but will not get him there.
67. **(D)** They will *meet at 7:00*. Choice (A) is confused with 3, the number of people already scheduled for dinner. Choice (B) is the time the man's meeting will end. Choice (C) is the time the woman suggests.
68. **(B)** A *wake-up call* will wake someone up. Choice (A) is incorrect because the man has to go to a meeting, but did not ask the clerk to take him. Choice (C) confuses *call* his home with wake-up *call*. Choice (D) is not mentioned.
69. **(C)** The man states that *he didn't get the job*. Choice (A) would have been true if he got the job. Choice (B) is not mentioned. Choice (D) is not mentioned.
70. **(C)** The meetings end *late* because they start *late*. Choice (A) is not mentioned. Choice (B) confuses everyone wants to *wait* with the solution *we won't wait for anyone*. Choice (D) is not mentioned.
71. **(D)** The room is *guaranteed until 9:00*. Choice (A) confuses the date (the third) with the check-in time, 3:00. Choice (B) is the standard check-in time. Choice (C) is the time the man will arrive.
72. **(B)** Since she is describing *a tour*, she is probably a *tour guide*. Choices (A), (C), and (D) are unlikely people to describe tours in detail.
73. **(D)** *Tied up* means *busy*. Choice (A) confuses *tied* with *tired*. Choice (B) confuses *discuss it tomorrow* with *don't want to discuss it*. Choice (C) confuses *fine* with *nine*.
74. **(C)** Choice (C) The *lost-and-found department* receives reports of *missing items*. Choice (A) is not mentioned. Choice (B) is not logical—there is no reason to make the cab hurry. Choice (D) confuses *tab* with *cab*.
75. **(D)** If he is complaining about *learning the software*, he probably can't use it very well. Choice (A) is not mentioned. Choice (B) is confusing *software program* with *watching a television program*. Choice (C) confuses *don't understand* with *can't stand up*.
76. **(B)** The man wants the woman to *congratulate her team*. Choices (A) and (D) have already happened; they worked on a *team project*. Choice (C) confuses *take credit* with *take a credit card*.
77. **(C)** *To be good at something* and *to do something well* are the same. Choice (A) is what the man is trying to do. Choices (B) and (D) are not mentioned.
78. **(B)** To *fix* something is to correct it. Choice (A) confuses a *date* on a letter and a *date* meaning an evening out. Choice (C) is incorrect because the woman will sign the letter after the assistant corrects it. Choice (D) confuses *leave* (as in *leaving*) with *leave it on my desk*.
79. **(A)** Her copies are due at noon, sooner than his at 4:00. Choice (B) confuses the time that his are due (*4:00*) with *making four copies*. Choice (C) is not true—she has to make *two hundred*. Choice (D) is incorrect; he doesn't have to leave at noon, her copies are *due at noon*.
80. **(B)** They are discussing *a place to eat*. Choice (A) confuses *something light* with

sunlight. Choice (C) is incorrect because they know the location—it's the *cafe on the corner*. Choice (D) confuses *good mood* with *in the mood for* and the reference to *good salads*.

Part IV: Short Talks

81. **(B)** *Businesspeople* are the most likely to *take business trips* and *carry briefcases*. Choice (A) is incorrect because *pilots* are at work when they are in airports. Choice (C) is incorrect because *tourists* don't work during their trips. Choice (D) is incorrect because *students* don't take business trips.

82. **(A)** It's *small* and *portable*. Choices (B) and (C) are not mentioned. Choice (D) confuses *easy to use* with *unfolds easily when you're ready to use it*.

83. **(C)** The report says *rain...turning to snow...will create ice hazards*. Choice (A) is true but not complete. Choice (B) is not mentioned. Choice (D) is incorrect because wind is not mentioned.

84. **(A)** People *go to and from work* during *rush hour*. Choices (B), (C), and (D) are not mentioned.

85. **(D)** If *office workers are less fit,* then an *accountant* would be less fit. Choices (A), (B), and (C) have active outdoor jobs.

86. **(C)** Going for walks during lunch is a way to keep fit. Choice (A) is a good way to get more exercise, but it is not mentioned. Choice (B) confuses *riding bicycles to work* with *riding stationary bicycles during breaks*. Choice (D) is not mentioned.

87. **(B)** The message is *on a personal telephone answering machine*. Choice (A), a *government telephone*, would announce the name of the agency. Choice (C) confuses an *answering machine recording* and a *recording studio*. Choice (D) is not used to record messages.

88. **(D)** You are instructed to leave a *brief* message. Choices (A) and (B) are not mentioned. Choice (C) is contradicted by *brief* since detailed messages are generally long.

89. **(A)** The ad states *if you hate to do your taxes, let us do them instead*. Choice (B) is incorrect because a company can prepare your return but cannot claim your return.

Choice (C) is incorrect because you have to provide them with your financial records. Choice (D) confuses *staff your accounting department* with *staff of accountants*.

90. **(D)** The ad states *fees are based on an hourly rate*. Choices (A), (B), and (C) are all possible ways of paying for services but are not mentioned here.

91. **(A)** The airlines *reduced fares*. Choices (B), (C), and (D) are all possible ways to improve service but are not mentioned here.

92. **(C)** Airlines are trying to *win customers from competing regional airlines*. Choices (A) and (B) are possible reasons to lose customers but are not mentioned here. Choice (D) is not mentioned.

93. **(B)** A computer user would call a computer helpline. Choices (A) and (C) are people you can reach by calling this number. Choice (D) might call if he or she is a computer user.

94. **(D)** The message says, *otherwise, stay on the line*. Choices (A), (B), and (C) are not mentioned.

95. **(B)** The flight is to *Houston*. Choices (A), (C), and (D) are not mentioned.

96. **(B)** The plane will be *at the gate at 4:47*. Choices (A), (C), and (D) are all times with similar sounds; Choices (C) and (D) may also be confused with a temperature of 70 degrees.

97. **(D)** The announcement says that the weather is *sunny*. Choices (A), (B), and (C) are all weather terms but are not mentioned.

98. **(B)** *Large amounts of rain have caused flooding*. Choice (A) is not likely to fill relief shelters. Choices (C) and (D) are similar disasters but are not the problem here.

99. **(A)** *Many people have had to stay in relief shelters until the flooding subsides*. The shelters must provide them with food. Choice (B) is not mentioned. Choice (C) refers to effects of past floods, not of present floods. Choice (D) must not be a problem if they can deliver food to collection centers and shelters.

100. **(D)** If people need the *address of the food collection center*, it is probably because they need to take the food there. Choice (A) is incorrect because food should go to the flood victims, not the public. Choice (B) is

incorrect because the shelters need food but may not collect it directly. Choice (C) is where donors should call to get the address of a collection center.

Part V: Incomplete Sentences

101. **(A)** *To* indicates destination. Choice (B) means *inside* or *within*. Choice (C) means movement past. Choice (D) indicates definite location.
102. **(B)** *Training period* can be modified by the past participle *extended*. Choice (A) is a verb. Choices (C) and (D) are nouns.
103. **(D)** *Before* establishes a logical time relationship between the two past tense verbs. Choices (A) and (B) would establish an illogical cause-and-effect relationship. Choice (C) would establish an illogical equal relationship.
104. **(C)** *Request* is followed by the simple form of the verb when it means that one person or group (*subscribers*) made another person or group (*we*) do something. Choice (A) is a present form. Choice (B) is a past form. Choice (D) is a progressive form.
105. **(A)** *After* indicates that the past tense *found* happened later; the other verb must be at least past tense. Choice (B) is present tense. Choice (C) would indicate a relationship to the present not expressed in the sentence. Choice (D) is present progressive.
106. **(D)** *Project* must be modified by an adjective. Choice (A) is an adverb. Choice (B) is an adjective, but it means *following in order*. Choice (C) is a noun.
107. **(B)** *Before* establishes a logical time relationship between the two verbs. Choices (A), (C), and (D) are not logical. Choice (C) is used with *neither*.
108. **(C)** *Has* requires the past participle *shortened* to complete the verb. Choice (A) is the simple form of the verb. Choice (B) is the progressive form. Choice (D) is a noun.
109. **(B)** A person can sit *by, beside, next to* or *with* another at a dinner, etc. Choice (A) means *in place of*. Choice (C) indicates destination. Choice (D) indicates source.
110. **(A)** *Mistakes* must be modified by an adjective. Choice (B) can be a noun (person) or a verb. Choice (C) is a noun (thing). Choice (D) is a verb.
111. **(C)** *For* means *with regard to*. Choices (A) and (B) illogically indicate location. Choice (D) means *through the means of*.
112. **(B)** The present tense indicates habit, which is logical here; this also requires an *-s* ending for the third person (store owner). Choice (A) is present but not third person. Choice (C) is the progressive. Choice (D) is the infinitive.
113. **(D)** *Assist* means *help*. Choice (A) means *guess*. Choice (B) means to *give a person work or responsibility*. Choice (C) means *agree* or *allow*.
114. **(B)** *Every week* can come after the verb. Choices (A), (C), and (D) should come between the auxiliary and the main verb.
115. **(C)** Present tense indicates *habit*, which is logical here; this also requires an *-s* ending for the third person (shift). Choice (A) is the progressive. Choice (B) is the infinitive. Choice (D) is present tense but not third person.
116. **(A)** *Was higher* is already past tense, so to establish an earlier past; use the past participle *had expected*. Choice (B) is the simple form. Choice (C) is the present progressive. Choice (D) is the future.
117. **(A)** *Sometimes* comes between the auxiliary and the main verb. Choice (B) has the main verb before the auxiliary. Choice (C) has *sometimes* and the main verb before the auxiliary. Choice (D) has *sometimes* before the verb.
118. **(B)** The adjective *popular* can modify *plan*; the adverb *especially* can modify *popular*. Choices (A) and (C) are verbs. Choice (D) is a noun.
119. **(D)** A specific date requires *on*. Choice (A) indicates purpose. Choice (B) indicates destination. Choice (C) indicates source.
120. **(C)** *When* establishes a logical time relationship between the two verbs. Choice (A) is not logical. Choice (B) is incomplete (*as soon as*). Choice (D) requires a contrast (*will not refund...until you cancel*).
121. **(B)** *Borrow* means *to take temporarily*. Choice (A) is *what you take* (*the reference*

526 EXPLANATORY ANSWERS

guide is a loan). Choice (C) means *to give temporarily*. Choice (D) means *gone away*.

122. **(A)** *Although* is a subordinate conjunction that indicates that one thing *(business cards not being printed)* happened in spite of another *(ordering the cards)*. Choices (B), (C), and (D) do not fit the context of the sentence.

123. **(A)** *Or* allows a choice between the items joined. Choice (B) would mean *both*. Choice (C) should be used with *or*. Choice (D) *but* would imply a contrast *(from the Madrid office but not from the Paris office)*.

124. **(A)** *Before* is an adverb and tells when the machine might be used. Choices (B), (C), and (D) do not fit the context of the sentence.

125. **(A)** An unreal condition requires past tense in the *if* clause to correspond with *would + verb* in the other clause. Choice (B) is present tense. Choice (C) is future tense. Choice (D) uses *would*.

126. **(B)** *Twice a day* can appear at the beginning or end of a sentence. Choice (A) links two events. Choices (C) and (D) should come between the auxiliary and main verb.

127. **(D)** *Holds* matches *receives (receives and holds)*. Choice (A) is present progressive. Choice (B) is past tense. Choice (C) is present tense but does not match the subject.

128. **(C)** *Help* is followed by the simple form (or the infinitive) when one thing *(the conference)* helps another *(employees)* do something. Choice (A) is past tense. Choice (B) is the gerund. Choice (D) is present progressive.

129. **(B)** Establishes a logical relationship between the two events. Choices (A) and (D) are illogical without a contrast *(Although we knew the city...; We knew the city, however,...)*. Choice (C) would belong in a result clause *(....therefore, Mr. Gutman drove...)*.

130. **(D)** The past progressive *had not been* requires the *-ing* form *depositing* to complete it. Choice (A) is the past tense. Choice (B) is the present tense. Choice (C) is the simple form.

131. **(B)** Present tense in a real condition in the *if* clause requires future tense in the other clause. Choice (A) is present tense. Choice (C) is present progressive. Choice (D) is present perfect.

132. **(A)** *Enter* matches drive *(drive and enter)*. Choice (B) is the past tense. Choice (C) is the gerund. Choice (D) is a noun.

133. **(D)** *Attending* forms the future progressive with *will be (will be attending)*. Choices (A), (B), and (C) do not form logical tenses with *attending*.

134. **(C)** *His* indicates a noun; expertise is logical. Choice (A) is an adverb. Choice (B) is a noun but refers to a person. Choice (D) is an adjective.

135. **(D)** Currency is a business/economic term that would be used with rates. Choice (A) *Money*, could be used, but is not. Choices (B) and (C) are inappropriate.

136. **(D)** Present tense and simple future are possible; only present is given. *Ms. Chang* requires third person *has*. Choice (A) is future perfect. Choice (B) is present progressive. Choice (C) is plural.

137. **(C)** The adjective *knowledgeable* modifies director; *quite* modifies *knowledgeable*. Choice (A) is the gerund. Choice (B) is a noun. Choice (D) is a verb.

138. **(B)** A time from past to present requires the present perfect *has been*. Choices (A) and (C) are present tenses and are illogical alone. Choice (D) is past tense.

139. **(D)** Past tense in the *if* clause of an unreal condition requires *would + simple verb* in the other clause. Choice (A) is future tense. Choice (B) is past perfect. Choice (C) is past tense.

140. **(A)** *Have* requires the simple form of the second verb when one person (trainers) have another (crew) do something. Choice (B) is the gerund. Choice (C) is noun. Choice (D) is past tense.

Part VI: Error Recognition

141. **(B)** (had her manager sign) *Had* requires *sign* in the present tense. Choice (A) is a correct subject. Choice (C) establishes a time relationship. Choice (D) is a correct verb.

142. **(B)** (and are or were pleased) The plural subject *managers* requires a plural verb *are*. Choice (A) is a past tense verb. Choice (C) is an infinitive after *pleased*. Choice (D) is a past tense verb.
143. **(C)** (branch, is) Main clause is *Ms. Wang is an experienced teller; she* repeats the subject. Choice (A) agrees with Ms. Wang. Choice (B) is the correct preposition. Choice (D) uses *an* before a vowel sound.
144. **(A)** (The proposed topic) Someone else *proposed* the *topic*; requires the past participle used as an adjective. Choice (B) is correct for a singular count noun. Choice (C) is the correct verb. Choice (D) is the correct possessive.
145. **(D)** (have handled) *Have* requires the past participle *handled* to complete the verb. Choice (A) correctly places *always* before the main verb. Choice (B) tells how many packages. Choice (C) makes a contrasting link between clauses.
146. **(C)** (she needs to) The subject *Ms. Gramm* requires *-s* for the third person present (*needs*). Choice (A) is a correct infinitive. Choice (B) is future progressive. Choice (D) noun phrase follows *during*.
147. **(A)** (The report) A specific report requires *the*. Choices (B) and (C) are correct verbs. Choice (D) is a correct superlative comparison form.
148. **(B)** (will be stuck) Future without *if* requires *will*, not *would*. Choice (A) is correct participle. Choice (C) means *during his trip home*. Choice (D) is a correct use of time of day.
149. **(D)** (are attending) Plural *guests* requires plural verb *are attending*. Choice (A) is a correct verb. Choice (B) is a correct question of quantity. Choice (C) is the correct infinitive after *know*.
150. **(D)** (he made the purchase) *Realized* is past tense; prior action must be at least past tense (*made the purchase*). Choice (A) correctly links two clauses. Choice (B) completes *should have verified*. Choice (C) correctly expresses a time relationship.

151. **(B)** (Much closer) *Much* is used with *-er* forms, not *-est* forms. Choice (A) is a correct singular verb. Choice (C) is a correct use of *than* in a comparison. Choice (D) is a correct pronoun use.
152. **(C)** (Has to leave) A future action *will return* can't happen before a past. Choice (A) indicates origin. Choice (B) establishes a correct time link between clauses. Choice (D) is a correct use of a pronoun.
153. **(B)** (Looking) Use the gerund *looking*; not the infinitive. Choice (A) is a correct verb form. Choice (C) is a correct verb for *job*. Choice (D) joins *advancement* and *salary*.
154. **(A)** (The passengers, who) Use *who* to refer to people (*passengers*). Choice (B) *frustrated by* the delays indicates the cause of the frustration. Choice (C) correctly expresses location. Choice (D) is a correct use of the infinitive.
155. **(B)** (As fast as) To complete the comparison use *as fast as*. Choice (A) is a gerund as the subject. Choice (C) is a correct noun phrase. Choice (D) is a correct comparison.
156. **(B)** (To smoke) The infinitive *to smoke* follows *requires*. Choice (A) is a correct noun. Choice (C) is a correct conjunction. Choice (D) is correct; use *the* with a specific building.
157. **(D)** (What she knew) *Where* refers to places; use *what*. Choice (A) is a correct verb. Choice (B) is correct; use *the* with a specific applicant. Choice (C) is correct; use *a* to mean any kind of chance.
158. **(A)** (Because; since) *Though* is illogical; use *because* or *since*. Choice (B) is a correct infinitive. Choice (C) is a correct pronoun for *clerks*. Choice (D) is a correct phrase to indicate exactness.
159. **(C)** (From the client) The specified singular count noun *client* needs an article, *the*. Choice (A) is a correct participle. Choices (B) and (D) are correct verbs.
160. **(B)** (An employee) Use *an* before a vowel sound. Choice (A) is a plural count noun used without an article. Choice (C) establishes time link between clauses. Choice (D) is correct; use *the* with a specific building.

Part VII: Reading Comprehension

161. **(C)** It reassures the public about safety. Choices (A) and (B) are not mentioned. Choice (D) is incorrect because the announcement doesn't say whether the policy is new or old.
162. **(A)** *Improve existing facilities with new safety information* means *continue to make them safe*. Choice (B) is not mentioned. Choice (C) is part of improving them. Choice (D) is implied if they are continuing to make them safe.
163. **(A)** The form is for a subscription to the magazine. Choice (B) confuses a *newspaper* with the name *News Events*. Choices (C) and (D) are not logical.
164. **(D)** The *newsstand price* of $2.25 is the *store price*. Choice (A) is half of the subscription price. Choice (B) is the subscription price. Choice (C) is twice the subscription price.
165. **(D)** Cash is not listed as acceptable. Choices (A), (B), and (C) are explicitly mentioned.
166. **(C)** *More than doubled* means *increased by more than twice as much*. Choices (A) and (D) are contradicted by doubled. Choice (B) omits *more than*.
167. **(A)** *Reduction of operating costs* means lower operating expenses. Choices (B) and (C) are possible but not mentioned. Choice (D) is unlikely.
168. **(D)** *Retail electronics* has the same meaning as electronics store. Choices (A), (B), and (C) are contradicted by electronics store.
169. **(B)** *Answering the phone* is not mentioned. Choices (A), (C), and (D) are explicitly mentioned.
170. **(B)** *Room to advance* means *opportunity for promotions*. Choice (A) is not mentioned. Choice (C) confuses *air* and *atmosphere*. Choice (D) is not mentioned.
171. **(B)** *Networking* means *talk to as many people as you can who work in your field or in related fields*. Choices (A), (C), and (D) are good practices but do not define *networking*.
172. **(D)** Discovering the salaries offered by companies is not mentioned as a benefit of networking. Choices (A), (B), and (C) are explicitly mentioned.
173. **(B)** It explains a safety rule so it is a *safety warning*. Choice (A) is incorrect because the memo *reminds* employees, so they must have heard the warning before. Choices (C) and (D) are not the subjects of the memo.
174. **(A)** The memo says fire doors *direct smoke away from areas where people are working*. Choices (B), (C), and (D) are not mentioned.
175. **(D)** If the *weather is hot* and the *air conditioner is not repaired*, employees were probably opening fire doors to let in cool air. Choices (A), (B), and (C) are all purposes of doors but do not relate to fire safety.
176. **(A)** All of the events are trade shows: shoes, furniture, autos, etc. Choices (B), (C), and (D) are not mentioned.
177. **(B)** The Shoe Fair is in Guangzhou, China. Choices (A), (C), and (D) are all held in Europe.
178. **(C)** You might want to look for dress material at the International Textile Fair in Moscow. Choice (A) will have a furniture fair. Choice (B) will have a jewelry fair. Choice (D) will have an art and antiques fair.
179. **(B)** An auction is a sale. Choices (A), (C), and (D) are contradicted by *estate auction*.
180. **(C)** Since jewelry is on the list of items to be auctioned, you will probably find bracelets for sale. Choice (A) confused Chinese antiques with china (dishes). Choice (B) is incorrect because a Porsche is a foreign car, but there is only one listed. Choice (D) confuses wall-to-wall carpeting and Oriental rugs.
181. **(D)** The preview starts at 10 A.M. on Saturday, October 3. Choice (A) is when the auction begins. Choice (B) is not mentioned. Choice (D) occurs when you can call Estate Planners with questions.
182. **(A)** The trend was *to grow larger*. Choice (B) is contradicted by *larger*. In Choice (C) the trend equated *success* with *large size*. Choice (D) is a current trend; wanting to grow larger is the historical trend.

183. **(B)** *Downsizing* contrasts with *growing larger*. Choice (A) is not logical: businesses are always interested in profits. Choices (C) and (D) do not contrast with *growing larger*.
184. **(A)** A company *cuts jobs* when it *downsizes*. Choice (B) is not mentioned. Choices (C) and (D) are not mentioned.
185. **(A)** The notice announces a *lecture series*. Choice (B) is incorrect; the university and business school organized the lectures. Choice (C) confuses a trade fair and a lecture on international trade. Choice (D) is incorrect; the notice does not try to recruit students.
186. **(B)** *Sims Lecture Hall* appears with the *date* and *time;* therefore it is the *place*. Choice (A) is sponsoring the events. Choice (C) is where to call for information. Choice (D) is the subject of the lecture.
187. **(D)** The phone number is given with the suggestion to call the Center for Professional Development. Choice (A) is sponsoring the lectures. Choice (B) is giving the lectures. Choice (C) is part of Beaumont University, which is sponsoring the lectures.
188. **(A)** *Tenants* and *leasing* indicate it's about *renting*. Choice (B) is incorrect; purchasing is not mentioned. Choice (C) confuses starting a business and office space. Choice (D) is incorrect; hotels are nearby.
189. **(B)** *They can occupy an entire floor.* Choice (A) is incorrect; *new* doesn't indicate it has to be good for small firms. Choices (C) and (D) are not mentioned.
190. **(C)** *Immediate occupancy* means *available right now*. Choices (A), (B), and (D) are contradicted by *immediate occupancy.*
191. **(A)** *Parks* are not mentioned. Choices (B), (C), and (D) are explicitly mentioned.
192. **(B)** Since more people mean less efficient discussion, fewer people will likely be more efficient. Choices (C) and (D) are not mentioned as ways to run meetings well.
193. **(D)** An *agenda keeps you focused.* Choices (A) and (C) may be additional advantages, but they are not mentioned. Choice (B) is incorrect; an agenda should *control* free discussion.
194. **(B)** *Thank them and move on*. Choice (A) would defeat the purpose of a meeting. Choice (C) makes the meeting inefficient. Choice (D) is not logical and is not mentioned.
195. **(A)** The author feels that real work does not happen in meetings; people are there as part of *primitive socializing behavior.* Choice (B) is contradicted when the author says *real work gets done after the meeting*. Choices (C) and (D) are not mentioned.
196. **(D)** This is the only valid option and is supported in the last paragraph: *What happens after a meeting is more important...; skills are more professional...; work that gets done after the meeting that is important*. Choices (A), (B), and (C) are not supported in the passage.
197. **(C)** The facility is in the *western United States*. Choices (A) and (D) are contradicted by *in a small town*. Choice (B) is contradicted by the *western United States*.
198. **(D)** Preparing employees for cultural changes is important. Choices (A), (B), and (C) are not the topics of the article.
199. **(B)** Their *families* are attending. Choices (A), (C), and (D) are all employees and would be attending with their families.
200. **(C)** The article mentions *cultural changes, cultural differences,* and *habits of Americans*. Choice (A) is incorrect; plans for moving are made by the company. Choices (B) and (D) are business topics.

Model Test 3

Part I: Picture

1. **(C)** Choice (C) identifies *the woman* and the action *watching the servers*. Choices (A) and (D) show negation: The plates are *not* empty; the menu is *not* on the table. Choice (B) has the related words *waiters* and *order* but does not describe the picture.
2. **(D)** Choice (D) identifies *the runners* and the action *passing a building*. Choice (A) identifies an incorrect action. Choice (B)

confuses similar sounds: *logger* with *jogger*; *can test* with *contest*. Choice (C) confuses different meanings: *races* (kind of people) with *races* (runs).

3. **(D)** Choice (D) identifies *technicians* and the action *standing next to the equipment*. Choice (A) confuses *laboratory* equipment with *sports* equipment and *set up* with *standing*. Choice (B) identifies an incorrect action. Choice (C) shows negation; the lab coats are *not* on the *hook* (technicians are wearing them).

4. **(A)** Choice (A) identifies the location *a highway under construction*. Choice (B) is incorrect because the picture shows traffic but no one is directing it. Choice (C) is incorrect because the workers are not moving anything. Choice (D) is incorrect because the workers are building with stone but there are no trucks loaded with stone.

5. **(B)** Choice (B) identifies *the passengers* and the action *ready to board a train*. Choice (A) confuses similar sounds: *rain* with *train*. Choice (C) is incorrect because if the train had departed, it would be farther away, not at the platform. Choice (D) confuses similar sounds: *grain* with *train*; *rye or* with *rider*.

6. **(C)** Choice (C) identifies the probable action *loading trucks*. Choice (A) is not able to be determined by the picture. Choice (B) cannot be confirmed from the picture. Choice (D) confuses similar sounds: *van* with *vandals* and related words: *tires* and *truck*.

7. **(D)** Choice (D) identifies the location of *cars in front of a factory*. Choice (A) confuses similar sounds: *carts* with *cars*. Choice (B) confuses different meanings: *plant* (flower) with *plant* (factory). Choice (C) is incorrect because the building is in good shape, not dilapidated.

8. **(A)** Choice (A) identifies the thing *all windows*. Choice (B) is incorrect because no one is talking to anyone. Choice (C) confuses *business team* with *sports team*. Choice (D) confuses *commuting* with *computing*.

9. **(C)** Choice (C) identifies *the waiters* and the action *setting the table*. Choice (A) is incorrect because guests haven't arrived yet. Choice (B) shows negation: dinner is not being served yet. Choice (D) is incorrect because the table is set for more than two.

10. **(B)** Choice (B) identifies the action *speaker addresses audience*. Choice (A) incorrectly identifies the place; it is a lecture hall, not a movie theater. Choice (C) is incorrect because the audience is listening, not demanding. Choice (D) is incorrect because the brick wall behind the speaker is not crumbling.

11. **(D)** Choice (D) makes assumptions: *the woman is a scientist performing an experiment*. Choice (A) confuses similar sounds: *washing* with *watching*. Choice (B) confuses similar sounds: *conductor* with *conduct* (an experiment). Choice (C) shows negation; the bottles are not on a shelf (they are in the equipment).

12. **(A)** Choice (A) identifies a thing: *stairs going up the tank*. Choice (B) is incorrect because the roof is round, not pointed. Choice (C) confuses the shape of the tank with the sun. Choice (D) confuses the railings with a fence.

13. **(B)** Choice (B) identifies the action *a flag hangs* and location *across the street*. Choice (A) confuses similar sounds: *elevator* and *escalator*. Choice (C) is incorrect because there is no parade in the picture. Choice (D) identifies an incorrect location.

14. **(B)** Choice (B) identifies the *service attendant* and his location *behind the car*. Choice (A) has the related word *smog*. Choice (C) incorrectly identifies the location as a *toll booth*. Choice (D) shows negation: the man is wearing a hat.

15. **(A)** Choice (A) identifies *students* and the action *study mathematics*. Choice (B) confuses similar sounds *equator* with *equation*. Choice (C) shows negation: the *chalkboard* is not blank (it has writing on it). Choice (D) confuses *officers* with *teachers*.

16. **(A)** Choice (A) identifies the *women;* the action *waiting;* and the location *by the phone*. Choice (B) mentions a *telephone* but in the wrong location *(on the table)*. Choice (C) incorrectly identifies *statues*. Choice (D) is incorrect because there are only three people in the station.
17. **(B)** Choice (B) identifies the action *talking on the phone*. Choice (A) confuses similar sounds: *talking* with *walking*. Choice (C) is too specific an action to be determined. Choice (D) confuses *phone wire* with *haywire*.
18. **(C)** Choice (C) identifies *the worker* and the action *inspecting the process*. Choice (A) confuses *bottling machine* with *soft drink machine*. Choice (B) shows negation: bottles are on a conveyor belt, not a shelf. Choice (D) is incorrect because the machine, not the worker, is filling the bottles.
19. **(A)** Choice (A) identifies the location of *the printers*. Choice (B) is incorrect because there are no switchboards. Choice (C) is incorrect because there are no chemicals in the picture. Choice (D) shows negation: there is no clutter in the picture.
20. **(A)** Choice (A) identifies the location of *the highways*. Choices (B) and (C) cannot be seen in the picture. Choice (D) is incorrect; there is no river in the picture.

Part II: Question-Response

21. **(A)** Choice (A) is a logical response to a question about *being hungry*. Choice (B) confuses similar sounds: *hungry* and *Hungary*. Choice (C) confuses *How hungry are you* with *How old are you?*
22. **(C)** Choice (C) is a logical response to a question about *playing basketball*. Choice (A) confuses similar sounds: *basketball* and *wastebasket*. Choice (B) has the related word *game* but is past tense and does not answer the question.
23. **(B)** Choice (B) is a logical response to a question about *who*. Choice (A) confuses *public relations* with *public address*. Choice (C) confuses similar sounds: *in charge* and *no charge* and related words: *public* and *public relations*.
24. **(B)** Choice (B) is a logical response to a question about *distance*. Choice (A) has the related words *paintings* and *modern* but does not give distance. Choice (C) answers a question about *when*.
25. **(A)** Choice (A) is a logical response to a question about *time*. Choice (B) tells *when they drove* by but not *when they bought*. Choice (C) answers the question *how much*, not *when*.
26. **(C)** Choice (C) is a logical response to a question about the *subject*. Choice (A) gives the location of the book, not *its subject*. Choice (B) gives the price.
27. **(A)** Choice (A) is a logical response to a question about *location*. Choice (B) has the related phrase *close the door* but does not give a location for the keys. Choice (C) has the related words *door* and *locked* but does not give a location for the keys.
28. **(C)** Choice (C) is a logical response to a question about *which train*. Choice (A) confuses similar sounds: *train* with *rain*. Choice (B) answers the incorrect question, *which class should I take*.
29. **(A)** Choice (A) is a logical response to a question about *copies*. Choice (B) confuses similar sounds: *copier is* with *cops; aren't* with *are on*. Choice (C) confuses similar sounds: *ready yet* with *already read it*.
30. **(C)** Choice (C) is a logical response to a question about *when*. Choice (A) tells *how long*, not *when*. Choice (B) confuses similar sounds: *is he* with *she;* and related words: *too long* and *when*.
31. **(C)** Choice (C) is a logical response to a question about *how much*. Choice (A) answers the question *how you paid*. Choice (B) answers the question *how many* (stories the hotel had).
32. **(A)** Choice (A) is a logical response to a question about *where one learns*. Choice (B) confuses *earn* with *learn*. Choice (C) answers the question *where*, but the verb does not match in tense or meaning.
33. **(B)** Choice (B) is a logical response to a question about a reason *why*. Choice (A) uses the word *watch* but the sense contradicts the question. Choice (C) confuses *lime* with *time*.

34. **(A)** Choice (A) is a logical response to a question about *going to the movies*. Choice (B) uses the related words *film* and *camera*; Choice (C) answers the *yes/no* question with a yes, but the verb is wrong.
35. **(C)** Choice (C) is a logical response to a question about *winning a tennis game*. Choice (A) has the related word *smoke* to another meaning of *match*. Choice (B) confuses *ten* with *tennis*. Only Choice (C) concerns the game, *tennis*.
36. **(B)** Choice (B) is a logical response to a question about *purpose of a visit*. Choice (A) uses related words: *visitors* and *visit*. Choice (C) confuses *proposal* with *purpose* and *list* with *visit*.
37. **(C)** Choice (C) is a logical response to a question about *seasonal preference*. Choice (A) confuses the related word *seasoning* with *season*. Choice (B) confuses the similar sounds *refer* and *prefer*.
38. **(A)** Choice (A) is a logical response to a question about *width*. Choice (B) confuses the sound of the word *slide* with *wide*. Choice (C) confuses the sound *wide* with *why*.
39. **(A)** Choice (A) is a logical response to a question about *when the mail comes*. Choice (B) confuses the similar sounds: *milk* with *mail c(ome)*. Choice (C) confuses the sound of *come* with *welcome*.
40. **(A)** Choice (A) is a logical response to a question about *where the bank is*. Choice (B) confuses the sound of *thank* with *bank*. Choice (C) confuses the similar sounds in *ink* and *bank*.
41. **(C)** Choice (C) is a logical response to a question about *the weather*. Choice (A) may seem close with its verb *is going* and the adverb *today*. Choice (B) confuses the sound *rain* with *complain*.
42. **(B)** Choice (B) is a logical response to a question about the *amount of a tip*. Choice (A) has related words *tip* (v) and *tip* (n). Choice (C) confuses *water* and *waded* with *waiter*, and has an answer to *how many*, not *how much*.
43. **(A)** Choice (A) is a logical response to a question about *who was the designer*. Choice (B) confuses *resign* with *design*. Choice (C) confuses *house* with *mouse*.
44. **(C)** Choice (C) is a logical response to a question about *your arrival time*. Choice (A) gives an arrival time in the *future*, not the *past* like the question. Choice (B) confuses the sounds *live* and *arrive*.
45. **(B)** Choice (B) is a logical response to a question about *the fabric a shirt is made of*. Choice (A) changes the preposition from *made of* to *made in*; Choice (C) confuses *this shirt* with *insert*.
46. **(A)** Choice (A) is a logical response to a question about *the reason a calculator doesn't work*. Choice (B) confuses *calculator* with *Calcutta*; Choice (C) refers to animate objects such as people (*no one*).
47. **(B)** Choice (B) is a logical response to a question about *where you study English*. Choice (A) confuses the related word *students* with *study* and *England* with *English*. Choice (C) answers *how long*.
48. **(C)** Choice (C) is a logical response to a question about *which sweater fits better*. Choice (A) confuses *sweater* with *sweat pants* and the concept of *fit* with something that is *too large*. Choice (B) confuses the word *sweater* with *weather*.
49. **(A)** Choice (A) is a logical response to a question about *the time*. Choice (B) answers another *do you have* question. Choice (C) answers *what time do you have to leave*.
50. **(A)** Choice (A) is a logical response to a request *to close the window*. Choice (B) confuses the word *close* with *clothes*; Choice (C) has the related word *open*.

Part III: Short Conversations
51. **(A)** *If closing at dark prevents them from going after work,* then *it must be dark after work*. Choice (B) is not necessarily a reason for not going. Choice (C) is not mentioned. Choice (D) confuses similar sounds *clothes* and *closes*.
52. **(C)** *The woman wants the person who can issue traveler's checks,* so *she must want to buy some*. Choice (A) is not mentioned. Choice (B) is not logical — she can get traveler's checks at the bank. Choice (D)

misses the point — she's only looking for the desk so she can find the person who issues traveler's checks.

53. **(B)** They *must locate the bus and wait*. Choice (A) contradicts *lost*. Choice (C) is incorrect; the market is where they may get lost. Choice (D) confuses *wait by the bus* and *take a bus*.

54. **(B)** *A roll of quarters will provide change*. Choice (A) is mentioned as a convenient time to get quarters. Choice (C) confuses *change for the bus* with *change buses*. Choice (D) confuses the noun *check* with the verb *check*.

55. **(D)** A *graphics program* can make graphs and charts. Choice (A) confuses *figure sales* with *sales figures*. Choice (B) confuses *illustrate programs* with *illustrate with a program*. Choice (C) confuses *sales trends* with *sell computers*.

56. **(B)** *Flight* and *rows designated for smoking* suggest a plane. Choices (A), (C), and (D) aren't consistent with restricted smoking on a flight.

57. **(A)** If the meeting is at 11:00, she'll have to clean it earlier. Choice (B) won't have the room clean for the meeting. Choice (C) is not logical; 11:00 is the scheduled time. Choice (D) confuses *2:35* with *Room 235*.

58. **(D)** *Resume* and *possible positions* suggest a job interview. Choices (A), (B), and (C) are all scheduled by appointment but would not involve a resume.

59. **(B)** *Fixing the leak* will solve the problem permanently. Choice (A) is suggested but rejected by the woman. Choice (C) confuses *stand* and *instead*. Choice (D) confuses *wetter*, *wet*, and *water*.

60. **(D)** If it takes *two weeks to get parts and one week to install them*, it will be *ready in three weeks*. Choice (A) is when they're sending the order. Choice (B) is the time to install parts. Choice (C) is the time to get parts.

61. **(C)** If you *introduce yourself*, you meet someone. Choice (A) confuses *managing director* with *manage the director*. Choice (B) is what the director is wearing. Choice (D) is incorrect; he is introducing himself to the director.

62. **(A)** A *morning paper* is a newspaper delivered in the morning. Choice (B) confuses *paper* stationery with news*paper*. Choice (C) confuses *more room* with staying in a hotel *room*. Choice (D) confuses *directly* and *directory*.

63. **(B)** *Address* can mean to *speak* to; *Mr. Chung will address a meeting*. Choice (A) confuses two meanings of *address*. Choice (C) is what they will do if Mr. Chung doesn't come. Choice (D) confuses similar sounds *date* and *late*.

64. **(B)** He'll pay *by check*. Choice (A) is what you do with your credit card. Choice (C) was used for identification, not payment. Choice (D) is a possible way to pay but is not used here.

65. **(D)** He asks for directions to the *history museum*. Choices (A), (B), and (C) are all places given as landmarks: *through the park, past the capitol, left at the train station*.

66. **(C)** He has *lunch*. Choices (A) and (B) are what the woman does during lunch. Choice (D) is the man's excuse for not exercising.

67. **(B)** *No street by that name* means *the street doesn't exist*. Choice (A) confuses mailing a *check* and *checking* for an error. Choice (C) is incorrect because the post office returned the letter; the company did not receive it or send it back. Choice (D) is not logical; the *post office returned it*, so it was mailed.

68. **(D)** *Never enough light before* means *it used to be dark*. Choice (A) is what the lobby has now. Choice (B) is not mentioned. Choice (C) is the current color of the walls.

69. **(C)** These are common phrases for *introductions*. Choice (A) is incorrect; *introducing yourself* is not working. Choice (B) confuses *meet* and *meeting*. Choice (D) is incorrect; *working here* suggests they are at the office, not at a party.

70. **(D)** If he wants *light*, he'll put it by *the window*. Choice (A) is the woman's suggestion. In Choice (B) *under the light* implies artificial light. Choice (C) confuses *entrance* and *who enters*.

534 EXPLANATORY ANSWERS

71. **(D)** The man wants to *hire temporary help*. Choice (A) is not mentioned. Choice (B) is not logical; they need *more*, not *fewer*. Choice (C) is incorrect; they're already working on a special project.

72. **(B)** No available room is appropriate. Choice (A) means *introducing himself to people*. Choice (C) confuses *schedule* (noun) and *schedule* (verb). Choice (D) contradicts the conversation: *if the conference room is not large enough, lots of people must be attending*.

73. **(C)** *Large* and *big* mean the same thing. Choice (A) is not mentioned. Choice (B) is not necessarily true. Choice (D) is contradicted by the conversation; she does have at least one bag.

74. **(A)** They are *taking a coffee break*. Choice (B) confuses *lake* and *break*. Choice (C) uses *loading* to make us think of *plane*. Choice (D) confuses *ring* and *rain*.

75. **(D)** This is probably a *tour of the city*. Choices (A) and (C) are incorrect; nothing in the conversation suggests a *convention* or a *meeting*. Choice (B) is not logical; the woman asks about *performances*, so she's not watching one.

76. **(C)** *Under warranty* means it is still guaranteed. Choice (A) is incorrect; the *copier* is working but the printer isn't. Choice (B) is not logical; if it is under warranty, it's probably not old. Choice (D) is incorrect; the *warranty* is still good but the printer is not.

77. **(B)** *Before we land* suggests they're on a plane, and the woman is answering questions. Choices (A) and (C) don't make sense; a *ticket agent* and a *baggage handler* wouldn't be on the flight. Choice (D) is incorrect; a *caterer* prepares food.

78. **(D)** The man has a *flat tire*. Choice (A) confuses *out of gas* with *gas station*. Choice (B) confuses *tired* and *tire*. Choice (C) confuses *a long road* and *along the road*.

79. **(B)** The man feels sleepy. Choice (A) is how he'll feel in the morning if he sleeps all night. Choices (C) and (D) are not mentioned.

80. **(A)** *Reading something* comes before commenting on it. Choice (B) is the second step, not the first. Choice (C) confuses *recommend* and *recommendations*. Choice (D) would also come after reading it.

Part IV: Short Talks

81. **(B)** *Not in service* means *not working*. Choice (A), *a wrong number,* means you misdialed. Choice (C) confuses the *recording* and an *answering machine*. Choice (D) means someone is using the phone.

82. **(C)** This is a person who helps *customers*. Choice (A) fixes broken phones. Choice (B) connects calls. Choice (D) makes decisions about the company.

83. **(C)** The water is *contaminated* with bacteria. Choice (A) is not logical; if there is no water, it can't be contaminated. Choice (B) is not sufficient reason to give an alert. Choice (D) is not mentioned.

84. **(A)** The announcement says to *boil water for five minutes*. Choice (B) involves cooling the water, the opposite of the advice. Choice (C) is not mentioned. Choice (D) would not make the water safe.

85. **(A)** A *computer school* provides *computer training*. Choice (B) is incorrect; the school trains in *business software*, not *business management*. Choice (C) confuses the ideas of *job placement* and *personnel*. Choice (D) is incorrect; the school *teaches*, it doesn't *train teachers*.

86. **(B)** The ad says *you can train* in *six months*. Choices (A), (C), and (D) are not mentioned.

87. **(D)** The train is bound for *New York and Boston*. Choice (A) confuses *Baltimore* and *Boston*. Choices (B) and (C) include other stops on the way to Boston but they are not mentioned here.

88. **(A)** New York passengers board *at the front*. Choice (B) is where Boston passengers board. Choices (C) and (D) are not mentioned as boarding sites.

89. **(C)** Those hours refer to *business hours*. Choices (A) and (B) are both contradicted; the hours given are for weekdays during

the day. Choice (D) is not logical; they are not open *before 8:00*.
90. **(B)** *To contact in writing* means *to write a letter*. Choices (A), (C), and (D) are possible solutions but not mentioned here.
91. **(B)** *Apply in person* means *go to the hotel*. Choice (A) is not required. Choices (C) and (D) are unnecessary if you apply in person.
92. **(D)** *Opportunity for advancement* means *possible promotions*. Choices (A) and (B) are not mentioned. Choice (C) is unlikely for these kinds of jobs.
93. **(B)** *The ad is selling an electronic office mail communication system*. Choice (A) is not mentioned. Choice (C) is incorrect; duplication (copying) is something buyers would save money on. Choice (D) is incorrect; distribution is already part of the electronic mail system.
94. **(C)** The ad mentions saving on *paper and wear and tear on the printer*. Choice (A) is not mentioned. Choice (B) is not probable; the system is unlikely to reduce the number of workers. Choice (D) is illogical; the system is for mailing interoffice mail, not for eliminating it.
95. **(B)** A *heat wave* means *hot weather*. Choices (A), (C), and (D) are possible problems but not true here.
96. **(D)** *The report says the weather will be over one hundred degrees*. Choices (A), (B), and (C) are all under one hundred degrees.
97. **(C)** To avoid heatstroke, residents should *drink lots of water*. Choice (A) is incorrect because residents are advised to wear light, not dark, clothes. Choice (B) is contradicted by *avoid strenuous exercise*. Choice (D) is not mentioned.
98. **(D)** Executives are advised to *establish a quiet hour*. Choices (A), (B), and (C) are not part of establishing a quiet hour.
99. **(B)** *Closing your office door* is probably to keep people out. Choice (A) would also keep you from getting work done. Choice (C) is not appropriate; these signs are found in hotels, not offices. Choice (D) is incorrect because emergencies are the exception to the do not disturb rule.
100. **(A)** *Difficult tasks* require *quiet time*. Choice (B) is possible but not mentioned.

Choice (C) is not mentioned. Choice (D) is contradicted by asking staff not to disturb you.

Part V: Incomplete Sentences
101. **(C)** The plural *contracts* requires a plural verb. Choices (A) and (B) are singular. Choice (D) is the simple form.
102. **(B)** *The* must be followed by a noun. Choice (A) is an adjective. Choices (C) and (D) are verbs.
103. **(A)** *On* is a preposition meaning *upon the surface of*. Choice (B) indicates movement across something. Choice (C) means *to place inside*. Choice (D) means *lacking*.
104. **(D)** Someone else sealed the bid; use the past participle. Choices (A) and (B) are verbs. Choice (C) is the present participle.
105. **(C)** Use the simple form for a command. Choice (A) is a gerund. Choice (B) is future tense. Choice (D) is past tense.
106. **(D)** Someone else *included* the taxes; use the past participle. Choice (A) is the present participle. Choice (B) and (C) are verbs.
107. **(B)** Complete the verb: *wants to finalize*. Choices (A) and (D) are nouns. Choice (C) is is an adverb.
108. **(A)** A comparison of two things uses *more + adjective* or the *-er* form. Choices (B) and (C) use *most*. Choice (D) uses *the*.
109. **(C)** Use *who* to refer to people. Choice (A) refers to things. Choice (B) is possessive. Choice (D) is objective.
110. **(D)** *On* is used with days of the week. Choice (A) indicates location. Choice (B) indicates source. Choice (C) is not logical.
111. **(B)** *Paint* and *pictures* are equal items joined with *and*. Choices (A), (C), and (D) join clauses, not nouns.
112. **(A)** *Aware* is the only adjective among the options. Choices (B), (C), and (D) do not fit the context of the sentence.
113. **(B)** The sentence requires a conjugated verb and past participle. Choices (A) and (D) use the present participle. Choice (C) uses the simple form of the verb.
114. **(A)** *Between* expresses beginning and ending points. Choice (B) indicates *in the company of* or *by means of*. Choice (C)

indicates movement across something. Choice (D) indicates source.

115. **(C)** The causative *had* requires the simple form of the following verb. Choice (A) is past tense. Choice (B) is past perfect. Choice (D) is present tense.

116. **(D)** Superlative comparisons use *the* + *-est* forms. Choices (A) and (B) are comparative forms. Choice (C) incorrectly uses *than*.

117. **(B)** The items are equal, so link with *and*. Choice (A) implies a choice. Choice (C) is not logical. Choice (D) cannot be followed by clause.

118. **(C)** Habitual action uses present tense; *head* requires third person singular forms. Choice (A) is the simple form. Choices (B) and (D) are the present progressive.

119. **(A)** The causative *ask* requires a following infinitive. Choice (B) is the gerund. Choice (C) is future tense. Choice (D) is present tense.

120. **(D)** An *office* isn't specified; don't specify the *administrative assistant* either. Remember the following vowel and use *an*. Choice (A) isn't used in place of *a*. Choice (B) is used only before consonant sounds. Choice (C) is specific.

121. **(C)** This sentence requires a conjugated verb and past participle. Choice (A) uses the simple form of the verb. Choice (B) is the gerund. Choice (D) is the present participle.

122. **(A)** The causative *got* requires a following infinitive. Choice (B) is the past progressive. Choice (C) is the simple form. Choice (D) is the simple past.

123. **(B)** The subject *variety* requires a singular verb. Choice (A) is plural. Choice (B) is the gerund. Choice (D) is the simple form.

124. **(A)** *Name* and *address* are equal; use *and*. Choice (B) implies a choice. Choice (C) links clauses, not nouns. Choice (D) is used with *neither*.

125. **(D)** *Beside* means *next to*. Choices (A) and (B) need more than one bus as a reference point. Choice (C) means *direction away*; it is not logical.

126. **(C)** Choice (C) is a correctly formed time link. Choices (A) and (B) are incomplete. Choice (D) incorrectly uses than.

127. **(D)** An unreal condition requires *would* in the clause without *if*. Choice (A) has *would* but is illogical. Choices (B) and (C) do not use *would*.

128. **(A)** Habitual action uses present tense; *handbook* requires third person singular forms. Choice (B) is the present progressive. Choice (C) is the simple form. Choice (D) is the gerund.

129. **(C)** The costs are rising themselves; use the present participle. Choices (A) and (D) must tell who raised costs. Choice (B) is the past participle.

130. **(B)** *Always* goes between the auxiliary verb and the main verb. In Choice (C) *always* is before the auxiliary verb. In choices (A) and (D) *always* is after the main verb.

131. **(D)** *Even though* establishes a logical link between clauses. Choices (A), (B), and (C) are not logical.

132. **(C)** *Make an appointment* is a common business expression. Choice (A) is incorrect; *make a meeting* means *be able to attend* the meeting. Choice (B) is not used for appointments. Choice (D) is incorrect; *a time* is not used for specific appointments.

133. **(A)** The sentence requires a conjugated verb and past participle. *Team* is singular. Choice (B) is plural. Choices (C) and (D) use the present participle.

134. **(B)** The subject *record* requires a singular verb. Choices (A) and (C) are plural. Choice (D) needs *been* to form the present perfect *has been kept*.

135. **(C)** Use *between* with two items. Choice (A) means *together*. Choice (B) indicates time. Choice (D) is used with three or more items.

136. **(D)** *Although* establishes a logical connection between events. Choice (A) cannot be followed by a clause. Choice (B) is not logical. Choice (C) cannot be followed by a clause.

137. **(B)** Match *collecting* with *organizing*. Choice (A) is a noun. Choices (C) and (D) are verbs.

138. **(C)** The present progressive is the only appropriate verb. Choice (A) uses the past participle. Choice (B) uses plural *have*. Choice (D) uses *has* instead of *be*.

139. **(B)** *Suggested* is followed by the gerund. Choice (A) is the simple form of the verb. Choice (C) is the past tense. Choice (D) is the infinitive.

140. **(D)** Days of the week require *on*. Choice (A) indicates source. Choice (B) means *inside* or *within*. Choice (C) indicates a recipient.

Part VI: Error Recognition

141. **(C)** (have been distributed) The plural subject *copies* requires *have*. Choice (A) is a correct preposition plus article. Choice (B) tells what kind of policy. Choice (D) correctly completes the verb.

142. **(B)** (is) The present tense *return* doesn't allow past tense in the *if* clause; use *is*. Choice (A) correctly uses *if* for a real condition. Choice (C) is a correct adverb. Choice (D) is logical.

143. **(B)** *Both* means *two*; use *and*. Choice (A) matches *handling*. Choice (C) matches *shipping charges*. Choice (D) is the past participle.

144. **(A)** (exciting advertisement) The advertisement is *exciting* other people; use the present participle. Choice (B) is a correct verb phrase. Choice (C) is the simple form after causative *make*. Choice (D) is correctly used with *pay attention*.

145. **(B)** (an interesting report) *Interesting* begins with a vowel sound; use *an*. Choice (A) modifies *assistant*. Choice (C) means *concerning*. Choice (D) is the correct word family.

146. **(A)** (Although; even though) *But* can start the second clause; or use *although* to begin the sentence. Choice (B) is a correct verb. Choice (C) is correctly placed between the auxiliary and main verb. Choice (D) is logical.

147. **(A)** (The visitor whose car) *His* repeats the subject *visitor*; use the relative pronoun *whose*. Choice (B) indicates location. Choice (C) is a past tense verb. Choice (D) modifies *signs*.

148. **(B)** The complete verb is *has been sitting*. Choice (A) correctly uses *the* for specified noun. Choice (C) matches *all afternoon*. Choice (D) is logical.

149. **(C)** (since) *During* isn't logical or grammatical; use *since*. Choice (A) is a correct plural. Choice (B) is a correct comparison. Choice (D) is a correct verb phrase.

150. **(A)** (advised going) *Advise* is followed by the gerund. Choice (B) is correct; use *the* with seasons. Choice (C) joins clauses by establishing a time relationship. Choice (D) is a logical comparative adjective.

151. **(B)** (that) *Who* refers to people; use *that*. Choice (A) correctly uses *the* with a specified noun. Choice (C) indicates origin. Choice (D) is a correct verb.

152. **(A)** (will have been) The future perfect uses *have*. Choice (B) indicates a period of time. Choice (C) uses *the* with a specified noun. Choice (D) is a correct preposition.

153. **(B)** *Careful* is an adjective. You must use the adverb *carefully*. Choice (A) is the subject. Choice (C) is a conjunction. Choice (D) is an adverb.

154. **(B)** (is easier than) Never use more with *-er* forms. Choice (A) is a gerund. Choice (C) is the correct comparative. Choice (D) is correct; use a with a general, singular count noun.

155. **(B)** (allowed Mr. Cooper to take) The causative *allowed* is followed by the infinitive. Choice (A) is a correct pronoun. Choice (C), *during*, is correctly followed by a noun phrase. Choice (D) is a superlative form.

156. **(B)** (that the intern typed had) *It* repeats the subject *letter* in main clause. Omit *it*. Choice (A) joins phrases; correctly refers to *letter*. Choice (C) tells how many mistakes. Choice (D) tells what kind of mistakes.

157. **(C)** (until) *While* is not logical; use *until*. Choice (A) is future tense. Choice (B) is a correct noun. Choice (D) is the past participle.

158. **(D)** (differently) *Treat* must be modified by an adverb *(differently)*. Choice (A) is

logical. Choice (B) is a correct possessive noun. Choice (C) is a correct verb.
159. **(A)** (is) Company names are singular; use a singular verb. Choice (B) joins equal terms. Choice (C) matches *largest*. Choice (D) is a correct preposition.
160. **(B)** (Once a week the president OR with the other employees once a week) Move the phrase to the beginning or end of the clause. Choice (A) modifies *president*. Choices (C) and (D) are correct prepositions.

Part VII: Reading Comprehension

161. **(D)** Product quality is improved by improvements in technology. The other options are not explicitly mentioned.
162. **(D)** *Hiring practices* are not mentioned. Choices (A), (B), and (C) are explicitly mentioned.
163. **(B)** It is *lowering costs by improving manufacturing processes*. Choice (A) is not linked to lowering costs. Choices (C) and (D) are not logical ways to lower costs.
164. **(C)** To find people to apply for jobs. Choice (A) is incorrect; they want to meet job applicants, not *new people*. Choices (B) and (D) might encourage people but do not describe the purpose of the ad.
165. **(A)** National Headquarters is mentioned with the *time* and *date*, so it must be the place. Choice (B) is not mentioned. Choice (C) is not a logical location for an open house. Choice (D) is incorrect; the airport is regional, not the office.
166. **(C)** The airline wants *representatives for sales and reservations*. Choices (A), (B), and (D) are all airline jobs but are not mentioned.
167. **(B)** It comes from an electric company, so the letter refers to *electrical service*. Choices (A), (C), and (D) are contradicted by *electrical*.
168. **(B)** Payment is due July 10. Choice (A) may be required later. Choices (C) and (D) are not mentioned.
169. **(C)** They will temporarily *interrupt service*. Choice (A) means *stop service*. Choice (B) means *install service again*. Choice (D) means *starting it* after interrupting it.
170. **(D)** The purpose of this letter is to notify the customer that the due date on the bill has passed and payment is delinquent. Choice (A) is incorrect because service has not yet been interrupted. Choice (B) is not mentioned. Choice (C) confuses rate changes with charges to be incurred if payment is not received.
171. **(D)** The first line of the letter gives the answer: *pleased to receive your fax*. The other choices are not mentioned.
172. **(D)** It sells through a *worldwide marketing network*. Choices (A), (B), and (C) are not logical.
173. **(A)** 25% are through *other channels* that are not direct. Choices (A) and (C), *direct sales* and *sales through other channels*, add up to 100%. Choice (B) is not mentioned. Choice (D) represents total sales.
174. **(C)** *Company distribution centers* ship goods. Choice (A) suggests the shipping method but does not ship. Choice (B) is incorrect; the distribution centers may *use* airlines. Choice (D) is incorrect; *headquarters* does not ship goods.
175. **(B)** The details in the fax answer the question about the company's distribution network. The other questions are not answered in the fax.
176. **(A)** It gives *etiquette rules for bus riders*. Choices (B), (C), and (D) are not the subjects of the notice.
177. **(D)** Drivers cannot *give riders change for fares*. Choice (A) is not logical; passengers would know anyway. Choice (B) is not necessarily true. Choice (C) is not relevant.
178. **(B)** *Senior citizens and disabled riders* means *elderly people and handicapped people*. Choices (A), (C), and (D) are not designated for priority seats.
179. **(C)** *Reading* is allowed. Choices (A), (B), and (D) are specifically listed as not allowed.
180. **(B)** It found out *how sales managers spend their time*. Choice (A) is not logical; the chart shows what they do. There may be other things they *should* do. Choice (C) is not mentioned. Choice (D)

is incorrect; the chart indicates *percentage of time*, not *actual* time.
181. **(C)** *Reviewing sales records* makes up 25%. Choice (A) makes up 15%. Choice (B) makes up 5%. Choice (D) makes up 22%.
182. **(C)** They spend *10%* of their time with the technical staff. Choice (A) is spent in *administrative duties*. Choice (B) is spent in *miscellaneous tasks*. Choice (D) is spent *training new salespeople*.
183. **(A)** If only 5% of each manager's time is spent dealing with customer problems, it can be assumed that there are few problems. Choice (B) is contradicted in the passage: *training sales personnel (15%), reviewing records (25%),* and *making sales assignments (22%)* show that sales are the highest priority. Choices (C) and (D) are also contradicted.
184. **(B)** The ad suggests you *return to school*. Choice (A) is not mentioned. Choice (C) might be the result of going to school. Choice (D) is to find out more about classes.
185. **(A)** The ad states *You will study with your peers*. Peers are defined here as *other experienced managers*. The other choices are not mentioned.
186. **(D)** The application must be accompanied by *three letters of recommendation*. The other choices are not specifically mentioned.
187. **(B)** The course is a *week-long* intensive one. The other periods of time are not mentioned.
188. **(A)** It guarantees the *lowest prices*. Choices (B), (C), and (D) are not mentioned.
189. **(C)** They will *beat any price* so they have the *lowest price*. Choices (A), (B), and (D) are not mentioned.
190. **(B)** They will *refund the difference*, which means *pay you the difference in price*. Choices (A) and (C) are not given as resolutions to the problem. Choice (D) is incorrect; the store will *refund the difference*, not refund all of your money.
191. **(D)** The *low price guarantee does not apply to limited quantity offers*. Choices (A), (B), and (C) do not have restrictions on the guarantee.
192. **(C)** It *allows employees to take paid time off for volunteer activities*. Choices (B), (C), and (D) concern other types of *time off*.
193. **(D)** They may take *up to eight hours of paid leave per month*. Choices (A), (B), and (C) are all less than the allowed time.
194. **(C)** They are *eligible* if they are *full-time* and have worked for *one year*. Choice (A) is incorrect; some employees may not be eligible even if their supervisor approves. Choice (B) is incorrect; part-time workers are not eligible. Choice (D) is incorrect; employees are not eligible merely because they are interested.
195. **(D)** Volunteer leave must be *requested in advance* and *approved by the supervisor*. Choices (A), (B), and (C) are not mentioned as requirements.
196. **(B)** This article describes *security problems*. Choices (B), (C), and (D) are not problems.
197. **(C)** It says that users *enter...by using a private password*. Choices (A), (B), and (D) are not ways to enter the system.
198. **(A)** The thief has to *discover the password*. Choices (B), (C), and (D) are probably true but are not mentioned.
199. **(D)** It says that *users should change their passwords often*. Choices (A), (B), and (C) are not ways to secure the system.
200. **(A)** Young adults who do "wrong" things just for the *fun* of it are *mischievous*. The other people are not mentioned.

Model Test 4

Part I: Picture
1. **(A)** Choice (A) identifies *the man* and the action *checking his bag*. Choice (B) is incorrect; the woman *weighs a bag*, not *the man*. Choice (C) confuses *standing close to the counter* and *closing a deal*. Choice (D) is incorrect because luggage is on the floor, not on a trolly.
2. **(C)** Choice (C) identifies *the waiter* and the action *puts the silverware*. Choice (A) shows negation; the table is set for two

(not four). Choice (B) is incorrect because the diners have not arrived yet. Choice (D) confuses *waiter* with *officer* and *bow tie* with *bowing*.

3. **(B)** Choice (B) describes the action *a meeting in session*. Choice (A) confuses homonyms *meat* and *meet*. Choice (C) is incorrect because more than four people attended. Choice (D) confuses *track meet* and *meeting*.

4. **(B)** Choice (B) identifies the location *of the pipeline*. Choice (A) is incorrect; the picture shows a *pipeline*, not *lumber*. Choice (C) is incorrect; you cannot assume the pipeline carries water. Choice (D) confuses related words: *pipeline oil tankers*.

5. **(D)** Choice (D) identifies the thing *X rays* and their location *behind the doctor*. Choice (A) incorrectly identifies the people and their clothing. Choice (B) confuses related word *examine* and gives an incorrect action. Choice (C) gives the incorrect action and misidentifies the doctor.

6. **(C)** Choice (C) identifies *the family* and the action *having dinner*. Choices (A) and (B) give incorrect locations; the lamp is above the table; the mother sits across from the father. Choice (D) confuses *eating food* with *throwing food*.

7. **(A)** Choice (A) makes assumptions: *it looks like a restaurant*, so *the customers must be holding a menu* and *ordering food*. Choice (B) confuses *reading a menu* and *learning to read*. Choice (C) is incorrect because the waiter has already approached the customer. Choice (D) is incorrect because the guest is ordering, not waiting to order.

8. **(C)** Choice (C) makes assumptions: *it could be an office, but the straight rows of computers indicate a classroom*. Choice (A) incorrectly describes the position of the computers. Choice (B) confuses *straight rows of corn* with *straight rows of computers*. Choice (D) cannot be determined by the picture.

9. **(B)** Choice (B) identifies the thing *protective clothing*. Choice (A) describes an incorrect occupation and action. Choice (C) is incorrect because there are no animals in the picture. Choice (D) confuses the jars with pharmaceuticals.

10. **(A)** Choice (A) identifies *the girls* and the action *playing soccer*. Choice (B) confuses related words: *(fish) net* with *goal*. Choice (C) is incorrect because the ball is on the ground, not being held. Choice (D) confuses different meanings: *(playing) field* and *field (with flowers)*.

11. **(C)** Choice (C) identifies *the doorman* and the action *carrying a bag*. Choice (A) confuses similar sounds: *ports are* with *porter* (person who carries bags). Choices (B) and (D) misidentify the people and the actions, and do not match the picture.

12. **(D)** Choice (D) identifies *the passengers* and the action *getting their luggage*. Choice (A) identifies an incorrect action *waiting for their flight*. Choice (B) is incorrect because the luggage is not scattered around. Choice (C) has the related word *trip* but identifies the wrong action.

13. **(A)** Choice (A) identifies the thing *tanker* and location *docked by the storage facility*. Choice (B) uses the related phrases *service station* and *pump gas* but does not describe the picture. Choice (C) has the related words *sailboat* and *harbor* but does not describe the picture. Choice (D) is incorrect because there are no waves in the picture.

14. **(A)** Choice (A) identifies the action *refers to the map*. Choice (B) is not able to be determined. Choice (C) is incorrect because the man's arm is bent, but his glasses are straight. Choice (D) is incorrect because he is gesturing downwards, not upwards.

15. **(C)** Choice (C) identifies *the messenger* and the action *knocking*. Choice (A) is incorrect; the messenger carries papers not a mailbag. Choice (B) is incorrect; the pants have a dark stripe. Choice (D) incorrectly identifies the man's occupation.

16. **(C)** Choice (C) identifies the action *unloading cargo*. Choices (A) and (B) misidentify the cargo *(shopping bags, pillows)*. Choice (D) does not match the picture.

17. **(B)** Choice (B) identifies the action *relaxing*. Choice (A) confuses *drinking tea* with *preparing A-V equipment*. Choice (C) has the related words: *waitress* and *food* but does not describe the picture. Choice (D) is incorrect because the woman is reading, not conversing.
18. **(C)** Choice (C) identifies the *pedestrians*. Choice (A) does not describe the picture. Choice (B) is incorrect; the street is crowded, but you cannot assume the store is crowded. Choice (D) confuses similar sounds: *repair* with *stair* and has the related word *bicycles,* but does not describe the picture.
19. **(B)** Choice (B) identifies a thing *gloves*. Choice (A) shows negation: the oil rig is not under water. Choice (C) misidentifies the action: they are talking *in person* not *over a distance*. Choice (D) has the related word *pipes* but does not describe the picture.
20. **(A)** Choice (A) identifies the *track with walls on both sides*. Choice (B) confuses similar sounds: *monopoly* with *monorail*. Choice (C) has the related words *train* and *track* but is incorrect: the train is above ground (elevated). Choice (D) confuses similar sounds: *elevator* with *elevated* and *grain* with *train* and has the related word *railroad* but does not describe the picture.

Part II: Question-Response

21. **(C)** Choice (C) is a logical response to a question about *who*. Choice (A) confuses similar sounds: *who's* and *whose* and indicates possession. Choice (B) confuses similar sounds: *there* with *here* and indicates location.
22. **(B)** Choice (B) is a logical response to a question about *thoughts*. Choice (A) confuses similar sounds: *thinking* and *sinking*. Choice (C) confuses similar sounds *think* with *ink*; *blue* with *about*.
23. **(A)** Choice (A) is a logical response to a question about *time*. Choice (B) confuses different meanings: *leave* (v) and *leaves* (n). Choice (C) confuses similar sounds: *leave her* and *lawyer*; *did* and *deed*.
24. **(A)** Choice (A) is a logical response to a question about *where*. Choice (B) confuses similar sounds: *stay* and *say*. Choice (C) confuses similar sounds: *stay* and *stain*.
25. **(B)** Choice (B) is a logical response to a question about *which*. Choice (A) confuses similar sounds: *number* and *numb*. Choice (C) confuses similar sounds: *fax* and *fast*.
26. **(B)** Choice (B) is a logical response to a question about *why no one is present*. Choice (A) shows negation: if the room is crowded, people are there. Choice (C) confuses similar sounds: *no one here* and *not hear*.
27. **(A)** Choice (A) is a logical response to a question about *weather*. Choice (B) contains the same verb *was* and might be related to *weather* (bad weather causes some people to wear hats) but does not describe the weather. Choice (B) also confuses similar sounds: *weather* and *wearing*. Choice (C) confuses similar sounds: *weather* and *wet*.
28. **(C)** Choice (C) is a logical response to a question about *coffee*. Choice (A) confuses similar sounds: *coffee* and *cough*. Choice (B) confuses similar sounds: *coffee* and *fee*.
29. **(C)** Choice (C) is a logical response to a question about *who*. Choice (A) confuses similar sounds: *letter* and *let her*; *open* and *opera*. Choice (B) confuses similar sounds: *open* and *pen*.
30. **(A)** Choice (A) is a logical response to a question about *when*. Choice (B) expresses future (*day after tomorrow*); the question indicates past tense (*did begin*). Choice (C) confuses similar sounds: *conf(erence)* and *can*; *begin* and *tin*.
31. **(B)** Choice (B) is a logical response to a question about *time*. Choice (A) confuses related words: *time* and *watch*. Choice (C) confuses related words: *morning* and *get up*.
32. **(B)** Choice (B) is a logical response to a question about *duration of time*. Choice (A) confuses similar sounds: *ride* and *bride* and related words: *long* with *tall*. Choice (C) describes *how long the train is* (ten cars) not *how long the ride is* (two hours).

33. **(A)** Choice (A) is a logical response to a question about *occupation*. Choice (B) confuses similar sounds: *occupation* and *attention*. Choice (C) confuses similar sounds: *occupied* with *occupation*.
34. **(B)** Choice (B) is a logical response to a question about *coming*. Choice (A) confuses *not coming* with *are coming* or *not* (coming) and does not match the subject (*you-he*). Choice (C) confuses *didn't come* with *are coming* or *not* (coming) and does not match subject (*you-they*) or tense.
35. **(A)** Choice (A) is a logical response to a question about *seat location*. Choice (B) confuses similar sounds: *sitting* and *city*. Choice (C) confuses similar sounds: *sitting* and *sitter*.
36. **(B)** Choice (B) is a logical response to a question about *being sleepy*. Choice (A) confuses similar sounds: *sleep* and *deep*. Choice (C) confuses similar sounds: *sweet pea* with *sleepy*.
37. **(A)** Choice (A) is a logical response to a question about *who*. Choice (B) confuses similar sounds: *phone* and *home*. Choice (C) has the full form *telephone* but answers location, not identity.
38. **(C)** Choice (C) is a logical response to a question about *quantity*. Choice (A) has the related word *supermarket* and gives *quantity of people* (crowded) but does not refer to quantity of food. Choice (B) confuses similar sounds: *food* and *mood*.
39. **(B)** Choice (B) is a logical response to a question about *how often*. Choice (A) tells *how often* but confuses similar sounds: *train* and *rain*. Choice (C) tells *how often* but confuses similar sounds: *plane* with *train*.
40. **(A)** Choice (A) is a logical response to a question about *what color*. Choice (B) confuses similar sounds: *hall* and *tall*. Choice (C) confuses related words: *paint* and *painting* and similar sounds: *wall* with *hall*.
41. **(C)** Choice (C) is a logical response to a question about *which*. Choice (A) confuses similar sounds: *my gray* and *migraine*. Choice (B) confuses similar sounds: *tie* and *tried*; *suit* and *do it*.
42. **(B)** Choice (B) is a logical response to a question about *who*. Choice (A) confuses similar sounds: *met* and *bet*. Choice (C) confuses *at the door* and *by the door* and tells *what* not *who*.
43. **(A)** Choice (A) is a logical response to a question about *when*. Choice (B) is incorrect; *finished* (past tense) does not match the tense of the question—*will be finished* (future). Choice (C) is incorrect; *thought* (past tense) does not match the tense of the question—*think* (present tense).
44. **(B)** Choice (B) is a logical response to a question about *not coming with us*. Choice (A) has the related word *go* but does not answer *why*. Choice (C) is incorrect; *didn't come* (past tense) does not match *aren't coming* (present tense) and does not answer *why*.
45. **(A)** Choice (A) is a logical response to a question about *being alone*. Choice (B) confuses different meanings: *alone* and *lonely*. Choice (C) should use *yes* instead of *no* (*Yes, I am alone because no one is here*).
46. **(C)** Choice (C) is a logical response to a question about *what page*. Choice (A) answers *when,* not *what page*. Choice (B) confuses *on* with *under* and does not answer *what page*.
47. **(B)** Choice (B) is a logical response to a question about *where*. Choice (A) confuses similar sounds: *wait* and *weigh*. Choice (C) is incorrect; *waited* (past tense) does not match *should wait* (present-future) and answers *how long* (an hour) but not *where*.
48. **(A)** Choice (A) is a logical response to a question about *duration*. Choice (B) confuses *on the phone* with *off the hook*. Choice (C) confuses *long* with *how much longer* and has the related word *cord*.
49. **(A)** Choice (A) is a logical response to a question about *sending a memo*. (*E-mail* means *electronic mail*, a way to send correspondence by computer.) Choice (B) confuses *sending* with *shipping department* (any department can send and

receive memos). Choice (C) confuses related words: *departments* with *department store.*

50. **(C)** Choice (C) is a logical response to a question about *the worst part.* Choice (A) confuses similar sounds: *trip* and *rip.* Choice (B) confuses similar sounds (and related words): *tip* with trip.

Part III: Short Conversations

51. **(C)** *It opens earlier on Saturdays.* Choices (A) and (B) have the same hours. Choice (D) is incorrect; the store is closed on Sunday.
52. **(A)** If the shoes are *soaked with rain*, they are *wet.* Choice (B) confuses *train* and *rain.* Choice (C) confuses *drop on the corner* with *drip on the carpet.* Choice (D) confuses *carpet* and *car.*
53. **(D)** *The woman didn't hear the phone ring.* Choices (A) and (B) are contradicted by *didn't hear the phone.* Choice (C) confuses *answering machine* with *answer.*
54. **(B)** *Didn't fly* means *didn't take a plane.* Choice (A) is not mentioned. Choice (C) confuses *country* and *countryside.* Choice (D) confuses *inside* and *countryside.*
55. **(C)** *Made a mistake* means *do something wrong.* Choice (A) is contradicted by *the supervisor wants to see you in his office.* Choice (B) confuses *see his office* with *see you in his office.* Choice (D) is contradicted by *been doing a good job.*
56. **(B)** The woman prefers *something quieter.* Choice (A) is how the man describes the new room. Choice (C) is how the man describes the original room. Choice (D) is contradicted by *quieter.*
57. **(D)** *Getting a check after dinner* means *a restaurant.* Choices (A), (B), and (C) are not places people typically eat dinner and wouldn't involve a check.
58. **(A)** *Expired* means *out of date.* Choice (B) means *lost.* Choice (C) is contradicted by *has expired.* Choice (D) is contradicted by the clerk accepting a credit card payment.
59. **(D)** *All other suggestions have been rejected.* Choice (A) is incorrect; the woman is *busy all day.* Choice (B) is not suggested except for Choice (C), *dinner,* when the man is *tied up.*
60. **(C)** *Two towels, two extra towels, and one remaining towel* means *three towels are missing.* Choice (A) is the number of towels remaining. Choice (B) is the number of extra towels that were brought up. Choice (D) is the total number of towels.
61. **(B)** *Tickets, hotel reservations, and rental cars* are all handled by travel agents. Choice (A) handles only hotel reservations. Choice (C) flies airplanes. Choice (D) handles booking tickets only.
62. **(C)** *To get seats* means *to sit down.* Choices (A) and (B) are not mentioned. Choice (D) is incorrect; both trains are going downtown.
63. **(B)** If he is *boiling water,* he's probably going to *make tea.* Choice (A) is illogical; the woman asks him not to make coffee. Choice (C) is incorrect; he's going to boil water. Choice (D) confuses *fish* and *fresh.*
64. **(A)** A *receptionist* receives visitors. Choice (B) is incorrect; *shipping clerks* handle shipments. Choice (C) is incorrect; *librarians* keep books. Choice (D) is incorrect; the *personnel director* sees job applicants.
65. **(D)** *Avoid heavy traffic* means *the traffic will get bad.* Choice (A) confuses *arrive early* and *three-thirty.* Choice (B) uses *early* and *airport* to suggest miss *the plane.* Choice (C) confuses *hurry* and *heavy.*
66. **(C)** *Natural light* comes in *the window.* Choice (A) is contradicted by *should hang it by the window.* Choice (B) is contradicted by *likes natural light.* Choice (D) is not a good choice if the plant likes natural light.
67. **(A)** *The woman got a round-trip ticket.* Choice (B) is contradicted by *round-trip.* Choices (C) and (D) are not mentioned.
68. **(D)** *One week and three weeks add up to four weeks.* Choice (A) confuses *one night* and *last night.* Choice (B) is the time to be spent in the hospital. Choice (C) is the time to be spent at home.
69. **(C)** The woman says *if you used a computer.* Choice (A) is the expected

544 EXPLANATORY ANSWERS

solution for fixing the typewriter. Choices (B) and (D) are not given as solutions.

70. **(A)** *Postpone* means *do later*. Choice (B) is true of everyone, due to the weather. Choice (C) is contradicted by *let's change our meeting*. Choice (D) is contradicted by *her suggestion to postpone*.

71. **(D)** *Turn down* means *lower the volume*. Choice (A) confuses *turn down* with *turn around*. Choice (B) suggests *practice* from *trying* and *music*. Choice (C) confuses *try harder* with *trying to work*.

72. **(C)** *Go back on your own* means *go alone*. Choice (A) is not suggested, and another tour may have the same problem. Choice (B) confuses *in a hurry* and *hurry up*. Choice (D) confuses *of her own* and *on your own*.

73. **(D)** The man got lost trying to find the restaurant. Choice (A) confuses *got lost* and *lost his map*. Choice (B) is incorrect because he doesn't even have a map. Choice (C) is not mentioned.

74. **(D)** The man says the *dealine is tomorrow*. Choice (A) is when he got the report. Choice (B) is when the woman has to leave. Choice (C) confuses *ten* and *then*.

75. **(D)** *She doesn't like to park her car in the city*. Choice (A) is not mentioned. Choice (B) is contradicted by *always take the subway*. Choice (C) confuses *like to drive* and *like to park*.

76. **(B)** *The man can't get calls if he's not near a phone*. Choice (A) is not relevant. Choice (C) is contradicted by the fact that he is talking to the receptionist. Choice (D) is not a logical reason for not leaving a message.

77. **(C)** Other suggestions were rejected. Choice (A) was rejected: *people will run into it* there. Choice (B) was not suggested. Choice (D) confuses *hall* and *wall*.

78. **(A)** *She suggests that he call the nurse*. Choice (B) is not logical; she can't walk if she hurt her ankle. Choice (C) confuses *chairs* and *stairs*. Choice (D) confuses *taking shoes* off with *buying shoes*.

79. **(A)** The man *hoped there was a post office closer*. Choice (B) confuses *closed* and *close*. Choice (C) confuses *round* and *around*. Choice (D) confuses *on the bus* and *bus route*.

80. **(C)** *Every two weeks* is approximately *twice a month*. Choice (A) is not given. Choice (B) contrasts with *every two weeks*. Choice (D) confuses *two weeks* and *two o'clock*.

Part IV: Short Talks

81. **(C)** Senior citizens should get on the plane during priority boarding. Choices (A), (B), and (D) are not mentioned.

82. **(B)** People may *request assistance from a flight attendant*. Choices (A), (C), and (D) are airline personnel but have other duties.

83. **(C)** This ad is for *professional* books. Choices (A) and (B) would not be sold at such a store. Choice (D) is incorrect; textbooks are for students who are not yet professionals.

84. **(D)** They will *order it*. Choice (A) is unnecessary if they can order it. Choice (B) would not help in getting the book. Choice (C) is not logical.

85. **(B)** It says *cloudiness is expected this afternoon*. Choice (A) is contradicted by *this morning will be partly sunny*. Choices (C) and (D) are incorrect; it will already be cloudy by evening and night.

86. **(A)** *Continue through the weekend* means *all weekend*. Choices (B), (C), and (D) are not logical ways to express *all weekend*.

87. **(D)** *3-5 days* is explicitly mentioned. Choices (A), (B), and (C) are all shorter periods of time.

88. **(B)** Drink plenty of *water* and *fruit juices*, which are *fluids*. Choices (A), (C), and (D) may help but are not mentioned.

89. **(B)** Since the ad concentrates on *meetings*, it is for businesspeople. Choice (A) is incorrect; do not have business meetings. Choices (C) and (D) do not set up business meetings.

90. **(C)** The advertisement discusses *food for business occasions*. Choice (A) confuses *conference planning* and *conference room*. Choices (B) and (D) are not provided by catering companies.

91. **(D)** The subway is *to the shopping mall and suburbs*. Choices (A) and (C) are

contradicted by *to the northern suburbs*. Choice (B) is not mentioned.

92. **(A)** The announcement says to catch *the gray line to the airport*. Choice (B) is the current line. Choices (C) and (D) are not mentioned.

93. **(C)** *Things will close* because of *the federal holiday*. Choice (A) is incorrectly suggested by *weekend schedule*. Choice (B) is contradicted by *public transportation will operate*. Choice (D) is not mentioned.

94. **(A)** The announcement says there will be *no additional buses or trains for rush hour service*. Choice (B) is confused with *operate on a weekend schedule*. Choices (C) and (D) are unlikely if transportation follows weekend service.

95. **(D)** This was a *survey of business travelers*. Choices (A), (B), and (C) do not travel much on business.

96. **(C)** Hotels should be located close to *shopping and entertainment facilities*. Choice (A) is where they don't want hotels located. Choices (B) and (D) are not mentioned.

97. **(A)** *To provide access* means that *facilities should be open*. Choice (B) is not mentioned. Choice (C) confuses *light snacks* and serving *lighter meals*. Choice (D) is not mentioned.

98. **(B)** The service helps people *find their way around the city by public transportation*. Choice (A) is not mentioned. Choice (C) is incorrect; they tell you how to use transportation but do not sell tickets. Choice (D) is incorrect; they tell you how to use transportation but do not tell you what to see.

99. **(D)** You should have the day and time of travel available in order to get help. Choices (A), (B), and (C) are not mentioned.

100. **(C)** The announcement tells you to have *a pencil and paper ready to write down information*. Choice (A) is not needed for this information service. Choices (B) and (D) might give you destinations but are not necessary or mentioned.

Part V: Incomplete Sentences

101. **(B)** The present tense in the *if* clause of a real condition can use future in the other clause. Choice (A) is past. Choice (C) is past perfect. Choice (D) is present progressive.

102. **(C)** *Until* joins the clauses; it is logical. Choices (A) and (D) are not logical. Choice (B) is used in relative clauses.

103. **(A)** *At* indicates location. Choice (B) means *together*. Choice (C) means *to place inside*. Choice (D) indicates a recipient.

104. **(D)** Someone else *enclosed* the envelope; use the past participle. Choice (A) has an unnecessary *is*. Choice (B) is the simple form of the verb. Choice (C) is the present participle.

105. **(C)** *Advice* is a noun and is logical. Choice (A) is a verb. Choice (B) is an adjective. Choice (D) is a noun, but it is not logical.

106. **(B)** Use *on* with days of the week. Choice (A) means *inside*. Choice (C) means *above*. Choice (D) indicates location.

107. **(B)** *Increase* is logical. Choice (A) is used for physical movement. Choice (C) includes increases in speed and volume. Choice (D) requires an object (*...expects circulation to raise ad revenues*).

108. **(A)** The adjective *effective* modifies *way*. Choices (B) and (C) are nouns. Choice (D) is an adverb.

109. **(D)** Join contrasting clauses with *but*. Choices (A), (B), and (C) are not logical.

110. **(C)** Specific times use *at*. Choice (A) is incorrect; an earlier action must be mentioned with *until*. Choice (B) indicates destination. Choice (D) indicates a recipient.

111. **(D)** *Head of operations* requires a singular verb. Choice (A) is a gerund. Choice (B) is plural. Choice (C) is the simple form.

112. **(B)** *Always* should come between the auxiliary and the main verb. In Choice (A) *always* is before the verb. In Choice (C) *always* is after the main verb. Choice (D) uses the wrong form of *be*.

113. **(C)** *Under* is logical. Choices (A), (B), and (D) require more than one item as a

reference point. Choice (B) generally indicates a specific area rather than a specific thing.
114. **(B)** Join equal terms with *and*. Choice (A) indicates a choice between terms. Choice (C) indicates a contrast. Choice (D) is used with *nor*.
115. **(D)** The causative *had* is followed by the simple form. Choice (A) is the gerund. Choice (B) is past tense. Choice (C) is the past participle.
116. **(C)** *Promises* is followed by the infinitive. Choice (A) is the future tense. Choice (B) is the gerund. Choice (D) is the present tense.
117. **(A)** The clauses contrast; use *although*. Choice (B) is not used with clauses. Choices (C) and (D) are not logical.
118. **(D)** The sentence requires a noun subject. Choice (A) is a noun but is not logical. Choice (B) is a verb. Choice (C) is a gerund.
119. **(A)** The causative *persuade* is followed by the infinitive. Choice (B) is the gerund. Choice (C) is past tense. Choice (D) is the past participle.
120. **(D)** *Repairs* is the only noun among the options. Choices (A), (B), and (C) do not fit the context of the sentence.
121. **(C)** Use *at* with specific times. Choice (A) is used with dates. Choice (B) indicates a recipient. Choice (D) means *inside*.
122. **(B)** The causative *suggest* is followed by the gerund. Choice (A) is the past tense. Choice (C) is present tense. Choice (D) is the infinitive.
123. **(A)** Use the idiomatic *on* with dates. Choice (B) means *inside*. Choice (C) indicates location. Choice (D) indicates destination.
124. **(C)** The comparative *more* is followed by an adjective and *than*. Choice (A) omits *than*. Choice (B) is an adverb. Choice (D) is an incomplete *as-as* comparison.
125. **(B)** *Because* establishes a cause-and-effect relationship. Choices (A), (C), and (D) are not logical.
126. **(C)** The causative *request* is followed by the simple form of the verb. Choice (A) is the gerund. Choice (B) is the present tense. Choice (D) is the infinitive.
127. **(D)** *Who* refers to the subject *person*. Choice (A) is possessive. Choice (B) refers to things. Choice (C) is objective.
128. **(C)** Equal comparisons use as + adjective + as; *the memo* is causing people to become confused, so the adjective must be the present participle. Choice (A) omits the second *as*. Choice (B) omits the first *as*. Choice (D) uses the past participle.
129. **(A)** Since *know* happened before *was*, it must also be past tense. Choice (B) is the past participle. Choice (C) is the present progressive. Choice (D) is the past perfect.
130. **(B)** Commands are in the simple form of the verb. Choice (A) is the present progressive. Choice (C) is the present tense. Choice (D) is the future tense.
131. **(A)** *On* is used for building, floor, or ship deck locations. Choice (B) means *below*. Choice (C) means *inside*. Choice (D) means *above*.
132. **(C)** *Effect* is a logical noun. Choice (A) is a verb. Choice (B) is a noun but is not logical. Choice (D) is an adjective.
133. **(B)** *Reservation* is the only noun among the options that matches a hotel context. Choices (A), (C), and (D) do not fit the context of the sentence.
134. **(C)** *And* joins equal terms. Choice (A) implies a contrast. Choice (B) implies a choice. Choice (D) is used with *or*.
135. **(D)** *Which* refers to *merger*. Choice (A) refers to time. Choice (B) is possessive. Choice (C) repeats the subject *merger*.
136. **(A)** Habitual action is expressed by the present tense. Choice (B) is past tense. Choice (C) is the simple form of the verb. Choice (D) is the past participle.
137. **(C)** Implies a past continuing action; use the past progressive. Choice (A) is the simple past and is not logical; she could not type if the typewriter was broken. Choice (B) is the present progressive. Choice (D) is present.
138. **(A)** *Tomorrow* uses the future tense. Choice (B) is past tense. Choice (C) is past perfect. Choice (D) is the present progressive.
139. **(B)** *Someone else surprised Mr. Hopper*; use the past participle. Choice (A) is the simple form. Choice (C) is the present participle. Choice (D) is the present tense.

140. **(D)** *And* joins equal terms. Choice (A) needs *neither* after the verb. Choice (B) implies a contrast. Choice (C) is used with *nor*.

Part VI: Error Recognition

141. **(B)** (will go) *Are* in the *if* clause requires future in the other clause. Choice (A) is a correct noun. Choice (B), (C), and (D) are correct adjectives.

142. **(A)** (A good salesperson) A singular count noun must have an article. Choice (B) is correct use of *always*. Choice (C) is a correct verb. Choice (D) is a correct verb.

143. **(A)** (Mr. Lee to give) The causative *ask* requires a following infinitive. Choice (B) is a correct phrase. Choice (C) is used with noun *demonstration*. Choice (D) is a correct superlative.

144. **(B)** (Twice a week new employees; training sessions twice a week) *Twice a week* must appear at the beginning or end. Choice (A) modifies *employees*. Choice (C) is the infinitive after *required*. Choice (D) modifies *sessions*.

145. **(B)** (sent from Toronto) *It* repeats the subject *fax*. Choice (A) joins two clauses. Choice (C) indicates origin. Choice (D) modifies *fax*.

146. **(D)** (to increase) *Increasing* should match *to decrease*. Choice (A) is a correct verb. Choice (B) is correct use of *during*. Choice (C) can join equal terms.

147. **(C)** (to buy) After *encourage*, use the infinitive. Choice (A) correctly uses *an* before a vowel sound. Choice (B) is a correct verb. Choice (D) is a correct noun.

148. **(C)** (is included) Someone else *included* the charge; use the past participle. Choice (A) is a correct noun. Choice (B) indicates purpose. Choice (D) is a correct noun.

149. **(D)** (rarely lasts) *Rarely* goes before the main verb. Choice (A) is a correct article. Choice (B) is a correct verb. Choice (C) is the comparative *than*.

150. **(B)** (have) The subject *items* requires a plural verb. Choice (A) is correct; use *on* for items on a list, invoice, etc. Choice (C) tells what kind of identification numbers. Choice (D) is a plural noun.

151. **(A)** (had already written) The adverb of frequency comes between the auxiliary and the verb. Choice (B) joins clauses in a time relationship. Choice (C) is a correct plural. Choice (D) *out* is used with *went* for sudden lack of light, power, heat, etc.

152. **(C)** (will answer) The real condition *if* clause is in the present tense. The main clause is in the future tense. Choice (B) means *not present*. Choice (D) is a correct prepositional phrase.

153. **(B)** (write) The causative *insist* is followed by the simple form of the verb. Choice (A) is a correct possessive pronoun. Choice (C) modifies *updates*. Choice (D) modifies *project*.

154. **(C)** (need) The plural subject *clerks* requires a plural verb. Choice (A) is correctly used with departments. Choice (B) tells which department. Choice (D) is correct; *need* requires a following infinitive.

155. **(D)** (allowed) An unreal condition uses past tense, not present. Choice (A) is a correct verb. Choice (B) modifies *manager*. Choice (C) is correct use of *if*.

156. **(A)** (If) Not logical; use *if, because* or *since* to express a cause and effect relationship. Choice (B) is a correct verb. Choice (C) is a common business expression. Choice (D) is a correct verb.

157. **(B)** (convincing) The argument *convinced* others; use the present participle. Choice (A) is a correct verb. Choice (C) joins two clauses. Choice (D) correctly uses the infinitive after *voted*.

158. **(A)** (who) *He* repeats the subject *salesman*. Choices (B) and (C) are correct verbs. Choice (D) modifies *sales*.

159. **(A)** (went) *Took* and *last* indicate past tense; replace future *will go* with past. Choice (B) indicates destination. Choice (C) joins clauses in a time relationship. Choice (D) is a correct time marker.

160. **(C)** (as hard as) Equal comparisons require *as* on both sides of the adverb. Choice (A) is correct; use *the* with a specified noun. Choice (B) is correctly used between the title and the department. Choice (D) is a correct verb.

Part VII: Reading Comprehension

161. **(C)** The practice of hiring temporary workers is increasing. Choice (A) is contradicted by *minimum staff*. Choice (B) does not refer to a hiring practice. Choice (D) is not given as a hiring practice.

162. **(A)** Temporary workers are hired *when the workload increases*. Choice (B) is not mentioned. Choices (C) and (D) are reasons to keep a minimum staff, not reasons to hire temporary workers.

163. **(C)** Since the reply states *we are no longer hiring full-time workers*, his letter must have concerned this topic. They may *hire temporary workers*. Choices (A), (B), and (D) may also interest him, but his letter apparently did not ask about these issues.

164. **(B)** This is a *boarding pass for an airline flight*. Choices (A), (C), and (D) are not consistent with the information on the coupon.

165. **(B)** *From New York (La Guardia Airport) to Los Angeles*. Choice (A) is incorrect; *Greece* is not mentioned. Choice (C) is incorrect; *Newfoundland* is not mentioned. Choice (D) is incorrect; *Los Alamos* and *Greenland* are not mentioned.

166. **(C)** Her seat is *12A*. Choice (A) confuses the *seat* and the *date*. Choice (B) confuses the *seat* and the *time*. Choice (D) confuses the *seat* and the *gate*.

167. **(D)** *Upon receipt* means when you receive them. Choice (A) confuses the *due date* with the *date when interest will start to accrue*. Choice (B) confuses *last day* and *first day*. Choice (C) confuses the date the invoice was issued with the date the invoice was received.

168. **(A)** Accounts *unpaid...shall accrue interest*. Choice (B) is incorrect; the bank only sets the interest rate. Choice (C) is incorrect; you will pay the invoice plus the interest, but this may not be *twice as much*. Choice (D) is not mentioned.

169. **(D)** Since the notice says interest is accrued at the Consumers Bank rate, we can assume it sets a base interest rate. Choices (A), (B), and (C) are not mentioned.

170. **(C)** A stockbroker is likely to attend to learn how he/she can better assist clients. Choice (A) is contradicted by *clients*. Choice (B) confuses *manager* and *management firm*. Choice (D) is not likely.

171. **(C)** The seminar will help you learn about how you can predict trends for successful investments. Choices (A), (B), and (C) are mentioned but are not what will be discussed.

172. **(B)** To reserve a seat, fill out the card and mail it with your registration fee. Choices (A) and (C) are not mentioned. Choice (D) is what you do to get more information.

173. **(A)** New Tech has cut jobs as part of its strategy to reorganize its money-losing business and become more profitable. Choice (B) is incorrect because the international offices are already opened and are more cost-effective. Choices (C) and (D) are not mentioned.

174. **(B)** The jobs will be cut in Brazil. Choices (A) and (D) will not have job cuts even though there are employees in these areas. Choice (C) is not mentioned.

175. **(D)** The company has had *two years of losses*. Choices (A), (B), and (C) are contradicted by *two years*.

176. **(C)** The analysts were surprised at the *reduction in labor*. Choices (A), (B), and (D) were all mentioned but not as surprises.

177. **(A)** Ms. Strube has made the international branches more cost-effective. The other choices are not mentioned in the passage.

178. **(B)** The new fares are *effective March 1*. Choices (A), (C), and (D) are contradicted by *March 1*.

179. **(C)** *8:00 P.M. Thursday* is off-peak. Choices (A), (B), and (D) are peak hours when everyone is traveling to or from work.

180. **(D)** The peak fare is *$1.70*. Choice (A) is the off-peak fare within one zone. Choice (B) is the peak fare within one zone. Choice (C) is the peak fare between zones 1 and 2, the off-peak fare between zones 1 and 3, and the peak fare between zones 2 and 3.

181. **(B)** *Consumer preferences* means *what consumers like*. Choices (A) and (C) are likely uses for this information but are not the duties of the Specialist. Choice (D) is incorrect; product testing is a way to discover consumer preferences but is not explicitly mentioned.
182. **(D)** The Specialist will write reports *for use within the company*. Choice (A) is incorrect; the reports will be *about* the consumer. Choices (B) and (C) are contradicted by *within the company*.
183. **(A)** The qualifications are *a college degree in research and experience in advertising*. Choice (B) is not logical. Choice (C) is not mentioned. Choice (D) is related but not necessary.
184. **(D)** This person has a morning full of meetings. Choice (A) is incorrect; breakfast is with the accountants. Choice (B) is incorrect; lunch is at 1:00. Choice (C) is incorrect; the person is working all morning it seems—no day off here.
185. **(B)** *On the half-hour* indicates every thirty minutes. Choices (A), (C), and (D) are other ways to organize a calendar that are not used here. *Minutes* is a little excessive.
186. **(D)** The new regulations *reduced port costs* and *increased efficiency*. Choices (A), (B), and (C) are not mentioned.
187. **(B)** The *Pacific Rim* is the only geographical region mentioned.
188. **(B)** Ports in recent years have been moving over half of their capacity. Choices (A), (C), and (D) refer to other statistics in the passage.
189. **(C)** The regulation requiring that 60% of all exports be carried by Peruvian-flag carriers has been abolished. Choice (A) is contradicted by competition. Choice (B) is true prior to the reforms. Choice (D) confuses *display their flag* and *Peruvian flag-carriers*.
190. **(B)** This is the best choice and is directly stated in the passage: *increase in traffic*. Choices (A), (C), and (D) may be true, but are not stated in the passages.
191. **(D)** The purpose of this notice is to encourage investors to keep their Southern Regional stock. Choice (A) associates *warning* with *alert*. Choice (B) confuses *suggesting a change in management* and *if present management does not change*. Choice (C) is mentioned, but it is not the purpose of the notice.
192. **(B)** *Reduced costs* and *lowered costs* have the same meaning; they also had a higher number of *profitable routes*. Choice (A), (C), and (D) are not mentioned.
193. **(C)** The airline lost *$112.4 million for all of this year*. Choices (A) and (D) are contradicted by the figure given. Choice (B) is the amount earned in the fourth quarter.
194. **(C)** The airline will focus on the *short-haul markets where it built its strong base*. Choice (B) is being eliminated. The other options are not mentioned.
195. **(B)** Guaranteed arrival allows you to get a room after check-in time. Choice (A) is not logical. Choice (C) is incorrect; you must arrive before 4:00 if you did *not* guarantee arrival. Choice (D) is incorrect because you still have to check in.
196. **(A)** You must pay for the *first night's room charge*. Choice (B) confuses *first choice* and *first night's charge*. Choices (C) and (D) are not logical.
197. **(B)** The memo is about *vacation time*. Choices (A), (C), and (D) are not mentioned. Also Choice (C) is a different kind of time off.
198. **(D)** The supervisor has to approve *vacation periods longer than one week*. Choices (A), (B), and (C) are one week or less.
199. **(D)** If you have frequent absences, your request could be denied. Choices (A), (B), and (C) are not mentioned.
200. **(D)** The Personnel Review Board can examine the vacation request. Choice (A) is incorrect; supervisors can approve vacations only for their own employees. Choices (B) and (C) may not be possible.

Model Test 5

Part I: Picture

1. **(C)** Choice (C) identifies the action *using a public phone*. Choice (A) confuses simi-

lar sounds: *phone* with *loan*. Choices (B) and (D) are not shown in the picture.

2. **(A)** Choice (A) identifies location. Choice (B) confuses *plane* with *train*. Choice (C) confuses similar sounds: *computer* with *commuter* and related words: *row* and *line*. Choice (D) cannot be assumed from the picture.

3. **(B)** Choice (B) identifies *dentist* and *patient*. Choice (A) confuses the similar sounds: *nose* and *toes*. Choice (C) has the related phrase *brushing his teeth* but does not describe the action in the picture. Choice (D) has the related word *drill* but does not describe the picture.

4. **(D)** Choice (D) identifies the *technician* and the action, *doing lab work*. Choice (A) shows negation: the counter is not under a window. Choice (B) confuses similar sounds: *printed at the mint* and *experiment*. Choice (C) confuses a *technician* with a *doctor*, who prescribes medicine.

5. **(A)** Choice (A) makes the assumption the group is a *family* and the action is *traveling*. Choice (B) misidentifies an action; the child is *talking, not reading*. Choice (C) shows negation: the meals have not been served. Choice (D) misidentifies location: the child sits *next to* the woman.

6. **(D)** Choice (D) identifies previous action: *the bed had been made*. Choice (A) shows negation: the maid is not even in the room. Choice (B) shows negation: no luggage is in the room. Choice (C) misidentifies location: the folded clothes are *on the table*, not *the bed*.

7. **(B)** Choice (B) makes an assumption: *a robot assembles a car on an automatic assembly line*. Choice (A) misidentifies the action *in an accident*. Choice (C) is not able to be determined. Choice (D) confuses *being assembled* and *under inspection*.

8. **(A)** Choice (A) identifies location: *The woman is in front of the camera*. Choice (B) misidentifies the action: *on TV* not *watching TV*. Choice (C) misidentifies things: he uses a *camera* not a *microscope;* she uses a *microphone* not a *microscope*. Choice (D) confuses *cameraman* and *camera being mobile*.

9. **(C)** Choice (C) identifies the action *making a (photo)copy*. Choice (A) confuses similar sounds: *photographer* with *photocopy*. Choice (B) confuses related words: *lid* and *cover*. Choice (D) has the related word *secretary* but confuses *photocopier* and *fax machine*.

10. **(C)** Choice (C) identifies the action *packing* and the thing *fish*. Choice (A) has the related words *chef* and *cook* but does not describe the picture. Choice (B) confuses related words: *fishing boats* and *sea* with *fish* and does not describe the picture. Choice (D) is incorrect because the meat is not canned.

11. **(B)** Choice (B) identifies the location *at his desk*. Choice (A) has the related phrase *conference in session* but does not describe the picture. Choice (C) misidentifies the action: he is not signing papers. Choice (D) is incorrect because the papers are neat and in order, not strewn about.

12. **(D)** Choice (D) identifies the workers; they are focused and intent. Choice (A) shows negation: their work station is *not* very tidy. Choice (B) cannot be assumed from the picture; pads of paper are on the table, but we don't know if pads of paper are in the drawer. Choice (C) confuses *microphones* with *telephones*.

13. **(A)** Choice (A) identifies things: *cars parked on the sidewalk*. Choice (B) shows negation: the buildings are *not* over ten stories tall. Choices (C) and (D) show negation: there are no pedestrians at the curb or traffic light at the corner.

14. **(C)** Choice (C) identifies the action: *watching the game*. Choice (A) confuses related words: *spectacles* with *spectators*. Choice (B) confuses different meanings of *match* (for fire) and *match* (game). Choice (D) does not match the picture.

15. **(D)** Choice (D) identifies *technicians* and the location *control room*. Choice (A) misidentifies the action: they are monitoring the screens, not punching a time clock. Choice (B) misidentifies location: this is a control room, not an elevator. Choice (C)

is incorrect because most of the screens have a picture, and are not blank.

16. **(A)** Choice (A) identifies the location: *in front of the mountain*. Choice (B) is incorrect; the smoke is from *smokestacks*, not from a *forest fire*. Choice (C) confuses similar sounds: *log* with *smog*. Choice (D) confuses different meanings: *plant (flower)* with *plant (factory)*.
17. **(B)** Choice (B) identifies things: *empty seats*. Choice (A) shows negation: overhead bins are *closed*, not *open*. Choice (C) confuses *middle class* with *business class*. Choice (D) shows negation: there are no flight attendants in the picture.
18. **(A)** Choice (A) identifies the action: *clearing the table*. Choice (B) confuses *placing a coffee cup on the table* with *brewing coffee*. Choice (C) associates *tip* with *server*, but does not match the picture. Choice (D) misidentifies the action: she is not accepting reservations.
19. **(C)** Choice (C) identifies the action: *pointing to the map*. Choice (A) is incorrect; he is in front of *a map* not *a window*. Choice (B) is incorrect; he is not wearing a suit. Choice (D) incorrectly associates the glasses case in the man's pocket with an optometrist lecturing on lenses.
20. **(A)** Choice (A) identifies a thing: *protective glasses*. Choice (B) is incorrect; the man is wearing *protective glasses*, not using *binoculars*. Choice (C) shows negation: the plant is *not* billowing smoke. Choice (D) has the related word *chemistry* but does not match the picture.

Part II: Question-Response

21. **(A)** Choice (A) is a logical response to a question about *location*. Choice (B) confuses similar sounds: *waiting* and *weigh the*. Choice (C) confuses similar sounds: *waiting* and *raining*.
22. **(B)** Choice (B) is a logical response to a question about *location*. Choice (A) confuses related words: *books* and *library*. Choice (C) confuses *read books* with *sell books*.
23. **(B)** Choice (B) is a logical response to a question about *a dinner invitation*. Choice (A) confuses similar sounds: *dinner* and *December*. Choice (C) confuses similar sounds: *join* and *coin*; *dinner* and *thinner*.
24. **(A)** Choice (A) is a logical response to a question about *finishing a project*. Choice (B) confuses similar sounds: *project* (n) and *projected* (v). Choice (C) has the word *finish* but does not answer the question.
25. **(B)** Choice (B) is a logical response to a question about *plans*. Choice (A) confuses similar sounds: *plans* and *plane*; *noon* and *afternoon*. Choice (C) has the related word *planning* but refers to the past (yesterday) not the present (*this afternoon*).
26. **(C)** Choice (C) is a logical response to a question about *which train*. Choice (A) confuses related words: *express train* and *express mail*. Choice (B) would answer *excuse me* when it means permission to leave a room but not when it is used before another question.
27. **(B)** Choice (B) is a logical response to a question about *delivery*. Choice (A) confuses similar sounds: *package* and *packed*. Choice (C) confuses similar sounds: *her age* with *package*.
28. **(C)** Choice (C) is a logical response to a question about *transportation*. Choice (A) has the related word *plane* but does not answer the question *how*. Choice (B) confuses similar sounds: *airport* and *port*; *get* and *met*.
29. **(C)** Choice (C) is a logical response to a question about *reading material*. Choice (A) confuses related words: *newspapers* and *newsstand*, *newspaper* and *magazine*. Choice (B) confuses related words: *book* with *newspaper* and similar sounds: *read* (present tense) and *read* (past tense).
30. **(A)** Choice (A) is a logical response to a question about *returning*. Choice (B) confuses relates words: *return* (come back) with *return* (bring something back). Choice (C) confuses similar sounds: *return* and *right turn*.
31. **(B)** Choice (B) is a logical response to a question about *frequency*. Choice (A) has the frequency word *usually* but confuses similar sounds: *stay* and *play*. Choice (C) confuses similar sounds: *added* with *often* and related words: *telephone bill* and *hotel bill*.

32. **(C)** Choice (C) is a logical response to a question about *movies*. Choice (A) confuses similar sounds: *movies* and *moving*. Choice (B) uses the word *like* but expresses a preference not related to movies.
33. **(A)** Choice (A) is a logical response to a question about *reasons for cancellation*. Choice (B) confuses similar sounds: *flight* and *fight* and gives the *duration*, not a *reason*. Choice (C) confuses similar sounds: *canceled* and *can sell*.
34. **(A)** Choice (A) is a logical response to a question about *possession*. Choice (B) confuses similar sounds: *suitcase* and *suit*. Choice (C) confuses different meanings: *case* (instance) and *case* (suitcase or bag).
35. **(B)** Choice (B) is a logical response to a question about *storage*. Choice (A) confuses similar sounds: *swept* with *kept*. Choice (C) confuses similar sounds: *supplies* and *supper*.
36. **(C)** Choice (C) is a logical response to a question about *opinions*. Choice (A) confuses similar sounds: *vacation* and *vacant*. Choice (B) confuses similar sounds: *nation* with *vacation*.
37. **(A)** Choice (A) is a logical response to a question about *computers*. Choice (B) confuses *turn off lights* with *turn off computer*. Choice (C) discusses the same object (computer) but does not answer the question.
38. **(B)** Choice (B) is a logical response to a question about *attendance*. Choice (A) confuses different meanings: *attend* (be present) and *attend* (take care of). Choice (C) confuses similar sounds: *attend* and *at ten* and answers *when*.
39. **(A)** Choice (A) is a logical response to a question about *a meal*. Choice (B) has the related words *lunch* and *at noon* but answers *when* not *what*. Choice (C) answers *who are we having for dinner* not *what are we having for dinner*.
40. **(A)** Choice (A) is a logical response to a question about *quantity*. Choice (B) gives the number of the room, not the number of chairs. Choice (C) is not a logical response.
41. **(B)** Choice (B) is a logical response to a question about *location*. Choice (A) confuses similar sounds: *software* and *soft*; *software* with *wearing*. Choice (C) confuses similar sounds: *manual* and *man you know well*.
42. **(C)** Choice (C) is a logical response to a question about *the last time*. Choice (A) confuses related words: *oil* with *gas*. Choice (B) confuses similar sounds: *last* and *elastic*; *car* and *far*.
43. **(B)** Choice (B) is a logical response to a question about *cause*. Choice (A) confuses different meanings: *fire* (take away someone's job) with *forest fire*. Choice (C) confuses similar sounds: *forest* and *for a rest*.
44. **(A)** Choice (A) is a logical response to a question about *transportation*. Choice (B) confuses similar sounds: *live in town* with *go downtown* and *us* with *bus*. Choice (C) has the word *go* but does not answer *which bus*.
45. **(C)** Choice (C) is a logical response to a question about *not writing*. Choice (A) has the related word *letters* but does not give a reason. Choice (B) is incorrect; *will write* (future) does not answer *haven't written* (present perfect). Choice (B) also reverses the pronoun references and does not give a reason.
46. **(B)** Choice (B) is a logical response to a question about *action*. Choice (A) confuses similar sounds: *leave* (v) and *leave* (n) and implies that the rain happened in the past. Choice (C) is incorrect; *didn't rain* (past) does not match the tense of *before it starts to rain*.
47. **(A)** Choice (A) is a logical response to a question about *frequency*. Choice (B) confuses *how often* (frequency) with *how* (in what manner) and confuses similar sounds: *international* and *information*. Choice (C) confuses related words: *calls* and *phones* and *how many* with *how often*.
48. **(B)** Choice (B) is a logical response to the question of *need*. The speaker did not bring a car, so she or he needs a ride. Choice (A) confuses similar sounds: *tide* and *ride*. Choice (C) confuses similar sounds: *tried* and *ride*.

49. **(A)** Choice (A) is a logical response to a question about *time*. Choice (B) confuses similar sounds: *would* and *wood*. Choice (C) confuses similar sounds: *could* with *wood*. Also in Choice (C), *came...could* (past tense) does not match *would be able to come* (future).

50. **(B)** Choice (B) is a logical response to a question about *permission*. Choice (A) confuses similar sounds: *may* (aux.) and *May* (n). Choice (C) confuses different meanings: (sit) *down* and *cushion...filled with down* (feathers).

Part III: Short Conversations

51. **(B)** *Put something in the trash* means *throw it away*. Choice (A) confuses *place* and *space*. Choice (C) is not suggested. Choice (D) confuses *sell books* with *bought books*.

52. **(D)** *Black* coffee means no cream or sugar. Choice (A) is not mentioned. Choice (B) confuses *dream* and *cream*. Choice (D) confuses *toast* and *most*.

53. **(C)** The brakes may be bad. Choices (A), (B), and (D) are not mentioned.

54. **(A)** *Reads a newspaper*. Choice (B) is not mentioned. Choice (C) confuses *rain* and *train*. Choice (D) is not mentioned.

55. **(B)** He'll *send someone up* to fix the TV. Choice (A) is unlikely. Choice (C) confuses *take away* and *right away*. Choice (D) is illogical; the TV is already in the right room.

56. **(A)** To *work through lunch* means to *not take a lunch hour*. Choice (B) is contradicted by the fact that it is scheduled at *11:00*. Choices (C) and (D) don't explain why they need sandwiches.

57. **(A)** *One night*. Choice (B) confuses *two nights* and *two hundred dollars*. Choice (C) is incorrect; she was *charged* for three nights. Choice (D) confuses *for* and *four*.

58. **(D)** She wants air-conditioning. Choice (A) contradicts the man's suggestion. Choices (B) and (C) are not mentioned.

59. **(A)** *Wash* means *clean*. Choice (B) confuses *shirt* and *dirty*. Choice (C) confuses *watch* and *wash*. Choice (D) confuses *sweep the floor* with *sixth floor*.

60. **(C)** *Suitcase*, *luggage*, and *baggage* have the same meaning. Choice (A) is incorrect; they have to get luggage first. Choice (B) is incorrect; his bags aren't mentioned. Choice (D) is incorrect; they're stuck *at the airport*, not *in the city*.

61. **(B)** He needs the *fax number* to *fax* something. Choice (A) cannot be used for faxes. Choice (C) confuses *check* (noun) with *check* (verb). Choice (D) confuses *dial* (noun) with *dial* (verb).

62. **(B)** They'll eat *in the park*. Choices (A) and (C) confuse *sidewalk* and *cafe* with *sidewalk cafe*. Choice (D) is incorrect; the woman brought her sandwich *from home*.

63. **(D)** He needs the *new* number for the *new office*. Choice (A) confuses *dictionary* and *directory*. Choice (B) has the old number. Choice (C) doesn't have the number.

64. **(B)** The camera is still *at the hotel*. Choice (A) is incorrect; the man's camera is not as good. Choice (C) confuses *still* and *stolen*. Choice (D) confuses *moment* and *monument*.

65. **(A)** She cooks, he eats; they have *food* in common. Choice (B) is incorrect; he isn't good at golf. Choice (C) is incorrect; *free time* is when you do what you have in common. Choice (D) confuses *books* and *cook*.

66. **(C)** She put it in a separate box. Choice (A) is incorrect; she should not throw it away. Choices (B) and (C) are not mentioned.

67. **(A)** *Books*, *loan* and *overdue* indicate a library. Choice (B) is incorrect; bookstores *sell* books; the don't *lend* them. Choice (C) is incorrectly suggested by *loan*. Choice (D) is not mentioned.

68. **(D)** She *prefers a different paper*. Choice (A) is incorrect; *through reading* means *finished reading*. Choice (B) is incorrect because she would like to buy a paper. Choice (C) is not given as a reason for declining the offer.

69. **(B)** They pay *at the cash register*. Choice (A) is incorrect; he leaves *a tip* on the table. Choice (C) is contradicted by *the waitress doesn't take the check*. Choice (D) is not logical.

70. **(B)** *Facing the parking lot* probably means she has *a view of the parking lot*. Choice (A) confuses *park* and *parking lot*. Choice (C) is not mentioned. Choice (D) confuses *overlooked* and *overlooking*.

71. **(A)** If she asked about her savings account, she might prefer a *combined statement*. Choices (B) and (C) are incorrect; she wants information about both accounts. Choice (D) confuses *activity statement* with *activity in your account*.

72. **(C)** The room had a *double bed*, not a *king-sized bed*. Choice (A) is incorrect; he wants a big *bed*, not a big *room*. Choice (B) is not mentioned. Choice (D) is incorrect; he reserved a room with a king-sized bed.

73. **(D)** An office is likely to have different printers on different floors. Choices (A), (B), and (C) are not places to make copies.

74. **(A)** Rent a car. Choice (B) is illogical; if he is flying, he already has tickets. Choice (C) is contradicted by *flying to the conference*. Choice (D) is illogical; if he knows he is going, his place is already reserved.

75. **(B)** *Set up* and *get ready* have the same meaning. Choice (A) is incorrect; the rooms are being cleaned now. Choice (C) is incorrect; the staff needs to help, not talk. Choice (D) is incorrect; they need people to *prepare*, not *serve*.

76. **(B)** *Job requirements* and *testing typing speed* indicate a job interview. Choice (A) is incorrect; introductions include names and occupations. Choice (C) is incorrect; students test for *assignments*, not *jobs*. Choice (D) confuses a *package in the mail* and a *software package*.

77. **(D)** *Missing* and *can't find* have the same meaning. Choice (A) confuses *can't catch their train* with *missing training film*. Choice (B) confuses *making copies* with *having a second copy*. Choice (C) is incorrect; they don't know if they can start on time.

78. **(C)** He's been walking today. Choice (A) confuses *hot weather* and *hot water*.

Choice (B) is incorrect; *walking*, not *shoes*, hurts his feet. Choice (D) confuses *socks* and *soak*.

79. **(C)** The tickets are for 5:00. Choice (A) is confused with the time the meeting might end. Choice (B) is the earlier flight he wants to catch. Choice (D) is confused with the arrival of the 5:00 flight.

80. **(A)** *Bus*, *drive*, and advice about an unfamiliar place indicate a tour guide. Choices (B), (C), and (D) are not jobs described by these terms.

Part IV: Short Talks

81. **(A)** *Your call will be answered* indicates a telephone message. Choice (B) is incorrect; at a reception desk, a person answers calls. Choices (C) and (D) are not places calls are answered.

82. **(D)** You are advised to *stay on the line*. Choices (A), (B), and (C) are not choices given.

83. **(B)** is a *transfer point*. Choices (A) and (D) are contradicted by *Downtown Central*. Choice (C) is contradicted by *transfer point*.

84. **(A)** The platform is on the *lower level*. Choice (B) is the opposite. Choice (C) is contradicted by *take the elevator or stairs*. Choice (D) is not mentioned.

85. **(B)** It will be *partly sunny*. Choices (A) and (C) are contradicted by *sunny*. Choice (D) is contradicted by *seventy-two degrees*.

86. **(C)** *Get stronger* means *increase*. Choice (A) is incorrect; it is sunny already. Choice (B) is contradicted by *sunny*. Choice (D) is not mentioned and is not logical if the temperature is seventy-two degrees.

87. **(B)** Delivery within *two days*. Choice (A) is not a new service. Choices (C) and (D) are not mentioned.

88. **(A)** Customers in Alaska pay *$19* instead of *$9*. Choices (B), (C), and (D) are contradicted by *the same two-day service*.

89. **(A)** The hotline tells about *events*. Choices (B), (C), and (D) are not considered events.

90. **(B)** The hotline provides information on special events as well as public transporta-

tion routes. Choices (A), (C), and (D) are not mentioned.

91. **(A)** *Hello* is the first thing the receptionist should say. Choices (B), (C), and (D) all occur afterward.

92. **(D)** He should wait *in the lobby*. Choices (A) and (C) are contradicted by *take a seat in the lobby*. Choice (B) is not logical.

93. **(B)** They'll arrive *later*. Choice (A) is incorrect; *sooner* is the opposite of *later*. Choices (C) and (D) are contradicted by *no change in the number of scheduled trips*.

94. **(C)** June 5. Choice (A) is incorrect; nothing will happen *immediately*. Choice (B) is incorrect; the announcement mentions current *times* but not current *changes*. Choice (D) is confused with *21A* the number of the route that will change.

95. **(D)** It handles groups to *two hundred*. Choice (A) is the smallest group it will serve. Choices (B) and (C) fall within the limits.

96. **(C)** The advertisement describes *our guest rooms*. Choices (A), (B), and (D) are not logical if the center provides rooms.

97. **(A)** If its guest rooms *overlook the countryside*, the conference center is located in the country. Choices (B) and (C) are contradicted by *countryside*. Choice (D) is incorrect; the countryside doesn't have parks.

98. **(A)** *Have lost electrical power* means a *power failure*. Choices (B) and (D) are possible but are not mentioned. Choice (C) is not the problem.

99. **(C)** It's due to the *violent thunderstorm*. Choices (A), (B), and (D) could cause power failures but are not the problem here.

100. **(D)** Residents should *turn off appliances*. Choices (A) and (B) are not mentioned. Choice (C) is contradicted by *service crews are already working*.

Part V: Incomplete Sentences

101. **(A)** The present tense in the *if* clause of a real condition requires future in the other clause. Choice (B) is present tense but third person. Choice (C) is present progressive. Choice (D) is past.

102. **(C)** *Because* establishes a cause-and-effect relationship between the clauses. Choices (A), (B), and (D) are not logical.

103. **(B)** Use *on* with days of the week. Choice (A) means *together*. Choice (C) is used with times, not days. Choice (D) indicates a recipient.

104. **(D)** The *results* surprise others; use the present participle. Choice (A) is the past participle. Choice (B) is the present tense. Choice (C) is the simple form.

105. **(B)** *Inventory* is logical; it means *stock*. Choice (A) invites a person to an event. Choice (C) is a new thing or procedure. Choice (D) is a summary of goods or services.

106. **(D)** *At* is used with specific times. Choice (A) means *inside*. Choice (B) is used with days. Choice (C) means *above*.

107. **(C)** *Quit* requires a following gerund. Choice (A) is the infinitive. Choice (B) is the simple form of the verb. Choice (D) is a noun.

108. **(D)** A comparison of two things uses *more* and *than*. Choice (A) has *as*. Choice (B) has *most*. Choice (C) has *the*.

109. **(B)** The clauses contrast; use *but*. Choices (A) and (D) denote cause and effect. Choice (C) indicates a choice.

110. **(A)** Use *between* for the limits of a time frame. Choice (B) is used with a specific time. Choice (C) is not used with a range of time. Choice (D) means together.

111. **(B)** *Technicians* requires a plural verb. Choices (A) and (D) are singular. Choice (C) is the infinitive.

112. **(A)** *Never* goes between the auxiliary and the main verb. In Choice (B) *never* is before the auxiliary. In Choice (C) *never* is after the main verb. Choice (D) uses the wrong form of the auxiliary.

113. **(C)** *Inside* is logical. Choice (A) is logical, but too formal. Choices (B) and (D) require more than one item as a reference point.

114. **(D)** *Tradition* and *experience* are equal items; use *and*. Choice (A) is used with *neither*. Choice (B) implies a contrast. Choice (C) implies a choice.

556 EXPLANATORY ANSWERS

115. **(A)** The causative *had* requires the simple form of the following verb. Choice (B) is the past tense. Choice (C) is the gerund. Choice (D) is the present tense.
116. **(C)** Equal comparisons require *as* on both sides of the adjective. Choice (A) omits the first *as*. Choice (B) omits the second *as*. Choice (D) uses *than*.
117. **(B)** *During* is logical and is used with noun phrases. Choice (A) is not logical. Choices (C) and (D) are used with clauses, not noun phrases.
118. **(B)** The causative *require* should be followed by the infinitive. Choice (A) is the present tense. Choice (C) is the gerund. Choice (D) is the simple form of the verb.
119. **(D)** Use an adjective to modify *hiring*. Choice (A) is a verb. Choice (B) is an adverb. Choice (C) is a noun.
120. **(A)** A comparison of two things uses *-er* and *than*. Choice (B) is an incomplete equal comparison. Choice (C) is a superlative form. Choice (D) incorrectly uses *than* with a superlative.
121. **(C)** *At* is used with specific times. Choice (A) means *inside*. Choice (B) is used with days. Choice (D) means *together*.
122. **(B)** *Because* expresses a cause-and-effect relationship. Choices (A), (C), and (D) are not logical.
123. **(C)** *In* is used for city locations. Choice (A) is used with days. Choice (B) indicates a recipient. Choice (D) indicates destination.
124. **(B)** *Market* must be modified by an adjective. Choice (A) is a noun (person). Choice (C) is a noun (thing). Choice (D) is an adverb.
125. **(A)** *Until* is logical and establishes a time relationship between clauses. Choices (B), (C), and (D) are not logical.
126. **(C)** Habitual action is expressed by the present tense. Choice (A) is a gerund. Choice (C) is a simple form of the verb. Choice (D) is the infinitive.
127. **(D)** *Who* replaces *salespeople*. Choice (A) is possessive. Choice (B) replaces things. Choice (C) is objective.
128. **(D)** A comparison of two things uses *more* and *than*. Choice (A) omits *than*. Choice (B) is an incomplete equal comparison. Choice (C) omits *more*.
129. **(B)** Habitual action is expressed by the present tense. Choices (A) and (C) are incorrect; *like* is never used in the progressive forms. Choice (D) is the simple form of the verb.
130. **(C)** The *change* is causing the ticketholders to be confused; use the past participle. Choice (A) is the present participle. Choice (B) is the simple form of the verb. Choice (D) is the present tense.
131. **(C)** *In* is used for locations within buildings. Choice (A) is used for floor locations within buildings. Choice (B) means *below*. Choice (D) means *above*.
132. **(D)** Comparisons of more than two things use *the* and the superlative form. Choice (A) uses the comparative form. Choice (B) uses the simple (equal) form. Choice (C) uses the superlative form but omits *the*.
133. **(B)** *For* is used with periods of time. Choice (A) means *inside*. Choice (C) means *together*. Choice (D) is used with specific times.
134. **(B)** Contrasting clauses may be joined by *but*. Choice (A) gives a choice between items. Choice (C) express an equal link. Choice (D) is used with *or*.
135. **(A)** *That* replaces *conference*. Choice (B) is possessive. Choice (C) repeats *conference*. Choice (D) is used with people, not things.
136. **(B)** *Was* indicates that *answer* also happened in the past; use the past tense. Choice (A) is the future tense. Choice (C) is the present tense. Choice (D) is the gerund.
137. **(C)** Continuous action is expressed by the progressive; *went* indicates past; use the past progressive. Choice (A) is the simple past tense. Choice (B) is the present progressive. Choice (D) is conditional.
138. **(B)** A comparison of three or more things (superlative) uses *the* and *-est* or *most*. Choice (A) is the comparative adjective, but omits *than*. Choice (C) is the complete

comparative with *than*. Choice (D) is an equal comparison.

139. **(B)** Someone else included the software; use the past participle. Choice (A) is the present tense. Choice (C) is the present progressive. Choice (D) is the past tense.

140. **(D)** Gives a choice between breakfasts; join with *or*. Choices (A) and (B) are illogical. Choice (C) is used with *or*.

Part VI: Error Recognition

141. **(C)** (were not) An unreal (contrary to fact) condition uses only the *were* form of *be* in the *if* clause. Choice (A) is a correct verb. Choice (B) is correct use of *if*. Choice (D) modifies project.

142. **(A)** (Even though; although) *Because* establishes incorrect cause and effect; use a contrast such as *even though*. Choices (B) and (C) are correct verbs. Choice (D) modifies premises.

143. **(C)** (and) He is having both meetings, not choosing between them; use *and*. Choice (A) is a correct future tense. Choice (B) is a correct noun. Choice (D) is used with days of the week.

144. **(B)** (are often required) *Often* goes between the auxiliary and the main verb. Choice (A) is correct; no article is needed. Choice (C) *require* is followed by the infinitive. Choice (D) is correctly followed by a noun phrase.

145. **(A)** (The attached brochure) Someone else attached the brochure; use the past participle. Choice (B) is a correct verb. Choice (C) replaces *tours*. Choice (D) modifies *tours*.

146. **(D)** (economical) *And* joins equal terms; attractive is matched by *economical*. Choice (A) is a correct verb. Choice (B) replaces *package*. Choice (C) is a correct verb.

147. **(A)** *Helpful* begins with a consonant sound; use *a*. Choice (B) is a correct verb. Choice (C) is a correct noun. Choice (D) is a correct adjective.

148. **(B)** (which appeared) *It* repeats *advertisement*. Choice (A) is correct; *which replaces advertisement* in the dependent clause. Choice (C) is used for information contained in newspapers, magazines, etc. Choice (D) is a correct adjective.

149. **(A)** (Who) *Who* should replace *they* to join clauses. Choices (B) and (C) are correct verbs. Choice (D) means an increase in wage.

150. **(D)** (rang) *Rang* is the past tense of *ring*. *Was leaving* is past tense; *ring* must be past also. Choice (A) is correct; a singular count noun requires an article. Choice (B) is a correct verb. Choice (C) joins the clauses in a time relationship.

151. **(B)** (had another salesperson make) The causative *had* is followed by the simple form of the verb. Choice (A) modifies *salesperson*. Choice (C) establishes a time relationship between clauses. Choice (D) is a correct verb.

152. **(A)** (Every day the president takes; during her lunch hour every day) *Every day* goes at the beginning or the end of the sentence. Choice (B) is a correct verb. Choice (C) modifies *walk*. Choice (D) is correctly followed by a noun phrase.

153. **(B)** (that the accountant reviewed is) *It* repeats *report;* omit *it*. Choice (A) replaces *report*. Choice (C) is a correct past participle. Choice (D) modifies *errors*.

154. **(C)** (The most efficient) Superlative comparisons use *most* or *-est*. Choice (A) is a correct pronoun. Choice (B) is a correct verb. Choice (D) is correct; *on the market* is a common business expression.

155. **(A)** (Software that uses) *A* is not used with non-count nouns. Choice (B) is a correct superlative. Choice (C) is a correct verb. Choice (D) is correct placement of *always*.

156. **(C)** (as soon as) Equal comparisons require *as* on both sides of the adverb. Choices (A) and (D) are correct verbs. Choice (B) is a correct article.

157. **(B)** (the enclosed report) Someone else enclosed the report; use the past participle. Choice (A) is a correct past participle. Choice (C) is a correct verb. Choice (D) means *concerning*.

158. **(D)** (competitive) *Prices* must be modified by an adjective. Choice (A) is a correct adjective. Choice (B) is a correct preposition. Choice (C) is a correct possessive pronoun.

159. **(A)** (made) *Was held* is past tense; *make* should be past also. Choice (B) is correct; a singular-count noun requires an article. Choice (C) is a correct verb. Choice (D) is used with days of the week.
160. **(B)** (is) *Product* is the subject of the sentence, not *countries*. A singular subject takes a singular verb. Choice (A) is a correct noun in the possessive case. Choice (C) is a verb. Choice (D) is a correct adverb.

Part VII: Reading Comprehension

161. **(A)** They spent $3 million, *half of $6 million*. Choices (B) and (D) are not mentioned. Choice (C) is the amount spent in two years.
162. **(B)** They'll *increase money spent by $2 million per year*; this makes $5 million total. Choice (A) is what they spent last year. Choice (C) is what they spent in two years. Choice (D) incorrectly adds $2 million to $6 million.
163. **(C)** It *depends upon pending environmental regulations*. Choices (A), (B), and (D) are not mentioned.
164. **(D)** Out to Asia is popular. Choices (A), (B), and (C) are not mentioned.
165. **(A)** We'll get names of past participants so you can get a firsthand impression. Choices (B), (C), and (D) would not give you a firsthand impression.
166. **(C)** They can pass on greater volume discounts, so your dollars can buy you more. Choices (A), (B), and (D) are not mentioned.
167. **(B)** You have to *change planes*. Choice (A) is incorrect; the table states that there are no refunds. Choice (C) is required only if you change an already scheduled flight. Choice (D) is not mentioned.
168. **(D)** The most inexpensive ticket is *based on a 14-day advance purchase*. Choices (A), (B), and (C) are less than 14 days.
169. **(C)** There is a *$25 fee* for changing flights after ticket purchase. Choices (A), (B), and (D) are not mentioned.
170. **(B)** This announcement informs users of a new phone system for ordering tickets. Choices (A) and (C) are not mentioned. Choice (D) is incorrect because a new system is already in place, not being proposed.
171. **(D)** The system was installed *to save you time*, so it is faster. Choices (A), (B), and (C) are not given as reasons.
172. **(C)** 2 is for *purchasing group tickets*. Choice (A) requires line 3. Choice (B) requires line 4. Choice (D) requires line 1.
173. **(A)** Line 5 is for *other information*. Choices (B), (C), and (D) are not options given.
174. **(A)** Delicious Goods will raise prices on jams and jellies, made of gelatin. Choices (B), (C), and (D) are not mentioned.
175. **(B)** The *second increase in eight months* means they've raised prices twice in eight months. Choices (A), (C), and (D) are contradicted by *twice in eight months*.
176. **(C)** The increases are due to *higher prices...due to the dry weather last spring*. Choice (A) may be true but is not mentioned directly. Choice (B) is contradicted by *dry weather*. Choice (D) is not mentioned.
177. **(D)** It has programs lasting *6–12 months*. Choices (A), (B), and (C) are shorter than the given time.
178. **(C)** *Upon completion means when you have finished your program*. Choices (A) and (B) are before completion. Choice (D) is not logical.
179. **(D)** It says to *call the school* for information. Choices (A) and (B) could not help you enroll. Choice (C) is not logical.
180. **(C)** *Enclosed are two documents* means the *packet contains the documents*. Choices (A), (B), and (D) are contradicted by *documents*.
181. **(B)** The welcome packet would most likely be given to new employees because it describes the company's compensation plan. Choices (A), (C), and (D) are not likely recipients.
182. **(B)** *Give these documents your full attention* means *read them carefully*. Choice (A) is incorrect because human resources would issue a packet like this one, but would expect you to read it before coming to them. Choices (C) and (D) are not mentioned.

183. **(A)** A *recession* means *the economy is weak*. Choice (B) is contradicted by recession. Choices (C) and (D) are not mentioned.
184. **(B)** The first 100 customers who spend $1,000 in a ten day period will get a 10% discount on their next purchase over $100. Choice (A) is not mentioned. Choice (C) confuses $100 cash and first 100 customers. Choice (D) is not mentioned.
185. **(C)** It shows the *information available* to customers. Choices (A), (B), and (D) are not options.
186. **(D)** Four of the five lines deal with fees and bills. Choices (A) and (B) are incorrect because only one line is dedicated to address changes and one to areas of dispute. Choice (C) is not mentioned.
187. **(C)** People *who have moved* would most likely want to *change their billing address*. Choices (A), (B), and (D) are less likely.
188. **(C)** The *value of the job to your career* is the most important. Choice (A) is incorrect; the article suggests you might have to move. Choice (B) is contradicted; the article suggests you might have to take a lower salary. Choice (D) confuses how much you will *like* it with how much you will *learn* from it.
189. **(B)** Lack of benefits is not mentioned as a necessary job sacrifice. Choices (A), (C), and (D) are explicitly mentioned.
190. **(A)** You should not accept jobs that are *not related to your career goals*. Choice (B) is not given as a reason for refusing jobs. Choice (C) is a possible consequence of taking a job that is not within your career path. Choice (D) is not given as a reason for refusing jobs.
191. **(B)** The author believes you will be *frustrated and will not perform your best*. The other options are not mentioned in this context.
192. **(D)** The last sentence advises the reader to *think carefully*. The other choices are not mentioned.
193. **(A)** This is a *hotel registration card*. Choices (B), (C), and (D) are not logical.

194. **(B)** A *double room* was requested. Choice (A) is contradicted by *double* and by the fact that two guests are listed. Choices (C) and (D) are characteristics of rooms but not kinds of rooms.
195. **(D)** *Tax not included* means you must add the tax to the room rate. Choices (A), (B), and (C) are not mentioned.
196. **(A)** The author of the memo is upset at all the individual questions; he or she wants to give one single response. The other choices are not mentioned.
197. **(B)** *Items in or on desk* are items *you should pack*. Choice (A) can apparently be packed by others. Choice (C) will be packed by the movers. Choice (D) is not moved.
198. **(A)** You should *clear messages from your phone*. Choice (B) confuses *get a new password* and *give your old password to the administrator*. Choice (C) is not mentioned. Choice (D) is incorrect because clients should be notified of your new location, not your replacement.
199. **(C)** You should turn in your computer *password* and *ID number*. Choice (A) will move with you; it is being packed by the movers. Choices (B) and (D) will probably move with you.
200. **(A)** *Clearly labeled boxes* make unpacking easier. Choice (B) should be done during packing, but it is not mentioned with unpacking. Choices (C) and (D) are not mentioned.

Model Test 6

Part I: Pictures
1. **(A)** Choice (A) identifies the action: *looking in a bookstore window*. Choice (B) incorrectly identifies the location of the books; they are *in a window*. Choice (C) is wrong: In the picture the man is *looking in the window,* he is not *cleaning it*. Choice (D) is incorrect because the man would have to go inside the store if he wants to purchase a book.

2. **(C)** Choice (C) identifies the location *bridges cross the river*. Choices (A) and (B) do not match the picture, although there are related words such as *island* and *water*. Choice (D) is incorrect because there does not appear to be much traffic.
3. **(A)** Choice (A) identifies the occupation *musician*. Choice (B) confuses the similar words *play* (v) and *play* (n). Choice (C) confuses the similar words *songbird* and *song*. Choice (D) confuses the similar words *notes* (writing) and *notes* (musical).
4. **(B)** Choice (B) identifies the occupation and actions of a person *waiter pouring water*. Choice (A) uses the related word *drink* but does not describe the picture. Choice (C) uses the related word *pouring*. Choice (D) confuses similar sounds: *water* with *order*.
5. **(D)** Choice (D) identifies someone by location: *technician on his knees*. Choice (A) is not able to be determined, but the tubes most likely transport electricity. Choice (B) is incorrect; no wires cross in mid-air. Choice (C) is incorrect because the worker is performing, not explaining, the procedure.
6. **(A)** Choice (A) identifies a person by occupation *the artist draws*. Choices (B), (C), and (D) are incorrect; the context clues for the other professions do not match the picture.
7. **(A)** Choice (A) describes a location *smoke from chimneys*. Choice (B) confuses different meanings: *refined* (v) with *refinery* (n). Choice (C) is contradicted by the smoke coming from the plant, which means it is in operation. Choice (D) confuses different meanings: *to iron* (v) with *iron* (n).
8. **(C)** Choice (C) identifies the person by occupation *a technician*. In Choices (A), (B), and (D), the context clues for the other occupations do not match the picture.
9. **(D)** Choice (D) describes the location *a harbor*. Choice (A) is incorrect; a *cruise ship* is a very large passenger ship, not a *small sailboat*. All ships, even those without sails, *set sail* (leave port). Choice (B) is incorrect because there is only one boat in the picture, so we can't tell if there is a race. Choice (C) confuses similar sounds: *boots* and *boats*, *sale* and *sail*.
10. **(B)** Choice (B) identifies the person by action *speaker using a microphone*. Choice (A) is contradicted by the man's smile. Choice (C) shows negation: no one is singing with the man. Choice (D) is incorrect because the man has his hand up and opened, but is not gesturing towards anything.
11. **(A)** Choice (A) identifies occupation and location *sellers sitting on ground*. Choice (B) uses related words: *(super)market* and *produce*. Choice (C) uses the related word *banana*. Choice (D) uses the related word *vegetables*. Choices (B), (C), and (D) do not match the picture.
12. **(C)** Choice (C) identifies action *person being rescued*. Choice (A) confuses the *pilot approaching the helicopter* and *the helicopter approaching the hangar*. Choice (B) confuses similar sounds: *cops* and *copters*. Choice (D) confuses *minimizing risk* and *a risky operation*.
13. **(A)** Choice (A) identifies action *assembly*. Choice (B) uses related words: *cars, stop,* and *traffic* but does not describe the picture. Choice (C) incorrectly identifies the action. Choice (D) is incorrect because the autos must first be assembled before they can be displayed for sale.
14. **(A)** Choice (A) describes location *on the disk*. Choice (B) describes an incorrect action: she is looking through papers, not collating them. Choice (C) does not identify people by occupation: She may be a manager, but she is not *sealing an envelope*. Choice (D) does not identify people by occupation; she may be a printer, but she is not *copying the forms*.
15. **(D)** Choice (D) makes an assumption about why the cars are on the dock; they are waiting to be shipped. Choice (A) is an incorrect assumption because a ship would not be found at an impound lot. Choice (B) is incorrect; we can't see the shoreline. Choice (C) is incorrect; we can't see any crew on the deck.

16. **(B)** Choice (B) identifies the person by description *worker wearing gloves*. Choice (A) is not logical; this does not seem the place to be reading a newspaper. Choice (C) incorrectly identifies an occupation and action. Choice (D) is incorrect because the man is standing on a ladder, not climbing it.
17. **(C)** Choice (C) identifies the person by action *man inputting data*. Choice (A) uses the related word *software*. Choice (B) confuses similar words: *computation* and *computer*. Choice (D) confuses *slot machine* with *computer*.
18. **(A)** Choice (A) describes the location *illuminated buildings*. Choice (B) uses the related words *electric, power plant*, and *river*. Choice (C) uses the related word *light bulbs*. Choice (D) uses the related word *lighting up*. Choices (B), (C), and (D) do not describe the picture.
19. **(B)** Choice (B) identifies the person by occupation and action *woman dusts furniture*. Choice (A) uses the related word *table*. Choice (C) confuses similar sounds: *made* with *maid*. Choice (D) shows negation: There are no patrons in the picture.
20. **(D)** Choice (D) identifies the buildings by description *modern*. Choice (A) is about the insides of buildings. Choice (B) confuses similar sounds: *cordoned* with *corner*. Choice (C) identifies a person by occupation, but there are no people in the picture.

Part II: Question-Response

21. **(A)** Choice (A) is a logical response to a question about *a telephone number*. Choice (B) answers what month you were born in and confuses similar sounds: *number* with *November*. Choice (C) confuses the numbers with clothing sizes.
22. **(C)** Choice (C) is a logical response to a question about *a location*. Choice (A) confuses *dress* with *address*. Choice (B) confuses *address* with *adding* and uses the related words *your* and *mine*.
23. **(A)** Choice (A) is a logical response to a question about *occupation*. Choice (B) repeats the word *office*. Choice (C) confuses *his voice* with *office*.
24. **(B)** Choice (B) is a logical response to a question about *location*. Choice (A) uses the related word *raining*. Choice (C) confuses *leave* with *leisure*.
25. **(C)** Choice (C) is a logical response to a question about *time*. Choices (A) and (C) both contain time markers, but only (C) answers the question about the arrival time of the electrician. Choice (B) uses related words: *generators* and *nuclear-powered*.
26. **(B)** Choice (B) is a logical response to a request for a *reason*. Choice (A) is a common thing to do with newspaper, but is not a reason. Choice (A) also confuses similar sounds: *newspaper* with *paper*; *wrapped* with *put an ad*. Choice (C) repeats the word *newspaper* but does not answer the question.
27. **(A)** Choice (A) is a logical response to a question about *number of visits*. Choice (B) confuses related words: *China* and *dishes*. Choice (C) repeats the word *time*.
28. **(A)** Choice (A) is a logical response to a question about *a past action*. Choice (B) confuses *fax* with *facts*; Choice (C) confuses *sent* with *rent*.
29. **(B)** Choice (B) is a logical response to a question about *identity*. Choice (A) confuses *marketing* with *market*. Choice (C) confuses the related phrases *develop a plan* and *develop film*.
30. **(C)** Choice (C) is a logical response to a question about *time*. Choice (A) confuses *purchase* with *purpose*. Choice (B) confuses *computer* with *commuter*; Choices (B) and (C) both have time markers, but only (C) refers to the question about a computer purchase.
31. **(B)** Choice (B) is a logical response to a question about *seasonal preference*. Choice (A) confuses *season* with *reason*. Choice (C) uses the related word *fall* (as a verb, not a season.)
32. **(C)** Choice (C) is a logical response to *a request for a reason*. Choice (A) confuses *eat* with *late*. Choice (B) confuses *late* with *date*. Only Choice (C) gives a reason *why* in the past tense.
33. **(C)** Choice (C) is a logical response to a question about *preference*. Choice (A) confuses *chair* and *there*, and *more com-*

fortable and *more coming*. Choice (B) confuses *comfortable* and *table*.

34. **(A)** Choice (A) is a logical response to a question about *length of study*. Choice (B) repeats the word *English* and uses the related word *books*. Choice (C) uses the similar word *England*. Choices (A) and (C) both have *year* time markers, but only (A) gives the duration of years asked in the question.

35. **(A)** Choice (A) is a logical response to a question about *location*. Choices (A) and (B) both use prepositions as location markers (*across from*, *delivered to*), but only the subject pronoun of (A) matches the question. Choice (C) uses the related word *postal*.

36. **(B)** Choice (B) is a logical response *to a request*. Choice (A) repeats the word *pass*. Choice (C) confuses *salt* with *insulted*.

37. **(C)** Choice (C) is a logical response to a question about *purpose*. Choice (A) uses the related word *visitors*. Choice (B) confuses *purpose* and *porpoise*. Only Choice (C) gives a reason for the visit.

38. **(B)** Choice (B) is a logical response to a question about *who*. Choice (A) confuses *break* with *broken*. Choice (C) confuses the expressions *take a break* and *take a walk*.

39. **(C)** Choice (C) is a logical response to a request *for a reason*. Choice (A) confuses *postponed* with *phone*. Choice (B) confuses *meeting* with *meat*.

40. **(C)** Choice (C) is a logical response to a question about *when*. Choice (A) confuses *menu* and *memo* and tells the language the menu was written in, but not when it was written. Choice (B) confuses *written* with *typewriter* and answers *how*, not *when*.

41. **(A)** Choice (A) is a logical response to a question about *location*. Choice (B) confuses *suitcases* with *in case*. Choice (C) confuses *where are our* with *they're on*. Choices (A) and (C) both have location markers, but only Choice (A) provides a logical location for the suitcases.

42. **(B)** Choice (B) is a logical response to a question about *time*. Choice (A) confuses *land* and *sand* and *plays* and *plane*. Choice (C) has a time marker but the context is wrong. Only Choice (B) answers the question *how soon will*.

43. **(A)** Choice (A) is a logical response to a yes/no question about number of languages spoken. Choice (B) confuses related words: *speak other languages* and *linguist*. Choice (C) confuses related words: *speak* and *say* and *doesn't* and *never*.

44. **(C)** Choice (C) is a logical response to a question about *the future*. Choice (A) confuses *retiring from work* and *retiring for the evening* (to go to bed). Choice (B) confuses the sounds of *tire* and *retire*. Although both Choice (A) and Choice (C) talk about a future action, only Choice (C) answers the question about life after quitting work.

45. **(B)** Choice (B) is a logical response to a question about *time*. Choice (A) uses the related word *exhibit*. Choice (C) confuses the words *clothes* and *close* and *closet*.

46. **(A)** Choice (A) is a logical response to a question about *a reason for high airfares*. Choice (B) confuses *hair* with *air* and continues to talk about *cost*. Choice (C) uses the related word *airport*. Only Choice (A) gives a logical reason *why*.

47. **(C)** Choice (C) is a logical response to a question about *location*. Choice (A) repeats the word *paper* but uses the past tense. Choice (B) has the related word *news*.

48. **(A)** Choice (A) is a logical response to a question about *identifying an object*. Choice (B) uses the past tense of *move*. Choice (C) uses the related word *removed*.

49. **(B)** Choice (B) is a logical response *to a suggestion*. Choice (A) repeats the word *let*. Choice (C) confuses the expression *take a walk* with *take it away*.

50. **(C)** Choice (C) is a logical response *to a question about time*. Choice (A) repeats the word *over*: *over* (adv.) and *over* (prep.). Choice (B) uses the related word *perform*. Choices (B) and (C) both have time markers, but only the subject of (C) matches the question.

Part III: Short Conversations

51. **(D)** At *8:00*. Choice (A) confuses *4:00* and *4:30*. Choice (B) is the time the meeting starts. Choice (C) is rejected in favor of *8:00*.

52. **(B)** He wants to *cash a check*. Choice (A) is incorrectly suggested by *driver's license*. Choice (C) confuses *open an account* with *account number*. Choice (D) confuses *identification* and *introduce*.

53. **(C)** *Not open to the public* means *no sightseers*. Choice (A) is contradicted by *then we'll see the plaza*. Choice (B) is contradicted by *they're not open to the public*. Choice (D) is not relevant.

54. **(A)** *Lunch* is part of *meal service*. Choice (B) confuses *launch* and *lunch*. Choice (C) is incorrect; the man talks about different arrival times. Choice (D) is not mentioned.

55. **(A)** *Steak with mushrooms* indicates *dinner*. Choice (B) confuses *maid service* with *room service*. Choice (C) confuses *larger room* with *mushroom*. Choice (D) is not mentioned.

56. **(C)** She asks *where Gate 23 is*. Choice (A) is incorrect; she asks *where*, not *when*. Choice (B) is incorrect; the man points out the signs. Choice (D) is not logical; she knows she is departing.

57. **(D)** *In the hall*. Choices (A) and (B) are contradicted by *not enough space in your office or mine*. Choice (C) confuses *another room* and *no room*.

58. **(B)** He needs light *by the file cabinet*. Choice (A) is contradicted by *enough light for reading*. Choice (C) confuses *dark ramp* with *desk lamp*. (C) also uses related (opposite) word *dark*. Choice (D) is not mentioned.

59. **(D)** She'll have to buy *a national paper*. Choice (A) is sold out or not available yet. Choices (B) and (C) are the local papers mentioned.

60. **(B)** Their *tire is flat*. Choice (A) confuses *tired* and *tire*. Choice (C) is past tense; they are *going to fix it*. Choice (D) confuses *took too long* and *won't take long*.

61. **(A)** He gave her a *brochure*. Choices (B) and (C) are contradicted by the fact that they don't have guided tours. Choice (D) is not logical; exhibits are displayed in museums, not given away.

62. **(C)** He suggests *two-day mail*. Choice (A) costs more than the woman wants to pay. Choice (B) confuses *two-day* mail and *today's* mail. Choice (D) is unlikely since she'd asked about fast service.

63. **(B)** She suggests discussing the *contract deadline*. Choice (A) confuses *contacts* and *contracts*. Choice (C) confuses *deadlines* and *bad phone lines*. Choice (D) confuses by combining *over(time)* and *project*.

64. **(D)** She requests that *he call her*. Choice (A) is contradicted by *call me*. Choice (B) is incorrect; she'll meet him in the lobby. Choice (C) is incorrect; the woman will come downstairs.

65. **(D)** *Sales* and *engineer* are jobs. Choice (A) is incorrect; *hobbies* are what you do in your free time. Choice (B) is incorrect; the woman mentions *computer software* but not *computers*. Choice (C) is incorrect; *colleagues* are other people in the same field.

66. **(C)** He will wear a raincoat. Choice (B) is incorrect; if he *walks* over, he won't use a car. Choices (A) and (D) are not mentioned.

67. **(B)** She wants to *attend a concert*. Choices (A) and (C) are activities the man wants to do. Choice (D) is what he does *not* have to do.

68. **(A)** *Haven't arrived* means *aren't here*. Choice (B) is contradicted by *ordered supplies last week*. Choice (C) is incorrect; they're late this time, but maybe not every time. Choice (D) isn't mentioned.

69. **(D)** *Bring back* and *return* have the same meaning. Choice (A) is not logical; if people borrow them, they use them. Choice (B) is contradicted by *people borrow them*. Choice (C) confuses *borrow* and *lend*.

70. **(B)** He should *get organized*. Choice (A) is not mentioned. Choice (C) confuses

writing a letter with *writing a list*. Choice (D) confuses *organize time* and *make time*.
71. **(A)** Reports are turned in on *Mondays*. Choice (B) is rejected as the due date. Choice (C) confuses *soon enough* with *as soon as*. Choice (D) confuses *twice a week* with *Monday and Friday*.
72. **(C)** The woman would *prefer the subway*. Choices (A), (B), and (D) are not mentioned.
73. **(B)** Figures that are *off* are *wrong*. Choice (A) is possible, but they could also be too high. Choice (C) confuses *check* (n.) and *check* (v.). Choice (D) confuses *fix* and *fax*.
74. **(A)** *Display* means *exhibit*. Choice (B) confuses *display* and *play*. Choice (C) is incorrect; the exhibit hall doesn't open until two. Choice (D) is not mentioned.
75. **(D)** Her *new office*. Choice (A) confuses *company* and *company health club*. Choice (B) is across from her office. Choice (C) is incorrect; her new office is compared to her old office.
76. **(C)** She's got *work to do*. Choice (A) is contradicted by *eat a sandwich*. Choice (B) is confused with the time her work is due. Choice (D) is incorrect; she's going to eat a sandwich at her desk.
77. **(A)** The woman will *mail a letter* for him. Choice (B) is incorrect; she has to attend; he doesn't. Choice (C) is not mentioned. Choice (D) confuses *three letters* with *letter in the mail by 3:00*.
78. **(A)** *Food that isn't good* and *slow waiters* mean a *bad restaurant*. Choice (B) is incorrect; they could come back (though they probably won't). Choice (C) is incorrect; the waiters are slow, not talkative. Choice (D) confuses *wait* and *waiters*.
79. **(D)** He left his *sunglasses at home*. Choice (A) is incorrect; he has his hat. Choice (B) confuses *son* and *sunglasses*. Choice (C) confuses *eyeglasses* and *sunglasses*.
80. **(B)** *Buying gas*, *checking oil* and *washing windshields* happen at *service stations*. Choice (A) is incorrectly suggested by *gas* and *oil*. Choice (C) would park your car, not put gas in it. Choice (D) would clean your house.

Part IV: Short Talks
81. **(B)** This is an *information service* that provides *news*. Choice (A) refers to *categories of news*. Choice (C) refers to *category codes*. Choice (D) refers to *a list of news categories*.
82. **(D)** Dialing *1000* provides a list of codes. Choices (A) and (B) are not given as choices. Choice (C) would provide an unknown category.
83. **(A)** *Secretaries are more efficient*. Choice (B) is contradicted by the study. Choice (C) is incorrect; managers have their secretaries' help. Choice (D) is possibly true but is not part of the study.
84. **(C)** Managers admit that work is easier with their secretaries' help. Choice (A) confuses *efficiency* with *hard work*. Choices (B) and (D) are not mentioned.
85. **(B)** *Fill out* means to *complete*. Choice (A) won't help you order faster. Choice (C) is only part of the information needed. Choice (D) confuses *item number* and *page number*.
86. **(D)** You should *have your credit card handy*. Choices (A), (B), and (C) are not logical methods for paying over the phone.
87. **(A)** The restaurant has *jobs available*. Choice (B) is incorrect; all restaurants have *food service*. Choices (C) and (D) are incorrect; nothing indicates that the phone number or the restaurant is new.
88. **(C)** Food service experience. Choices (A) and (B) may be useful but are not mentioned. Choice (D) confuses *food service* and *grocery store*.
89. **(B)** Snow. Choices (A) and (C) will fall in the morning. Choice (D) is not mentioned.
90. **(C)** *Low visibility* is a *visibility hazard*. Choices (A) and (B) are probably true but are not mentioned. Choice (D) is incorrectly suggested by *drivers*.
91. **(A)** *Landing* suggests a *plane*. Choices (B) and (C) are not mentioned. Choice (D) is incorrectly suggested by *cabin*.
92. **(B)** Passengers are asked to *put their baggage under the seat*. Choice (A) is

incorrectly suggested by *luggage*. Choice (C) confuses *change your seat* and *return to your seat*. Choice (D) is not logical.

93. **(A)** They have the *lowest prices* available. Choice (B) is not mentioned. Choice (C) location cannot be determined. Choice (D) is not mentioned.

94. **(B)** Talk to their design specialist. Choice (A) is not mentioned. Choice (C) is not likely to be suggested in an ad. Choice (D) is contradicted by *consult one of our design specialists*.

95. **(A)** *Broken* means *not in service*. Choices (B) and (C) are contradicted in the announcement: *to use the escalators and stairs* suggests both are working and open. Choice (D) is not mentioned.

96. **(C)** They can take a bus. Choices (A), (B), and (D) are not mentioned.

97. **(B)** *We regret* means *we apologize*. Choices (A) and (C) are not logical. Choice (D) is incorrect; passengers have already been advised of the problem.

98. **(B)** It is *due to the extremely cold weather*. Choice (A) is contradicted by *cold weather*. Choice (C) is not mentioned. Choice (D) is not logical.

99. **(A)** *Reduce consumption* means *use less*. Choices (B), (C), and (D) are not mentioned.

100. **(D)** Residents are *asked* to help avoid this situation. Choices (A), (B), and (C) are not the purpose of the announcement.

Part V: Incomplete Sentences

101. **(B)** *Price* requires a singular verb. Choice (A) is the infinitive. Choice (C) is the gerund. Choice (D) is plural.

102. **(C)** *Because* establishes a cause and effect relationship. Choices (A) and (B) are not logical. Choice (D) does not show the relationship between clauses.

103. **(A)** The causative *request* is followed by the simple form of the verb. Choice (B) is the present tense. Choice (C) is the past tense. Choice (D) is the gerund.

104. **(C)** *Were loading* is past tense; use *fell*. Choice (A) is the present perfect. Choice (B) is the present. Choice (D) is the present progressive.

105. **(D)** *Who* replaces *manager* in the dependent clause. Choices (A) and (B) are subject pronouns. Choice (C) replaces things, not people.

106. **(B)** The past perfect in the *if* clause of an unreal condition requires *would have + verb* in the other clause. Choice (A) uses the present form of the verb. Choices (C) and (D) use *will*.

107. **(C)** The subject must be an animate noun. Choice (A) is a noun, but not animate. Choice (B) is an adjective. Choice (D) is an adverb.

108. **(D)** Superlative comparisons use *most* or *-est* forms. Choice (A) is an incorrect comparative form. Choice (B) is the simple (positive) form of the adjective. Choice (C) is the comparative form.

109. **(B)** The causative *get* requires a following infinitive. Choice (A) is the gerund. Choice (C) is the past tense. Choice (D) is the present tense.

110. **(D)** Use *by* with deadlines or schedules. Choices (A) means *together*. Choice (B) means *inside*. Choice (C) indicates a recipient.

111. **(A)** *Beside* means *next to*. Choices (B) and (C) require more than one item as a reference point. Choice (D) should be *across from*.

112. **(D)** The superlative comparison in the sentences uses *the* and *-est* form. Choice (A) is the simple (positive) form of the adjective. Choice (B) omits *the*. Choice (C) is the comparative form.

113. **(D)** *Every month* can follow the main verb. Choices (A), (B), and (C) cannot.

114. **(B)** *After* establishes a logical time reference. Choices (A), (C), and (D) are not logical.

115. **(B)** Comparisons of two things use *more* or *-er* forms and *than*. Choice (A) is the superlative form. Choices (C) and (D) are equal comparisons that omit one *as*.

116. **(A)** *Adapt* means to modify. A good chef must be able to modify recipes. Choices (B), (C), and (D) do not fit the context of the sentence.

117. **(D)** *Before* establishes the time relationship between clauses. Choices (A), (B), and (C) are not logical.

566 EXPLANATORY ANSWERS

118. **(C)** *On* is used with specific dates. Choice (A) indicates purpose. Choice (B) indicates destination. Choice (D) means *inside*.
119. **(D)** *Was giving* is in the past; *when* indicates simultaneous action; use the past tense. Choice (A) is the present progressive. Choice (B) is the present tense. Choice (C) is the past perfect, not simultaneous with the past tense.
120. **(D)** *From* is used with *borrow*. Choice (A) uses *to*, not *from*. Choice (B) is an infinitive. Choice (C) uses *to*, not *from*.
121. **(B)** *Both* indicates joining equal items; use *and*. Choice (A) gives a choice between items. Choice (C) contrasts items. Choice (D) is used with *neither*.
122. **(A)** *Will* + the simple form of a verb is the future tense. Choice (B) is an adjective. Choice (C) is a noun. Choice (D) is the gerund.
123. **(B)** *Never* goes between the auxiliary and the main verb. Choices (A) and (D) place *never* after the verb. Choice (C) places *never* before the auxiliary.
124. **(A)** Use *were* in unreal condition; *if* clauses for the past tense of *be*. Choice (B) is singular past tense. Choice (C) is future. Choice (D) uses *would*.
125. **(A)** *From* indicates the departure point (*to* indicates the arrival point). Choices (B), (C), and (D) are not logical.
126. **(C)** *And* implies a verb to match *turns*; use *brews*. Choice (A) is the gerund. Choice (B) is the simple form. Choice (D) is the past tense.
127. **(A)** The speech made the audience bored; use the present participle. Choice (B) is the past participle. Choice (C) is the present tense. Choice (D) is the simple form of the verb.
128. **(D)** Use *in* with city locations. Choice (A) is used with dates. Choice (B) indicates a recipient. Choice (C) indicates location.
129. **(B)** *Because* establishes a cause and effect relationship. Choice (A) contrasts information. Choices (C) and (D) are used with clauses expressing a result.
130. **(A)** Commands require the simple form of the verb. Choice (B) is the present tense. Choice (C) is the present participle. Choice (D) is the future.
131. **(D)** Use *were* in unreal condition; *if* clauses for the past tense of *be*. Choice (A) is the first person present tense. Choice (B) is singular present tense. Choice (C) is singular past tense.
132. **(D)** Someone else designated the spaces; use the past participle. Choices (A) and (B) use the present participle. Choice (C) is the past tense.
133. **(B)** *Who* joins the clauses by replacing *participants* (people). Choice (A) repeats *participants*. Choice (C) refers to things. Choice (D) refers to people but is objective.
134. **(B)** *With* needs a noun object; *experience* is logical. Choice (A) is a noun but is not logical. Choices (C) and (D) are adjectives.
135. **(D)** Commands require the simple form of the verb. Choice (A) is the present tense. Choice (B) is the future. Choice (C) is the present progressive.
136. **(A)** Items joined by *and* take a plural verb. Choices (B) and (C) are singular. Choice (D) is first person present.
137. **(A)** Use an adjective to match *knowledgeable*. Choices (B) and (D) are nouns. Choice (C) is a an adjective but is not logical with people.
138. **(B)** An action that started in the past and continues to the present uses the present perfect. Choice (A) is the present tense. Choice (C) is the past perfect. Choice (D) is the past tense.
139. **(C)** *On* is used with answering machines, tapes, etc. Choice (A) means *inside*. Choice (B) indicates possession. Choice (D) indicates destination.
140. **(A)** The causative *get* requires a following infinitive. Choice (B) is the gerund. Choice (C) is the simple form. Choice (D) is the past tense.

Part VI: Error Recognition

141. **(A)** (More responsible) A comparison of two things uses *more* or *-er*. Choices (B) and (D) are correct gerunds. Choice (C) establishes a time relationship between clauses.
142. **(A)** (The person who lost) *Who* replaces the subject *person*. Choice (B) is correct; a singular count noun needs an article.

Choice (C) refers to *briefcase*. Choice (D) indicates location.

143. **(B)** (as eager as) Equal comparisons require *as* on both sides of the adjective. Choice (A) is correct; a singular-count noun needs an article. Choice (C) is a correct infinitive. Choice (D) is the correct preposition; *be part of* is a common expression.

144. **(C)** (had been waiting) The earlier action in the past requires the past perfect *had been waiting*. Choice (A) establishes a time relationship between the clauses. Choice (B) is a correct past tense. Choice (D) is used with periods of time.

145. **(C)** (that the orders be sent) The causative *request* is followed by the simple form of the verb, *be*. Choice (A) modifies *subscribers*. Choice (B) joins the clauses. Choice (D) is a correct noun phrase.

146. **(A)** (The enclosed information) Someone else enclosed the information; use the past participle. Choice (B) is a correct verb. Choice (C) means *concerning*. Choice (D) is a correct noun.

147. **(D)** (for many years) *For* is used with range of time. Choice (B) is a correct past participle. Choice (C) indicates association. Choice (A) is a correct verb.

148. **(A)** (was preparing) A continuous past action requires the past progressive *was preparing*. Choice (B) is used with days of the week. Choice (C) establishes a time relationship between clauses. Choice (D) is a correct past participle.

149. **(C)** (cannot get) *If Ms. Weiss has missed* involves the present; *tomorrow* is future; the verb can't be past tense. Use *cannot get*. Choice (A) is correct use of *if*. Choice (B) modifies *flight*. Choice (D) shows the relationship to *tomorrow*.

150. **(B)** (suggested hiring) The causative *suggest* is followed by the gerund *hiring*. Choice (A) is a correct article and adjective describing *committee*. Choice (C) means *in the position of*. Choice (D) is a correct preposition.

151. **(C)** (because) *Although* is not logical; establish cause and effect with *because*. Choice (A) is a correct verb. Choice (B) is a correct noun. Choice (D) modifies *salary*.

152. **(B)** (and) *But* implies a contrast; use *and* to include both items. Choice (A) is a correct article and adjective describing *all*. Choice (C) modifies *charge*. Choice (D) is a correct verb.

153. **(B)** (Once a week Mr. Wang reviews; reviews the progress of the...committee once a week) *Once a week* comes at the beginning or end of the sentence. Choice (A) is a correct verb. Choice (C) indicates possession. Choice (D) describes *committee*.

154. **(A)** (suggested leaving) *Suggest* is followed by the gerund *leaving*. Choice (B) establishes a cause-and-effect relationship. Choice (C) is a correct verb. Choice (D) is a correct adverb.

155. **(B)** (The report that you are looking for is) *It* repeats the subject *report*. Omit *it*. Choice (A) replaces *report*. Choice (C) means *above*. Choice (D) indicates position.

156. **(A)** (Ms. Ericson seldom leaves) *Seldom* goes before the main verb. Choice (B) establishes a time relationship between clauses. Choice (C) is a correct verb. Choice (D) is a commonly used phrase meaning "for the rest of the day."

157. **(A)** (and) *Nor* is used with neither; the items should be joined with *and*. Choice (B) indicates possession. Choice (C) indicates the recipient. Choice (D) indicates location.

158. **(B)** (better) A comparison of two things uses the comparative form. Choice (A) is the past participle. Choice (C) is correct use of *than*. Choice (D) joins the clauses.

159. **(D)** *Morning* and *afternoon* are used with *in*. Choice (A) is used with days of the week. Choice (B) is used with cities. Choice (C) is used with specific times.

160. **(B)** (discussed delaying) *Discuss* is followed by the gerund *delaying*. Choice (A) is a correct noun. Choice (C) establishes a time relationship. Choice (D) is a correct verb.

Part VII: Reading Comprehension

161. **(B)** Car services are for trips *too short for a rental car and too long for a taxi*. Choice (A) includes taxis and rental cars. Choice (C) is not mentioned. Choice (D) is not logical.

162. **(C)** They are also called *limousine services*. Choice (A) includes all types. Choice (B) means taxi service. Choice (D) means any transportation that goes to the airport.

163. **(D)** Business travelers will need ground transportation. Choices (A) and (B) are not mentioned. Choice (C) is contradicted by *business travel*.

164. **(B)** This card notifies others of your *new address*. Choice (A) is incorrect; the business would send you a card. Choice (C) is not logical. Choice (D) is not logical; the card would have their address, not yours.

165. **(B)** The new address is *effective immediately*, so they should start when they get the card. Choices (A), (C), and (D) are all contradicted by *immediately*.

166. **(D)** The *fourth quarter* means the *last quarter of the year*. Choice (A) confuses *last year* and *last quarter*. Choices (B) and (C) are contradicted by *the fourth quarter*.

167. **(D)** Tarstan earned $8 million after a significant loss the previous year, which verifies an impressive comeback. Choice (A) is how it did last year. Choices (B) and (C) are contradicted by its impressive comeback.

168. **(C)** A portable stereo cassette player is offered when you buy the language program. Choice (A) confuses foreign language textbook and Language Wizard Program. Choice (B) is what the ad is selling, but the free gift is what's being offered when you buy the program. Choice (D) is not mentioned.

169. **(D)** When you order the language program, they'll send you the gift. Choice (A) is what you will have to do after you order the program. Choices (B) and (C) are not mentioned.

170. **(A)** Travel arrangements are not mentioned. Choices (B), (C), and (D) are explicitly mentioned.

171. **(B)** The ad says *if you enjoy people*. Choice (A) is contradicted by *like people*. Choice (C) is not logical; a convention center is unlikely to be quiet. Choice (D) is contradicted by *good with details*.

172. **(C)** The ad says to *come by City Hall for an application*. Choices (A), (B), and (D) are all contradicted by *come by City Hall*.

173. **(C)** Lawyers would be likely to attend Legal Education seminars. Choice (A) confuses workers with the subject of workers compensation. Choices (B) and (D) are not likely to be interested.

174. **(A)** Workers compensation is payment to injured employees. Choices (B), (C), and (D) are not mentioned.

175. **(A)** The faculty will show you how to anticipate new trends in defense. Choices (B), (C), and (D) are not mentioned.

176. **(A)** Students might not need this book at this time. The other choices would make likely use of an Office Writer's Handbook.

177. **(A)** It describes English grammar rules *accurately and clearly*. Choices (B) and (C) are incorrect; books do not present things at different speeds. Choice (D) is not mentioned.

178. **(D)** The special section covers *common writing mistakes*. Choices (A), (B), and (C) are covered in other sections of the book.

179. **(B)** *Landscape architects* work with gardens. Choice (A) confuses *designing skyscrapers* and *designing gardens*. Choices (C) and (D) are what Guy Williams is doing.

180. **(D)** *We have decided not to place an ad in the December issue*. Choices (A) and (B) aren't mentioned and Choice (C) is contradicted.

181. **(D)** *Quarterly* means *every three months*. If this issue is *December* and the *next issue* is *March*, the magazine comes out every three months.

182. **(C)** Foods *account for the largest portion of* agricultural exports. Choices (A), (B), and (D) are not foods.

183. **(A)** It's increased because of *increased interest among consumers in more exotic food products*. Choices (B) and (C) are not mentioned. Choice (D) may be another result of (A) but is not mentioned.
184. **(B)** *Exports of native tropical fruits and root vegetables have increased . . . . growth is expected to continue*. Choice (A) is incorrect; not all agricultural exports show a trend. Choices (C) and (D) are results of the trend.
185. **(B)** His *country of citizenship* is *Bulgaria*. Choices (A), (C), and (D) are not mentioned.
186. **(A)** *First name* and *given name* have the same meaning. Choice (B) is his family name. Choice (C) is the name of a city. Choice (D) is not a name.
187. **(D)** If he is traveling for *pleasure*, he is probably on vacation. Choices (A) and C are not pleasure trips. Choice (B) is possible but not the only purpose of his trip.
188. **(C)** Business travelers would most likely read this article since it is about them. Choices (A), (B), and (D) are not likely to be interested in an article related to business travelers.
189. **(A)** It says *their schedules are suddenly changed*. Choice (B) is not mentioned. Choice (C) is contradicted by *hotel exercise rooms*. Choice (D) is not mentioned.
190. **(B)** The article says you can exercise *in your airplane seat*. Choice (A) is not logical. Choices (C) and (D) are not mentioned.
191. **(D)** The article suggests that you *run in place for a good aerobic workout*. Choice (A) is not mentioned. Choice (B) confuses *work your abdomen* and *stretch your abdominal muscles*. Choice (C) is what you should do on the airplane.

192. **(A)** People who exercise regularly perform *more efficiently at work*. The other options, though true, are not mentioned.
193. **(A)** Darla works at a law firm, has a law degree, is a member of the Bar Association, and represents clients, so she must be a lawyer. Choice (B) confuses *professor* and her giving a talk at the continuing education foundation. Choice (C) is incorrect because she is a member of the New York Bar Association, not an employee. Choice (D) confuses similar words *bar* (place to drink) and *Bar* (legal association).
194. **(D)** Darla received a doctorate from Harvard University in 1987. Choice (A) is normally a four-year degree, which she got in 1980. Choices (B) and (C) are not mentioned.
195. **(B)** Darla's practice emphasizes the representation of corporate interests in libel suits. Choices (A), (C), and (D) are not mentioned.
196. **(D)** Mr. Horsta writes that he was *so impressed with the product that he decided to share it with others*. The other options are not mentioned.
197. **(D)** *To purchase new software*—specifically *KleanIt*. Choices (A), (B), and (C) are not mentioned.
198. **(C)** It says that *electronic mail messages pile up*. Choices (A), (B), and (C) are not mentioned; they are usually part of the software rather than user files.
199. **(A)** The computer will operate *inefficiently*, which for computers means *slowly*. Choice (B) is possible but not mentioned. Choices (C) and (D) are not mentioned.
200. **(B)** The only files should be for *current projects* and *routine tasks*. Choices (A), (C), and (D) are examples of files you might delete.

Appendix

TRANSCRIPTS FOR LISTENING COMPREHENSION EXERCISES, MINI-TEST, AND MODEL TESTS 1–6

Transcripts for the Listening Comprehension Sections

The transcripts for the Listening Comprehension exercises, the Mini-Test for Listening Comprehension, and the Listening Comprehension sections of the six Model Tests in this book follow. Each Listening Comprehension section has four parts and each part has separate instructions.

You should use the compact discs when you take the Listening Comprehension sections. If you do not have the compact discs available, someone can read the Listening Comprehension sections to you. The reader should have a stopwatch or a watch with a second hand to keep track of the timed pauses between questions. The length of the pause is noted in the transcript. The TOEIC uses two male voices and one female voice, so it would be advisable to have more than one reader. The reader or readers should speak clearly at a normal speed.

Listening Comprehension Exercises

Problem 1
Part I

(A) The pharmacist serves his customers.
(B) The technicians are conducting experiments.
(C) The laboratory animals are in a cage.
(D) The shelves are empty.

Problem 2
Part I

(A) Four people are looking at a map.
(B) The men are wearing suits.
(C) Both women are taller than the men.
(D) The man with glasses is pointing to a chart.

Problem 3
Part I

(A) The children are playing on the floor.
(B) The television is off.
(C) The father is playing the piano.
(D) The curtains are open.

GO ON TO THE NEXT PAGE

Problem 4

Part I

- (A) The men are smoking pipes.
- (B) The earth is planted with crops.
- (C) The trench is being dug.
- (D) The workers are laying pipeline.

Problem 5

Part I

- (A) Some shoppers want to buy new luggage.
- (B) Passengers are passing through airport security.
- (C) The police guard the bank.
- (D) The flight attendant seats the passengers.

Problem 6

Part I

- (A) The waiters are beside the table.
- (B) The man with glasses is next to the woman.
- (C) A bottle is under the table.
- (D) There are four people in front of the first table.

Problem 7

Part I

- (A) The fair operates all night.
- (B) The freight train is in the station.
- (C) The car door is open.
- (D) The men are loading cargo onto the plane.

Part II

Was the letter delivered today?
- (A) Yes, it came this morning.
- (B) The ladder was on the delivery truck.
- (C) He was late on Tuesday.

Part III

Man: How new is your boat?
Woman: It's brand new. I'm really having fun with it.
Man: Let's both go sailing one day.

Part IV

Attention shoppers. The market will be closing in ten minutes. Please proceed to the checkout counters.

Problem 8
Part I

(A) The man is shoveling snow.
(B) The skiers are on the mountain.
(C) The iceberg is very cold.
(D) The voters went to the polls.

Part II

How long have you been married?
(A) Almost ten years.
(B) About five feet.
(C) The bride is my cousin.

Part III

Man: Please return to your seat and fasten your seat belt.
Woman: Are we getting ready to land?
Man: No, but there is some turbulence in the air.

Part IV

The weather this weekend will be perfect for those who want to play golf or do outside chores such as gardening. The temperature will be in the low 70s and the humidity will also be low.

Problem 9
Part I

(A) They're rushing down the stairs.
(B) They're being trained.
(C) They're boarding the windows.
(D) They're staring at the train.

Part II

He leaves next week, doesn't he?
(A) No, he's going tomorrow.
(B) Yes, he's very weak.
(C) The leaves are turning yellow.

Part III

Woman: Will you sew this button on for me?
Man: I don't have time now.
Woman: I'll be glad to wait.

Part IV

The sun will shine this morning, but rain is likely by this afternoon. There may be some strong winds, too. Spring weather is unpredictable.

Problem 10
Part I

(A) Math is the first class of the day.
(B) There is more room in first class.
(C) This is a middle-class neighborhood.
(D) The documents are classified.

Part II

Is this bed too hard?
(A) Yes, it's very difficult.
(B) Not for me. I like it firm.
(C) The flower bed needs water.

Part III

Man: Why didn't you call this summer?
Woman: I was working on my bachelor's degree.
Man: Now that summer's over, I'll give you a ring next week.

Part IV

Tennis fans will not want to miss the final match at Forest Lawn tomorrow. This championship match will be sponsored by Sporting Goods Company, the maker of Big Blue Racquets, a racquet without equal.

Problem 11
Part I

(A) After the firefighters arrived, they extinguished the fire with water.
(B) Before the fire started, the firefighters arrived.
(C) Prior to extinguishing the fire, the firefighters put away their hoses.
(D) While the fire blazed, the firefighters rested.

Part II

When did you leave the office?
(A) Before it started to rain.
(B) After tomorrow.
(C) While you were speaking.

Part III

Man   We have decided not to bid on the project.
Woman: Did you decide before or after you heard about your competition?
Man: Our decision was made prior to their announcement.

Part IV

Mr. Ahmed Saleh, Chairman and CEO, will retire at the end of the next quarter. He has been with the company for over twenty years and has been the Chairman since the company merged with Rotel International, five years ago.

Problem 12

Part I

(A) None of the seats is occupied.
(B) No one is sitting down.
(C) Not one of the men is wearing a tie.
(D) No one is wearing glasses.

Part II

He hasn't done anything illegal, has he?
(A) No, of course not. He's a law-abiding citizen.
(B) He's a legal secretary, I think.
(C) There is something illegible in this letter.

Part III

Man: Do you have everything you need for your trip?
Woman: I even have what I don't need.
Man: You can never take too much.

Part IV

At no time in the history of our company have we had such sales. Our profit margins are unprecedented. Our total revenues, unimaginable. This unparalleled success is due to the selfless dedication of our employees.

Problem 13

Part I

(A) What a lot of brochures there are!
(B) How many restaurants are there?
(C) How delicious the food looks!
(D) There is no food left.

Part II

Nobody does as much as you.
(A) No one does it better.
(B) I won't do it again.
(C) I like to stay busy.

GO ON TO THE NEXT PAGE

Part III

Man: I'm going to Europe this summer.
Woman: Isn't that great! How I envy you!
Man: I'm trying not to think about it more than twenty hours a day.

Part IV

How the weather changes! Yesterday morning, it was hot and sunny. By noon, the temperature was falling. Last night, it began to rain. And this morning, it has never been so windy.

Problem 14

Part I

(A) The man on the right is dressed more warmly.
(B) Both men are wearing the same glasses.
(C) Neither man has a beard.
(D) Their pants are the same color.

Part II

What is the fastest way to your home?
(A) At rush hour, a train is the fastest.
(B) Take a plane to Rome.
(C) My home is farther than yours.

Part III

Man: This meeting will never end!
Woman: It's even longer than yesterday's, and I thought that was long.
Man: This one holds the world's record for being the longest and the most boring.

Part IV

There never used to be as many cars on the road as there are today. It seems that as we improve the roads, more people want to drive. The more roads there are, the more cars there are on them.

Problem 15

Part I

(A) They might be going on a business trip.
(B) They have checked their bags.
(C) The plane should be on time.
(D) The passengers will check in.

Part II

I'd rather go first class than economy.
(A) I would too, but I can't afford it.
(B) This is my first time here.
(C) You'll save some money.

Part III

Man: Did you attend the reception last night?
Woman: I would have gone if I had been free.
Man: I wish I had been someplace else.

Part IV

The presentation could have been more interesting if the speakers had used some visuals. Colorful visuals projected on a screen would have made it easier for the audience to follow the main points. Without this support, most of us felt lost.

Problem 16

Part I

(A) The chefs are used to the heat.
(B) I used to cook on Sunday.
(C) The pans are used to mix paint.
(D) The food used to be better.

Part II

I'm used to working all night.
(A) Me, too. I don't need much sleep.
(B) When did you stop working at night?
(C) I used all my sick days.

Part III

Man: I used to be a frequent speaker at conferences.
Woman: On what subject?
Man: Anything that people wanted to hear.

Part IV

Before the photocopier, people used to type multiple copies of their letters using carbon paper inserted between white pages. These copies would be called "cc's," which stands for "carbon copies." We are now used to making many copies of our correspondence, when before we would have been satisfied with one.

Problem 17

Part II

What did you say her title was?
(A) She's the Marketing Director.
(B) She's worked here for ten years.
(C) She's been talking about her book.

Part III

Man: Sand this wall until it is smooth.
Woman: Then I'll put the first coat of paint on, right?
Man: Yes, but I'll mix the color for you.

GO ON TO THE NEXT PAGE

Part IV

Our flight attendants will be passing through the cabin now, passing out immigration forms. These forms must be completed by everyone before we land. Please present these forms with your passport at customs.

Problem 18

Part II

We need more towels in Room 233. Whom should we call?
(A) The housekeeper will bring them to you.
(B) I'll call the plumber for you, sir.
(C) How about the restaurant manager?

Part III

Man: I'd like you to put one in each room.
Woman: I'll have to run wires along the baseboard.
Man: No problem. I don't want to run every time the phone rings.

Part IV

It is a state law that all employees who handle food must wash their hands before leaving the rest room.

Problem 19

Part II

What should we do, son, while we wait for Father?
(A) Judge, I am innocent.
(B) Let's browse in this store, Mom.
(C) I finished my homework.

Part III

Man: Would you like more coffee?
Woman: No, just the check please.
Man: Here you are. Please pay at the cashier.

Part IV

The library's representative is authorized to collect a fine for each day that a borrowed book is overdue. If a book is not returned, the borrower may lose his or her library privileges.

Problem 20

Part II

Where will you be waiting?
(A) On the corner.
(B) In the envelope.
(C) Under the cushion.

Part III

Man: I left the letter here on top of these books.
Woman: You mean the books on the shelf?
Man: No, the stack on the desk.

Part IV

Mail that is important for everyone is routed to every office. Please initial the routing next to your name and pass the communication to the next person on the routing list.

Problem 21

Part II

When does your train leave?
(A) At 5:42.
(B) By car.
(C) With my colleague.

Part III

Man: I need to go in about ten minutes.
Woman: Please stay for another hour.
Man: Let's compromise. I'll leave in a half-hour.

Part IV

Snow has fallen every day now for the last week. If it keeps up, we will have accumulated over sixty inches in the last two months.

Problem 22

Part II

What are you doing with this report?
(A) I love watching sports on TV.
(B) I'm going to read it over the weekend.
(C) We're going to the movies.

Part III

Man: I think we're lost. Turn left here.
Woman: I can't. This is a one-way street.
Man: I knew we should have bought a map.

Part IV

In the event of rain, the picnic will not be postponed. It will be held as scheduled but will take place in the office cafeteria.

GO ON TO THE NEXT PAGE

582 TRANSCRIPTS

Problem 23

Part II

What happened to you last night?
(A) I had to work late.
(B) It was last Friday.
(C) About 8 P.M.

Part III

Man: The shipment is still in customs.
Woman: If it isn't released by Friday, production will be delayed.
Man: That means we will have to redo our advertising plan.

Part IV

This past week there have been floods in the Midwest, fires in the Northwest, earthquakes in the West, hurricanes in the Southeast, and a blizzard in the Northeast. Never have so many disasters happened at one time.

Problem 24

Part II

How are you today?
(A) Fine, thanks.
(B) My name is Bob.
(C) I'm by the window.

Part III

Man: I'm starving. My stomach is growling.
Woman: Me, too. I haven't eaten all day.
Man: Let's go find something to eat.

Part IV

Our neighbors have requested that employees park their cars on the street or in designated parking areas. They are not pleased that some of you have been leaving your cars on their lawns.

Problem 25

Part II

Why don't you use milk in your coffee?
(A) I take milk for my cough.
(B) I prefer it black.
(C) Tea, thank you.

Part III

Man: I can't read when I travel by car.
Woman: Me, neither. That's why I travel by plane or train.
Man: I get a lot of work done on the train.

Part IV

Because of a work slowdown, all flights will be delayed. We apologize to our passengers for the inconvenience and hope to have them on their way as soon as possible.

Problem 26

Part II

I only had 10 minutes to finish the task, but you gave Tim three times as much time.
(A) Tim had a half-hour to finish.
(B) I did three times as much as Tim.
(C) Tim finished in ten minutes.

Part III

Man: It's almost thirty degrees outside.
Woman: Yes. This is a record low temperature for this late in the winter.
Man: At least it's not snowing.

Part IV

When ordering supplies it is advisable to order in quantity. Products sold in bulk are cheaper. Buying a gross of pencils is less expensive than buying 144 individual pencils. Often suppliers will take off an additional ten percent when the total order exceeds $100.00.

Problem 27

Part II

Did you like the book?
(A) No, it was too violent.
(B) I bought the book.
(C) Yes, we always do.

Part III

Man: That speaker was really funny.
Woman: I never laughed so hard.
Man: Where did he find those jokes?

GO ON TO THE NEXT PAGE

Part IV

Moviegoers, take out your handkerchiefs. This is a four-hanky movie. You will start crying within ten minutes of the opening credits and will continue until the lights go up at the end.

Problem 28
Part II

What are you talking about?
(A) We're listening to the radio.
(B) I'm talking about my vacation.
(C) It's about over.

Part III

Man: Would you consider yourself a generous person?
Woman: Not at all. I'm very tight with money.
Man: What a shame. I won't ask for your help then.

Part IV

I regret to announce that as of this afternoon I will no longer serve as your Managing Director. The Board of Directors asked me to submit my letter of resignation and I have done so. They told me to leave by the close of business today. I want to thank you for the privilege of having worked with you all.

Problem 29
Part II

If you can get up early, we leave at dawn.
(A) Sure. I'll set my alarm clock.
(B) We left in the afternoon.
(C) If we had thought about it.

Part III

Man: If we had asked for less money, the budget would have been approved.
Woman: But then we wouldn't have had enough to complete the project.
Man: Now, we don't have money or a way to complete the project.

Part IV

If the prices of stock continue to fall, investors will wait for the prices to hit bottom and then begin to buy. A down market has a positive side.

Problem 30
Part II

Shouldn't we leave more time to get there?
(A) I left my watch at home.
(B) I don't drive anymore.
(C) Yes, let's leave earlier.

Part III

Man: Maybe we should start with your report?
Woman: What if we save mine for last?
Man: No, I want yours to be first.

Part IV

With the unemployment figures rising and the number of homeless increasing, it is important for all of us to consider those less fortunate. Shouldn't we all try to help those in need as much as we can?

Problem 31

Part II

Let me know if you need any help.
(A) They helped me a lot.
(B) Thanks, I will.
(C) My knees hurt.

Part III

Woman: Why is this train so late? It's cold on this platform.
Man: Let me get you some hot coffee.
Woman: Would you? Thanks. That'll get us warm.

Part IV

Anyone who is traveling with small infants or who needs extra time to find his or her seat may board the aircraft at this time. First class passengers and our Frequent Flyer cardholders are invited to board at this time as well.

Problem 32

Part II

Would you mind opening the window?
(A) Not at all. It is warm in here.
(B) I opened the door.
(C) The curtains are new.

Part III

Man: Do you think you would have time to mail this letter?
Woman: Yes. I could do it on my way to the bank.
Man: I appreciate it. I really wanted to stay home and finish this novel.

GO ON TO THE NEXT PAGE

586 TRANSCRIPTS

Part IV

Ladies and gentlemen: The management would like to thank you for your cooperation in using only the lobby area for cigarette and cigar smoking. We would also like to thank you for your enthusiastic reception to Act I. Now, would you kindly return to your seats? The second act is about to begin.

Problem 33

Part III

Man: Don't be mad at me. I'm only five minutes late.
Woman: This is the last time I'm waiting for you.
Man: But you know I always have a good excuse.

Part IV

When completing the form, it is important to use a black ballpoint pen and to press firmly. You will be making four copies which will be distributed to the departments that will track your loan application. You will be contacted by each department head individually after they have reviewed your case.

This is the end of the Listening Comprehension Exercises.

Mini-Test for Listening Comprehension Parts I, II, III, and IV

> **Part I: Picture**
>
> Directions: In your test book, you will see a picture. On the compact disc, you will hear four statements. Choose the statement that most closely matches the picture and fill in the corresponding oval on your answer sheet.

1. Look at the picture marked number 1 in your test book.
   (A) There are plates on the tray.
   (B) Guests are tasting the appetizers.
   (C) The men are discussing the buffet.
   (D) They are in charge of the bus.

2. Look at the picture marked number 2 in your test book.
   (A) They wrote the check in the bank.
   (B) The trees are by the flowers.
   (C) The hall is very large.
   (D) The passengers are on the plane.

3. Look at the picture marked number 3 in your test book.
   (A) The sheep are in the meadow.
   (B) Water gathered around the bucket.
   (C) Most of the votes are headed in.
   (D) The ship is leaving the harbor.

4. Look at the picture marked number 4 in your test book.
   (A) The man is enunciating clearly.
   (B) The announcer is leading a panel.
   (C) The man is holding a headset.
   (D) The flipchart contains the data.

5. Look at the picture marked number 5 in your test book.
   (A) The operator pushes a button.
   (B) The man is fixing the elevator.
   (C) He's putting a button on his shirt.
   (D) Stocks are going up.

6. Look at the picture marked number 6 in your test book.
   (A) The crane is on the truck.
   (B) Building materials are being unloaded.
   (C) The plans are on the table.
   (D) The engineers are on the site.

GO ON TO THE NEXT PAGE

588 TRANSCRIPTS

7. Look at the picture marked number 7 in your test book.
   (A) The wires carry electricity.
   (B) The laundry hangs from poles.
   (C) The light fixtures are tall.
   (D) The polls are open for the election.

8. Look at the picture marked number 8 in your test book.
   (A) The jewels are in the safe.
   (B) The woman works with her hands.
   (C) The optician is grinding lenses.
   (D) The woman saws metal.

9. Look at the picture marked number 9 in your test book.
   (A) The nurses are administering medication.
   (B) There are two purses at the reception desk.
   (C) The pharmacists are conferring.
   (D) The nurses are in front of the window.

10. Look at the picture marked number 10 in your test book.
    (A) The attendant offers a newspaper.
    (B) The passenger is sleeping.
    (C) The tourists are taking photos.
    (D) The newsstand is crowded.

Part II: Question-Response

<u>Directions:</u> On the compact disc, you will hear a question and three possible answers. Choose the answer that most closely answers the question and fill in the corresponding oval on your answer sheet.

11. Where do you live?
    (A) About five o'clock.
    (B) On Third Avenue.
    (C) In ten minutes.

12. Why are you late?
    (A) My watch stopped.
    (B) I ate already.
    (C) I'll call you later.

13. Who are you waiting for?
    (A) I've lost a lot of weight.
    (B) I don't know the way.
    (C) My wife; she is meeting me here.

14. What are you going to do now?
    (A) I went home early.
    (B) I didn't do anything then.
    (C) I plan to take a vacation.

15. Which chair is yours?
    (A) Mine is the one on the left.
    (B) We need to cheer loudly.
    (C) This exam is not fair.

16. When did he arrive?
    (A) By train.
    (B) Shortly after lunch.
    (C) In the mail.

17. How long have you worked here?
    (A) Only for a few months.
    (B) I work on Tuesdays.
    (C) She can't hear if you sing along.

18. Where did you park your car?
    (A) In the darkroom.
    (B) The park is easy to get to.
    (C) In the lot across the street.

GO ON TO THE NEXT PAGE

19. What should I do now?
    (A) Why don't you make some coffee?
    (B) The wood is on the fire.
    (C) You were the first one here.

20. When does the meeting start?
    (A) The meat is frozen.
    (B) The car won't start.
    (C) At 10 A.M. sharp.

21. Who delivered the letter?
    (A) A messenger brought it.
    (B) The ladder is in the closet.
    (C) I'll let her leave sooner or later.

22. How large is your company?
    (A) It's about 10 inches.
    (B) It's as big as a penny.
    (C) We have offices in ten countries.

23. Where would you like to eat?
    (A) Let's go to an Italian restaurant.
    (B) The heat is very bad in here.
    (C) I always eat at eight.

24. Why is there no electricity today?
    (A) I prefer to cook with gas.
    (B) The power company shut it off for an hour.
    (C) The elections are Saturday.

25. Which is taller—this building or the one next door?
    (A) Both are the same height.
    (B) This cabinet is well-built.
    (C) The construction crew stops at noon.

Part III: Short Conversations

<u>Directions</u>: On the compact disc, you will hear a short conversation. In your test book, you will see a question and four possible answers. Choose the best answer to the question and fill in the corresponding oval on your answer sheet.

26. Man: This should be a fun evening.
    Woman: Yes, I've been looking forward to seeing the play.
    Man: The reviews haven't been that good though.

27. Man: What seems to be the matter with your forearm?
    Woman: I was getting off the bus and I fell down the stairs.
    Man: It looks swollen. Let me take an X ray.

28. Man: If we leave now, we can be there at six.
    Woman: It's rush hour now. Let's wait an hour.
    Man: Alright, but don't blame me if we're late.

29. Man: Oh no! The golf course is covered with snow.
    Woman: It's going to snow through the weekend.
    Man: I wish my sport were skiing rather than golf.

30. Man: Did I have any calls?
    Woman: Yes—about twenty. I left all the messages in your desk.
    Man: Thanks. Would you get me a purchase order form, please?

31. Man: Are you too busy to see me sometime next week?
    Woman: Any day but Wednesday. Would Friday afternoon be OK?
    Man: Actually, it's not. Let's meet the following week.

32. Man: Last year thirty percent of our budget was spent on advertising.
    Woman: Was that all in TV advertising?
    Man: No, half of it was in print.

33. Man: I'm really exhausted.
    Woman: I've never worked so hard in my life.
    Man: We deserve a bonus for this.

34. Man: How many more letters do I have to sign?
    Woman: There are only a few more and we'll be finished.
    Man: I'm going to need a new pen after this.

35. Man: I'd like to exchange this shirt, please.
    Woman: Of course, sir. What would you like instead?
    Man: I'd prefer one with long sleeves and in blue.

GO ON TO THE NEXT PAGE

592   TRANSCRIPTS

36. **Man:** I'm almost finished doing the invoices and the payroll.
    Woman: I needed the tax statement for this quarter first.
    Man: I can't compute the taxes without the salary information.

37. **Man:** Are you going to New York or Paris this fall?
    Woman: Neither. I want to go to some place warmer.
    Man: Why don't you stay home then?

38. **Man:** I can't get this printer to work. The paper always jams.
    Woman: Let me see if I can fix it.
    Man: Thanks. I really need to get these letters in the mail.

39. **Man:** Excuse me. But does this bus go to 75th Street?
    Woman: No. This one turns at 57th. You need the M5 bus.
    Man: I've waited long enough for this one. I think I'll just walk.

40. **Man:** Did you see that bird?
    Woman: No, what kind was it?
    Man: I don't know, but it flew by really fast.

Part IV: Short Talks

<u>Directions:</u> On the compact disc, you will hear a short talk. In your test book, you will see several questions on the talk and four possible answers. Choose the best answer to the question and fill in the corresponding oval on your answer sheet.

Questions 41 and 42 refer to the following announcement.

Man: This train makes all stops between Grand Central Station and 125th (one-hundred-twenty-fifth) Street. The express train is across the station. Please step in and watch the closing doors.

Now read question 41 in your test book and answer it.

Now read question 42 in your test book and answer it.

Questions 43 and 44 refer to the following weather report.

Man: At six A.M. the temperature at National Airport is 53 degrees. Today's forecast calls for rain early in the morning with skies clearing by noon. The rest of the day will be seasonably mild with winds developing in the evening.

Now read question 43 in your test book and answer it.

Now read question 44 in your test book and answer it.

Questions 45 and 46 refer to the following announcement.

Man: Due to the extremely hot weather, the electric company is planning to turn off power in certain districts during the day. This will reduce the total demand for electricity and prevent a city-wide shutdown of electrical services. Power will not be out longer than two hours in your area.

Now read question 45 in your test book and answer it.

Now read question 46 in your test book and answer it.

Questions 47 and 48 refer to the following announcement.

Man: Good morning, ladies and gentlemen. This is your cruise director speaking. It's 7:30 and it's a beautiful day at sea. We have a lot planned for you both on ship and on shore. The first shore excursion will depart from the Main Deck at 9:00 A.M. Anyone wishing to go ashore at this time should report to the lounge for a ticket. Enjoy your breakfast.

Now read question 47 in your test book and answer it.

Now read question 48 in your test book and answer it.

GO ON TO THE NEXT PAGE

594 TRANSCRIPTS

Questions 49 and 50 refer to the following advertisement.

Man: Are you tired of getting up to turn off the television? Tired of getting up to turn down the radio? Turn on the video recorder? Our new remote control will let you operate any electronic appliance in your home from a comfortable chair. Call our toll-free number for more information. No sales personnel will call your home.

Now read question 49 in your test book and answer it.

Now read question 50 in your test book and answer it.

This is the end of the Mini-Test for Listening Comprehension.

Model Test 1 Listening Comprehension

> **Part I: Picture**
>
> Directions: In your test book, you will see a picture. On the compact disc, you will hear four statements. Choose the statement that most closely matches the picture and fill in the corresponding oval on your answer sheet.

1. Look at the picture marked number 1 in your test book.
   (A) The doctor is examining a patient.
   (B) The technician is working.
   (C) The chemist is setting the meter.
   (D) The expert is logging new data.

2. Look at the picture marked number 2 in your test book.
   (A) Sympathy is visible in their faces.
   (B) The audience is applauding.
   (C) The conductor leads the orchestra.
   (D) The musicians are dealing with cancer.

3. Look at the picture marked number 3 in your test book.
   (A) The negotiators are meeting.
   (B) The participants are washing their glasses.
   (C) Preparations for the banquet have begun.
   (D) Vacant seats fill the room.

4. Look at the picture marked number 4 in your test book.
   (A) They are going to the show.
   (B) The leader is scouting the terrain.
   (C) The hikers have chosen their campsite.
   (D) The skiers walk across the mountain.

5. Look at the picture marked number 5 in your test book.
   (A) The policeman is giving a ticket.
   (B) The emergency crew is at the scene.
   (C) The accident victim is at the hospital.
   (D) The boy is riding his bicycle.

6. Look at the picture marked number 6 in your test book.
   (A) The delivery man brought a fan.
   (B) This plant does light manufacturing.
   (C) The worker is in an automobile factory.
   (D) The chauffeur is in the car.

GO ON TO THE NEXT PAGE

596   TRANSCRIPTS

7. Look at the picture marked number 7 in your test book.
   (A) The cowboys are setting up for the rodeo.
   (B) The vines are full of ripe fruit.
   (C) The straw is very dry.
   (D) The men are loading the truck.

8. Look at the picture marked number 8 in your test book.
   (A) The staff look at their computers.
   (B) The terminal is full of customers.
   (C) Each worker has a private office.
   (D) Several technicians are working on the problem.

9. Look at the picture marked number 9 in your test book.
   (A) The man is signing his name.
   (B) The electric bill is overdue.
   (C) The equipment uses laser beams.
   (D) The technician checks the circuitry.

10. Look at the picture marked number 10 in your test book.
    (A) The gymnasium is primarily for racquet sports.
    (B) The athletes are boarding the train.
    (C) The people are exercising.
    (D) The people are examining the monitors.

11. Look at the picture marked number 11 in your test book.
    (A) The flags fly from the roof.
    (B) The court is in session.
    (C) The ceiling is very low.
    (D) The yard is full of tourists.

12. Look at the picture marked number 12 in your test book.
    (A) There's standing room only left on the bus.
    (B) People were trampled at the fair.
    (C) The conductor is wearing a pouch.
    (D) The bus stopped at the corner.

13. Look at the picture marked number 13 in your test book.
    (A) The robot runs automatically.
    (B) The man is pulling a lever.
    (C) The worker is recording data.
    (D) The worker is explaining the details.

14. Look at the picture marked number 14 in your test book.
    (A) The horses are racing.
    (B) The hoarse announcer can't catch up.
    (C) The writer is very fast.
    (D) The jockey has a twin.

15. Look at the picture marked number 15 in your test book.
    (A) The medicine is in the cabinet.
    (B) The technician stands beside the patient.
    (C) The woman scanned the newspaper.
    (D) The patient is completely submerged.

16. Look at the picture marked number 16 in your test book.
    (A) The trolley car is late.
    (B) The street cart vendor sells fruit.
    (C) The women are carrying dresses.
    (D) The cafe is near the street.

17. Look at the picture marked number 17 in your test book.
    (A) There are two banks on the hill.
    (B) The field has been plowed.
    (C) The pipelines cross the field.
    (D) Pale limestone covers the site.

18. Look at the picture marked number 18 in your test book.
    (A) The garden requires maintenance.
    (B) He is cleaning the floor.
    (C) He is sweeping with a broom.
    (D) The vacuum is stored securely.

19. Look at the picture marked number 19 in your test book.
    (A) A boat passes under the bridge.
    (B) The waterways are impassable.
    (C) The sailors went along the ridge.
    (D) The card game is called bridge.

20. Look at the picture marked number 20 in your test book.
    (A) The gardeners are cutting flowers.
    (B) The bridegroom is in the middle.
    (C) The husband is waving.
    (D) The newlyweds are posing.

GO ON TO THE NEXT PAGE

Part II: Question-Response

Directions: On the compact disc, you will hear a question and three possible answers. Choose the answer that most closely answers the question and fill in the corresponding oval on your answer sheet.

21. Good evening. How are you?
    (A) It's time for bed.
    (B) Fine, thank you.
    (C) I'm not Mr. Goode.

22. Is this your pen?
    (A) No, it's not mine.
    (B) I don't know what will happen.
    (C) Yes, he's European.

23. Why are you late?
    (A) Since about three o'clock.
    (B) My car wouldn't start.
    (C) There are more than eight.

24. Who is coming with us?
    (A) She came after us.
    (B) Mitch is combing his hair.
    (C) My sister wants to.

25. When does the meeting begin?
    (A) At nine A.M.
    (B) The windows are open.
    (C) The track meet is on Friday.

26. What's for dinner?
    (A) We're having steak.
    (B) My wife and her mother.
    (C) After I get home.

27. Where were you last week?
    (A) I was on vacation.
    (B) This weekend I'm at home.
    (C) The event will last a week.

28. How often do you play golf?
    (A) The play will be over at 10.
    (B) Get off the golf course.
    (C) Almost every Sunday.

29. Which way is faster?
    (A) The coast road is quicker.
    (B) My horse came in last.
    (C) I weigh 180 pounds.

30. Are there any messages?
    (A) The massage room is over there.
    (B) Any of us could do it.
    (C) Your brother called three times.

31. What did the customer buy?
    (A) The customs officer is busy.
    (B) A pair of gloves.
    (C) He is nearby.

32. How much paper do we need?
    (A) Enough for ten copies.
    (B) The newspaper costs 25 cents.
    (C) I need to pay more.

33. When does the plane leave?
    (A) At the airport.
    (B) Before we take off.
    (C) In about 45 minutes.

34. Why don't you take a coffee break?
    (A) The cup was broken.
    (B) I have too much work.
    (C) The car brakes won't work.

35. Have you finished eating?
    (A) She finished the report.
    (B) The eggs haven't been beaten.
    (C) Yes, it was delicious.

36. Where is the hotel?
    (A) It's across from the park.
    (B) Rooms are $200 a night.
    (C) The elevator is around the corner.

37. Who painted this picture?
    (A) We paid for the picture frame.
    (B) She's a great photographer.
    (C) I forgot the artist's name.

38. Which desk is ours?
    (A) The hours are very long.
    (B) The one by the window.
    (C) Have a seat please.

GO ON TO THE NEXT PAGE

39. When did you join the company?
    (A) I prefer to be alone.
    (B) In 19__.
    (C) My knee is out of joint.

40. How near is your office?
    (A) My earache is better.
    (B) My office is closed today.
    (C) It's only a few blocks from here.

41. Is this your pen or mine?
    (A) I'll open it when you want.
    (B) I think it's yours.
    (C) It's European.

42. What kind of books do you like to read?
    (A) I enjoy historical novels.
    (B) It looks like it's OK to proceed.
    (C) I couldn't find my book.

43. Why don't you buy a house?
    (A) I don't have room in my house.
    (B) Should I sell my house?
    (C) It's more economical to rent one.

44. Where did you have lunch?
    (A) I thought we were meeting for lunch tomorrow.
    (B) At the restaurant across the street.
    (C) Yes, let's go at noon.

45. Shouldn't we ask your father to join us?
    (A) He'd rather not come.
    (B) It's not that far.
    (C) The task was not finished.

46. Who was at the conference?
    (A) Our neighbors put up the fence.
    (B) The conference was yesterday.
    (C) Only people from our office attended.

47. Which shoes are more comfortable?
    (A) These sandals are more comfortable.
    (B) Use more tables on these charts.
    (C) Take off your shoes and be comfortable.

48. Where can I leave my coat?
    (A) I live on 14th Street.
    (B) Just hang it in the hall closet.
    (C) You can leave a note if you want.

49. When did you place the order?
    (A) The race started at ten.
    (B) I'll place it by the door.
    (C) I sent the order by fax last night.

50. Are we almost done?
    (A) Yes, this is the last one.
    (B) I like my steak well-done.
    (C) We won't have much fun.

GO ON TO THE NEXT PAGE

Part III: Short Conversations

Directions: On the compact disc, you will hear a short conversation. In your test book, you will see a question and four possible answers. Choose the best answer to the question and fill in the corresponding oval on your answer sheet.

51. Man: Can we meet at 3:00 or 4:00?
    Woman: I'm busy until 5:00.
    Man: Let's meet then.

52. Man: I'd like to make a deposit.
    Woman: Is your account at this branch?
    Man: Yes, my checking account is.

53. Man: The first stop on today's tour is the museum.
    Woman: Then are we going to the commercial district?
    Man: No, next we'll tour the government buildings.

54. Man: You must change planes in Chicago.
    Woman: Is there a direct flight?
    Man: No, but you could change planes in Denver instead.

55. Man: Could you please bring two extra towels to Room 603?
    Woman: Certainly, sir. The housekeeper will bring them right away.
    Man: I'd like some more soap, too.

56. Man: I can't find a taxi.
    Woman: There is a taxi stand at the corner.
    Man: Thank you. I'll get one there.

57. Man: Good evening. Are you ready to order yet?
    Woman: The menu looks wonderful. What do you recommend?
    Man: The chicken with rice is a local dish. It's very good.

58. Man: I'm calling about the ad for the catering position.
    Woman: Do you have any experience?
    Man: Yes, I've worked in the food and beverage industry for five years.

59. Man: Have you called the repairperson?
    Woman: Yes. He'll be here between 2:00 and 2:30.
    Man: Oh, no! I have to make 50 copies by 1:00.

60. Woman: We need to have this report ready for the meeting.
    Man: I can finish it on the plane.
    Woman: I can only work at home or at the office—not when I'm traveling.

MODEL TEST 1

61. **Woman:** Your room is number 439. It has a view of the city.
    Man: What about my bags?
    Woman: The bellman will bring them up.

62. **Woman:** You always arrive late!
    Man: Sorry. The bus was late.
    Woman: Buses are always late in the rain. You should leave earlier in bad weather.

63. **Man:** I'm waiting for my wife and we're going shopping for the kids.
    Woman: I never shop during lunch. There's not enough time.
    Man: When it's just the two of us, without the kids, we shop quickly.

64. **Man:** Should we send it special delivery?
    Woman: It needs to get there as soon as possible.
    Man: Overnight mail would be better, then.

65. **Man:** There were too many people at this convention.
    Woman: I know. All of the presentations were overcrowded.
    Man: Next year, they should get bigger rooms.

66. **Man:** I'm taking a train to Brussels tonight.
    Woman: Flying is much faster.
    Man: Yes, but the airport is too far away. The train station is right downtown.

67. **Woman:** The brochures are back from the printers.
    Man: Good. They're right on schedule.
    Woman: Now I just have to address them and mail them.

68. **Man:** What do I owe you?
    Woman: It's eight dollars on the meter, plus a dollar fifty for your bags.
    Man: Here you are, driver. Keep the change.

69. **Man:** Why do you keep dialing that number?
    Woman: I want to leave a message, but the answering machine turns off too soon.
    Man: You'll just have to learn to talk faster!

70. **Man:** Would you like a window seat, or an aisle seat?
    Woman: A window seat, please. Is that a dinner flight?
    Man: Yes, and they'll show a movie, too.

71. **Man:** Drive past the park and turn right. There is a bank on the corner.
    Woman: Does it have a drive-in window?
    Man: Yes, and there's a parking lot, too.

72. **Man:** Work is slow because everyone has to wait to use the printer.
    Woman: What should we do about it?
    Man: The first thing is to buy more printers.

GO ON TO THE NEXT PAGE

604 TRANSCRIPTS

73. Man: I'm tired of all the rain.
    Woman: They've been predicting rain all week.
    Man: Then I guess I won't be able to play golf tomorrow.

74. Man: You had a message at ten o'clock, from Mr. Green.
    Woman: What does it say?
    Man: He'd like to make one change to the proposal. He'll be in his office after four.

75. Man: We'd like to offer you the position of human resources assistant.
    Woman: Thank you. I'm happy to accept.
    Man: I'm sure you'll like working here.

76. Man: I'm out of stationery. Do you need anything from the supply room?
    Woman: Yes, I'm out of pens and paper clips.
    Man: I'll bring you a box of each.

77. Man: This chair is really uncomfortable!
    Woman: I think that chair is designed for someone taller than you.
    Man: Maybe I'll ask for a new one.

78. Man: I tried to call you, but I got a busy signal.
    Woman: I'm sorry. I left the phone off the hook.
    Man: You could miss important calls that way.

79. Woman: Do you have the banking report?
    Man: No, I don't. I loaned it to Mr. Smith.
    Woman: Okay. I'll get it from him.

80. Man: Stay away from the building and move out of the street.
    Woman: What's wrong, officer?
    Man: There's smoke coming from one of the windows. The fire department is on the way.

Part IV: Short Talks

Directions: On the compact disc, you will hear a short talk. In your test book, you will see several questions on the talk and four possible answers. Choose the best answer to the question and fill in the corresponding oval on your answer sheet.

Questions 81 and 82 refer to the following announcement.

Man: This train provides service to all arrival and departure gates, baggage claims, and ticketing areas. Color-coded maps and signs are posted within each car. Please move to the center of the car and away from the doors.

Now read question 81 in your test book and answer it.

Now read question 82 in your test book and answer it.

Questions 83 and 84 refer to the following recording.

Woman: Thank you for calling the City Museum. We are open to the public from ten until six Monday through Saturday, and from one until five on Sundays. Information about special exhibits, classes, and lectures can be obtained by calling our Education Office at 548-6251.

Now read question 83 in your test book and answer it.

Now read question 84 in your test book and answer it.

Questions 85 and 86 refer to the following announcement.

Man: Organizing your workday is the key to getting things done. Start every morning by making a list of things you need to do during the day. Next, rank each task on the list according to its importance. Work on the most important task first, and stay with it until it is completed. Then, move on to the next task.

Now read question 85 in your test book and answer it.

Now read question 86 in your test book and answer it.

Questions 87 and 88 refer to the following advertisement.

Woman: Our holiday sale offers you great savings on new office furniture. All desks, chairs, tables, and filing cabinets are on sale. We also have sale prices on office accessories like lamps and bookcases. Now is the time to give your office a great new look at a low, low price.

Now read question 87 in your test book and answer it.

Now read question 88 in your test book and answer it.

GO ON TO THE NEXT PAGE

Questions 89 and 90 refer to the following advertisement.

Woman: Are you successful? Pass some of that success along to a new generation by serving as a volunteer tutor. With as little as two hours a week, you can help a child with his schoolwork and share your love of learning. Children of all ages are waiting for your help. Call your local school system today.

Now read question 89 in your test book and answer it.

Now read question 90 in your test book and answer it.

Questions 91 and 92 refer to the following weather report.

Woman: Here's today's weather report. Temperatures will be in the mid sixties with breezes of ten to fifteen miles per hour. The sun will shine all day with no clouds expected. It's a great day to spend some time outdoors.

Now read question 91 in your test book and answer it.

Now read question 92 in your test book and answer it.

Questions 93 and 94 refer to the following advertisement.

Woman: Our special ski weekend is a great value. One terrific price includes two nights at our mountain lodge with continental breakfast and gourmet dinner. Ski equipment is available from the hotel's rental shop for an additional fee. Certified ski instructors provide classes for all ability levels. Spend your next ski vacation with us.

Now read question 93 in your test book and answer it.

Now read question 94 in your test book and answer it.

Questions 95 through 97 refer to the following announcement.

Woman: We are experiencing delays of up to forty-five minutes on the inbound subway line, due to damage to the tracks. Trains are currently running every fifteen minutes. In addition, special buses are available to carry commuters around the damaged portions of the track.

Now read question 95 in your test book and answer it.

Now read question 96 in your test book and answer it.

Now read question 97 in your test book and answer it.

Questions 98 through 100 refer to the following news item.

Man: There was an underground explosion today at the corner of Main Street and Central Avenue. Authorities do not yet know the cause, but they suspect a leaking gas pipe. Streets in the area were closed, and workers were evacuated from nearby office buildings. In spite of the force of the explosion, no injuries were reported.

Now read question 98 in your test book and answer it.

Now read question 99 in your test book and answer it.

Now read question 100 in your test book and answer it.

This is the end of the Listening Comprehension portion of the test.

Model Test 2 Listening Comprehension

> **Part I: Picture**
>
> Directions: In your test book, you will see a picture. On the compact disc, you will hear four statements. Choose the statement that most closely matches the picture and fill in the corresponding oval on your answer sheet.

1. Look at the picture marked number 1 in your test book.
   (A) The men are discussing the documents.
   (B) Two men are signing their names.
   (C) Negotiations have come to a standstill.
   (D) The man on the left has reading glasses.

2. Look at the picture marked number 2 in your test book.
   (A) The sign is pointing the way.
   (B) The kitchen staff is chopping vegetables.
   (C) Guests can see the kitchen through a glass window.
   (D) The cooks prepare a meal.

3. Look at the picture marked number 3 in your test book.
   (A) The pilot turns the dials.
   (B) The technician pushes the buttons.
   (C) The switchboard is flooded with incoming calls.
   (D) A panel of experts made the decision.

4. Look at the picture marked number 4 in your test book.
   (A) The couple is viewing art.
   (B) The paintings are all the same size.
   (C) Pictures are stacked on the floor.
   (D) The sculptures stand out.

5. Look at the picture marked number 5 in your test book.
   (A) The majority of the passengers are females.
   (B) The concourse is virtually empty.
   (C) The passengers wait at the airport.
   (D) The bags are on the truck.

6. Look at the picture marked number 6 in your test book.
   (A) Both players want the puck.
   (B) The athletes rest after the game.
   (C) The tackle is a success.
   (D) A player carries the ball.

7. Look at the picture marked number 7 in your test book.
   (A) The man watches the monitors.
   (B) His swivel chair is in the corner.
   (C) The men are analyzing computer code.
   (D) The man is projecting the outcome.

8. Look at the picture marked number 8 in your test book.
   (A) The dentist is using a drill.
   (B) The automobile is in the showroom.
   (C) The woman works on a car interior.
   (D) The worker is assembling the engine.

9. Look at the picture marked number 9 in your test book.
   (A) White cranes are in the water.
   (B) The trains pass on a bridge.
   (C) Narrow carts went through the tunnel.
   (D) Skyscrapers clutter the city.

10. Look at the picture marked number 10 in your test book.
    (A) The umbrellas shade the guest rooms.
    (B) The passage has an arch.
    (C) There's seating in front of the hotel.
    (D) Many of the windows have shutters.

11. Look at the picture marked number 11 in your test book.
    (A) Passengers are watching the takeoff.
    (B) A man is walking toward the counter.
    (C) Many visitors are at the border.
    (D) Bellboys wait in the lobby.

12. Look at the picture marked number 12 in your test book.
    (A) Ten of us are playing.
    (B) The player hits the ball.
    (C) There are matches on the table.
    (D) The tennis player is struggling with an injury.

13. Look at the picture marked number 13 in your test book.
    (A) Most of the riders are reading.
    (B) New writers are hard to train.
    (C) The hanging straps are well utilized.
    (D) Everyone must stand inside.

14. Look at the picture marked number 14 in your test book.
    (A) The space is for rent.
    (B) It's a new rocking chair.
    (C) The bird flies through the air.
    (D) The rocket lifts off.

GO ON TO THE NEXT PAGE

15. Look at the picture marked number 15 in your test book.
    (A) The auditorium is crowded.
    (B) The audience interacts with the panel.
    (C) People are watching a slide presentation.
    (D) The chairs are by the door.

16. Look at the picture marked number 16 in your test book.
    (A) Both men are wearing pinstripes.
    (B) Both men are reading the news.
    (C) The speakers are standing at their booth.
    (D) The men are seated around a table.

17. Look at the picture marked number 17 in your test book.
    (A) The satellite dish points upward.
    (B) The dish counts passing aircraft.
    (C) The saucer is being installed by a technician.
    (D) The radio antennae is on the truck.

18. Look at the picture marked number 18 in your test book.
    (A) The woman is measuring gloves.
    (B) The factory worker repairs a machine.
    (C) The robot is assembling telephones.
    (D) Produce is next to canned goods.

19. Look at the picture marked number 19 in your test book.
    (A) The hold is full of gas.
    (B) The cruise ship is in port.
    (C) The tanker moves through the water.
    (D) The crew are releasing the lines.

20. Look at the picture marked number 20 in your test book.
    (A) The office worker uses his computer.
    (B) There are keys in his hand.
    (C) The man is wearing glasses.
    (D) His printer is jammed.

Part II: Question-Response

Directions: On the compact disc, you will hear a question and three possible answers. Choose the answer that most closely answers the question and fill in the corresponding oval on your answer sheet.

21. Did you have a good trip?
    (A) Yes, thank you. It was very pleasant.
    (B) My vacation is in August.
    (C) We are good friends.

22. How long will you stay?
    (A) There are twenty-four hours in a day.
    (B) I always stay at a hotel.
    (C) Only one week.

23. Who wrote this letter?
    (A) I did, and I typed it, too.
    (B) She can read better than I.
    (C) The exchange rate is better today.

24. What color shirt are you wearing?
    (A) I need a long-sleeve shirt.
    (B) It's a light blue.
    (C) Everyone knows where I am.

25. When will she call me?
    (A) She said after lunch.
    (B) I'll return this call soon.
    (C) She called me lazy.

26. Why are you waiting in here?
    (A) It's too cold to wait outside.
    (B) I knew my way there.
    (C) The waiter is new here.

27. Where is your family from?
    (A) All her books made her famous.
    (B) My children are at school.
    (C) My parents were born here.

28. How soon will you be ready?
    (A) In about ten minutes.
    (B) Her son left early.
    (C) We said we wanted red.

GO ON TO THE NEXT PAGE

612 TRANSCRIPTS

29. Which restaurant shall we go to?
    (A) It's closed tonight.
    (B) I have reservations at a steak house.
    (C) We restored this hall last year.

30. What time does the train leave?
    (A) It stopped raining at 4.
    (B) The train is on time.
    (C) It departs every hour on the hour.

31. All lines are busy. Will you hold?
    (A) No, I'll call back.
    (B) I'm not busy this evening.
    (C) She's not very old.

32. Who is working late this evening?
    (A) Good night. Sleep well.
    (B) All of us—until we finish this report.
    (C) I always eat after ten.

33. When was the invoice sent?
    (A) Two weeks ago.
    (B) My voice is very soft.
    (C) We went in March.

34. How many times have you been to Asia?
    (A) I have a Chinese watch.
    (B) It takes about 14 hours.
    (C) This is my first trip.

35. Why don't you come over tonight?
    (A) Thank you. I'd like to.
    (B) His pants are too tight.
    (C) There's more light over here.

36. Which team is your favorite?
    (A) I prefer tea with milk.
    (B) I like them both.
    (C) Your fee seems right.

37. Have you met my new assistant?
    (A) No, I don't have a new chair.
    (B) Yes, I introduced myself earlier.
    (C) The newspaper is wet.

38. Where is the fax machine?
    (A) It's next to the photocopier.
    (B) All the facts are true.
    (C) The magazine is on the desk.

39. What day is she coming?
    (A) She left yesterday.
    (B) He will come next month.
    (C) On Tuesday, I think.

40. Who made the reservation?
    (A) You need to reserve a table.
    (B) My travel agent.
    (C) The housekeeper made the beds.

41. Do we have to use a pen?
    (A) No, use a pencil if you want.
    (B) I'll tell you when.
    (C) We are used to having it open.

42. What is the deadline for this project?
    (A) He died last week.
    (B) We need to finish it this week.
    (C) The bid was rejected.

43. Why are you laughing?
    (A) The staffing policies are under review.
    (B) I laughed until I cried.
    (C) I just heard a joke.

44. Who is standing by the window?
    (A) That's a client of mine.
    (B) The plant is by the window.
    (C) The carpenter is sanding the chair.

45. Where did you find your address book?
    (A) Address this envelope, please.
    (B) Just yesterday.
    (C) I found it at the office.

46. How can I get my pants pressed?
    (A) Don't be depressed.
    (B) Send them to the cleaners.
    (C) I got a new pair last week.

47. When are you going to start exercising?
    (A) I start my day with a healthful breakfast.
    (B) The exercises are at the end of the book.
    (C) I'll start when I have more free time.

48. What kept you so long?
    (A) I'm sorry. I couldn't get off the phone.
    (B) I think I'll keep the long one.
    (C) She wept a long time.

GO ON TO THE NEXT PAGE

49. Could you summarize the article for me?
    (A) I've never liked that size art.
    (B) You should read the article yourself.
    (C) Summer is my favorite season, too.

50. Where would you recommend I go?
    (A) At this time of year, I would go south.
    (B) I'll go sometime soon.
    (C) You should comment on this memo.

Part III: Short Conversations

<u>Directions</u>: On the compact disc, you will hear a short conversation. In your test book, you will see a question and four possible answers. Choose the best answer to the question and fill in the corresponding oval on your answer sheet.

51. Man: When do you take your lunch break?
    Woman: I wait until one. A late lunch makes the afternoon seem shorter.
    Man: I'm always so hungry, I eat promptly at twelve.

52. Woman: Could you leave this package with the receptionist for me?
    Man: Of course. I'll pass by her desk on my way out.
    Woman: Thanks. It will save me a trip to the lobby.

53. Man: Can you type this memo for me?
    Woman: I'll be glad to, but I must finish these letters first.
    Man: That's OK. I'll ask Mr. Brown to type it.

54. Man: May I help you find something?
    Woman: I'm looking for a souvenir to take home.
    Man: Perhaps you'd like a carved box by a local artist.

55. Man: Are you going to the evening session at the convention hall?
    Woman: I'm too tired. I'm going to order room service and go to bed early.
    Man: OK, but you'll miss a great speaker.

56. Man: Would you like to order one of the house specialties?
    Woman: What would you suggest?
    Man: The fish with mushrooms is very good here.

57. Man: Will this be cash or charge?
    Woman: Charge. Here is my card.
    Man: That comes to forty-two dollars even. Please sign here.

58. Man: I look forward to seeing you again in Tokyo.
    Woman: Likewise. I've enjoyed working with you.
    Man: Thanks. Have a good trip.

59. Woman: I'm afraid Mr. Wu is out at the moment. May I take a message?
    Man: Yes. Please tell him I called.
    Woman: May I have your name and number, please?

60. Man: Did you get a copy of the report?
    Woman: No, but I'd like to see one.
    Man: I sent you one. I wonder what happened to it.

GO ON TO THE NEXT PAGE

61. **Man:** We got the environmental proposal today.
    Woman: Great! That's a terrific contract for our company.
    Man: Yes. I hope we can get others like it.

62. **Woman:** I'd like to return this coffeemaker. It doesn't work.
    Man: Of course. Would you like a refund, or a replacement?
    Woman: A refund, please.

63. **Man:** Do you play golf?
    Woman: Not really. My best games are tennis and bowling.
    Man: I enjoy tennis, but I don't have the skill for bowling.

64. **Man:** Oh, no. The flight to Chicago is delayed two hours.
    Woman: That's a long time to wait.
    Man: From now on we'll call about the flight before we leave for the airport.

65. **Man:** How do you turn the computer on?
    Woman: The switch is at the back.
    Man: There, I found it. Thanks for your help.

66. **Man:** How can I get from the airport to my hotel?
    Woman: You can take the subway or a taxi. But your hotel has an airport shuttle bus.
    Man: Thank you. The shuttle will be the easiest way.

67. **Man:** Can you join the three of us for dinner?
    Woman: Thank you, I will. Is six-thirty all right?
    Man: I'm in a meeting until six. Let's make it seven.

68. **Man:** I'll need a wake-up call, please.
    Woman: Certainly, sir. What time?
    Man: Six o'clock. I have an early meeting.

69. **Man:** I didn't get the clerk's job I applied for.
    Woman: That's okay. The salary was too low.
    Man: Maybe my luck will be better next time.

70. **Man:** Our meetings always seem to run late.
    Woman: We never start until the latecomers arrive.
    Man: Let's start our next meeting on time. We won't wait for anyone.

71. **Woman:** Your room is confirmed for the third. Our check-in time is five o'clock.
    Man: I won't be arriving until seven P.M.
    Woman: That's all right. We'll guarantee your room for late arrival until nine.

72. **Woman:** You have your choice of the walking tour or the bus tour.
    Man: How long does the walking tour take?
    Woman: The walking tour takes a full day; the bus tour takes half a day.

MODEL TEST 2   617

73. Man: Let's discuss this tomorrow. How about nine?
    Woman: I can't. I'm tied up all day tomorrow.
    Man: Okay. We'll do it on Wednesday.

74. Man: Where's my briefcase? It's got my notes in it.
    Woman: You probably left it in the cab.
    Man: Hurry! Let's call their lost-and-found department.

75. Man: I'll never learn this new software!
    Woman: Yes, you will. It just takes practice.
    Man: Even if I practice, I'll never understand this program.

76. Man: You did an excellent job on the project.
    Woman: Thank you. I can't take all the credit. The entire team worked hard.
    Man: Then give them my congratulations.

77. Woman: What kind of job are you looking for?
    Man: I'm not sure.
    Woman: You should think about what you are good at, and start from there.

78. Woman: There's a typo in this letter. You left off the date.
    Man: I'll fix it right away.
    Woman: Just leave it on my desk to sign.

79. Man: Do you need the copier?
    Woman: Yes. I have to make two hundred copies by noon. Do you need it, too?
    Man: Yes, but go ahead. My copies don't have to be ready until four.

80. Man: Where would you like to eat?
    Woman: I'm in the mood for something light.
    Man: We'll go to the cafe on the corner. They serve good salads.

GO ON TO THE NEXT PAGE

Part IV: Short Talks

<u>Directions:</u> On the compact disc, you will hear a short talk. In your test book, you will see several questions on the talk and four possible answers. Choose the best answer to the question and fill in the corresponding oval on your answer sheet.

<u>Questions 81 and 82</u> refer to the following advertisement.

Woman: Don't you hate to waste time waiting in airports? On your next business trip, put that time to use with our new portable computer. It's small enough to fit in your briefcase, and unfolds easily when you're ready to use it. Stop wasting time. Call us today.

Now read question 81 in your test book and answer it.

Now read question 82 in your test book and answer it.

<u>Questions 83 and 84</u> refer to the following weather report.

Man: A winter storm warning is in effect for this area through midnight tonight. Heavy rain is expected, turning to snow by late this afternoon. This will create ice hazards tonight as the rain and snow freeze over. This means dangerous icy conditions for rush hour tomorrow.

Now read question 83 in your test book and answer it.

Now read question 84 in your test book and answer it.

<u>Questions 85 and 86</u> refer to the following news item.

Man: A study out today suggests that people who have office jobs are less fit than people who have more active jobs. Sitting all day at a desk simply reduces opportunities for exercise. Experts suggest that office workers incorporate more activity into their day by climbing stairs, going for walks during lunch, and riding bicycles to work.

Now read question 85 in your test book and answer it.

Now read question 86 in your test book and answer it.

<u>Questions 87 and 88</u> refer to the following recording.

Woman: You have reached 479-8526. I am not able to take your call right now. Please leave your name, your number, the date and time of your call, and a brief message at the sound of the tone. I will get back to you as soon as I can.

Now read question 87 in your test book and answer it.

Now read question 88 in your test book and answer it.

MODEL TEST 2 619

Questions 89 and 90 refer to the following advertisement.

Man: It's tax time again. And if you hate to do your taxes, let us do them instead. Just provide us with your financial records. Our qualified staff of accountants can prepare your return for you, quickly and easily. Fees are based on an hourly rate.

Now read question 89 in your test book and answer it.

Now read question 90 in your test book and answer it.

Questions 91 and 92 refer to the following news item.

Woman: Several airlines reduced fares today in an attempt to increase ticket sales. Some fares were slashed by as much as fifty percent for round-trip tickets. This is seen in the industry as an attempt to win customers from competing regional airlines.

Now read question 91 in your test book and answer it.

Now read question 92 in your test book and answer it.

Questions 93 and 94 refer to the following recording.

Man: Thank you for calling our computer helpline. If you need assistance with one of our software packages, press one. If you need the names of qualified service personnel in your area, press two. If you would like an update on our newest products, press three. Otherwise, stay on the line and a customer service representative will assist you.

Now read question 93 in your test book and answer it.

Now read question 94 in your test book and answer it.

Questions 95 through 97 refer to the following announcement.

Man: Welcome aboard Flight six-two-seven to Houston. We'll be flying today at a cruising altitude of thirty-five thousand feet. Our flying time will be two hours and forty minutes, putting us at our gate at four forty-seven Houston time. The weather there is sunny and seventy degrees. Please sit back, relax, and enjoy your trip.

Now read question 95 in your test book and answer it.

Now read question 96 in your test book and answer it.

Now read question 97 in your test book and answer it.

GO ON TO THE NEXT PAGE

620 TRANSCRIPTS

Questions 98 through 100 refer to the following news item.

Man: Due to the large amounts of rain in the area, many people have had to leave their homes and stay in relief shelters until the flooding subsides. Food supplies at the relief centers are running low. We are asking for help from the public to increase our food supplies. If you can donate food, contact this radio station for the address of the food collection center nearest you.

Now read question 98 in your test book and answer it.

Now read question 99 in your test book and answer it.

Now read question 100 in your test book and answer it.

This is the end of the Listening Comprehension portion of the test.

Model Test 3 Listening Comprehension

> **Part I: Picture**
>
> Directions: In your test book, you will see a picture. On the compact disc, you will hear four statements. Choose the statement that most closely matches the picture and fill in the corresponding oval on your answer sheet.

1. Look at the picture marked number 1 in your test book.
   (A) All the plates are empty.
   (B) The waiter's taking an order.
   (C) The woman is watching the servers.
   (D) The menu is on the table.

2. Look at the picture marked number 2 in your test book.
   (A) The joggers are stretching.
   (B) Loggers can test their skills with a saw.
   (C) Many races live here.
   (D) The runners pass the building.

3. Look at the picture marked number 3 in your test book.
   (A) The sports equipment is all set up.
   (B) The couple is reading the radar.
   (C) The laboratory coats are on the hook.
   (D) The technicians are standing next to the equipment.

4. Look at the picture marked number 4 in your test book.
   (A) The highway is under construction.
   (B) The officer directs traffic.
   (C) The workers are moving heavy equipment.
   (D) The trucks are loaded with stone.

5. Look at the picture marked number 5 in your test book.
   (A) The people are standing in the rain.
   (B) The passengers are ready to board.
   (C) The train has just departed.
   (D) The grain is rye or wheat.

6. Look at the picture marked number 6 in your test book.
   (A) The trucks are being weighed.
   (B) Shoppers are in the supermarket.
   (C) The trucks are being loaded.
   (D) Vandals have removed the tires.

GO ON TO THE NEXT PAGE

7. Look at the picture marked number 7 in your test book.
   (A) Several carts are in the field.
   (B) The plant grows tall in the sun.
   (C) The building is dilapidated.
   (D) Cars are parked in front of the factory.

8. Look at the picture marked number 8 in your test book.
   (A) One side of the office is all windows.
   (B) The supervisor is explaining the procedure.
   (C) The team is on the field.
   (D) The workers are commuting.

9. Look at the picture marked number 9 in your test book.
   (A) Guests are being seated.
   (B) Dinner is being served.
   (C) The waiters set the table.
   (D) The table is set for two.

10. Look at the picture marked number 10 in your test book.
    (A) The movie theater is empty.
    (B) The speaker addresses the audience.
    (C) The audience is demanding answers.
    (D) The brick wall is worn and crumbling.

11. Look at the picture marked number 11 in your test book.
    (A) The woman is washing beakers.
    (B) The conductor takes a bow.
    (C) The bottles are on the shelf in the laboratory.
    (D) The scientist performs an experiment.

12. Look at the picture marked number 12 in your test book.
    (A) Stairs go up the storage tank.
    (B) The roof is pointed.
    (C) It's a scientific model of the sun.
    (D) The barbed wire fence keeps out trespassers.

13. Look at the picture marked number 13 in your test book.
    (A) The elevator is going down.
    (B) A flag hangs across the street.
    (C) A parade is passing by.
    (D) The cathedral is elegant.

14. Look at the picture marked number 14 in your test book.
    (A) Smog covers the city.
    (B) The service attendant is behind the car.
    (C) Both cars stopped at the toll booth.
    (D) The man isn't wearing a hat.

15. Look at the picture marked number 15 in your test book.
    (A) The students study mathematics.
    (B) The equator circles the globe.
    (C) The chalkboard is blank.
    (D) The officers are discussing chemistry.

16. Look at the picture marked number 16 in your test book.
    (A) The women are waiting by the phone.
    (B) The telephone is on the table.
    (C) The statues stand in front of the building.
    (D) The station is crowded.

17. Look at the picture marked number 17 in your test book.
    (A) The operator is walking away.
    (B) The man is talking on the phone.
    (C) The captain is issuing orders.
    (D) The panel is going haywire.

18. Look at the picture marked number 18 in your test book.
    (A) The soft drink machine offers good variety.
    (B) Bottles are stored on shelves.
    (C) The worker inspects the process.
    (D) The worker is filling the bottles with syrup.

19. Look at the picture marked number 19 in your test book.
    (A) The printers are behind the men.
    (B) The men are operating a switchboard.
    (C) The laboratory is used to store chemicals.
    (D) The clutter is distracting.

20. Look at the picture marked number 20 in your test book.
    (A) The highways pass over one another.
    (B) Pedestrians are waiting.
    (C) The roads are under repair.
    (D) The road parallels a river.

GO ON TO THE NEXT PAGE

Part II: Question-Response

<u>Directions:</u> On the compact disc, you will hear a question and three possible answers. Choose the answer that most closely answers the question and fill in the corresponding oval on your answer sheet.

21. How hungry are you?
    (A) Not very. I had a late lunch.
    (B) I've never been to Hungary.
    (C) I'm thirty years old.

22. Do you play basketball?
    (A) Yes, I emptied the wastebasket.
    (B) The game was already over.
    (C) Actually, swimming is my sport.

23. Who is in charge of public relations?
    (A) The public address system is on.
    (B) The marketing manager is.
    (C) There is no charge to the public.

24. How far is the museum from here?
    (A) Most of the paintings are modern.
    (B) It's about a ten-minute walk.
    (C) It was about a decade ago.

25. When did you buy your house?
    (A) When we got married.
    (B) We drove by it this morning.
    (C) It was very expensive.

26. What is the book about?
    (A) The book is on the shelf.
    (B) It costs about five dollars.
    (C) It's a war story.

27. Where are the keys to the front door?
    (A) They're in the receptionist's desk.
    (B) Close the door if you're cold.
    (C) I locked the door.

28. Which train should we take?
    (A) It won't rain today.
    (B) They teach a good class at the local college.
    (C) Let's take the express.

29. Why aren't these copies ready yet?
    (A) The copier is out of paper.
    (B) The cops are on the corner.
    (C) I already read it.

30. When is he expected?
    (A) For a month.
    (B) She waited too long.
    (C) Around 2 P.M.

31. How much was your hotel bill?
    (A) I paid with a credit card.
    (B) Over thirty stories.
    (C) Just under $500.

32. Where did you learn to program computers?
    (A) I learned on the job.
    (B) I earned enough.
    (C) You can purchase a computer through the mail.

33. Why are you always on time?
    (A) I don't have a watch.
    (B) I hate to be late.
    (C) I always prefer lime to lemon.

34. Have you seen this film?
    (A) No, I never go to the movies.
    (B) My camera is out of film.
    (C) Yes, I've been there.

35. Who won the tennis match?
    (A) I don't smoke.
    (B) No, there were nine not ten.
    (C) The game was canceled.

36. What was the purpose of this visit?
    (A) The visitors left early.
    (B) He just wanted to say hello.
    (C) The proposal was on the list.

37. Which season do you prefer?
    (A) I always use salt and pepper.
    (B) I referred them to you.
    (C) Summer is my favorite.

38. How wide is this room?
    (A) About fourteen feet.
    (B) The slides are in the next room.
    (C) I don't know why.

GO ON TO THE NEXT PAGE

39. When does the mail come?
   (A) Every morning at eleven.
   (B) Milk is served at three.
   (C) You're welcome.

40. Where's the bank?
   (A) It's across from the post office.
   (B) You needn't thank me.
   (C) The ink is in the top drawer.

41. Is it going to rain today?
   (A) He's going tomorrow.
   (B) Why don't you complain?
   (C) I don't think so. The sky is clear.

42. How much should I tip the waiter?
   (A) I tipped the boat over.
   (B) Fifteen percent is sufficient.
   (C) Ten children waded in the water.

43. Who designed your house?
   (A) The same architect that did our office building.
   (B) I resigned this morning.
   (C) I use a mouse with my computer.

44. When did you arrive?
   (A) I'll be there around midnight tomorrow.
   (B) Last night's telecast was live from New York.
   (C) I got in early last night.

45. What is this shirt made of?
   (A) It was made in Hong Kong.
   (B) It's made of cotton.
   (C) Insert the cassette into the recorder.

46. Why doesn't this calculator work?
   (A) Maybe the batteries are dead.
   (B) Calcutta is in India.
   (C) No one works on Sunday.

47. Where did you study English?
   (A) The students are not going to England.
   (B) I studied it at school.
   (C) For six years.

48. Which sweater fits me better?
   (A) These sweat pants are too large for you.
   (B) The weather is better in the south.
   (C) The wool one fits you perfectly.

49. What time do you have?
    (A) I'm sorry. I don't have a watch.
    (B) I have both yours and mine.
    (C) In about twenty minutes.

50. Would you close the window please?
    (A) Of course. Are you cold?
    (B) Here take my clothes.
    (C) All teller windows are open.

GO ON TO THE NEXT PAGE

Part III: Short Conversations

Directions: On the compact disc, you will hear a short conversation. In your test book, you will see a question and four possible answers. Choose the best answer to the question and fill in the corresponding oval on your answer sheet.

51. Man: There's an art show in the park.
    Woman: That sounds like fun. Can we go after work?
    Man: No, it closes at dark. Let's plan it for Sunday.

52. Man: Ms. Noor can issue you some traveler's checks.
    Woman: Thank you. Where do I find her?
    Man: That's her desk on the left.

53. Man: Please stay with the tour. It's easy to get lost in the market district.
    Woman: What should we do if we get separated?
    Man: You should wait by the tour bus at Market Street and Main Street.

54. Woman: I never have exact change for the bus.
    Man: Next time you cash a check, ask for a roll of quarters.
    Woman: That's a good idea. Then I'll always have enough coins.

55. Woman: We need a chart to illustrate these market trends.
    Man: I'll do that. My computer has an excellent graphics program.
    Woman: Great. You can do the graph of the sales figures, too.

56. Man: I'm sorry. You can't smoke here.
    Woman: I thought the last three rows were designated for smoking.
    Man: No. This entire flight is nonsmoking.

57. Man: Could you clean room two-thirty-five, please?
    Woman: Of course. It's on my schedule at eleven o'clock.
    Man: Can you do it earlier? That guest is having a business meeting then.

58. Man: I have your resume and I'd like to talk to you about possible positions.
    Woman: That will be fine. When would you like to meet?
    Man: How about Thursday at nine-thirty?

59. Man: The carpet is wet here. I'll call the janitor to mop the water up.
    Woman: Call the building engineer instead.
    Man: Good idea. Then he can fix the leak if there is one.

60. Man: How long will the repairs to the television set take?
    Woman: We'll send the order today. It will take two weeks to get the replacement parts, and another week to install them.
    Man: That's longer than I expected.

61. Man: Isn't that the new managing director?
    Woman: The man with the glasses? Yes, that is.
    Man: I'll introduce myself.

62. Man: Here is your room key. The elevators are on your left.
    Woman: Can I get a morning paper tomorrow?
    Man: Certainly. A paper can be delivered directly to your room.

63. Man: Where is Mr. Chung? He's due to address the meeting this morning.
    Woman: He's probably caught in traffic.
    Man: We can show the film first if he's late.

64. Man: I'd like to pay for this sweater by check.
    Woman: I'll need to see two forms of identification.
    Man: Here are a driver's license and a credit card.

65. Man: How do I get to the history museum?
    Woman: Go through the park, past the capitol building, and turn left at the train station.
    Man: Thank you. That sounds easy to find.

66. Man: I try to exercise, but I don't have the time. I'm too busy working.
    Woman: Exercise during your lunch hour. I usually take a walk.
    Man: I always use my lunch hour to eat lunch!

67. Man: The post office returned this letter I mailed to the Harris Company.
    Woman: No wonder. There is no street by that name.
    Man: Oh. I'll have to check the address again.

68. Man: I like the way they redecorated the lobby.
    Woman: The white walls make it brighter.
    Man: Yes. It never had enough light before.

69. Man: I'm pleased to meet you.
    Woman: The pleasure is mine.
    Man: I'm sure you'll enjoy working here.

70. Man: Should the desk go by the door or by the window?
    Woman: By the door. You'll be able to see who enters the office.
    Man: Yes, but there's more light by the window.

71. Man: The special project is behind schedule. We need more people on it.
    Woman: Who is available to work on it?
    Man: No one. We should hire some temporary help.

GO ON TO THE NEXT PAGE

630 TRANSCRIPTS

72. **Man:** We need the auditorium for a meeting Tuesday morning.
    Woman: I'm sorry. It's scheduled all day. Can you use the conference room?
    Man: No, that's not really big enough.

73. **Man:** Do you have any bags to check?
    Woman: No, I'll carry my suitcase onto the plane.
    Man: I'm sorry, but that suitcase is too big. You'll have to let us take it.

74. **Man:** I've let the phone ring, but there's no answer from the loading dock.
    Woman: It's ten o'clock. That's when they take their coffee break.
    Man: Oh, that explains it. I'll call back in fifteen minutes.

75. **Man:** This is the oldest theater in the city.
    Woman: Is it still being used?
    Man: Yes. They have special productions here twice a year.

76. **Man:** The copier is working, but the printer isn't.
    Woman: Should I call a repairperson?
    Man: No, I'll call the manufacturer. It's still under warranty.

77. **Woman:** Our flying time today will be two hours and twenty minutes.
    Man: Will we make our connecting flights?
    Woman: Yes. I'll have a list of gates before we land.

78. **Man:** I have a flat tire. Where is the nearest garage?
    Woman: There is a gas station about half a mile along the road.
    Man: Thank you. I hope it's open.

79. **Man:** The motion of the train always makes me sleepy.
    Woman: You should be rested by morning, then.
    Man: Yes, I'll probably sleep all night.

80. **Man:** What do you think of the recommendations in the report?
    Woman: I'll have to read them before I can comment.
    Man: I thought you'd seen them already.

Part IV: Short Talks

<u>Directions:</u> On the compact disc, you will hear a short talk. In your test book, you will see several questions on the talk and four possible answers. Choose the best answer to the question and fill in the corresponding oval on your answer sheet.

<u>Questions 81 and 82</u> refer to the following announcement.

Man: The telephone number you have called is not in service. Please check the number in your telephone directory. Or, stay on the line and a customer service representative will be with you shortly.

Now read question 81 in your test book and answer it.

Now read question 82 in your test book and answer it.

<u>Questions 83 and 84</u> refer to the following announcement.

Woman: A contaminated-water alert has been issued for this area. It is possible that agricultural bacteria have invaded the water supply. Residents are asked to boil water for five minutes before using it for drinking or cooking. This will make the water safe.

Now read question 83 in your test book and answer it.

Now read question 84 in your test book and answer it.

<u>Questions 85 and 86</u> refer to the following advertisement.

Woman: Are you bored with your current job? Get computer training and start a new career. Our computer school can train you in just six months on the most popular business software. Job placement assistance is available at the end of the course.

Now read question 85 in your test book and answer it.

Now read question 86 in your test book and answer it.

<u>Questions 87 and 88</u> refer to the following announcement.

Man: The Northeast train bound for New York and Boston is leaving in ten minutes from Track 27. Passengers for New York should board at the front of the train. Passengers for Boston should board at the rear.

Now read question 87 in your test book and answer it.

Now read question 88 in your test book and answer it.

GO ON TO THE NEXT PAGE

632 TRANSCRIPTS

Questions 89 and 90 refer to the following recording.

Man: You have reached the Smith Company. Our business hours are eight A.M. to six P.M. Monday through Friday. If you call back during those hours, we will be happy to assist you. Or, you may contact us in writing at one-seven-one-one Northwood Parkway, Greenville, California, 97286.

Now read question 89 in your test book and answer it.

Now read question 90 in your test book and answer it.

Questions 91 and 92 refer to the following announcement.

Woman: The Royal Hotel currently has positions open for desk clerks, waiters, and housekeepers. No experience is required; we will train new employees. Apply in person to the hotel manager. Good starting wage and opportunity for advancement.

Now read question 91 in your test book and answer it.

Now read question 92 in your test book and answer it.

Questions 93 and 94 refer to the following advertisement.

Man: Our efficient electronic office mail communication system saves you both time and money. Forget about making copies and checking distribution lists. Send memos almost instantly to your entire staff. Send entire documents to colleagues without spending time at the printer. Save on paper and wear and tear on the printer.

Now read question 93 in your test book and answer it.

Now read question 94 in your test book and answer it.

Questions 95 through 97 refer to the following announcement.

Woman: A heat-wave alert has been issued for the city and outlying suburbs. Temperatures are expected to be over one hundred degrees. Residents should follow these simple precautions to avoid heatstroke. Wear light-colored, loose-fitting clothes. Drink plenty of water, stay out of direct sunlight, and avoid strenuous exercise.

Now read question 95 in your test book and answer it.

Now read question 96 in your test book and answer it.

Now read question 97 in your test book and answer it.

Questions 98 through 100 refer to the following announcement.

Man: Many busy executives get work done by establishing a quiet hour. Ask your staff not to disturb you during this time, except in emergencies. Ask your secretary to hold telephone calls. Close your office door. Use this time to concentrate on demanding tasks.

Now read question 98 in your test book and answer it.

Now read question 99 in your test book and answer it.

Now read question 100 in your test book and answer it.

This is the end of the Listening Comprehension portion of the test.

Model Test 4 Listening Comprehension

> **Part I: Picture**
>
> Directions: In your test book, you will see a picture. On the compact disc, you will hear four statements. Choose the statement that most closely matches the picture and fill in the corresponding oval on your answer sheet.

1. Look at the picture marked number 1 in your test book.
   (A) The man checks his bag.
   (B) The woman weighs the man.
   (C) The clients are closing the deal.
   (D) The luggage is on a trolley.

2. Look at the picture marked number 2 in your test book.
   (A) The table is set for four.
   (B) The diners seem pleased.
   (C) The waiter puts the silverware on the table.
   (D) The officer is bowing.

3. Look at the picture marked number 3 in your test book.
   (A) The meat is on display.
   (B) The meeting is in session.
   (C) Only four people attended.
   (D) The track meet is held today.

4. Look at the picture marked number 4 in your test book.
   (A) The trees are cut into lumber.
   (B) The pipeline runs down the mountain.
   (C) Water comes from the well.
   (D) Oil is transported by tankers.

5. Look at the picture marked number 5 in your test book.
   (A) The laboratory workers are in lab coats.
   (B) The doctor is examining the chart.
   (C) The woman is reading to the patient.
   (D) X rays are behind the doctor.

6. Look at the picture marked number 6 in your test book.
   (A) The lamp is on the table.
   (B) The mother sits next to the father.
   (C) The family is having dinner.
   (D) The boys are throwing food.

7. Look at the picture marked number 7 in your test book.
   (A) The customer is ordering a meal.
   (B) They are learning to read.
   (C) The waiter is approaching the customer.
   (D) The guests are waiting to order.

8. Look at the picture marked number 8 in your test book.
   (A) The terminals are set back-to-back.
   (B) The rows of corn are straight.
   (C) The students learn how to use computers.
   (D) They're all on the same page of the manual.

9. Look at the picture marked number 9 in your test book.
   (A) The surgeon gives himself an injection.
   (B) The man wears protective clothing.
   (C) The scientist experiments with guinea pigs.
   (D) The pharmacy serves hospital patients.

10. Look at the picture marked number 10 in your test book.
    (A) The girls are playing soccer.
    (B) The fish net is drying.
    (C) The goalie is holding the ball.
    (D) The field is covered with flowers.

11. Look at the picture marked number 11 in your test book.
    (A) The port handles heavy traffic.
    (B) The police officer stops the thief at the door.
    (C) The doorman carries a bag.
    (D) The pilot prepares to take off.

12. Look at the picture marked number 12 in your test book.
    (A) People are waiting for their flight to board.
    (B) Luggage is scattered throughout the hall.
    (C) People are planning for their trip.
    (D) Passengers get their luggage.

13. Look at the picture marked number 13 in your test book.
    (A) The tanker is docked by the storage facility.
    (B) The service station attendant is pumping gas.
    (C) The sailboat is in the harbor.
    (D) The island is being pounded by waves.

14. Look at the picture marked number 14 in your test book.
    (A) The man refers to the map.
    (B) The storm is approaching rapidly.
    (C) His glasses are bent and crooked.
    (D) The speaker is gesturing upwards.

GO ON TO THE NEXT PAGE

15. Look at the picture marked number 15 in your test book.
    (A) The messenger carries a mailbag.
    (B) The pants have a white stripe.
    (C) The messenger knocks on the door.
    (D) The manager delivers the bill.

16. Look at the picture marked number 16 in your test book.
    (A) The shopping bags are large.
    (B) The pillows are stuffed with cotton.
    (C) The cargo is being unloaded.
    (D) The ship is going through customs.

17. Look at the picture marked number 17 in your test book.
    (A) The clients are preparing A-V equipment.
    (B) The people are relaxing.
    (C) The waitress serves the food.
    (D) The woman is conversing with the men.

18. Look at the picture marked number 18 in your test book.
    (A) The laborers are eating lunch.
    (B) The store is crowded.
    (C) There are many pedestrians.
    (D) The shopkeeper repairs bicycles.

19. Look at the picture marked number 19 in your test book.
    (A) The oil rig is under water.
    (B) Both men are wearing gloves.
    (C) The workers are talking over a distance.
    (D) The plumbers repair the pipes.

20. Look at the picture marked number 20 in your test book.
    (A) There are walls on both sides of the track.
    (B) The company has a monopoly.
    (C) The train track runs underground.
    (D) The grain elevator is near the railroad.

Part II: Question-Response

<u>Directions</u>: On the compact disc, you will hear a question and three possible answers. Choose the answer that most closely answers the question and fill in the corresponding oval on your answer sheet.

21. Who's there?
    (A) It's mine.
    (B) Over here.
    (C) It must be Joan.

22. What are you thinking about?
    (A) The boat is sinking.
    (B) I'm thinking about my vacation.
    (C) Your ink pad is blue.

23. When did he leave her?
    (A) Sometime last night.
    (B) The leaves turn yellow in the fall.
    (C) Her lawyer signed the deed.

24. Where are you staying?
    (A) At a hotel.
    (B) Even if they say no.
    (C) I got a stain here.

25. Which is your fax number—this one or that one?
    (A) My back feels numb.
    (B) The one that ends in fifty-six.
    (C) I'm not very fast.

26. Why is no one here?
    (A) The room is crowded.
    (B) We're just too early.
    (C) I cannot hear very well.

27. How was the weather?
    (A) It rained every day.
    (B) She was wearing a hat.
    (C) The clothes are still wet.

28. Would you like milk in your coffee?
    (A) Milk is good for your cough.
    (B) The fee was approved.
    (C) Just sugar.

GO ON TO THE NEXT PAGE

29. Who opened this letter?
    (A) He let her come to the opera.
    (B) She used this pen.
    (C) I opened it by mistake.

30. When did the conference begin?
    (A) It started last Monday.
    (B) The day after tomorrow.
    (C) The can is made of tin.

31. Which time is better for you—morning or afternoon?
    (A) This watch is better.
    (B) I'm free after lunch.
    (C) It's time to get up.

32. How long is the train ride?
    (A) The bride is very tall.
    (B) It's very short—only two hours.
    (C) There are ten cars on the train.

33. What is your occupation?
    (A) I'm an accountant.
    (B) I'll pay close attention.
    (C) The room is occupied.

34. Are you coming or not?
    (A) He is not coming.
    (B) Yes, but I'll be late.
    (C) They didn't come last night.

35. Where are you sitting?
    (A) My seat is on the aisle.
    (B) I live in New York City.
    (C) The baby-sitter is at home.

36. Why are you so sleepy?
    (A) The water is very deep.
    (B) I was awake all night.
    (C) I love sweet peas.

37. Who was on the phone?
    (A) It was the travel agent calling about our trip.
    (B) I left my work at home.
    (C) The telephone is on the desk.

38. Is there any more food?
    (A) The supermarket is crowded.
    (B) He is still in a bad mood.
    (C) There's more in the kitchen.

39. How often do you travel by train?
    (A) It rains frequently.
    (B) I take the train every day.
    (C) A plane leaves every hour.

40. What color shall we paint the hall?
    (A) Let's leave it white.
    (B) He's over six feet tall.
    (C) The painting hangs on the wall.

41. Which tie should I wear with my gray suit?
    (A) I always get migraines at work.
    (B) I tried, but I couldn't do it.
    (C) Either the red or the blue one.

42. Who met you at the door?
    (A) They bet me I wouldn't come.
    (B) The security guard was at the front door.
    (C) The table is by the door.

43. When do you think you'll be finished?
    (A) In about an hour.
    (B) They finished after me.
    (C) I thought about it yesterday.

44. Why aren't you coming with us?
    (A) We won't go with you.
    (B) I don't feel well.
    (C) I didn't come with you.

45. Are you alone?
    (A) Yes, everyone has gone to lunch.
    (B) Yes, you're lonely.
    (C) No, no one is here.

46. What page is the article on?
    (A) It's on Wednesday.
    (B) Did you look under the bed?
    (C) It's on page two at the bottom of the page.

47. Where should I wait for you?
    (A) You weigh too much already.
    (B) Wait for me on the corner.
    (C) I waited for an hour for you.

48. How much longer will you be on the phone?
    (A) I'll be off in a minute.
    (B) The phone is off the hook.
    (C) The cord is five feet long.

GO ON TO THE NEXT PAGE

49. Has this memo been sent to all departments?
    (A) Yes, it was sent by e-mail.
    (B) The shipping department is on the first floor.
    (C) No, the department store is closed.

50. What was the worst part of your trip?
    (A) The rip was mended by the tailor.
    (B) Don't forget to give a big tip.
    (C) We missed the plane. That was the worst.

Part III: Short Conversations

<u>Directions</u>: On the compact disc, you will hear a short conversation. In your test book, you will see a question and four possible answers. Choose the best answer to the question and fill in the corresponding oval on your answer sheet.

51. Man: What are your store hours?
    Woman: We're open from ten until six, Monday through Friday, and from nine until eight on Saturdays. We're closed on Sundays.
    Man: Thank you.

52. Woman: I'm going to buy some new shoes. These are soaked with rain.
    Man: They certainly are! They're dripping on the carpet.
    Woman: I'll buy shoes that will keep my feet dry.

53. Man: I tried to call you, but there was no answer.
    Woman: I'm sorry. I didn't hear the phone ring.
    Man: You should turn the volume up.

54. Man: It's a beautiful day for a drive.
    Woman: Yes, I'm glad we didn't fly.
    Man: We can see some of the countryside instead.

55. Man: The supervisor would like to see you in his office.
    Woman: Oh, no. I wonder what I did wrong.
    Man: Don't worry. You've been doing a good job.

56. Man: Room three-sixty-five is large and overlooks the hotel pool.
    Woman: Actually, I'd prefer something quieter.
    Man: I'll move you to five-seventeen. It's smaller, but very quiet.

57. Man: Would you like any dessert?
    Woman: No, thank you. I'm full after that delicious dinner.
    Man: I'll just get the check, then.

58. Man: I'll pay with a credit card. Here you are.
    Woman: I'm sorry, sir. This card has expired.
    Man: Put it on this other card, then.

59. Man: Are you free to meet for lunch at twelve?
    Woman: No, I'm busy all day. How about dinner on Tuesday?
    Man: No. I'm tied up then. Let's have breakfast on Wednesday.

GO ON TO THE NEXT PAGE

642 TRANSCRIPTS

60. **Man:** There are three towels missing from room four-sixteen.
    Woman: Are you sure? There are only supposed to be two towels per room.
    Man: Yes, but they asked for two extras last night. This morning, there was just one.

61. **Man:** Here are your tickets and your hotel reservations. Will you need anything else for your trip?
    Woman: Yes, I'd like a rental car.
    Man: We reserved one for you already. Enjoy your trip.

62. **Man:** This subway car is too crowded. Let's wait for the next train.
    Woman: We'll be later getting into the city.
    Man: But at least we'll be able to get seats during the ride.

63. **Man:** This coffee isn't fresh. I'll make a new pot for you.
    Woman: Please don't bother. I'd prefer tea.
    Man: In that case, I'll boil some water.

64. **Man:** May I help you?
    Woman: Yes, I have a ten o'clock appointment with Ms. White.
    Man: Ms. White is expecting you. Her office is on the tenth floor.

65. **Man:** I'd like to leave for the airport by three-thirty.
    Woman: Isn't that a little early?
    Man: Yes, but we will avoid heavy traffic.

66. **Man:** Don't you think this plant will look nice on my desk?
    Woman: You should hang it by the window. It likes natural light.
    Man: Oh, dear. I thought it was a plant for artificial light.

67. **Man:** Would you like a round-trip ticket or one way?
    Woman: Round-trip, please. Is it a direct flight?
    Man: Yes, it's nonstop.

68. **Man:** Mr. Tan was in an accident last night.
    Woman: Is he all right?
    Man: He's going to be fine. But he'll spend one week in the hospital and another three weeks at home.

69. **Man:** My typewriter ribbon broke again!
    Woman: That wouldn't happen if you used a computer.
    Man: Maybe, but some jobs are still easier to do on a typewriter.

70. **Man:** It's very icy this morning. The roads are terrible!
    Woman: Let's change our nine o'clock meeting until one o'clock.
    Man: That's a good idea. With this weather, everyone will be late.

71. **Man:** Could you please turn your radio down a little?
    Woman: Of course. Don't you like music?
    Man: Yes, but not when I'm trying to work.

72. Man: Did you enjoy the museum?
    Woman: Yes, but the tour guide was in such a hurry, I hardly got to see the paintings.
    Man: Maybe you can go back there on your own.

73. Man: I'm sorry I'm late. I got lost trying to find the restaurant.
    Woman: We'll buy you a map of the city after lunch.
    Man: Maybe that will keep me from getting lost next time.

74. Man: Can you help me type this report? I just got it this afternoon, and the deadline is tomorrow.
    Woman: Sure, but I can only stay until seven.
    Man: That's fine. I hope we'll be done by then.

75. Man: Do you drive to work?
    Woman: No, I take the subway. I don't like to park in the city.
    Man: I always drive. I like having the car nearby if I need it.

76. Man: May I speak to Ms. Kim, please?
    Woman: I'm sorry. She's not in. May I have her return your call?
    Man: No, thank you. I won't be near a phone. I'll call back later.

77. Man: Can I help you set up the display?
    Woman: Sure. Let's put it by the door.
    Man: No, people will run into it. We'll put it along the wall.

78. Woman: Ow! I think I hurt my ankle on the stairs.
    Man: Take off your shoe. Can I do anything?
    Woman: Just call the company nurse. It really hurts a lot.

79. Man: Is there a post office around here?
    Woman: Not very close. Go two stops on the bus and turn right.
    Man: I know where that one is. I hoped there was one closer.

80. Man: How often are paychecks issued?
    Woman: Paychecks are given out every two weeks.
    Man: Good. I think that's better than once a month.

Part IV: Short Talks

Directions: On the compact disc, you will hear a short talk. In your test book, you will see several questions on the talk and four possible answers. Choose the best answer to the question and fill in the corresponding oval on your answer sheet.

Questions 81 and 82 refer to the following recording.

Woman: This is the first call for priority boarding for Flight two-nine-four to Minneapolis. Persons with disabilities, senior citizens, and persons traveling with small children are invited to board at this time. Anyone needing extra help may request assistance from a flight attendant.

Now read question 81 in your test book and answer it.

Now read question 82 in your test book and answer it.

Questions 83 and 84 refer to the following advertisement.

Man: Can't find the information you need? Come see our wide selection of technical and professional books. We cover a variety of topic areas in over fifty fields, including computer science, psychology, economics, and international law. If it's not in stock, we'll order it for you!

Now read question 83 in your test book and answer it.

Now read question 84 in your test book and answer it.

Questions 85 and 86 refer to the following weather report.

Woman: This morning will be partly sunny with temperatures in the upper fifties. Increasing cloudiness is expected this afternoon, giving us some rain by early evening and into the night. The rain will continue through the weekend.

Now read question 85 in your test book and answer it.

Now read question 86 in your test book and answer it.

Questions 87 and 88 refer to the following news item.

Man: This is the season when everyone catches colds. Although there is no cure, most colds last only three to five days. To recover as quickly as possible, you can follow a few simple steps. Drink plenty of water and fruit juice. Get lots of rest, and make sure you eat healthy meals.

Now read question 87 in your test book and answer it.

Now read question 88 in your test book and answer it.

MODEL TEST 4 645

Questions 89 and 90 refer to the following advertisement.

Woman: Let Office Caterers take care of your next lunch meeting. We can provide a gourmet box lunch for each of the participants, or set up an elegant buffet right in your conference room. We can also cater your next office party, reception, or breakfast meeting!

Now read question 89 in your test book and answer it.

Now read question 90 in your test book and answer it.

Questions 91 and 92 refer to the following announcement.

Man: This is the green line subway to the shopping mall and northern suburbs. If you want to go to the airport, you're on the wrong train. Get off at this station and catch the next gray line train to the airport.

Now read question 91 in your test book and answer it.

Now read question 92 in your test book and answer it.

Questions 93 and 94 refer to the following announcement.

Woman: Because of the federal holiday, all government offices will be closed on Monday. Schools, banks, and libraries will also be closed. Buses, subways, and other public transportation will operate on a weekend schedule, with no additional buses or trains for rush hour service.

Now read question 93 in your test book and answer it.

Now read question 94 in your test book and answer it.

Questions 95 through 97 refer to the following news item.

Man: The latest survey shows that business travelers have some suggestions for improving hotel service. Most travelers would like hotels to be located closer to shopping and entertainment facilities, rather than in the business district. They also suggest that the hotel restaurants include lighter meals, such as fresh salads and vegetable plates. They request that exercise and recreation facilities at the hotels be open at night as well as during the day, to accommodate business travelers' hectic schedules.

Now read question 95 in your test book and answer it.

Now read question 96 in your test book and answer it.

Now read question 97 in your test book and answer it.

GO ON TO THE NEXT PAGE

Questions 98 through 100 refer to the following recording.

Man: Thank you for calling the City Transit Authority Helpline. We will be glad to help you find your way around the city by public transportation. Please have the following information available: your point of departure, where you are going, and the day of the week and time you would like to travel. You will want to have a pencil and paper handy to write down the bus numbers, subway lines, and transfer points.

Now read question 98 in your test book and answer it.

Now read question 99 in your test book and answer it.

Now read question 100 in your test book and answer it.

This is the end of the Listening Comprehension portion of the test.

Model Test 5 Listening Comprehension

Part I: Picture

Directions: In your test book, you will see a picture. On the compact disc, you will hear four statements. Choose the statement that most closely matches the picture and fill in the corresponding oval on your answer sheet.

---

1. Look at the picture marked number 1 in your test book.
   (A) The woman is getting a loan.
   (B) She's using small change to pay.
   (C) She is using a public phone.
   (D) There's a long line at the phone.

2. Look at the picture marked number 2 in your test book.
   (A) The train is in the station.
   (B) The passengers are waiting for the plane.
   (C) The computers are in a row.
   (D) Most people commute by bus.

3. Look at the picture marked number 3 in your test book.
   (A) The doctor examines his toes.
   (B) The dentist is with a patient.
   (C) The man is brushing his teeth.
   (D) The carpenter has a new drill.

4. Look at the picture marked number 4 in your test book.
   (A) The counter is under a window.
   (B) Money is printed at the mint.
   (C) The man prescribes medicine.
   (D) The technician does lab work.

5. Look at the picture marked number 5 in your test book.
   (A) A family is traveling together.
   (B) The child is reading a book.
   (C) Their meals have been served.
   (D) The child sits between the parents.

6. Look at the picture marked number 6 in your test book.
   (A) The maid is finishing the room.
   (B) The luggage is on the floor.
   (C) The clothes are folded on the bed.
   (D) The bed is made.

GO ON TO THE NEXT PAGE

7. Look at the picture marked number 7 in your test book.
    (A) The car is in an accident.
    (B) A robot assembles a car.
    (C) The machinery is locked.
    (D) The vehicle is under inspection.

8. Look at the picture marked number 8 in your test book.
    (A) The woman is in front of the camera.
    (B) The couple are watching TV.
    (C) The technician uses a microscope.
    (D) The cameraman looks very mobile.

9. Look at the picture marked number 9 in your test book.
    (A) The photographer takes a picture.
    (B) The lid covers the bin.
    (C) The woman photocopies a document.
    (D) The secretary is using the fax machine.

10. Look at the picture marked number 10 in your test book.
    (A) The chef cooks the fish.
    (B) The fishing boat sets off to sea.
    (C) The fish is packed for export.
    (D) The meat is canned for sale.

11. Look at the picture marked number 11 in your test book.
    (A) The conference is in session.
    (B) The man is at his desk.
    (C) The worker is signing papers.
    (D) The papers are strewn about randomly.

12. Look at the picture marked number 12 in your test book.
    (A) Their work station is very tidy.
    (B) There are pads of paper in the drawer.
    (C) They're talking on microphones.
    (D) The workers are intent.

13. Look at the picture marked number 13 in your test book.
    (A) Cars are parked on the sidewalk.
    (B) The buildings are over ten stories tall.
    (C) The pedestrians are waiting at the curb.
    (D) The traffic light is at the corner.

14. Look at the picture marked number 14 in your test book.
    (A) The woman needs new spectacles.
    (B) The smoker wants a match.
    (C) The crowd watches the game.
    (D) The players accept their trophies.

15. Look at the picture marked number 15 in your test book.
    (A) The technicians are punching in on a time clock.
    (B) The elevator button is pressed.
    (C) Most of the screens are blank.
    (D) Two technicians work in the control room.

16. Look at the picture marked number 16 in your test book.
    (A) Smoke rises in front of the mountain.
    (B) The forest is on fire.
    (C) The campers burn a small log.
    (D) The plant blooms at sunset.

17. Look at the picture marked number 17 in your test book.
    (A) The overhead bins are open.
    (B) There are a few empty seats.
    (C) The middle class will be taxed.
    (D) The flight attendants are seated.

18. Look at the picture marked number 18 in your test book.
    (A) The woman is clearing the table.
    (B) She's brewing a pot of coffee.
    (C) She is taking her tip.
    (D) The clerk accepts reservations.

19. Look at the picture marked number 19 in your test book.
    (A) The speaker is in front of a window.
    (B) The man is putting on his suit.
    (C) The speaker points to the map.
    (D) The optometrist is lecturing on lenses.

20. Look at the picture marked number 20 in your test book.
    (A) The worker is wearing protective glasses.
    (B) The man is using binoculars.
    (C) The plant is billowing smoke.
    (D) Chemistry class meets today.

GO ON TO THE NEXT PAGE

Part II: Question-Response

Directions: On the compact disc, you will hear a question and three possible answers. Choose the answer that most closely answers the question and fill in the corresponding oval on your answer sheet.

21. Where were you waiting?
    (A) I was waiting on the corner.
    (B) I weigh the same as you.
    (C) Because it was raining.

22. Which shop sells children's books?
    (A) The library has lots of books.
    (B) There's a children's bookstore in the shopping center.
    (C) I read books to my children.

23. Why don't you join us for dinner?
    (A) I didn't join the club until December.
    (B) Thank you. I'd love to.
    (C) These coins are thinner.

24. When did you finish the project?
    (A) Late last night.
    (B) The slide was projected on the screen.
    (C) The horse finished the race.

25. What are your plans for this afternoon?
    (A) The plane leaves at noon.
    (B) I think I'll play golf.
    (C) The planning meeting was yesterday.

26. Excuse me. Is this the express train?
    (A) Express mail is a one-day service.
    (B) You may leave the room.
    (C) No, it's across the platform.

27. Who delivered the package?
    (A) The housekeeper packed the bags.
    (B) A messenger brought it this morning.
    (C) She won't tell her age.

28. How will we get to the airport?
    (A) The plane is late.
    (B) They met us at the port.
    (C) We'll take a taxi.

29. Which newspapers do you read?
    (A) The magazine is at the newsstand.
    (B) I already read that book.
    (C) I only read the morning papers.

30. When will you return?
    (A) I'll be back after lunch.
    (B) She returned the book.
    (C) Take the first right turn.

31. Do you often stay at this hotel?
    (A) No, usually I play at my club.
    (B) Yes, I always stay here.
    (C) I added this telephone bill.

32. What type of movies do you like?
    (A) I'm moving to a quiet neighborhood.
    (B) I like my meat rare.
    (C) I prefer comedies.

33. Why was the flight canceled?
    (A) There was some mechanical problem.
    (B) The fight lasted only five minutes.
    (C) She can sell anything.

34. Which suitcase is yours?
    (A) Mine is the black one on the left.
    (B) This suit is Italian.
    (C) I spoke to her about this case.

35. Where are the supplies kept?
    (A) The floor was swept this morning.
    (B) In the room at the end of the hall.
    (C) We had supper after work.

36. How was your vacation?
    (A) The room was vacant.
    (B) There are flags from all nations.
    (C) Very relaxing, thank you.

37. Did you turn your computer off?
    (A) No, I always leave it on.
    (B) The lights are turned off at midnight.
    (C) This is my first computer.

38. Who attended the seminar?
    (A) The doctor attended to the patients.
    (B) All senior management went.
    (C) They came at ten.

GO ON TO THE NEXT PAGE

39. What's for lunch?
    (A) I think it's chicken salad.
    (B) It's at noon.
    (C) We're having two guests.

40. How many chairs are in the room?
    (A) There are ten.
    (B) The room number is six-o-two.
    (C) About six feet high.

41. Where is the software manual?
    (A) This shirt I'm wearing is soft.
    (B) It's on the bookshelf.
    (C) He's a man you know well.

42. When did you last put gas in the car?
    (A) The oil refinery opened in December.
    (B) The elastic stretches far.
    (C) I filled the tank two days ago.

43. What caused the forest fire?
    (A) We fired the receptionist last week.
    (B) Lightning struck a tree.
    (C) Because he went away for a rest.

44. Which bus goes downtown?
    (A) The number 4 bus goes downtown.
    (B) Most of us live in town.
    (C) We must go soon.

45. Why haven't you written me?
    (A) The letters are on the desk.
    (B) You will write me soon.
    (C) I haven't had time to write.

46. Shouldn't we leave before it starts to rain?
    (A) The rain caused the leaves to fall.
    (B) Yes, let's take an umbrella with us.
    (C) It didn't rain the night we left.

47. How often do you make international calls?
    (A) I telephone my international clients almost every day.
    (B) I'll call information for the number.
    (C) We have about ten phones.

48. Who needs a ride?
    (A) The tide comes in at six P.M.
    (B) I didn't bring my car today, so I do.
    (C) They tried to finish on time.

49. When would you be able to come?
    (A) I can come any day next week.
    (B) The table is made of wood.
    (C) We came as soon as we could.

50. May I sit down?
    (A) Yes, I went in May.
    (B) Please do. This seat isn't occupied.
    (C) The cushion is filled with down.

654 TRANSCRIPTS

Part III: Short Conversations

<u>Directions</u>: On the compact disc, you will hear a short conversation. In your test book, you will see a question and four possible answers. Choose the best answer to the question and fill in the corresponding oval on your answer sheet.

51. Man: I bought another book, but I can't fit it into my bookcase.
    Woman: You should put some of your old magazines in the trash.
    Man: You're right. Or maybe I should sell them.

52. Man: I'd like to order eggs, toast, and coffee.
    Woman: Certainly, sir. Cream and sugar?
    Man: No, thank you. I'll drink it black.

53. Woman: My car makes a loud noise when I slow down.
    Man: The brakes may be bad. I'll have our mechanic take a look.
    Woman: Thank you. It sounds like a dangerous problem.

54. Man: I hate waiting for the subway. It's a waste of time.
    Woman: I always look at the newspaper while I wait for the train.
    Man: That's a good idea.

55. Man: Front desk.
    Woman: I'm in room six-two-four. I'm afraid the television set doesn't work.
    Man: We'll send someone up right away.

56. Woman: Can you order some sandwiches for the meeting?
    Man: I thought the meeting was at eleven, not at noon.
    Woman: It is, but we'll need to work through lunch.

57. Man: There seems to be a mistake in my hotel bill.
    Woman: What is the problem?
    Man: I was charged two hundred dollars for three nights, but I only stayed for one.

58. Woman: It's hot and stuffy in here.
    Man: I'll open the window.
    Woman: That will help some. But we need air-conditioning.

59. Man: This coffeepot is really dirty.
    Woman: There's a small kitchen on the sixth floor.
    Man: Oh, good. I can wash it there.

60. Man: I'm glad to be off that plane. Shall we catch a cab?
    Woman: First I have to get my suitcase at the baggage claim.
    Man: That means we'll be stuck here for a while.

61. Man: I can't get this fax to go through.
    Woman: Make sure you are dialing the fax number, not the phone number.
    Man: Maybe that's the problem. I'll check the number.

62. Man: It's a beautiful day. Let's have lunch at the sidewalk cafe.
    Woman: I brought a sandwich from home. I'm going to eat it in the park.
    Man: I'll buy a sandwich and meet you there.

63. Man: Do you have the number for the sales manager in your phone log?
    Woman: No, I don't. Look it up in the company directory.
    Man: He's moved to a new office. The directory has the old number.

64. Man: Can you take a picture of that monument?
    Woman: Oh, no! I must have left my camera at the hotel.
    Man: We can still use mine, even though it's not as good as yours.

65. Man: What do you do in your spare time?
    Woman: I like to cook and play golf.
    Man: I'm no good at golf, but I do like to eat!

66. Man: Don't throw the white paper away. Put it in this box and recycle it.
    Woman: What should I do with this green paper?
    Man: That goes in a separate box here.

67. Man: Here is your book. The loan period is two weeks.
    Woman: What if I don't bring it back on time?
    Man: The fine is twenty-five cents for each day the book is overdue.

68. Woman: I'd like to buy a newspaper. Is there a newsstand nearby?
    Man: No, there isn't. Please take my paper. I'm through reading it.
    Woman: No, thank you. I prefer a different paper.

69. Man: Does the waitress take the check?
    Woman: No, we pay at the register.
    Man: I'll leave her a tip at the table, though.

70. Woman: What a beautiful view!
    Man: Yes, I'm lucky to have this office overlooking the park.
    Woman: My office faces the parking lot!

71. Man: The monthly statement details the activity in your checking account.
    Woman: What about my savings account?
    Man: We can send you a combined statement about both accounts.

72. Man: I reserved a room with a king-sized bed. This room has two double beds.
    Woman: I'm sorry sir. We'll move you to another room immediately.
    Man: Thank you. I would appreciate it.

GO ON TO THE NEXT PAGE

73. Man: This copy came out in black and white. It should be in color.
    Woman: This printer is black and white only. The color printer is on the fourth floor.
    Man: Then I'll try printing it there.

74. Man: I must remember to reserve a rental car.
    Woman: Oh, I thought you were flying to the conference.
    Man: I am, but I'll need a car while I'm there.

75. Man: The waiters need extra help setting up for the banquet.
    Woman: Ask the housekeeper if her staff can help.
    Man: I don't think so. They are still busy cleaning the rooms.

76. Woman: The secretarial job requires word-processing skills.
    Man: I know the two most popular word-processing packages.
    Woman: Good. Then the next thing we'll do is test your typing speed.

77. Man: The training film is missing.
    Woman: Oh, no. The training session starts in half an hour.
    Man: Let's call human resources. They'll have a second copy.

78. Man: My feet hurt after all the walking we did today.
    Woman: Why don't you soak them in some hot water?
    Man: I will, as soon as I take my shoes off.

79. Man: I have tickets for the five o'clock flight.
    Woman: Then you'll arrive here at seven. That's a little late.
    Man: Yes, but if the meeting ends by two maybe I can catch the four o'clock flight.

80. Woman: Meet me at the bus at eight tomorrow for a drive through the river valley.
    Man: Do we need to bring anything with us?
    Woman: No, but dress warmly. It will be cold on the river.

Part IV: Short Talks

Directions: On the compact disc, you will hear a short talk. In your test book, you will see several questions on the talk and four possible answers. Choose the best answer to the question and fill in the corresponding oval on your answer sheet.

Questions 81 and 82 refer to the following recording.

Man: Hello. You have reached the Financial Information Service. All of our lines are busy right now. Please stay on the line, and your call will be answered in turn by one of our qualified financial advisors.

Now read question 81 in your test book and answer it.

Now read question 82 in your test book and answer it.

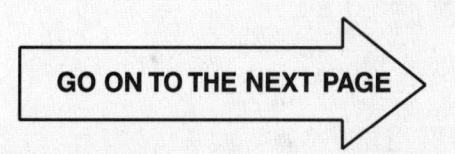

Questions 83 and 84 refer to the following announcement.

Woman: This station is Downtown Central, transfer point for the East-West subway line. Take the elevator or the stairs to the transfer platform on the lower level.

Now read question 83 in your test book and answer it.

Now read question 84 in your test book and answer it.

Questions 85 and 86 refer to the following weather report.

Man: We are expecting partly sunny weather for the area with a high of seventy-two degrees. The wind will be getting stronger this afternoon, with gusts of up to twenty-five miles per hour, calming down again by early evening.

Now read question 85 in your test book and answer it.

Now read question 86 in your test book and answer it.

Questions 87 and 88 refer to the following advertisement.

Woman: Our catalogue now offers even faster service through the Express Delivery Company. For an additional nine-dollar handling charge we guarantee delivery anywhere in the continental United States within two business days. The same two-day service is offered to our customers in Alaska and Hawaii for nineteen dollars.

Now read question 87 in your test book and answer it.

Now read question 88 in your test book and answer it.

GO ON TO THE NEXT PAGE

658 TRANSCRIPTS

Questions 89 and 90 refer to the following announcement.

Man: For the latest information on upcoming events in and around the city, call the City Events Hotline. We can provide you with the times and places of special events, as well as the most convenient public transportation routes to get you there.

Now read question 89 in your test book and answer it.

Now read question 90 in your test book and answer it.

Questions 91 and 92 refer to the following instructions.

Woman: It's very easy to greet a visitor at the reception desk. First, say hello. Then, ask his name, and the name of the person he is here to see. Have him sign the guest book and take a seat in the lobby. Then, call the person he is visiting.

Now read question 91 in your test book and answer it.

Now read question 92 in your test book and answer it.

Questions 93 and 94 refer to the following recording.

Man: Please note the following change in local bus service. Buses on Route 21A will continue to start their route at the current time, but will arrive at the final stop four minutes later. There will be no change in the number of scheduled trips. June fifth is the effective date for this service change.

Now read question 93 in your test book and answer it.

Now read question 94 in your test book and answer it.

Questions 95 through 97 refer to the following advertisement.

Man: Greenway Conference Center can take the problems out of planning your next conference. We can accommodate groups from ten to two hundred. Our meeting rooms can be set up with your choice of state-of-the-art audio-visual equipment. A cafeteria and catering services on-site provide meals and snacks at your request. Our comfortable guest rooms overlook beautiful countryside. Both indoor and outdoor recreation facilities are available.

Now read question 95 in your test book and answer it.

Now read question 96 in your test book and answer it.

Now read question 97 in your test book and answer it.

Questions 98 through 100 refer to the following announcement.

Man: We interrupt this program for a special news bulletin. Due to the violent thunderstorm, neighborhoods throughout the city have lost electrical power. Service crews are already working to restore power in some of these areas, and additional crews are on their way to other sites. Residents are asked to turn off all electrical appliances to prevent potential hazards until power has been restored.

Now read question 98 in your test book and answer it.

Now read question 99 in your test book and answer it.

Now read question 100 in your test book and answer it.

This is the end of the Listening Comprehension portion of the test.

Model Test 6 Listening Comprehension

> **Part I: Picture**
>
> Directions: In your test book, you will see a picture. On the compact disc, you will hear four statements. Choose the statement that most closely matches the picture and fill in the corresponding oval on your answer sheet.

1. Look at the picture marked number 1 in your test book.
   (A) The man is looking in the window.
   (B) The books are under the window.
   (C) The man is cleaning the windows.
   (D) The man is purchasing a textbook.

2. Look at the picture marked number 2 in your test book.
   (A) The island is in the ocean.
   (B) There is water on the floor.
   (C) The bridges cross the river.
   (D) Traffic is tangled in the city.

3. Look at the picture marked number 3 in the test book.
   (A) The musicians are playing.
   (B) They must cancel the play.
   (C) The songbird is on the edge of his chair.
   (D) The players took notes.

4. Look at the picture marked number 4 in your test book.
   (A) The carpenter takes a drink.
   (B) The waiter is pouring water.
   (C) It's pouring down rain.
   (D) The waiter is filling an order.

5. Look at the picture marked number 5 in your test book.
   (A) The tubes transport liquids.
   (B) The wires cross in mid-air.
   (C) The worker is explaining the procedure.
   (D) The technician is on his knees.

6. Look at the picture marked number 6 in your test book.
   (A) The artist draws a portrait.
   (B) The magician does a trick.
   (C) The optician repairs his glasses.
   (D) The tailor stitches a suit.

7. Look at the picture marked number 7 in your test book.
   (A) Clouds of smoke come from the chimneys.
   (B) Their manners are being refined.
   (C) The plant is no longer in operation.
   (D) The clothes will be ironed by five o'clock.

8. Look at the picture marked number 8 in your test book.
   (A) The woman is playing chess.
   (B) The clerk completes the form.
   (C) The technician wears a mask.
   (D) The seamstress sews a dress.

9. Look at the picture marked number 9 in your test book.
   (A) The cruise ship set sail.
   (B) The race is close.
   (C) These boots are on sale.
   (D) The sailboat is in the harbor.

10. Look at the picture marked number 10 in your test book.
    (A) The announcer looks serene.
    (B) The speaker is using a microphone.
    (C) Everyone is singing in harmony.
    (D) The speaker is gesturing towards the chart.

11. Look at the picture marked number 11 in your test book.
    (A) The food sellers are sitting on the ground.
    (B) The supermarket has lots of produce.
    (C) The banana trees are on the hillside.
    (D) The cook chops the vegetables.

12. Look at the picture marked number 12 in your test book.
    (A) The pilot is approaching the helicopter.
    (B) The cops are on the beat.
    (C) A person is being rescued.
    (D) Investors are better off minimizing risk.

13. Look at the picture marked number 13 in your test book.
    (A) The assembly is done by robots.
    (B) The cars are stopped at the traffic light.
    (C) The car wash is very thorough.
    (D) The autos are displayed for sale.

14. Look at the picture marked number 14 in your test book.
    (A) There are two calculators on the desk.
    (B) The worker is collating papers.
    (C) The manager is sealing an envelope.
    (D) The printer copies the forms.

GO ON TO THE NEXT PAGE

15. Look at the picture marked number 15 in your test book.
    (A) The automobiles are being impounded.
    (B) The shoreline is covered with spectators.
    (C) The crew is on the deck.
    (D) Exports wait for shipment.

16. Look at the picture marked number 16 in your test book.
    (A) The man is opening a newspaper.
    (B) The worker is wearing rubber gloves.
    (C) The painter is testing the temperature.
    (D) The worker is climbing a ladder.

17. Look at the picture marked number 17 in your test book.
    (A) The clerk is selling software.
    (B) The computation is not accurate.
    (C) The man inputs data into the computer.
    (D) The technician is repairing the slot machine.

18. Look at the picture marked number 18 in your test book.
    (A) The buildings are illuminated at night.
    (B) The electric power plant is by the river.
    (C) This store has lots of light bulbs.
    (D) Smokers are lighting up.

19. Look at the picture marked number 19 in your test book.
    (A) The customer shops for a table.
    (B) The woman dusts the furniture.
    (C) The mistake has already been made.
    (D) Patrons are milling in the lobby.

20. Look at the picture marked number 20 in your test book.
    (A) The rooms are very large.
    (B) The entrances have been cordoned.
    (C) The architects draw the plans.
    (D) The buildings are very modern.

Part II: Question-Response

Directions: On the compact disc, you will hear a question and three possible answers. Choose the answer that most closely answers the question and fill in the corresponding oval on your answer sheet.

21. Is this 237–1280?
    (A) No, you have the wrong number.
    (B) I was born in November.
    (C) I wear a smaller size.

22. What is your address?
    (A) The woman's dress is blue.
    (B) The adding machine is mine.
    (C) I live on Wilson Boulevard.

23. Who cleans the offices?
    (A) A cleaning company comes in at night.
    (B) The office is closed.
    (C) His voice is awful.

24. Where did you leave your umbrella?
    (A) It's raining now.
    (B) Probably on the bus.
    (C) My leisure time is spent at home.

25. When did the electrician arrive?
    (A) The light bulb burnt out last night.
    (B) The generators are nuclear-powered.
    (C) He came around ten this morning.

26. Why didn't you put an ad in the newspaper?
    (A) They wrapped the food in paper.
    (B) That would have been a good idea.
    (C) I'll put the newspaper on the table.

27. How many times have you been to China?
    (A) Only once.
    (B) We bought several sets of dishes.
    (C) It's time to go.

28. Has the fax been sent?
    (A) Yes, it was sent this morning.
    (B) The facts were not checked.
    (C) The rent was paid on time.

GO ON TO THE NEXT PAGE

MODEL TEST 6   663

29. Who developed the marketing plan?
    (A) The market sells vegetables.
    (B) Our sales staff.
    (C) The film was developed overnight.

30. When will you purchase a computer?
    (A) The purpose is for education.
    (B) The commuter train leaves at 6 A.M.
    (C) When the prices go down.

31. What is the best season to visit?
    (A) There's only one reason.
    (B) I think summer is best.
    (C) The stock prices may fall.

32. Why were you late?
    (A) I'll eat when I'm hungry.
    (B) The date has not been set.
    (C) My watch was slow.

33. Which chair is more comfortable?
    (A) There are more coming.
    (B) The table by the window is wider.
    (C) I like this big, soft one.

34. How many years did you study English?
    (A) For six years in school.
    (B) I had several English books.
    (C) I will visit England next year.

35. Where is the post office?
    (A) It's across from the bank.
    (B) The letter was delivered to the office.
    (C) The postal workers are on duty.

36. Would you pass the salt, please?
    (A) Cars must not pass on hills.
    (B) Certainly. Here you are.
    (C) The woman was insulted.

37. What is the purpose of your visit?
    (A) The visitors are in the next room.
    (B) Porpoises are sea mammals.
    (C) I'm here on business.

38. Who would like to take a break?
    (A) All of the rules were broken.
    (B) Let's all rest for a while.
    (C) We take a walk every week.

39. Why was the meeting postponed?
    (A) Use the mail or the phone.
    (B) The meat market is across from the post office.
    (C) Because the participants were ill.

40. When was this memo written?
    (A) The menu was in French.
    (B) The typewriter was electric.
    (C) The same day it was sent.

41. Where are our suitcases?
    (A) In the hall closet.
    (B) I came in case you needed me.
    (C) They're on the phone now.

42. How soon will this plane land?
    (A) He always plays in the sand.
    (B) We should be landing in twenty minutes.
    (C) They landed in June.

43. Doesn't your receptionist speak other languages?
    (A) No, only English.
    (B) The linguist's lecture was well-received.
    (C) She never says what she's thinking.

44. What will you do when you retire?
    (A) I'll read this book before going to bed.
    (B) These are new tires on the car.
    (C) I plan to play a lot of golf.

45. When will the exhibition close?
    (A) The models are on exhibit.
    (B) It will be open for another two weeks.
    (C) I put my clothes in the closet.

46. Why are airfares so expensive?
    (A) Because there is no competition.
    (B) A haircut doesn't cost very much.
    (C) The airport isn't far from town.

47. Where can I buy a newspaper?
    (A) I knew where the paper was.
    (B) The radio has the news every hour.
    (C) At the newsstand in the lobby.

48. Which desk do you want moved?
    (A) The desk by the window.
    (B) We moved here last year.
    (C) I removed the stain.

GO ON TO THE NEXT PAGE

49. Let's take a walk.
    (A) He let them make it up.
    (B) Yes, let's. I can use the exercise.
    (C) I took it away already.

50. When is the concert over?
    (A) It's over the river.
    (B) The doctor performed the operation yesterday.
    (C) It will be over by ten o'clock.

Part III: Short Conversations

<u>Directions:</u> On the compact disc, you will hear a short conversation. In your test book, you will see a question and four possible answers. Choose the best answer to the question and fill in the corresponding oval on your answer sheet.

51. Man: Let's get together for dinner at six.
    Woman: I have a four-thirty meeting. It may last a while.
    Man: Then we'll meet at eight.

52. Man: I'd like to cash a check.
    Woman: May I see some identification?
    Man: Yes, here are my driver's license and my account number.

53. Man: First we'll tour the museum, and then we'll see the plaza.
    Woman: Will we get to go inside the houses along the plaza?
    Man: No, I'm sorry. They're not open to the public.

54. Man: You can take the ten o'clock flight, which arrives at one.
    Woman: Is that a lunch flight?
    Man: No, but there is a lunch flight leaving at twelve.

55. Man: I'd like to order room service for room five-seven-four.
    Woman: Of course, sir. What would you like?
    Man: The steak with mushrooms, please.

56. Man: Your flight departs from Gate 23.
    Woman: Where is that?
    Man: Turn left and follow the signs.

57. Man: There's not enough space for the printer in your office or in mine.
    Woman: We'll have to set it up in the hall.
    Man: You're right. There's no room anywhere else.

58. Man: There's not enough light in this room.
    Woman: Why don't you get a desk lamp?
    Man: I have enough light for reading. I need more light by the file cabinet.

59. Woman: I'd like to buy a local newspaper, please.
    Man: I'm sorry. The morning paper is sold out, and the evening edition isn't available yet.
    Woman: Then I guess I'll have to take a national paper.

60. Woman: It looks like we have a flat tire.
    Man: Oh, no. We'll certainly be late now.
    Woman: It's OK. It won't take long to fix.

GO ON TO THE NEXT PAGE

668 TRANSCRIPTS

61. Man: Welcome to the Museum of Contemporary Art.
    Woman: Do you have guided tours?
    Man: No, but here is a brochure, with a map and a description of each exhibit.

62. Man: This package will cost eighteen dollars for one-day service.
    Woman: That's more than I expected.
    Man: If two-day mail is convenient, that's only nine dollars.

63. Woman: What's the agenda for the staff meeting?
    Man: We need to discuss overtime and project assignments.
    Woman: We need to go over the contract deadline, too.

64. Woman: I'm expecting a client at eleven this morning.
    Man: Shall I send him up when he arrives?
    Woman: No, just call me. I'll come down to meet him.

65. Man: What do you do?
    Woman: I sell computer software. What about you?
    Man: I'm a petrochemical engineer.

66. Man: I'm getting this folder ready for my sales appointment at three.
    Woman: It looks like rain. You should wear your raincoat when you walk over.
    Man: I should probably take an umbrella, too.

67. Man: I don't have to work this weekend.
    Woman: Then let's attend the concert in the park.
    Man: Actually, I'd like to see the art exhibit and try that new restaurant.

68. Man: Didn't you order office supplies last week?
    Woman: Yes, but they aren't here yet.
    Man: Call the supplier and find out why the order is delayed.

69. Man: We used to have three dictionaries here. What happened?
    Woman: People borrow them and forget to bring them back.
    Man: Maybe the manager can send a memo about returning them.

70. Man: I can never get everything done!
    Woman: You should learn to organize your time better.
    Man: Maybe you're right. I'll write a list of everything I need to do today.

71. Man: The team leaders submit job status reports every Monday.
    Woman: Do you think they should be turned in on Fridays instead?
    Man: I think Mondays are soon enough.

72. Man: Shall we go in your car or in my car?
    Woman: Actually, I'd prefer to take the subway.
    Man: I think a car would be best.

73. Man: The total on these sales figures is off.
    Woman: I'm sorry. I'll fix it right away.
    Man: Thank you. And please check more carefully next time.

74. Man: Do you need help setting up that display?
    Woman: Thank you. The exhibit hall opens at two.
    Man: That gives us forty-five minutes to get ready.

75. Man: I like your new office.
    Woman: Thank you. It has more room than my old one.
    Man: And it's across from the company health club.

76. Woman: I've got a lot of work to get done by five.
    Man: Aren't you stopping for lunch in the cafeteria?
    Woman: No, I'm going to eat a sandwich at my desk.

77. Man: This letter needs to be in the mail by three.
    Woman: The mailroom is on the way to my next meeting. I can take it for you.
    Man: Thank you. That will save me time.

78. Man: The food in this restaurant isn't very good.
    Woman: The waiters are slow, too.
    Man: We certainly won't come here again.

79. Man: I left my sunglasses at home.
    Woman: That's too bad. The sun is really bright today.
    Man: Maybe my hat will provide enough shade.

80. Man: I need five gallons of gas, please.
    Woman: Certainly. Shall I check the oil, too?
    Man: The oil is fine, but the windshield needs washing.

GO ON TO THE NEXT PAGE

Part IV: Short Talks

<u>Directions:</u> On the compact disc, you will hear a short talk. In your test book, you will see several questions on the talk and four possible answers. Choose the best answer to the question and fill in the corresponding oval on your answer sheet.

<u>Questions 81 and 82</u> refer to the following recording.

Woman: Thank you for calling the News in a Minute information service. If you already know the category code number for the information you want, please press that number now. If you do not know the category code, press 1000 for a list of news categories and their corresponding code numbers.

Now read question 81 in your test book and answer it.

Now read question 82 in your test book and answer it.

<u>Questions 83 and 84</u> refer to the following news item.

Man: A new study suggests that secretaries may be more efficient than their managers. Evidence comes from the fact that secretaries have to keep track of the schedules of several managers, control the department record-keeping, type letters, and coordinate events such as meetings and conferences. Even managers admit that work is easier with their secretaries' help.

Now read question 83 in your test book and answer it.

Now read question 84 in your test book and answer it.

<u>Questions 85 and 86</u> refer to the following announcement.

Man: We will be happy to take your catalogue order by phone. For faster ordering, complete the order form in the catalogue, including size, color, and item number. Please have your credit card number handy.

Now read question 85 in your test book and answer it.

Now read question 86 in your test book and answer it.

<u>Questions 87 and 88</u> refer to the following advertisement.

Woman: Joe's Restaurant has job openings for waiters, cooks, and hostesses. If you have experience in the food service industry, one of these jobs is right for you. Good pay and benefits for full-time employees. Call today at 843-2000.

Now read question 87 in your test book and answer it.

Now read question 88 in your test book and answer it.

Questions 89 and 90 refer to the following weather report.

Woman: We can expect rain and sleet this morning, with snow developing by noon and continuing throughout the afternoon. Strong winds tonight with falling snow will create a visibility hazard for drivers.

Now read question 89 in your test book and answer it.

Now read question 90 in your test book and answer it.

Questions 91 and 92 refer to the following announcement.

Man: We have been confirmed for landing at Gate 29 in fifteen minutes. We ask that you prepare by putting your luggage under the seat in front of you and returning your seat to its upright position. Cabin attendants will collect any trash you may wish to throw away.

Now read question 91 in your test book and answer it.

Now read question 92 in your test book and answer it.

Questions 93 and 94 refer to the following advertisement.

Woman: Visit us for all your printing needs. We offer the lowest prices available for business cards, stationery, and brochures. If you don't know what you want, consult one of our design specialists who can help you pick the right look for your business from our samples.

Now read question 93 in your test book and answer it.

Now read question 94 in your test book and answer it.

Questions 95 through 97 refer to the following announcement.

Man: Please be advised that the elevator from the subway platform to the street level is not in service at this station. Passengers with disabilities who are unable to use the escalators or stairs should stay on the train, exit at the next station, and use the elevators there. Buses are available to take these passengers to their destinations. We regret any inconvenience this may cause our passengers.

Now read question 95 in your test book and answer it.

Now read question 96 in your test book and answer it.

Now read question 97 in your test book and answer it.

GO ON TO THE NEXT PAGE

672 TRANSCRIPTS

Questions 98 through 100 refer to the following announcement.

Man: Because of the high demand for electrical power due to the extremely cold weather, the city is in danger of consuming its entire power supply. We are asking residents to help us avoid this situation. Please reduce your power consumption as much as possible. Lower household heat to sixty degrees. Turn off all unnecessary appliances. Postpone energy-consuming tasks such as doing the laundry.

Now read question 98 in your test book and answer it.

Now read question 99 in your test book and answer it.

Now read question 100 in your test book and answer it.

This is the end of the Listening Comprehension portion of the test.

ANSWER SHEET

Mini-Test for Listening Comprehension Parts I, II, III, and IV

1 Ⓐ Ⓑ Ⓒ Ⓓ	14 Ⓐ Ⓑ Ⓒ	27 Ⓐ Ⓑ Ⓒ Ⓓ	40 Ⓐ Ⓑ Ⓒ Ⓓ
2 Ⓐ Ⓑ Ⓒ Ⓓ	15 Ⓐ Ⓑ Ⓒ	28 Ⓐ Ⓑ Ⓒ Ⓓ	41 Ⓐ Ⓑ Ⓒ Ⓓ
3 Ⓐ Ⓑ Ⓒ Ⓓ	16 Ⓐ Ⓑ Ⓒ	29 Ⓐ Ⓑ Ⓒ Ⓓ	42 Ⓐ Ⓑ Ⓒ Ⓓ
4 Ⓐ Ⓑ Ⓒ Ⓓ	17 Ⓐ Ⓑ Ⓒ	30 Ⓐ Ⓑ Ⓒ Ⓓ	43 Ⓐ Ⓑ Ⓒ Ⓓ
5 Ⓐ Ⓑ Ⓒ Ⓓ	18 Ⓐ Ⓑ Ⓒ	31 Ⓐ Ⓑ Ⓒ Ⓓ	44 Ⓐ Ⓑ Ⓒ Ⓓ
6 Ⓐ Ⓑ Ⓒ Ⓓ	19 Ⓐ Ⓑ Ⓒ	32 Ⓐ Ⓑ Ⓒ Ⓓ	45 Ⓐ Ⓑ Ⓒ Ⓓ
7 Ⓐ Ⓑ Ⓒ Ⓓ	20 Ⓐ Ⓑ Ⓒ	33 Ⓐ Ⓑ Ⓒ Ⓓ	46 Ⓐ Ⓑ Ⓒ Ⓓ
8 Ⓐ Ⓑ Ⓒ Ⓓ	21 Ⓐ Ⓑ Ⓒ	34 Ⓐ Ⓑ Ⓒ Ⓓ	47 Ⓐ Ⓑ Ⓒ Ⓓ
9 Ⓐ Ⓑ Ⓒ Ⓓ	22 Ⓐ Ⓑ Ⓒ	35 Ⓐ Ⓑ Ⓒ Ⓓ	48 Ⓐ Ⓑ Ⓒ Ⓓ
10 Ⓐ Ⓑ Ⓒ Ⓓ	23 Ⓐ Ⓑ Ⓒ	36 Ⓐ Ⓑ Ⓒ Ⓓ	49 Ⓐ Ⓑ Ⓒ Ⓓ
11 Ⓐ Ⓑ Ⓒ	24 Ⓐ Ⓑ Ⓒ	37 Ⓐ Ⓑ Ⓒ Ⓓ	50 Ⓐ Ⓑ Ⓒ Ⓓ
12 Ⓐ Ⓑ Ⓒ	25 Ⓐ Ⓑ Ⓒ	38 Ⓐ Ⓑ Ⓒ Ⓓ	
13 Ⓐ Ⓑ Ⓒ	26 Ⓐ Ⓑ Ⓒ Ⓓ	39 Ⓐ Ⓑ Ⓒ Ⓓ	

Mini-Test for Reading Part V and VI

1 Ⓐ Ⓑ Ⓒ Ⓓ	9 Ⓐ Ⓑ Ⓒ	17 Ⓐ Ⓑ Ⓒ	25 Ⓐ Ⓑ Ⓒ Ⓓ
2 Ⓐ Ⓑ Ⓒ Ⓓ	10 Ⓐ Ⓑ Ⓒ	18 Ⓐ Ⓑ Ⓒ	26 Ⓐ Ⓑ Ⓒ Ⓓ
3 Ⓐ Ⓑ Ⓒ Ⓓ	11 Ⓐ Ⓑ Ⓒ	19 Ⓐ Ⓑ Ⓒ	27 Ⓐ Ⓑ Ⓒ Ⓓ
4 Ⓐ Ⓑ Ⓒ Ⓓ	12 Ⓐ Ⓑ Ⓒ	20 Ⓐ Ⓑ Ⓒ	28 Ⓐ Ⓑ Ⓒ Ⓓ
5 Ⓐ Ⓑ Ⓒ Ⓓ	13 Ⓐ Ⓑ Ⓒ	21 Ⓐ Ⓑ Ⓒ	29 Ⓐ Ⓑ Ⓒ Ⓓ
6 Ⓐ Ⓑ Ⓒ Ⓓ	14 Ⓐ Ⓑ Ⓒ	22 Ⓐ Ⓑ Ⓒ	30 Ⓐ Ⓑ Ⓒ Ⓓ
7 Ⓐ Ⓑ Ⓒ Ⓓ	15 Ⓐ Ⓑ Ⓒ	23 Ⓐ Ⓑ Ⓒ	
8 Ⓐ Ⓑ Ⓒ Ⓓ	16 Ⓐ Ⓑ Ⓒ	24 Ⓐ Ⓑ Ⓒ	

Mini-Test for Reading Part VII

1 Ⓐ Ⓑ Ⓒ Ⓓ	11 Ⓐ Ⓑ Ⓒ Ⓓ	21 Ⓐ Ⓑ Ⓒ Ⓓ	31 Ⓐ Ⓑ Ⓒ Ⓓ
2 Ⓐ Ⓑ Ⓒ Ⓓ	12 Ⓐ Ⓑ Ⓒ Ⓓ	22 Ⓐ Ⓑ Ⓒ Ⓓ	32 Ⓐ Ⓑ Ⓒ Ⓓ
3 Ⓐ Ⓑ Ⓒ Ⓓ	13 Ⓐ Ⓑ Ⓒ Ⓓ	23 Ⓐ Ⓑ Ⓒ Ⓓ	33 Ⓐ Ⓑ Ⓒ Ⓓ
4 Ⓐ Ⓑ Ⓒ Ⓓ	14 Ⓐ Ⓑ Ⓒ Ⓓ	24 Ⓐ Ⓑ Ⓒ Ⓓ	34 Ⓐ Ⓑ Ⓒ Ⓓ
5 Ⓐ Ⓑ Ⓒ Ⓓ	15 Ⓐ Ⓑ Ⓒ Ⓓ	25 Ⓐ Ⓑ Ⓒ Ⓓ	35 Ⓐ Ⓑ Ⓒ Ⓓ
6 Ⓐ Ⓑ Ⓒ Ⓓ	16 Ⓐ Ⓑ Ⓒ Ⓓ	26 Ⓐ Ⓑ Ⓒ Ⓓ	36 Ⓐ Ⓑ Ⓒ Ⓓ
7 Ⓐ Ⓑ Ⓒ Ⓓ	17 Ⓐ Ⓑ Ⓒ Ⓓ	27 Ⓐ Ⓑ Ⓒ Ⓓ	37 Ⓐ Ⓑ Ⓒ Ⓓ
8 Ⓐ Ⓑ Ⓒ Ⓓ	18 Ⓐ Ⓑ Ⓒ Ⓓ	28 Ⓐ Ⓑ Ⓒ Ⓓ	38 Ⓐ Ⓑ Ⓒ Ⓓ
9 Ⓐ Ⓑ Ⓒ Ⓓ	19 Ⓐ Ⓑ Ⓒ Ⓓ	29 Ⓐ Ⓑ Ⓒ Ⓓ	39 Ⓐ Ⓑ Ⓒ Ⓓ
10 Ⓐ Ⓑ Ⓒ Ⓓ	20 Ⓐ Ⓑ Ⓒ Ⓓ	30 Ⓐ Ⓑ Ⓒ Ⓓ	40 Ⓐ Ⓑ Ⓒ Ⓓ

BARRON'S BOOKS AND CASSETTES TO HELP YOU SUCCEED IN ESL AND TOEFL EXAMS

Where the Action Is: An Easy ESL Approach to Pure Regular Verbs • A clear, easy-to-follow guide complete with charts that instruct ESL students to use and understand pure regular verbs in speaking, reading and writing. Six practice test and answer keys are included. $7.95, Canada $10.50.

Barron's ESL Guide to American Business English • Focused to fit the needs of ESL students. Paperback handbook describes a variety of business writings and sample correspondence. Review section covers the basics of English grammar. $13.95, Canada $17.95.

Write English Right • This workbook presents exercises, assignment worksheets, and drills for TOEFL and ESL students. $9.95, Canada $13.50.

American Accent Training • Concentrates on spoken English, American style, with exercises in American speech rhythms and inflections. Exercises prompt ESL students to listen and imitate, in order to be better understood by Americans, while also increasing listening comprehension. Package consists of book and three 90-minute cassettes in a durable case. $39.95, Canada $49.95.

Writing a Research Paper American Style: An ESL/EFL Handbook • Instructs advanced high school, college, and graduate students who have little experience in writing academic papers in English. Explains and illustrates documentation rules using Modern Language Association parenthetical style and using endnotes, outlines documentation techniques, gives helpful grammar tips, and much more.
$9.95, Canada $12.95.

Minimum Essentials of English, 2nd • A concise 72-page summary of English grammar, rules, and language forms. Explains MLA, APA, and CMS documentation. An indispensable aid and style sheet to help with all written assignments. Pages are punched to fit a three-ring notebook binder.
$6.95, Canada $9.50.

Please send me the following titles:

____ Where the Action Is,
(0-7641-0509-4), $7.95, Canada $10.50.

____ Barron's ESL Guide to American Business English,
(0-7641-0594-9), $13.95, Canada $17.95.

____ Write English Right
(0-8120-1462-6), $9.95, Canada $13.50.

____ American Accent Training,
(0-8120-7763-6), $39.95, Canada $49.95.

____ Writing a Research Paper American Style,
(0-8120-9637-1), $9.95, Canada $12.95.

____ Minimum Essentials of English, 2nd,
(0-7641-0745-3), $6.95, Canada $9.50.

BARRON'S EDUCATIONAL SERIES, INC.
250 Wireless Blvd. • Hauppauge, NY 11788
In Canada: Georgetown Book Warehouse
34 Armstrong Ave. • Georgetown, Ontario
L7G 4R9

I am enclosing a check or money order for $_____ which includes an additional 18% for postage and shipping (minimum charge $5.95). New York State residents add sales tax to total.
Charge To My: ☐ Mastercard ☐ Visa ☐ American Express

Account # _____ Exp. Date _____
Signature_____
Name_____
Address_____
City _____ State_____ Zip_____
Phone _____

If not satisfied, please return books within 15 days of the date of purchase for full refund. Prices are subject to change without notice. All books are paperback editions, and may be purchased at local bookstores or direct from Barron's.

Visit our web site at: www.barronseduc.com

(#6a) R 7/01